Monographs in Theoretical Computer Science
An EATCS Series

Editors: W. Brauer G. Rozenberg A. Salomaa

On behalf of the European Association
for Theoretical Computer Science (EATCS)

Advisory Board: G. Ausiello M. Broy S. Even
J. Hartmanis N. Jones T. Leighton M. Nivat
C. Papadimitriou D. Scott

T0189611

Springer
Berlin
Heidelberg
New York
Barcelona
Hong Kong
London
Milan
Paris
Tokyo

Stéphane P. Demri   Ewa S. Orłowska

Incomplete Information: Structure, Inference, Complexity

Springer

Authors

Dr. Stéphane P. Demri
Laboratoire Spécification
et Vérification
CNRS UMR 8643, ENS de Cachan
61, avenue du Président Wilson
94235 Cachan Cedex, France

and

Laboratoire Leibniz
46, avenue Felix Viallet
38000 Grenoble, France
demri@lsv.ens-cachan.fr

Prof. Dr. Ewa S. Orłowska
National Institute
of Telecommunications
Szachowa 1
04-894 Warszawa, Poland
orlowska@itl.waw.pl

Series Editors

Prof. Dr. Wilfried Brauer
Institut für Informatik
Technische Universität München
Arcisstrasse 21
80333 München, Germany
brauer@informatik.tu-muenchen.de

Prof. Dr. Grzegorz Rozenberg
Leiden Institute
of Advanced Computer Science
University of Leiden
Niels Bohrweg 1
2333 CA Leiden, The Netherlands
rozenber@liacs.nl

Prof. Dr. Arto Salomaa
Data City
Turku Centre for Computer Science
20500 Turku, Finland
asolomaa@utu.fi

ISBN 978-3-642-07540-7

ACM Computing Classification (1998): F.2.2, F.4.1, H.1.1, H.2.1, H.2.4, I.2.3–4

Library of Congress Cataloging-in-Publication Data
Demri, Stéphane., 1967–
    Incomplete information: structure, inference, complexity/Stéphane P. Demri, Ewa S. Orłowska
    p.cm. – (Monographs in theoretical computer science)
    Includes bibliographical references and index.

    1. Soft computing. 2. Fuzzy sets. 3. Rough sets. I. Orłowska, Ewa. II. Title. III. Series
QA76.9.S63 D46 2001
006.3–dc21   2001055106

Springer-Verlag Berlin Heidelberg New York,
a member of BertelmannSpringer Science+Business Media GmbH
http://www.springer.de

© Springer-Verlag Berlin Heidelberg 2010
Printed in Germany

Cover design: KünkelLopka, Heidelberg

To Magdalena, Michał, and Noam

Preface

The construction of any broadly understood theory of information or information processing system involves two major methodological processes: (1) abstraction and analysis, (2) reasoning and computing. This monograph is a realisation of these two processes in relation to the study of incompleteness of information. The paradigm we are working with is inspired by a rough-set approach to data analysis: the formalisms we develop enable the use of a non-invasive data representation. This means that the only information which is and must be used in the process of analysis is the actual information that is to be analysed; we do not require any additional sources of information.

An abstraction is formed in the process of conception, design, and development of structures. Then analysis leads to a selection of a class of structures. In this book we delineate a class of informational structures that enable us to represent both numerical and non-numerical information and we analyse various manifestations of its incompleteness. We discuss several general types of incompleteness of information which are grounded in a rough-set-style view of imprecision and uncertainty. Manifestations of these types of incompleteness in information systems are investigated.

Reasoning is concerned both with verification of assertions and also with inference processes. With both these aspects in mind, we put forward a general perspective on reasoning with incomplete information and on handling uncertain knowledge. We develop several classes of deductive systems which allow us to make inferences from incomplete information with an explicit indication of a kind and a source of incompleteness. Computing in its traditional sense is centred on a manipulation of numbers. The underlying formal theories are the theory of arithmetic or the theory of reals. However, in a more general setting computing refers to a methodology in which the objects of computation are not necessarily numbers, but rather elements of some abstract algebras, like groups, rings, etc. In the book we present algebras that underlie computing with information items.

This monograph presents a systematic, exhaustive and up-to-date overview of formal methods and theories related to data analysis and inference inspired by the concept of rough sets. It is self-contained to a large degree. Chapter 1 is introductory and presents the basic mathematical notions and facts used throughout the book. The remaining 14 chapters are grouped into five parts.

Part I is a realisation of the abstraction component. We present and discuss informational structures that enable us to represent the most essential and general ingredients of a variety of data sets. In Chap. 2 we introduce the structures that employ the notions of object, attribute, and value of attribute as the basic pieces of information and we discuss relationships between them. The most fundamental of these structures is an information system with incomplete information. In database terms an information system is a multi-set of tuples, referred to as objects, whose elements are not necessarily entities, but rather subsets of a domain. The notion of an information system is then extended to the notion of a fuzzy information system. Given an information system or a fuzzy information system, we show how additional information can be derived from its content. This information is not stated explicitly in the system but is available as implicit information. More precisely, we can derive relations reflecting relationships among objects, referred to as "information relations", and operators acting on sets of objects, referred to as "information operators". These two classes of derived information are studied in Chaps. 3 and 4, respectively. We present an exhaustive list of the classes of information relations derived from information systems, and a catalogue of their abstract counterparts referred to as "information frames". An extension of information relations and information operators to their fuzzy counterparts is also discussed in this part. In all subsequent parts we study formal methods for the analysis of data from information systems based on processing of information relations and operators.

Part II provides a formal background for the reasoning component. We present a general framework for the development and the study of information logics. The term "information logic" refers to any logical system developed both for the representation of and also for the reasoning with data presented in the form of an information system. In the two chapters of this part we present the concepts, techniques, and methods of logic which are needed for the development and study of information logics and their deductive systems. Some of these techniques originated in connection with problems specific to information logics. In Chap. 5 we recall the basics of classical logic and standard modal logics. Next, we introduce some extensions of those standard logical systems needed both for getting a means of explicit representation of all the ingredients of information given in an information system or a fuzzy information system, and also for making inferences by exploiting exclusively and exhaustively the information from the system. In Chap. 6 the techniques underlying the methodology of information logics are presented.

Part III is a proper realisation of the reasoning component. We develop and investigate deductive systems that enable us to make inferences from data specified in the form of the structures discussed in Part II. The logics and deduction mechanisms presented allow us to represent and make inferences both from information given explicitly in an information system and also from the implicit information derived from the system in the way discussed in Chaps. 3 and 4. The logics presented in this part are modal logics with rather rich languages. Each logic enables us to give a direct representation of some of the following information items: individual objects, sets of objects, individual attributes, sets of attributes and their Boolean combinations, indiscernibility relations, their intersections and transitive closure of unions, and approximation operators determined by those relations. The deductive systems of these logics have either of two forms: Hilbert-style or Rasiowa–Sikorski-style. Each of the proofs of completeness of the given deductive systems employs one of three different methods. More precisely, we present an algebraic proof of completeness, a proof based on the copying method, and a Rasiowa–Sikorski-style proof. Thus we provide, on the one hand, an overview of various techniques of the theory of modal logics and, on the other hand, an insight into the extensions of these methods which are needed due to the specific features of information logics. In this part we study both important individual information logics that are typical examples within some groups of logics and also some general classes of information logics. In all the cases the focus is on the adequacy of the formalisms we present for dealing with information systems with incomplete information. On the side of formal methods we present a broad spectrum of useful techniques that provide a means for dealing with most important methodological problems of information logics.

In Part IV the computational aspects of formal systems developed in Part III are studied. Most of the information logics are shown to be decidable. The methods of proving these results, although inspired by the respective developments for standard modal systems, require several extensions and novel constructions that take into account the specific features of information logics. In Chap. 10 translations between information logics and some standard modal logics are investigated. On the one hand they provide a deeper insight into essential characteristics of information logics that make them distinct from other modal logics. On the other hand they enable us to transfer several methodological results, in particular decidability and complexity results from those standard logics, to information logics. In Chap. 11 we present decidability results for information logics. In proving these results we employ two major methods: the method based on the filtration construction and the method based on interpretability of the logic under consideration in a logic whose decidability status is known. For the latter method we extensively use the translations developed in Chap. 10. Chapter 12 contains a systematic study of the complexity of formal systems developed in Part III. The complexity classes **NP**, **PSPACE**, **EXPTIME**, and **NEXPTIME** are relevant to the satisfiability problems of information logics.

Part V is concerned both with algebraic approaches to information systems with incomplete information and also with some methodological issues that rely on relationships between algebraic and logical systems. In Chap. 13 the concept of the informational representability of structures is introduced and discussed. Intuitively, we say that a class of frames or a class of algebras is informationally representable if any member of the class is sufficiently similar to a frame or, respectively, to an algebra, derived from an information system. The property of being informationally representable is meant to provide a criterion of the adequacy of a formal model for the meaningful representation of incomplete information. In Chap. 14 we present several informational representability results for various classes of algebras that play an important role in the field of algebraic logic. We also present and discuss some classes of algebras that have been introduced in connection with information systems with incomplete information; in particular, we present, among others, the classes of rough relation algebras and fuzzy relation algebras. In Chap. 15 we present and discuss algebraic structures, referred to as "information algebras", that are closely related to information logics. As with information frames, we give a full catalogue of information algebras. We present the recent developments of their theory, in particular a duality theory, and we outline open problems.

The last section of every chapter of the book contains notes which provide a historical perspective on the subject of the chapter and references to the literature where the underlying issues have originated or have been pursued. In the notes we also mention some open problems.

The researchers, lecturers, and graduate students who wish to get acquainted with the rough-set-style theory of information systems with incomplete information and active researchers in the field will, we hope, find in this book inspiration for challenging new research issues.

Acknowledgements. Our work on incomplete information and its methodology was shaped by a long process of interaction and/or cooperation with many colleagues. We are grateful to: Zdzislaw Pawlak, Lotfi Zadeh, Carlos Areces, Philippe Balbiani, Wiktor Bartol, Patrick Blackburn, Wojtek Buszkowski, Ricardo Caferra, Mihir Chakraborty, Antonio Di Nola, Didier Dubois, Ivo Düntsch, Francesc Esteva, Luis Fariñas del Cerro, Dov Gabbay, Günther Gediga, lluis Godo, Rajeev Goré, Petr Hájek, Luisa Iturrioz, Tadeusz Iwinski, Jouni Järvinen, Beata Konikowska, Maarten Marx, Daniele Mundici, Akira Nakamura, Miroslav Novotný, Piero Pagliani, Janusz Pomykała, Henri Prade, Anna Radzikowska, Eric SanJuan, Ulrike Sattler, Andrzej Skowron, Magnus Steinby, Jarosław Stepaniuk, Helmut Thiele, Dimiter Vakarelov, Anita Wasilewska, Rudolf Wille, and Urszula Wybraniec-Skardowska. We would like also to thank the colleagues who read and commented on parts of the earlier versions of this book: John Addison, Ivo Düntsch, Rajeev Goré, Yasuo Kawahara, Wendy MacCaull, Janusz Pomykała, Anna Radzikowska, Eric SanJuan, Magnus Steinby, Andrzej Szałas, and Dimiter Vakarelov.

We thank the institutions where we worked on this book: the Institute of Telecommunications (Warsaw), the Laboratoire Leibniz (Grenoble), the Laboratoire Spécification et Vérification (Cachan), and the Centre Scientifique de l'Académie Polonaise des Sciences (Paris). We are also indebted to the LSV for a stimulating atmosphere while writing the final version of the book.

We acknowledge financial support from the Polish Science Commission (KBN), Warsaw (Grant No. 8T11C04010, Grant No. 8T11C01617, POLONIUM project No. 7004), the French Foreign Office (POLONIUM project No. 7004), Ecole Normale Supérieure de Cachan (ENS de Cachan), Centre National de la Recherche Scientifique (CNRS), and the European Union (COST Action No. 15 in Informatics).

We thank the members of our families, Suzana, Henryk, Maciek, and Teresa, for their support and encouragement.

Cachan and Warsaw, March 2002 *S. Demri   E. Orłowska*

Contents

Part V. Representability and Duality

14. Informational Interpretation of Standard Algebraic Structures ... 321

15. Information Algebras ... 355

1. Mathematical Prerequisites

1.1 Set-theoretical Notions

Throughout this book we use the standard notation for set-theoretical notions: membership ($\in$), inclusion ($\subseteq$), strict (or proper) inclusion ($\subset$), union of sets ($\cup$), intersection of sets ($\cap$), difference of sets ($\backslash$), and product of sets ($\times$). By X^n we denote the product $X \times \cdots \times X$ with n factors. A disjoint union $\dot{\cup}$ of the sets X and Y is the set $X \dot{\cup} Y = (X \times \{1\}) \cup (Y \times \{2\})$. The union and the intersection of an indexed family $(X_i)_{i \in I}$ of sets are denoted by $\bigcup_{i \in I} X_i$ and $\bigcap_{i \in I} X_i$, respectively. Sometime, we also write $\bigcap \{X_i : i \in I\}$ [resp. $\bigcup \{X_i : i \in I\}$] to denote $\bigcap_{i \in I} X_i$ [resp. $\bigcup_{i \in I} X_i$]. The empty set is denoted by $\emptyset$. $\mathbb{N}$, $\mathbb{R}$, and $\mathbb{Q}$ denote the sets of all natural numbers, real numbers, and rational numbers, respectively. $[0, 1]$ and $[0, 1]_{\mathbb{Q}}$ are the closed intervals of real and rational numbers between 0 and 1, respectively. By $\mathcal{P}(X)$ we denote the powerset of the set X, that is the family of all subsets of X, and by $\mathcal{P}_f(X)$ we denote the family of all finite subsets of X. The powerset hierarchy is generated by any set X as follows: $\mathcal{P}^0(X) \overset{\text{def}}{=} X$, $\mathcal{P}^i(X) \overset{\text{def}}{=} \mathcal{P}(\mathcal{P}^{i-1}(X))$ for every $i \geq 1$. By $\text{card}(X)$ we denote the cardinality of the set X. A family $(X_i)_{i \in I}$ of subsets of Y is a *cover* of Y $\overset{\text{def}}{\Leftrightarrow}$ $\bigcup_{i \in I} X_i = Y$. A family $(X_i)_{i \in I}$ of subsets of Y is a *partition* of Y $\overset{\text{def}}{\Leftrightarrow}$ it is a cover of Y such that for all $i, j \in I$, $i \neq j$ implies $X_i \cap X_j = \emptyset$.

1.2 Relations

An *n-ary relation* on a set W is a subset R of W^n, $n \geq 1$. If R is an n-ary relation on W, $n \geq 1$, and $W' \subseteq W$, then $R_{|W'} \overset{\text{def}}{=} R \cap (W')^n$. If $n = 2$, then R is a *binary* relation. The *relative product* (or *composition*) of two binary relations R and S on a set W is the relation $R; S \overset{\text{def}}{=} \{\langle x, y \rangle \in W \times W :$ there is a $z \in W$ such that $\langle x, z \rangle \in R$ and $\langle z, y \rangle \in S\}$. The *converse* of a binary relation R is the relation $R^{-1} \overset{\text{def}}{=} \{\langle y, x \rangle : \langle x, y \rangle \in R\}$. The *identity* on a set W (or the *diagonal relation*) is the relation $Id_W \overset{\text{def}}{=} \{\langle x, x \rangle : x \in W\}$ and the *universal relation* on W is $W \times W$. The *reflexive and transitive closure* of a binary relation R on W is the relation $R^* \overset{\text{def}}{=} \bigcup_{i \in \mathbb{N}} R^i$, where

$R^0 \stackrel{\text{def}}{=} Id_W$ and $R^i \stackrel{\text{def}}{=} R; R^{i-1}$ for every $i \geq 1$. Similarly, the *transitive closure* of a binary relation R on W is the relation $R^+ \stackrel{\text{def}}{=} \bigcup_{i \geq 1} R^i$. If R is a binary relation on W, $X \subseteq W$ and $x \in W$, then $R(x) \stackrel{\text{def}}{=} \{y \in W : \langle x, y \rangle \in R\}$ and $R(X) \stackrel{\text{def}}{=} \bigcup_{x \in X} R(x)$.

For every binary relation R on a set W, $\text{dom}(R) \stackrel{\text{def}}{=} \{x : \langle x, y \rangle \in R\}$ is the *domain* of R and $\text{ran}(R) \stackrel{\text{def}}{=} \{y : \langle x, y \rangle \in R\}$ is the *range* of R. For all $w, u \in W$, an *R-path between w and u* is a sequence $w_0, \ldots, w_s \in W$ for some $s \geq 0$ such that $w_0 = w$, $w_s = u$ and for every $i \in \{0, \ldots, s-1\}$, $\langle w_i, w_{i+1} \rangle \in R$. By an *$R$-path*, we mean an R-path between w and u for some $w, u \in W$. The length of an R-path $w_0, \ldots, w_s$ is s. An *R-cycle* is an R-path of length greater than 1 such that $w = u$. By extension, an *infinite R-path* is an infinite sequence such that every one of its finite initial segments is an R-path.

We say that a binary relation R on a set W is:

* *reflexive* $\stackrel{\text{def}}{\Leftrightarrow}$ for every $x \in W$, $\langle x, x \rangle \in R$ (i.e., $Id_W \subseteq R$);
* *symmetric* $\stackrel{\text{def}}{\Leftrightarrow}$ for all $x, y \in W$, if $\langle x, y \rangle \in R$, then $\langle y, x \rangle \in R$ (i.e., $R \subseteq R^{-1}$);
* *antisymmetric* $\stackrel{\text{def}}{\Leftrightarrow}$ for all $x, y \in W$, if $\langle x, y \rangle \in R$ and $\langle y, x \rangle \in R$, then $x = y$ (i.e., $R \cap R^{-1} \subseteq Id_W$);
* *transitive* $\stackrel{\text{def}}{\Leftrightarrow}$ for all $x, y, z \in W$, if $\langle x, y \rangle \in R$ and $\langle y, z \rangle \in R$, then $\langle x, z \rangle \in R$ (i.e., $R; R \subseteq R$);
* *n-transitive* , $n \geq 2$ $\stackrel{\text{def}}{\Leftrightarrow}$ for all $x_1, \ldots, x_{n+1} \in W$ if for every $i \in \{1, \ldots, n\}$, $\langle x_i, x_{i+1} \rangle \in R$, then $\langle x_1, x_{n+1} \rangle \in R$ (i.e., $R; \cdots ; R$ (with n factors) $\subseteq R$); it follows that R is transitive iff R is 2-transitive;
* *weakly reflexive* $\stackrel{\text{def}}{\Leftrightarrow}$ for all $x, y \in W$, if $\langle x, y \rangle \in R$, then $\langle x, x \rangle \in R$ (i.e., $(Id_W \cap (R; (W \times W))) \subseteq R$);
* *irreflexive* $\stackrel{\text{def}}{\Leftrightarrow}$ for every $x \in W$, $\langle x, x \rangle \notin R$ (i.e., $Id_W \subseteq W \times W \setminus R$);
* *intransitive* $\stackrel{\text{def}}{\Leftrightarrow}$ for all $x, y, z \in W$, if $\langle x, y \rangle \in R$ and $\langle y, z \rangle \in R$, then $\langle x, z \rangle \notin R$ (i.e., $R; R \subseteq W \times W \setminus R$);
* *connected* $\stackrel{\text{def}}{\Leftrightarrow}$ $(R \cup R^{-1})^* = W \times W$;
* *totally connected* $\stackrel{\text{def}}{\Leftrightarrow}$ for all $x, y \in W$, either $\langle x, y \rangle \in R$ or $\langle y, x \rangle \in R$ (i.e., $R \cup R^{-1} = W \times W$);
* *serial* $\stackrel{\text{def}}{\Leftrightarrow}$ for every $x \in W$, there is a $y \in W$ such that $\langle x, y \rangle \in R$;
* *atomic* $\stackrel{\text{def}}{\Leftrightarrow}$ for every $x \in W$, there is a $y \in W$ such that $\langle x, y \rangle \in R$ and for every $z \in W$, if $\langle y, z \rangle \in R$, then $z = y$;
* *weakly dense* $\stackrel{\text{def}}{\Leftrightarrow}$ for all $x, y \in W$, if $\langle x, y \rangle \in R$, then there is a $z \in W$ such that $\langle x, z \rangle \in R$ and $\langle z, y \rangle \in R$;
* *discrete* $\stackrel{\text{def}}{\Leftrightarrow}$ for all $x, y \in W$, if $\langle x, y \rangle \in R$, then there is a $z \in W$ such that $\langle x, z \rangle \in R$ and there is no z' such that $\langle x, z' \rangle \in R$ and $\langle z', z \rangle \in R$;
* an *equivalence relation* $\stackrel{\text{def}}{\Leftrightarrow}$ R is reflexive, symmetric, and transitive;
* a *tolerance relation* $\stackrel{\text{def}}{\Leftrightarrow}$ R is reflexive and symmetric;

⋆ a *partial order* $\overset{\text{def}}{\Leftrightarrow}$ R is reflexive, antisymmetric, and transitive;

⋆ a *linear order* $\overset{\text{def}}{\Leftrightarrow}$ R is a totally connected partial order;

⋆ a *well-ordering* $\overset{\text{def}}{\Leftrightarrow}$ R is a linear order such that for every non-empty subset W' of W there is a $w \in W'$ such that for every $w' \in W'$ $\langle w, w' \rangle \in R$.

If Π is any property of binary relations on a set W, then we say that a relation R has the property coΠ iff $W \times W \setminus R$ has the property Π. For example, R is coreflexive iff $W \times W \setminus R$ is reflexive (or equivalently R is irreflexive).

If R is an equivalence relation on a set W, then any set $|x|_R \overset{\text{def}}{=} \{y \in W : \langle x, y \rangle \in R\}$ is said to be an *equivalence class* of R generated by x. For every equivalence relation R, the equivalence classes of R are sometimes called *R-clusters* . Throughout the book we often write $|x|$ if it is clear from the context which relation determines this equivalence class. The equivalence classes of an equivalence relation on W are non-empty, pairwise disjoint and their union equals W, that is to say, they form a partition of W (or in other words a classification of the elements of W). Observe also that for all equivalence relations R and R' on a set W, for every $x \in W$, $R \subseteq R'$ implies $|x|_R \subseteq |x|_{R'}$.

A *function* (or a *mapping*) f from a set X to a set Y, denoted by $f : X \to Y$, is a subset of $X \times Y$ such that for every $x \in X$, there is at most one $y \in Y$ such that $\langle x, y \rangle \in f$. The usual notation for this fact is $f(x) = y$. Y^X denotes the set of all the functions $f : X \to Y$. The function f is *n-ary* $\overset{\text{def}}{\Leftrightarrow}$ $X = X_1 \times \cdots \times X_n$, $n \geq 1$. By the *domain* [resp. *range*] of a function f we mean the set $\text{dom}(f) \overset{\text{def}}{=} \{x \in X : \text{ there is a } y \in Y \text{ such that } f(x) = y\}$ [resp. $\text{ran}(f) \overset{\text{def}}{=} \{y \in Y : \text{ there is an } x \in X \text{ such that } f(x) = y\}$]. The function $f : X \to Y$ is *total* $\overset{\text{def}}{\Leftrightarrow}$ $\text{dom}(f) = X$. The function f is *injective* (or *one-to-one*) $\overset{\text{def}}{\Leftrightarrow}$ $f(x_1) = f(x_2)$ implies $x_1 = x_2$ and it is *surjective* (or *onto*) $\overset{\text{def}}{\Leftrightarrow}$ for every $y \in Y$ there exists an $x \in X$ such that $f(x) = y$. A function is *bijective* $\overset{\text{def}}{\Leftrightarrow}$ it is both injective and surjective. The image $f(Z)$ of a set $Z \subseteq X$ is the set $\{f(x) : x \in Z\}$. The *inverse image* $f^{-1}(Z)$ of a set $Z \subseteq Y$ is defined as $\{x \in X : f(x) \in Z\}$. The function f is *constant* $\overset{\text{def}}{\Leftrightarrow}$ there is a $c \in Y$ such that $f(x) = c$ for every $x \in X$ and then we write $f = c$. The *membership function* of a subset $Y \subseteq W$ is the function $f_Y : W \to \{0, 1\}$ such that $f_Y(x) \overset{\text{def}}{=} 1$ if $x \in Y$, otherwise $f_Y(x) \overset{\text{def}}{=} 0$. For every finite set X, a *permutation* of X is a bijective map $f : X \to X$.

1.3 Strings

For every set X, we write X^* [resp. X^+] to denote the set of [resp. the set of non-empty] finite strings (or sequences) built from elements of X. X is often referred to as an *alphabet*. λ denotes the empty string and, as usual, $s \cdot s'$ denotes the concatenation of two strings. Usually the concatenation sign is dropped and the string is written ss'. For every finite string s, we write $|s|$ [resp. $last(s)$] to denote its length [resp. the last element of s]. For every $s \in X^*$, we write s^k to denote the string composed of k copies of s. For instance, $(1 \cdot 2)^2 = 1 \cdot 2 \cdot 1 \cdot 2$ and $|(1 \cdot 2)^2| = 4$. For every finite string s, we write $set(s)$ to denote the set of elements occurring in s. For example $set(1 \cdot 2 \cdot 3 \cdot 3 \cdot 4) = \{1, 3, 2, 4\}$. For all $s, s' \in X^*$, s is a *prefix* of s' [resp. s is a substring of s'] $\overset{\text{def}}{\Leftrightarrow}$ s' is of the form $s \cdot s_1''$ [resp. $s_1'' \cdot s \cdot s_2''$], where s_i'', $i = 1, 2$, are strings in X^*. If $s = x_1 \cdot \ \cdots \ \cdot x_n$ is a string such that $n \geq 0$, then we mean that, in the case $n = 0$, the string s is empty.

1.4 Trees and Orders

A *tree* is defined as a pair $\mathcal{T} = \langle W, R \rangle$, where W is a non-empty set of *nodes* and R is a binary relation on W such that R is connected and there is a designated element r of W (the *root*) such that $R^{-1}(r) = \emptyset$ and for every $w \in W \setminus \{r\}$, $\text{card}(R^{-1}(w)) = 1$. If $\langle w, w' \rangle \in R$, then we say that w is the *parent* of w' and w' is a *child* of w. If $\langle w, w' \rangle \in R^+$, then we say that w is an *ancestor* of w'. The elements of W are called the *nodes* of the tree $\mathcal{T} = \langle W, R \rangle$. A *branch* $\text{BR} = w_0, w_1, \ldots$ of a tree $\mathcal{T} = \langle W, R \rangle$ is a maximal sequence of elements of W such that $w_0 = r$ and for every $i \geq 1$, $\langle w_i, w_{i+1} \rangle \in R$. As a consequence, either BR is infinite or no proper extension of BR is a branch. Note that a branch BR can be finite or infinite. The *level* of $w \in W$, denoted by $|w|$, is the distance from the root. In particular, $|r| = 0$. Equivalently, $|w| = n$ iff there is a branch $\text{BR} = w_0, w_1, \ldots, w_n, \ldots$ such that $w = w_n$. The nodes w of W such that $R(w) = \emptyset$ are called the *leaves*.

A tree $\mathcal{T} = \langle W, R \rangle$ over $\mathbb{N}$ is a tree such that W is a subset of $\mathbb{N}^*$ and if $s \cdot i \in W$, where $s \in \mathbb{N}^*$ and $i \in \mathbb{N}$, then $\langle s, s \cdot i \rangle \in R$ and $s \cdot (i - 1) \in W$ if $i > 1$.

Let X be a set. An *X-labelled tree* is a pair $\langle \mathcal{T}, f \rangle$ such that $\mathcal{T} = \langle W, R \rangle$ is a tree and f is a map $f : W \to X$. We often refer to f as a labelled tree leaving its domain implicit.

The partial orders are usually denoted by $\leq$. If $\leq$ is a partial order, then $\geq \overset{\text{def}}{=} \leq^{-1}$ and $x < y$ is an abbreviation for $x \leq y$ and $x \neq y$. $\langle W, \leq \rangle$ is a partially ordered set (or *poset*) [resp. well-ordered set] $\overset{\text{def}}{\Leftrightarrow}$ $\leq$ is a partial order [resp. well-ordering] defined on W. The *well ordering principle* says that every set can be well ordered. It is known that the axiom of choice is equivalent to the well ordering principle. A *chain* is a poset $\langle W, \leq \rangle$ such that $\leq$ is a linear order.

Let $\langle W, \leq \rangle$ be a poset and let $X \subseteq W$. An element $a \in X$ is a *maximal* [resp. *minimal*] element of X $\overset{\text{def}}{\Leftrightarrow}$ for every $x \in X$, $a \leq x$ [resp. $x \geq a$] implies $x = a$. An element $a \in X$ is the *greatest* [resp. the *least*] element of X $\overset{\text{def}}{\Leftrightarrow}$ for every $x \in X$, $x \leq a$ [resp. $a \leq x$]. The greatest [resp. the least] element is also called the *top* [resp. *bottom*] element. An element $a \in W$ is an *upper* [resp. *lower*] *bound* of $X \subseteq W \overset{\text{def}}{\Leftrightarrow}$ for every $x \in X$, $x \leq a$ [resp. $a \leq x$]. The *least upper bound* [resp. *greatest upper bound*] of X is the least [resp. greatest] element in the set of all upper [resp. lower] bounds of X. The least upper bound [resp. the greatest lower bound] of X is called *supremum* [resp. *infimum*] of X and is denoted by $sup(X)$ [resp. $inf(X)$].

Let $L = \langle W, \leq \rangle$ be a poset. A mapping $f : W \rightarrow W$ is said to be:

★ *idempotent* $\overset{\text{def}}{\Leftrightarrow} f(f(x)) = f(x)$ for every $x \in W$;

★ *extensive* $\overset{\text{def}}{\Leftrightarrow} x \leq f(x)$ for every $x \in W$;

★ *isotone* $\overset{\text{def}}{\Leftrightarrow} x \leq y$ implies $f(x) \leq f(y)$ for all $x, y \in W$;

★ *antitone* $\overset{\text{def}}{\Leftrightarrow} x \leq y$ implies $f(y) \leq f(x)$ for all $x, y \in W$;

★ a *closure operator* $\overset{\text{def}}{\Leftrightarrow} f$ is idempotent, extensive, and isotone.

If for some $x \in W$, $f(x) = x$, then x is said to be a *closed element* of W. Let $\langle W, \leq \rangle$ be a poset, then for every $x \in W$, we define $\uparrow x \overset{\text{def}}{=} \{y \in W : x \leq y\}$.

Let $L^d = \langle W, \geq \rangle$ be a poset with the order relation $\geq$. A mapping d on W is a *dual closure operator* in $L \overset{\text{def}}{\Leftrightarrow}$ it is a closure operator in L^d. A disjoint union of posets $L_1 = \langle W_1, \leq_1 \rangle$ and $L_2 = \langle W_2, \leq_2 \rangle$ is the poset $L_1 \dot{\cup} L_2 = \langle W, \leq \rangle$ such that $W = W_1 \cup W_2$ and for all $\langle x, j \rangle, \langle y, k \rangle \in W$, $j, k = 1, 2$, $\langle x, j \rangle \leq \langle y, k \rangle$ iff $j = k$, $x, y \in W_j$, and $x \leq_j y$.

1.5 Algebras

An *n-ary operation* on a set X is a function $f : X^n \rightarrow X$, $n \geq 0$. If $n = 0$, then X^0 is a set consisting of the empty string and we identify the function f with an element of X which is its unique value. A subset $Y \subseteq X$ is *closed under the operation* $f \overset{\text{def}}{\Leftrightarrow}$ for all $x_1, \ldots, x_n \in Y$, $f(x_1, \ldots, x_n) \in Y$. Let f and g be operations on X and Y, respectively, where $Y \subseteq X$. If for all $x_1, \ldots, x_n \in Y$, $f(x_1, \ldots, x_n) = g(x_1, \ldots, x_n)$, then f is an *extension* of g to X and g is a *restriction* of f to Y.

A *signature* Σ is a set of operation symbols such that with every operation symbol there is associated a natural number (including 0) expressing the arity of the operation. An *algebra* of the signature Σ is a structure $\mathcal{A} = \langle A, \Sigma^{\mathcal{A}} \rangle$, where A is a non-empty set referred to as a *carrier set* or *universe* of $\mathcal{A}$, and $\Sigma^{\mathcal{A}}$ is a set of operations on A consisting of n-ary operations $f^{\mathcal{A}}$ for every n-ary symbol $f \in \Sigma$. If $\Sigma = \{f_1, \ldots, f_k\}$, $k \geq 1$, is finite, then we write $\langle A, f_1^{\mathcal{A}}, \ldots, f_k^{\mathcal{A}} \rangle$ for $\langle A, \Sigma^{\mathcal{A}} \rangle$. We shall usually omit the superscript $\mathcal{A}$ and write $\langle A, f_1, \ldots, f_k \rangle$. An algebra is *finite* $\overset{\text{def}}{\Leftrightarrow} card(A)$ is finite and $\mathcal{A}$ is *non-degenerate* $\overset{\text{def}}{\Leftrightarrow} card(A) \geq 2$.

Two algebras are *similar* $\overset{\text{def}}{\Leftrightarrow}$ they are of the same signature. From now on, let $\mathcal{A} = \langle A, \Sigma^{\mathcal{A}} \rangle$ and $\mathcal{B} = \langle B, \Sigma^{\mathcal{B}} \rangle$ be similar algebras. $\mathcal{B}$ is a *subalgebra* of

$\mathcal{A} \overset{\text{def}}{\Leftrightarrow} B \subseteq A$ and every operation of $\mathcal{B}$ is the restriction of the corresponding operation in $\mathcal{A}$ to B. It follows that B is closed under the operations of $\mathcal{A}$.

A mapping $h : \mathcal{A} \to \mathcal{B}$ is a *homomorphism* from the algebra $\mathcal{A}$ to the algebra $\mathcal{B}$ $\overset{\text{def}}{\Leftrightarrow}$ for every n-ary operation $f \in \Sigma$ and for all $a_1, \ldots, a_n \in A$, we have $h(f^{\mathcal{A}}(a_1, \ldots, a_n)) = f^{\mathcal{B}}(h(a_1), \ldots, h(a_n))$. A homomorphism h is an *embedding* (or *monomorphism*) $\overset{\text{def}}{\Leftrightarrow}$ h is injective, and h is an *isomorphism* $\overset{\text{def}}{\Leftrightarrow}$ it is bijective. We say that the algebra $\mathcal{A}$ is *embeddable in* [resp. *isomorphic to*] the algebra $\mathcal{B}$ $\overset{\text{def}}{\Leftrightarrow}$ there is an embedding [resp. isomorphism] from $\mathcal{A}$ to $\mathcal{B}$. It follows that $\mathcal{A}$ is embeddable in $\mathcal{B}$ iff $\mathcal{A}$ is isomorphic to a subalgebra of $\mathcal{B}$.

The *(direct) product* $\mathcal{A}_1 \times \mathcal{A}_2$ of algebras $\mathcal{A}_1$ and $\mathcal{A}_2$ is the algebra whose universe is the set $A_1 \times A_2$ and for all $a_1, \ldots, a_n \in A_1$ and $b_1, \ldots, b_n \in A_2$,

$$f^{\mathcal{A}_1 \times \mathcal{A}_2}(\langle a_1, b_1 \rangle, \ldots, \langle a_n, b_n \rangle) \overset{\text{def}}{=} \langle f^{\mathcal{A}_1}(a_1, \ldots, a_n), f^{\mathcal{A}_2}(b_1, \ldots, b_n) \rangle.$$

The mapping $\Pi_i : \mathcal{A}_1 \times \mathcal{A}_2 \to \mathcal{A}_i$, $i = 1, 2$, defined by $\Pi_i(\langle a_1, a_2 \rangle) = a_i$ and $\Pi_i(f^{\mathcal{A}_1}, f^{\mathcal{A}_2}) = f^{\mathcal{A}_i}$ is called the *i*th *projection map* of $\mathcal{A}_1 \times \mathcal{A}_2$. The notions of direct product and projection map are generalised in a natural way to any indexed family $(\mathcal{A}_i)_{i \in I}$ of algebras. The product of $(\mathcal{A}_i)_{i \in I}$ is denoted by $\Pi_{i \in I} \mathcal{A}_i$. An algebra $\mathcal{A}$ is a *subdirect product* of an indexed family $(\mathcal{A}_i)_{i \in I}$ of algebras if $\mathcal{A}$ is a subalgebra of $\Pi_{i \in I} \mathcal{A}_i$ and $\Pi_i(\mathcal{A}) = \mathcal{A}_i$ for each $i \in I$. An embedding $h : \mathcal{A} \to \Pi_{i \in I} \mathcal{A}_i$ is *subdirect* if $h(\mathcal{A})$ is a subdirect product of the $(\mathcal{A}_i)_{i \in I}$. An algebra $\mathcal{A}$ is *subdirectly irreducible* if for every subdirect embedding $h : \mathcal{A} \to \Pi_{i \in I} \mathcal{A}_i$ there is an $i \in I$ such that $h; \Pi_i : \mathcal{A} \to \mathcal{A}_i$ is an isomorphism.

Theorem 1.5.1. *Every algebra is isomorphic to a subdirect product of subdirectly irreducible algebras.*

Let f be an operation on a set X and let R be an equivalence relation on X. R is a *congruence* with respect to f $\overset{\text{def}}{\Leftrightarrow}$ for all $x_1, \ldots, x_n, y_1, \ldots, y_n \in X$, if for every $i \in \{1, \ldots, n\}$, $\langle x_i, y_i \rangle \in R$, then $\langle f(x_1, \ldots, x_n), f(y_1, \ldots, y_n) \rangle \in R$. An equivalence relation R is a *congruence* on an algebra $\mathcal{A}$ $\overset{\text{def}}{\Leftrightarrow}$ it is a congruence with respect to every operation of $\mathcal{A}$.

An algebra $\mathcal{A}$ is *simple* if the only congruences on $\mathcal{A}$ are the identity relation and the universal relation. $\mathcal{A}$ is *semisimple* if it is isomorphic to a subdirect product of simple algebras.

A binary operation $\cdot$ on a set X is:

⋆ *associative* $\overset{\text{def}}{\Leftrightarrow}$ $(x \cdot y) \cdot z = x \cdot (y \cdot z)$, for all $x, y, z \in X$;
⋆ *commutative* $\overset{\text{def}}{\Leftrightarrow}$ $x \cdot y = y \cdot x$, for all $x, y \in X$;
⋆ *idempotent* $\overset{\text{def}}{\Leftrightarrow}$ $x \cdot x = x$, for all $x \in X$.

Let $+$ and $\cdot$ be binary operations on X. The operation $\cdot$ *left-distributes* over $+$ $\overset{\text{def}}{\Leftrightarrow}$ for all $x, y, z \in X$, $x \cdot (y + z) = (x \cdot y) + (x \cdot z)$. In a similar way we define *right-distributivity* of $\cdot$ over $+$, and we say that $\cdot$ *distributes* over $+$ if it both left-distributes and right-distributes over $+$. An element $e \in X$ is said to be a *zero element* [resp. *unit element*] of an algebra $\langle X, \cdot \rangle \overset{\text{def}}{\Leftrightarrow} x \cdot e = e \cdot x = e$ [resp. $x \cdot e = e \cdot x = x$] for every $x \in X$.

Let $\mathcal{A} = \langle A, \Sigma^{\mathcal{A}} \rangle$ be an algebra and let R be a congruence on $\mathcal{A}$. The algebra $\mathcal{A}/R = \langle A/R, \{f^{\mathcal{A}/R} : f \in \Sigma^{\mathcal{A}}\}\rangle$, where A/R is the family of equivalence classes of R, and

$$f^{\mathcal{A}/R}(|a_1|_R, \ldots, |a_n|_R) = |f^{\mathcal{A}}(a_1, \ldots, a_n)|_R$$

is referred to as the *quotient algebra* of $\mathcal{A}$ determined by R.

Theorem 1.5.2. *(Homomorphism Theorem) Let h be a homomorphism from an algebra $\mathcal{A}$ onto an algebra $\mathcal{B}$. Let R be a congruence on $\mathcal{A}$ induced by h: $\langle x, y \rangle \in R$ iff $h(x) = h(y)$. Then $\mathcal{A}/R$ is isomorphic to $\mathcal{B}$ and an isomorphism f is given by $f(|x|_R) = h(x)$ for every x in the universe of $\mathcal{A}$.*

Let T_0 be a set of variables and let Σ be a signature. The set T of Σ-*terms* is the smallest set such that $T_0 \subseteq T$ and if $t_1, \ldots, t_n \in T$, $n \geq 0$, and $f \in \Sigma$ is an n-ary operation symbol, then $f(t_1, \ldots, t_n) \in T$. An *identity* is an expression of the form $t_1 = t_2$, where t_1, t_2 are Σ-terms.

Let $\mathcal{A} = \langle A, \Sigma^{\mathcal{A}} \rangle$ be an algebra, and let $t(x_1, \ldots, x_n)$, $n \geq 0$, be a Σ-term such that all the variables appearing in t are among $x_1, \ldots, x_n$. We define a mapping $t^{\mathcal{A}} : A^n \to A$ as follows:

- $\star$ if t is a variable x, then $t^{\mathcal{A}}(a) \overset{\text{def}}{=} a$;
- $\star$ if t is of the form $f(t_1, \ldots, t_m)$ for $f \in \Sigma$ and $t_1, \ldots, t_m \in T$, $m \geq 0$, then $t^{\mathcal{A}}(a_1, \ldots, a_n) = f^{\mathcal{A}}(t_1^{\mathcal{A}}(a_1, \ldots, a_n), \ldots, t_m^{\mathcal{A}}(a_1, \ldots, a_n))$.

An identity $t_1(x_1, \ldots, x_n) = t_2(x_1, \ldots, x_n)$ is *true* (or holds) in $\mathcal{A}$ if for every choice of elements $a_1, \ldots, a_n$ of A, we have $t_1^{\mathcal{A}}(a_1, \ldots, a_n) = t_2^{\mathcal{A}}(a_1, \ldots, a_n)$.

1.6 Lattices

A *lattice* can be defined either as an ordered set or as an algebra. A nonempty ordered set $\langle W, \leq \rangle$ is a *lattice* $\overset{\text{def}}{\Leftrightarrow}$ for all $x, y \in W$, $sup(\{x, y\})$ and $inf(\{x, y\})$ exist. A lattice may or may not have a greatest or a least element. Simple examples of such lattices are intervals of real numbers with or without endpoints. A lattice is *bounded* $\overset{\text{def}}{\Leftrightarrow}$ it has a greatest and a least element. These elements are denoted by 1 and 0 (or $\top$ and $\bot$), respectively. A lattice is *complete* $\overset{\text{def}}{\Leftrightarrow}$ for every $X \subseteq W$, $inf(X)$ and $sup(X)$ exist. It is known that if $inf(X)$ exists in an ordered set $\langle W, \leq \rangle$ for every non-empty $X \subseteq W$, then $sup(X)$ exists in $\langle W, \leq \rangle$ for every non-empty $X \subseteq W$ which has an upper bound in W, namely $sup(X)$ is the infimum of the set of all upper bounds of X.

Lemma 1.6.1. *An ordered set in which all infima exist is a complete lattice.*

Alternatively, a lattice is an algebra $L = \langle W, +, \cdot \rangle$ with two binary operations which are associative, commutative, idempotent, and satisfy the absorption laws $(x \cdot y) + y = y$ and $x \cdot (x + y) = y$. If $\langle W, \leq \rangle$ is a lattice, then $\langle W, +, \cdot \rangle$ such that $x + y = sup(\{x, y\})$ and $x \cdot y = inf(\{x, y\})$ is a lattice. If $\langle W, +, \cdot \rangle$ is a lattice, then $\langle W, \leq \rangle$ such that $x \leq y$ iff $x + y = y$ (or equivalently $x \cdot y = y$) is a lattice. $\leq$ is referred to as a natural ordering of $\langle W, +, \cdot \rangle$. The lattice is *distributive* $\overset{\text{def}}{\Leftrightarrow}$ $\cdot$ distributes over $+$ and $+$ distributes over $\cdot$. It is known that in every lattice, $\cdot$ distributes over $+$ iff $+$ distributes over $\cdot$.

Example 1.6.1. An example of a lattice is the family of intervals of real numbers with the operations of intersection (meet) and of taking the smallest interval including the given two intervals (join).

Let $L = \langle W, +, \cdot \rangle$ be a lattice. A non-empty set $F \subseteq W$ is a *filter* of L $\overset{\text{def}}{\Leftrightarrow}$ for all $x, y \in W$, $x \cdot y \in F$ iff $x \in F$ and $y \in F$. Equivalently, F is a filter when the two following conditions are satisfied for all $x, y \in W$:

⋆ if $x, y \in F$, then $x \cdot y \in F$;
⋆ if $x \in F$ and $x \leq y$, then $y \in F$.

A non-empty set $I \subseteq W$ is an *ideal* of L $\overset{\text{def}}{\Leftrightarrow}$ for all $x, y \in W$, $x + y \in I$ iff $x \in I$ and $y \in I$. Equivalently, I is an ideal when the following two conditions are satisfied for all $x, y \in W$:

⋆ if $x, y \in I$, then $x + y \in I$;
⋆ if $y \in I$ and $x \leq y$, then $x \in I$.

The set W is both a filter and an ideal. The notion of ideal is dual, in some sense, to that of filter. In what follows, we recall some basic notions and facts concerning filters. The corresponding properties of ideals can be obtained by duality through the replacement of $+, \cdot, \leq, 1, 0$ by $\cdot, +, \geq, 0, 1$, respectively.

Let $L = \langle W, +, \cdot \rangle$ be a lattice. A filter $F(X)$ of L generated by a non-empty set $X \subseteq W$ is the least (with respect to inclusion) filter of L containing X. It follows that $F(X) = \{x \in W : \text{ there are } x_1, \ldots, x_n \in X, \text{ such that } x_1 \cdot \ldots \cdot x_n \leq x, n \geq 1\}$. A filter F of L is a *proper* filter $\overset{\text{def}}{\Leftrightarrow}$ it is a proper subset of W. If L has a bottom element 0, then a filter F is proper iff $0 \notin F$. A filter F of L is *maximal* $\overset{\text{def}}{\Leftrightarrow}$ it is proper and is not a proper subset of any proper filter of L. F is a *prime* filter $\overset{\text{def}}{\Leftrightarrow}$ it is proper and if $x + y \in F$, then either $x \in F$ or $y \in F$.

Lemma 1.6.2. *For every lattice L, the following assertions hold:*

(I) if L has a bottom element, then every proper filter of L is contained in a maximal filter;
(II) if L has a bottom element 0, then for every $x \neq 0$, there is a maximal filter F of L such that $x \in F$;
(III) if L is distributive, then every maximal filter of L is prime.

Example 1.6.2. Consider the closed unit interval $[0, 1]$ of real numbers and let a be a number satisfying $0 \leq a < 1$. Then the set $\{x : a < x \leq 1\}$ is a prime filter and $\{x : 0 < x \leq 1\}$ is a maximal filter.

Let $L = \langle W, +, \cdot \rangle$ be a lattice with a bottom element 0. The *pseudo-complement* x^* of an element $x \in W$ is the greatest element in the set $\{y \in W : x \cdot y = 0\}$. That is, we have $y \leq x^*$ iff $x \cdot y = 0$. In particular, $x \cdot x^* = 0$. Let $L = \langle W, +, \cdot \rangle$ be a lattice with a top element 1. The *dual pseudo-complement* x^+ of the element x of L is the least element in the set $\{y \in W : x + y = 1\}$. That is, we have $x^+ \leq y$ iff $x + y = 1$. In particular, $x + x^+ = 1$. It follows from these definitions that the pseudo-complement x^* and the dual pseudo-complement x^+, if they exist, are uniquely determined by x.

Let $L = \langle W, +, \cdot \rangle$ be a lattice. The *pseudo-complement of x relative to y*, denoted by $x \to y$, is the greatest element in the set $\{z \in W : x \cdot z \leq y\}$. That is, we have $z \leq x \to y$ iff $x \cdot z \leq y$. If L has a bottom element 0, then $x^* = x \to 0$. If L has a top element 1, then $x \to x$ exists and $x \to x = 1$, $x \leq y$ iff $x \to y = 1$, $1 \to y = y$. A *complement* $-x$ of x is an element that is both the pseudo-complement of x and the dual pseudo-complement of x. If a lattice L is bounded, then 0 is the complement of 1 and 1 is the complement of 0. If L is distributive, then for every $x \in L$, if $-x$ exists, then it is unique.

The following results are standard.

Lemma 1.6.3. *For every distributive lattice $L = \langle W, +, \cdot \rangle$ and for all $x, y \in W$, the following assertions hold:*

(I) if x, y have complements, then $x \leq y$ iff $-y \leq -x$;
(II) if x has the complement $-x$, then $-x$ has the complement $--x = x$;
(III) if x, y have complements, then $x + y$ and $x \cdot y$ have complements, and $-(x + y) = -x \cdot -y$ and $-(x \cdot y) = -x + -y$.

A *semilattice* is an algebra $\langle W, \cdot \rangle$ such that $\cdot$ is a binary associative, commutative, and idempotent operation. A poset $\langle W, \leq \rangle$ is a join-semilattice [resp. meet-semilattice] $\overset{\text{def}}{\Leftrightarrow}$ for all $x, y \in W$, the join $sup(\{x, y\})$ [resp. the meet $inf(\{x, y\})$] exists in W. If $\langle W, \cdot \rangle$ is a semilattice, then the condition $x \leq y$ iff $x \cdot y = y$ [resp. $x \cdot y = x$] defines a partial order on W such that $\langle W, \leq \rangle$ is a join-semilattice [resp. meet-semilattice], where $x +_{\langle W, \leq \rangle} y = x \cdot y$ [resp. $x \cdot_{\langle W, \leq \rangle} y = x \cdot y$].

Let L be a lattice with a bottom element 0. An *atom* of L is an element $x \neq 0$ such that for every y, if $0 \leq y \leq x$, then either $y = 0$ or $y = x$. L is *atomic* if for each $y \in L$, if $y \neq 0$, then there is an atom x of L such that $x \leq y$. L is *atomistic* if every $x \neq 0$ is a supremum of atoms. L is atomistic implies that L is atomic, but not conversely.

1.7 Boolean Algebras

A *Boolean algebra* is a distributive lattice such that each of its elements has a complement. This means also that every Boolean algebra has a top element and a bottom element. Hence, Boolean algebras can be understood as the structures of the form

$$\mathcal{B} = \langle W, +, \cdot, -, 1, 0 \rangle,$$

where

* $\langle W, +, \cdot \rangle$ is a distributive lattice;
* $-$ is the unary complement operation, that is $x \cdot -x = 0$ and $x + -x = 1$ for every $x \in W$;
* 1 and 0 are the elements that satisfy $x \cdot 0 = 0$ and $x + 1 = 1$ for every $x \in W$.

A natural partial order in $\mathcal{B}$ is determined by the operations, as in the corresponding lattice: for all $x, y \in W$, $x \leq y \stackrel{\text{def}}{\Leftrightarrow} x + y = y$ (or equivalently $x \cdot y = x$). It is known that a Boolean algebra is atomic iff it is atomistic. Filters in Boolean algebras have the following properties.

Lemma 1.7.1. *Let* F *be a filter of a Boolean algebra* $\mathcal{B} = \langle W, +, \cdot, -, 1, 0 \rangle$. *Then the following statements are equivalent:*

(I) F *is maximal;*
(II) F *is prime;*
(III) F *is proper and for every element* $x \in W$, *either* $x \in$ F *or* $-x \in$ F*;*
(IV) *for every* $x \in W$, *exactly one of* x *and* $-x$ *belongs to* F.

Lemma 1.7.2. *Let* F *be a filter of a Boolean algebra* $\mathcal{B} = \langle W, +, \cdot, -, 1, 0 \rangle$. *Then the following assertions hold:*

(I) *for every* $x \in W$, *the filter generated by* $F \cup \{-x\}$ *is proper iff* $x \notin$ F*;*
(II) *if* $x \notin$ F, *then there is a maximal filter* G *such that* $F \subseteq$ G *and* $x \notin$ G.

Let $\mathcal{B} = \langle W, +, \cdot, -, 1, 0 \rangle$ be a Boolean algebra. For every $X \subseteq W$, we define $-X \stackrel{\text{def}}{=} \{-x : x \in X\}$.

Lemma 1.7.3. *For every Boolean algebra* $\mathcal{B}$, *the following assertions hold:*

(I) *if* F *is a filter of* $\mathcal{B}$, *then* $-$F *is an ideal of* $\mathcal{B}$*;*
(II) *if* I *is an ideal of* $\mathcal{B}$, *then* $-$I *is a filter of* $\mathcal{B}$.

Example 1.7.1. The well known example of a Boolean algebra is the Boolean algebra $\langle \mathcal{P}(X), \cup, \cap, -, X, \emptyset \rangle$ of the subsets of a set X. The respective operations are the union, intersection, and complement of sets.

A Boolean algebra is *complete* if it is complete as a lattice. A Boolean algebra is *representable* $\stackrel{\text{def}}{\Leftrightarrow}$ it is isomorphic to a Boolean algebra of sets. It is known that every Boolean algebra is representable.

Theorem 1.7.1. *(Stone Representation Theorem) Let $\mathcal{B}$ be a Boolean algebra and let $U_{\mathcal{B}}$ be the family of the maximal filters of $\mathcal{B}$. Then $\mathcal{B}$ is isomorphic to a subalgebra of $\mathcal{P}(U_{\mathcal{B}})$. The isomorphism f is given by $f(x) = \{F \in U_{\mathcal{B}} : x \in F\}$.*

1.8 Algebras of Relations

The *full algebra of binary relations* on a set W is the structure

$$Rel(W) \stackrel{\text{def}}{=} \langle \mathcal{P}(W \times W), \cup, \cap, -, W \times W, \emptyset, ;, ^{-1}, Id_W \rangle,$$

where $\langle \mathcal{P}(W \times W), \cup, \cap, -, W \times W, \emptyset \rangle$ is the Boolean algebra of subsets of $W \times W$, ; and $^{-1}$ are the relational operations of composition and converse, respectively, and Id_W is the identity relation on W. Every subalgebra of $Rel(W)$ is referred to as an algebra of binary relations on W.

Lemma 1.8.1. *For all relations R and R' in $Rel(W)$ the following conditions are satisfied (1 stands for $W \times W$):*

(I) $R \neq 1$ iff $1; (-R); 1 = 1$,
(II) $R = 1$ or $R' = 1$ iff $1; -(1; (-R); 1); 1 \cup R' = 1$,
(III) $R = 1$ implies $R' = 1$ iff $1; (-R); 1 \cup R' = 1$.

A generalisation of algebras of binary relations is provided by the notion of relation algebra. A *relation algebra* is a structure of the form

$$\langle W, +, \cdot, 1, 0, ;, ^{-1}, 1' \rangle,$$

where

(1) $\langle W, +, \cdot, 1, 0 \rangle$ is a Boolean algebra,
(2) ; is an associative binary operation that distributes over $+$,
(3) $^{-1}$ is an unary operation that distributes over $+$ and satisfies $(x^{-1})^{-1} = x$ and $(x; y)^{-1} = y^{-1}; x^{-1}$,
(4) $1'; x = x; 1' = x$,
(5) for all $x, y, z \in W$ the following equalities are equivalent:

$$(x; y) \cdot z = 0, \quad (x^{-1}; z) \cdot y = 0, \quad (z; y^{-1}) \cdot x = 0.$$

Let RA be the class of relation algebras. Every algebra of binary relations is in RA. A relation algebra is said to be *representable* $\stackrel{\text{def}}{\Leftrightarrow}$ it is isomorphic to a product of algebras of binary relations. It is known that not every member of the class RA is representable.

1.9 Notes

An introductory exposition of the mathematical concepts and facts useful for reading this monograph can be found in [Ras73]. [BS81] is a useful introduction to universal algebra. The basic information about lattices and Boolean algebras can be found in [RS63, BS81]. The theory of lattices is presented in [Bir84, BD74]. The comprehensive exposition of the theory of Boolean algebras can be found in [Mon89]. An introduction to the calculus of relations and a theory of relation algebras is presented in [Tar41]. A survey of the theory can be found in [Jón82, Mad97].

Part I

Structures with Incomplete Information

2. Structures of Information

2.1 Introduction and Outline of the Chapter

Different application areas use different conceptual means for representation of information about the domains they deal with. It can be observed that a great variety of informational structures and data employ the notions of "object" and "property" as the most elementary pieces of information. Often the notion of property is split into two components: an attribute and its value. These notions are fundamental, for example in the theory of databases. Similarly, it is well established in cognitive science and logic that an analysis of concepts is based on these notions. A concept is determined by its extension (or denotation) and intension (or connotation). The extension of a concept consists of the objects that are instances of this concept and the intension of a concept consists of the properties that are characteristic for the objects to which this concept applies. In this chapter we present several structures of information that employ "object" and "property" as their basic notions.

In Sect. 2.2 we present the notion of information systems with incomplete information and we briefly discuss several examples of such systems. Information systems are the fundamental informational structures dealt with in the book. All the results presented in the subsequent chapters of the book are focused on developing concepts and methods for reasoning about or computing with information from an information system. In the remaining sections of this chapter we present other structures for representing incomplete information and we compare them with information systems. In Sect. 2.3 we discuss property systems and their relationship to consequence systems. It is shown that a similar relationship holds between information systems and bi-consequence systems. In Sect. 2.4 we discuss formal contexts. They are the informational structures underlying formal concept analysis. In Sect. 2.5 we show that decision tables can be understood as information systems with an additional attribute having a special status of a decision. In Sect. 2.6 we present a general form of structures with information which forms a hierarchy having the form of a tree. Subject classification systems are typical examples of such information representations. We show how hierarchical information can be represented as a family of information systems. The specific features of those information systems inspire some developments of the subsequent chapters. In Sect. 2.7 we introduce the notion of fuzzy information system. The range of fuzziness is modelled by the class of double residuated lattices.

2.2 Information Systems

Information systems are collections of information items that have the form of descriptions of some objects in terms of their properties. More formally, an *information system* is a structure of the form

$$\langle OB, AT, (VAL_a)_{a \in AT}, f \rangle,$$

where OB is a non-empty set of *objects*, AT is a non-empty set of *attributes*, VAL_a is a non-empty set of *values* of the attribute a, and f is a total function $OB \times AT \to \bigcup_{a \in AT} \mathcal{P}(VAL_a)$ such that for every $\langle x, a \rangle \in OB \times AT$, $f(x, a) \subseteq VAL_a$. We shall often use the more concise notation

$$\langle OB, AT \rangle$$

instead of $\langle OB, AT, (VAL_a)_{a \in AT}, f \rangle$. With that short notation, each attribute $a \in AT$ is considered as a map $a : OB \to \mathcal{P}(VAL_a)$ that assigns subsets of values to objects. If we need a direct reference to the ranges of the attributes, we write $\langle OB, AT, (VAL_a)_{a \in AT} \rangle$ for an information system in question. Although the shorthand $\langle OB, AT \rangle$ suggests that $OB \cap AT$ is empty (a map cannot take itself as an argument), in a structure $\langle OB, AT, (VAL_a)_{a \in AT}, f \rangle$, $OB \cap AT \cap \bigcup \{VAL_a : a \in AT\}$ is not necessarily empty.

An information system $\langle OB, AT \rangle$ is *total* [resp. *deterministic*] $\stackrel{\text{def}}{\Leftrightarrow}$ for every $a \in AT$ and for every $x \in OB$, $f(x, a) \neq \emptyset$ [resp. $\text{card}(f(x, a)) \leq 1$]. If S is not deterministic then it is said to be *non-deterministic*. If $a(x)$ is a singleton set, say $\{v\}$, then we often omit the parentheses and we write $a(x) = v$. In the literature, information systems are also called *attribute systems* or *A-systems*.

Let A be a subset of attributes. The set of *A-deterministic* objects is defined as follows:

$$D(A) \stackrel{\text{def}}{=} \{x \in OB : \text{card}(a(x)) \leq 1 \text{ for every } a \in A\}.$$

The set $D(AT)$ is referred to as the set of *deterministic objects* of the information system S. So S is deterministic iff $D(AT) = OB$.

Every set $a(x)$ can be viewed as the given set of properties of an object x corresponding to the attribute a. For example, if the attribute a is "colour" and $a(x) = \{green\}$, then x possesses the property of "being green". If a is "age" and x is 25 years old, then $a(x) = \{25\}$ and this means that x possesses the property of "being 25 years old". If a is "languages spoken" and if a person x speaks, say, Polish (Pl), German (D), and French (F), then $a(x) =$

$\{Pl, D, F\}$, and x possesses the properties of "speaking Polish", "speaking German", and "speaking French". In this setting any set $a(x)$ is referred to as the set of *a-properties* of the object x and its complement $VAL_a \setminus a(x)$ is said to be the set of *negative a-properties* of x. If in an information system S for some object x and some attribute a the set $a(x)$ is empty, then it may be interpreted as the fact that a-properties of x are unknown in S. This is one possible interpretation that is often used in practice.

Example 2.2.1. Consider a simple file presented in Table 2.1.

	Colour
x_1	Green
x_2	Green
x_3	Blue
x_4	Blue
x_5	Red

Table 2.1. Simple file

In this file we have $OB = \{x_1, \ldots, x_5\}$, $AT = \{colour\}$, and $VAL_{colour} = \{green, blue, red\}$.

A description of an object of the form (attribute, a subset of values) may have several intuitive meanings. For instance, if the age of a person is known approximately, say, to be between 20 and 25, then this information may be represented as the pair $\langle age, \{20, \ldots, 25\}\rangle$. In this case the given subset of values provides a non-deterministic description of the age of object x in the disjunctive sense: the age of x equals one of the numbers between 20 and 25. With another interpretation a pair (attribute, a subset of values) can be viewed as conjunctive information, as in the following example.

Example 2.2.2. In Table 2.2 we consider a file containing information about the degrees of some persons $P_1, \ldots, P_6$ and the languages that these persons speak.

	Language	Degree
P_1	$\{F, D\}$	$\{BS, MS, PhD\}$
P_2	$\{H, R\}$	$\{BS\}$
P_3	$\{F, D, S\}$	$\{BS, MS\}$
P_4	$\{F\}$	$\{BS, MS\}$
P_5	$\{F, D\}$	$\{BS\}$
P_6	$\{R\}$	$\{BS\}$

Table 2.2. Degrees and languages

In that file we are given a set $OB = \{P_1, ..., P_6\}$ of objects. Properties of these objects are of the form "having some degree" and "speaking some language". "Degree" and "language" play the role of attributes; they determine these properties, that is, each of the properties can be expressed by an attribute and a value of this attribute. Hence, we have the set $AT = \{Degree\ (Deg), Language\ (Lan)\}$ of attributes, and the sets

$$VAL_{Deg} = \{BS, MS, PhD\}, \quad VAL_{Lan} = \{D, F, H, R, S\}$$

of values of these attributes. According to the information given in our file, the object P_2 possesses properties $\{H, R\}$ of speaking Hungarian and Romanian; the object P_3 does not possess those properties. Since the attributes are treated as mappings $a : OB \rightarrow \mathcal{P}(VAL_a)$ from the set of objects into the family of subsets of their values, we may write, for example, $Lan(P_2) = \{H, R\}$. This set is also the set of negative Lan-properties of P_3.

The content of an information system does not enable us to distinguish between conjunctive and disjunctive interpretation of sets of properties attributed to the objects. All the developments of this book are general enough to be meaningful for either one of these interpretations.

In some systems of knowledge representation and data analysis the pairs of the form (attribute, set of values) are referred to as *symbolic objects*.

Example 2.2.3. Consider a file from the catalogue of sleeping bags presented in Table 2.3, where F, T, W, P, M denote fabricator, minimal temperature in degrees Celsius, weight in grams, price in DM and material, respectively. This file is an information system whose objects are listed in the first column, and the subsequent columns are labelled with attributes and contain the values of these attributes, respectively.

Suppose we are interested in bags that are filled with either goose-downs or duck-downs and whose price is between 250 and 400 DM. Then one of the steps of the information processing method based on symbolic objects is to adjoin to the given file an object x, referred to as a symbolic object, with $M(x) = \{\text{goose-downs, duck-downs}\}$, $P(x) = \{250, ..., 400\}$, and $a(x) = VAL_a$ for the remaining attributes $a \in \{F, T, W\}$. The resulting structure is a non-deterministic information system.

An information system $S = \langle OB, AT \rangle$ is said to be *A-separable* for $A \subseteq AT \overset{\text{def}}{\Leftrightarrow}$ for every $a \in A$ and for all $v, v' \in VAL_a$ (for every $x \in OB$, $v \in a(x)$ iff $v' \in a(x)$) iff $v = v'$. The information system S is said to be *separable* $\overset{\text{def}}{\Leftrightarrow}$ S is AT-separable.

For every pair $\langle W, V \rangle$ such that W is a non-empty set and $V \subseteq \mathcal{P}(\mathcal{P}(W))$, the *set-theoretical information system* $S = \langle OB, AT \rangle$ under $\langle W, V \rangle$ is the information system defined as follows:

	F	T	W	P	M
One Kilo Bag	Wolfskin	7	940	149	Litelof
Sund	Kodiak	3	1880	139	Hollow fibre
Kompakt Basic	Ajungilak	0	1280	249	MTI Loft
Finmark Tour	Finmark	0	1750	179	Hollow fibre
Interlight Lyx	Caravan	0	1900	239	Thermolite
Kompakt	Ajungilak	-3	1490	299	MTI Loft
Touch the Cloud	Wolfskin	-3	1550	299	Liteloft
Cat's Meow	The North Face	-7	1450	339	Polarguard
Igloo Super	Ajungilak	-7	2060	279	Terraloft
Donna	Ajungilak	-7	1850	349	MTI Loft
Tyin	Ajungilak	-15	2100	399	Ultraloft
Travellers Dream	Yeti	3	970	379	Goose-downs
Yeti Light	Yeti	3	800	349	Goose-downs
Climber	Finmark	-3	1690	329	Duck-downs
Viking	Warmpeace	-3	1200	369	Goose-downs
Eiger	Yeti	-3	1500	419	Goose-downs
Climber Light	Finmark	-7	1380	349	Goose-downs
Cobra	Ajungilak	-7	1460	449	Duck-downs
Cobra Comfort	Ajungilak	-10	1820	549	Duck-downs
Foxfire	The North Face	-10	1390	669	Goose-downs
Mont Blanc	Yeti	-15	1800	549	Goose-downs

Table 2.3. Catalogue of sleeping bags

$\star$ $OB \stackrel{\text{def}}{=} W$;

$\star$ $AT \stackrel{\text{def}}{=} \{at^X : X \in V\}$, where $at^X : W \to \mathcal{P}(\mathcal{P}(W))$ and for every $x \in V$ $at^X(x) \stackrel{\text{def}}{=} \{Y : Y \in X, \ x \in Y\}$.

A set-theoretical information system $\langle OB, AT \rangle$ under $\langle W, V \rangle$ is sometimes denoted by $\langle W, V \rangle$ itself. Set-theoretical information systems play an important role in Chap. 13.

The notion of information system is very general and many structures of information can be viewed as its instances. In Sects. 2.3, 2.4, 2.5, and 2.6 we present various information structures known in the literature and we show how they are related to the information systems defined above.

2.3 Property Systems

A *property system* (P-system) is a structure of the form

$$S = \langle OB, PR, f \rangle,$$

where OB is a non-empty set of objects, PR is a non-empty set of properties (here the properties are not necessarily expressed in terms of attributes and their values), and $f : OB \to \mathcal{P}(PR)$ is a mapping that assigns sets of properties to objects.

Any property system S and the information system $\langle OB, AT \rangle$ such that $AT = \{f\}$ and $VAL_f = PR$ provide the same information about objects from OB. It is a usual practice to identify a property with the set of objects that possess this property. To reflect this intuition, for a given P-system $S = \langle OB, PR, f \rangle$, we define the P-system $/S/ = \langle OB_{/S/}, PR_{/S/}, f_{/S/} \rangle$ as follows:

$\star$ $OB_{/S/} \stackrel{\text{def}}{=} OB$;
$\star$ $PR_{/S/} \stackrel{\text{def}}{=} \{/v/ : v \in PR\}$, where $/v/ \stackrel{\text{def}}{=} \{x \in OB : v \in f(x)\}$;
$\star$ $f_{/S/}(x) \stackrel{\text{def}}{=} \{/v/ : x \in /v/ \in PR_{/S/}\}$.

The following fact follows from the given definition.

Lemma 2.3.1. *For every P-system $S = \langle OB, PR, f \rangle$, for every $x \in OB$, and for every $v \in PR$, $v \in f(x)$ iff $/v/ \in f_{/S/}(x)$.*

Hence, an object x possesses a property v in the P-system S iff x possesses the property $/v/$ in the system $/S/$, and $/v/$ coincides with the set of objects that possess the property v.

In the following, we present a relationship between property systems and broadly understood logical systems.

Definition 2.3.1. *A consequence system (C-system) is a pair*

$$S = \langle Sen, \vdash \rangle,$$

where Sen is a non-empty set whose elements are referred to as sentences and $\vdash$ is a binary relation on the set $\mathcal{P}_f(Sen)$ of finite subsets of Sen, referred to as a consequence relation, and satisfying the following conditions. For all $X, X', Y, Y' \in \mathcal{P}_f(Sen)$ and for every $x \in Sen$:

(1) if $X \cap Y \neq \emptyset$, then $X \vdash Y$ (reflexivity);
(2) if $X \vdash Y$, $X \subseteq X'$, and $Y \subseteq Y'$, then $X' \vdash Y'$ (monotonicity);
(3) if $X \vdash Y \cup \{x\}$ and $\{x\} \cup X \vdash Y$, then $X \vdash Y$ (cut).

Given a P-system $S = \langle OB, PR, f \rangle$, we construct a C-system $C(S) \stackrel{\text{def}}{=} \langle Sen_{C(S)}, \vdash_{C(S)} \rangle$ as follows:

$\star$ $Sen_{C(S)} \stackrel{\text{def}}{=} OB$;
$\star$ for all finite subsets $X = \{a_1, \ldots, a_m\}$ and $Y = \{b_1, \ldots, b_n\}$ of OB, $n, m \geq 0$, $X \vdash_{C(S)} Y \stackrel{\text{def}}{\Longleftrightarrow} f(a_1) \cap \ldots \cap f(a_m) \subseteq f(b_1) \cup \ldots \cup f(b_n)$.

For $m = 0$ [resp. $n = 0$], we adopt the convention that $f(a_1) \cap \ldots \cap f(a_m) = PR$ [resp. $f(b_1) \cup \ldots \cup f(b_n) = \emptyset$]. It is easy to verify that $C(S)$ is a C-system. It is referred to as a *C-system over S*.

Lemma 2.3.2. *For every P-system S, $C(S) = C(/S/)$.*

It follows that every property system may be considered as a certain C-system whose consequence relation is determined by the properties of the objects in the following way: a set Y of objects is a consequence of a set X of objects whenever the properties that are shared by all the objects from X are possessed by some objects from Y.

Conversely, given a C-system $S = \langle Sen, \vdash \rangle$, we construct a P-system $P(S) \stackrel{\text{def}}{=} \langle OB_{P(S)}, PR_{P(S)}, f_{P(S)} \rangle$ as follows:

* $OB_{P(S)} \stackrel{\text{def}}{=} Sen$;
* $PR_{P(S)} \stackrel{\text{def}}{=} \{X \subseteq Sen : \text{ for all } Y, Z \in \mathcal{P}_f(Sen), \text{ if } Y \vdash Z \text{ and } Y \subseteq X, \text{ then } Z \cap X \neq \emptyset\}$;
* for every $x \in OB_{P(S)}$, $f_{P(S)}(x) \stackrel{\text{def}}{=} \{X \in PR_{P(S)} : x \in X\}$.

Theorem 2.3.1. *For every C-system S, $S = C(P(S))$.*

The above theorem provides a kind of informational representation of consequence systems. It says that every consequence system can be constructed over a certain property system.

Now let us take as a starting point a property system $S = \langle OB, PR, f \rangle$, and consider the property system $P(C(S))$. By the respective definitions, $OB_{P(C(S))} = OB$. The following theorem provides a relationship between S and $P(C(S))$.

Theorem 2.3.2. *For every P-system $S = \langle OB, PR, f \rangle$, for every $x \in OB$, and for every $v \in PR$, we have $v \in f(x)$ iff $/v/ \in f_{P(C(/S/))}(x)$.*

A natural question arises whether there is a relationship between information systems and consequence systems. It is known that information systems are related to *bi-consequence systems*.

Definition 2.3.2. *A bi-consequence system (B-system) is a triple*

$$S = \langle Sen, \vdash, |\sim \rangle,$$

where $\langle Sen, \vdash \rangle$ is a C-system and $|\sim$ is a binary relation on the set $\mathcal{P}_f(Sen)$ of finite subsets of Sen, referred to as a weak consequence relation, and satisfying the following conditions. For all $X, X', Y, Y' \in \mathcal{P}_f(Sen)$ and for every $x \in Sen$:

(1) if $X \cap Y \neq \emptyset$, then $X |\sim Y$ (reflexivity);
(2) if $X |\sim Y$, $X \subseteq X'$, and $Y \subseteq Y'$, then $X' |\sim Y'$ (monotonicity);
(3) if $X |\sim Y \cup \{x\}$ and $\{x\} \cup X |\sim Y$, then $X |\sim Y$ (cut);
(4) if $X \cup \{x\} \vdash Y$ and $X |\sim \{x\} \cup Y$, then $X |\sim Y$;
(5) if $X \vdash Y$, then $X |\sim Y$.

Observe that in a B-system $S = \langle Sen, \vdash, |\!\sim\rangle$, both $\langle Sen, \vdash\rangle$ and $\langle Sen, |\!\sim\rangle$ are C-systems.

Example 2.3.1. Let $(\langle Sen, \vdash_i\rangle)_{i \in I}$ be a family of C-systems sharing the set of sentences. We define $\vdash$ and $|\!\sim$ on $\mathcal{P}_f(Sen)$ as follows:

* $X \vdash Y \overset{\text{def}}{\Leftrightarrow}$ for every $i \in I$, $X \vdash_i Y$;
* $X |\!\sim Y \overset{\text{def}}{\Leftrightarrow}$ for some $i \in I$, $X \vdash_i Y$.

The structure $\langle Sen, \vdash, |\!\sim\rangle$ is a B-system.

The relationships between information systems and bi-consequence systems are analogous to those between property systems and consequence systems.

Let $S = \langle OB, AT, (VAL_a)_{a \in AT}, f\rangle$ be an information system. We define the information system

$$\backslash S\backslash = \langle OB_{\backslash S\backslash}, AT_{\backslash S\backslash}, (VAL_{\backslash S\backslash, b})_{a \in AT_{\backslash S\backslash}}, f_{\backslash S\backslash}\rangle$$

determined by S in the following way. For every $a \in AT$ and for every $v \in VAL_a$, define $g_a(v) \overset{\text{def}}{=} \{x \in OB : v \in f(x, a)\}$. Let $\backslash a\backslash \overset{\text{def}}{=} \{g_a(v) : v \in VAL_a\}$. Then:

* $OB_{\backslash S\backslash} \overset{\text{def}}{=} OB$;
* $AT_{\backslash S\backslash} \overset{\text{def}}{=} \{\backslash a\backslash : a \in AT\}$;
* $VAL_{\backslash S\backslash, \backslash a\backslash} \overset{\text{def}}{=} \backslash a\backslash$;
* $f_{\backslash S\backslash}(x, \backslash a\backslash) \overset{\text{def}}{=} \{X \in \backslash a\backslash : x \in X\}$.

Lemma 2.3.3. *For all $x \in OB$, $a \in AT$, and $v \in VAL_a$, we have $v \in f(x, a)$ iff $g_a(v) \in f_{\backslash S\backslash}(x, \backslash a\backslash)$.*

Hence, the systems $\backslash S\backslash$ and S provide the same information, in a sense, about their objects.

Let $S = \langle OB, AT, (VAL_a)_{a \in AT}, f\rangle$ be an information system. We construct the bi-consequence system $B(S) = \langle Sen_{B(S)}, \vdash_{B(S)}, |\!\sim_{B(S)}\rangle$ as follows:

* $Sen_{B(S)} \overset{\text{def}}{=} OB$;
* for all finite subsets $X = \{x_1, \ldots, x_n\}$ and $Y = \{y_1, \ldots, y_m\}$ of OB, $n, m \geq 0$, we define the respective consequence relations:
    * $X \vdash_{B(S)} Y \overset{\text{def}}{\Leftrightarrow}$ for every $a \in AT$, $f(x_1, a) \cap \ldots \cap f(x_n, a) \subseteq f(y_1, a) \cup \ldots \cup f(y_m, a)$;
    * $X |\!\sim_{B(S)} Y \overset{\text{def}}{\Leftrightarrow}$ there is an $a \in AT$ such that $f(x_1, a) \cap \ldots \cap f(x_n, a) \subseteq f(y_1, a) \cup \ldots \cup f(y_m, a)$.

It is easy to verify that $B(S)$ is a bi-consequence system.

Lemma 2.3.4. *For every information system S, $B(S) = B(\backslash S\backslash)$.*

Given a B-system $S = \langle Sen, \vdash, |\sim \rangle$, we construct the information system $A(S) = \langle OB_{A(S)}, AT_{A(S)}, (VAL_{A(S),a})_{a \in AT_{A(S)}}, f_{A(S)} \rangle$ as follows:

* $OB_{A(S)} \overset{\text{def}}{=} Sen$;
* $AT_{A(S)} \overset{\text{def}}{=} \{a \subseteq \mathcal{P}(Sen) :$ for all $X, Y \in \mathcal{P}_f(Sen)$, if $X \vdash Y$ then there is a $Z \in a$ such that $X \subseteq Z$ implies $Y \cap Z \neq \emptyset$, and if $X |\sim Y$ then there is a $Z \in a$ such that $X \subseteq Z$ and $Y \cap Z = \emptyset\}$;
* $VAL_{A(S),a} \overset{\text{def}}{=} a$;
* $f_{A(S)}(x, a) \overset{\text{def}}{=} \{X \in a : x \in X\}$.

Theorem 2.3.3. *For every B-system S, $S = B(A(S))$.*

Now let $S = \langle OB, AT, (VAL_a)_{a \in AT}, f \rangle$ be an information system, and consider the system $A(B(S))$. We clearly have $OB = OB_{A(B(S))}$.

Theorem 2.3.4. *For all $x \in OB$, $a \in AT$, and $v \in VAL_a$, we have $v \in f(x, a)$ iff $g_a(v) = f_{A(B(S))}(x, \backslash a \backslash)$.*

2.4 Formal Contexts

A *formal context* is a structure of the form

$$C = \langle G, M, I \rangle,$$

where G and M are non-empty sets whose elements are interpreted as objects and features, respectively, and $I \subseteq G \times M$ is a binary relation. If $g \in G$, $m \in M$ and $\langle g, m \rangle \in I$, then the object g is said to have the feature m. If G is finite, then the relation I can be naturally represented as a matrix $(c_{\langle g,m \rangle})_{g \in G, m \in M}$ such that the rows and the columns are labelled with objects and features, respectively, and if $\langle g, m \rangle \in I$, then $c_{\langle g,m \rangle} = 1$, otherwise $c_{\langle g,m \rangle} = 0$.

In the theory of formal contexts the following two mappings $i : \mathcal{P}(G) \to \mathcal{P}(M)$ and $e : \mathcal{P}(M) \to \mathcal{P}(G)$ play important roles. For all $X \subseteq G$ and $Y \subseteq M$ we define:

* $i(X) \overset{\text{def}}{=} \{y \in M : \langle x, y \rangle \in I$, for every $x \in X\}$;
* $e(Y) \overset{\text{def}}{=} \{x \in G : \langle x, y \rangle \in I$, for every $y \in Y\}$.

$i(X)$ and $e(Y)$ are referred to as the *intent* of X and the *extent* of Y, respectively.

Lemma 2.4.1. *For all $X, X_1, X_2 \subseteq G$ and $Y, Y_1, Y_2 \subseteq M$, the following conditions are satisfied:*

(I) if $X_1 \subseteq X_2$, then $i(X_2) \subseteq i(X_1)$;
(II) $X \subseteq e(i(X))$;
(III) if $Y_1 \subseteq Y_2$, then $e(Y_2) \subseteq e(Y_1)$;
(IV) $Y \subseteq i(e(Y))$.

Each formal context can be viewed as a deterministic information system. Given a formal context $C = \langle G, M, I \rangle$, we define the information system $\langle OB, AT, (VAL_a)_{a \in AT}, f \rangle$ determined by C as follows:

* $OB \stackrel{\text{def}}{=} G$;
* $AT \stackrel{\text{def}}{=} M$;
* for every $a \in AT$ and for every $x \in OB$, $f(x, a) \stackrel{\text{def}}{=} \{1\}$ if $\langle x, a \rangle \in I$, otherwise $f(x, a) \stackrel{\text{def}}{=} \{0\}$.

Following the terminology of formal contexts, attributes whose sets of values are included in $\{0, 1\}$ are referred to as *features*.

Sometimes, a formal context can be represented as an information system with a set of attributes smaller than M.

Example 2.4.1. Consider the following formal context. Let G be the set of planets G = {Mercury (Me), Venus (V), Earth (E), Mars (Ma), Jupiter (J), Saturn (Sa), Uranus (U), Neptune (N), Pluto (P)}. The set M of features is {small size, medium size, large size, near to Sun, far from Sun, having a Moon, no Moon}. The relation I is represented in Table 2.4.

	Size			Distance from Sun		Moon	
	Small	Medium	Large	Near	Far	Yes	No
Me	1	0	0	1	0	0	1
V	1	0	0	1	0	0	1
E	1	0	0	1	0	1	0
Ma	1	0	0	1	0	1	0
J	0	0	1	0	1	1	0
Sa	0	0	1	0	1	1	0
U	0	1	0	0	1	1	0
N	0	1	0	0	1	1	0
P	1	0	0	0	1	1	0

Table 2.4. Planets

This formal context can be represented as the following information system. The set AT of attributes consists of three attributes: D = "distance from the Sun", S = "size", and M = "possession of a Moon". The values of the attribute D are "near" and "far", the values of the attribute S are "small", "medium", "large", and the values of the attribute M are "yes", "no". The respective information system is given in Table 2.5.

In Sect. 3.6 we discuss relationships between features and arbitrary attributes in a formal way. There is also an inverse relationship between contexts and information systems, namely every information system determines a context such that both structures provide the same information about the underlying objects. For a given information system $\langle OB, AT \rangle$, we define the

	S	D	M
Me	Small	Near	No
V	Small	Near	No
E	Small	Near	Yes
Ma	Small	Near	Yes
J	Large	Far	Yes
S	Large	Far	Yes
U	Medium	Far	Yes
N	Medium	Far	Yes
P	Small	Far	Yes

Table 2.5. Planets (bis)

context $C = \langle OB \times OB, AT, I \rangle$, where $\langle \langle x, y \rangle, a \rangle \in I$ iff $a(x) = a(y)$ for all $x, y \in OB$ and $a \in AT$. Then we have the following lemma.

Lemma 2.4.2. *For every $A \subseteq AT$ and for every $R \subseteq OB \times OB$ we have:*

(I) $e(A) = \{\langle x, y \rangle : a(x) = a(y)$ for every $a \in A\}$;
(II) $i(R) = \{a \in AT : R \subseteq \{\langle x, y \rangle : a(x) = a(y)\}\}$.

Every formal context $\langle G, M, I \rangle$ can also be viewed as a property system $\langle G, M, f \rangle$ such that $f(g) = \{m \in M : \langle g, m \rangle \in I\}$ for every $g \in G$. Conversely, given a property system $\langle OB, PR, f \rangle$, the system $\langle OB, PR, I \rangle$ such that $\langle x, p \rangle \in I$ iff $p \in f(x)$, for every $x \in OB$ and every $p \in PR$, is a formal context.

2.5 Decision Tables and Decision Rules

A *decision table* is an information system

$$\langle OB, AT \cup \{d\}, (VAL_a)_{a \in AT}, VAL_d, f \rangle$$

with a special attribute d adjoined, referred to as a *decision attribute*. Usually, it is assumed that $d(x)$ is a singleton set for every object x. The values $d(x)$ are referred to as decisions. The attributes from AT are referred to as condition attributes.

Example 2.5.1. Consider the (decision) Table 2.6.
    In this table, "not green" stands for $VAL_{colour} \setminus \{green\}$.

Every row of a decision table determines a decision rule. Assume that $AT = \{a_1, \ldots, a_n\}$, $n \geq 1$. By the rule determined by an object $x \in OB$, we mean the following statement:

r_x: for every y, if the value of a_1 for y is $f(x, a_1)$ and ... and the value of a_n for y is $f(x, a_n)$, then decide $d(x)$.

	Colour	Size	d (select)
x_1	Green	Small	Yes
x_2	Not green	Small	Yes
x_3	Blue	medium	No

Table 2.6. Colour and size

We abbreviate such a rule as follows:

$$\langle a_1, f(x, a_1)\rangle \& \ldots \& \langle a_n, f(x, a_n)\rangle \to d(x).$$

Hence, the rules are statements determining a decision that depends on the properties of objects.

Example 2.5.2. The rules determined by the table from Example 2.5.1 are:

r_{x_1}: $\langle colour, green\rangle \& \langle size, small\rangle \to$ select;
r_{x_2}: $\langle colour, not\ green\rangle \& \langle size, small\rangle \to$ select;
r_{x_3}: $\langle colour, blue\rangle \& \langle size, medium\rangle \to$ do not select.

We will use this example in Sect. 3.8 for explaining the reduction of decision rules in the framework of information systems.

We say that a decision table is *inconsistent* $\overset{\text{def}}{\Leftrightarrow}$ it contains two objects x and y such that $a(x) = a(y)$ for every $a \in AT$ and $d(x) \neq d(y)$. Otherwise, the table is *consistent*. Hence, inconsistency appears whenever under the same conditions we could make two different decisions.

2.6 Hierarchical Information

A typical example of hierarchical information is a subject classification system.

Example 2.6.1. Consider a part of a subject classification system.

1 Computing Methodologies
  1.1 Algebraic Manipulation
    1.1.1 Algorithms
      1.1.1.1 Algebraic Algorithms
      1.1.1.2 Analysis of Algorithms
    1.1.2 Languages and Systems
      1.1.2.1 Evaluation Strategies
      1.1.2.2 Non-procedural Languages
      1.1.2.3 Special-purpose Hardware
  1.2 Artificial Intelligence
    1.2.1 Applications and Expert Systems

This system consists of keywords grouped into classes in such a way that each class is given a name which is a keyword more general than its members. Such a classification system can be viewed as an X-labelled tree $\mathcal{T}^l = \langle \langle W, R \rangle, f \rangle$, where $\mathcal{T} = \langle W, R \rangle$ is a tree over $\mathbb{N}$ and

$$X = \{ \text{ ``Computing Methodologies'', ``Algebraic Manipulation'', } \dots \}.$$

For instance, $f(1.2.1) = $ "Applications and Expert Systems".

Hierarchical information has the form of a finite tree. In the general case, let $\mathcal{T}^l = \langle \langle W, R \rangle, f \rangle$ be a X-labelled tree for some set X of labels such that W is finite. We write $\mathcal{T}$ to denote the tree $\langle W, R \rangle$. Any such X-labelled tree can be represented as a family of information systems in the following way. For the sake of simplicity assume that all the branches in the tree are of the same length. Let $|\mathcal{T}|$ be the length of the branches of $\mathcal{T}$, that is to say, every branch of $\mathcal{T}$ has exactly $|\mathcal{T}| + 1$ nodes. The X-labelled tree $\mathcal{T}^l$ determines a family of $|\mathcal{T}|$ information systems, referred to as systems of degree $i = 1, \dots, |\mathcal{T}|$. The set OB_1 of the objects of the system of the lowest degree 1 consists of the leaves of $\mathcal{T}_1$. Its attributes are subsets of leaves such that each of these subsets is the set of children of a node of level $|\mathcal{T}| - 1$ in the tree. They can be identified with the membership functions of these subsets. The objects of the systems of any higher degree, say i, are the attributes of the system of degree $i - 1$, and a is an attribute of the system of degree i iff it is a member of $\mathcal{P}^i(OB_1)$ and there is a node of level $|\mathcal{T}| - i$ in $\mathcal{T}$ whose children coincide with the elements of a. More precisely, we have:

⋆ OB_1 is the set of leaves of $\mathcal{T}^l$, that is the nodes of level $|\mathcal{T}^l|$;
⋆ for every $i \geq 1$, $AT_i \subseteq \mathcal{P}^i(OB_1)$, $a(x) \stackrel{\text{def}}{=} 1$ if $x \in a$, otherwise $a(x) = 0$ and $a \in AT_i$ iff there is a node of level $|\mathcal{T}| - i$ in $\mathcal{T}$ whose children coincide with the elements of a;
⋆ for every $i > 1$, $OB_i \stackrel{\text{def}}{=} AT_{i-1}$.

The information provided by an information system of a higher index is less detailed and hence, in a sense, more abstract. Consequently, an arrangement of data into a hierarchy of information systems enables us to organise a process of information retrieval with a varying degree of detail. Hierarchical information is a motivation for considering information systems whose attributes are not necessarily individuals, but elements of a powerset hierarchy. Those information systems are the basis for the developments of Sects. 3.9, 3.10, and 5.4.

2.7 Fuzzy Information Systems

All the information structures presented in the preceding sections are based on crisp sets, whose membership function is two-valued. In this section we present the notion of fuzzy information systems, based on a concept of fuzzy sets. The original formulation of fuzzy sets is based on the generalised notion of a membership function. Namely, the membership function of a fuzzy set X is a mapping $f_X : X \to [0, 1]$, that is a degree of membership of an object to a fuzzy set is a real number from the unit interval. For defining the membership function of the union and intersection of fuzzy sets, the unit interval is equipped with the two operations referred to as a triangular norm (t-norm) and a triangular conorm (t-conorm). In a more general setting, the ranges of a membership function are sets of elements of various algebraic systems. All of these algebras are situated between the class of lattices additionally equipped with a structure of a monoid, and Boolean algebras. The monoid operator is an abstract counterpart of the t-norm. The counterpart of the t-conorm is usually defined as an operator dual to the monoid operator, but this is not general enough for capturing the class of t-conorms. In this section we present a class of double residuated lattices, where both t-norm and t-conorm receive an abstract counterpart. This class of algebras provides an arithmetic of degrees of fuzziness, and as a consequence a general concept of a fuzzy set can be defined. Based on such a notion of a fuzzy set we introduce in this section a generalisation of information systems to fuzzy information systems. Next, in Sect. 3.11 and Sect. 4.11 we discuss fuzzy information relations and fuzzy information operators derived from fuzzy information systems.

A *monoid* is a structure of the form

$$\langle W, \circ, e \rangle,$$

where W is a non-empty set, $\circ$ is an associative binary operation on W, and e is the unit element.

A *double residuated lattice* is a structure of the form

$$\langle W, +, \cdot, \odot, \rightarrow, \oplus, \leftarrow, 1, 0 \rangle,$$

where

(1) $\langle W, +, \cdot, 1, 0 \rangle$ is a lattice with the top element 1 and the bottom element 0 and with the natural ordering $\leq$;
(2) $\langle W, \odot, 1 \rangle$ and $\langle W, \oplus, 0 \rangle$ are monoids;
(3) $\odot$ and $\oplus$ are commutative;
(4) $\rightarrow$ is a *residuum* of $\odot$, that is $z \leq x \rightarrow y$ iff $x \odot z \leq y$ for all $x, y, z \in W$;
(5) $\leftarrow$ is a *dual residuum* of $\oplus$, that is $x \leftarrow y \leq z$ iff $y \leq x \oplus z$ for all $x, y, z \in W$.

The operations $\odot$ and $\oplus$ are referred to as *product* and *sum*, respectively. Condition (4) is referred to as a *residuation condition* and condition (5) is a *dual residuation condition*. Clearly $\rightarrow$ and $\leftarrow$ are uniquely determined by the residuation condition and the dual residuation condition, respectively. Furthermore, it follows from these conditions that $x \rightarrow y$ is the greatest element in the set $\{z : x \odot z \leq y\}$ and $x \leftarrow y$ is the least element in the set $\{z : y \leq x \oplus z\}$.

We shall use the following operations definable in terms of monoid operators and their residua:

$$\neg x \overset{\text{def}}{=} x \rightarrow 0, \qquad \ulcorner x \overset{\text{def}}{=} x \leftarrow 1.$$

They are generalisations of the pseudo-complement and the dual pseudo-complement defined in Sect. 1.6.

Double residuated lattices are the weakest structures that provide an algebraic framework for degrees of membership to fuzzy sets and, in a more general setting, degrees of certainty of assertions in fuzzy theories. The other classes of algebras may be obtained from the double residuated lattices by postulating some additional axioms. A double residuated lattice is linearly ordered if its natural ordering is linear, which means that $x \cdot y = x$ or $x \cdot y = y$ for all x, y (or equivalently $x + y = x$ or $x + y = y$).

We list some properties of the operations in double residuated lattices.

Lemma 2.7.1. *In every double residuated lattice* $\langle W, +, \cdot, \odot, \rightarrow, \oplus, \leftarrow, 1, 0 \rangle$ *for all* $x, y, z \in W$ *the following conditions hold:*

(I) $x \odot (x \rightarrow y) \leq y,$ $\qquad\qquad y \leq x \oplus (x \leftarrow y);$
(II) $y \leq x \rightarrow (x \odot y),$ $\qquad\qquad x \leftarrow (x \oplus y) \leq y;$
(III) $x \leq y$ *iff* $x \rightarrow y = 1$ *iff* $y \leftarrow x = 0;$
(IV) $z \leq x \rightarrow y$ *iff* $x \leq z \rightarrow y,$ $\quad x \leftarrow y \leq z$ *iff* $z \leftarrow y \leq x.$

Proof. (I) and (II) follow from the residuation condition and the dual residuation condition, respectively and reflexivity of $\leq$.

(III) Let $x \leq y$. It follows that $1 \odot x \leq y$. By the residuation condition the latter is equivalent to $1 \leq x \rightarrow y$. Similarly, by the assumption we get $x \leq y \oplus 0$. By the dual residuation condition $y \leftarrow x \leq 0$, and hence $y \leftarrow x = 0$.

(IV) follows directly from the residuation and dual residuation conditions. Q.E.D.

Lemma 2.7.2. *In every double residuated lattice* $\langle W, +, \cdot, \odot, \rightarrow, \oplus, \leftarrow, 1, 0 \rangle$ *for all* $x, y, z \in W$ *the following conditions hold:*

(I) if $x \leq y$, *then* $y \# z \leq x \# z$ *and* $z \# x \leq z \# y$ *for* $\# = \rightarrow, \leftarrow$;
(II) $1 \rightarrow x = x$, $x \rightarrow 1 = 1$, $x \rightarrow x = 1$, $0 \rightarrow x = 1$;
(III) $0 \leftarrow x = x$, $x \leftarrow 0 = 0$, $x \leftarrow x = 0$, $1 \leftarrow x = 0$;
(IV) if $x \leq y$, *then* $x \# z \leq y \# z$ *and* $z \# x \leq z \# y$ *for* $\# = \odot, \oplus$.

Proof. (IV) Let $x \leq y$, then by Lemma 2.7.1(II) and transitivity of $\leq$ we have $x \leq z \rightarrow (y \odot z)$. By the residuation condition we obtain $x \odot z \leq y \odot z$. Observe that since $\odot$ is commutative, we also have $z \odot x \leq z \odot y$. For the operation $\oplus$ the proof is similar.   Q.E.D.

Lemma 2.7.3. *In every double residuated lattice* $\langle W, +, \cdot, \odot, \rightarrow, \oplus, \leftarrow, 1, 0 \rangle$ *for all* $x, y, z \in W$ *the following conditions hold:*

(I) $x \odot y \leq x \cdot y$, $x + y \leq x \oplus y$;
(II) $y \leq x \rightarrow y$, $x \leftarrow y \leq y$;
(III) $x \odot (x \rightarrow y) \leq x \cdot y$, $x + y \leq x \oplus (x \leftarrow y)$;
(IV) $x \odot x = 1$ *iff* $x = 1$, $x \oplus y = 0$ *iff* $x = 0$;
(V) $(x \odot y) \rightarrow z = x \rightarrow (y \rightarrow z)$, $(x \oplus y) \leftarrow z = x \leftarrow (y \leftarrow z)$;
(VI) $(x \rightarrow y) \odot (y \rightarrow z) \leq (x \rightarrow z)$, $(x \leftarrow z) \leq (x \leftarrow y) \oplus (y \leftarrow z)$.

Proof. (I) We prove the second assertion. By Lemma 2.7.2(III) we have $x \leftarrow x \leq y$. By the dual residuation condition we obtain $x \leq x \oplus y$. In a similar way we get $y \leq x \oplus y$. Hence, $x + y \leq x \oplus y$.

(VI) We prove the second assertion. By associativity of $\oplus$ and Lemma 2.7.1(I) we have: $x \oplus ((x \leftarrow y) \oplus (y \leftarrow z)) = (x \oplus (x \leftarrow y)) \oplus (y \rightarrow z) \geq y \oplus (y \leftarrow z) \geq z$. By the dual residuation condition we get $x \leftarrow z \leq (x \leftarrow y) \oplus (y \leftarrow z)$. Q.E.D.

The following lemma shows how the monoid operators and their residua act with the lattice operations.

Lemma 2.7.4. *In every double residuated lattice* $\langle W, +, \cdot, \odot, \rightarrow, \oplus, \leftarrow, 1, 0 \rangle$ *for all* $x, y, z \in W$ *the following conditions hold:*

(I) $x \odot (y + z) = (x \odot y) + (x \odot z)$, $x \oplus (y \cdot z) = (x \oplus y) \cdot (x \oplus z)$;
(II) $x \rightarrow (y \cdot z) = (x \rightarrow y) \cdot (x \rightarrow z)$, $x \leftarrow (y + z) = (x \leftarrow y) + (x \leftarrow z)$;
(III) $(x + y) \rightarrow z = (x \rightarrow z) \cdot (y \rightarrow z)$, $(x \cdot y) \leftarrow z = (x \leftarrow z) + (y \leftarrow z)$;
(IV) $(x \rightarrow z) + (y \rightarrow z) \leq (x \cdot y) \rightarrow z$, $(x + y) \leftarrow z \leq (x \leftarrow z) \cdot (y \leftarrow z)$;
(V) $(x \rightarrow y) + (x \rightarrow z) \leq x \rightarrow (y + z)$, $x \leftarrow (y \cdot z) \leq (x \leftarrow y) \cdot (x \leftarrow z)$.

Proof. (II) We prove the second assertion.

($\leq$) Since $x \leftarrow y \leq (x \leftarrow y) + (x \leftarrow z)$ and $x \leftarrow z \leq (x \leftarrow y) + (x \leftarrow z)$, by the dual residuation condition we get $y \leq x \oplus ((x \leftarrow y) + (x \leftarrow z))$ and $z \leq x \oplus ((x \leftarrow y) + (x \leftarrow z))$. It follows that $y + z \leq x \oplus ((x \leftarrow y) + (x \leftarrow z))$. Using the dual residuation condition again, we obtain $x \leftarrow (y + z) \leq (x \leftarrow y) + (x \leftarrow z)$.

($\geq$) Since $y \leq y + z$ and $z \leq y + z$, by Lemma 2.7.2(I) we get $x \leftarrow y \leq x \leftarrow (y + z)$ and $x \leftarrow z \leq x \leftarrow (y + z)$. It follows that $(x \leftarrow y) + (x \leftarrow z) \leq x \leftarrow (y + z)$.

The following lemma presents the properties of the complement operators.

Lemma 2.7.5. *In every double residuated lattice* $\langle W, +, \cdot, \odot, \rightarrow, \oplus, \leftarrow, 1, 0 \rangle$ *for all* $x, y, z \in W$ *the following conditions hold:*

(I)   *if* $x \leq y$, *then* $\neg y \leq \neg x$ *and* $^\ulcorner y \leq {^\ulcorner x}$;

(II) $x \odot \neg x = 0$, $x \oplus {^\ulcorner x} = 1$;

(III) $x \leq \neg\neg x$, $^{\ulcorner\ulcorner} x \leq x$;

(IV) $x \rightarrow y \leq \neg y \rightarrow \neg x$, $^\ulcorner x \leftarrow {^\ulcorner y} \leq y \leftarrow x$.

Proof. (I) follows from Lemma 2.7.2(I). (II) follows from Lemma 2.7.1(I). (III) follows from (II) and the residuation and dual residuation conditions, respectively.

(IV) By Lemma 2.7.1(I), we have $x \odot (x \rightarrow y) \leq y$. By Lemma 2.7.2(IV), $(x \odot (x \rightarrow y)) \odot \neg y \leq y \odot \neg y = 0$. Due to associativity and commutativity of product we get $(x \odot \neg y) \odot (x \rightarrow y) \leq 0$. By the residuation condition we obtain $(x \rightarrow y) \leq (x \odot \neg y) \rightarrow 0$. In view of Lemma 2.7.3(V), we have $(x \rightarrow y) \leq \neg y \rightarrow (x \rightarrow 0) = \neg y \rightarrow \neg x$. The proof of the second condition is similar.   *Q.E.D.*

A double residuated lattice $\langle W, +, \cdot, \odot, \rightarrow, \oplus, \leftarrow, 1, 0 \rangle$ is complete if the lattice $\langle W, +, \cdot, 1, 0 \rangle$ is complete. In a complete double residuated lattice $x \rightarrow y = sup(\{z \in W : x \odot z \leq y\})$ and $x \leftarrow y = inf(\{z \in W : y \leq x + z\})$. In what follows we write $inf_i\ x_i$ [resp. $sup_i\ x_i$] instead of $inf(\{x_i : i \in I\})$ [resp. $sup(\{x_i : i \in I\})$], where I is any set of indices.

The following lemma shows how the join and meet operations act with the elements of the form $sup_i\ x_i$ and $inf_i\ x_i$.

Lemma 2.7.6. *In every double residuated lattice* $\langle W, +, \cdot, \odot, \rightarrow, \oplus, \leftarrow, 1, 0 \rangle$ *for all indexed families* $(x_i)_{i \in I}$ *and* $(y_i)_{i \in I}$ *of elements of* W, *and for every* $z \in W$ *if the respective infima and suprema exist, then the following assertions hold:*

(I)   *if* $x_i \leq y_i$ *for every* $i \in I$, *then* $sup_i\ x_i \leq sup_i\ y_i$ *and* $inf_i\ x_i \leq inf_i\ y_i$;

(II) $sup_i\ (z \cdot x_i) \leq z \cdot sup_i\ x_i$, $z + inf_i\ x_i \leq inf_i\ (z + x_i)$;

(III) $sup_i\ (z + x_i) = z + sup_i\ x_i$, $inf_i\ (z \cdot x_i) = z \cdot inf_i\ x_i$;

(IV) $z + inf_i\ x_i \leq inf_i\ (z + x_i)$, $sup_i\ (z \cdot x_i) \leq z \cdot sup_i\ x_i$;

(V) $sup_i\ (x_i + y_i) = sup_i\ x_i + sup_i\ y_i$, $inf_i\ (x_i \cdot y_i) = inf_i\ x_i \cdot inf_i\ y_i$.

Proof. (III) We prove the second assertion. Since for every i, $z \cdot inf_i \, x_i \leq z \cdot x_i$, we get $z \cdot inf_i \, x_i \leq inf_i \, (z \cdot x_i)$. Moreover, $z \cdot x_i \leq z$ and $z \cdot x_i \leq x_i$ for every i. Hence, $inf_i \, (z \cdot x_i) \leq z$ and $inf_i \, (z \cdot x_i) \leq inf_i \, x_i$. We conclude that $inf_i \, (z \cdot x_i) \leq z \cdot inf_i \, x_i$.

(IV) Since for every i, $z + inf_i \, x_i \leq z + x_i$, we get $z + inf_i \, x_i \leq inf_i \, (z + x_i)$. The proofs of the remaining conditions are similar.   *Q.E.D.*

Lemma 2.7.7. *In every double residuated lattice* $\langle W, +, \cdot, \odot, \rightarrow, \oplus, \leftarrow, 1, 0 \rangle$ *for all indexed families* $(x_i)_{i \in I}$ *and* $(y_i)_{i \in I}$ *of elements of* W, *and for every* $z \in W$ *if the respective infima and suprema exist then the following assertions hold:*

(I) $sup_i \, (x_i \odot z) = (sup_i \, x_i) \odot z$, $inf_i \, (x_i \oplus z) = (inf_i \, x_i) \oplus z$;
(II) $(inf_i \, x_i) \odot z \leq inf_i \, (x_i \odot z)$, $sup_i \, (x_i \oplus z) \leq (sup_i \, x_i) \oplus z$.

Proof. (I) We prove the first assertion. By Lemma 2.7.2(IV), $x_i \odot z \leq (sup_i \, x_i) \odot z$. Therefore, $sup_i \, (x_i \odot z) \leq (sup_i \, x_i) \odot z$. Furthermore, for every i, $x_i \odot z \leq sup_i \, (x_i \odot z)$. By the residuation condition we get $x_i \leq z \rightarrow sup_i \, (x_i \odot z)$. This implies $sup_i \, x_i \leq z \rightarrow sup_i \, (x_i \odot z)$. Applying the residuation condition we obtain $(sup_i \, x_i) \odot z \leq sup_i \, (x_i \odot z)$.
The proofs of the remaining conditions are similar.   *Q.E.D.*

Lemma 2.7.8. *In every double residuated lattice* $\langle W, +, \cdot, \odot, \rightarrow, \oplus, \leftarrow, 1, 0 \rangle$ *for all indexed families* $(x_i)_{i \in I}$ *and* $(y_i)_{i \in I}$ *of elements of* W, *and for every* $z \in W$ *if the respective infima and suprema exist then the following assertions hold:*

(I) $inf_i \, (z \rightarrow x_i) = z \rightarrow inf_i \, x_i$, $z \leftarrow sup_i \, x_i = sup_i \, (z \leftarrow x_i)$;
(II) $inf_i \, (x_i \rightarrow z) = sup_i \, x_i \rightarrow z$, $inf_i \, x_i \leftarrow z = sup_i \, (x_i \leftarrow z)$;
(III) $sup_i \, (z \rightarrow x_i) \leq z \rightarrow sup_i \, x_i$, $z \leftarrow inf_i \, x_i \leq inf_i \, (z \leftarrow x_i)$;
(IV) $sup_i \, (x_i \rightarrow z) \leq inf_i \, x_i \rightarrow z$, $sup_i \, x_i \leftarrow z \leq inf_i \, (x_i \leftarrow z)$;
(V) $sup_i \, x_i \leq \neg inf_i \, \neg x_i$, $^\ulcorner sup_i \, ^\ulcorner x_i \leq inf_i \, x_i$;
(VI) $\neg sup_i \, x_i = inf_i \, \neg x_i$, $^\ulcorner inf_i \, x_i = sup_i \, ^\ulcorner x_i$.

Proof. (I) We show the second equality.
($\leq$) By Lemma 2.7.1(I), we have $x_i \leq z \oplus (z \leftarrow x_i)$ for every i. Hence, $sup_i \, x_i \leq sup_i \, (z \oplus (z \leftarrow x_i))$. By Lemma 2.7.7(IV), we have $sup_i \, (z \oplus (z \leftarrow x_i)) \leq sup_i \, (z \leftarrow x_i) \oplus z$. Hence, $sup_i \, x_i \leq sup_i \, (z \leftarrow x_i) \oplus z$. By the dual residuation condition, we get $z \leftarrow sup_i \, x_i \leq sup_i \, (z \leftarrow x_i)$.
($\geq$) Since for every i, $x_i \leq sup_i \, x_i$, by Lemma 2.7.2(I), we get $z \leftarrow x_i \leq z \leftarrow sup_i \, x_i$. Hence, $sup_i \, (z \leftarrow x_i) \leq z \leftarrow sup_i \, x_i$.

(II) We show the first equality.
($\leq$) $inf_i \, (x_i \rightarrow z) \leq x_i \rightarrow z$ for every i. By Lemma 2.7.1(IV), we get $x_i \leq inf_i \, (x_i \rightarrow z) \rightarrow z$ for every i. It follows that $sup_i \, x_i \leq inf_i \, (x_i \rightarrow z) \rightarrow z$. Applying again Lemma 2.7.1(IV) we get $inf_i \, (x_i \rightarrow z) \leq sup_i \, x_i \rightarrow z$.
($\geq$) Since for every i, $x_i \leq sup_i \, x_i$, by Lemma 2.7.2(I), we get $sup_i \, x_i \rightarrow z \leq x_i \rightarrow z$ for every i. Therefore $sup_i \, x_i \rightarrow z \leq inf_i \, (x_i \rightarrow z)$.

(IV) By Lemma 2.7.3(V) we have (i) $(sup_i \; (x_i \to z)) \odot inf_i \; x_i = sup_i \; (x_i \to z) \odot inf_k \; x_k$. Since the product is isotone, we obtain $(x_i \to z) \odot inf_k \; x_k \leq (x_i \to z) \odot x_i$ for every i. So $sup((x_i \to z)) \odot inf_k \; x_k \leq sup_i \; (x_i \to z) \odot x_i = sup_i \; (x_i \odot (x_i \to z)) \leq z$ by Lemma 2.7.1(I). Hence, by (i) we get $(sup_i \; (x_i \to z)) \odot inf_i \; x_i \leq z$. By the residuation condition, $sup_i \; (x_i \to z) \leq inf_i \; x_i \to z$.
(V) We show the second condition. Since for every i, $x_i \leftarrow 1 \leq sup_i \; (x_i \leftarrow 1)$, by the dual residuation condition we get $sup((x_i \leftarrow 1)) \leftarrow 1 \leq x_i$ for every i. Hence, $sup_i \; (x_i \leftarrow 1) \leftarrow 1 \leq inf_i \; x_i$.
The proofs of the remaining conditions are similar.   *Q.E.D.*

Now we show that the converse inequalities in Lemma 2.7.8(IV) do not hold. Consider a lattice such that $+ = \oplus = max$, $\odot = \cdot = min$, and $x \to y = 1$ if $x \leq y$, otherwise $x \to y = y$. Consider a sequence $(x_i)_{i \in \mathbb{N}}$ such that $x_i = 1/2 + 1/2^i$. Clearly, $inf_i \; x_i = 1/2$. We also have $inf(x_i) \to 1/2 = 1/2 \to 1/2 = 1$. However, we have $x_i \to 1/2 = 1/2$ for every i. So $sup_i \; (x_i \to 1/2) = 1/2$. Then we have $sup_i \; (x_i \to 1/2) = 1/2 < 1 = inf_i \; x_i \to 1/2$. To obtain a counterexample for the second part we take $y \leftarrow x = 0$ if $x \leq y$ and $y \leftarrow x = x$ otherwise, and the family $(x_i)_{i \in \mathbb{N}}$ such that $x_i = 1/2 - 1/2^i$.

Given a double residuated lattice $L = \langle W, +, \cdot, \odot, \to, \oplus, \leftarrow, 1, 0 \rangle$ and a universe U of objects, any mapping $X : U \to L$ is an *L-fuzzy subset* of U. The family of L-fuzzy subsets of U is denoted by $\mathcal{F}_L \mathcal{P}(U)$. By a *fuzzy set* we mean an L-fuzzy set for some double residuated lattice L. The operations on L-fuzzy sets are defined in the following way, for all $X, Y \in \mathcal{F}_L \mathcal{P}(U)$ and for every $x \in U$:

$(\neg_L X)(x) \stackrel{\text{def}}{=} \neg X(x);$
$(\ulcorner_L X)(x) \stackrel{\text{def}}{=} \ulcorner X(x);$
$(X \cup_L Y)(x) \stackrel{\text{def}}{=} X(x) \oplus Y(x);$
$(X \cap_L Y)(x) \stackrel{\text{def}}{=} X(x) \odot Y(x).$

The empty fuzzy set $\emptyset_L$ is defined as $\emptyset_L(x) = 0$ for every $x \in U$. L-inclusion and L-equality of L-fuzzy sets are defined as follows:

$X \subseteq_L Y \stackrel{\text{def}}{\Leftrightarrow}$ for every $x \in U$, $X(x) \leq Y(x);$
$X =_L Y \stackrel{\text{def}}{\Leftrightarrow} X \subseteq_L Y$ and $Y \subseteq_L X.$

L-fuzzy sets X and Y are *L-compatible* $\stackrel{\text{def}}{\Leftrightarrow}$ there is an $x \in U$ such that $X(x) \odot Y(x) = 1$ and *L-exhaustive* $\stackrel{\text{def}}{\Leftrightarrow}$ for every $x \in U$, $X(x) \oplus Y(x) = 1$.

Typical examples of monoid operators which play an important role in the fuzzy set theory are t-norms and t-conorms. A *t-norm* is a mapping $* : [0,1]^2 \to [0,1]$ satisfying the following conditions:

(1) $*$ is commutative and associative;

(2) $*$ is isotone in both arguments, that is if $x_1 \leq x_2$, then $x_1 * y \leq x_2 * y$ and if $y_1 \leq y_2$, then $x * y_1 \leq x * y_2$, where $\leq$ is the natural ordering of reals;

(3) for every $x \in [0,1]$, $1 * x = x$.

A *t-conorm* is a mapping $\bullet : [0,1]^2 \rightarrow [0,1]$ satisfying the following conditions:

(1) $\bullet$ is commutative and associative;
(2) $\bullet$ is isotone in both arguments;
(3) for every $x \in [0,1]$, $0 \bullet x = 0$.

A t-norm is left-continuous [resp. right-continuous] if it is continuous as a one-argument function of its left [resp. right] argument.

Lemma 2.7.9.

(I) A t-norm has a residuum iff it is left-continuous and a t-conorm has a dual residuum iff it is right-continuous;

(II) if $*$ is a left-continuous t-norm and $\bullet$ is a right-continuous t-conorm, then the structure $L = \langle [0,1], +, \cdot, *, \rightarrow, \bullet, \leftarrow, 1, 0 \rangle$ such that $\rightarrow$ is the residuum of $*$, $\leftarrow$ is a dual residuum of $\bullet$, $x \cdot y = min(x, y)$, and $x + y = max(x, y)$ is a double residuated lattice;

(III) in the lattice L from (II), the identities $(x \rightarrow y) + (y \rightarrow x) = 1$, $(x \leftarrow y) \cdot (y \leftarrow x) = 0$, $x + y = ((x \rightarrow y) \rightarrow y) \cdot ((y \rightarrow x) \rightarrow x)$, and $x \cdot y = ((x \leftarrow y) \leftarrow y) + ((y \leftarrow x) \leftarrow x)$ hold;

(IV) if $*$ is a continuous t-norm, then the identity $x * (x \rightarrow y) = x \cdot y$ holds in the lattice L from (II);

(V) if $\bullet$ is a continuous t-conorm, then the identity $x \bullet (x \leftarrow y) = x + y$ holds in the lattice from (II).

The smallest t-norm is the function defined as:

$$x * y \stackrel{\text{def}}{=} \begin{cases} x \text{ if } y = 1; \\ y \text{ if } x = 1; \\ 0 \text{ otherwise.} \end{cases}$$

The greatest t-norm is the function defined as $x * y = min(x, y)$. The other typical examples include the Lukasiewicz t-norm defined as $x * y = max(0, x + y - 1)$, and the multiplication of reals.

The smallest t-conorm is the maximum operation. The greatest t-conorm is defined as:

$$x \bullet y \stackrel{\text{def}}{=} \begin{cases} x \text{ if } y = 0; \\ y \text{ if } x = 0; \\ 1 \text{ otherwise.} \end{cases}$$

The Lukasiewicz t-conorm is defined as $x \bullet y = min(1, x + y)$.

Now we introduce the notion of a fuzzy information system which is a generalisation of the notion of information system presented in Sect. 2.2. In fuzzy information systems objects are characterised in terms of fuzzy properties.

A *fuzzy information system* is a structure of the form

$$\langle OB, L, AT, (VAL_a)_{a \in AT} \rangle,$$

where OB is a non-empty set of objects, L is a double residuated lattice, and every attribute $a \in AT$ is a mapping $a : OB \to \mathcal{F}_L \mathcal{P}(VAL_a)$ which assigns an L-fuzzy subset of VAL_a to an object. Intuitively, $a(x)(v)$ is a degree to which an object x assumes the value v of the attribute a. In Sects. 3.11 and 4.11 we present information relations and information operators derived from fuzzy information systems.

2.8 Notes

Information systems. The notion of (deterministic) information system employed in this book is introduced in [Paw82]. Non-deterministic information systems are introduced in [Lip76, Lip79]. Every non-deterministic information system can be viewed as a generalisation of a relational database where, first, the tuples may be strings of sets of values of attributes, not necessarily of single values and, second, a database relation is a multi-set of generalised tuples rather than a set. Such a generalisation is motivated, on the one hand, by the need to model incompleteness of information and, on the other hand, by recent needs for modelling multi-media information. A distinction between various forms of non-determinism in information systems such that the sets of values of attributes in the generalised tuples receive various interpretations, for example conjunctive (all the values from the given set are attributed to the respective object) or disjunctive (some values from the given set are attributed to the respective object) is discussed in [DGO01]. Generalised tuples can be useful in modelling multi-media databases, where the characteristics of objects may have a variety of forms. For that purpose some additional structures in sets of values of attributes under consideration should be assumed relevant to the type of the attributes.

Property systems. The notion of P-systems is introduced in [Vak98]. In the early papers on information systems they are defined as attribute systems; however, the name "attribute system" appeared for the first time in [Vak98]. The content of Sect. 2.3 is based on that paper and the proofs of all the theorems can be found there. C-systems satisfy the standard Scott's axioms and similar structures are introduced in [Sco82] (see also [DP90a]).

Contexts. The notion of context and the theory of concept analysis in contexts were originated in [Wil82]. A discussion of relationships between formal contexts and information systems as well as the related methods of data analysis can be found in [Pag93, Pag98, Ken93]. Example 2.4.1 is from [Wil82].

Decision tables. An origin of techniques and applications of decision tables can be found in [Mon74]. Decision tables understood as information systems are presented in [Paw85, Paw87, Paw91]. Various problems relevant to decision tables, for example discretisation of continuous attributes, grouping of symbolic values of attributes, searching for classifiers, and generation of decision rules, have also been studied in relation to information systems with incomplete information; for a comprehensive survey see [PSe99].

Algebraic structures of fuzziness. The theory of fuzzy sets originated in [Zad65] and since then fuzzy logic has been a well established and rapidly developing field of research with a great variety of practical applications. The notions of t-norm and t-conorm are introduced in [SS83]. A generalisation of fuzzy sets to the sets whose membership functions are lattice-valued is due to [Gou67]. Residuated lattices of the form $\langle W, +, \cdot, \odot, \backslash, /, 1, 0, e \rangle$ where $\langle W, +, \cdot, 1, 0 \rangle$ is a lattice, $\langle W, \odot, e \rangle$ is a monoid such that its unit element e is not necessarily an element of the lattice and $\odot$ is not necessarily commutative, $/$ and $\backslash$ are the residua of $\odot$, that is $x/y = sup(\{z \in W : x \odot z \leq y\})$ and $x \backslash y = sup(\{z \in W : z \odot x \leq y\})$ were introduced in [WD39]. If the monoid operation is commutative, then the two residua coincide. Residuated lattices with a commutative monoid operation and its residuum are investigated in [Höh96]. In [EG01] a survey of fuzzy logics is presented. Double residuated lattices are introduced and investigated in [OR01]. A logic based on double residuated Heyting algebras is investigated in [Rau74].

Fuzzy information system. The concept of fuzzy information systems considered in this section is a generalisation of the notion of information system introduced in [RK01a]. In that paper the range of fuzziness is the real interval $[0, 1]$, while here we use double residuated lattices. Another version of the notion of fuzzy information system which is a generalisation of deterministic information systems is presented in [Orło99].

3. Information Relations Derived from Information Systems

3.1 Introduction and Outline of the Chapter

In this chapter we explore information that is not explicitly given in an information system but can be derived from its content. This information reflects relationships among objects of the information system and has the form of relations determined by the attributes from the system. Each relation is referred to as an information relation. These relations are intended to reflect either the differentiation or separation of objects, or the similarity or sameness of objects. In both cases the respective relations are obtained from information about the attributes of objects; no external information is used.

In Sect. 3.2 we present two families of information relations reflecting the two types of features of objects mentioned above. In Sect. 3.3 we discuss properties of these relations. The remaining sections indicate various applications of the given relations. In Sect. 3.4 we show how properties of objects in an information system can be expressed using indiscernibility relations derived from the system. Sect. 3.5 is devoted to the representation of database dependencies in terms of indiscernibility relations. We show that several dependencies considered in database theory, like functional dependencies, multivalued dependencies, etc., can be uniformly represented with indiscernibility relations. We also present some natural generalisations of those dependencies. The generalisations employ the indiscernibility relations as a principal tool. Sect. 3.6 is devoted to the study of the processes of decomposition and contraction of attributes. We discuss how these two processes influence the indiscernibility relations determined by the respective attributes. Sect. 3.7 explains the role of diversity relations in the algorithms for finding reducts of sets of attributes. Sect. 3.8 indicates the application of complementarity relations in the algorithms for the simplification of decision rules and for the reduction of sets of rules. Sect. 3.9 presents the notion of relative relation. This notion was introduced in connection with relations derived from an information system as defined in Sect. 3.2. Each of these relations is determined by a set of attributes. Hence, any means of representing these relations must be capable of expressing both which objects are related and with respect to which attributes they are related. Therefore, any relative relation is defined, first, by specifying a set of pairs of objects which are related; hence, it is a usual binary relation and, second, by specifying a set of parameters representing the attributes with respect to which the objects are related. By saying that a relation is relative we mean that it is determined relative to the specified parameters. In this section we also present several properties specific to relative relations. They are referred to as global conditions, since they are relevant not to a single relation but to the whole family of relations determined by subsets of a set of parameters. In Sect. 3.10 we present the classes of systems with relative relations, referred to as relative frames, that are intended to be the abstract counterparts of families of relations derived from information systems. The classes are defined by sets of local and global conditions. In Sect. 3.11 we present the notions of fuzzy relation and fuzzy relative relation. Then, we define some fuzzy information relations derived from a fuzzy information system.

3.2 Information Relations

Any information system $S = \langle OB, AT \rangle$ contains some implicit information about relationships among the objects from the set OB. These relationships are determined by the properties of objects. Typically, the relationships have the form of binary relations. They are referred to as information relations derived from the information system S. There are two major groups of information relations: the relations that reflect various forms of indistinguishability of objects in terms of their properties and the relations that indicate distinguishability of the objects. Below we present a list of the classes of atomic relations that generate a whole family of *information relations*. To each of these classes we assign a name that suggests the intuitive meaning and/or the role of the respective relations.

Now we present a list of *indistinguishability relations* derived from an information system. The relations reflect various kinds of "sameness" of objects. Let $S = \langle OB, AT \rangle$ be an information system. For every $A \subseteq AT$, we define the following binary relations on OB:

* the *strong* [resp. *weak*] *indiscernibility relation* $ind(A)$ [resp. $wind(A)$] is a relation such that for all $x, y \in OB$, $\langle x, y \rangle \in ind(A)$ [resp. $\langle x, y \rangle \in wind(A)$] $\overset{\text{def}}{\Leftrightarrow}$ for all [resp. some] $a \in A$, $a(x) = a(y)$;
* the *strong* [resp. *weak*] *similarity relation* $sim(A)$ [resp. $wsim(A)$] is a relation such that for all $x, y \in OB$, $\langle x, y \rangle \in sim(A)$ [resp. $\langle x, y \rangle \in wsim(A)$] $\overset{\text{def}}{\Leftrightarrow}$ for all [resp. some] $a \in A$, $a(x) \cap a(y) \neq \emptyset$;
* the *strong* [resp. *weak*] *forward inclusion relation* $fin(A)$ [resp. $wfin(A)$] is a relation such that for all $x, y \in OB$, $\langle x, y \rangle \in fin(A)$ [resp. $\langle x, y \rangle \in wfin(A)$] $\overset{\text{def}}{\Leftrightarrow}$ for all [resp. some] $a \in A$, $a(x) \subseteq a(y)$;
* the *strong* [resp. *weak*] *backward inclusion relation* $bin(A)$ [resp. $wbin(A)$] is a relation such that for all $x, y \in OB$, $\langle x, y \rangle \in bin(A)$ [resp. $\langle x, y \rangle \in wbin(A)$] $\overset{\text{def}}{\Leftrightarrow}$ for all [resp. some] $a \in A$, $a(y) \subseteq a(x)$;

⋆ the *strong* [resp. *weak*] *negative similarity relation* $nim(A)$
  [resp. $wnim(A)$] is a relation such that for all $x, y \in OB$, $\langle x, y \rangle \in nim(A)$
  [resp. $\langle x, y \rangle \in wnim(A)$] $\overset{\text{def}}{\Leftrightarrow}$ for all [resp. some] $a \in A$, $-a(x) \cap -a(y) \neq \emptyset$
  where $-$ is the complement with respect to VAL_a;
⋆ the *strong* [resp. *weak*] *incomplementarity relation* $icom(A)$
  [resp. $wicom(A)$] is a relation such that for all $x, y \in OB$, $\langle x, y \rangle \in icom(A)$
  [resp. $\langle x, y \rangle \in wicom(A)$] $\overset{\text{def}}{\Leftrightarrow}$ for all [resp. some] $a \in A$, $a(x) \neq -a(y)$.

If A is a singleton, then the respective strong and weak relations coincide.
Intuitively, two objects are A-indiscernible whenever their sets of a-properties
determined by the attributes $a \in A$ are the same. In other words, up to dis-
criminative resources provided by properties determined by A, these objects
are the same. For example, in the file given in Example 2.2.2, P_3 and P_4
are Deg-indiscernible, since we have $Deg(P_3) = Deg(P_4)$. Objects are weakly
A-indiscernible whenever their properties determined by some members of
A are the same. Objects are A-similar [resp. weakly A-similar] whenever
all [resp. some of] the sets of their properties determined by the attributes
from A are not disjoint, in other words the objects share some properties.
For example, $\langle P_1, P_3 \rangle \in sim(Lan)$. A similar intuitive interpretation can
be given to all the remaining information relations. We have, for example,
$\langle P_2, P_5 \rangle \in icom(Lan)$, which means that, up to our present knowledge, P_2
and P_5 are not "completely" distinct with respect to the attribute Lan, because the set of Lan-properties of P_2 does not equal to the set of negative
Lan-properties of P_5.

Now we present a list of *distinguishability relations* derived from an information system:

⋆ the *strong* [resp. *weak*] *diversity relation* $div(A)$ [resp. $wdiv(A)$] is a relation
  such that for all $x, y \in OB$, $\langle x, y \rangle \in div(A)$ [resp. $\langle x, y \rangle \in wdiv(A)$] $\overset{\text{def}}{\Leftrightarrow}$ for
  all [resp. some] $a \in A$, $a(x) \neq a(y)$;
⋆ the *strong* [resp. *weak*] *right orthogonality relation* $rort(A)$ [resp. $wrort(A)$]
  is a relation such that for all $x, y \in OB$, $\langle x, y \rangle \in rort(A)$ [resp. $\langle x, y \rangle \in$
  $wrort(A)$] $\overset{\text{def}}{\Leftrightarrow}$ for all [resp. some] $a \in A$, $a(x) \subseteq -a(y)$;
⋆ the *strong* [resp. *weak*] *left orthogonality relation* $lort(A)$ [resp. $wlort(A)$]
  is a relation such that for all $x, y \in OB$, $\langle x, y \rangle \in lort(A)$ [resp. $\langle x, y \rangle \in$
  $wlort(A)$] $\overset{\text{def}}{\Leftrightarrow}$ for all [resp. some] $a \in A$, $-a(x) \subseteq a(y)$;
⋆ the *strong* [resp. *weak*] *right negative similarity relation* $rnim(A)$ [resp.
  $wrnim(A)$] is a relation such that for all $x, y \in OB$, $\langle x, y \rangle \in rnim(A)$
  [resp. $\langle x, y \rangle \in wrnim(A)$] $\overset{\text{def}}{\Leftrightarrow}$ for all [resp. some] $a \in A$, $a(x) \cap -a(y) \neq \emptyset$;
⋆ the *strong* [resp. *weak*] *left negative similarity relation* $lnim(A)$ [resp.
  $wlnim(A)$] is a relation such that for all $x, y \in OB$, $\langle x, y \rangle \in lnim(A)$
  [resp. $\langle x, y \rangle \in wlnim(A)$] $\overset{\text{def}}{\Leftrightarrow}$ for all [resp. some] $a \in A$, $-a(x) \cap a(y) \neq \emptyset$;

⋆ the *strong* [resp. *weak*] *complementarity relation* $com(A)$ [resp. $wcom(A)$] is a relation such that for all $x, y \in OB$, $\langle x, y \rangle \in icom(A)$ [resp. $\langle x, y \rangle \in wcom(A)$] $\overset{\text{def}}{\Leftrightarrow}$ for all [resp. some] $a \in A$, $a(x) = -a(y)$.

Objects are A-orthogonal [resp. weakly A-orthogonal] when all [resp. some of] sets of their properties (or negative properties) determined by attributes from A are disjoint, and they are A-diverse [resp. weakly A-diverse] if all [resp. some of] sets of their properties determined by members of A are different. Objects are A-complementary if their respective sets of properties are complements of each other. In Example 2.2.2, we have $Lan(P_3) = -Lan(P_2)$, hence $\langle P_2, P_3 \rangle \in com(Lan)$. Moreover, $Lan(P_3) \subseteq -Lan(P_6)$, so $\langle P_3, P_6 \rangle \in rort(Lan)$.

A more general method of defining information relations is as follows. Let $Bool(x, y)$ be an expression built from the set variables x and y using the Boolean set operators $\cup, \cap$, and $-$. For every information system $S = \langle OB, AT \rangle$ and for every $A \subseteq AT$, the binary relation $R^{=,\forall}_{Bool(x,y)}(A)$ [resp. $R^{\neq,\forall}_{Bool(x,y)}(A)$] is defined as follows: for all $x, y \in OB$,

$\langle x, y \rangle \in R^{=,\forall}_{Bool(x,y)}(A)$ [resp. $\langle x, y \rangle \in R^{\neq,\forall}_{Bool(x,y)}(A)$] $\overset{\text{def}}{\Leftrightarrow}$ for every $a \in A$, $Bool(a(x), a(y)) = \emptyset$ [resp. $Bool(a(x), a(y)) \neq \emptyset$].

Similarly, the binary relation $R^{=,\exists}_{Bool(x,y)}(A)$ [resp. $R^{\neq,\exists}_{Bool(x,y)}(A)$] is defined as follows: for all $x, y \in OB$,

$\langle x, y \rangle \in R^{=,\exists}_{Bool(x,y)}(A)$ [resp. $\langle x, y \rangle \in R^{\neq,\exists}_{Bool(x,y)}(A)$] $\overset{\text{def}}{\Leftrightarrow}$ there is an $a \in A$ such that $Bool(a(x), a(y)) = \emptyset$ [resp. $Bool(a(x), a(y)) \neq \emptyset$].

Clearly all the strong [resp. weak] relations derived from information systems are of the form $R^{=,\forall}_{Bool(x,y)}(A)$ or $R^{\neq,\forall}_{Bool(x,y)}(A)$ [resp. $R^{=,\exists}_{Bool(x,y)}(A)$ or $R^{\neq,\exists}_{Bool(x,y)}(A)$] for a suitable $Bool(x, y)$. In Sect. 13.3 we introduce a more general framework for defining information relations by treating information systems as classical first order structures.

3.3 Properties of Information Relations

The information relations derived from an information system satisfy several properties listed in Sect. 2.2.

Lemma 3.3.1. *For every information system $S = \langle OB, AT \rangle$, for every $A \subseteq AT$, the following assertions hold:*

(I) $ind(A)$ is an equivalence relation;
(II) $sim(A)$ and $nim(A)$ are weakly reflexive and symmetric;
(III) if S is total, then $sim(A)$ is a tolerance relation;
(IV) $fin(A)$ and $bin(A)$ are reflexive and transitive;

(V) icom(A) is symmetric and if $A \neq \emptyset$, then icom(A) is reflexive; for every $a \in AT$, icom(a) is co-3-transitive.

Lemma 3.3.2. *For every information system $S = \langle OB, AT \rangle$ and for every $A \subseteq AT$, the following assertions hold:*

(I) wind(A) is a tolerance relation and for every $a \in AT$, wind(a) is transitive;
(II) wsim(A) is a tolerance relation;
(III) wnim(A) is weakly reflexive and symmetric;
(IV) wicom(A) is reflexive, symmetric, and co-3-transitive;
(V) wfin(A) and wbin(A) are reflexive; for every $a \in AT$, wfin(a) and wbin(a) are transitive.

Lemma 3.3.3. *For every information system $S = \langle OB, AT \rangle$, and for every $A \subseteq AT$, the following assertions hold:*

(I) div(A) is symmetric; if $A \neq \emptyset$, then div(A) is irreflexive; for every $a \in AT$, div(a) is cotransitive;
(II) rort(A) is symmetric; if $A \neq \emptyset$, then rort(A) is irreflexive;
(III) lort(A) is coweakly reflexive and symmetric;
(IV) com(A) is symmetric and 3-transitive; if $A \neq \emptyset$, then com(A) is irreflexive;
(V) rnim(A) and lnim(A) are irreflexive for every $A \neq \emptyset$; for every $a \in AT$, rnim(a) and lnim(a) are cotransitive.

Lemma 3.3.4. *For every information system $S = \langle OB, AT \rangle$, and for every $A \subseteq AT$, the following assertions hold:*

(I) wdiv(A) is irreflexive, symmetric, and cotransitive;
(II) wrort(A) is symmetric; if S is total, then wrort(A) is irreflexive;
(III) wlort(A) is coweakly reflexive and symmetric;
(IV) wcom(A) is irreflexive and symmetric; for every $a \in A$, wcom(a) is 3-transitive;
(V) wrnim(A) and wlnim(A) are irreflexive and cotransitive.

The following lemma states some relationships between information relations of different kinds.

Lemma 3.3.5. *For every information system $S = \langle OB, AT \rangle$, for every $A \subseteq AT$, and for all $x, y, z \in OB$, the following assertions hold:*

(I) $\langle x, y \rangle \in sim(A)$ and $\langle x, z \rangle \in fin(A)$ imply $\langle z, y \rangle \in sim(A)$;
(II) $\langle x, y \rangle \in ind(A)$ implies $\langle x, y \rangle \in fin(A)$;
(III) $\langle x, y \rangle \in fin(A)$ and $\langle y, x \rangle \in fin(A)$ imply $\langle x, y \rangle \in ind(A)$.

The following lemma presents some relationships between information relations and sets of deterministic objects.

Lemma 3.3.6. *For every information system $S = \langle OB, AT \rangle$, for every $A \subseteq AT$, and for all $x, y \in OB$, the following assertions hold:*

(I) $y \in D(A)$ and $\langle x, y \rangle \in fin(A)$ imply $x \in D(A)$;
(II) $x \in D(A)$ and $\langle x, y \rangle \in sim(A)$ imply $\langle x, y \rangle \in fin(A)$;
(III) $x \in D(A)$, $y \in D(A)$, and $\langle x, y \rangle \in sim(A)$ imply $\langle x, y \rangle \in ind(A)$.

The following two lemmas state some properties of the classes of information relations.

Lemma 3.3.7. *For every information system $S = \langle OB, AT \rangle$, for all $A, B \subseteq AT$, and for every $R \in \{R^{=,\forall}_{Bool(x,y)}, R^{\neq,\forall}_{Bool(x,y)}\}$, the following conditions are satisfied:*

(I) $R(\emptyset) = OB \times OB$;
(II) $R(A \cup B) = R(A) \cap R(B)$;
(III) $A \subseteq B$ implies $R(B) \subseteq R(A)$.

Proof. (I) For all $x, y \in OB$, $\langle x, y \rangle \in R(\emptyset)$ iff for every $a \in \emptyset$, we have $Bool(a(x), a(y)) = \emptyset$ [resp. $Bool(a(x), a(y)) \neq \emptyset$]. This guarantees that $R(\emptyset) = OB \times OB$.
(II) Let $A, B \subseteq AT$. We have $\langle x, y \rangle \in R(A \cup B)$ iff for every $a \in A \cup B$, $Bool(a(x), a(y)) = \emptyset$ [resp. $Bool(a(x), a(y)) \neq \emptyset$] iff for every $a \in A$, $Bool(a(x), a(y)) = \emptyset$ [resp. $Bool(a(x), a(y)) \neq \emptyset$], and for every $a \in B$, $Bool(a(x), a(y)) = \emptyset$ [resp. $Bool(a(x), a(y)) \neq \emptyset$]. Hence, $\langle x, y \rangle \in R(A \cup B)$ iff $\langle x, y \rangle \in R(A)$ and $\langle x, y \rangle \in R(B)$.
(III) Let $A \subseteq B \subseteq AT$. Assume that $\langle x, y \rangle \in R(B)$. For every $a \in B$, $Bool(a(x), a(y)) = \emptyset$ [resp. $Bool(a(x), a(y)) \neq \emptyset$]. Since $A \subseteq B$, for every $a \in A$, $Bool(a(x), a(y)) = \emptyset$ [resp. $Bool(a(x), a(y)) \neq \emptyset$], that is $\langle x, y \rangle \in R(A)$.   *Q.E.D.*

Lemma 3.3.8. *For every information system $S = \langle OB, AT \rangle$, for all $A, B \subseteq AT$, and for every $R \in \{R^{=,\exists}_{Bool(x,y)}, R^{\neq,\exists}_{Bool(x,y)}\}$, the following conditions are satisfied:*

(I) $R(\emptyset) = \emptyset$;
(II) $R(A \cup B) = R(A) \cup R(B)$;
(III) $A \subseteq B$ implies $R(A) \subseteq R(B)$.

The proof is similar to the proof of the previous lemma.

Lemma 3.3.9. *For every information system $S = \langle OB, AT \rangle$, for every $A \subseteq AT$, and for every $x \in OB$, if S is A-separable, then $x \notin D(A)$ implies that there is a $y \in OB$ such that $\langle x, y \rangle \notin fin(A)$.*

Proof. Let S be an A-separable system and $x \notin D(A)$. So there is an $a \in A$ such that $\text{card}(a(x)) \geq 2$. Let v and v' be two distinct elements of $a(x)$. Since S is A-separable, there is a $y \in OB$ such that not $(v \in a(y)$ iff $v' \in a(y))$. If $\{v, v'\} \cap a(y) = \{v\}$ [resp. $\{v, v'\} \cap a(y) = \{v'\}$], then $v' \in a(x)$ [resp. $v \in a(x)$] and $v' \notin a(y)$ [resp. $v \notin a(y)$]. So $a(x) \not\subseteq a(y)$, which implies $\langle x, y \rangle \notin fin(A)$. Q.E.D.

The following lemma states the basic properties of set-theoretical information systems.

Lemma 3.3.10. *Let $S = \langle W, V \rangle$ be a set-theoretical information system and let AT be its set of attributes. Then the following conditions are satisfied:*

(I) S is separable;
(II) $\langle x, y \rangle \in fin(AT)$ iff for every $a \in V$ and for every $v \in a$, $x \in v$ implies $y \in v$;
(III) $\langle x, y \rangle \in ind(AT)$ iff for every $a \in V$ and for every $v \in a$, $x \in v$ iff $y \in v$;
(IV) $\langle x, y \rangle \in sim(AT)$ iff for every $a \in V$, there is a $v \in a$ such that $\{x, y\} \subseteq v$;
(V) $x \in D(AT)$ iff for every $a \in V$, for all $v, v' \in a$, $x \in v \cap v'$ implies $v = v'$.

3.4 Representation of Properties of Objects with Indiscernibility Relations

Given an information system $S = \langle OB, AT \rangle$, the family $(ind(A))_{A \subseteq AT}$ of indiscernibility relations derived from S enables us to represent properties of objects. For the sake of simplicity, we assume that the system S is deterministic and total. In other words, for all $x \in OB$ and $a \in AT$, $\text{card}(f(x, a)) = 1$. Any equivalence class $|x|_{ind(a)}$ for every $a \in AT$ consists of those objects that possess an a-property v such that $a(x) = v$. Hence, an information system provides both intensional and extensional information. A property can be represented intensionally with an attribute and its value as a certain a-property v, or extensionally as the set of those objects that possess the a-property v. In this section we shall discuss some aspects of the latter interpretation of properties. We list the following simple observations.

Lemma 3.4.1. *For all $A, B \subseteq AT$, for every $x \in OB$, and for every $a \in AT$, the following conditions are satisfied:*

(I) $|x|_{ind(A)} = \bigcap_{a \in A} |x|_{ind(a)}$;
(II) $|x|_{ind(a)} = a^{-1}(a(x))$;
(III) $|x|_{ind(A \cup B)} = |x|_{ind(A)} \cap |x|_{ind(B)}$.

It follows that by making intersections of indiscernibility relations we form new properties from some given properties. Properties obtained by means of intersection from some other properties can provide a finer (and never a coarser) partition of the set of objects than the properties which are the components of the intersection. It can be illustrated with the following example.

Example 3.4.1. Consider the information system given in Example 2.4.1. The equivalence classes determined by the indiscernibility relations corresponding to the given attributes are as follows:

* $ind(S)$: $X_1 = \{Me, V, E, Ma, P\}$, $X_2 = \{J, S\}$, $X_3 = \{U, N\}$;
* $ind(D)$: $Y_1 = \{Me, V, E, Ma\}$, $Y_2 = \{J, S, U, N, P\}$;
* $ind(M)$: $Z_1 = \{Me, V\}$, $Z_2 = \{E, Ma, J, S, U, N, P\}$;
* $ind(M, D)$: $T_1 = \{Me, V\}$, $T_2 = \{E, Ma\}$, $T_3 = \{J, S, U, N, P\}$;
* $ind(S, D)$: $W_1 = \{Me, V, E, Ma\}$, $W_2 = \{J, S\}$, $W_3 = \{U, N\}$, $W_4 = \{P\}$;
* $ind(S, D, M)$: $\{Me, V\}$, $\{E, Ma\}$, $\{J, Sa\}$, $\{U, N\}$, $\{P\}$.

Equivalence classes of these indiscernibility relations correspond to the following properties:

* X_1 : being of small size;
* X_2: being of large size;
* X_3: being of medium size;
* Y_1: being near to Sun;
* Y_2: being far from Sun;
* Z_1: having no Moon;
* Z_2: having a Moon;
* $T_2 = Y_1 \cap Z_2$: being near to Sun and having a Moon;
* $W_4 = X_1 \cap Y_2$: being small and far from Sun;

The other operation which enables us to define new properties from the given ones is the transitive closure of the union of indiscernibility relations. We recall that for a binary relation R on a set W, $R^* = \bigcup_{j \in \mathbb{N}} R^j$ where $R^0 = Id_W$ and $R^{j+1} = R; R^j$. Sometimes we write $R \cup^* R'$ instead of $(R \cup R')^*$. If R and R' are equivalence relations on a set W, then so is $R \cup^* R'$. For every $x \in W$, $|x|_R \subseteq |x|_{R \cup^* R'}$ and $|x|_{R'} \subseteq |x|_{R \cup^* R'}$. Hence, properties determined by $ind(A) \cup^* ind(B)$ can provide a coarser (and never a finer) partition of objects than properties determined by $ind(A)$ or $ind(B)$.

Example 3.4.2. Assume that we are given seven objects consisting of circles or crosses. We have $OB = \{x_1, \ldots, x_7\}$ and $AT = \{$number of circles (o), number of crosses (+)$\}$. Consider the information system given in Table 3.1.

The equivalence classes of the relations $ind(o)$ and $ind(+)$ are as follows:

* $ind(o)$: $\{x_1, x_2\}$, $\{x_3, x_4\}$, $\{x_5, x_6, x_7\}$;
* $ind(+)$: $\{x_1, x_3\}$, $\{x_2, x_4\}$, $\{x_5\}$, $\{x_6, x_7\}$.

The transitive closure of the union of these relations provides the following equivalence classes:

	o	+
x_1	1	1
x_2	1	2
x_3	2	1
x_4	2	2
x_5	3	3
x_6	3	4
x_7	3	4

Table 3.1. Crosses and circles

⋆ $ind(o) \cup^* ind(+)$: $\{x_1, x_2, x_3, x_4\}, \{x_5, x_6, x_7\}$.

We conclude that while performing operations on indiscernibility relations we form new properties from the primitive properties given in the information system under consideration. Formally, we can extend a given system by assuming that the new relation becomes an attribute, say R; its values are the objects of the system and R treated as a mapping from the set of objects into the powerset of the set of values is defined as $R(x) \stackrel{\text{def}}{=} |x|_R$ for every object x.

3.5 Application of Indiscernibility Relations to the Representation of Data Dependencies

Dependencies between information items play an important role in knowledge representation with information systems. Dependencies express constraints that the data must satisfy. Intuitively, a dependency says that if some information items exist in an information system, then either they are somehow related to each other, or some other information items must exist in the information system.

Below we recall some basic notions relevant to dependency theory. Given a finite set AT of attributes, and a set VAL of values of attributes, by a *tuple* we mean a mapping $t : AT \to VAL$. For every $A \subseteq AT$, $t[A]$ denotes the restriction of the tuple t to the set A. Every set of tuples with a common domain AT is called a *database relation*. It can be easily seen that the notion of database relation is very similar to the notion of information system. Given a database relation M, by AT_M we denote the set of attributes that is the domain of the tuples from M.

For every $A \subseteq AT_M$, by the *projection* of relation M onto the set A we mean the relation:

$$pr_A(M) \stackrel{\text{def}}{=} \{t[A] : t \in M\}.$$

Two tuples $t : AT \to VAL$ and $t' : AT' \to VAL'$ are *compatible* if $a \in AT \cap AT'$ always implies $t(a) = t'(a)$. By the *join* $M \natural N$ of database relations M and N we mean the following relation:

$M \sharp N \overset{\text{def}}{=} \{t : \text{ domain of } t \text{ is } AT_M \cup AT_N, t[AT_M] \in M, t[AT_N] \in N, \text{and}$

$t[AT_M] \text{ and } t[AT_N] \text{ are compatible}\}.$

Let M be a database relation, and let $A \subseteq AT_M$. Two tuples $t, t' \in M$ are indiscernible in M with respect to A whenever their restrictions to A are equal. We define the corresponding indiscernibility relation in the set M as follows:

$$\langle t, t' \rangle \in ind_M(A) \overset{\text{def}}{\Leftrightarrow} t[A] = t'[A].$$

Clearly, for every A the relation $ind_M(A)$ is an equivalence relation on M. In the sequel we often omit the subscript, and write $ind(A)$ when a database relation in question is clear from the context or immaterial.

Example 3.5.1. Consider a database relation M with attributes a, b, and c and with the tuples $t_1, \ldots, t_4$ of Table 3.2. The indiscernibility relation $ind(a)$

	a	b	c
t_1	u	v	w
t_2	u$'$	v$'$	w$'$
t_3	u$'$	v$'$	w
t_4	u	v$'$	w$'$

Table 3.2. Example of database relation

determined by the attribute a consists of the following pairs of tuples:

$$ind(a) = \{\langle t_1, t_1 \rangle, \langle t_2, t_2 \rangle, \langle t_3, t_3 \rangle, \langle t_4, t_4 \rangle, \langle t_1, t_4 \rangle, \langle t_4, t_1 \rangle, \langle t_2, t_3 \rangle, \langle t_3, t_2 \rangle\}.$$

The indiscernibility relation $ind(\{b, c\})$ determined by the attributes b and c consists of the following pairs of tuples:

$$ind(\{b, c\}) = \{\langle t_1, t_1 \rangle, \langle t_2, t_2 \rangle, \langle t_3, t_3 \rangle, \langle t_4, t_4 \rangle, \langle t_1, t_2 \rangle, \langle t_2, t_1 \rangle\}.$$

Let a database relation M be given. Various attribute dependencies in M can be defined in terms of indiscernibility relations. We recall the standard definitions of those dependencies and we give their representation in terms of indiscernibility relations. Let A, B, C be subsets of AT_M.

A *functional dependency* $A \to B$ holds in M $\overset{\text{def}}{\Leftrightarrow}$ for all tuples $t, t' \in M$, if $t[A] = t'[A]$, then $t[B] = t'[B]$.

Lemma 3.5.1. *The following conditions are equivalent:*

(I) the functional dependency $A \to B$ holds in M;
(II) $ind(A) \subseteq ind(B)$.

	a	b	c
t_1	0	0	0
t_2	1	1	1
t_3	2	1	0
t_4	2	2	1

Table 3.3. Example of database relation

Example 3.5.2. Consider a database relation M with attributes a, b, and c and with the tuples $t_1, \ldots, t_4$ of Table 3.3. The equivalence classes of the indiscernibility relations determined by attributes a, b, and c are as follows:

* $ind(a)$: $\{t_1\}, \{t_2\}, \{t_3, t_4\}$;
* $ind(b)$: $\{t_1\}, \{t_2, t_3\}, \{t_4\}$;
* $ind(c)$: $\{t_1, t_3\}, \{t_2, t_4\}$.

The relations $ind(\{a, b\})$, $ind(\{b, c\})$, and $ind(\{a, c\})$ are identity relations on the set $\{t_1, \ldots, t_4\}$. The following functional dependencies hold in M:

$$\{a, b\} \to c, \quad \{b, c\} \to a, \quad \{a, c\} \to c.$$

A *multi-valued dependency* $A \twoheadrightarrow B$ holds in M $\overset{\text{def}}{\Leftrightarrow}$ for all tuples $t, t' \in M$, if $t[A] = t'[A]$, then there is a $t'' \in M$ such that $t[A \cup B] = t''[A \cup B]$ and $t''[AT_M \setminus (A \cup B)] = t'[AT_M \setminus (A \cup B)]$.

Lemma 3.5.2. *The following conditions are equivalent:*

(I) the multi-valued dependency $A \twoheadrightarrow B$ holds in M;
(II) $ind(A) \subseteq (ind(A \cup B); ind(AT_M \setminus (A \cup B)))$.

Example 3.5.3. Consider a database relation M with attributes a, b, and c and with the tuples $t_1, \ldots, t_4$ of Table 3.4. It is easy to see that multi-valued

	a	b	c
t_1	u	v	w
t_2	u	v	w'
t_3	u'	v	w
t_4	u'	v	w'

Table 3.4. Example of database relation

dependency $b \twoheadrightarrow a$ holds in M.

An *embedded multi-valued dependency* $A \twoheadrightarrow B \mid C$ holds in M $\overset{\text{def}}{\Leftrightarrow}$ $A \twoheadrightarrow B$ holds in $pr_{A \cup B \cup C}(M)$.

Lemma 3.5.3. *The following conditions are equivalent:*

(I) the embedded multi-valued dependency $A \twoheadrightarrow B \mid C$ holds in M;
(II) $ind(A) \subseteq (ind(A \cup B); ind(C \setminus (A \cup B)))$.

A *decomposition* $\langle A, B \rangle$ holds in $M \overset{\text{def}}{\Leftrightarrow} A \cup B = AT_M$ and for all $t, t' \in M$, if $t[A \cap B] = t'[A \cap B]$, then there exists a $t'' \in M$ such that $t''[A] = t[A]$ and $t''[B] = t'[B]$.

Lemma 3.5.4. *The following conditions are equivalent:*

(I) the decomposition $\langle A, B \rangle$ holds in M;
(II) $A \cup B = AT_M$ and $ind(A \cap B) \subseteq ind(A); ind(B)$.

Example 3.5.4. Consider a database relation M with attributes a, b, and c and with the tuples $t_1, \ldots, t_5$ of Table 3.5. The decomposition $\langle \{a, b\}, \{b, c\} \rangle$

	a	b	c
t_1	0	0	0
t_2	0	0	1
t_3	1	0	1
t_4	1	1	1
t_5	1	0	0

Table 3.5. Example of database relation

holds in M.

A *join dependency* $*(A_1, \ldots, A_n)$ holds in $M \overset{\text{def}}{\Leftrightarrow} A_1 \cup \ldots \cup A_n = AT_M$ and M is the join of the relations $pr_{A_i}(M)$, $i = 1, \ldots, n$.

Lemma 3.5.5. *If a join dependency $*(A_1, \ldots, A_n)$, $n \geq 1$, holds in M, then $ind(A_1 \cap \cdots \cap A_n) \subseteq (ind(A_1); \cdots ; ind(A_n))$.*

The proofs of the above lemmas are by an easy verification.
A dependency defined by the condition

$$ind(A_1 \cap \cdots \cap A_n) \subseteq ind(A_1); \cdots ; ind(A_n)$$

for $A_1, \ldots, A_n$ such that $A_1 \cup \cdots \cup A_n = AT_M$ will be called a *generalised join dependency* and denoted by $\sharp(A_1, \ldots, A_n)$.

We introduce the following abbreviations. Let X be a finite set of binary relations on a set W, let R, R' be binary relations on W, and let $1 = W \times W$. Then we define:

$\star$ $con(X) \overset{\text{def}}{=} 1$ if $X = \emptyset$, otherwise $con(X) \overset{\text{def}}{=} \bigcap X$.
$\star$ $neg(R) \overset{\text{def}}{=} 1; (1 \setminus R); 1$.
$\star$ $imp(R, R') \overset{\text{def}}{=} neg(R) \cup R'$.

It is easy to see that these operations satisfy the following conditions.

Lemma 3.5.6. *For all binary relations R and R', the following conditions are satisfied:*

(I) $con(R, R') = 1$ iff $R = 1$ and $R' = 1$;
(II) $neg(R) = 1$ iff $R \neq 1$;
(III) $imp(R, R') = 1$ iff $R = 1$ implies $R' = 1$.

If R is of the form $ind(A)$ for some $A \subseteq AT$, then we define $AT(R) \stackrel{\text{def}}{=} A$ and if $X = \{ind(A) : A \in Z \subseteq \mathcal{P}(AT)\}$, then $AT(X) \stackrel{\text{def}}{=} \bigcup Z$.

Let X, Y be finite sets of indiscerniblity relations. Consider the relations of the form:

(FD) $-con(X) \cup con(Y)$,
(EMVD) $-con(X) \cup (con(X \cup Y); con(Z \setminus (X \cup Y))$,
(GJD) $-con(X_1 \cap \ldots \cap X_n) \cup (con(X_1); \ldots; con(X_n))$,
(GDC) $-con(X \cap Y) \cup (con(X); con(Y))$,
(B) any relation built from indiscernibility relations with $-, \cup, \cap$.

They are referred to as functional dependency relations (FD-relations), embedded multi-valued dependency relations (EMVD-relations), generalised join dependency relations (GJD-relations), generalised decomposition relations (GDC-relations), and Boolean dependency relations (B-relations), respectively.

Lemma 3.5.7. *Let M be a database relation and $1 = M \times M$. Then the following conditions hold:*

(I) $(FD) = 1$ iff the functional dependency $AT(X) \to AT(Y)$ holds in M;
(II) $(EMVD) = 1$ with $AT(Z) = AT_M$ iff the multi-valued dependency $AT(X) \to\to AT(Y)$ holds in M;
(III) $(EMVD) = 1$ iff the embedded multi-valued dependency $AT(X) \to\to AT(Y) \mid AT(Z)$ holds in M;
(IV) $(GDC) = 1$ with $AT(X \cup Y) = AT_M$ iff the decomposition $\langle AT(X), AT(Y) \rangle$ holds in M;
(V) $(GJD) = 1$ with $AT(X_1 \cup \ldots \cup X_n) = AT_M$ iff the generalised join dependency $\natural(AT(X_1), \ldots, AT(X_n))$ holds in M.

Proof. The proof is based on the following facts that can be easily derived from the properties of indiscernibility relations. Let X, Y be finite sets of indiscernibility relations. Then:

⋆ $con(X) = ind(AT(X))$;
⋆ $AT(X \cup Y) = AT(X) \cup AT(Y)$;
⋆ $AT(X \cap Y) = AT(X) \cap AT(Y)$;
⋆ $AT(X \setminus Y) = AT(X) \setminus AT(Y)$.

Q.E.D.

In a more general setting every relation generated by indiscernibility relations with the standard relational operations may be seen as a generalised dependency. A dependency D holds in a database relation M if $D = 1$ is true in M. The implication problem for dependencies consists in showing that if the dependencies D_i, $i = 1, \ldots, n$, hold in M, then the dependency D holds in M. This problem can be equivalently represented as follows.

Lemma 3.5.8. *The following conditions are equivalent:*

(I) dependencies D_i, $i = 1, \ldots, n$, imply dependency D in a database relation M;

(II) $imp(con(\{D_i : i = 1, \ldots, n\}), D) = 1$ in M.

The proof is based on Lemma 3.5.6.

3.6 Contraction of Attributes

In order to explain in a formal way a relationship between formal contexts and deterministic information systems, in this section we discuss a decomposition of attributes into features and the formation of attributes from features. Let $S = \langle OB, AT, (VAL_a)_{a \in AT} \rangle$ be an information system such that for every $a \in AT$,

(1) $VAL_a = a(OB)$ is a finite non-empty set;
(2) for every $x \in OB$, $\operatorname{card}(a(x)) = 1$.

For all $a \in AT$ and $v \in VAL_a$ we define the map $a_v : OB \to \{0, 1\}$ such that $a_v(x) \stackrel{\text{def}}{=} 1$ if $a(x) = \{v\}$, otherwise $a_v(x) \stackrel{\text{def}}{=} 0$. We define the information system $S' = \langle OB, AT' \rangle$ such that $AT' \stackrel{\text{def}}{=} \{a_v : a \in AT, v \in VAL_a\}$. Since for every object x, there is a unique v such that $a(x) = v$, we have $|x|_{ind(a)} = a^{-1}(v) = a_v^{-1}(1) = |x|_{ind(a_v)}$. It follows that $ind(a) = ind(\{a_v : v \in VAL_a\})$. The set

$$F(a) = \{a_v : v \in VAL_a\}$$

is referred to as a decomposition of the attribute a into features. We clearly have $ind(a) = ind(b)$ iff $F(a) = F(b)$. It follows that an attribute and its associated set of features provide the same classification of objects. Observe that $\operatorname{card}(F(a)) \geq 2$ for every non-constant attribute a, and that if a is a constant attribute, then $\operatorname{card}(F(a)) = 1$. In view of the assumptions on the information systems under consideration, for every attribute a, the set $F(a)$ is finite.

Let $f : W \to \{0, 1\}$ be a feature on a set W. We define W_f as the set $\{x \in W : f(x) = 1\}$. Given the features f and g on W, we define the new features $-f$, $f + g$, $f \times g$ and $f * g$ as follows. Let $x \in W$, then:

$\star$ $(-f)(x) \stackrel{\text{def}}{=} 1 - f(x)$;

$\star$ $(f+g)(x) \stackrel{\text{def}}{=} min(1, f(x)+g(x))$;

$\star$ $(f \times g)(x) \stackrel{\text{def}}{=} f(x) \times g(x)$;

$\star$ $(f * g)(x) \stackrel{\text{def}}{=} (f+g)(x)$ if $f(x) \times g(x) = 0$, otherwise undefined.

For the first three features, on the right-hand side of the above equalities we have the usual arithmetic operations. The operation $*$ is called the *disjoint sum of features*. We conclude that $W_{-f} = W \setminus W_f$, $W_{f+g} = W_f \cup W_g$, and $W_{f \times g} = W_f \cap W_g$. If f is a non-constant feature, then $F(f) = \{f, -f\}$.

Lemma 3.6.1. *Let* $X = \{f_1, \ldots, f_n\}$, $n \geq 1$, *be a finite set of features on a set* W. *Then* X *is a decomposition of a non-constant attribute* a *iff the following conditions are satisfied:*

(I) $\text{card}(X) \geq 2$;
(II) for all $i, j \in \{1, \ldots, n\}$, *if* $i \neq j$, *then* $f_i \times f_j = 0$;
(III) $f_1 + \ldots + f_n = 1$.

Proof. ($\rightarrow$) Clear from the definition of decomposition.
($\leftarrow$) Define an attribute $a : W \rightarrow \{1, \ldots, n\}$ as follows: $a(x) = i$ iff $f_i(x) = 1$. Clearly, $X = F(a)$.   *Q.E.D.*

Example 3.6.1. In Example 2.4.1 the set of features {small size, medium size, large size} is the decomposition of attribute "size"; {near to Sun, far from Sun} is the decomposition of "distance from Sun"; {having a Moon, no Moon} is the decomposition of "possession of a Moon".

Lemma 3.6.2. *Let* a *be an attribute on a set* W *and let* $F(a) = \{a_1, \ldots, a_n\}$, $n \geq 1$, *be its decomposition into features. Let* X *be a set obtained from* $F(a)$ *by making disjoint sums of some of its elements. Then either there is an attribute* b *on* W *such that* $X = F(b)$ *or* $\text{ind}(X) = W \times W$.

Proof. If a is a constant attribute, then $\text{card}(F(a)) = 1$ and the operator of disjoint sums is not applicable.
If $\text{card}(F(a)) = 2$, then $X = \{a_1 * a_2\}$ and $a_1 * a_2$ is a constant feature such that $a_1 * a_2(x) = 1$ for every $x \in W$. Hence, $\text{ind}(X) = W \times W$. Now let $\text{card}(F(a)) > 2$. Let $\{I_1, \ldots, I_m\}$ be a partition of $\{1, \ldots, n\}$, $n, m \geq 1$, and let $X = \{*(a_k)_{k \in I_j} : j = 1, \ldots, m\}$. If $m = 1$, then $X = \{a_1 * \ldots * a_n\}$ and then $\text{ind}(X) = W \times W$. If $m > 1$, then $\text{card}(X) \geq 2$, and hence condition (I) of Lemma 3.6.1 is satisfied. The conditions (II) and (III) are also satisfied because for every $i \in \{1, \ldots, n\}$, a_i is an element of $F(a)$.   *Q.E.D.*

Let $S = \langle OB, AT, (VAL_a)_{a \in AT} \rangle$ be an information system such that for every $a \in AT$,

(1) $VAL_a = a(OB)$ is a finite non-empty set;
(2) for every $x \in OB$, $\text{card}(a(x)) = 1$.

Let a, b be attributes of AT. We say that b is a *contraction* of a (written $b \leq_c a$) $\overset{\text{def}}{\Leftrightarrow}$ there is a map $g : VAL_a \to VAL_b$ such that for every $x \in OB$, $b(x) = g(a(x))$. The mapping g is referred to as a *contractor* of a to b. It follows from this definition that $\text{card}(VAL_b) \leq \text{card}(VAL_a)$. If $b \leq_c a$ and $\text{card}(VAL_b) < \text{card}(VAL_a)$, then b is a *proper contraction* of a (written $b <_c a$). If $\text{card}(VAL_b) = \text{card}(VAL_a) - 1$, then b is an *elementary contraction* of a. The corresponding contractors are a *proper* and an *elementary contractor*, respectively. It is easy to see that if $b \leq_c a$, then $ind(a) \subseteq ind(b)$.

Lemma 3.6.3. *If b is an elementary contraction of a, then there exists a pair $\langle f, g \rangle$ of features such that $\{f, g\} \subseteq F(a)$ and $ind(b) = ind((F(a) \setminus \{f, g\}) \cup \{f * g\})$.*

Proof. If a is a constant attribute, then there are no elementary contractions. Therefore, $\text{card}(VAL_a) \geq 2$. Let $VAL_a = \{v_1, \ldots, v_n\}$, $n \geq 1$, and $VAL_b = \{w_1, \ldots, w_{n-1}\}$ and let α be the corresponding contractor. Hence, there exist two values $v, v' \in VAL_a$ and a value $w \in VAL_b$ such that $\alpha(v) = \alpha(v') = w$. Without any loss of generality we may assume that $v = v_{n-1}$, $v' = v_n$, and $w = w_{n-1}$. Since α is an elementary contractor, it is injective on $VAL_a \setminus \{v_{n-1}, v_n\}$ and without any loss of generality we may assume that $\alpha(v_i) = w_i$ for every $i \in \{1, \ldots, n-2\}$. Therefore:

(i) for every $i \in \{1, \ldots, n-2\}$, $b^{-1}(w_i) = a^{-1}(v_i)$;
(ii) $b^{-1}(w_{n-1}) = a^{-1}(v_{n-1}) \cup a^{-1}(v_n)$.

Let $F(a) = \{a_1, \ldots, a_n\}$, $n \geq 1$, and $F(b) = \{b_1, \ldots, b_{n-1}\}$ be a decomposition into features of a and b, respectively. It follows from (i) that $a_i = b_i$ for every $i \in \{1, \ldots, n-2\}$. The statement (ii) is equivalent to $b_{n-1} = a_{n-1} * a_n$. Consequently, $F(b) = (F(a) \setminus \{a_{n-1}, a_n\}) \cup \{a_{n-1} * a_n\}$. Putting $f = a_{n-1}$ and $g = a_n$ completes the proof.   *Q.E.D.*

Lemma 3.6.4. *For every attribute a, the following conditions are satisfied:*

(I) every contraction of a can be obtained by making disjoint sums of features from $F(a)$;

(II) every disjoint sum of features from $F(a)$ is a contraction of a.

Proof. (I) It is easy to see that any proper contractor is a composition of a finite number of elementary contractors. Hence we apply step-wise Lemma 3.6.2 and Lemma 3.6.3.
(II) Observe that if b is a feature obtained by performing a disjoint sum of some elements from $F(a)$, then for every $v \in VAL_a$, either (i) $a^{-1}(v) \subseteq b^{-1}(1)$ or (ii) $a^{-1}(v) \subseteq b^{-1}(0)$. If (i) holds, then define $g(v) = 1$, if (ii) holds, then define $g(v) = 0$.   *Q.E.D.*

Let $A, B \subseteq AT$. We say that B is a *contraction* of A (written $B \leq_c A$) $\overset{\text{def}}{\Leftrightarrow}$ there is an injective map $g : B \to A$ such that for every $b \in B$, b is a contraction of $g(a)$.

Example 3.6.2. Consider a set of four objects and the attributes "colour" and "c" from Table 3.6. If we are not interested in distinguishing tints of

	Colour	c
x_1	Light green	Green
x_2	Red	Red
x_3	Blue	Blue
x_4	Dark green	Green

Table 3.6. Colours

colours, then we define a contraction c of attribute "colour" and we possibly replace the column labelled by "colour" by the column labelled by c in an information system.

3.7 Applications of Diversity Relations

Let $S = \langle OB, AT \rangle$ be an information system and $B \subseteq AT$. We say that an attribute $a \in B$ is *indispensable* in $B \overset{\text{def}}{\Leftrightarrow} ind(B) \neq ind(B \setminus \{a\})$. It follows that if a is indispensable in B, then the classification of objects with respect to attributes from B is properly finer than the classification based on $B \setminus \{a\}$. The set B of attributes is *independent* $\overset{\text{def}}{\Leftrightarrow}$ every element of B is indispensable in B, otherwise B is *dependent*. The set of all the elements indispensable in B is referred to as the *core* of B in the system S:

$$CORE_S(B) \overset{\text{def}}{=} \{a \in B : ind(B) \neq ind(B \setminus \{a\})\}.$$

A set $C \subseteq B$ is a *reduct* of B in the system $S \overset{\text{def}}{\Leftrightarrow} C$ is independent and $ind(C) = ind(B)$. The family of reducts of B in S is denoted by $RED_S(B)$.

Let S be an information system. By the *discernibility matrix* of S we mean the family $(c_{x,y})_{x,y \in OB}$ of sets such that $c_{x,y} = \{a \in AT : \langle x, y \rangle \in div(a)\}$. Clearly, for all $x, y \in OB$, $c_{x,y} = c_{y,x}$ and $c_{x,x} = \emptyset$. In the case of finite OB, the family is usually represented as a table whose columns and rows are labelled with objects and whose entries are the sets $c_{x,y}$.

Lemma 3.7.1. *Let $S = \langle OB, AT \rangle$ be an information system and let $C \subseteq B \subseteq AT$. Then the following assertions hold:*

(I) $\langle x, y \rangle \in ind(B)$ iff $c_{x,y} \cap B = \emptyset$;
(II) $ind(C) \subseteq ind(B)$ iff for all $x, y \in OB$, $(c_{x,y} \cap B \neq \emptyset$ implies $c_{x,y} \cap C \neq \emptyset$);
(III) $ind(C) = ind(B)$ iff for all $x, y \in OB$, $(c_{x,y} \cap B \neq \emptyset$ iff $c_{x,y} \cap C \neq \emptyset$);
(IV) if $C \subseteq B$, then $ind(C) = ind(B)$ iff for all $x, y \in OB$, $c_{x,y} \cap B \neq \emptyset$ implies $c_{x,y} \cap C \neq \emptyset$.

Proof. (I) and (II) can be easily verified.
(III) follows from (II).
(IV) follows from (III) and Lemma 3.3.7(III).   *Q.E.D.*

The above lemma enables us to establish a method of computing the core and the reducts of a set of attributes; namely we have the following theorem.

Theorem 3.7.1. *Let $S = \langle OB, AT \rangle$ be an information system and let $B \subseteq AT$. Then the following assertion holds:*

$$CORE_S(B) = \{a \in B : c_{x,y} \cap B = \{a\} \text{ for some } x, y \in OB\}.$$

Proof. Let $a \in B$. Since $B \setminus \{a\} \subset B$, by Lemma 3.7.1(IV), $ind(B \setminus \{a\}) = ind(B)$ iff for all $x, y \in OB$, $c_{x,y} \cap B \neq \emptyset$ implies $c_{x,y} \cap (B \setminus \{a\}) \neq \emptyset$. Hence, $ind(B \setminus \{a\}) \neq ind(B)$ iff there are $x_0, y_0 \in OB$ such that $c_{x_0,y_0} \cap B \neq \emptyset$ and $c_{x_0,y_0} \cap (B \setminus \{a\}) = \emptyset$. So $ind(B \setminus \{a\}) \neq ind(B)$ iff there are $x_0, y_0 \in OB$ such that $c_{x_0,y_0} \cap B = \{a\}$.   *Q.E.D.*

Theorem 3.7.1 says that $a \in CORE_S(B)$ iff there are $x, y \in OB$ such that a is the only attribute that enables us to distinguish between x and y. In other words, the only distinction between x and y is provided by their a-properties.

Lemma 3.7.2. *Let $S = \langle OB, AT \rangle$ be an information system and $B \subseteq AT$. Then $C \in REDS(B)$ iff C is a minimal (with respect to inclusion) subset of AT such that:*

(i) for all $x, y \in OB$, if $c_{x,y} \cap B \neq \emptyset$, then $C \cap c_{x,y} \cap B \neq \emptyset$.

Proof. ($\rightarrow$) Let $C \in REDS(B)$. Then $C \subseteq B$ and $ind(C) = ind(B)$. By Lemma 3.7.1(IV), for all $x, y \in OB$, $c_{x,y} \cap B \neq \emptyset$ implies $c_{x,y} \cap C \neq \emptyset$. So, if $c_{x,y} \cap B \neq \emptyset$, then $C \cap c_{x,y} \cap B = c_{x,y} \cap C \neq \emptyset$. Now suppose C is not a minimal subset of AT satisfying (i). This means that there is a $C' \subset C$ such that if $c_{x,y} \cap B \neq \emptyset$, then $C' \cap c_{x,y} \cap B \neq \emptyset$. Since $C' \subset C \subseteq B$, $C' \cap c_{x,y} \cap B = c_{x,y} \cap (B \cap C') = c_{x,y} \cap C'$. So, if $c_{x,y} \cap B \neq \emptyset$, then $c_{x,y} \cap C' \neq \emptyset$. By Lemma 3.7.1(II), $ind(C') \subseteq ind(B)$. Since $C' \subseteq B$, $ind(B) \subseteq ind(C')$. Hence, $ind(C') = ind(B) = ind(C)$, a contradiction.
($\leftarrow$) Let C be a minimal subset of AT satisfying (i). Suppose $C \not\subseteq B$. So, if $c_{x,y} \cap B \neq \emptyset$, then $(B \cap C) \cap c_{x,y} \cap B = C \cap c_{x,y} \cap B \neq \emptyset$, a contradiction. Indeed, $(B \cap C)$ satisfies (i) and $B \cap C \subset C$. Hence $C \subseteq B$. Since for all $x, y \in OB$, $(c_{x,y} \cap C) = C \cap (c_{x,y} \cap B)$, we get $ind(C) = ind(B)$. Indeed, assume that $\langle x, y \rangle \in ind(C)$ and $\langle x, y \rangle \notin ind(B)$. By Lemma 3.7.1(I), $c_{x,y} \cap C = \emptyset$ and $c_{x,y} \cap B \neq \emptyset$. So by (i), $C \cap (c_{x,y} \cap B) = c_{x,y} \cap C \neq \emptyset$, a contradiction. Finally, suppose that C is not independent. So there is a $C' \subset C$ such that $ind(C') = ind(C) = ind(B)$. Since $C' \subseteq B$, this implies that if $c_{x,y} \cap B \neq \emptyset$, then $C' \cap c_{x,y} \cap B \neq \emptyset$, a contradiction by minimality of C.   *Q.E.D.*

Lemma 3.7.2 says that a reduct of a set B of attributes is a minimal subset C of B which enables us to pairwise distinguish all those objects which can be distinguished with respect to the attributes from B.

Example 3.7.1. Consider the information system described in Table 3.7.

	a	b	c	d	e
x_1	$-$	$+$	$+$	$+$	$+$
x_2	$+$	0	$-$	$-$	$-$
x_3	$+$	$-$	$-$	$-$	0
x_4	0	$-$	$-$	0	$-$
x_5	$+$	$-$	$-$	$-$	$-$
x_6	0	$+$	$-$	0	$+$

Table 3.7. An information system

The equivalence classes of indiscernibility relations derived from this information system are:

* $ind(a)$: $\{x_1\}$, $\{x_2, x_3, x_5\}$, $\{x_4, x_6\}$;
* $ind(b)$: $\{x_1, x_6\}$, $\{x_2\}$, $\{x_3, x_4, x_5\}$;
* $ind(c)$: $\{x_1\}$, $\{x_2, \ldots, x_6\}$;
* $ind(d)$: $\{x_1\}$, $\{x_2, x_3, x_5\}$, $\{x_4, x_6\}$;
* $ind(e)$: $\{x_1, x_6\}$, $\{x_2, x_4, x_5\}$, $\{x_3\}$.

Moreover, we have $ind(\{b, e\})$: $\{x_1, x_6\}$, $\{x_2\}$, $\{x_3\}$, $\{x_4, x_5\}$.

The discernibility matrix for the system is presented in Table 3.8. Since in

	x_1	x_2	x_3	x_4	x_5	x_6
x_1	$\emptyset$					
x_2	$\{a,b,c,d,e\}$	$\emptyset$				
x_3	$\{a,b,c,d,e\}$	$\{b,e\}$	$\emptyset$			
x_4	$\{a,b,c,d,e\}$	$\{a,b,d\}$	$\{a,d,e\}$	$\emptyset$		
x_5	$\{a,b,c,d,e\}$	$\{b\}$	$\{e\}$	$\{a,d\}$	$\emptyset$	
x_6	$\{a,c,d\}$	$\{a,b,d,e\}$	$\{a,b,d,e\}$	$\{b,e\}$	$\{a,b,d,e\}$	$\emptyset$

Table 3.8. Discernibility matrix

the discernibility matrix $c_{x,y} = c_{y,x}$, we can represent it with the left–lower triangle only. Using the previous lemmas, we conclude that in our system $CORE_S(AT) = \{b, e\}$ and the reducts of AT are the sets $B = \{a, b, e\}$ and $C = \{b, d, e\}$. Indeed, both $ind(B)$ and $ind(C)$ are the identity relation on OB. We conclude that a situation represented by our information system can be represented with the smaller sets B or C of attributes and in both cases the reduction does not change the classification of objects determined by the attributes from AT.

3.8 Applications of Complementarity Relations

Complementarity relations derived from a decision table provide criteria for reduction of both individual rules and sets of rules determined by the table. An analysis of complementarity constitutes a fundamental principle of many methods and algorithms developed for machine learning and rule-based knowledge representation. Let $S = \langle OB, AT \cup \{d\}, (VAL_a)_{a \in AT}, VAL_d, f \rangle$ be a decision table. We say that a condition attribute a is *redundant* in the rule r_x determined by $S \overset{\text{def}}{\Leftrightarrow}$ there is an object $y \in OB$ such that the following conditions are satisfied:

(1) $\langle x, y \rangle \in com(a)$;
(2) $\langle x, y \rangle \in ind(AT \setminus \{a\})$;
(3) for every $z \in OB$, if $\langle x, z \rangle \in div(d)$, then there is an attribute $b \in AT \setminus \{a\}$ such that $\langle x, z \rangle \in div(b)$.

In other words, a condition attribute a is redundant in the rule r_x whenever the decision $d(x)$ does not depend on a. As a consequence, when a is redundant in the rule r_x we may delete the part of this rule that contains a. Moreover, we may delete from the set of rules determined by S all the rules r_y such that the objects x and y satisfy the conditions (1)–(3) above and this will not change the classification of objects determined by the decision attribute d.

Example 3.8.1. Consider the decision rules from Example 2.5.2. We observe that $\langle x_1, x_2 \rangle \in com(colour)$ and $\langle x_1, x_2 \rangle \in ind(AT - colour)$. Moreover, $\langle x_1, x_3 \rangle \in div(colour)$ and $\langle x_1, x_3 \rangle \in div(size)$. We conclude that the attribute "colour" is redundant in the rules r_{x_1} and r_{x_2}.

3.9 Relative Relations

An information system constitutes explicit information available in an application domain, while the information provided by information relations is implicit. These relations enable us to identify some aspects of incompleteness of explicit information. The relational systems consisting of a family of relations on a set are referred to as frames.

Definition 3.9.1. *Let S be an information system and let $(\mathcal{R}_A^i)_{A \subseteq AT}$, $i = 1, \ldots, t$, $t \geq 1$ be families of information relations derived from S. The structure $\langle OB, (\mathcal{R}_A^1)_{A \subseteq AT}, \ldots, (\mathcal{R}_A^t)_{A \subseteq AT} \rangle$ is said to be an information frame derived from S.*

If $(\mathcal{R}_A)_{A \subseteq AT}$ is a family of indiscernibility relations derived from an information system $S = \langle OB, AT \rangle$, then the frame $\langle OB, (\mathcal{R}_A)_{A \subseteq AT} \rangle$ is denoted by $D_{ind}(S)$. The analogous notation indicating the type of relations will be used for the other information frames.

The relations in the frames derived from an information system depend on subsets of the set AT. In a general setting, the elements of these subsets play the role of parameters which provide a means for representing an intensional part of information included in an information system. From a technical point of view, we deal with families of relations indexed with subsets of a set. The fact that the relations derived from information systems are indexed with subsets of the set of attributes suggests that in a general setting a hierarchy of relative relations may be constructed which is determined by the powerset hierarchy of a set of parameters. Thus we can consider families of relations indexed with the elements of $\mathcal{P}^n(PAR)$ for every $n \in \mathbb{N}$.

Definition 3.9.2. *A relative frame is a structure*

$$F = \langle W, (\mathcal{R}_P^1)_{P \in \mathcal{P}^n(PAR)}, \ldots, (\mathcal{R}_P^t)_{P \in \mathcal{P}^n(PAR)} \rangle$$

such that $t \geq 1$, *W and PAR are non-empty sets, $n \in \mathbb{N}$, and for every $h \in \{1, \ldots, t\}$, $(\mathcal{R}_P^h)_{P \in \mathcal{P}^n(PAR)}$ is a family of binary relations on W.*

Any such frame is said to be a frame of level n. If $n = 1$, then the corresponding relative frame is denoted by $\langle W, (\mathcal{R}_P^1)_{P \subseteq PAR}, \ldots, (\mathcal{R}_P^t)_{P \subseteq PAR} \rangle$. If $n = 0$, then F is a frame in its classical understanding. Clearly, every frame derived from an information system is a relative frame. The relations in relative frames with $n \geq 1$ will be denoted by calligraphic $\mathcal{R}$. The notion of relative frame can be extended to m-ary relations for every $m \geq 2$, but in the book we deal with binary relations.

Example 3.9.1. The powerset hierarchy of attributes which appears naturally in the representation of a hierarchical subject classification system (see an example in Sect. 2.6) leads to information relations of any finite level. Relations indexed with the elements of $\mathcal{P}^0(PAR)$ form a usual family of relations whose indices are individuals. Information relations defined in Sect. 3.2 are examples of relations indexed with the elements of $\mathcal{P}^1(PAR)$, where PAR is the set of attributes of an information system.

Apart from the usual properties of relations (for example those listed in Sect. 1.2) relative relations may satisfy conditions that say how a relation indexed with a compound set depends on the relations indexed with the component sets. These conditions refer to the family of relations as a whole, and therefore they are referred to as the *global conditions*. In what follows we define several examples of global conditions. The conditions referring to a single relation are called the *local conditions*. Examples of local conditions can be found in Sect. 1.2.

Definition 3.9.3. *A relation predicate ρ of arity $ar \geq 2$ is a map such that for every set W, $\rho(W)$ is a subset of $\mathcal{P}(W^{i_1}) \times \cdots \times \mathcal{P}(W^{i_{ar}})$, where $i_1, \ldots, i_{ar} \geq 1$, and $i_1, \ldots, i_{ar}$ do not depend on W. $\langle i_1, \ldots, i_{ar} \rangle$ is said to be the profile of ρ. Moreover, we assume that for every bijection $g : W \to W'$ and for every $\langle X_1, \ldots, X_{ar} \rangle \in \mathcal{P}(W^{i_1}) \times \cdots \times \mathcal{P}(W^{i_{ar}})$,*

$$\rho(W') = \{\langle g(X_1), \ldots, g(X_{ar}) \rangle : \langle X_1, \ldots, X_{ar} \rangle \in \rho(W)\}.$$

The above definition captures the following standard binary relation predicates: $=, \subseteq, \supseteq, \subset, \supset$. They are of arity 2, with $i_1 = i_2 = 2$.

Definition 3.9.4. *A relation predicate ρ of arity $ar \geq 2$ is functional $\overset{\text{def}}{\Leftrightarrow}$ for every set W and for every $\langle X_1, \ldots, X_{ar-1} \rangle \in \mathcal{P}(W^{i_1}) \times \cdots \times \mathcal{P}(W^{i_{ar-1}})$, there is a unique $X_{ar} \subseteq W^{i_{ar}}$ such that $\langle X_1, \ldots, X_{ar} \rangle \in \rho(W)$. $\rho(W)$ is also simply written ρ.*

Clearly, $=$ is functional. A functional relation predicate is referred to as a *relation operation*. Relation operations enable us to represent uniformly both the operations acting on relations, for instance the operations mentioned in Sect. 1.2, and also various properties of relations, for example many of the properties listed in Sect. 1.2. In Table 3.9, we present several unary relation operations.

Definition of $\rho(W)(R)$
R
$R \cup \{(x,x) : x \in W\}$
$R \cup \{(x,x) : x \in W, (x,y) \in R \text{ for some } y \in W\}$
$R \cup \{(y,y) : y \in W, (x,y) \in R \text{ for some } x \in W\}$
$\{(x,y) : \text{ either } (x,y) \in R \text{ or } (y,x) \in R\}$
$\{(x,y) : x,y \in W, \exists x_1, \ldots, x_n \in W \text{ such that } n \geq 2, x_1 = x, x_n = y, \text{ and } \forall i \in \{1,\ldots,n-1\}, (x_i, x_{i+1}) \in R\}$
$R \cup \{(x,y) : \exists x_1, \ldots, x_n \text{ such that } n \geq 2, (x_1, x) \in R, (x_n, y) \in R, \text{ and } \forall i \in \{1,\ldots,n-1\} \text{ either } (x_i, x_{i+1}) \in R \text{ or } (x_{i+1}, x_i) \in R\}$
$W \times W$
$\text{dom}(R) \times (\text{dom}(R) \cup \text{ran}(R))$

Table 3.9. Examples of relation operations

A *set operation* f is a relation operation such that for every set W, $f(W)$ has the profile $\langle 1, \ldots, 1 \rangle$.

A general form of a global condition is as follows. Let f_1, f_2, ρ be a set operation, a relation operation, and a relation predicate in $\{=, \subseteq, \supseteq\}$, respectively. f_1 and f_2 are assumed to be of the same arity ar. Then we consider the conditions of the form:

$$\rho(\mathcal{R}_{f_1(P_1, \ldots, P_{ar})}, f_2(\mathcal{R}_{P_1}, \ldots, \mathcal{R}_{P_{ar}})),$$

where W and PAR are non-empty sets, $P_1, \ldots, P_{ar} \subseteq PAR$, and for every $j \in \{1, \ldots, ar\}$, $\mathcal{R}_{P_j} \subseteq W^{i_j}$.

Definition 3.9.5. *Let f_1 be a set operation of arity $n \geq 2$ and f_2 be a relation operation of profile $\langle 2, \ldots, 2 \rangle$ and of arity $n+1$. Let $\langle W, (\mathcal{R}_P)_{P \subseteq PAR} \rangle$ be a relative frame. We say that $(\mathcal{R}_P)_{P \subseteq PAR}$ satisfies condition $(C_{[f_1, f_2]}) \stackrel{\text{def}}{\Leftrightarrow}$ for all $P_1, \ldots, P_n \subseteq PAR$, $\mathcal{R}_{f_1(P_1, \ldots, P_n)} = f_2(\mathcal{R}_{P_1}, \ldots, \mathcal{R}_{P_n})$.*

In the sequel, we list several conditions of that kind which play an important role in the characterisation of the classes of relative relations derived from information systems. Let W and PAR be non-empty sets and $(\mathcal{R}_P)_{P \in \mathcal{P}^n(PAR)}$, $n \geq 1$, be a family of binary relations on W. We say that $(\mathcal{R}_P)_{P \in \mathcal{P}^n(PAR)}$ satisfies condition (C_i), $i = 1, \ldots, 9 \stackrel{\text{def}}{\Leftrightarrow}$

(C_0): true;
(C_1): $\mathcal{R}_{P \cup Q} = \mathcal{R}_P \cap \mathcal{R}_Q$ for all $P, Q \in \mathcal{P}^n(PAR)$;
(C_2): $\mathcal{R}_P = \bigcap_{p \in P} \mathcal{R}_{\{p\}}$ for every $P \in \mathcal{P}^n(PAR)$;
(C_3): $\mathcal{R}_{P \cup Q} = \mathcal{R}_P \cup \mathcal{R}_Q$ for all $P, Q \in \mathcal{P}^n(PAR)$;
(C_4): $\mathcal{R}_P = \bigcup_{p \in P} \mathcal{R}_{\{p\}}$ for every $P \in \mathcal{P}^n(PAR)$;
(C_5): $\mathcal{R}_{P \cup Q} = \mathcal{R}_P \cup^* \mathcal{R}_Q$ for all $P, Q \in \mathcal{P}^n(PAR)$;
(C_6): $\mathcal{R}_{P \cap Q} = \mathcal{R}_P \cap \mathcal{R}_Q$ for all $P, Q \in \mathcal{P}^n(PAR)$;
(C_7): $\mathcal{R}_{P \cap Q} = \mathcal{R}_P \cup \mathcal{R}_Q$ for all $P, Q \in \mathcal{P}^n(PAR)$;
(C_8): $\mathcal{R}_P = \mathcal{R}_{(PAR \setminus P)}$ for every $P \in \mathcal{P}^n(PAR)$;
(C_9): $\mathcal{R}_P = W^2 \setminus \mathcal{R}_{(PAR \setminus P)}$ for every $P \in \mathcal{P}^n(PAR)$.

Condition (C_2) implies condition (C_1), but the converse is not true. Here is a counterexample. Let $\langle W, (\mathcal{R}_P)_{P \subseteq PAR} \rangle$ be the relative frame such that $W = PAR = \mathbb{N}$, and for every $P \subseteq \mathbb{N}$,

$$\mathcal{R}_P \stackrel{\text{def}}{=} \left\{ \begin{array}{l} \{\langle i, i \rangle \in \mathbb{N}^2 : 0 \leq i \leq \min P\} \text{ if } P \text{ is finite and non-empty;} \\ \emptyset \text{ if } P \text{ is infinite.} \end{array} \right.$$

Clearly, for all $P, Q \subseteq \mathbb{N}$, $\mathcal{R}_{P \cup Q} = \mathcal{R}_P \cap \mathcal{R}_Q$, that is (C_1) holds. By contrast, (C_2) does not hold, since $\mathcal{R}_{\mathbb{N} \setminus \{0\}} = \emptyset$ by definition and $\bigcap_{i \in \mathbb{N} \setminus \{0\}} \mathcal{R}_{\{i\}} = \{\langle 0, 0 \rangle\}$.

Our convention here is that a global condition which is satisfied by any family of relative relations (which means no restriction on the family) is denoted by "true". We make this convention for the sake of uniformity of presentation.

The characterisation of a family of relative relations often requires special postulates for the relations indexed with the empty set and the given set PAR. The typical conditions for these relations are:

(C_1'): $\mathcal{R}_\emptyset = W^2$;
(C_2'): $\mathcal{R}_\emptyset = \emptyset$;
(C_3'): $\mathcal{R}_{PAR} = W^2$;
(C_4'): $\mathcal{R}_{PAR} = \emptyset$.

One can easily imagine other constraints on a family of relative relations, for instance:

* $\langle\{\mathcal{R}_P : P \in \mathcal{P}^n(PAR)\}, \subseteq\rangle$ is a complete lattice, $n \geq 1$;
* $\langle\{\mathcal{R}_P : P \in \mathcal{P}^n(PAR)\}, \cup, \cap, -, \emptyset, \bigcup\{R_P : P \subseteq PAR\}\rangle$ is a Boolean algebra.

3.10 Abstract Information Relations

In this section we define information relations in an abstract way, without assuming that they are derived from an information system. In this way we obtain several families of relative frames.

We define the following classes of relative frames.

* FS is the class of relative frames in which the families of relative relations satisfy conditions (C_1) and (C'_1). The members of FS are called FS-*frames* or *relative frames with strong relations*.

* FVS is the class of relative frames in which the families of relative relations satisfy conditions (C_2) and (C'_1). The members of FVS are called FVS-*frames* or *relative frames with very strong relations*.

* FW is the class of relative frames in which the families of relative relations satisfy conditions (C_3) and (C'_2). The members of FW are called FW-*frames* or *relative frames with weak relations*.

* FVW is the class of relative frames in which the families of relative relations satisfy conditions (C_4) and (C'_2). The members of FVW are called FVW-*frames* or *relative frames with very weak relations*.

We say that a frame $F = \langle W, (\mathcal{R}^1_P)_{P \subseteq PAR}, \ldots, (\mathcal{R}^t_P)_{P \subseteq PAR}\rangle$ is a *reflection* of a frame $F' = \langle W, (\mathcal{R}'^1_P)_{P \subseteq PAR}, \ldots, (\mathcal{R}'^t_P)_{P \subseteq PAR}\rangle$ iff for every $P \subseteq PAR$ and for every $h \in \{1, \ldots, t\}$, $\mathcal{R}^h_P = W \times W \setminus \mathcal{R}'^h_P$, and then we write $F = (F')^{\neg}$. We say that the frame F is a *conversion* of the frame F' iff for every $P \subseteq PAR$ and for every $h \in \{1, \ldots, t\}$, $\mathcal{R}^h_P = (\mathcal{R}'^h_P)^{-1}$, and then we write $F = (F')^{-1}$.

Lemma 3.10.1. *For all frames F, F', the following conditions are satisfied:*

(I) $F \in$ FS iff $F^{\neg} \in$ FW;
(II) $F \in$ FS [resp. $F \in$ FW] iff $F^{-1} \in$ FS [resp. $F^{-1} \in$ FW];
(III) $F = (F')^{\neg}$ iff $F' = F^{\neg}$;
(IV) $((F)^{\neg})^{\neg} = F$;
(V) $F = (F')^{-1}$ iff $F' = F^{-1}$;
(VI) $(F^{-1})^{-1} = F$.

Lemma 3.10.1 also holds if we replace FS by FVS and FW by FVW.

We define more specific classes of frames postulating some conditions that the relations are supposed to satisfy. The properties of relations in the frames are intended to characterise information relations derived from information systems. We introduce four groups of classes of relative frames, each containing the frames with at most two families of relations of level 1:

⋆ FS-frames with indistinguishability relations;
⋆ FW-frames with indistinguishability relations;
⋆ FS-frames with distinguishability relations;
⋆ FW-frames with distinguishability relations.

In each group, we introduce the classes that are abstract counterparts of the corresponding classes of frames derived from information systems.

3.10.1 FS-frames with Indistinguishability Relations

⋆ FS-IND is the class of FS-frames $\langle W, (\mathcal{R}_P)_{P \subseteq PAR} \rangle$ such that for every $p \in PAR$, $\mathcal{R}_{\{p\}}$ is an equivalence relation. Consequently, for every $P \subseteq PAR$, $\mathcal{R}_P$ is an equivalence relation, since reflexivity, symmetry, and transitivity are preserved under intersection. The members of FS-IND are called *strong indiscernibility frames*.

⋆ FS-FIN is the class of FS-frames $\langle W, (\mathcal{R}_P)_{P \subseteq PAR} \rangle$ such that for every $p \in PAR$, $\mathcal{R}_{\{p\}}$ is reflexive and transitive. Consequently, for every $P \subseteq PAR$, $\mathcal{R}_P$ is reflexive and transitive since reflexivity and transitivity are preserved under intersection. The members of FS-FIN are called *strong forward inclusion frames*.

⋆ FS-SIM-TOT is the class of FS-frames $\langle W, (\mathcal{R}_P)_{P \subseteq PAR} \rangle$ such that for every $p \in PAR$, $\mathcal{R}_{\{p\}}$ is a tolerance relation. Consequently, for every $P \subseteq PAR$, $\mathcal{R}_P$ is a tolerance relation. The members of FS-SIM-TOT are called *strong total similarity frames*.

⋆ FS-SIM is the class of FS-frames $\langle W, (\mathcal{R}_P)_{P \subseteq PAR} \rangle$ such that for every $p \in PAR$, $\mathcal{R}_{\{p\}}$ is weakly reflexive and symmetric. Consequently, for every $P \subseteq PAR$, $\mathcal{R}_P$ is weakly reflexive and symmetric. The members of FS-SIM are called *strong similarity frames*.

⋆ FS-ICOM is the class of FS-frames $\langle W, (\mathcal{R}_P)_{P \subseteq PAR} \rangle$ such that for every $p \in PAR$, $\mathcal{R}_{\{p\}}$ is reflexive, symmetric, and co-3-transitive. Consequently, for every $P \subseteq PAR$, $\mathcal{R}_P$ is reflexive and symmetric. The property of co-3-transitivity is not preserved under intersection. The members of FS-ICOM are called *strong incomplementarity frames*.

⋆ FS-IN is the class of relative FS-frames $\langle W, (\mathcal{R}_P)_{P \subseteq PAR}, (\mathcal{Q}_P)_{P \subseteq PAR} \rangle$ with two families of relative relations such that for every $p \in PAR$, $\mathcal{R}_{\{p\}}$ and $\mathcal{Q}_{\{p\}}$ are reflexive and transitive, and $\mathcal{R}_{\{p\}} = \mathcal{Q}_{\{p\}}^{-1}$. Consequently, for every $P \subseteq PAR$, $\mathcal{R}_P$ and $\mathcal{Q}_P$ are reflexive and transitive, and $\mathcal{R}_P = \mathcal{Q}_P^{-1}$. The members of FS-IN are called *strong inclusion frames*.

3.10.2 FW-frames with Indistinguishability Relations

⋆ FW-IND is the class of FW-frames $\langle W, (\mathcal{R}_P)_{P \subseteq PAR} \rangle$ such that for every $p \in PAR$, $\mathcal{R}_{\{p\}}$ is an equivalence relation. Consequently, for every $\emptyset \neq P \subseteq PAR$, $\mathcal{R}_P$ is reflexive and symmetric. Transitivity is not preserved under union. The members of FW-IND are called *weak indiscernibility frames*.

⋆ FW-SIM-TOT is the class of FW-frames $\langle W, (\mathcal{R}_P)_{P \subseteq PAR} \rangle$ such that for every $p \in PAR$, $\mathcal{R}_{\{p\}}$ is a tolerance relation. Consequently, for every $\emptyset \neq P \subseteq PAR$, $\mathcal{R}_P$ is a tolerance relation. The members of FS-SIM-TOT are called *weak total similarity frames*.

⋆ FW-SIM is the class of FW-frames $\langle W, (\mathcal{R}_P)_{P \subseteq PAR} \rangle$ such that for every $p \in PAR$, $\mathcal{R}_{\{p\}}$ is weakly reflexive and symmetric. Consequently, for every $P \subseteq PAR$, $\mathcal{R}_P$ is weakly reflexive and symmetric. The members of FW-SIM are called *weak similarity frames*.

⋆ FW-ICOM is the class of FW-frames $\langle W, (\mathcal{R}_P)_{P \subseteq PAR} \rangle$ such that for every $p \in PAR$, $\mathcal{R}_{\{p\}}$ is reflexive, symmetric, and co-3-transitive. Consequently, for every $\emptyset \neq P \subseteq PAR$, $\mathcal{R}_P$ is reflexive, symmetric, and co-3-transitive. The property of co-3-transitivity is preserved under union. The members of FW-ICOM are called *weak incomplementarity frames*.

⋆ FW-IN is the class of relative FW-frames $\langle W, (\mathcal{R}_P)_{P \subseteq PAR}, (\mathcal{Q}_P)_{P \subseteq PAR} \rangle$ with two families of relative relations such that for every $p \in PAR$, $\mathcal{R}_{\{p\}}$ and $\mathcal{Q}_{\{p\}}$ are reflexive and transitive, and $\mathcal{R}_{\{p\}} = \mathcal{Q}_{\{p\}}^{-1}$. Consequently, for every $P \subseteq PAR$, $\mathcal{R}_P = \mathcal{Q}_P^{-1}$ and if $P \neq \emptyset$, then $\mathcal{R}_P$ and $\mathcal{Q}_P$ are reflexive. Transitivity is not preserved under union. The members of FW-IN are called *weak inclusion frames*.

3.10.3 FS-frames with Distinguishability Relations

⋆ FS-DIV is the class of FS-frames $\langle W, (\mathcal{R}_P)_{P \subseteq PAR} \rangle$ such that for every $p \in PAR$, $\mathcal{R}_{\{p\}}$ is irreflexive, symmetric, and cotransitive. Consequently, for every $P \subseteq PAR$, $\mathcal{R}_P$ is symmetric, and if $P \neq \emptyset$, then $\mathcal{R}_P$ is irreflexive. Cotransitivity is not preserved under intersection. The members of FS-DIV are called *strong diversity frames*.

* **FS-RORT-TOT** is the class of FS-frames $\langle W, (\mathcal{R}_P)_{P \subseteq PAR} \rangle$ such that for every $p \in PAR$, $\mathcal{R}_{\{p\}}$ is irreflexive and symmetric. Consequently, for every $P \subseteq PAR$, $\mathcal{R}_P$ is irreflexive and symmetric. The members of FS-RORT-TOT are called *strong total right orthogonality frames*.

* **FS-RORT** is the class of FS-frames $\langle W, (\mathcal{R}_P)_{P \subseteq PAR} \rangle$ such that for every $p \in PAR$, $\mathcal{R}_{\{p\}}$ is coweakly reflexive and symmetric. Consequently, for every $P \subseteq PAR$, $\mathcal{R}_P$ is coweakly reflexive and symmetric. The members of FS-RORT are called *strong right orthogonality frames*.

* **FS-COM** is the class of FS-frames $\langle W, (\mathcal{R}_P)_{P \subseteq PAR} \rangle$ such that for every $p \in PAR$, $\mathcal{R}_{\{p\}}$ is irreflexive, symmetric, and 3-transitive. Consequently, for every $P \subseteq PAR$, $\mathcal{R}_P$ is symmetric and 3-transitive, and if $P \neq \emptyset$, then $\mathcal{R}_P$ is irreflexive. The members of FS-COM are called *strong complementarity frames*.

* **FS-RLNIM** is the class of relative FS-frames $\langle W, (\mathcal{R}_P)_{P \subseteq PAR}, (\mathcal{Q}_P)_{P \subseteq PAR} \rangle$ with two families of relative relations such that for every $p \in PAR$, $\mathcal{R}_{\{p\}}$ and $\mathcal{Q}_{\{p\}}$ are irreflexive and cotransitive, and $\mathcal{R}_{\{p\}} = \mathcal{Q}_{\{p\}}^{-1}$. Consequently, for every $P \subseteq PAR$, $\mathcal{R}_P = \mathcal{Q}_P^{-1}$ and if $P \neq \emptyset$, then $\mathcal{R}_P$ and $\mathcal{Q}_P$ are irreflexive. Cotransitivity is not preserved under intersection. The members of FS-RLNIM are called *strong right–left negative similarity frames*.

3.10.4 FW-frames with Distinguishability Relations

* **FW-DIV** is the class of FW-frames $\langle W, (\mathcal{R}_P)_{P \subseteq PAR} \rangle$ such that for every $p \in PAR$, $\mathcal{R}_{\{p\}}$ is irreflexive, symmetric, and cotransitive. Consequently, for every $P \subseteq PAR$, $\mathcal{R}_P$ is irreflexive, symmetric, and cotransitive. Cotransitivity is preserved under union. The members of FW-DIV are called *weak diversity frames*.

* **FW-RORT-TOT** is the class of FW-frames $\langle W, (\mathcal{R}_P)_{P \subseteq PAR} \rangle$ such that for every $p \in PAR$, $\mathcal{R}_{\{p\}}$ is irreflexive and symmetric. Consequently, for every $P \subseteq PAR$, $\mathcal{R}_P$ is irreflexive and symmetric. The members of FW-RORT-TOT are called *weak total right orthogonality frames*.

* **FW-RORT** is the class of FW-frames $\langle W, (\mathcal{R}_P)_{P \subseteq PAR} \rangle$ such that for every $p \in PAR$, $\mathcal{R}_{\{p\}}$ is coweakly reflexive and symmetric. Consequently, for every $P \subseteq PAR$, $\mathcal{R}_P$ is coweakly reflexive and symmetric. The members of FW-RORT are called *weak right orthogonality frames*.

⋆ FW-COM is the class of FW-frames $\langle W, (\mathcal{R}_P)_{P \subseteq PAR} \rangle$ such that for every $p \in PAR$, $\mathcal{R}_{\{p\}}$ is irreflexive, symmetric, and 3-transitive. Consequently, for every $P \subseteq PAR$, $\mathcal{R}_P$ is irreflexive and symmetric. 3-transitivity is not preserved under union. The members of FW-COM are called *weak complementarity frames*.

⋆ FW-RLNIM is the class of FW-frames $\langle W, (\mathcal{R}_P)_{P \subseteq PAR}, (\mathcal{Q}_P)_{P \subseteq PAR} \rangle$ with two families of relative relations such that for every $p \in PAR$, $\mathcal{R}_{\{p\}}$ and $\mathcal{Q}_{\{p\}}$ are irreflexive and cotransitive, and $\mathcal{R}_{\{p\}} = \mathcal{Q}_{\{p\}}^{-1}$. Consequently, for every $P \subseteq PAR$, $\mathcal{R}_P$ and $\mathcal{Q}_P$ are irreflexive and cotransitive, and $\mathcal{R}_P = \mathcal{Q}_P^{-1}$. Cotransitivity is preserved under union. The members of FW-RLNIM are called *weak right–left negative similarity frames*.

The relations in the families of frames defined above will be named according to the name of the respective class of frames. For example, if $\langle W, (\mathcal{R}_P)_{P \subseteq PAR} \rangle$ is an indiscernibility frame, then the relations $\mathcal{R}_P$ are referred to as indiscernibility relations.

For every class FS-C [resp. FW-C] defined above, we write FVS-C [resp. FVW-C] to denote the class FS-C ∩ FVS [resp. FW-C ∩ FVW] of relative frames.

We have the following result.

Lemma 3.10.2. *For every information system S, the following conditions are satisfied:*

(I) $D_{ind}(S) \in$ FS-IND, $D_{sim}(S) \in$ FS-SIM, $D_{nim}(S) \in$ FS-SIM,
   $D_{icom}(S) \in$ FS-ICOM, $D_{fin,bin}(S) \in$ FS-IN, *and the analogous conditions hold for the respective FW-frames;*

(II) $D_{div}(S) \in$ FS-DIV, $D_{rort}(S) \in$ FS-RORT, $D_{lort}(S) \in$ FS-RORT,
   $D_{com}(S) \in$ FS-COM, $D_{rnim,lnim}(S) \in$ FW-RLNIM, *and the analogous conditions hold for the respective FW-frames;*

(III) $F \in$ FS-IND *[resp.* FS-SIM, FS-SIM-TOT, FS-ICOM, FS-IN*] iff* $F^{\neg} \in$ FW-DIV *[resp.* FW-RORT, FW-RORT-TOT, FW-COM, FW-RLNIM*]*;

(IV) $F \in$ FW-IND *[resp.* FW-SIM, FW-SIM-TOT, FW-ICOM, FW-IN*] iff* $F^{\neg} \in$ FS-DIV *[resp.* FS-RORT, FS-RORT-TOT, FS-COM, FS-RLNIM*]*.

Proof. Conditions (I) and (II) follow from Lemmas 3.3.1, 3.3.2, 3.3.3, and 3.3.4. Observe that left orthogonality relations derived from an information system satisfy the same conditions as right orthogonality relations. The same concerns similarity and negative similarity. Conditions (III) and (IV) can be easily verified.   *Q.E.D.*

Lemma 3.10.2 also holds for the classes of very strong frames and very weak frames, respectively.

3.11 Fuzzy Information Relations

In this section we define several fuzzy relations analogous to information relations. Let $L = \langle W, +, \cdot, \odot, \rightarrow, \oplus, \leftarrow, 1, 0 \rangle$ be a double residuated lattice and let U be a universe of objects. An L-fuzzy relation on U is a mapping $R : U^n \rightarrow L$, $n \geq 1$. By a *fuzzy relation* we mean an L-fuzzy relation for some double residuated lattice L. Clearly, every fuzzy relation on a set U is a fuzzy subset of U^n for some $n \geq 1$, so the operations on fuzzy sets apply to fuzzy relations. The family of all L-fuzzy binary relations on U is denoted by $\mathcal{F}_L Rel(U)$.

From now on we assume that L is a complete double residuated lattice. The operations on L-fuzzy binary relations analogous to the composition and converse of ordinary relations are defined as follows. Let $R, R' \in \mathcal{F}_L Rel(U)$, then for all $x, y \in U$:

* $(R ;_L R')(x, y) \overset{\text{def}}{=} sup(\{R(x, z) \odot R'(z, y) : y \in U\})$;
* $R^{-1_L}(x, y) \overset{\text{def}}{=} R(y, x)$.

We also define the relational constants $1'_L$, 1_L, and 0_L:

* $1'_L(x, y) = 1$ if $x = y$, otherwise $1'_L(x, y) = 0$;
* $1_L(x, y) = 1$, $0_L(x, y) = 0$.

Fuzzy relations may satisfy various properties analogous to the properties of ordinary relations. We say that an L-fuzzy binary relation R on a set U is:

* *reflexive* $\overset{\text{def}}{\Leftrightarrow}$ $R(x, x) = 1$ for every $x \in U$;
* *weakly reflexive* $\overset{\text{def}}{\Leftrightarrow}$ $R(x, x) = sup(\{R(x, y) : y \in U\})$ for every $x \in U$;
* *irreflexive* $\overset{\text{def}}{\Leftrightarrow}$ $R(x, x) = 0$ for every $x \in U$;
* *weakly irreflexive* $\overset{\text{def}}{\Leftrightarrow}$ $R(x, x) = inf(\{R(x, y) : y \in U\})$ for every $x \in U$;
* *symmetric* $\overset{\text{def}}{\Leftrightarrow}$ $R(x, y) = R(y, x)$ for all $x, y \in U$;
* *n-transitive*, $n \geq 2$ $\overset{\text{def}}{\Leftrightarrow}$ $R(x_1, x_2) \odot R(x_2, x_3) \odot \ldots \odot R(x_n, x_{n+1}) \leq R(x_1, x_{n+1})$ for all $x_1, x_2, \ldots, x_n, x_{n+1} \in U$;
* *transitive* $\overset{\text{def}}{\Leftrightarrow}$ 2-transitive;
* *strongly transitive* $\overset{\text{def}}{\Leftrightarrow}$ $sup(\{R(x, y) \odot R(y, z) : y \in W\}) = R(x, z)$ for all $x, z \in U$;
* *n-cotransitive*, $n \geq 2$ $\overset{\text{def}}{\Leftrightarrow}$ $R(x_1, x_2) \oplus R(x_2, x_3) \oplus \ldots \oplus R(x_n, x_{n+1}) \geq R(x_1, x_{n+1})$ for all $x_1, x_2, \ldots, x_n, x_{n+1} \in U$;
* *cotransitive* $\overset{\text{def}}{\Leftrightarrow}$ 2-cotransitive.

Although the names of these properties are the same as the names of the properties of the ordinary binary relations, it is always clear from the context which relations they are referred to.

We define several L-fuzzy binary relations on a family $\mathcal{F}_L \mathcal{P}(U)$ for every set U. These relations provide patterns for fuzzy relative relations. Let $X, Y \in \mathcal{F}_L \mathcal{P}(U)$, then:

* $In_L(X, Y) \overset{\text{def}}{=} inf(\{X(x) \to Y(x) : x \in U\})$ (inclusion relation);
* $Ni_L(X, Y) \overset{\text{def}}{=} sup(\{Y(x) \leftarrow X(x) : x \in U\})$ (negative inclusion relation);
* $Sim_L(X, Y) \overset{\text{def}}{=} sup(\{X(x) \odot Y(x) : x \in U\})$ (similarity relation);
* $Exh_L(X, Y) \overset{\text{def}}{=} inf(\{X(x) \oplus Y(x) : x \in U\})$ (exhaustiveness relation);
* $Ind_L(X, Y) \overset{\text{def}}{=} In_L(X, Y) \odot In_L(Y, X)$ (indiscernibility relation);
* $Div_L(X, Y) \overset{\text{def}}{=} Ni_L(X, Y) \oplus Ni_L(Y, X)$ (diversity relation).

The following lemma shows that the relations defined above may be understood as a representation of the degrees of inclusion, non-inclusion, compatiblity, exhaustiveness, equality, and non-equality of fuzzy sets, respectively.

Lemma 3.11.1. *For all $X, Y \in \mathcal{F}_L \mathcal{P}(U)$, the following assertions hold:*

(I) $X \subseteq_L Y$ iff $In_L(X, Y) = 1$ iff $Ni_L(X, Y) = 0$;
(II) $X =_L Y$ iff $Ind_L(X, Y) = 1$ iff $Div_L(X, Y) = 0$;
(III) X and Y are L-compatible iff $Sim_L(X, Y) = 1$;
(IV) X and Y are L-exhaustive iff $Exh_L(X, Y) = 1$.

The proof is by an easy verification.
The relations defined above have the following properties.

Lemma 3.11.2.

(I) In_L is reflexive and transitive;
(II) Ni_L is irreflexive and cotransitive;
(III) Sim_L and Exh_L are symmetric;
(IV) Ind_L is reflexive, symmetric, and transitive;
(V) Div_L is irreflexive and symmetric.

The proof follows easily from the arithmetic of double residuated lattices presented in Sect. 2.7.

Fuzzy information systems induce families of fuzzy information relations analogous to the information relations derived from ordinary information systems. Let $\langle OB, L, AT, (VAL_a)_{a \in AT} \rangle$ be a fuzzy information system, let $L = \langle W, +, \cdot, \odot, \to, \oplus, \leftarrow, 1, 0 \rangle$ be a double residuated lattice, and let R_L be any of the set relations defined above. For every $a \in AT$, we define a family of fuzzy information relations $r_L : OB \times OB \to L$ determined by the attribute a as follows. For all $x, x' \in W$,

$$r_L(a)(x, x') \overset{\text{def}}{=} R_L(a(x), a(x')).$$

For example, if $R_L = Ind_L$, then $ind_L(a)(x, x') = Ind_L(a(x), a(x'))$ is the fuzzy indiscernibility relation derived from a fuzzy information system. According to the definition of Ind_L and Lemma 2.7.1(II), $ind_L(a)$ represents a degree of equality of the fuzzy sets of values of attribute a assigned to objects

x and x', respectively. In a similar way, we can obtain the other relations derived from a fuzzy information system, analogous to the classical information relations presented in Sect. 3.2. For a finite set A of attributes we define strong and weak fuzzy information relations:

$$r_L^s(A) \stackrel{\text{def}}{=} \cap_L \{r_L(a) : a \in A\}, \quad r_L^w(A) \stackrel{\text{def}}{=} \cup_L \{r_L(a) : a \in A\}.$$

We conclude that the methodology of deriving information relations from an information system can be applied to fuzzy information systems.

In a general setting, relative fuzzy relations are defined as follows. We confine ourselves to binary relations. Let X and Y be sets and let PAR be a family of mappings $p : X \to \mathcal{F}_L \mathcal{P}(Y)$ assigning an L-fuzzy subset of Y to every element of X. It follows that for every $x \in X$, $p(x)$ is an L-fuzzy subset of Y, that is $p(x) : Y \to L$. Let $\mathcal{R}_L : \mathcal{F}_L \mathcal{P}(Y) \times \mathcal{F}_L \mathcal{P}(Y) \to L$ be an L-fuzzy binary relation on a family of L-fuzzy subsets of X.

A relative binary L-fuzzy relation on X determined by $P \subseteq PAR$ and $\mathcal{R}_L$ is any relation $r_{L,P}$ such that for all $x, y \in X$:

⋆ $r_{L,p}(x,y) = \mathcal{R}_L(p(x),p(y))$ for every $p \in PAR$;
⋆ $r_{L,P} = f(\{r_{L,p} : p \in P\})$, where f is an operation on fuzzy binary relations.

In particular, if $f = \cap_L$, then we say that $r_{L,P}$ is strong, and if $f = \cup_L$, then $r_{L,P}$ is said to be weak.

3.12 Notes

Information relations. Indiscernibility relations derived from information systems are introduced in [KOP81]. Similarity and forward inclusion are introduced in [Orło85a]. Negative similarity is introduced in [Vak91a]. The applications of discernibility relations presented in Sect. 3.5 are developed in [RS91]. The set-theoretical formulation of this method presented in Sect. 3.7 is from [Jär97]. The information system in Example 3.7.1 is a part of an information system presented in [Paw91]. A general concept of complementarity is introduced in [Boh58]. Applications of complementarity relations mentioned in Sect. 3.8 are developed in [DO98a].

Relative relations. Frames with relative (parameterised) relations have been suggested in [Orło88a] in the context of a rough-set analysis of data, and they were investigated, among others, in [Kon87, Bal96a, Kon98, Kon97, Bal98]. Often we are interested in studying relationships between information relations that belong to different families. Hence, it is natural to consider frames with families of relations of different types. A great variety of such frames is studied in the literature; see for example [Orło84a, Orło85a, Orło87b, Vak87, Orło89, Vak89, Vak89, Vak91c, Vak91a, DO96, Dem96a, Oe98a, Dem97a, Bal01]. For every information system the information relations derived from the system are defined according to a certain common pattern. It leads to a closure property on the set of relations generated by the information relations with the standard operations of union, intersection, complement, and converse of relations. This closure property is expressed in the form of derivability in a certain logical system related to syllogistics [Wed48, She56]. The details can be found in [Orło99]. The discussion of methods of construction of "full" classes of information relations (in some precisely defined sense) can also be found in [Vak98].

Hierarchy of relative relations. Apart from information systems relative relations of level 2 appear naturally in data concerning social activities. Such a knowledge is usually represented in the form of rules that express imperatives, permissions, prohibitions, norms, actions, etc. In some applications these rules are grouped into families of sets of rules referred to as *rule complexes*. They are investigated in [BG00]. Dealing with rule complexes provides us with a formal means of expressing an idea that some rules are tied to one another with respect to their functions. In a natural way, the rules determine binary relations in a set of agents. These relations are defined in a similar way as information relations determined by attributes in an information system. For example, given a rule r, an indiscernibility relation $ind(r)$ in a set of agents may be defined as follows: $\langle x, y \rangle \in ind(r)$ iff (r is a rule of x iff r is a rule of y). These relations generalise to relations parameterised by sets of rules and rule complexes, leading to relations of levels 1 and 2, respectively. Deontic logic is another source of examples of relative relations of levels 2 and 3. Such a deontic logic can be found in [Bro96]. The logic includes modal operators that express degrees of urgency of obligation, with each such degree construed as a set of obligations, and each obligation construed as a non-empty set of possible worlds.

Dependencies of attributes. The study of dependencies of attributes began with the introduction of the notion of functional dependency in relational databases [Cod70]. This opened up the possibility of specifying data in the form of facts and constraints. In this connection the problem arose of development of formal systems for proving implications of dependencies. In those systems any set of dependencies is identified with a set of sentences of a formal language, and a proof system for the language serves as an inference tool for proving dependencies and various relationships between them. The first formal system for dependencies was given in [Arm74]; a survey of dependency theory can be found in [FV86b]. Relational representation of dependencies presented in Sect. 3.5 is developed in [Orło87a]. In [BO98] a relational deduction system for generalised database dependencies is developed and decidability issues are discussed. Relational formalisation of some other types of data dependencies can be found in [Mac00, Mac01]. Dependencies of attributes in information systems are also studied in [Paw85, DG97, Rau85, Rau88]. Dependencies of attributes in contexts are studied, among others, in [Wil88, Lux98].

Decomposition and contraction of attributes. The notion of decomposition of an attribute into features and the notion of contraction of attributes are introduced in [Iwi88]. The material of Sect. 3.6 is from that paper.

Fuzzy information relations. Fuzzy information relations were suggested in [Orło99]. Some fuzzy information relations with the values in the unit interval [0, 1] are introduced and investigated in [RK01c]. Here we consider more general information relations with the values in a double residuated lattice. In many cases the properties of these two classes of relations are similar and we follow the developments in [RK01c].

4. Information Operators Derived from Information Systems

4.1 Introduction and Outline of the Chapter

In Chap. 3 we have shown that every information system contains an implicit information which may have the form of information relations. In the present chapter we discuss an implicit information of another kind. We show how an information system induces various families of operators acting on sets of objects, we present their applications, and we study their properties.

There are two major groups of those operators. The first group contains the operators that enable us to represent sets of objects which may be characterised – precisely or approximately – in terms of information from a given information system. These operators are presented in Sect. 4.2 and they are referred to as approximation operators. In Sect. 4.3 we introduce some useful operators definable with approximation operators. In Sect. 4.4 we present a classification of sets of objects of an information system. The classification reflects non-numerical degrees of definability of the sets in terms of the informational resources provided by the information system. In Sect. 4.5 we illustrate the application of approximation operators to approximate information retrieval.

The second group of operators consists of knowledge operators; they are discussed in Sect. 4.6. These operators enable us to represent sets of objects which may be considered as known or approximately known in view of information provided by the given information system. We present a hierarchy of non-numerical degrees of knowing the sets of objects.

In Sect. 4.7 we discuss some structural properties of the whole family of information operators derived from an information system, including both approximation and knowledge operators. In Sect. 4.8 we briefly discuss ways of generalising the notion of approximation operator and we present some generalised approximation operators. In Sect. 4.9 we show how properties of information relations can be expressed with information operators. We present several examples of such correspondences both for local and global properties of relations. In Sect. 4.10 we present the fundamental structures that can be derived from an information system, namely, its approximation space, the family of rough subsets of an approximation space, and the knowledge structure of an approximation space. We conclude the chapter by presenting in Sect. 4.11 the information operators derived from any fuzzy information system.

4.2 Approximation Operators

We begin with a simple example.

Example 4.2.1. Consider the information system from Example 2.2.1. Suppose that we are interested in defining the set $X = \{x_1, x_3, x_4\}$ in terms of the properties of objects available in the system. We easily observe that the statement, which at first glance seems to be the description of the given set, is not true: $x \in X$ iff x is either green or blue. This description is true not only of the objects from X but also of x_2.

The above observation is the starting point of the rough set theory that deals with approximate definability of sets by means of their approximations. Let $S = \langle OB, AT \rangle$ be an information system and $(ind(A))_{A \subseteq AT}$ be the family of indiscernibility relations derived from the system S. The approximation operators derived from S are functions on the set $\mathcal{P}(OB)$ defined as follows. The *lower $ind(A)$-approximation* $L_{ind(A)}(X)$ of a set X of objects is the union of those equivalence classes of $ind(A)$ that are included in X and the *upper $ind(A)$-approximation* $U_{ind(A)}(X)$ of a set X is the set of those equivalence classes that have an element in common with X:

$\star$ $L_{ind(A)}(X) \overset{\text{def}}{=} \bigcup \{|x|_{ind(A)} : x \in OB, \ |x|_{ind(A)} \subseteq X\}$
$\quad = \{x \in OB : \text{ for every } y \in OB, \text{ if } \langle x, y \rangle \in ind(A),$
$\quad \text{then } y \in X\};$

$\star$ $U_{ind(A)}(X) \overset{\text{def}}{=} \bigcup \{|x|_{ind(A)} : x \in OB, |x|_{ind(A)} \cap X \neq \emptyset\}$
$\quad = \{x \in OB : \text{ there is a } y \in OB \text{ such that } \langle x, y \rangle \in ind(A)\}.$

In the following we list the fundamental properties of these approximation operators. Throughout this chapter we will drop the symbol of information relation from the name of the underlying operations whenever there is no danger of confusion.

Lemma 4.2.1. *For every information system* $S = \langle OB, AT \rangle$ *and for all* $A, B \subseteq AT$, *if* $A \subseteq B$, *then:*

(I) $ind(B) \subseteq ind(A)$;
(II) $L_{ind(A)}(X) \subseteq L_{ind(B)}(X)$ for every $X \subseteq OB$;
(III) $U_{ind(B)}(X) \subseteq U_{ind(A)}(X)$ for every $X \subseteq OB$.

It follows that the smaller $ind(A)$ relation is, the closer to X the approximations $L_{ind(A)}(X)$ and $U_{ind(A)}(X)$ are.

Lemma 4.2.2. *Let* $S = \langle OB, AT \rangle$ *be an information system and let* $L = L_{ind(A)}$ *and* $U = U_{ind(A)}$ *be the approximation operators associated with a given set* $A \subseteq AT$ *of attributes. Then for all* $X, Y \subseteq OB$, *we have:*

(I) $L(X) \subseteq X \subseteq U(X)$;

(II) $L(X \cap Y) = L(X) \cap L(Y)$, $\qquad\qquad U(X \cup Y) = U(X) \cup U(Y)$;

(III) $L(L(X)) = L(X)$, $\qquad\qquad\qquad U(U(X)) = U(X)$;

(IV) $L(OB) = OB$, $\qquad\qquad\qquad\qquad U(\emptyset) = \emptyset$;

(V) $L(X) = OB \setminus U(OB \setminus X)$.

Lemma 4.2.2 enables us to deduce the properties of the approximations determined by the Boolean structure of $\mathcal{P}(OB)$. The following lemma shows how the properties of lower approximations depend on the Boolean structure of the subsets of attributes that determine the underlying indiscernibility relation.

Lemma 4.2.3. *Let $S = \langle OB, AT \rangle$ be an information system and let $A, B \subseteq AT$. For every $X \subseteq OB$, the following assertions hold:*

(I) $L_{ind(A \cup B)}(X) \supseteq L_{ind(A)}(X) \cup L_{ind(B)}(X)$;

(II) $L_{ind(A \cap B)}(X) \subseteq L_{ind(A)}(X) \cap L_{ind(B)}(X)$;

(III) $L_{ind(\emptyset)}(X) = \emptyset$ *if* $X \neq OB$ *and* $L_{ind(\emptyset)}(OB) = OB$.

The corresponding properties of the upper approximations can be deduced using Lemma 4.2.2(V).

Example 4.2.2. Consider the information system S from Example 2.4.1 and let $X = \{Me, V, J, Sa, P\}$.
We have $L_{ind(AT)}(X) = \{J, Sa\}$ and $U_{ind(AT)}(X) = X \cup \{E, Ma\}$.

Let $S = \langle OB, AT \rangle$ be an information system and let $L = L_{ind(A)}$ and $U = U_{ind(A)}$ be the approximation operators associated to a set $A \subseteq AT$. For all $X, Y \subseteq OB$, we define *rough equalities, rough inclusions*, and *rough intersections* as follows:

$\star\ X \underset{\sim}{\subseteq} Y \overset{\text{def}}{\Leftrightarrow} L(X) \subseteq L(Y)$ $\qquad\qquad$ (rough bottom inclusion);

$\star\ X \overset{\sim}{\subseteq} Y \overset{\text{def}}{\Leftrightarrow} U(X) \subseteq U(Y)$ $\qquad\qquad$ (rough top inclusion);

$\star\ X \overset{\sim}{\underset{\sim}{\subseteq}} Y \overset{\text{def}}{\Leftrightarrow} X \overset{\sim}{\subseteq} Y$ and $X \underset{\sim}{\subseteq} Y$ $\qquad$ (rough inclusion);

$\star\ X \underset{\sim}{=} Y \overset{\text{def}}{\Leftrightarrow} L(X) = L(Y)$ $\qquad\qquad$ (rough bottom equality);

$\star\ X \overset{\sim}{=} Y \overset{\text{def}}{\Leftrightarrow} U(X) = U(Y)$ $\qquad\qquad$ (rough top equality);

$\star\ X \overset{\sim}{\underset{\sim}{=}} Y \overset{\text{def}}{\Leftrightarrow} X \underset{\sim}{=} Y$ and $X \overset{\sim}{=} Y$ $\qquad$ (rough equality);

$\star\ X \underset{\sim}{\cap} Y \overset{\text{def}}{=} L(X) \cap L(Y)$ $\qquad\qquad$ (rough bottom intersection);

$\star\ X \overset{\sim}{\cap} Y \overset{\text{def}}{=} U(X) \cap U(Y)$ $\qquad\qquad$ (rough top intersection).

We may speak of the rough intersection of X and Y, in analogy to rough inclusion and rough equality defined above, but it would be equal to rough bottom intersection and so the notion is redundant.

Lemma 4.2.4. *Let $Z = \{X_1, \ldots, X_k\}$, $k \geq 1$, be a (finite) set of equivalence classes of an indiscernibility relation on a set OB. Let $k' \leq k$ be the number of one-element sets in Z. Then:*

(I) $\operatorname{card}(\{|Y|_{\underset{\sim}{=}} : Y \in \mathcal{P}(OB)\}) = 2^k$;

(II) $\operatorname{card}(\{|Y|_{\cong} : Y \in \mathcal{P}(OB)\}) = 2^k$;

(III) $\operatorname{card}(\{|Y|_{\underset{\sim}{\cong}} : Y \in \mathcal{P}(OB)\}) = 2^{k'} \times 3^{k-k'}$.

Proof. Without any loss of generality, we may assume that $X_1, \ldots, X_{k'}$ are the one-element sets in Z. Let $\mathcal{X}_1$ be the set of maps $f : \{1, \ldots, k\} \to \{0, 1\}$ and $\mathcal{X}_2$ be the set of maps $f : \{1, \ldots, k\} \to \{-1, 0, 1\}$ such that for every $i \in \{1, \ldots, k'\}$, $f(i) \in \{-1, 1\}$. Obviously, $\operatorname{card}(\mathcal{X}_1) = 2^k$ and $\operatorname{card}(\mathcal{X}_2) = 2^{k'} \times 3^{k-k'}$. For every $X \in \mathcal{P}(OB)$, we write f_1^X [resp. f_2^X, f_3^X] to denote the element of $\mathcal{X}_1$ [resp. $\mathcal{X}_1$, $\mathcal{X}_2$] defined as follows. For every $i \in \{1, \ldots, k\}$:

* $f_1^X(i) \overset{\text{def}}{=} 0$ if $X \cap X_i = \emptyset$, otherwise $f_1^X(i) \overset{\text{def}}{=} 1$;
* $f_2^X(i) \overset{\text{def}}{=} 0$ if $X_i \not\subseteq X$, otherwise $f_2^X(i) \overset{\text{def}}{=} 1$;
* $f_3^X(i) \overset{\text{def}}{=} -1$ if $f_1^X(i) = 0$;
* $f_3^X(i) \overset{\text{def}}{=} 1$ if $f_2^X(i) = 1$;
* $f_3^X(i) \overset{\text{def}}{=} 0$ if $i \notin \{1, \ldots, k'\}$ and $\langle f_1^X(i), f_2^X(i) \rangle = \langle 1, 0 \rangle$.

Observe that for every $i \in \{1, \ldots, k'\}$, either $f_1^X(i) = 0$ or $f_2^X(i) = 1$. One can show that for all $X, Y \in \mathcal{P}(OB)$,

* $X \cong Y$ iff $f_1^X = f_1^Y$;
* $X \underset{\sim}{=} Y$ iff $f_2^X = f_2^Y$;
* $X \underset{\sim}{\cong} Y$ iff $f_3^X = f_3^Y$.

Moreover, one can easily check that:

$$\{f_1^X : X \in \mathcal{P}(OB)\} = \{f_2^X : X \in \mathcal{P}(OB)\} = \mathcal{X}_1$$

and

$$\{f_3^X : X \in \mathcal{P}(OB)\} = \mathcal{X}_2,$$

which entails (I), (II), and (III).   Q.E.D.

The notions defined in this section will be used in the subsequent chapters.

4.3 Regions of Certainty

Given an information system $S = \langle OB, AT \rangle$, a set $X \subseteq OB$ of objects, and a set $A \subseteq AT$ of attributes, the question arises whether the A-properties are sufficient to classify all the elements of OB either as members or as non-members of X. As is shown in Example 4.2.1, it is not always the case. Since A might not enable us to distinguish sufficiently between individual objects, we are usually able to characterise just clusters of objects rather than individual objects. In our example the property of "being green" enables us to distinguish the group $\{x_1, x_2\}$ from the remaining objects, but it tells nothing about the differences between x_1 and x_2. Since it is the only available property of these objects, in the given information system the objects x_1 and x_2 behave as they were identical. We conclude that, in general, only the equivalence classes of indiscernibility relations are the entities that can be distinguished in terms of the given attributes, not necessarily the individual objects.

It follows that we can assert the membership of an object in a set up to an indiscernibility relation. Instead of looking for the definite classification of objects as members or non-members of a set, we should rather admit a weaker classification into definite members, definite non-members, and borderline instances.

Example 4.3.1. Consider the information system from Example 2.2.1 and the set X from Example 4.2.1. The objects x_3 and x_4 are definitely members of X on the basis of their colour, the object x_5 is definitely not a member of X, and both x_1 and x_2 are in the region of uncertainty.

Given sets $X \subseteq OB$ and $A \subseteq AT$, we consider four regions of certainty of X determined by $ind(A)$, namely the sets of *positive, negative, lower borderline*, and *upper borderline instances* of X:

* $Pos_{ind(A)}(X) \stackrel{\text{def}}{=} L_{ind(A)}(X)$;
* $Neg_{ind(A)}(X) \stackrel{\text{def}}{=} OB \setminus U_{ind(A)}(X)$;
* $Bl_{ind(A)}(X) \stackrel{\text{def}}{=} X \setminus L_{ind(A)}(X)$;
* $Bu_{ind(A)}(X) \stackrel{\text{def}}{=} U_{ind(A)}(X) \setminus X$.

In terms of lower borderline and upper borderline instances, we define *borderline instances*:

$$B_{ind(A)}(X) \stackrel{\text{def}}{=} Bl_{ind(A)}(X) \cup Bu_{ind(A)}(X).$$

The elements of $Pos_{ind(A)}(X)$ definitely, relative to A-properties, belong to X. The elements of $Neg_{ind(A)}(X)$, in view of these properties, do not belong to X. $B_{ind(A)}(X)$ is a region of doubt; its elements possibly belong to X, but we cannot decide it for certain considering only the A-properties.

Lemma 4.3.1. *Let $S = \langle OB, AT \rangle$ be an information system and let $A \subseteq B$.*
Then $Bl_{ind(B)}(X) \subseteq Bl_{ind(A)}(X)$ for every $X \subseteq OB$.

The following lemma states how the operators Bl and Bu act on compound sets.

Lemma 4.3.2. *Let $S = \langle OB, AT \rangle$ be an information system and let $Bl = Bl_{ind(A)}$ and $Bu = Bu_{ind(A)}$ be the borderline operators associated with a set $A \subseteq AT$. Then, for all $X, Y \subseteq OB$, we have:*

(I) $Bl(X \cup Y) \subseteq Bl(X) \cup Bl(Y)$;
(II) $Bl(X \cap Y) \supseteq Bl(X) \cap Bl(Y)$;
(III) $Bl(\emptyset) = \emptyset$, $Bl(OB) = \emptyset$;
(IV) $Bl(X) = Bu(OB \setminus X)$.

The following lemma states how borderline instances depend on varying sets of attributes.

Lemma 4.3.3. *Let $S = \langle OB, AT \rangle$ be an information system. For all $A, B \subseteq AT$ and for every $X \subseteq OB$, the following assertions hold:*

(I) $Bl_{ind(A \cup B)}(X) \subseteq Bl_{ind(A)}(X) \cup Bl_{ind(B)}(X)$;
(II) $Bl_{ind(A \cap B)}(X) \supseteq Bl_{ind(A)}(X) \cap Bl_{ind(B)}(X)$;
(III) $Bl_{ind(\emptyset)}(X) = X$ if $X \neq OB$, $Bl_{ind(\emptyset)}(OB) = \emptyset$;
(IV) $Bl_{ind(AT)}(X) \subseteq Bl_{ind(A)}(X) \subseteq Bl_{ind(\emptyset)}(X)$.

4.4 Definability of Sets

The following types of definability/indefinability of sets are defined in a natural way in terms of the approximations. Let $S = \langle OB, AT \rangle$ be an information system. A set $X \subseteq OB$ is said to be:

* $ind(A)$-*definable* $\overset{\text{def}}{\Leftrightarrow}$ $L_{ind(A)}(X) = X$;
* *roughly* $ind(A)$-*definable* $\overset{\text{def}}{\Leftrightarrow}$ $L_{ind(A)}(X) \neq \emptyset$, $U_{ind(A)}(X) \neq OB$, and $B_{ind(A)}(X) \neq \emptyset$;
* *bottom* $ind(A)$-*indefinable* $\overset{\text{def}}{\Leftrightarrow}$ $L_{ind(A)}(X) = \emptyset$;
* *top* $ind(A)$-*indefinable* $\overset{\text{def}}{\Leftrightarrow}$ $U_{ind(A)}(X) = OB$;
* *totally* $ind(A)$-*indefinable* $\overset{\text{def}}{\Leftrightarrow}$ X is both bottom $ind(A)$-indefinable and top $ind(A)$-indefinable.

We say that X is bottom [resp. top] $ind(A)$-definable $\overset{\text{def}}{\Leftrightarrow}$ X is not bottom [resp. top] $ind(A)$-indefinable. Observe that the empty set and OB are $ind(A)$-definable for every $A \subseteq AT$. If a set is totally $ind(A)$-indefinable, then it is not $ind(A)$-definable.

The following lemma provides a characterisation of degrees of definability listed above.

Lemma 4.4.1. *Let $S = \langle OB, AT \rangle$ be an information system. For every $A \subseteq AT$ and for every $X \subseteq OB$, the following statements are equivalent:*

(I) X is $ind(A)$-definable;
(II) $U_{ind(A)}(X) = X$;
(III) $Bl_{ind(A)}(X) = Bu_{ind(A)}(X) = \emptyset$;
(IV) $Pos_{ind(A)}(X) = OB \setminus Neg_{ind(A)}(X)$;
(V) $X = \bigcup_{x \in X} |x|_{ind(A)}$.

Lemma 4.4.2. *Let $S = \langle OB, AT \rangle$ be an information system. For every $A \subseteq AT$ and for every $X \subseteq OB$, the following statements are equivalent:*

(I) X is roughly $ind(A)$-definable;
(II) $Bl_{ind(A)}(X) \notin \{X, \emptyset\}$ and $Bu_{ind(A)}(X) \notin \{OB \setminus X, \emptyset\}$.

Proof. We obtain the required equivalence by observing that the following conditions hold:

★ $Bu(X) = \emptyset$ iff $U(X) = X$;
★ $Bl(X) = \emptyset$ iff $L(X) = X$.

In both cases, the set X is $ind(A)$-definable. Moreover, we have:

★ $Bu(X) = -X$ iff $U(X) = OB$;
★ $Bl(X) = X$ iff $L(X) = \emptyset$.

$Q.E.D.$

Lemma 4.4.3. *Let $S = \langle OB, AT \rangle$ be an information system. For every $A \subseteq AT$ and for every $X \subseteq OB$, the following statements are equivalent:*

(I) X is top $ind(A)$-indefinable;
(II) $Bu_{ind(A)}(X) = OB \setminus X$ and $X \neq OB$;
(III) $B_{ind(A)}(X) = OB \setminus Pos_{ind(A)}(X)$ and $X \neq OB$;
(IV) $Neg_{ind(A)}(X) = \emptyset$ and $X \neq OB$.

Lemma 4.4.4. *Let $S = \langle OB, AT \rangle$ be an information system. For every $A \subseteq AT$ and for every $X \subseteq OB$, the following statements are equivalent:*

(I) X is totally $ind(A)$-indefinable;
(II) $Bl_{ind(A)}(X) = X$ and $Bu_{ind(A)}(X) = OB \setminus X$;
(II) $B_{ind(A)}(X) = OB$.

Example 4.4.1. Continuing Example 4.2.1, we observe that:

★ $L_{ind(colour)}(X) = \{x_3, x_4\}$;
★ $U_{ind(colour)}(X) = \{x_1, x_2, x_3, x_4\}$;
★ $Bl_{ind(colour)}(X) = \{x_2\}$;
★ $Bu_{ind(colour)}(X) = \{x_1\}$.

We conclude that $X = \{x_1, x_2, x_4\}$ is not definable in terms of colour. Clearly, X cannot be expressed as the union of any of the equivalence classes $\{x_1, x_2\}$, $\{x_3, x_4\}$, and $\{x_5\}$ of $ind(colour)$.

4.5 Approximate Information Retrieval

In this section we present an application of approximation operations to information retrieval. Assume that we are given a set D of documents and that for every document $d \in D$, there is a corresponding set K_d of index terms, or keywords, that represent the document d. We also assume that *queries* are defined as sets of keywords. Usually, keywords are grouped into classes of conceptually similar words. Assume that these classes form a partition of the set W of all keywords used for indexing and let R be the corresponding equivalence relation.

We present document retrieval strategies in response to a query such that it is not necessarily required that the document matches the query; approximate matchings are permitted. The strategies are expressed in terms of relationships between approximations of a query and approximations of the documents proposed as a response to the query, where the approximations are defined with respect to the relation R mentioned above. For every query $Q \subseteq W$, we define the following retrieval strategies:

$(Str =)$ $\{d : K_d = Q\}$. This strategy retrieves those and only those documents that are about all topics mentioned in the query and none others.

$(Str \subseteq)$ $\{d : K_d \subseteq Q\}$. The retrieved documents are about some, possibly all, topics mentioned in the query.

$(Str \supseteq)$ $\{d : K_d \supseteq Q\}$. The retrieved documents are about all topics in the query and possibly some other.

$(Str\cap)$ $\{d : K_d \cap Q \neq \emptyset\}$. The retrieved documents are about some, possibly all, topics in the query and possibly about others besides.

$(Str \underset{\sim}{\subseteq})$ $\{d : K_d \subseteq \underset{\sim}{Q}\}$. If Q is bottom definable, the retrieval condition means that for every document retrieved all the keywords included in K_d are also included in Q. Hence, the retrieved documents are definitely about some subjects in which the user is definitely interested, and not definitely about any other subject (although possibly about some other subjects). Observe that if for some document d, K_d is bottom indefinable, then d is automatically retrieved regardless of its connection to the query, so in this situation some additional constraints are needed.

$(Str \underset{\sim}{\supseteq})$ $\{d : K_d \supseteq \underset{\sim}{Q}\}$. If Q is bottom definable, then the strategy returns those documents that are definitely about all subjects in which the user has a definite interest, and maybe (even definitely) about other subjects besides. If Q is bottom indefinable, any document meets the retrieval criterion and in this situation some additional constraints are required.

$(Str\underset{\sim}{\cap})$ $\{d : K_d \cap \underset{\sim}{Q} \neq \emptyset\}$. The retrieved documents are definitely about some, possibly all, subjects that the user is definitely interested in and maybe also about some other topics.

$(Str \underset{\sim}{=})$ $\{d : K_d \underset{\sim}{=} Q\}$. The retrieved documents here are definitely about those and only those subjects that the user definitely has in mind, and maybe about some others besides.

$(Str \underset{\sim}{\subseteq})$ $\{d : K_d \overset{\sim}{\subseteq} Q\}$. The documents retrieved are definitely not about anything that the user is definitely not interested in. With this strategy and the remaining ones undesirable effects are obtained from top indefinable queries, and they require some additional constraints.

$(Str \overset{\sim}{\supseteq})$ $\{d : K_d \overset{\sim}{\supseteq} Q\}$. The user is definitely not interested in those topics that the retrieved documents definitely do not cover.

$(Str\overset{\sim}{\cap})$ $\{d : K_d \overset{\sim}{\cap} Q \neq \emptyset\}$. The retrieved documents may be about some (possibly all) subjects in which the user may be interested, and maybe (even definitely) about others besides.

$(Str \overset{\sim}{=})$ $\{d : K_d \overset{\sim}{=} Q\}$. The retrieved documents may be about all and no other subjects in which the user may be interested.

$(Str \underset{\sim}{\overset{\sim}{\subseteq}})$ $\{d : K_d \underset{\sim}{\overset{\sim}{\subseteq}} Q\}$. The documents retrieved here all are definitely about some (possibly all) of the subjects in which the user definitely is interested, and not definitely about anything else, but maybe about other subjects provided that the user may have them in mind too.

$(Str \underset{\sim}{\overset{\sim}{\supseteq}})$ $\{d : K_d \underset{\sim}{\overset{\sim}{\supseteq}} Q\}$. The documents yielded here are definitely about everything that the user is definitely interested in, and maybe about everything that the user may have in mind, and maybe (even definitely) some other things besides.

$(Str \underset{\sim}{\overset{\sim}{=}})$ $\{d : K_d \underset{\sim}{\overset{\sim}{=}} Q\}$. The documents retrieved are definitely about all of that in which the user definitely is interested (and not definitely about anything else) and maybe about everything that the user may have in mind, but can admit no subjects besides.

The retrieval strategies discussed above employ the approximation operators determined by an equivalence (indiscernibility) relation. Similarity relations are used for information retrieval in response to a query that has the form of a symbolic object. Consider the information system of sleeping bags in Example 2.2.3. Let the query q be the following symbolic object:

	F	T	W	P	M
q	VAL_F	VAL_T	VAL_W	$\{250, \ldots, 400\}$	$\{goose\text{-}downs, duck\text{-}downs\}$

The required answer is the set of those objects that are in the relation $sim(P, M)$ with q, that is $\{x \in OB : \langle x, q \rangle \in sim(P, M)\}$.

4.6 Knowledge Operators

In this section we consider knowledge operators derived from an information system. It is commonly accepted that knowledge of an agent is manifested in his ability to find patterns and regularities in a set of data. Therefore knowledge operators should reflect degrees of certainty with which an agent classifies objects. In view of the discussion presented in the preceding sections of this chapter we may assume that his knowledge depends on an indiscernibility relation in the set of objects.

Given an information system $S = \langle OB, AT \rangle$, for every $A \subseteq AT$, we define knowledge operators determined by the indiscernibility relations $ind(A)$ as follows. For every $X \subseteq OB$, we set:

$$K_{ind(A)}(X) \overset{\text{def}}{=} Pos_{ind(A)}(X) \cup Neg_{ind(A)}(X).$$

We say that knowledge about the set X determined by the indiscernibility relation $ind(A)$ is:

* *complete* $\overset{\text{def}}{\Leftrightarrow}$ $K_{ind(A)}(X) = OB$;
* *rough* $\overset{\text{def}}{\Leftrightarrow}$ $Pos_{ind(A)}(X) \neq \emptyset$, $Neg_{ind(A)}(X) \neq \emptyset$, and $B_{ind(A)}(X) \neq \emptyset$;
* *pos-empty* $\overset{\text{def}}{\Leftrightarrow}$ $Pos_{ind(A)}(X) = \emptyset$;
* *neg-empty* $\overset{\text{def}}{\Leftrightarrow}$ $Neg_{ind(A)}(X) = \emptyset$;
* *empty* $\overset{\text{def}}{\Leftrightarrow}$ both pos-empty and neg-empty.

Observe that $Pos_{ind(A)}(\emptyset) = L_{ind(A)}(\emptyset) = \emptyset$ and $Neg_{ind(A)}(\emptyset) = OB \setminus U_{ind(A)}(\emptyset) = OB$. This means that $K(\emptyset)$ is complete, which is in agreement with the fact that $\emptyset$ is $ind(A)$-definable for every $A \subseteq AT$.

The following lemma provides a characterisation of the types of knowledge listed above.

Lemma 4.6.1. *Let* $S = \langle OB, AT \rangle$ *be an information system. For every* $A \subseteq AT$ *and for every* $X \subseteq OB$, *the following assertions hold:*

(I) $K_{ind(A)}(X)$ *is complete iff* X *is* $ind(A)$-*definable;*
(II) $K_{ind(A)}(X)$ *is rough iff* X *is roughly* $ind(A)$-*definable;*
(III) $K_{ind(A)}(X)$ *is pos-empty iff* X *is bottom* $ind(A)$-*indefinable;*
(IV) $K_{ind(A)}(X)$ *is neg-empty iff* X *is top* $ind(A)$-*indefinable;*
(V) $K_{ind(A)}(X)$ *is empty iff* X *is totally* $ind(A)$-*indefinable.*

The following lemma states some important facts about interaction of information operators. Axiomatisation of logics with these operators presented in Chap. 9 relies on these facts.

Lemma 4.6.2. *Let* $S = \langle OB, AT \rangle$ *be an information system. For every* $X \subseteq OB$, *the following assertions hold:*

(I) $Pos(K(X)) = K(X)$, $Neg(K(X)) = B(X)$;
(II) $Bl(K(X)) = Bu(K(X)) = \emptyset$;
(III) $K(Pos(X)) = OB$, $K(Neg(X)) = OB$;

(IV) $K(Bl(X)) = K(Bu(X)) = K(X)$;
(V) $K(K(X)) = OB$, $K(X) = K(OB \setminus X)$, $K(\emptyset) = OB$.

Observe that the knowledge operators defined in this section do not have the unwanted properties of omniscience, positive introspection, and negative introspection.

Lemma 4.6.3. *None of the following conditions hold in any information system* $\langle OB, AT \rangle$:

(I) $K(X) \subseteq X$ *for every* $X \subseteq OB$,	*(omniscience)*;
(II) $K(X) \subseteq K(K(X))$ *for every* $X \subseteq OB$,	*(positive introspection)*;
(III) $-K(X) \subseteq K(-K(X))$ *for every* $X \subseteq OB$,	*(negative introspection)*.

4.7 A Clone of Information Operators

Let $S = \langle OB, AT \rangle$ be an information system. In the preceding sections we associated with each set $A \subseteq AT$ of attributes various operators on $\mathcal{P}(OB)$. Instead of defining the operators one by one, we shall see that the set $\{Pos, Neg, Bl, Bu\}$ has a special status and that many other operators can be generated from its members. In this section, we define a family $Clo_{ind(A)}$ of information operators determined by an indiscernibility relation $ind(A)$ derived from an information system. The family $Clo_{ind(A)}$ includes the already defined operators Pos, Neg, Bl, Bu, B, and K determined by $ind(A)$. Moreover, $Clo_{ind(A)}$ includes the following operators:

⋆	$H_0(X) \stackrel{\text{def}}{=} \emptyset$	(constant operator);
⋆	$H_1(X) \stackrel{\text{def}}{=} OB$	(constant operator);
⋆	$Id(X) \stackrel{\text{def}}{=} X$	(identity);
⋆	$(-Id)(X) \stackrel{\text{def}}{=} OB \setminus X$	(complement);
⋆	$H_{ind(A)}(X) \stackrel{\text{def}}{=} Pos_{ind(A)}(X) \cup Bu_{ind(A)}(X)$.	

We define $Clo_{ind(A)}$ and $Gen_{ind(A)}$ as follows:

* ⋆ $Gen_{ind(A)} \stackrel{\text{def}}{=} \{f_{ind(A)} : f \in \{Pos, Neg, Bl, Bu\}\}$;
* ⋆ $Clo_{ind(A)} \stackrel{\text{def}}{=} Gen_{ind(A)} \cup \{f_{ind(A)} :$
  $f \in \{K, Id, H, H_0, -Pos, -Neg, -Bl, -Bu, B, -Id, -H, H_1\}\}$

where for every operation f, $-f \stackrel{\text{def}}{=} (-Id); f$. In the rest of this section, we omit the parameter $ind(A)$ in the names of the operators. Let $+$ be the binary operation on Clo such that $(f + g)(X) \stackrel{\text{def}}{=} f(X) \cup g(X)$ for every $X \subseteq OB$.

Lemma 4.7.1. *The set* Clo *is the smallest set including* Gen *and closed with respect to the operation* $+$.

Proof. It is easy to see that the following equalities hold:

$\star$ $Id = Pos + Bl$; $-Id = Neg + Bu$; $K = Pos + Neg$; $-K = B = Bl + Bu$;
$\star$ $H = Pos + Bu$; $-H = Neg + Bl$; $-Bl = Pos + Neg + Bu$; $-Bu = Pos + Neg + Bl$;
$\star$ $-Neg = Pos + Bl + Bu$; $-Pos = Neg + Bl + Bu$; $H_1 = Pos + Neg + Bl + Bu$.

$$Q.E.D.$$

Lemma 4.7.2. *The set Clo is closed with respect to the composition of operators.*

Proof. We present a part of the composition table for the operators from Clo in Table 4.1. An operator f in a cell of the table situated at the crossing of a column labelled by an operator g and a row labelled by an operator h is defined as $f = g; h$.

	Pos	Neg	Bl	Bu
Pos	Pos	$-Pos$	H_0	H_0
Neg	Neg	$-Neg$	H_0	H_0
Bl	H_0	K	Bl	Bu
Bu	H_0	K	Bu	Bl
K	K	B	H_0	H_0
H	Pos	H_1	Bu	Bl
H_0	H_0	H_W	H_0	H_0
$-Id$	Neg	Pos	Bu	Bl

Table 4.1. Composition of information operators

The full table can be easily obtained from the part given above using the representation of the operators presented in the proof of Lemma 4.7.1. *Q.E.D.*

4.8 Generalised Approximation Operators

Approximation operators are intended to reflect an intuition of approximating a set from the "bottom" and from the "top" using some atomic sets. A minimal rationality postulate concerning the atomic sets is that they form a cover of the given universe OB of objects and minimal rationality postulates concerning approximation operators L and U are $L(X) \subseteq X \subseteq U(X)$ and duality of the operators, that is $U(X) = OB \setminus L(OB \setminus X)$.

Let $(X_i)_{i \in I}$ be a cover of the set OB. If we define a lower approximation operation as

$$L(X) \stackrel{\text{def}}{=} \bigcup \{X_i : i \in I, \ X_i \subseteq X\}$$

then the dual operation of upper approximation should be

$$U(X) \overset{\text{def}}{=} \{x \in OB : \text{ for every } i \in I, \text{ if } x \in X_i, \text{ then } X_i \cap X \neq \emptyset\}.$$

If we define an upper approximation as:

$$U(X) \overset{\text{def}}{=} \bigcup\{X_i : i \in I, X_i \cap X \neq \emptyset\}$$

then the dual operation of lower approximation should be

$$L(X) \overset{\text{def}}{=} \{x \in OB : \text{ for every } i \in I, \text{ if } x \in X_i, \text{ then } X_i \subseteq X\}.$$

Let R be a tolerance relation on a set W. A *tolerance class* of R is a maximal (with respect to inclusion) subset X of W such that $X \times X \subseteq R$. The tolerance classes of R are non-empty and their union equals W, that is to say, they form a cover of W. The set of tolerance classes is denoted by $tol(R)$. It is known that tolerance relations satisfy the following conditions.

Lemma 4.8.1. *For every tolerance relation R on a set W, the following assertions hold:*

(I) $X \subseteq W$ is a tolerance class of R iff $X = \bigcap_{x \in X} R(x)$;
(II) $R(x)$ is a tolerance class of R iff $R(x) = \bigcup\{X : X \in tol(R) \text{ and } x \in X\}$;
(III) a tolerance class X of R is of the form $R(x)$ for some $x \in W$ iff X is the only class containing x;
(IV) for every $X \subseteq W$, $R(X) = \bigcup\{Y \in tol(R) : X \cap Y \neq \emptyset\}$.

Example 4.8.1. Let a tolerance relation R on a set OB be given. The natural covers of OB determined by R are: the family $(R(x))_{x \in OB}$ and the family of tolerance classes of R. They are characterised in Lemma 4.8.1. In general, these two covers do not coincide, contrary to the case when R is an equivalence relation. It follows that they may lead to different approximation operations.

Let R be a tolerance relation on a set OB and consider the family $(R(x))_{x \in OB}$. The approximation operations satisfying the rationality postulates mentioned above are defined as follows:

(1) $L(X) \overset{\text{def}}{=} \{x \in OB : R(x) \subseteq X\}$;
(2) $U(X) \overset{\text{def}}{=} \{x \in OB : R(x) \cap X \neq \emptyset\}$.

In Sect. 14.9 we present generalised approximation operators on partially ordered sets.

4.9 Information Operators and Properties of Information Relations

Information operators enable us to express properties of information relations. Observe that the information operators introduced in the previous sections suggest a more general notion of an operator acting on sets of objects. In this section we consider operators that are defined as the approximation operators but without using any particular information relation for defining the operators. We also present operators of sufficiency and impossibility which are needed for representing the properties of relations from the distinguishability group. Anticipating the developments of the subsequent chapters, the notation and the names of these operators are adopted from modal logic. We consider the following operators.

Definition 4.9.1. *Let R be a binary relation on a non-empty set W and let $X \subseteq W$.*

* $\langle R \rangle(X) \stackrel{\text{def}}{=} \{x \in W : \text{ there is a } y \in X \text{ such that } \langle x, y \rangle \in R\}$
  (possibility);
* $[R](X) \stackrel{\text{def}}{=} \{x \in W : \text{ for every } y \in W, \text{ if } \langle x, y \rangle \in R, \text{ then } y \in X\}$
  (necessity);
* $\langle\langle R \rangle\rangle(X) \stackrel{\text{def}}{=} \{x \in W : \text{ there is a } y \in W \text{ such that } y \notin X \text{ and } \langle x, y \rangle \notin R\}$
  (impossibility).
* $[[R]](X) \stackrel{\text{def}}{=} \{x \in W : \text{ for every } y \in W, \text{ if } y \in X, \text{ then } \langle x, y \rangle \in R\}$
  (sufficiency).

The following properties of these operators follow directly from the corresponding definitions.

Lemma 4.9.1. *For every binary relation R on a non-empty set W and for every $X \subseteq W$ the following conditions are satisfied:*

(I) $\langle R \rangle(X) = W \setminus [R](W \setminus X)$;
(II) $\langle\langle R \rangle\rangle(X) = W \setminus [[R]](W \setminus X)$;
(III) $\langle R \rangle(X) = \langle\langle (W \times W \setminus R) \rangle\rangle(W \setminus X)$;
(IV) if $X \subseteq Y$, then $[[R]](Y) \subseteq [[R]](X)$.

In the following lemmas we show how the properties of information relations defined in Sect. 3.10 can be expressed with these operators.

Lemma 4.9.2. *Let R be a binary relation on a non-empty set W.*

(I) R is reflexive iff $X \subseteq \langle R \rangle(X)$ for every $X \subseteq W$;
(II) R is weakly reflexive iff $\langle R \rangle(W) \cap [R](X) \subseteq X$ for every $X \subseteq W$;
(III) R is symmetric iff $X \subseteq [R](\langle R \rangle(X))$ for every $X \subseteq W$;
(IV) R is transitive iff $\langle R \rangle(\langle R \rangle(X)) \subseteq \langle R \rangle(X)$ for every $X \subseteq W$;
(V) R is 3-transitive iff $\langle R \rangle(\langle R \rangle(\langle R \rangle(X))) \subseteq \langle R \rangle(X)$ for every $X \subseteq W$.

Proof. By way of example we prove (II).
($\rightarrow$) Suppose that there is an x such that $x \in \langle R \rangle(W)$, $x \in [R](X)$, and $x \notin X$. Then (i) there is a $z \in W$ such that $\langle x, z \rangle \in R$ and (ii) for every $t \in W$ if $\langle x, t \rangle \in R$, then $t \in X$. From (i) and the assumption we get $\langle x, x \rangle \in R$. From (ii) we obtain $x \in X$, a contradiction.
($\leftarrow$) Suppose that (i) there are $x, y \in W$ such that $\langle x, y \rangle \in R$ and that (ii)

$\langle x, x \rangle \notin R$. It follows from (i) that $x \in \langle R \rangle(W)$. Consider $X = \{z \in W : \langle x, z \rangle \in R\}$. Clearly, $x \in [R](X)$. Hence, $x \in \langle R \rangle(W) \cap [R](X)$. So by the assumption $x \in X$. It follows that $\langle x, x \rangle \in R$, a contradiction with (ii). The proofs of the remaining assertions are similar.   *Q.E.D.*

Lemma 4.9.3. *Let R be a binary relation on a set W.*

(I) R is irreflexive iff $[[R]](X) \subseteq -X$ for every $X \subseteq W$;
(II) R is coweakly reflexive iff $X \cap [[R]](X) \subseteq [[R]](W)$ for every $X \subseteq W$;
(III) R is cotransitive iff $[[R]](X) \subseteq [[R]](-[[R]](X))$ for every $X \subseteq W$;
(IV) R is co-3-transitive iff $[[R]](X) \subseteq [[R]](-[[R]](-[[R]](X)))$ for every $X \subseteq W$;
(V) R is symmetric iff $X \subseteq [[R]][[R]](X)$ for every $X \subseteq W$;
(VI) R is cosymmetric iff R is symmetric.

Proof. By way of example, we prove (I).
($\rightarrow$) Let R be an irreflexive relation and suppose that for some $X \subseteq W$ the condition does not hold. Hence, there is an $x \in W$ such that $x \in [[R]](X)$ and $x \in X$. It follows that for every $y \in W$, if $y \in X$, then $\langle x, y \rangle \in R$. In particular $\langle x, x \rangle \in R$, a contradiction.
($\leftarrow$) Suppose that for some $x \in W$ we have $\langle x, x \rangle \in R$. Consider the set $X = \{y \in W : \langle x, y \rangle \in R\}$. Then we have $x \in X$. Hence, by the assumption we must also have $x \notin [[R]](X)$. We conclude that there is a $y \in W$ such that $y \in X$ and $\langle x, y \rangle \notin R$, a contradiction.
In the remaining cases the proofs are similar.   *Q.E.D.*

Lemma 4.9.4. *Let $F = \langle W, (\mathcal{R}_P)_{P \subseteq PAR} \rangle$ be a relative frame.*

(I) F satisfies condition (C_1) iff for all $P, Q \subseteq PAR$, for every $X \subseteq W$,
$[[\mathcal{R}_{P \cup Q}]](X) = [[\mathcal{R}_P]](X) \cap [[\mathcal{R}_Q]](X)$;
(II) F satisfies condition (C_1') iff for every $X \subseteq W$, $[[\mathcal{R}_\emptyset]](X) = W$;
(III) F satisfies condition (C_3) iff for all $P, Q \subseteq PAR$, for every $X \subseteq W$,
$\langle \mathcal{R}_{P \cup Q} \rangle(X) = \langle \mathcal{R}_P \rangle(X) \cup \langle \mathcal{R}_Q \rangle(X)$;
(IV) F satisfies condition (C_2') iff for every set $X \subseteq W$, $\langle \mathcal{R}_\emptyset \rangle(X) = \emptyset$.

Proof. We recall that the conditions (C_1), (C_1'), (C_3), and (C_2') are defined in Sect. 3.9. By way of example we prove $\mathcal{R}_P \cap \mathcal{R}_Q \subseteq \mathcal{R}_{P \cup Q}$ iff $[[\mathcal{R}_{P \cup Q}]](X) \supseteq [[\mathcal{R}_P]](X) \cap [[\mathcal{R}_Q]](X)$.
($\rightarrow$) Suppose there is an $x \in W$ such that (i) for every $y \in W$, if $y \in X$, then $\langle x, y \rangle \in \mathcal{R}_P$, (ii) for every $t \in W$, if $t \in X$, then $\langle x, t \rangle \in \mathcal{R}_Q$, and (iii) there is a $z \in X$ such that $\langle x, z \rangle \notin \mathcal{R}_{P \cup Q}$. From (i) and (ii) we get $\langle x, z \rangle \in \mathcal{R}_P$ and $\langle x, z \rangle \in \mathcal{R}_Q$. But then by the assumption $\langle x, z \rangle \in \mathcal{R}_{P \cup Q}$, a contradiction.
($\leftarrow$) Suppose there are $x, y \in W$ such that $\langle x, y \rangle \in \mathcal{R}_P$, $\langle x, y \rangle \in \mathcal{R}_Q$, and $\langle x, y \rangle \notin \mathcal{R}_{P \cup Q}$. Consider the set $X = \{z \in W : \langle x, z \rangle \in \mathcal{R}_P \cap \mathcal{R}_Q\}$. Then we have $x \in [[\mathcal{R}_P]](X)$ and $x \in [[\mathcal{R}_Q]](X)$. So by the assumption $x \in [[\mathcal{R}_{P \cup Q}]](X)$. Since $y \in X$, we must have $\langle x, y \rangle \in \mathcal{R}_{P \cup Q}$, a contradiction.
In the remaining cases the proof are similar.   *Q.E.D.*

Properties of a relation R expressible with the operators $\langle R \rangle$ and $[R]$ are related to its properties expressible with the operators $\langle\langle R \rangle\rangle$ and $[[R]]$. Let Π be a property of R expressible with $\langle R \rangle$ and $[R]$ and let $expr(\Pi)$ be the respective expression. Let $expr'(\Pi)$ be the expression obtained from $expr(\Pi)$ through replacement of $\langle R \rangle$ by $\langle\langle R \rangle\rangle-$ and $[R]$ by $[[R]]-$, respectively. In many cases, R possesses the property Π expressed with $expr(\Pi)$ iff R possesses the property coΠ expressed with $expr'(\Pi)$. An abstract setting for the correspondences of that kind is developed in Chap. 15.

Example 4.9.1. Reflexivity of a relation R on W is expressible with an expression *expr* of the form "for every $X \subseteq W$, $X \subseteq \langle R \rangle X$". Let *expr'* be the expression "for every $X \subseteq W$, $X \subseteq \langle\langle R \rangle\rangle - X$". It is easy to see that *expr'* is equivalent to "for every $X \subseteq W$, $[[R]]X \subseteq -X$", which expresses the irreflexivity of R.

A general problem of expressibility of properties of relations with expressions of modal logics is a subject of modal correspondence theory.

4.10 Structures with Information Operators

If R is an equivalence relation on a set W, then the frame $\langle W, R \rangle$ is referred to as an *approximation space*. Consequently, for every $X \subseteq W$, we shall often write $L_R(X)$, $U_R(X)$ instead of $[R](X)$, $\langle R \rangle(X)$, respectively, keeping in mind the analogy with approximation operations. Similarly, we define positive $(Pos_R(X))$, negative $(Neg_R(X))$, and borderline $(B_R(X))$ instances of subsets of W with respect to R as in Sect. 4.3.

Definition 4.10.1. *A rough subset of W with respect to R is a pair*

$$\langle L_R(X), U_R(X) \rangle$$

for some $X \subseteq W$.

For a given approximation space $\langle W, R \rangle$ the family of rough subsets of W with respect to R is denoted by $\mathcal{P}_r(W, R)$.

Definition 4.10.2. *A knowledge structure of $\langle W, R \rangle$ is the set*

$$K(W, R) \stackrel{\text{def}}{=} \{\langle Pos_R(X), Neg_R(X) \rangle : X \subseteq W\}.$$

Given an information system $S = \langle OB, AT \rangle$, we refer to the frame $\langle OB, ind(AT) \rangle$ as *approximation space derived from S*. Similarly, the *family of rough sets derived from S* is

$$\{\langle L_{ind(AT)}(X), U_{ind(AT)}(X) \rangle : X \subseteq OB\}$$

and the *knowledge structure derived from S* is

$$\{\langle Pos_{ind(AT)}(X), Neg_{ind(AT)}(X)\rangle : X \subseteq OB\}.$$

The structures defined here play an essential role in developing an informational representation theory for various classes of algebras presented in Chap. 14.

4.11 Fuzzy Information Operators

In this section we present generalisations of some of the information operators introduced in the preceding sections of this chapter. The key feature of the information operators investigated in this chapter is that they are determined by the information relations. In an analogous way the fuzzy information operators are determined by the fuzzy information relations.

By a *fuzzy approximation space* we mean a structure $\langle W, L, R\rangle$, where W is a non-empty set, L is a double residuated lattice, and R is an L-fuzzy binary relation on W. Let $X \in \mathcal{F}_L P(W)$. We define the L-fuzzy approximations of a set X with respect to the relation R as follows:

* $(L_{L,R}(X))(x) \stackrel{\text{def}}{=} inf(\{R(x,y) \to X(y) : y \in W\})$
  (L-lower approximation);
* $(U_{L,R}(X))(x) \stackrel{\text{def}}{=} sup(\{R(x,y) \odot X(y) : y \in W\})$
  (L-upper approximation).

Lemma 4.11.1. *For every fuzzy approximation space $\langle W, L, R\rangle$ the following conditions hold:*

(I) $L_{L,R}(W) = W$;
(II) $U_{L,R}(\emptyset) = \emptyset$;
(III) if $X \subseteq_L Y$, then $L_{L,R}(X) \subseteq_L L_{L,R}(Y)$ and $U_{L,R}(X) \subseteq_L U_{L,R}(Y)$.

Proof. (II) $(U_{L,R}(\emptyset))(x) = sup(\{R(x,y)\odot\emptyset(y) : y \in W\}) = sup(\{R(x,y)\odot 0 : y \in W\}) = 0 = \emptyset(x).$
(III) We show the second inclusion.

$$\begin{aligned}(U_{L,R}(X))(x) &= sup(\{R(x,y) \odot X(y) : y \in W\})\\ &\leq sup(\{R(x,y) \odot Y(y) : y \in W\}) \text{ by Lemma 2.7.2(IV)}\\ &= (U_{L,R}(Y))(x).\end{aligned}$$

The proofs of the remaining conditions are similar.   *Q.E.D.*

Lemma 4.11.2. *For every fuzzy approximation space $\langle W, L, R\rangle$ such that R is reflexive the following conditions hold:*

(I) $L_{L,R}(\emptyset) = \emptyset$;
(II) $U_{L,R}(W) = W$;
(III) $L_{L,R}(X) \subseteq X \subseteq U_{L,R}(X)$;

(IV) $L_{L,R}(X) \subseteq U_{L,R}(L_{L,R}(X))$;
(V) $L_{L,R}(U_{L,R}(X)) \subseteq U_{L,R}(X)$.

Proof. (II) $(U_{L,R}(W))(x) = sup(\{R(x,y) \odot 1 : y \in W\}) = sup(\{R(x,y) : y \in W\})$. Since R is reflexive, $sup(\{R(x,y) : y \in W\}) = 1$.
(III) $(L_{L,R}(W))(x) = inf(\{R(x,y) \to X(y) : y \in W\}) \leq R(x,x) \to X(x) = 1 \to X(x) = X(x)$. Similarly, $(U_{L,R}(W))(x) = sup(\{R(x,y) \odot X(y) : y \in W\}) \geq R(x,x) \odot X(x) = 1 \odot X(x) = X(x)$.
The proofs of the remaining conditions are similar.   *Q.E.D.*

Lemma 4.11.3. *For every fuzzy approximation space $\langle W, L, R \rangle$ such that R is strongly transitive the following conditions hold:*

(I) $U_{L,R}(U_{L,R}(X)) = U_{L,R}(X)$;
(II) $L_{L,R}(L_{L,R}(X)) = L_{L,R}(X)$.

Proof. (II)

$$
\begin{aligned}
L_{L,R}(L_{L,R}(X)) &= inf(\{R(x,y) \to inf(\{R(y,z) \to X(z) : z \in W\}) : y \in W\}) \\
&= inf(\{inf(\{R(x,y) \to (R(y,z) \to X(z)) : z \in W\}) : y \in W\}) \\
&\quad \text{(by Lemma 2.7.8(I))} \\
&= inf(\{inf(\{(R(x,y) \odot R(y,z)) \to X(z)) : z \in W\}) : y \in W\}) \\
&\quad \text{(by Lemma 2.7.3(V))} \\
&= inf(\{sup(\{R(x,y) \odot R(y,z) : y \in W\}) \to X(z) : z \in W\}) \\
&\quad \text{(by Lemma 2.7.8(II))} \\
&= inf(\{R(x,z) \to X(z) : z \in W\}) \text{ (by strong transitivity)} \\
&= L_{L,R}(X).
\end{aligned}
$$

The proof of (I) is similar.   *Q.E.D.*

Let $R \in \mathcal{F}_L Rel(U)$. A fuzzy set $X \in \mathcal{F}_L P(U)$ is *R-definable* iff $L_{L,R}(X) = X = U_{L,R}(X)$.

Example 4.11.1. Let $\xi \in L$ and let X_ξ be an L-fuzzy subset of U defined as $X_\xi(x) = \xi$ for every $x \in U$. We show that X_ξ is R-definable for every reflexive L-fuzzy relation R. Since $\xi \leq R(x,y) \to \xi$ for all x, y, we have $(L_{L,R}(X_\xi))(x) = inf(\{R(x,y) \to \xi : y \in U\}) \geq \xi$. Hence, $X_\xi \subseteq_L L_{L,R}(X_\xi)$. By Lemma 4.11.3(III) we have $L_{L,R}(X_\xi) = X_\xi$.
$(U_{L,R}(X_\xi))(x) = sup(\{R(x,y) \odot \xi : y \in U\}) = (sup(\{R(x,y) : y \in U\}) \odot \xi)$ (by Lemma 2.7.7(I)). Since R is reflexive, $sup(\{R(x,y) : y \in U\}) = 1$. Since 1 is the unit element of the respective monoid, we get $(U_{L,R}(X_\xi))(x) = \xi$ which means that $U_{L,R}(X_\xi) = X_\xi$.

Clearly, the operators of L-lower approximation and L-upper approximation may be treated as generalised modal-like operators of L-necessity and L-possibility:

$$[R]_L(X) \overset{\text{def}}{=} L_{L,R}(X), \quad \langle R \rangle_L(X) \overset{\text{def}}{=} U_{L,R}(X).$$

The other meaningful operators are the operators of L-copossibility and L-conecessity defined as follows:

$co[R]_L(X)(x) \overset{\text{def}}{=} inf(\{R(x,y) \oplus X(y) : y \in U\});$
$co\langle R\rangle_L(X)(x) \overset{\text{def}}{=} sup(\{R(x,y) \leftarrow X(y) : y \in U\}).$

Observe that if the lattice L is such that $\oplus = +$, $\odot = \cdot$, and the negations $\neg$ and $\ulcorner$ coincide and equal the complement $-$, then we have:

$$co[R]_L = [-R]_L, \quad co\langle R\rangle_L = \langle -R\rangle_L.$$

Fuzzy information operators enable us to express the properties of fuzzy relations. The following lemma provides one such example.

Lemma 4.11.4. *For every fuzzy relation R on a set U, $L_{L,R}(X) \subseteq_L X$ for every $X \in \mathcal{F}_L P(U)$ iff R is reflexive.*

Proof. $(\rightarrow)$ Suppose that R is not reflexive, that is there is an $x_0 \in U$ such that $R(x_0, x_0) < 1$. Take an L-fuzzy set X such that $X(z) = R(x_0, z)$. Then we have $(L_{L,R}(X))(x_0) = inf(\{R(x_0, y) \rightarrow X(y) : y \in U\}) = inf(\{R(x_0, y) \rightarrow R(x_0, y) : y \in U\}) = 1 > X(x_0)$, a contradiction.
$(\leftarrow)$ Now assume that $R(x, x) = 1$ for every $x \in U$. Then we have $inf(\{R(x, y) \rightarrow X(y) : y \in U\}) \leq R(x, x) \rightarrow X(x) = 1 \rightarrow X(x) = X(x)$ for every $x \in U$.   Q.E.D.

4.12 Notes

Approximation operations. Approximation operations are intended to reflect the limits of tolerance of membership of an element in a set, given some granularity of the universe of objects. Approximation operations determined by indiscernibility relations, where the granularity is due to the equivalence classes of those relations, are introduced in [KOP81] and [Paw81a, Paw82]. Approximation operations based on similarity relations are originated in [Ž83]. Various classes of approximation operators determined by tolerance relations or covers of a set of objects can be found in [Pom87, Pom88]. In Sect. 14.9 a general concept of approximation operation is discussed. Within the logical framework approximation operations are the modal connectives. Logical aspects of approximations are discussed in Chaps. 7 and 8.

Approximate retrieval of information. The content of Sect. 4.5 is based on [GHOS96]. Approximate equalities of sets determined by an indiscernibility relation are introduced in [Paw82] and investigated, among others, in [NP85b, NP85a, WV95]. Representation of information with symbolic objects is discussed in [Did87].

Knowledge operators. Regions of certainty are introduced in [Orło83]. Knowledge operators considered in Sect. 4.6 are introduced in [Orło89]. Semantic properties of operator K can be found in [Orło89, Rau92]. The material of Sect. 4.7 is based on the developments in [Che92]. Logical aspects of operator K are discussed in Chap. 9.

Fuzzy information operators. The idea of combining the concepts from fuzzy logic and rough set theory is due to [DP90b, DP91]. Some ideas in this direction can also be found in [Thi97]. Fuzzy approximation operations determined by *t*-norms and *t*-conorms on the unit interval are investigated in [RK01a, RK01b].

Correspondence theory. The theory studies expressibility of properties of relations in terms of formulae of modal logics. A survey of the correspondence theory within the framework of classical modal logic can be found in [Ben84]. Some further correspondence results are presented in [NS98]. In [Gor90b] properties of relations expressible with the operators of sufficiency or impossibility are discussed. In Chaps. 7, 8, and 9 we present some correspondence results related to the corresponding logics.

Part II

Introduction to Information Logics

5. Towards Information Logics

5.1 Introduction and Outline of the Chapter

The information operators presented in Chap. 4 are intensional operators in that the result of applying an operator to a compound set of objects depends not only on the component sets but also on an information relation. From a logical perspective, it follows that information operators have the status of modal connectives. It is therefore natural to postulate that information logics be modal-like logics. However, reasoning about the objects and relations of an information system often requires more subtle means than ordinary mono-modal logics can offer. For example, we might need an explicit representation of compound information relations obtained by performing some relational operations on the component relations. This is needed, for instance, for reasoning about definability of sets of objects in information systems. Similarly, it might not be sufficient to consider only the modal connectives analogous to possibility and necessity. For instance, the operators of sufficiency needed for a characterisation of complementarity relations are not among the classical modal connectives. In this chapter we present a general scheme of modal logics. The scheme captures the classes of information logics considered in this book as well as most modal logics from the literature. Our definition of modal logics is semantic. This enables us to stress the links between the logics under consideration and their intended use in information systems.

Before developing a framework for studying information logics, we recall in Sect. 5.2 basic definitions and facts about the classical propositional calculus and first-order logic. In Sect. 5.3 and Sect. 5.4 we present a general notion of modal logic. This notion is intended to capture the most essential features of various logics that have been developed in connection with information systems with incomplete information. The key characteristics of these logics are the following. In their languages, the modal operators are the abstract counterparts of information operators discussed in Chap. 4. The semantic structures of the logics are the information frames presented in Chap. 3. Moreover, if the respective frames consist of relative relations, then the logical language contains expressions representing the underlying sets of attributes; these are referred to as parameter expressions. These logics belong to the family of Rare-logics – logics with relative accessibility relations. The family is defined in a general way; it includes logics with parameter expressions interpreted as elements of any level of the powerset hierarchy of a set. The relations in the semantic structures of Rare-logics may satisfy some local and/or global conditions. In some logics, the families of relations are endowed with an algebraic structure. In Sect. 5.5 we discuss a general concept of fuzzy information logic. Most of the logics mentioned in this chapter as examples illustrating the concepts introduced in the chapter, are investigated in the subsequent chapters.

5.2 Classical Logic

5.2.1 Classical Propositional Logic PC

The language of classical propositional logic is a system $PC = \langle FOR_0, O_{FOR} \rangle$ such that FOR_0 is a countable set of propositional variables and $O_{FOR} = \{\neg, \wedge\}$ is the set of propositional connectives of negation and conjunction, respectively. The set FOR of PC-formulae is the smallest set including FOR_0 and closed with respect to the logical connectives from O_{FOR}. We admit the connectives of disjunction ($\vee$), implication ($\Rightarrow$), equivalence ($\Leftrightarrow$) and the constants $\top$, $\bot$ as the standard abbreviations. For all $\phi, \psi \in FOR$:

⋆ $\phi \vee \psi \overset{\text{def}}{=} \neg(\neg\phi \wedge \neg\psi)$;
⋆ $\phi \Rightarrow \psi \overset{\text{def}}{=} \neg(\phi \wedge \neg\psi)$;
⋆ $\phi \Leftrightarrow \psi \overset{\text{def}}{=} (\phi \Rightarrow \psi) \wedge (\psi \Rightarrow \phi)$;
⋆ $\top \overset{\text{def}}{=} \neg(p \wedge \neg p)$ and $\bot \overset{\text{def}}{=} p \wedge \neg p$ for some fixed propositional variable p.

The operators $\neg$ and $\wedge$ (as are $\vee$, $\Rightarrow$, $\Leftrightarrow$) are said to be *Boolean*. We write $\bigvee$ and $\bigwedge$ to denote the extension of $\vee$ and $\wedge$ to a finite number of arguments, respectively. The connectives $\vee$ and $\wedge$ are right-associative, that is the expression $\phi \vee \psi \vee \varphi$ is read as $\phi \vee (\psi \vee \varphi)$ and similarly for $\wedge$. We shall also use the convention that $\neg$ [resp. $\wedge$, $\vee$, $\Rightarrow$] binds more strongly than $\wedge$ [resp. $\vee$, $\Rightarrow$, $\Leftrightarrow$]. For example, the formula $\neg\phi \wedge \psi \vee \varphi \Rightarrow \phi$ is actually $(((\neg\phi) \wedge \psi) \vee \varphi) \Rightarrow \phi$.

Let $\{0, 1\}$ be the set of truth-values "false" and "true", respectively. By a *valuation* we mean any mapping $v : FOR_0 \rightarrow \{0, 1\}$. The valuation v is extended to FOR as follows:

⋆ $v(\neg\phi) \overset{\text{def}}{=} 1 - v(\phi)$;
⋆ $v(\phi \wedge \psi) \overset{\text{def}}{=} min(v(\phi), v(\psi))$.

A formula ϕ is a *tautology* (or ϕ is PC-valid) [resp. PC-satisfiable] whenever $v(\phi) = 1$ for every valuation v [resp. for some valuation v].

We will often use the following tautologies.

Lemma 5.2.1. *For all formulae ϕ, ψ, φ, the following are tautologies of PC:*

(I) $(\phi \Rightarrow (\psi \vee \varphi)) \Leftrightarrow ((\phi \Rightarrow \psi) \vee (\phi \Rightarrow \varphi))$;

(II) $((\phi \vee \psi) \Rightarrow \varphi) \Leftrightarrow ((\phi \Rightarrow \varphi) \wedge (\psi \Rightarrow \varphi))$;
(III) $(\phi \Rightarrow (\psi \wedge \varphi)) \Leftrightarrow ((\phi \Rightarrow \psi) \wedge (\phi \Rightarrow \varphi))$;
(IV) $((\phi \wedge \psi) \Rightarrow \varphi) \Leftrightarrow ((\phi \Rightarrow \varphi) \vee (\psi \Rightarrow \varphi))$;
(V) $(\phi \wedge \psi \Rightarrow \varphi) \Leftrightarrow (\phi \Rightarrow (\psi \Rightarrow \varphi))$;
(VI) $\neg(\phi \vee \psi) \Leftrightarrow \neg\phi \wedge \neg\psi$;
(VII) $\neg(\phi \wedge \psi) \Leftrightarrow \neg\phi \vee \neg\psi$.

5.2.2 Classical First-order Logic

In this section we present the first-order predicate logic FOL without function symbols. The vocabulary of FOL consists of:

⋆ the symbols $\neg$, $\wedge$ for propositional connectives;
⋆ the symbol $\forall$ for the universal quantifier;
⋆ for every $j \geq 1$, a countable set PRE_j of j-ary predicate symbols;
⋆ a countable set VAR of individual variables;
⋆ the binary predicate symbol = interpreted as identity.

An *atomic formula* of FOL has one of the following forms: $P(x_1, \ldots, x_j)$ or $x=x'$, where $P \in PRE_j$, $j \geq 1$, and $x_1, \ldots, x_j, x, x' \in$ VAR.
     The set of FOL-formulae is the smallest set containing the set of atomic formulae and closed under the following rules:

⋆ if ϕ is an FOL-formula, then $\neg\phi$ is an FOL-formula;
⋆ if ϕ, ψ are FOL-formulae, then $\phi \wedge \psi$ is an FOL-formula;
⋆ if ϕ is an FOL-formula and x is an individual variable, then $\forall x \, \phi$ is an FOL-formula.

The existential quantifier $\exists$ is defined by $\exists x \, \phi \overset{\text{def}}{=} \neg\forall x \, \neg\phi$.

As usual we assume that in every formula the different (occurrences of) quantifiers bind different variables.

A *structure for FOL* is a pair $\mathcal{M} = \langle D, m \rangle$ such that D is a non-empty set (the domain) and m is a meaning function such that for every $j \in \mathbb{N}$,

⋆ $m(P) \subseteq D^j$ for every $P \in PRE_j$;
⋆ $m(=) = \{\langle a, a \rangle : a \in D\}$.

A valuation in $\mathcal{M}$ is a map $v : \text{VAR} \to D$. We write $\mathcal{M}, v \models \phi$ to denote that ϕ is satisfied in $\mathcal{M}$ by v. The relation $\models$ is inductively defined as follows:

⋆ $\mathcal{M}, v \models P(x_1, \ldots, x_j) \overset{\text{def}}{\Leftrightarrow} \langle v(x_1), \ldots, v(x_j) \rangle \in m(P)$;
⋆ $\mathcal{M}, v \models x=x' \overset{\text{def}}{\Leftrightarrow} v(x) = v(x')$;
⋆ $\mathcal{M}, v \models \neg\phi \overset{\text{def}}{\Leftrightarrow}$ not $\mathcal{M}, v \models \phi$;
⋆ $\mathcal{M}, v \models \phi \wedge \psi \overset{\text{def}}{\Leftrightarrow} \mathcal{M}, v \models \phi$ and $\mathcal{M}, v \models \psi$;
⋆ $\mathcal{M}, v \models \forall x \, \phi \overset{\text{def}}{\Leftrightarrow}$ for every valuation v' in $\mathcal{M}$ such that v and v' coincide on VAR $\setminus \{x\}$, $\mathcal{M}, v' \models \phi$.

A formula ϕ is true in $\mathcal{M} \overset{\text{def}}{\Leftrightarrow} \mathcal{M}, v \models \phi$ for every valuation v in $\mathcal{M}$. ϕ is a *tautology of FOL* (or ϕ is *FOL-valid*) $\overset{\text{def}}{\Leftrightarrow}$ ϕ is true in all the structures for FOL. A *closed* FOL-formula is an FOL-formula such that all the occurrences of any individual variable are in the scope of a quantifier; otherwise, a formula is said to be *open*. If ϕ is closed, then the satisfaction of ϕ in a structure $\mathcal{M}$ does not depend on a valuation and we may write $\mathcal{M} \models \phi$.

Lemma 5.2.2. *The following formulae are tautologies of FOL:*

(I) $(\forall x \phi(x) \lor \forall x \psi(x)) \Rightarrow \forall x (\phi(x) \lor \psi(x))$;
(II) $\exists x (\phi(x) \land \psi(x)) \Rightarrow (\exists x \phi(x) \land \exists x \psi(x))$;
(III) $\exists x \forall y \phi(x, y) \Rightarrow \forall y \exists x \phi(x, y)$.

In this book we need a fragment of FOL with equality, with unary and binary predicate symbols only, and without function symbols. We shall abbreviate this fragment by FOL-M ("M" refers to the modal aspect of the fragment). We shall denote the unary predicate symbols by P and the binary predicate symbols by R. The other fragments of FOL used in the book are FOL$_n$ (Chap. 12, Chap. 13), the fragments of FOL with n individual variables, $n \geq 1$. We also consider a first-order language for information systems, FOL-IS, in Sect. 13.3.1.

5.3 Modal Logics

In this section we present a general notion of modal logic. The notion subsumes the definition of modal logic existing in the literature as well as the notion of information logic discussed in this book. Roughly speaking, any logic is determined by its syntax, its semantics, and a function which links the two. This function is determined by the maps which assign semantic objects to syntactic objects. The notion of modal logic presented in this section is developed according to this methodological principle.

5.3.1 Modal Language

Syntax of a modal logic is presented in the form of a modal language.

Definition 5.3.1. *A modal language is a system of the form*

$$L = \langle M_0, O_M, M, FOR_0, O_{FOR} \rangle$$

such that:

* M_0 *is a countable set of basic modal expressions;*
* O_M *is a finite set of modal operators of (fixed) non-zero finite arities;*
* *the set of modal expressions is the smallest set including M_0 and closed with respect to the operators from O_M;*

⋆ M *is a (possibly empty) subset of the set of modal expressions, closed under subexpressions. This means that if* $\oplus$ *is an n-ary connective from* O_M *and* $\oplus(a_1, \ldots, a_n) \in M$, *then for every* $i \in \{1, \ldots, n\}$, $a_i \in M$;
⋆ FOR_0 *is a countable set of basic formulae;*
⋆ O_{FOR} *is a set of logical connectives such that*

$$\{\neg, \wedge\} \subseteq O_{FOR} \subseteq \{\neg, \wedge\} \cup \{[a], K(a), [[a]] : a \in M\}.$$

We write OM_{FOR} to denote the set of modal connectives from O_{FOR}, that is $OM_{FOR} = O_{FOR} \setminus \{\neg, \wedge\}$.

Standard abbreviations include $\langle a \rangle$ and $\langle\langle a \rangle\rangle$:

$$\langle a \rangle \phi \stackrel{\text{def}}{=} \neg[a]\neg\phi, \quad \langle\langle a \rangle\rangle\phi \stackrel{\text{def}}{=} \neg[[a]]\neg\phi.$$

The connectives $[a]$, $\langle a \rangle$, $[[a]]$, and $\langle\langle a \rangle\rangle$ are referred to as *necessity, possibility, sufficiency,* and *impossibility*, respectively. The standard assumption is that the modal connectives bind more strongly than the binary Boolean connectives. If the elements of M_0 are atomic (entities without any structure), then they are referred to as *modal constants*. In the modal languages defined in Sect. 5.4 basic modal expressions are structured objects.

Modal expressions in M are intended to represent (indices of) binary relations that determine modal connectives. Consequently, modal operators from the set O_M represent operations on binary relations. In most of the modal languages considered in this book the set M [resp. O_{FOR}] is exactly the set of all the modal expressions generated from M_0 with the operators from O_M [resp. is exactly $\{\wedge, \neg\} \cup \{[a] : a \in M\}$]. If M [resp. O_{FOR}] is not defined explicitly, we mean that this is the case. The set FOR_0 contains propositional variables and/or propositional constants. The constants which will be interpreted as singletons are referred to as *object nominals*. They are treated as names of the respective objects. By default, FOR_0 is a countably infinite set of propositional variables. A *literal* is either a basic formula or a negated basic formula.

As a notational convention, for every syntactic category X and for every syntactic object O, we write X(O) to denote the set of elements of X occurring in O. For instance, $FOR_0(\phi)$ denotes the set of basic formulae that occur in the formula ϕ.

Definition 5.3.2. *Let* $L = \langle M_0, O_M, M, FOR_0, O_{FOR} \rangle$ *be a modal language. The set* FOR *of L-formulae is the smallest set including* FOR_0 *and closed with respect to the logical connectives from* O_{FOR}.

Observe that, contrary to a common practice, we do not include the set FOR of L-formulae in the formal system of the modal language L. This is because FOR is completely and uniquely determined by the components of L. Hence, in the subsequent chapters the presentation of any particular language will require only a specification of modal expressions and propositional connectives.

If M = {a} (a singleton), then the unary modal connectives are written $\Box, \Diamond, K, [[]], \langle\langle\rangle\rangle$, respectively. Clearly, the modal languages are extensions of the classical propositional language.

The set sub(ϕ) of *subformulae* of the formula ϕ is the smallest (with respect to inclusion) set of L-formulae satisfying the following conditions:

⋆ $\phi \in \text{sub}(\phi)$;
⋆ if $\neg\psi \in \text{sub}(\phi)$, then $\psi \in \text{sub}(\phi)$;
⋆ if $\psi_1 \wedge \psi_2 \in \text{sub}(\phi)$, then $\psi_1, \psi_2 \in \text{sub}(\phi)$;
⋆ for every $\oplus \in \text{OM}_{\text{FOR}}$, if $\oplus\psi \in \text{sub}(\phi)$ then $\psi \in \text{sub}(\phi)$.

A set X of L-formulae is said to be *closed under subformulae* $\overset{\text{def}}{\Leftrightarrow}$ $X = \bigcup\{\text{sub}(\phi) : \phi \in X\}$. The *modal weight* of ϕ, written $\text{mw}(\phi)$, is the number of occurrences of the elements of OM_{FOR} in ϕ. The *modal depth* of an occurrence of a formula ψ in ϕ is the number of occurrences of elements of OM_{FOR} in ϕ such that ψ is in their scope. We write $\text{md}(\phi)$ to denote the *modal degree* of ϕ, that is, the maximum of the modal depths of the subformulae of ϕ. md is naturally extended to finite sets of formulae, understood as conjunctions of their elements, and by convention $\text{md}(\emptyset) = 0$.

A *universal* [resp. *existential*] modality is a finite (possibly empty) sequence of elements of OM_{FOR} of the form [a] [resp. $\langle a \rangle$], for a $\in$ M. Let ϕ, ψ, and φ be L-formulae. We write $\phi[\psi \leftarrow \varphi]$ to denote the formula obtained from ϕ by simultaneously replacing every occurrence of ψ by φ. A set X of L-formulae is *closed under (uniform) substitution* in L $\overset{\text{def}}{\Leftrightarrow}$ for all L-formulae ϕ, ψ, and for every propositional variable p of L, if $\phi \in X$, then $\phi[\text{p} \leftarrow \psi] \in X$.

5.3.2 Semantics of Modal Languages

The following definition of a model for a modal language is reminiscent of the definition of a first-order structure over a restricted vocabulary with unary and binary predicate symbols only. Actually, the intensional connectives used in the modal logics investigated here can be viewed as restricted quantifiers from first-order classical logic. The choice we make here for the notion of model is motivated by this standard analogy. More importantly, it fits all the logics studied in this volume and it combines simplicity with generality.

Definition 5.3.3. *Let* L *be a modal language. An* L-*model is a structure* $\mathcal{M} = \langle W, m \rangle$ *such that* W *is a non-empty set and* m *is a meaning function, that is, a map* $m : \text{FOR}_0 \cup M \to \mathcal{P}(W) \cup \mathcal{P}(W \times W)$ *such that:*

⋆ $m(\text{p}) \subseteq W$ *for every* p $\in \text{FOR}_0$;
⋆ $m(\text{a}) \subseteq W \times W$ *for every* a $\in$ M.

Traditionally, the relations $m(a)$ are referred to as the accessibility relations. If FOR_0 includes object nominals, then for every object nominal x, $m(x)$ is a singleton set. If the restriction of m to the set of nominals is a bijection, then the nominals of L are said to be *strong nominals*. By the *cardinality of a model* $\langle W, m \rangle$, we mean the cardinality of the set W.

Definition 5.3.4. *An L-frame is a structure* $F = \langle W, m \rangle$ *such that W is a non-empty set and m is a map* $m : M \to \mathcal{P}(W \times W)$.

An L-model $\mathcal{M} = \langle W, m \rangle$ is said to be *based on* an L-frame $F = \langle W, m' \rangle$ $\overset{\text{def}}{\Leftrightarrow}$ m' is the restriction of m to the set M of modal expressions. Any L-frame $F = \langle W, m \rangle$ can be presented in an equivalent manner as in Definition 3.9.2. If M is finite, say $M = \{a_1, \ldots, a_n\}$, $n \geq 1$, then we write $\langle W, R_{a_1}, \ldots, R_{a_n} \rangle$ where $R_{a_i} = m(a_i)$ for every $i \in \{1, \ldots, n\}$. In a similar way, we write $\langle W, (R_a)_{a \in M} \rangle$ [resp. $\langle W, (R_a)_{a \in M}, m \rangle$] to denote the L-frame [resp. L-model] $\langle W, m \rangle$ such that for every $a \in M$, $m(a) = R_a$.

We say that a formula ϕ is satisfied in the model $\mathcal{M}$ by the object x (written $\mathcal{M}, x \models \phi$) if the following conditions are satisfied:

* $\mathcal{M}, x \models p \overset{\text{def}}{\Leftrightarrow} x \in m(p)$ for $p \in FOR_0$;
* $\mathcal{M}, x \models \phi \wedge \psi \overset{\text{def}}{\Leftrightarrow} \mathcal{M}, x \models \phi$ and $\mathcal{M}, x \models \psi$;
* $\mathcal{M}, x \models \neg\phi \overset{\text{def}}{\Leftrightarrow}$ not $\mathcal{M}, x \models \phi$;
* $\mathcal{M}, x \models [a]\phi \overset{\text{def}}{\Leftrightarrow}$ for every $y \in m(a)(x)$, $\mathcal{M}, y \models \phi$;
* $\mathcal{M}, x \models [[a]]\phi \overset{\text{def}}{\Leftrightarrow}$ for every $y \in W$ if $\mathcal{M}, y \models \phi$, then $y \in m(a)(x)$;
* $\mathcal{M}, x \models K(a)\phi \overset{\text{def}}{\Leftrightarrow}$ either for every $y \in m(a)(x)$, $\mathcal{M}, y \models \phi$ or for every $y \in m(a)(x)$, not $\mathcal{M}, y \models \phi$.

If $\mathcal{M}, x \models \langle a \rangle \phi$, $\langle x, y \rangle \in R_a$, and $\mathcal{M}, y \models \phi$, we say that y is a *witness* for $\mathcal{M}, x \models \langle a \rangle \phi$. We extend the meaning function m to all the formulae:

$$m(\phi) \overset{\text{def}}{=} \{w \in W : \mathcal{M}, w \models \phi\}.$$

The L-satisfiability relation $\models$ might be understood as associating to each model and to each object $x \in W$ of the model, a truth-value for each L-formula. Namely, if $\mathcal{M}, x \models \phi$ holds, then the truth-value of ϕ at $\mathcal{M}$ and x is "true", and "false" otherwise.

An L-formula ϕ is said to be *true in the L-model* $\mathcal{M} = \langle W, m \rangle$ (written $\mathcal{M} \models \phi$) $\overset{\text{def}}{\Leftrightarrow}$ for every $x \in W$, we have $\mathcal{M}, x \models \phi$. An L-formula ϕ is said to be *true in the L-frame* F (written $F \models \phi$) $\overset{\text{def}}{\Leftrightarrow}$ ϕ is true in all the L-models based on F. It is easy to see that in every L-model $\mathcal{M}$ and for every object x the connectives $\neg$ and $\wedge$ receive their standard meaning as classical negation and conjunction, respectively.

Let X be a set of L-frames. We write $\text{TFOR}(X)$ to denote the set of L-formulae that are true in all the frames belonging to X. Similarly, for every set X of L-formulae, we write $\mathrm{TFR}(X)$ to denote the set of L-frames F such that for every formula $\phi \in X$, ϕ is true in F.

Let $\mathcal{M} = \langle W, (R_\mathrm{a})_{\mathrm{a} \in \mathrm{M}}, m \rangle$ be an L-model. If W is a set of objects of an information system, R_a is an information relation from the class of indistinguishability relations derived from an information system, and $m(\phi)$ is a subset of objects, then the formulae $[\mathrm{a}]\phi$ and $\langle \mathrm{a} \rangle \phi$ represent the lower and upper approximations of $m(\phi)$ with respect to the relation R_a, respectively. Hence, approximation operators are examples of necessity and possibility connectives. The result of the application of the operators Bl and Bu (defined in Sect. 4.3) determined by the relation R_a to a set $m(\phi)$ of objects can be represented by modal formulae as follows: $\phi \wedge \neg[\mathrm{a}]\phi$, $\langle \mathrm{a} \rangle \phi \wedge \neg \phi$. Similarly, the information operators $[[R]]$ and $\langle\langle R \rangle\rangle$ defined in Sect. 4.9 are examples of the sufficiency and impossibility connectives, and knowledge operators defined in Sect. 4.6 are examples of knowledge connectives.

It follows that modal languages enable us to represent all the information operators presented in Chap. 4. Moreover, since in the modal languages we explicitly represent the relations that determine modal connectives (by means of modal expressions), we are able to represent relationships among the information operators determined by different information relations.

Definition 5.3.5. *A class X of L-frames is said to be first-order definable* $\overset{\mathrm{def}}{\Longleftrightarrow}$

(1) there is a set Y of closed FOL-M-formulae containing no unary predicate symbols and
(2) there is an injective map $f : \mathrm{M} \to \mathrm{PRE}_2$

such that for every L-frame $F = \langle W, (R_\mathrm{a})_{\mathrm{a} \in \mathrm{M}} \rangle$, the following statements are equivalent:

* $F \in X$;
* *for every FOL-M-model $\mathcal{M} = \langle W, m \rangle$ such that $m(f(\mathrm{a})) = R_\mathrm{a}$ for every $\mathrm{a} \in \mathrm{M}$, we have $\mathcal{M} \models \phi$ for every $\phi \in Y$.*

Observe that we admit here a generalised concept of first-order definability, since we do not assume that Y is finite. This enables us to state that a modal logic with a countably infinite set of modal expressions has a first-order definable class of frames.

Example 5.3.1. Let L be the modal language such that the only modal expressions are a and b. The class of L-frames $\langle W, R_\mathrm{a}, R_\mathrm{b} \rangle$ such that R_a is reflexive and $R_\mathrm{a} \subseteq R_\mathrm{b}$ is first-order definable. Indeed, let f be a map such that $f(\mathrm{a}) = \mathrm{R}_0$, $f(\mathrm{b}) = \mathrm{R}_1$, and Y consists of the formula

$$\forall x\, \mathrm{R}_0(x, x) \wedge \forall x, y\, (\mathrm{R}_0(x, y) \Rightarrow \mathrm{R}_1(x, y)).$$

It is easy to check that f and Y satisfy the required conditions. By contrast, the class of frames $\langle W, R_a \rangle$ such that there are no infinite R_a-paths is not first-order definable. Similarly, there is no first-order formula stating that a relation is the transitive closure of another relation.

A formula is *positive* [resp. *negative*] $\overset{\text{def}}{\Leftrightarrow}$ every basic formula occurs under an even [resp. odd] number of negation symbols.

Definition 5.3.6. *A simple Sahlqvist formula of* L *is of the form* $\phi \Rightarrow \psi$, *where*

* ψ *is positive;*
* ϕ *is built from*
  * *negative formulae, or*
  * *formulae built from* $\top$ *and* $\bot$, *or*
  * *formulae of the form* σp, *where* σ *is a universal modality and* $p \in FOR_0$ *using only* $\wedge, \vee$ *and the existential modalities.*

A Sahlqvist formula is a conjunction of formulae of the form $\sigma(\phi \Rightarrow \psi)$ *where* σ *is a universal modality and* $\phi \Rightarrow \psi$ *is a simple Sahlqvist formula.*

Example 5.3.2. Let L be a modal language such that [a] and [b] are logical connectives and p, q are basic formulae. The following are examples of simple Sahlqvist formulae:

* $[a]p \Rightarrow [b]q$;
* $\langle a \rangle [a][a][b]q \Rightarrow [a](q \wedge \langle b \rangle p)$;
* $[b]p \Rightarrow [b][b]p$.

By contrast, $[a]([a]p \Rightarrow p) \Rightarrow [a]p$ is not a Sahlqvist formula, since $[a]([a]p \Rightarrow p)$ is not negative.

Theorem 5.3.1. *Let* X *be a set of Sahlqvist formulae. Then the class* $TFR(X)$ *of frames is first-order definable.*

Sahlqvist formulae satisfy other interesting properties; see Sect. 5.6 for references. In the subsequent chapters the proofs of some particular instances of Theorem 5.3.1 relevant to information logics will be presented.

Let $L = \langle M_0, O_M, M, FOR_0, O_{FOR} \rangle$ be a modal language. In the general definition of semantics of modal languages given so far, we did not postulate any relationship between the meaning of modal expressions defining compound relations and the meanings of their subexpressions denoting the component relations. The obvious requirement is that the meaning of the complex expressions can be computed from the meanings of their components. The notions of relation operation (see Sect. 3.9) and operator interpretation enable us to make this requirement precise.

Definition 5.3.7. *Let* L *be a modal language. By a modal operator interpretation for* L *we mean a mapping* $\mathcal{I}$ *from the set* O_M *into a family of relation operations such that for every* $\oplus \in O_M$, $\oplus$ *and* $\mathcal{I}(\oplus)$ *have the same arity* n, $n \geq 1$, *and the profile of* $\mathcal{I}(\oplus)$ *is the* $n+1$-*tuple* $\langle 2, \ldots, 2, 2 \rangle$.

Now we can state in a formal way how the meaning of compound modal expressions is defined.

Definition 5.3.8. *Let* L *be a modal language, let* $\mathcal{M} = \langle W, (R_a)_{a \in M}, m \rangle$ *be an* L-*model, and let* $\mathcal{I}$ *be a modal operator interpretation for* L. *We say that the meaning function* m *respects* $\mathcal{I} \overset{\text{def}}{\Leftrightarrow}$ *for every* $\oplus(a_1, \ldots, a_{ar(\oplus)}) \in M$, $m(\oplus(a_1, \ldots, a_{ar(\oplus)})) = \mathcal{I}(\oplus)(m(a_1), \ldots, m(a_{ar(\oplus)}))$. *By extension, we say that the model* $\mathcal{M}$ *respects* $\mathcal{I}$ *whenever the underlying meaning function* m *respects* $\mathcal{I}$.

If $O_M = \{\oplus_1, \ldots, \oplus_s\}$, $s \geq 1$, then the structure

$$\langle \{R_a : a \in M\}, \mathcal{I}(\oplus_1), \ldots, \mathcal{I}(\oplus_s) \rangle$$

is an algebra of relations generated from $\{R_c : c \in M_0\}$ with the operations $\mathcal{I}(\oplus_1), \ldots, \mathcal{I}(\oplus_s)$. However, the operations of this algebra may not be the standard relational operations defined in Sect. 1.8; see Example 5.4.4.

5.3.3 Modal Logic

The following definition of modal logic will be used throughout the book. It enables us to present information logics in a uniform framework.

Definition 5.3.9. *A modal logic is a pair* $\mathcal{L} = \langle L, \mathcal{S} \rangle$, *where* L *is a modal language and* $\mathcal{S}$ *is a non-empty class of* L-*models respecting* $\mathcal{I}$ *for some modal operator interpretation* $\mathcal{I}$ *for* L.

Such a logic $\mathcal{L}$ is often denoted by $\langle L, \mathcal{I}, \mathcal{S} \rangle$. Observe that the map $\mathcal{I}$ may introduce a first-order feature to the semantics of modal logic. The need for extending semantic structures of information logics beyond the purely propositional level is a consequence of a high expressive power of their languages which, in turn, are intended to reflect the expressiveness of information systems.

The class $\mathcal{S}$ of models of $\mathcal{L}$ is usually defined in terms of properties that the relations in the models of $\mathcal{S}$ are supposed to satisfy. For example, properties of relations listed in Sect. 1.2 are often used.

If the set M of modal expressions of L is not a singleton set, the logic $\mathcal{L}$ is often referred to as a *multi-modal* (or *polymodal*) logic. In $\mathcal{L} = \langle L, \mathcal{S} \rangle$, L is called the $\mathcal{L}$-*language* (also denoted by $\mathrm{LAN}(\mathcal{L})$) and $\mathcal{S}$ is called the set of $\mathcal{L}$-*models* (also denoted by $\mathrm{MOD}(\mathcal{L})$). The set of formulae of the logic $\mathcal{L}$ is defined as the set of formulae of $\mathrm{LAN}(\mathcal{L})$ and it is denoted by $\mathrm{FOR}(\mathcal{L})$. An

$\mathcal{L}$-frame F is a LAN($\mathcal{L}$)-frame for which there is an $\mathcal{L}$-model based on F. A modal logic can be viewed as being obtained from FOL by restricting both the language and the class of semantic structures. However, it is inaccurate to state that each modal logic is a fragment of FOL. Indeed, the class of models of a given modal logic is not necessarily first-order definable.

The methodology of modal logics is concerned with the following concepts. Let $\mathcal{L} = \langle L, S \rangle$ be a modal logic.

* An L-formula ϕ is $\mathcal{L}$-satisfiable $\overset{\text{def}}{\Leftrightarrow}$ there is an $\mathcal{L}$-model $\mathcal{M} = \langle W, m \rangle \in S$ and $x \in W$ such that $\mathcal{M}, x \models \phi$. We write SAT($\mathcal{L}$) to denote the set of $\mathcal{L}$-satisfiable formulae.
* An L-formula ϕ is satisfiable in an L-model $\mathcal{M}$ $\overset{\text{def}}{\Leftrightarrow}$ there is a $w \in W$ such that $\mathcal{M}, w \models \phi$.
* An L-formula ϕ is $\mathcal{L}$-valid $\overset{\text{def}}{\Leftrightarrow}$ for every $\mathcal{L}$-model $\mathcal{M} \in S$, ϕ is true in $\mathcal{M}$. We write VAL($\mathcal{L}$) to denote the set of $\mathcal{L}$-valid formulae.
* $\mathcal{L}$ has the *finite model property* $\overset{\text{def}}{\Leftrightarrow}$ for every $\mathcal{L}$-satisfiable formula ϕ, there exist an $\mathcal{L}$-model $\langle W, m \rangle$ and a $w \in W$ such that W is finite and $\mathcal{M}, w \models \phi$.
* Let X be a set of $\mathcal{L}$-formulae and ϕ be an $\mathcal{L}$-formula. ϕ is a *semantic consequence* of X in $\mathcal{L}$ (in symbols $X \models \phi$) $\overset{\text{def}}{\Leftrightarrow}$ for every $\mathcal{L}$-model $\mathcal{M}$, if for every $\psi \in X$, $\mathcal{M} \models \psi$, then $\mathcal{M} \models \phi$. We write CONS($\mathcal{L}$) to denote the set of non-empty sequences $\langle \phi_1, \ldots, \phi_n \rangle$ of L-formulae such that $\{\phi_1, \ldots, \phi_{n-1}\} \models \phi_n$. CONS($\mathcal{L}$) is called the *logical $\mathcal{L}$-consequence problem*.
* Let O_1 and O_2 be syntactic objects of the same kind (for example modal expressions, formulae, etc.) that may occur in L-formulae. O_1 and O_2 are said to be *$\mathcal{L}$-equivalent* (in symbols $O_1 \sim_{\mathcal{L}} O_2$) $\overset{\text{def}}{\Leftrightarrow}$ for every $\mathcal{L}$-model $\langle W, m \rangle$, $m(O_1) = m(O_2)$.

Definition 5.3.10. *Let $\mathcal{L}$ be a logic and let* b *be a modal expression such that* [b] *is a modal connective of* LAN($\mathcal{L}$). [b] *is said to be a universal modal connective in $\mathcal{L}$* $\overset{\text{def}}{\Leftrightarrow}$ *for every $\mathcal{L}$-model $\mathcal{M} = \langle W, (R_a)_{a \in M}, m \rangle$, $R_b = W \times W$.*

Example 5.3.3. The basic modal logics are K, T, B, S4, and S5. Their common language LAN(K) is defined as follows:

* $M_0 = \{a\}$ is a singleton set;
* $O_M = \emptyset$;
* $M = M_0$;
* FOR_0 is a countably infinite set of propositional variables;
* $O_{FOR} = \{\neg, \wedge, [a]\}$.

The models of these logics are the LAN(K)-models $\mathcal{M} = \langle W, R, m \rangle$ (we write R instead of R_a) such that:

* $\mathcal{M}$ is a K-model $\overset{\text{def}}{\Leftrightarrow}$ R is any binary relation on W;

$\star$ $\mathcal{M}$ is a T-model $\overset{\text{def}}{\Leftrightarrow}$ R is a reflexive relation on W;

$\star$ $\mathcal{M}$ is a B-model $\overset{\text{def}}{\Leftrightarrow}$ R is a tolerance relation on W;

$\star$ $\mathcal{M}$ is an S4-model $\overset{\text{def}}{\Leftrightarrow}$ R is a reflexive and transitive relation on W;

$\star$ $\mathcal{M}$ is an S5-model $\overset{\text{def}}{\Leftrightarrow}$ R is an equivalence relation on W.

In the following, we present some examples of valid formulae.

Lemma 5.3.1.

(I) $\sigma \Box \phi \Leftrightarrow \Box \phi$ is S5-valid for every sequence σ of modal connectives in $\{\Box, \Diamond\}^*$;

(II) $\Box \phi \Rightarrow \sigma \phi$ is S4-valid for every universal modality σ;

(III) $\Box \phi \Rightarrow (\Box(\phi \Rightarrow \psi) \Rightarrow \Box \psi)$ is K-valid.

In Example 5.3.3, the simplicity of the standard modal logics hides the generality of the notion of modal logic we use. The following example is more relevant to illustrate our definition of modal logic.

Example 5.3.4. We present the data analysis logic DAL. This logic is discussed in Chaps. 8, 10, and 12. The language LAN(DAL) is a modal language such that:

$\star$ the countably infinite set M_0 of basic modal expressions consists of modal constants;

$\star$ $O_M = \{\cup^*, \cap\}$ (both binary);

$\star$ $O_{FOR} = \{\wedge, \neg\} \cup \{[a] : a \in M\}$.

For every LAN(DAL)-model $\mathcal{M} = \langle W, (R_a)_{a \in M}, m \rangle$, $\mathcal{M} \in$ MOD(DAL) iff

(1) for every $a \in M$, R_a is an equivalence relation on W;

(2) for all $a, b \in M$, $R_{a \cup^* b} = (R_a \cup R_b)^*$, where * is the reflexive and transitive closure operation and $R_{a \cap b} = R_a \cap R_b$, where on the right-hand side of the equality, $\cap$ is the set intersection.

It can be easily seen that, in view of the respective definitions, the modal connectives [a] and $\langle a \rangle$ of the language of DAL can be regarded as generalised operations of upper approximation and lower approximation with respect to relation R_a, respectively (see Sect. 4.2). It follows that the logic DAL and its variants may be useful in an analysis of and reasoning about data which are incomplete in that they are determined up to an equivalence relation. The inclusion of relational operations $\cup^*$ and $\cap$ in the language of DAL is motivated by their applications to formation of properties of objects (see Sect. 3.4). A variant of the logic DAL, called DALLA, is investigated in details in Chap. 8.

Definition 5.3.11. *A standard modal logic is a modal logic $\langle L, S \rangle$ with*

$$L = \langle M_0, O_M, M, FOR_0, O_{FOR} \rangle$$

such that:

⋆ M_0 *is a countable (possibly finite) set of modal constants;*
⋆ *the modal connectives are of the form* [a], *for every* a ∈ M.

The logic DAL defined in Example 5.3.4 is a standard modal logic.

Example 5.3.5. In this example, we define various PDL-like logics. The propositional dynamic logic PDL is a standard modal logic whose language LAN(PDL) satisfies the following conditions:

⋆ M_0 is a countably infinite set of modal constants, referred to as *program constants*;
⋆ $O_M = \{*, ;, \cup\}$ where $*$ is unary and ;, $\cup$ are binary;
⋆ $O_{FOR} = \{\wedge, \neg\} \cup \{[a] : a \in M\}$.

For every LAN(PDL)-model $\mathcal{M} = \langle W, (R_a)_{a \in M}, m \rangle$, $\mathcal{M} \in$ MOD(PDL) iff for all a, b ∈ M

(1) $R_{a\cup b} = R_a \cup R_b$,
(2) $R_{a;b} = R_a; R_b$,
(3) $R_{a^*} = R_a^*$;

that is the modal operators are interpreted as the corresponding relation operations. The propositional dynamic logic PDL with converse (PDL + converse) [resp. PDL with intersection (PDL + intersection), PDL with complement (PDL + complement)] is defined as PDL except that the unary modal operator $^{-1}$ [resp. the binary modal operator $\cap$, the unary modal operator $-$] is added to the set O_M and there is an extra condition on models: $R_{a^{-1}} = R_a^{-1}$ [resp. $R_{a\cap b} = R_a \cap R_b$, $R_{-a} = (W \times W) \setminus R_a$]. Combinatory PDL is an extension of PDL obtained by adding a universal modal connective [U] to the set O_{FOR} and a countably infinite set of object nominals to the set FOR_0 of basic formulae.

In the rest of the book, the modal operators $*$, ;, and $\cup$ are always interpreted in the standard way as in PDL-like logics. Furthermore, $\cup^*$ is interpreted as the transitive and reflexive closure of the union as in the logic DAL. We will refer to the PDL-like logics in connection with the decidability issues discussed in Chaps. 10 and 11.

Finally, we introduce some modal logics that are needed in the subsequent chapters.

Definition 5.3.12. *Let* c ∈ {0, U} *and let* $\mathcal{L}$ *be a standard modal logic (in the sense of Definition 5.3.11) such that* c *is not a part of its language* LAN($\mathcal{L}$). *We write* $\mathcal{L}^c$ *to denote the standard modal logic obtained from* $\mathcal{L}$ *by adding a distinguished modal constant* c *to* M_0 *and by assuming that in every* $\mathcal{L}^c$*-model* $R_0 = \emptyset$ *and* $R_U = W \times W$. *By* $\mathcal{L}^{c^-}$ *we denote the logic obtained from* $\mathcal{L}^c$ *by allowing the occurrences of* c *only in the connective* [c] *(*c *cannot occur in a structured modal expression).*

It follows that in the language of $\mathcal{L}^{c^-}$, there are no modal expressions, where the operators from O_M are applied to c.

Example 5.3.6. DAL^U is an extension of DAL with the modal connective [U] such that $\mathcal{M} \in MOD(DAL^U) \overset{\text{def}}{\Leftrightarrow}$ (1) and (2) from Example 5.3.4 hold and $R_U = W \times W$. Clearly, [U] is a universal modal connective. DAL^U is investigated in Sect. 11.3.

For every $c \in \{0, U\}$, $\mathcal{L}^c$ is said to be c-*simplifiable* $\overset{\text{def}}{\Leftrightarrow}$ for every formula ϕ of $\mathcal{L}^c$ there is a formula ψ in $\mathcal{L}^{c^-}$ such that $\phi \sim_{\mathcal{L}^c} \psi$. For instance, the logic DAL^U obtained from the standard modal logic DAL is U-simplifiable. This is due to the fact that for every $R \subseteq (W \times W)$, $R \cup^* (W \times W) = (W \times W) \cup^* R = (W \times W)$ and $R \cap (W \times W) = (W \times W) \cap R = R$.

5.4 Modal Logics with Relative Accessibility Relations

In Sect. 3.2 we have shown that information relations derived from information systems are relative relations determined by subsets of attributes and that there are several relevant families of those relations. Then, in Sect. 3.9 we discussed relative relations determined by members of any level n, $n \in \mathbb{N}$, of the powerset hierarchy of a set. For each $n \in \mathbb{N}$ these relations are referred to as relative relations of level n. It follows that logics with modal connectives determined by these relations should have in their models several families of relative relations of some level n. Consequently, the language of these logics should include the expressions that represent the indices of the families of relations and the expressions that represent indices of the relations within each family. Usually, the relations in any given family are of the same kind. For instance, we can have a family of relative indiscernibility relations, relative similarity relations, etc. Therefore the indices of the families of relations are referred to as relation types. The indices of relations in a family of relations are called parameter expressions. The indices of relative relations may be complex objects (sets, families of sets, etc.) and we should be able to perform the operations on these indices, for instance the set operations, in order to form compound parameter expressions. Parameter expressions representing sets of parameters and their unions, intersections, and complements are needed, for example, for expressing global conditions on families of information relations (Sect. 3.9) or dependencies of attributes in information systems (Sect. 3.5).

5.4.1 Parameter Expressions

The syntax of parameter expressions is defined as follows:

⋆ P_0 is a countable set of *basic parameter expressions*;

⋆ O_P is a finite set of operators referred to as P-*operators*;
⋆ the set P of *parameter expressions* is the smallest set including P_0 and
  closed under the operators from O_P.

If the elements of P_0 are atomic entities, they are referred to as *parameter constants*. Semantics of parameter expressions is defined in a similar way as semantics of modal expressions (Sect. 5.3.2). To define the meaning of parameter expressions, first, we have to interpret the operators from the set O_P. Since the parameter expressions represent members of different levels of the powerset hierarchy, we have to interpret the P-operators accordingly. For that purpose we need the notion of set operation of level n, $n \in \mathbb{N}$.

Let $h : W \to W'$ be a 1–1 mapping from a non-empty set W onto a set W'. For every $j \in \mathbb{N}$, we define a map $h^j : \mathcal{P}^j(W) \to \mathcal{P}^j(W')$ such that $h^0 \stackrel{\text{def}}{=} h$ and for every $X \in \mathcal{P}^{j+1}(W)$, $h^{j+1}(X) = \{h^j(x) : x \in X\}$. The maps h^n, $n \geq 0$, are needed in Definition 5.4.1.

Definition 5.4.1. *A set operation of level $n \in \mathbb{N}$ and of arity $ar \geq 1$ is a map f such that for every non-empty set W, $f(W)$ is a map*

$$f(W) : (\mathcal{P}^n(W))^{ar} \to \mathcal{P}^n(W)$$

and for every bijection $h : W \to W'$, for all $X_1, \ldots, X_{ar} \in \mathcal{P}^n(W)$,

$$f(W')(h^n(X_1), \ldots, h^n(X_{ar})) = h^n(f(W)(X_1, \ldots, X_{ar})).$$

As in Definition 3.9.4, $f(W)(X_1, \ldots, X_{ar})$ is also written $f(X_1, \ldots, X_{ar})$.

Example 5.4.1. Let $\cup$ be the binary set operation of level 1 such that for every set W and for all $X, Y \subseteq W$, $\cup(X, Y)$ is the standard union of the sets X and Y. Now, let $\cup'$ be the binary set operation of level 2 such that for every set W and for all $X, Y \in \mathcal{P}^2(W)$,

$$\cup'(X, Y) \stackrel{\text{def}}{=} \{\cup(x, y) : x \in X, \; y \in Y\}.$$

For instance,

$$\cup'(\{\{1, 2\}, \{3\}\}, \{\{0\}, \{1\}\}) = \{\{0, 1, 2\}, \{1, 2\}, \{0, 3\}, \{1, 3\}\}.$$

Now we define an interpretation of parameter operators. In order to distinguish it from the interpretation of modal operators (Definition 5.3.7) we refer to it as parameter operator interpretation.

Definition 5.4.2. *A parameter operator interpretation is a function $\mathcal{I}$ from the set O_P into a family of set operations of level n, for some $n \in \mathbb{N}$, such that for every $\oplus \in O_P$, $\oplus$ and $\mathcal{I}(\oplus)$ are of the same arity.*

Often we use the same symbol for $\oplus$ and $\mathcal{I}(\oplus)$. If the range of $\mathcal{I}$ is a family of set operations of level n, then $\mathcal{I}$ is said to be a parameter operator interpretation of level n.

Semantics of parameter expressions is defined as follows.

Definition 5.4.3. *Let PAR be a non-empty set. By a* P-*meaning function we mean a map* $m : \mathrm{P} \to \mathcal{P}^n(PAR)$ *for some* $n \in \mathbb{N}$. *The function* m *is said to be a* P-*meaning function of level* n *provided that the range of* m *is* $\mathcal{P}^n(PAR)$.

As with the semantics of modal expressions, we must add a postulate that the meaning of any compound parameter expression can be computed from the meanings of its components.

Definition 5.4.4. *Let* $\mathcal{I}$ *be a parameter operator interpretation. We say that the* P-*meaning function* m *respects* $\mathcal{I} \overset{\text{def}}{\Leftrightarrow}$ *for every* $\oplus(\mathrm{A}_1, \ldots, \mathrm{A}_{ar(\oplus)}) \in \mathrm{P}$, *the following holds:*

$$m(\oplus(\mathrm{A}_1, \ldots, \mathrm{A}_{ar(\oplus)})) = \mathcal{I}(\oplus)(m(\mathrm{A}_1), \ldots, m(\mathrm{A}_{ar(\oplus)})).$$

For the sake of simplicity we make the convention that if P_0 is a countably infinite set of parameter constants and $\mathrm{O_P} = \{\cup, \cap, -\}$ of arities 2,2,1, respectively, then we shall always interpret these operations as set operations of union, intersection, and complement respectively. Such a set P of parameter expressions is said to be a *standard set of parameter expressions*. The respective P-meaning function is said to be a *standard P-meaning function*.

Following the convention from Sect. 5.3.3, for all $\mathrm{A}, \mathrm{B} \in \mathrm{M}$, we write $\mathrm{A} \sim \mathrm{B}$ [resp. $\mathrm{A} \sim \top$, $\mathrm{A} \sim \perp$] to mean that for every P-meaning function $m : \mathrm{P} \to \mathcal{P}^n(PAR)$ respecting some $\mathcal{I}$, $m(\mathrm{A}) = m(\mathrm{B})$ [resp. $m(\mathrm{A}) = \emptyset$, $m(\mathrm{A}) = \mathcal{P}^{n-1}(PAR)$].

Sometimes there is a need to represent individual parameters. In that case, the set P_0 of basic parameter expressions includes the constants referred to as *parameter nominals* and every P-meaning function is assumed to satisfy the following conditions. For all parameter nominals E, E′:

⋆ $m(\mathrm{E})$ is of the form $\{p\}$ for some $p \in PAR$;
⋆ if $\mathrm{E} \neq \mathrm{E}'$, then $m(\mathrm{E}) \neq m(\mathrm{E}')$.

In the rest of this section, we shall present normal forms for standard parameter expressions. The normal forms are extensions of normal forms for the formulae of PC. They play an important role in Chaps. 10 and 11.

Let $c_1, \ldots, c_n$ be basic parameter expressions in a set P of standard parameter expressions. For every $k \in \{0, \ldots, 2^n - 1\}$, let B'_k be defined as $\mathrm{A}'_1 \cap \ldots \cap \mathrm{A}'_n$ where, for every $s \in \{1, \ldots, n\}$, $\mathrm{A}'_s = c_s$ if $bit_s(k) = 0$, and $\mathrm{A}'_s = -c_s$ otherwise, where $bit_s(k)$ denotes the sth bit in the binary representation of k. One can show that for every standard P-meaning function $m : \mathrm{P} \to \mathcal{P}(PAR)$ the family

$$\{m(\mathrm{B}'_k) : k \in \{0, \ldots, 2^n - 1\}\}$$

is a partition of PAR. If there are parameter nominals among $c_1, \ldots, c_n$, some of the B'_k can be simplified, since for any two distinct parameter nominals E and E', we have $m(\text{E} \cap \text{E}') = \emptyset$ and $m(\text{E} \cap -\text{E}') = m(\text{E})$. This leads to the following definitions.

Let $E_1, \ldots, E_l$, $l \geq 0$, be distinct parameter nominals and let $C_1, \ldots, C_n$, $n \geq 0$, be distinct parameter constants. If $n \geq 1$, then for every integer $k \in \{0, \ldots, 2^n - 1\}$, we define the standard parameter expression

$$B_k \overset{\text{def}}{=} A_1 \cap \ldots \cap A_n,$$

where for every $s \in \{1, \ldots, n\}$, $A_s = C_s$ if $bit_s(k) = 0$, and $A_s = -C_s$ otherwise.

If $l \geq 1$, then for every integer $k' \in \{0, \ldots, l\}$, we define the standard parameter expression

$$D_{k'} \overset{\text{def}}{=} \begin{cases} -E_1 \cap \ldots \cap -E_l & \text{if } k' = 0; \\ E_{k'} & \text{otherwise.} \end{cases}$$

Furthermore, for all $n, l \geq 1$, $k \in \{0, \ldots, 2^n - 1\}$, and $k' \in \{0, \ldots, l\}$, we define

$$A_{k,k'} \overset{\text{def}}{=} B_k \cap D_{k'}.$$

We have introduced three types of parameter expressions:

* $A_{k,k'}$ built from both parameter constants and parameter nominals;
* B_k built only from parameter constants;
* $D_{k'}$ built only from parameter nominals.

In the subsequent chapters, whenever we refer to normal forms from the present section, $A_{k,k'}$, B_k, and $D_{k'}$ are the parameter expressions defined above.

Let $X = \{C_1, \ldots, C_n\}$, $n \geq 0$, be a set of parameter constants and let $Y = \{E_1, \ldots, E_l\}$, $l \geq 0$, be a set of parameter nominals. The set $\text{Comp}(X, Y)$ of $\langle X, Y \rangle$-*components* is defined as follows:

$$\text{Comp}(X, Y) \overset{\text{def}}{=} \begin{cases} \{A_{k,k'} : k \in \{0, \ldots, 2^n - 1\}, k' \in \{0, \ldots, l\}\} & \text{if } n, l \geq 1; \\ \{B_k : k \in \{0, \ldots, 2^n - 1\}\} & \text{if } X \neq \emptyset \text{ and } Y = \emptyset; \\ \{D_{k'} : k' \in \{0, \ldots, l\}\} & \text{if } Y \neq \emptyset \text{ and } X = \emptyset; \\ \emptyset & \text{otherwise.} \end{cases}$$

We write $\text{Comp}(X)$ [resp. $\text{Comp}(Y)$] when Y [resp. X] is empty.

Example 5.4.2. Let $X = \{C_1, C_2, C_3\}$ and $Y = \{E_1, E_2\}$. We have:

* $B_1 = -C_1 \cap C_2 \cap C_3$;
* $B_5 = -C_1 \cap C_2 \cap -C_3$;
* $D_0 = -E_1 \cap -E_2$; $D_1 = E_1$; $D_2 = E_2$;
* $A_{5,2} = -C_1 \cap C_2 \cap -C_3 \cap E_2$.

The set $\text{Comp}(X,Y)$ of $\langle X, Y \rangle$-components enables us to partition any set of parameters, namely we have the following lemma.

Lemma 5.4.1. *For all finite sets* $X = \{C_1, \ldots, C_n\}$, $n \geq 0$, *and* $Y = \{E_1, \ldots, E_l\}$, $l \geq 0$, *of parameter constants and parameter nominals, respectively, for every standard* P-*meaning function* $m : P \to \mathcal{P}(PAR)$, *the family* $\{m(A) : A \in \text{Comp}(X,Y)\}$ *is a partition of* PAR.

Proof. By way of example, we consider the case when $n \times l \neq 0$. The proof extends easily to the case when one of l or n is 0. Let m be a standard P-meaning function $m : P \to \mathcal{P}(PAR)$. It is easy to show that $\{m(D_{k'}) : k' \in \{1, \ldots, l\}\}$ is a partition of PAR and $\{m(B_k) : k \in \{0, \ldots, 2^n - 1\}\}$ is a partition of PAR. Consequently,

$$\{m(D_{k'}) \cap m(B_k) : k' \in \{1, \ldots, l\}, k \in \{0, \ldots, 2^n - 1\}\}$$

is also a partition of PAR. Since $m(D_{k'}) \cap m(B_k) = m(A_{k,k'})$, we get the required result.   *Q.E.D.*

As a consequence of Lemma 5.4.1, we obtain the following result.

Lemma 5.4.2. *Let* X *and* Y *be finite sets of parameter constants and parameter nominals, respectively. Let* A *be a standard parameter expression built from* $X \cup Y$ *with* $\cap$, $\cup$, $-$. *Then either* $A \sim -A \cap A$ *or there is a unique non-empty subset* $\{A'_1, \ldots, A'_u\}$, $u \geq 1$, *of* $\text{Comp}(X,Y)$ *such that* $A \sim A'_1 \cup \ldots \cup A'_u$.

Lemma 5.4.2 enables us to define normal forms of standard parameter expressions built from parameter constants.

Definition 5.4.5. *Let* A *be a standard parameter expression built from parameter constants of* $X = \{C_1, \ldots, C_n\}$, $n \geq 1$, *with the operations* $\cup$, $\cap$, *and* $-$. *The normal form of* A *with respect to* X, *written* $N_X(A)$, *is defined as follows:*

$$N_X(A) \stackrel{\text{def}}{=} \begin{cases} C_1 \cap -C_1 \ \textit{if } A \sim C_1 \cap -C_1; \\ B_{k_1} \cup \ldots \cup B_{k_u} \ \textit{if } A \sim B_{k_1} \cup \ldots \cup B_{k_u} \\ \textit{with } k_1, \ldots, k_u \subseteq \{0, \ldots, 2^n - 1\}, u \geq 1. \end{cases}$$

It is worth observing that $N_X(A)$ is defined modulo associativity and commutativity of $\cap$ and $\cup$. It is possible to overcome this ambiguity but for the sake of simplicity we will not give further details, since it is harmless in the sequel. Clearly, there exists an effective procedure for computing $N_X(A)$ from A. This normal form applies to parameter expressions without nominals. For the parameter expressions with nominals the normal forms depend on a logic under consideration. Therefore those normal forms will be defined separately in the corresponding chapters.

Theorem 5.4.1. *Let* A *be a standard parameter expression built from parameter constants of* $X = \{C_1, \ldots, C_n\}$, $n \geq 1$, *with the operations* $\cup$, $\cap$ *and* $-$. *Then,* $A \sim N_X(A)$.

The proof is by an easy verification and uses Lemma 5.4.2.

5.4.2 Rare-logics

Throughout the book the logics with relative accessibility relations will be referred to as Rare-logics. The parameter expressions introduced in the previous section are an important part of a language for the Rare-logics.

Definition 5.4.6. *By a language for Rare-logics (a Rare-language), we mean a modal language*

$$L = \langle M_0, O_M, M, FOR_0, O_{FOR} \rangle$$

such that $M_0 = \{r(A) : r \in T, A \in P\}$ *for some finite set* T *of relation types and for some set* P *of parameter expressions.*

If $\text{card}(T) = 1$ and $O_M = \emptyset$, then we assume that $M_0 = P$ and we write, for example, [A] instead of [r(A)]. In Rare-languages the basic modal expressions are not necessarily entities, but they receive a structure reflected by the respective parameter expressions and relation types.

Definition 5.4.7. *Let* L *be a Rare-language. By an operator interpretation for* L *we mean a function* $\mathcal{I}$ *whose domain is* $O_M \cup O_P$ *and such that* $\mathcal{I}$ *restricted to* O_M *is a modal operator interpretation (Definition 5.3.7) and* $\mathcal{I}$ *restricted to* O_P *is a parameter operator interpretation (Definition 5.4.2).*

We shall often say informally the "M-part of $\mathcal{I}$" or the "P-part of $\mathcal{I}$" while referring to the respective restrictions of $\mathcal{I}$. If the P-part of $\mathcal{I}$ is a parameter operator interpretation of level n, $n \geq 1$, then we say that $\mathcal{I}$ is of level n.

Definition 5.4.8. *Let* L *be a Rare-language such that* $T = \{1, \ldots, t\}$ *with* $t \geq 1$. *An* L-*model of level* n, $n \geq 1$, *is a structure*

$$\mathcal{M} = \langle W, (\mathcal{R}_P^1)_{P \in \mathcal{P}^n(PAR)}, \ldots, (\mathcal{R}_P^t)_{P \in \mathcal{P}^n(PAR)}, m \rangle$$

such that W *is a non-empty set of objects,* PAR *is a non-empty set of parameters, and* $m : FOR_0 \cup M \cup P \to \mathcal{P}(W) \cup \mathcal{P}(W \times W) \cup \mathcal{P}^n(PAR)$ *is a meaning function such that:*

* $m(p) \subseteq W$ *for every* $p \in FOR_0$;
* $m(a) \subseteq W \times W$ *for every* $a \in M$;
* $m(A) \in \mathcal{P}^n(PAR)$ *for every* $A \in P$;
* $\mathcal{R}_{m(A)}^r = m(r(A))$ *for every* $r \in T$ *and for every* $A \in P$.

Observe that each L-model of level n for a Rare-language is based on a relative frame in the sense of Definition 3.9.2. Similarly to the case of general modal languages, models for a Rare-language L should respect some operator interpretation for L.

Definition 5.4.9. *Let* L *be a Rare-language,* $\mathcal{M} = \langle W, (\mathcal{R}_P^1)_{P \in \mathcal{P}^n(PAR)}, \cdots,$ $(\mathcal{R}_P^t)_{P \in \mathcal{P}^n(PAR)}, m \rangle$ *be an* L-*model of level* n, *and* $\mathcal{I}$ *be an operator interpretation for* L *of level* n, $n \geq 1$. *We say that* $\mathcal{M}$ *respects* $\mathcal{I}$ $\stackrel{\text{def}}{\iff}$ *the restriction of* m *to* P *respects the* P-*part of* $\mathcal{I}$ *and the restriction of* m *to* M *respects the* M-*part of* $\mathcal{I}$.

For the sake of simplicity, we confine ourselves to a finite set T of relation types and we assume that for every $s \in$ T the relations in families $(\mathcal{R}_P^s)_{P \in \mathcal{P}^n(PAR)}$ are indexed with the subsets of the same set PAR. However, most of the forthcoming developments can be easily formulated in a general case of arbitrary T and varying PAR. Finally, we introduce the notion of Rare-logic in a formal way.

Definition 5.4.10. *By a Rare-logic we mean a modal logic* $\mathcal{L} = \langle L, \mathcal{S} \rangle$ *such that* L *is a Rare language and* $\mathcal{S}$ *is a family of* L-*models that respect some operator interpretation* $\mathcal{I}$ *for* L.

As usual, the family $\mathcal{S}$ of models is defined by postulating conditions that the families of relative relations in the models from $\mathcal{S}$ are supposed to satisfy. Since those relations are relative relations, the conditions may be both local and global. Several examples of global conditions are given in Sect. 3.9. If $\mathcal{S}$ is a family of models of level n, $n \in \mathbb{N}$, then the logic is said to be a Rare-logic of level n.

Definition 5.4.11. *A standard Rare-logic is a Rare-logic of level 1 such that its set of relation types is a singleton set, its set of parameter expressions is standard, and the* P-*parts of the meaning functions in its models are standard.*

A standard Rare-logic $\mathcal{L}$ has the *finite parameter set property* $\stackrel{\text{def}}{\iff}$ for every $\mathcal{L}$-satisfiable formula ϕ, there exist an $\mathcal{L}$-model $\mathcal{M} = \langle W, (\mathcal{R}_P)_{P \subseteq PAR}, m \rangle$ and a $w \in W$ such that PAR is finite and $\mathcal{M}, w \models \phi$. In what follows we present several examples of Rare-logics.

Example 5.4.3. We present the logic of indiscernibility relations (LIR). LIR is a Rare-logic of level 1. The LIR-language is a Rare-language such that:

⋆ the set M_0 of basic modal expressions is built from a single relational type r and from a standard set of parameter expressions;

⋆ $O_M = \{\cap, \cup^*\}$;

⋆ $O_{FOR} = \{\neg, \wedge\} \cup \{[a] : a \in M\}$.

The LIR-models are based on relative frames $\langle W, (R_P)_{P \subseteq PAR} \rangle$, where the relations satisfy the conditions:

* $\mathcal{R}_P$ is an equivalence relation for every $P \subseteq PAR$;
* $\mathcal{R}_\emptyset = W \times W$ (condition (C_1'));
* $\mathcal{R}_{P \cup Q} = \mathcal{R}_P \cap \mathcal{R}_Q$ for all $P, Q \in \mathcal{P}(PAR)$ (condition (C_1)).

An example of a LIR-formula is $[r(C_1 \cup C_2) \cup^* r(C_3)]p \Rightarrow [r(C_1 \cup C_2)]p$.

The logic LIR is investigated in Chap. 10. Several results on relationships between LIR and DAL are presented there.

Example 5.4.4. We define the Rare-logic $S5_{L2}$ of level 2 as follows. The set P of parameter expressions includes a set P_0 of basic parameter expressions and is closed under the binary operators from $O_P = \{\text{⋒}, \text{⋓}\}$. Furthermore, $M_0 = M = \{r(A) : A \in P\}$, where r is a single relation type. The set FOR_0 of basic formulae is a countably infinite set of propositional variables and the set of logical connectives is $\{\neg, \wedge\} \cup \{[A] : A \in P\}$. The operator interpretation $\mathcal{I}$ of the logic $S5_{L2}$ interprets ⋒ as the set union and ⋓ as the operator $\cup'$ defined in Example 5.4.1. Hence, a P-meaning function m respecting $\mathcal{I}$ is a map $m : P \to \mathcal{P}^2(PAR)$ such that for all $A_1, A_2 \in P$:

* $m(A_1 \text{ ⋒ } A_2) = \cup(\mathcal{P}(PAR))(m(A_1), m(A_2))$;
* $m(A_1 \text{ ⋓ } A_2) = \cup'(PAR)(m(A_1), m(A_2))$.

The $S5_{L2}$-models are based on relative frames $\langle W, (\mathcal{R}_P)_{P \in \mathcal{P}^2(PAR)} \rangle$, where the relations satisfy the conditions:

* $\mathcal{R}_P$ is an equivalence relation for every $P \subseteq \mathcal{P}^2(PAR)$;
* $\mathcal{R}_{P \cup Q} = \mathcal{R}_P \cap \mathcal{R}_Q$ for all $P, Q \in \mathcal{P}^2(PAR)$;
* $\mathcal{R}_{\cup'(P,Q)} = \mathcal{R}_P \cup \mathcal{R}_Q$ for all $P, Q \in \mathcal{P}^2(PAR)$.

Examples of $S5_{L2}$-valid formulae are:

* $\phi \Rightarrow [A]\langle A \rangle \phi$;
* $[A \text{ ⋓ } B]\phi \Rightarrow \sigma\phi$ for every sequence σ of modal connectives in $\{[A], [B]\}^*$;
* $[A]\phi \Rightarrow [A \text{ ⋒ } B]\phi$.

5.5 Fuzzy Modal Logics

In this section we briefly outline a construction of fuzzy modal logics for reasoning about fuzzy information systems. For that purpose we suitably modify the developments of Sect. 5.3.

The language of fuzzy modal logics differs from the modal language introduced in Sect. 5.3.1 only in the propositional connectives. Namely, the Boolean connectives are replaced by the connectives corresponding to the operations of double residuated lattices, and the modal connectives are the abstract counterparts of the information operators derived from fuzzy information systems defined in Sect. 4.11. The formulae are interpreted as fuzzy sets. In this way, in the logics we can represent sets of objects and their algebraic structure determined by the fuzzy set operators defined in Sect. 4.11.

More precisely, the language for fuzzy modal logics is a system of the form $L = \langle M_0, O_M, M, FOR_0, O_{FOR}\rangle$ such that M_0, O_M, M, and FOR_0 are defined as in Definition 5.3.1, and

$$\{\wedge, \vee, \leftarrow, \rightarrow\} \subseteq O_{FOR} \subseteq \{\wedge, \vee, \leftarrow, \rightarrow, \neg, \ulcorner\} \cup \{[a], co[a] : a \in M\}.$$

An L-model is a structure $\mathcal{M} = \langle W, L, m\rangle$ such that W is a non-empty set, L is a double residuated lattice, and m is a meaning function that assigns an L-fuzzy subset of W to every basic formula and a binary L-fuzzy relation on W to every modal expression, namely

* $m(p) \in \mathcal{F}_L \mathcal{P}(W)$ for every $p \in FOR_0$;
* $m(a) \in \mathcal{F}_L Rel(W)$ for every $a \in M$.

A *value* of a formula ϕ in a model $\mathcal{M} = \langle W, L, m\rangle$ is an L-fuzzy set $(\phi)_{\mathcal{M}}$ defined as follows. For every $w \in W$:

* $(p)_{\mathcal{M}}(w) = m(p)(w)$ for every $p \in FOR_0$;
* $(\phi \vee \psi)_{\mathcal{M}}(w) = (\phi)_{\mathcal{M}}(w) \oplus (\psi)_{\mathcal{M}}(w)$;
* $(\phi \wedge \psi)_{\mathcal{M}}(w) = (\phi)_{\mathcal{M}}(w) \odot (\psi)_{\mathcal{M}}(w)$;
* $(\phi \leftarrow \psi)_{\mathcal{M}}(w) = (\phi)_{\mathcal{M}}(w) \leftarrow (\psi)_{\mathcal{M}}(w)$;
* $(\phi \rightarrow \psi)_{\mathcal{M}}(w) = (\phi)_{\mathcal{M}}(w) \rightarrow (\psi)_{\mathcal{M}}(w)$;
* $(\neg\phi)_{\mathcal{M}}(w) = \neg(\phi)_{\mathcal{M}}(w)$;
* $(\ulcorner\phi)_{\mathcal{M}}(w) = \ulcorner(\phi)_{\mathcal{M}}(w)$;
* $([a]\phi)_{\mathcal{M}}(w) = ([m(a)]_L(\phi)_{\mathcal{M}})(w)$;
* $(co[a]\phi)_{\mathcal{M}}(w) = (co[m(a)]_L(\phi)_{\mathcal{M}})(w)$.

Clearly, on the right-hand side of those equalities, we have the operations of the lattice L. This semantics is a most general one, where the formulae are interpreted as fuzzy sets, and the relations determining modal connectives are fuzzy relations. One can also imagine semantics where fuzziness is attributed only to the formulae or only to the relations. In Sect. 8.5 we present a logic which illustrates yet another way of introducing fuzziness. Every model of this logic is based on a fuzzy relation but the modal connectives are not determined directly by those fuzzy relations. Instead, for each of the fuzzy relations and for every element λ of the underlying lattice, there is a family of crisp relations such that a pair of objects belongs to the crisp relation if it belongs to the fuzzy relation to degree λ. Then, the modal connectives are determined by the crisp relations.

Truth of a formula of a fuzzy logic can be either absolute or graded. A formula ϕ is true in a model $\mathcal{M} = \langle W, L, m\rangle$ if $(\phi)_{\mathcal{M}}(w) = 1$ for every $w \in W$. For every $l \in L$ we say that ϕ is *l-true* in $\mathcal{M} = \langle W, L, m\rangle$ if $(\phi)_{\mathcal{M}}(w) \geq l$ for every $w \in W$.

As in the crisp case, a fuzzy modal logic is defined as a pair consisting of a language L for fuzzy modal logics and of a class of L-models. This analogy can be extended to fuzzy Rare-logics. They are defined in a way similar to what is presented in Sect. 5.4. The only difference is that the interpretation of parameter expressions is more involved. Each of them is interpreted as a mapping from X into $\mathcal{F}_L \mathcal{P}(Y)$ for some sets X and Y. The meaningful parameter operators are, for example, fuzzy set operations $\cup_L, \cap_L, \neg_L, \ulcorner_L$ defined in Sect. 2.7. The models of fuzzy Rare-logics are based on frames with fuzzy relative relations defined in Sect. 3.11.

5.6 Notes

Classical logic. General introductions to first-order logic are, for instance, [End72, CK73, Hod84].

Modal logic. We refer the reader to [BS84, Mak90] for fairly complete historical notes about modal logic. Introductions to modal logic can be found in [LS77, HC68, Seg71, HC84, CZ97, BRV01]. Semantics presented in Sect. 5.3.2 is derived from the possible worlds semantics of modal logic. The origin of the possible worlds semantics of modern modal logic can be found in [Kan57, Hin62, Kri63]. [JT51] can be viewed as an algebraic counterpart to the possible worlds semantics.

Knowledge connective. The definability of $K(a)$ in terms of [a] is provided by taking $K(a)\phi \overset{\text{def}}{=} [a]\phi \vee [a]\neg\phi$. The definability of [a] in terms of $K(a)$ and the Boolean connectives is studied in [Cre88]. Axiomatisations of the basic modal logic with the connectives $K(a)$ are presented in [Hum95, Kuh95].

Sufficiency connective [[]]. The modal connective of sufficiency is studied in [Hum83, Hum87, GPT87, GP90, Gor90b, Gor90a]. In [PT91] a historical analysis of the introduction of this modal connective is presented.

Universal modal connective. It is known that adding the universal modal connective to the language of a logic may increase its expressive power (see for example [GP92]) but it may also modify its decidability status (see for example [GP92, Spa93a, Hem96]).

Nominals. Prior and Bull considered the concept of nominals around 1960; see for example [Pri67, Bul70, PF77]. The use of nominals in modal logic originated in the papers [PT85, GPT87, PT91, GG93]. Since then the inclusion of nominals to the languages of various logics is the usual practice; see for example [Bla90, Bla93, Gia95, Are00, Bla00b]. The addition of nominals usually increases the expressive power of the logic under consideration. For instance, in a multi-modal logic with nominals intersection of relations from a model is definable with a formula of the logic [PT91], while it is not expressible without nominals [GT75]. The use of nominals in the languages of information logics can be found in [Orło84a, Gar86, Kon98, Kon97]. If the language of a logic includes the difference operator (introduced in [Seg76]), then the object nominals are definable with formulae of the logic [Sai88, Koy92, GG93]. Hybrid logics make also an extensive use of nominals, see for example [Bla00b, BRV01, AB01].

Information logics. The first formalisation of a rough set in the framework of formal logic is given in [OP81], where a modal logic is designed that uses lower and upper approximations as necessity and possibility connectives, respectively. The modal system defined there is a polymodal version of S5 with intersection as a modal operator. This, roughly speaking, is DAL without ∪*. Then more sophisticated systems have been defined. The data analysis logic DAL has been introduced in [FdCO85] to model reasoning in the presence of incomplete information. The upper and lower approximations with respect to indiscernibility relations are the core modal operations of the logic. The logic LIR from Example 5.4.3 has been introduced in [Orło93b] (see also [Orło84b]). The axiomatisation of DAL with nominals can be found in [Gar86]. The axiomatisation of DAL without nominals is an open problem. However, the axiomatisation of logics similar to DAL can be found in [FdCO85, Gar86, AT89, Bal96a]. The axiomatisation of DAL is closely related to the axiomatisation of the epistemic logic $S5_k(CDE)$ [HM97, HM99] with k independent S5 modal connectives, the common knowledge operator C, the everybody knows operator E, and the distributed knowledge operator D.

PDL-like logics. PDL was introduced in [Pra76] (see also [FL79, Pra80]). An exhaustive presentation of PDL-like logics can be found in [HKT00]. The version of PDL used in this book (defined in Example 5.3.5) is weaker than the one in [FL79] since the test operator "?" is not included in its language. Description logics, also known as terminological logics, form a large class of PDL-like logics (see for instance [HST00, CDGLN01]).

Rare-logics of level n. Classes of frames with relations indexed by sets of parameters have been studied in, for example, [Orło88a, Bal98, BO99].

Fuzzy modal logics. Fuzzy modal logics are considered, among others, in [HHE+94, EGGR97, GHE01].

6. Techniques for Information Logics

6.1 Introduction and Outline of the Chapter

This chapter presents the methodological concepts and formal techniques that are employed throughout the book for studying information logics. We present in detail only the core elements and steps of each of these techniques. Any variations or extensions that are needed in connection with a particular logic are usually presented in the chapter where the logic is discussed. In Sect. 6.2 we present model theoretic constructions, including filtration and copying. The method of copying has a special status since it has been introduced in relation to problems specific to information logics. Copying is useful in the situation when some properties of relations from semantic structures of a logic are not expressible in the language of the logic. Sect. 6.3 presents a general framework for deductive systems of information logics. We recall Hilbert-style proof systems for standard modal logics and the notion of canonical structure together with its principal properties. In Sect. 6.4 we present basic definitions and facts related to computational complexity. We recall the major complexity classes relevant to modal logics and we present logical problems that are complete with respect to those classes. The material of this section provides a basis for the developments of Chap. 12.

6.2 Model-theoretic Constructions

In this section we recall the definitions of various constructions on L-models for a fixed modal language L. These constructions are mainly needed in proofs of completeness of Hilbert-style proof systems and in decidability proofs. Although the different constructions admit a quite simple definition, we shall see that the concrete constructions for given information logics are rather sophisticated. Throughout this section we assume that the modal connectives in the logics under consideration are of the form [a], for a modal expression a, and the basic formulae are propositional variables.

6.2.1 Disjoint Unions and Isomorphic Copies

The following definitions introduce the notion of disjoint union of models and isomorphism between models.

Definition 6.2.1. *Let* L *be a modal language. Let* $\mathcal{M}_1 = \langle W_1, (R_a^1)_{a \in M}, m_1 \rangle$ *and* $\mathcal{M}_2 = \langle W_2, (R_a^2)_{a \in M}, m_2 \rangle$ *be* L-*models. The* disjoint union *of* $\mathcal{M}_1$ *and* $\mathcal{M}_2$ *is the* L-*model* $\mathcal{M} = \langle W, (R_a)_{a \in M}, m \rangle$ *defined as follows:*

* $W \overset{\text{def}}{=} W_1 \,\dot\cup\, W_2 = W_1 \times \{1\} \cup W_2 \times \{2\}$;
* *for every basic formula* p, $m(p) \overset{\text{def}}{=} m_1(p) \,\dot\cup\, m_2(p)$;
* *for every* a $\in$ M *and for all* $\langle x, j \rangle, \langle y, k \rangle \in W$, $\langle \langle x, j \rangle, \langle y, k \rangle \rangle \in R_a \overset{\text{def}}{\Leftrightarrow}$ $j = k$ *and* $\langle x, y \rangle \in R_a^j$.

A modal logic $\mathcal{L} = \langle L, \mathcal{S} \rangle$ is said to be *closed under disjoint unions* $\overset{\text{def}}{\Leftrightarrow}$ for all $\mathcal{L}$-models $\mathcal{M}_1 = \langle W_1, (R_a^1)_{a \in M}, m_1 \rangle$ and $\mathcal{M}_2 = \langle W_2, (R_a^2)_{a \in M}, m_2 \rangle$, the disjoint union of $\mathcal{M}_1$ and $\mathcal{M}_2$ is an $\mathcal{L}$-model.

Example 6.2.1. The logic DAL is closed under disjoint unions.

Let $f : W \to W'$ be a 1–1 mapping. We extend f to $\mathcal{P}(W) \cup \mathcal{P}(W^2)$ in a usual way:

* for every $X \subseteq W$, $f(X) \overset{\text{def}}{=} \{f(x) : x \in X\}$;
* for every $R \subseteq W^2$, $f(R) \overset{\text{def}}{=} \{\langle f(x), f(y) \rangle : \langle x, y \rangle \in R\}$.

Definition 6.2.2. *Let* $\mathcal{M} = \langle W, (R_a)_{a \in M}, m \rangle$ *and* $\mathcal{M}' = \langle W', (R_a')_{a \in M}, m' \rangle$ *be* L-*models.* $\mathcal{M}$ *and* $\mathcal{M}'$ *are said to be* isomorphic $\overset{\text{def}}{\Leftrightarrow}$ *there is a bijection* $f : W \to W'$ *such that:*

* *for every basic formula* p, $m'(p) = f(m(p))$;
* *for every* a $\in$ M, $R_a' = f(R_a)$.

In that case, $\mathcal{M}'$ *is said to be an isomorphic copy of* $\mathcal{M}$.
$\mathcal{M}$ *and* $\mathcal{M}'$ *are said to be* isomorphic modulo *a formula* ϕ $\overset{\text{def}}{\Leftrightarrow}$ *there is a bijection* $f : W \to W'$ *such that:*

* *for every basic formula* p *occurring in* ϕ, $m'(p) = f(m(p))$;
* *for every modal expression* a *occurring in* ϕ, $R_a' = f(R_a)$.

A modal logic $\mathcal{L} = \langle L, \mathcal{S} \rangle$ is said to be *closed under isomorphic copies* $\overset{\text{def}}{\Leftrightarrow}$ for every model $\mathcal{M} \in \mathcal{S}$, if $\mathcal{M}'$ is an isomorphic copy of $\mathcal{M}$, then $\mathcal{M}' \in \mathcal{S}$. The assumption that a modal logic is closed under disjoint unions and isomorphic copies is not a strong assumption. All the logics studied in this book are closed under isomorphic copies.

6.2.2 Restriction

The notion of restriction of a model coincides with the notion of a submodel in model theory of classical first-order structures. Intuitively, we shall use the restriction construction in order to remove superfluous objects from large models while preserving frame conditions.

Definition 6.2.3. *Let* $\mathcal{M} = \langle W, (R_a)_{a\in M}, m \rangle$ *be an L-model for a modal language* L. *A restriction of* $\mathcal{M}$ *to* W' *is an L-model* $\mathcal{M}_{|W'} = \langle W', (R'_a)_{a\in M}, m' \rangle$ *such that*

⋆ $\emptyset \neq W' \subseteq W$;
⋆ *for every basic formula* p, $m'(p) = m(p) \cap W'$;
⋆ *for every* $a \in M$, $R'_a = R_a \cap (W' \times W')$.

Similarly, let $F = \langle W, (R_a)_{a\in M} \rangle$ *and* $F' = \langle W', (R'_a)_{a\in M} \rangle$ *be L-frames.* F' *is a restriction of* F $\overset{\text{def}}{\Leftrightarrow}$ $\emptyset \neq W' \subseteq W$ *and for every* $a \in M$, $R'_a = R_a \cap (W' \times W')$.

A modal logic $\mathcal{L} = \langle L, \mathcal{S} \rangle$ is said to be *closed under restrictions* $\overset{\text{def}}{\Leftrightarrow}$ for every $\mathcal{L}$-model $\mathcal{M} = \langle W, (R_a)_{a\in M}, m \rangle$ and for every $\emptyset \neq W' \subseteq W$, $\mathcal{M}_{|W'} \in \mathcal{S}$. In the following we present a typical application of the restriction construction.

Example 6.2.2. Let $\mathcal{M} = \langle W, R, m \rangle$ be an S5-model, that is R is an equivalence relation. Let $w \in W$ and let ϕ be a formula such that $\mathcal{M}, w \models \phi$. Let $\mathcal{M}' = \langle W', R', m' \rangle$ be the restriction of $\mathcal{M}$ to the set $R(w)$ of objects. One can show that $\mathcal{M}', w \models \phi$. Now let X^ϕ be the set

$$X^\phi = \{\psi : \Box\psi \in \text{sub}(\phi), \ \mathcal{M}', w \not\models \Box\psi\}.$$

For every $\psi \in X^\phi$, there is a $w^\psi \in W'$ such that $\mathcal{M}', w^\psi \not\models \psi$. We say that w^ψ is a witness for $\mathcal{M}', w \not\models \Box\psi$. Let $\mathcal{M}'' = \langle W'', R'', m'' \rangle$ be the restriction of $\mathcal{M}'$ to $W'' = \{w\} \cup \{w^\psi : \psi \in X^\phi\}$. One can show by induction on the structure of the formulae that for every $\psi \in \text{sub}(\phi)$ and for every $w' \in W''$, $\mathcal{M}'', w' \models \psi$ iff $\mathcal{M}', w' \models \psi$. Consequently, $\mathcal{M}'', w \models \phi$ and $\mathcal{M}''$ is an S5-model. So, every S5-satisfiable formula ϕ has an S5-model $\mathcal{M} = \langle W, R, m \rangle$ such that $R = W \times W$ and $\text{card}(W) \leq \text{mw}(\phi) + 1$.

6.2.3 Filtration

Intuitively, a filtration of a model $\mathcal{M}$ is a construction that generates a partition of the universe of $\mathcal{M}$ such that two elements are in the same class iff they behave similarly with respect to the satisfaction of the formulae of a given set. This construction is used to generate finite models by "gluing" together as many objects as possible.

Let $\mathcal{M} = \langle W, (R_a)_{a\in M}, m \rangle$ be an L-model and let Γ be a set of L-formulae closed under subformulae. Let $\approx_{\mathcal{M},\Gamma}$ be the binary relation on W defined as follows: for all $x, y \in W$, $x \approx_{\mathcal{M},\Gamma} y$ $\overset{\text{def}}{\Leftrightarrow}$ for every $\psi \in \Gamma$, $\mathcal{M}, x \models \psi$ iff $\mathcal{M}, y \models \psi$. It is easy to check that $\approx_{\mathcal{M},\Gamma}$ is an equivalence relation.

Definition 6.2.4. *Let* $\mathcal{M} = \langle W, (R_a)_{a \in M}, m \rangle$ *be an* L-*model and let* Γ *be a set of* L-*formulae closed under subformulae. The* L-*model* $\langle W', (R'_a)_{a \in M}, m' \rangle$ *is a* Γ-*filtration of* $\mathcal{M}$ $\overset{\text{def}}{\Longleftrightarrow}$

(Fil1) $W' = \{|x| : x \in W\}$, *where* $|x|$ *is an equivalence class of* x *with respect to* $\approx_{\mathcal{M}, \Gamma}$;

(Fil2) *for every* $\mathrm{p} \in \Gamma \cap \mathrm{FOR}_0$, $m'(\mathrm{p}) = \{|x| : x \in m(\mathrm{p})\}$;

(Fil3) *for all* $x, y \in W$ *and for every* $\mathrm{a} \in \mathrm{M}(\Gamma)$, *if* $\langle x, y \rangle \in R_a$, *then* $\langle |x|, |y| \rangle \in R'_a$;

(Fil4) *for all* $x, y \in W$ *and for every* $[\mathrm{a}]\psi \in \Gamma$, *if* $\langle |x|, |y| \rangle \in R'_a$ *and* $\mathcal{M}, x \models [\mathrm{a}]\psi$, *then* $\mathcal{M}, y \models \psi$.

The following theorem is a direct consequence of the fact that the conditions in Definition 6.2.4 guarantee the preservation of a "local modal behaviour" of the Γ-filtration of a given model.

Theorem 6.2.1. *Let* $\mathcal{M}'$ *be a* Γ-*filtration of* $\mathcal{M} = \langle W, (R_a)_{a \in M}, m \rangle$. *For every* $x \in W$ *and for every* $\psi \in \Gamma$, $\mathcal{M}, x \models \psi$ *iff* $\mathcal{M}', |x| \models \psi$.

Proof. The proof is by induction on the structure of ψ. If ψ is a basic formula or the outermost connective of ψ is either $\neg$ or $\wedge$, then the proof can be easily obtained. Now assume that $\psi = [\mathrm{a}]\varphi$.

$(\rightarrow)$ Assume that $\mathcal{M}, x \models \psi$ and suppose that there is $|y| \in R'_a(|x|)$ such that $\mathcal{M}', |y| \not\models \varphi$. By condition (Fil4) in Definition 6.2.4, we get $\mathcal{M}, y \models \varphi$ and by the induction hypothesis $\mathcal{M}', |y| \models \varphi$, which leads to a contradiction.

$(\leftarrow)$ Assume that $\mathcal{M}', |x| \models \psi$ and suppose that there is a $y \in R_a(x)$ such that $\mathcal{M}, y \not\models \varphi$. By condition (Fil3) in Definition 6.2.4, $|y| \in R'_a(|x|)$ and therefore $\mathcal{M}', |y| \models \varphi$. By the induction hypothesis, we obtain $\mathcal{M}, y \models \varphi$, which leads to a contradiction.   Q.E.D.

In the following example we show an application of the filtration construction.

Example 6.2.3. We consider the modal logic S4 presented in Example 5.3.3. Using the filtration construction we show that if a formula has an S4-model, then it has an S4-model of the size exponential in the number of subformulae of the formula. Let $\mathcal{M} = \langle W, R, m \rangle$ be an S4-model, let $w \in W$, and let ϕ be a formula such that $\mathcal{M}, w \models \phi$. Let $\mathcal{M}' = \langle W', R', m' \rangle$ be the following model:

⋆ $W' \overset{\text{def}}{=} \{|x| : x \in W\}$, where $|x|$ is the equivalence class of x with respect to $\approx_{\mathcal{M}, \mathrm{sub}(\phi)}$;

⋆ for every $\mathrm{p} \in \mathrm{FOR}_0$, $m'(\mathrm{p}) \overset{\text{def}}{=} \{|x| : x \in m(\mathrm{p}), \mathrm{p} \in \mathrm{sub}(\phi)\}$;

⋆ for all $x, y \in W$, $\langle |x|, |y| \rangle \in R' \overset{\text{def}}{\Longleftrightarrow}$ for every $\Box\psi \in \mathrm{sub}(\phi)$, $\mathcal{M}, x \models \Box\psi$ implies $\mathcal{M}, y \models \Box\psi$.

One can show that $\mathcal{M}'$ is a sub(ϕ)-filtration of $\mathcal{M}$ and $\mathcal{M}'$ is an S4-model. By way of example, we check that condition (Fil3) holds. So assume $\langle x, y \rangle \in R$. Since R is reflexive and transitive, $R(y) \subseteq R(x)$ and therefore for every $\Box \psi \in$ sub(ϕ), if $\mathcal{M}, x \models \Box \psi$, then $\mathcal{M}, y \models \Box \psi$. Hence, by the definition of R', $\langle |x|, |y| \rangle \in R'$. It follows that every S4-satisfiable formula ϕ has an S4-model $\mathcal{M} = \langle W, R, m \rangle$ such that card(W) $\leq 2^{\text{card}(\text{sub}(\phi))}$.

6.2.4 Copying

Informally, the existence of a copying map from an L-model $\mathcal{M}$ into an L-model $\mathcal{M}'$ guarantees that every condition involving the relations of $\mathcal{M}$ can be matched with a similar condition in $\mathcal{M}'$. Moreover, the meaning of basic formulae is preserved. The copying construction is used when we need to "repair defects" of some model and construct a model without "defects". This new model is made out of a copy or multiple copies of the original model.

Definition 6.2.5. Let $\mathcal{M} = \langle W, (R_a)_{a \in \text{M}}, m \rangle$ and $\mathcal{M}' = \langle W', (R'_a)_{a \in \text{M}}, m' \rangle$ be L-models. A class COP of maps $f : W \to W'$ is a copying from $\mathcal{M}$ into $\mathcal{M}'$ $\overset{\text{def}}{\Leftrightarrow}$

(Cop1) $W' = \{ f(x) : f \in \text{COP}, x \in W \}$;
(Cop2) for all $x, y \in W$, and for all $f, g \in \text{COP}$, if $f(x) = g(y)$, then $x = y$;
(Cop3) for every a $\in$ M, for all $x, y \in W$, and for every $f \in \text{COP}$, if $\langle x, y \rangle \in R_a$, then there is a $g \in \text{COP}$ such that $\langle f(x), g(y) \rangle \in R'_a$;
(Cop4) for every a $\in$ M, for all $x \in W$, $y' \in W'$, and for every $f \in \text{COP}$, if $\langle f(x), y' \rangle \in R'_a$, then there are a $g \in \text{COP}$ and a $y \in W$ such that $g(y) = y'$ and $\langle x, y \rangle \in R_a$;
(Cop5) for every basic formula p, $m'(\text{p}) = \{ f(x) : x \in m(\text{p}), f \in \text{COP} \}$.

The term "copying" comes from the fact that for every $f \in \text{COP}$, $\mathcal{M}'_{|\{ f(x) : x \in W \}}$ can be viewed as a copy of $\mathcal{M}$. However, $\mathcal{M}'$ is not necessarily a disjoint union of copies; the relations in $\mathcal{M}'$ may link objects from different copies.

Theorem 6.2.2. *(Copying Theorem)* Let $\mathcal{M} = \langle W, (R_a)_{a \in \text{M}}, m \rangle$ and $\mathcal{M}' = \langle W', (R'_a)_{a \in \text{M}}, m' \rangle$ be L-models and let COP be a copying from $\mathcal{M}$ into $\mathcal{M}'$. For every $x \in W$, for every $f \in \text{COP}$, and for every L-formula ψ, $\mathcal{M}, x \models \psi$ iff $\mathcal{M}', f(x) \models \psi$.

Proof. The proof is by induction on the structure of ψ. The cases when ψ is a basic formula or the outermost connective of ψ is either $\neg$ or $\wedge$ are omitted. Now assume that $\psi = [\text{a}]\varphi$.
($\to$) Assume $\mathcal{M}, x \models \psi$ and suppose that there is a $y \in R'_a(f(x))$ such that $\mathcal{M}', y \not\models \varphi$. By condition (Cop4) in Definition 6.2.5, there are a $g \in \text{COP}$ and a $y' \in W$ such that $g(y') = y$ and $\langle x, y' \rangle \in R_a$. By the induction hypothesis,

$\mathcal{M}, y' \not\models \varphi$, which leads to a contradiction, since $\langle x, y' \rangle \in R_a$ and $\mathcal{M}, x \models \psi$. ($\leftarrow$) Assume $\mathcal{M}', f(x) \models \psi$ and suppose that there is a $y \in R_a(x)$ such that $\mathcal{M}, y \not\models \varphi$. By condition (Cop3) in Definition 6.2.5, there is a $g \in \text{COP}$ such that $\langle f(x), g(y) \rangle \in R'_a$. So, $\mathcal{M}', g(y) \models \varphi$, since $\mathcal{M}', f(x) \models \psi$ and $\langle f(x), g(y) \rangle \in R_a$. By the induction hypothesis, $\mathcal{M}, y \models \varphi$, which leads to a contradiction. $\hspace{2cm}$ Q.E.D.

The following theorem is a direct consequence of the fact that the conditions in Definition 6.2.5 guarantee the preservation of the "modal behaviour" of a copy of the given model.

Theorem 6.2.3. *Let $\mathcal{L}_1 = \langle L, S_1 \rangle$ and $\mathcal{L}_2 = \langle L, S_2 \rangle$ be logics having the same language and such that $S_1 \subseteq S_2$. If for every $\mathcal{M} \in S_2$ there are an $\mathcal{M}' \in S_1$ and a copying from $\mathcal{M}$ into $\mathcal{M}'$, then $\text{SAT}(\mathcal{L}_1) = \text{SAT}(\mathcal{L}_2)$.*

The proof of Theorem 6.2.3 follows easily from Theorem 6.2.2.

Example 6.2.4. We consider the modal logic K presented in Example 5.3.3. We illustrate applications of the copying construction by showing that if a formula has a [resp. finite] K-model, then it has a [resp. finite] K-model such that the binary relation in the model is irreflexive. Let $\mathcal{M} = \langle W, R, m \rangle$ be a K-model and $\mathcal{M}' = \langle W', R', m' \rangle$ be the following model:

* $W' \stackrel{\text{def}}{=} W \times \{0, 1\}$;
* for every $p \in \text{FOR}_0$, $m'(p) \stackrel{\text{def}}{=} \{\langle x, i \rangle : x \in m(p), \ i \in \{0, 1\}\}$;
* for every $\langle x, i \rangle, \langle y, j \rangle \in W'$, $\langle\langle x, i \rangle, \langle y, j \rangle\rangle \in R' \stackrel{\text{def}}{\Leftrightarrow} \langle x, y \rangle \in R$ and $i + j = 1$.

Let $\text{COP} = \{f_0, f_1\}$ be the set of maps $f_i : W \to W'$, $i \in \{0, 1\}$, such that for every $x \in W$, $f_i(x) = \langle x, i \rangle$. One can show that COP is a copying from $\mathcal{M}$ into $\mathcal{M}'$ and R' is irreflexive. It is easy to show that the conditions (Cop1), (Cop2), and (Cop5) are satisfied. We check the conditions (Cop3) and (Cop4).

Proof of (Cop3): let $i \in \{0, 1\}$ and let $\langle x, y \rangle \in R$. By definition, $\langle\langle x, i \rangle, \langle y, 1 - i \rangle\rangle \in R'$.

Proof of (Cop4): let $x \in W$, let $i \in \{0, 1\}$, and let $y' \in W'$ be such that $\langle\langle x, i \rangle, y' \rangle \in R'$. By the definition of W', there exist a $j \in \{0, 1\}$ and a $y \in W$ such that $y' = \langle y, j \rangle$. So $\langle\langle x, i \rangle, \langle y, j \rangle\rangle \in R'$. By the definition of R', $\langle x, y \rangle \in R$ and $i + j = 1$. Consequently, $f_{1-i}(y) = y'$.

6.3 Hilbert-style Proof Systems

In this section we present a general framework for developing proof systems for modal logics. The common core of all of them is a Hilbert-style proof system for PC.

6.3.1 General Formulation of Hilbert-style Proof Systems

A Hilbert-style proof system $H(L) = \langle Ax, Ru \rangle$ for a modal language L consists of a set Ax of L-formulae referred to as *axioms*, such that Ax is closed under uniform substitution and of a set Ru of *rules* that provide patterns of inferences admissible in L. The rules are of the form

$$\frac{\phi_1 \ \ldots \ \phi_n}{\phi} \ ,$$

where $\phi_1 \ldots \phi_n, \phi$ are L-formulae. Usually, $\phi_1 \ldots \phi_n$ are referred to as *premises* of the rule and ϕ is referred to as the *conclusion* of the rule. We shall often omit L and write simply H for a proof system when it will be clear from the context which language is H concerned with.

A *derivation* of a formula ϕ in H from a set X of L-formulae is a finite sequence $\langle \psi_1, \ldots, \psi_n \rangle$ of L-formulae such that $\psi_n = \phi$ and for every $i \in \{1, \ldots, n\}$:

★ either $\psi_i \in X$;
★ or ψ_i is an axiom from Ax;
★ or ψ_i is the conclusion of some inference rule in Ru whose premises are in $\{\psi_1, \ldots, \psi_{i-1}\}$.

We say that ϕ is derivable in H from X (in symbols $X \vdash_H \phi$) $\overset{\text{def}}{\Leftrightarrow}$ there is a derivation of ϕ in H from X. ϕ is a *theorem* of H (in symbols $\vdash_H \phi$ or $\phi \in \text{THM}(H)$) if ϕ is derivable in H from the empty set of formulae. In that case, ϕ is called an H-theorem. The formulae ϕ and ψ are said to be *equivalent in* H $\overset{\text{def}}{\Leftrightarrow}$ $\vdash_H \phi \Leftrightarrow \psi$. This is obviously a "syntactic" equivalence.

Definition 6.3.1. *Let $\mathcal{L}$ be a logic and let H be a Hilbert-style system in the language of $\mathcal{L}$. We say that:*

★ H *is $\mathcal{L}$-sound* $\overset{\text{def}}{\Leftrightarrow}$ $\text{THM}(H) \subseteq \text{VAL}(\mathcal{L})$;
★ H *is strongly $\mathcal{L}$-sound* $\overset{\text{def}}{\Leftrightarrow}$ *for every L-formula ϕ and for every set X of L-formulae, $X \vdash_H \phi$ implies ϕ is a semantic consequence of X in $\mathcal{L}$;*
★ H *is $\mathcal{L}$-complete* $\overset{\text{def}}{\Leftrightarrow}$ $\text{VAL}(\mathcal{L}) \subseteq \text{THM}(H)$;
★ H *is strongly $\mathcal{L}$-complete* $\overset{\text{def}}{\Leftrightarrow}$ *for every L-formula ϕ and for every set X of L-formulae, ϕ is a semantic consequence of X in $\mathcal{L}$ implies $X \vdash_H \phi$;*
★ H *is closed under uniform substitution* $\overset{\text{def}}{\Leftrightarrow}$ *the set $\text{THM}(H)$ is closed under uniform substitution;*
★ H *is a proof system for $\mathcal{L}$* $\overset{\text{def}}{\Leftrightarrow}$ $\text{THM}(H) = \text{VAL}(\mathcal{L})$.

Let $H = \langle Ax, Ru \rangle$ be a proof system in a language L. Let L' be a modal language whose set of formulae includes the formulae of L. Let X be a set of L'-formulae. By $H(L') + X$ we mean the smallest set of L'-formulae which includes $Ax \cup X$ and is closed under uniform substitution in L'. We may also add new rules defined from formulae of the language L' to H. Any such system H(L') is said to be an *extension* of H.

A rule is said to be *admissible* in a system H $\overset{\text{def}}{\Leftrightarrow}$ the extension of H with the rule has the same set of theorems as H.

Throughout the book, Hilbert-style proof systems for a given logic $\mathcal{L}$ will be denoted by H$\mathcal{L}$. However, within any particular section dealing with an information logic, we shall often write simply H and $\vdash \phi$, because it will always be clear that the system refers to the logic considered in that section.

6.3.2 A Hilbert-style Proof System for PC

In this section we present one of the most popular proof systems for PC. The set of axioms consists of the formulae of the following form:

(AxPC1) $\phi \Rightarrow (\psi \Rightarrow \phi)$ (law of simplification);
(AxPC2) $(\phi \Rightarrow (\psi \Rightarrow \varphi)) \Rightarrow ((\phi \Rightarrow \psi) \Rightarrow (\phi \Rightarrow \varphi))$ (law of Frege);
(AxPC3) $\neg\phi \Rightarrow (\phi \Rightarrow \psi)$ (law of Duns Scotus);
(AxPC4) $(\neg\phi \Rightarrow \phi) \Rightarrow \phi$ (law of Clavius).

The only rule of inference is:

$$\frac{\phi \quad \phi \Rightarrow \psi}{\psi} \text{ (modus ponens)}.$$

This proof system is referred to as HPC. In what follows we recall basic notions and facts concerning HPC.

Theorem 6.3.1. *(Deduction Theorem) For every set X of formulae of PC and for all formulae ϕ, ψ, $X \cup \{\phi\} \vdash_{\text{HPC}} \psi$ implies $X \vdash_{\text{HPC}} \phi \Rightarrow \psi$.*

Theorem 6.3.2. *(Soundness and Completeness) For every formula ϕ, $\phi \in$ THM(HPC) iff ϕ is a tautology of PC.*

Lemma 6.3.1. *If $\vdash_{\text{HPC}} \phi \Leftrightarrow \phi'$, then $\vdash_{\text{HPC}} \psi \Leftrightarrow \psi'$ where ψ' is obtained from ψ by replacing an occurrence of ϕ by ϕ'.*

In the rest of this section, let H be a Hilbert-style proof system for a language L that extends the system HPC by adding axioms and/or rules.

Lemma 6.3.2. *For all L-formulae ϕ, ψ, and φ the following assertions hold:*

(I) If $\phi \lor \psi$, $\phi \Rightarrow \varphi$, and $\psi \Rightarrow \varphi \in$ THM(H), then $\varphi \in$ THM(H);
(II) If $\phi \Rightarrow \psi$, $\phi \Rightarrow \varphi \in$ THM(H), then $\phi \Rightarrow \psi \land \varphi \in$ THM(H);
(III) If $\phi \Rightarrow \psi \in$ THM(H), then $\phi \land \varphi \Rightarrow \psi \in$ THM(H);
(IV) if $\phi \Rightarrow \psi$, $\psi \land \varphi \Rightarrow \phi' \in$ THM(H), then $\phi \land \varphi \Rightarrow \phi' \in$ THM(H).

Theorem 6.3.3. *(Compactness Theorem) For every set X of L-formulae and for every L-formula ϕ, if $X \vdash_{\text{H}} \phi$, then there is a finite subset X_0 of X such that $X_0 \vdash_{\text{H}} \phi$.*

Definition 6.3.2. *A set X of L-formulae is said to be H-consistent $\overset{\text{def}}{\Leftrightarrow}$ for every L-formula ϕ, neither $X \vdash_{H} \phi$ nor $X \vdash_{H} \neg\phi$. The set X is H-inconsistent $\overset{\text{def}}{\Leftrightarrow}$ X is not H-consistent.*

The following lemma presents some facts equivalent to consistency.

Lemma 6.3.3. *Let X be a set of L-formulae. The following statements are equivalent:*

(I) X is H-consistent;
(II) it is not the case that for some L-formula ϕ, $X \vdash_{H} \phi$ and $X \vdash_{H} \neg\phi$;
(III) there is no finite subset $\{\phi_1, \ldots, \phi_n\}$ of X such that $X \vdash_{H} \neg(\phi_1 \wedge \ldots \wedge \phi_n)$;
(IV) there is an L-formula ϕ such that not $X \vdash_{H} \phi$.

A set X of L-formulae is said to be a *maximal* H-consistent set $\overset{\text{def}}{\Leftrightarrow}$ X is H-consistent and for every L-formula ϕ, either $X \vdash_{H} \phi$ or $X \vdash_{H} \neg\phi$.

Lemma 6.3.4. *Let X be a set of L-formulae. The following statements are equivalent:*

(I) X is a maximal H-consistent set;
(II) for every set of L-formulae Y such that $X \subset Y$, Y is H-inconsistent.

Lemma 6.3.5. *Let X be a maximal H-consistent set. Then for all L-formulae ϕ and ψ:*

(I) exactly one member of $\{\phi, \neg\phi\}$ is in X;
(II) $\phi \vee \psi \in X$ iff either $\phi \in X$ or $\psi \in X$;
(III) $\phi \wedge \psi \in X$ iff $\{\phi, \psi\} \subseteq X$;
(IV) if $\phi \in \text{THM(H)}$, then $\phi \in X$;
(V) if $\{\phi, \phi \Rightarrow \psi\} \subseteq X$, then $\psi \in X$;
(VI) if $\phi \in X$ and $\phi \Rightarrow \psi \in \text{THM(H)}$, then $\psi \in X$.

Theorem 6.3.4. *(Lindenbaum Lemma) Every H-consistent set of L-formulae can be extended to a maximal H-consistent set.*

6.3.3 Hilbert-style Proof Systems for Classical Modal Logics

In this section we consider multi-modal versions of the standard modal logics K, T, B, S4, and S5 presented in Example 5.3.3. Let L be a modal language such that the set of logical connectives is $O_{\text{FOR}} = \{\neg, \wedge\} \cup \{[a] : a \in M\}$. The set M of modal expressions is not necessarily a singleton set. The Hilbert-style system HK(L) is an extension of HPC with the following axiom:

(AxK) $[a]\phi \Rightarrow ([a](\phi \Rightarrow \psi) \Rightarrow [a]\psi)$ for every $a \in M$;

and the inference rule:

$$\frac{\phi}{[\mathrm{a}]\phi} \text{ for every a} \in \mathrm{M}, \text{ (necessitation rule).}$$

The following rule will often be used:

$$\frac{\phi \Rightarrow \psi}{[\mathrm{a}]\phi \Rightarrow [\mathrm{a}]\psi} \text{ for every a} \in \mathrm{M}, \text{ (regular rule).}$$

The following lemma states the admissibility of the regular rule in any extension of HK(L).

Lemma 6.3.6. *Let H be an extension of* HK(L). *For all L-formulae ϕ and ψ, if $\phi \Rightarrow \psi \in$ THM(H), then $[\mathrm{a}]\phi \Rightarrow [\mathrm{a}]\psi \in$ THM(H) for every a $\in$ M.*

Proof. Assume $\phi \Rightarrow \psi \in$ THM(H). By application of the necessitation rule, $\varphi_0 = [\mathrm{a}](\phi \Rightarrow \psi) \in$ THM(H). The formula $(\mathrm{p} \Rightarrow (\mathrm{q} \Rightarrow \mathrm{q}')) \Rightarrow (\mathrm{q} \Rightarrow (\mathrm{p} \Rightarrow \mathrm{q}'))$ is a tautology of PC, so the formula

$$\varphi_1 = ([\mathrm{a}]\phi \Rightarrow ([\mathrm{a}](\phi \Rightarrow \psi) \Rightarrow [\mathrm{a}]\psi)) \Rightarrow ([\mathrm{a}](\phi \Rightarrow \psi) \Rightarrow ([\mathrm{a}]\phi \Rightarrow [\mathrm{a}]\psi))$$

belongs to THM(H). Using the axiom (AxK), $\varphi_2 = ([\mathrm{a}]\phi \Rightarrow ([\mathrm{a}](\phi \Rightarrow \psi) \Rightarrow [\mathrm{a}]\psi)) \in$ THM(H). Applying modus ponens to φ_1 and φ_2, we get $\varphi_3 = ([\mathrm{a}](\phi \Rightarrow \psi) \Rightarrow ([\mathrm{a}]\phi \Rightarrow [\mathrm{a}]\psi)) \in$ THM(H). Applying modus ponens to φ_0 and φ_3, we have $[\mathrm{a}]\phi \Rightarrow [\mathrm{a}]\psi \in$ THM(H).   *Q.E.D.*

The distributivity of [a] over $\wedge$ can be shown in HK(L).

Lemma 6.3.7. *Let H be an extension of* HK(L). *For every a $\in$ M and for all L-formulae ϕ and ψ, we have $[\mathrm{a}](\phi \wedge \psi) \Leftrightarrow ([\mathrm{a}](\phi) \wedge [\mathrm{a}](\psi)) \in$ THM(H).*

Lemma 6.3.8 enables us to prove the soundness of HK(L).

Lemma 6.3.8. *For all L-formulae ϕ and ψ and for every modal expression a of L we have:*

(I) if ϕ is a theorem of HPC, *then* TFR($\{\phi\}$) *is the set of all the L-frames;*
(II) TFR($\{[\mathrm{a}]\phi \Rightarrow ([\mathrm{a}](\phi \Rightarrow \psi) \Rightarrow [\mathrm{a}]\psi)\}$) *is the set of all the L-frames;*
(III) TFR(ϕ) $\subseteq$ TFR($[\mathrm{a}]\phi$).

Proof. By way of example, we show (III). Assume $F = \langle W, (R_\mathrm{b})_{\mathrm{b} \in \mathrm{M}} \rangle \in$ TFR(ϕ). By the definition of TFR(ϕ), $F \models \phi$; that is for every L-model $\mathcal{M} = \langle W, (R_\mathrm{b})_{\mathrm{b} \in \mathrm{M}}, m \rangle$ based on F and for every $w \in W$, $\mathcal{M}, w \models \phi$. So for every $w \in W$, $\mathcal{M}, w \models [\mathrm{a}]\phi$, since $R_\mathrm{a}(w) \subseteq W$. Hence, for every L-model $\mathcal{M} = \langle W, (R_\mathrm{b})_{\mathrm{b} \in \mathrm{M}}, m \rangle$ based on F and for every $w \in W$, $\mathcal{M}, w \models [\mathrm{a}]\phi$. This means that $F \in$ TFR($[\mathrm{a}]\phi$).   *Q.E.D.*

Theorem 6.3.5. TFR(THM(HK(L))) *is the set of all the L-frames.*

Proof. The proof is a consequence of Lemma 6.3.8.   *Q.E.D.*

In the book we shall often use extensions of HK(L) defined as follows:

* $\star$ HT(L) $\overset{\text{def}}{=}$ HK(L) + [a]$\phi \Rightarrow \phi$;
* $\star$ HB(L) $\overset{\text{def}}{=}$ HT(L) + $\phi \Rightarrow$ [a]$\langle$a$\rangle\phi$;
* $\star$ HS4(L) $\overset{\text{def}}{=}$ HT(L) + [a]$\phi \Rightarrow$ [a][a]ϕ;
* $\star$ HS5(L) $\overset{\text{def}}{=}$ HS4(L) + $\phi \Rightarrow$ [a]$\langle$a$\rangle\phi$.

In each of the above systems the added axiom corresponds to the specific property of the accessibility relation from the models of the respective logic. By way of example, we show such a correspondence theorem for [a]$\phi \Rightarrow$ [a][a]ϕ.

Lemma 6.3.9. *For every* a $\in$ M, *TFR(*[a]p $\Rightarrow$ [a][a]p*) is the class of L-frames* $\langle W, (R_b)_{b \in M} \rangle$ *such that* R_a *is transitive.*

Proof. Let $F = \langle W, (R_b)_{b \in M} \rangle$ be an L-frame such that [a]p $\Rightarrow$ [a][a]p is true in F for some a $\in$ M. Suppose R_a is not transitive. There exist $x_1, x_2, x_3 \in W$ such that $\langle x_1, x_2 \rangle \in R$, $\langle x_2, x_3 \rangle \in R$, and $\langle x_1, x_3 \rangle \notin R$. Let $\mathcal{M}_0 = \langle W, (R_b)_{b \in M}, m \rangle$ be the L-model based on F such that

$$m(\text{p}) \overset{\text{def}}{=} \{w \in W : \langle x_1, w \rangle \in R_a\}.$$

By definition, $\mathcal{M}_0, x_1 \models$ [a]p, and therefore $\mathcal{M}_0, x_1 \models$ [a][a]p since, by assumption, $\mathcal{M}_0, x_1 \models$ [a]p $\Rightarrow$ [a][a]p. Thus, $\mathcal{M}_0, x_3 \models$ p, since $\langle x_1, x_3 \rangle \in R_a; R_a$ which leads to a contradiction by the definition of $m(\text{p})$.
Now let $\mathcal{M} = \langle W, (R_b)_{b \in M}, m \rangle$ be an L-model such that R_a is transitive. Let $x \in W$ and assume $\mathcal{M}, x \models$ [a]p. So, for every $w \in R_a(x)$, $\mathcal{M}, w \models$ p. Since R_a is transitive, $R_a; R_a \subseteq R_a$. So, in particular, for every $w \in (R_a; R_a)(x)$, $\mathcal{M}, w \models$ p. Hence, $\mathcal{M}, x \models$ [a][a]p.   *Q.E.D.*

6.3.4 Canonical Structure

Let L be a modal language such that the set of modal connectives is $\{$[a] : a $\in$ M$\}$ and let H be an extension of HK(L). For every set X of L-formulae and for every modal expression a $\in$ M, we define the set [a]X as follows:

$$[a]X \overset{\text{def}}{=} \{\phi : [a]\phi \in X\}.$$

Definition 6.3.3. *The canonical structure for* H *is an* L-*model*

$$\mathcal{M}^c = \langle W^c, (R_a^c)_{a \in M}, m^c \rangle$$

defined as follows:

* $\star$ W^c *is the family of all the maximal* H-*consistent sets of formulae;*

⋆ *for all* $X, Y \in W^c$ *and for every* $a \in M$, $\langle X, Y \rangle \in R_a^c \overset{\text{def}}{\Leftrightarrow} [a]X \subseteq Y$;
⋆ *for every* $p \in FOR_0$, $m^c(p) \overset{\text{def}}{=} \{X \in W^c : p \in X\}$.

The structure $\langle W^c, (R_a^c)_{a \in M} \rangle$ is called the *canonical frame* for H.

Lemma 6.3.10. *If* $X \cup \{\neg [a]\phi\}$ *is H-consistent, then* $[a]X \cup \{\neg \phi\}$ *is H-consistent.*

Proof. Assume $X \cup \{\neg [a]\phi\}$ is H-consistent and suppose $[a]X \cup \{\neg \phi\}$ is not. So there is a finite subset $\{\phi_1, \dots, \phi_n\} \subseteq [a]X$ such that $\neg(\phi_1 \wedge \dots \wedge \phi_n \wedge \neg \phi) \in THM(H)$, which means that $(\phi_1 \wedge \dots \wedge \phi_n) \Rightarrow \phi \in THM(H)$. Using Lemma 6.3.6, $[a](\phi_1 \wedge \dots \wedge \phi_n) \Rightarrow [a]\phi \in THM(H)$. By Lemma 6.3.7, $[a](\phi_1 \wedge \dots \wedge \phi_n) \Rightarrow [a](\phi_1) \wedge \dots \wedge [a](\phi_n) \in THM(H)$. It follows that $([a](\phi_1) \wedge \dots \wedge [a](\phi_n)) \Rightarrow [a]\phi \in THM(H)$. So $\neg([a]\phi_1 \wedge \dots \wedge [a]\phi_n \wedge \neg [a]\phi) \in THM(H)$, which means that $X \cup \{\neg [a]\phi\}$ is not H-consistent, since $\{[a]\phi_1, \dots, [a]\phi_n\} \subseteq X$, a contradiction.   *Q.E.D.*

The following theorem is one of the fundamental results in modal logic.

Theorem 6.3.6. *For every* $X \in W^c$ *and for every* L-*formula* ϕ, $\mathcal{M}^c, X \models \phi$ *iff* $\phi \in X$.

Proof. The proof is by induction on the structure of ϕ. If ϕ is a basic formula, the theorem holds by definition of $\mathcal{M}^c$.
Induction step.
We omit the case when the outermost connective of ϕ is Boolean. Assume $\phi = [a]\psi$.
($\rightarrow$) Assume $\mathcal{M}^c, X \models [a]\psi$ and suppose $[a]\psi \notin X$. By Lemma 6.3.5(I), $\neg [a]\psi \in X$. By Lemma 6.3.10, $[a]X \cup \{\neg \psi\}$ is H-consistent. By Theorem 6.3.4, there is a $Y \in W^c$ such that $[a]X \cup \{\neg \psi\} \subseteq Y$. Hence $\langle X, Y \rangle \in R_a^c$, and, by the induction hypothesis, $\mathcal{M}^c, Y \not\models \psi$. So $\mathcal{M}^c, X \not\models [a]\psi$, a contradiction.
($\leftarrow$) Assume $[a]\psi \in X$ and take $Y \in R_a^c(X)$. Since $[a]X \subseteq Y$, $\psi \in Y$. By the induction hypothesis, $\mathcal{M}^c, Y \models \psi$. Hence $\mathcal{M}^c, X \models [a]\psi$.   *Q.E.D.*

The importance of Sahlqvist formulae is reflected by the following theorem.

Theorem 6.3.7. *Let* H *be an extension of* HK(L) *obtained by adding a set* X *of Sahlqvist formulae. Then the canonical frame* $F^c = \langle W^c, (R_a^c)_{a \in M} \rangle$ *for* H *belongs to* TFR(X).

Some particular cases of Theorem 6.3.7 are presented in the following lemma.

Lemma 6.3.11. *Let* H *be an extension of* HK(L). *Then for all* $a, b \in M$:

(I) *if* $[a]\phi \Rightarrow \phi \in THM(H)$ *for every* L-*formula* ϕ, *then* R_a^c *is reflexive;*
(II) *if* $\phi \Rightarrow [a]\langle a \rangle \phi \in THM(H)$ *for every* L-*formula* ϕ, *then* R_a^c *is symmetric;*

(III) if $[a]\phi \Rightarrow [a][a]\phi \in \mathrm{THM(H)}$ *for every L-formula* ϕ, *then* R_a^c *is transitive;*

(IV) if $\langle a \rangle \top \wedge [a]\phi \Rightarrow \phi \in \mathrm{THM(H)}$ *for every L-formula* ϕ, *then* R_a^c *is weakly reflexive;*

(V) if $[a]\phi \Rightarrow [b]\phi \in \mathrm{THM(H)}$ *for every L-formula* ϕ, *then* $R_b^c \subseteq R_a^c$;

(VI) if $\phi \Rightarrow [a]\langle b \rangle \phi \in \mathrm{THM(H)}$ *for every L-formula* ϕ, *then* $(R_a^c)^{-1} \subseteq R_b^c$.

Proof. We prove (III), (IV), and (V).

(III) Suppose there exist $x, y, z \in W^c$ such that (i) $\langle x, y \rangle \in R_a^c$, (ii) $\langle y, z \rangle \in R_a^c$, and $\langle x, z \rangle \in R_a^c$. So there is $[a]\phi \in x$ such that $\phi \notin z$. By assumption, $[a]\phi \Rightarrow [a][a]\phi \in x$ and by Lemma 6.3.5(V), $[a][a]\phi \in x$. By (i), $[a]\phi \in y$. By (ii), $\phi \in z$, a contradiction.

(IV) Suppose there exist $x, y \in W^c$ such that (i) $\langle x, y \rangle \in R_a^c$ and $\langle x, x \rangle \notin R_a^c$. So there is $[a]\phi \in x$ such that $\phi \notin x$. Since $\neg\top \notin y$ and (i), we obtain $\neg[a]\neg\top \in x$. By Lemma 6.3.5(III), $[a]\phi \wedge \neg[a]\neg\top \in x$. By assumption, $[a]\phi \wedge \neg[a]\neg\top \Rightarrow \phi \in x$. By Lemma 6.3.5(V), $\phi \in x$, a contradiction.

(V) Suppose there exist $x, y \in W^c$ such that (i) $\langle x, y \rangle \in R_b^c$ and (ii) $\langle x, y \rangle \notin R_a^c$. So, there is $[a]\phi \in x$ such that $\phi \notin y$. By assumption, $[a]\phi \Rightarrow [b]\phi \in x$. By Lemma 6.3.5(V), $[b]\phi \in x$. By (i), $\phi \in y$, a contradiction. $\qquad$ Q.E.D.

We refer the reader to Sect. 5.6 for useful pointers to the literature on Sahlqvist results and their applications.

6.4 Basics of Computational Complexity

The aim of this section is to recall some basic definitions from complexity theory needed for presentation of the complexity results stated in this volume (mainly in Chap. 12). We shall be rather succinct; Sect. 6.5 contains references to general introductions to complexity theory.

Complexity theory provides a means of assigning a measure to algorithms described in a given computation model. This measure is supposed to express how difficult a problem is, for instance by comparing its measure with the measure of other problems. A *decision problem*, or simply *problem*, is a subset of Σ^* for some finite alphabet Σ. For instance, the set of L-formulae of a given modal language L can be seen as a problem. Similarly, the set $\mathrm{VAL}(\mathcal{L})$ of $\mathrm{LAN}(\mathcal{L})$-formulae for some logic $\mathcal{L}$ can be considered to be a problem. More generally, a decision problem is usually defined as the problem of recognising some specific set of mathematical objects (formulae, finite models, etc.). This requires encoding of each object as a string of symbols over some finite alphabet. Obviously, the set of L-formulae is already a set of strings. The two most common measures of complexity are time (a number of elementary steps of a computation) and space (a size of the memory used during a computation). It is worth mentioning that these two measures are asymptotic functions in the length of the inputs and in this book we deal with worst-case complexity.

There are various other measures and they usually depend on the model of computation.

In order to determine the complexity of a problem $\mathcal{P}$, first, we have to choose a model of computation, that is to define a class of (abstract) machines that will be used for solving $\mathcal{P}$. In this book we shall use Turing machines (TMs) mainly because of the simplicity of their definition. However, to be honest, we shall not directly work with Turing machines but with a more intuitive model of computation (close to RAMs) for which our complexity results transfer easily to TMs. It is a standard result that RAMs and TMs can simulate each other. Such a simulation preserves time bounds modulo a polynomial, and space bounds modulo a constant. We follow a standard practice and discuss algorithms in an almost model-independent manner. Our informal demonstrations should be taken as an indication of how this could be done formally.

We briefly recall the informal description of a Turing machine. Turing machines compute by manipulating finite strings of symbols. A Turing machine usually consists of the following elements.

* An infinite memory is represented by $k \geq 1$ tapes, each with an infinite amount of cells. Each cell contains a symbol of some alphabet. In the simplest model of a Turing machine, there is only one tape. In more elaborated models, one can distinguish the input tape, the output tape, and the work tapes. The power of computation is not increased by adding work tapes.
* With each tape there is associated a head moving along the tape. The input tape (if any) works in the read-only mode whereas the work tapes usually work in the read/write mode.
* The behaviour of a machine is described in terms of a finite set of control states and a transition function which assigns to each state a successor state. An initial state and an accepting state are distinguished control states.
* For every control state and for every k-tuple of symbols (from the appropriate alphabets) viewed as the symbols on which currently the heads are, a transition function indicates
  * the next state;
  * for each tape, the new symbol to be written instead of the symbol read by the head;
  * the movement of each tape head (move one cell left, move one cell right, no move).

An execution on a Turing machine can be described as follows.

* Initially, the input word (over the input alphabet) is on the input tape, possibly delineated by end-markers. The other symbols of the input tape are blank symbols (not belonging to the input alphabet). The other tapes contain only blank symbols. The input tape head is on the first symbol of

the input word. The other tape heads are on the first cells of the respective tapes. The control state is the initial state.

⋆ At each step of the computation the machine performs the following actions:
  * reads the symbols under the head tapes;
  * replaces these symbols by those specified by the transition function;
  * moves the heads according to the transition function;
  * changes the control state according to the transition function.

An input word is accepted whenever after an execution the machine reaches the accepting state.

Below we provide a more formal definition of Turing machines. A *non-deterministic Turing machine* M (NDTM) is specified by:

⋆ a finite set Q of control states;
⋆ a finite input alphabet Σ;
⋆ a finite work tape alphabet Γ;
⋆ an initial state q_0;
⋆ an accepting state $q_a \notin Q$;
⋆ an end-marker $\S \notin \Sigma$ and a blank symbol $b \notin \Sigma$;
⋆ k work tapes for some $k \geq 1$ and an input tape;
⋆ a transition function δ

$$\delta : Q \times (\Sigma \cup \S) \times \Gamma^k \to \mathcal{P}((Q \cup \{q_a\}) \times \Gamma^k \times \{\leftarrow, \rightarrow, -\}^{k+1}).$$

If the machine is in the state q, scanning σ on the input tape, and scanning γ_i on the ith work tape for every $i \in \{1, \ldots, k\}$, and if

$$\langle q', \gamma'_1, \ldots, \gamma'_k, m_1, \ldots, m_{k+1} \rangle \in \delta(q, \sigma, \gamma_1, \ldots, \gamma_k),$$

then the machine M can do the following actions in one step:

⋆ changing its state to q';
⋆ printing γ'_i on the i–th work tape;
⋆ moving the ith head in direction m_i;
⋆ moving the input head in direction m_{k+1}.

If $\delta(q, \sigma, \gamma_1, \ldots, \gamma_k)$ contains at most one element for all q, σ, γ_1, ..., γ_k, then M is said to be *deterministic*.

A *configuration* of M is specified by:

⋆ the non-blank contents of all the tapes;
⋆ the positions of all the heads;
⋆ the control state.

We write $C \vdash_M C'$ $\overset{\text{def}}{\Leftrightarrow}$ the configuration C' can be obtained from C in one step of M. The machine cannot continue from a given configuration C whenever the state is the accepting state q_a. Given an input word $x \in \Sigma^*$, the initial configuration $C(x)$ of M with input x is defined by specifying that:

* $\S x \S$ is on the input tape with the head scanning the first symbol of x;
* the control state is q_0;
* all the work tapes are blank.

An *accepting computation* is a finite sequence $\langle C_1, \ldots, C_n \rangle$ of configurations such that:

* $n \geq 1$ and $C_1 = C(x)$;
* for every $i \in \{1, \ldots, n-1\}$, $C_i \vdash_M C_{i+1}$;
* the state in the configuration C_n is the accepting state q_a.

We say that M *accepts* x $\overset{\text{def}}{\Leftrightarrow}$ there is an accepting computation of M on x. We write $L(M)$ to denote the subset of Σ^* accepted by M. The *time* t of an accepting computation $\langle C_1, \ldots, C_n \rangle$ is $n-1$ and the *space* s is the number of work tape cells visited by heads on work tapes during the computation. For every NDTM with k work-tapes and for every accepting computation $\langle C_1, \ldots, C_n \rangle$ of M, $s \leq n \times k$ since at each step at most k work-tape cells can be visited. Let $f : \mathbb{N} \to \mathbb{R}$ be a map from the set $\mathbb{N}$ of natural numbers to the set $\mathbb{R}$ of real numbers. The TM M *accepts within time* [resp. *within space*] $f(n)$ if for each $x \in L(M)$, there is an accepting computation of M on x such that the time [resp. the space] of the computation is not greater than $f(|x|)$.

A deterministic Turing machine (DTM) with a single work tape can perform only a quite limited amount of work in a single step, but anyway it can perform any computation that can be made on an ordinary computer, maybe more slowly. However, throughout the book, we will present algorithms possibly independent of the models of computation.

For every map $f : \mathbb{N} \to \mathbb{R}$, we write $\mathcal{O}(f(n))$ to denote the class of maps $g : \mathbb{N} \to \mathbb{N}$ such that there exist an n_0 and a $c \in \mathbb{N}$ such that for all $n > n_0$, $g(n) < c \times f(n)$. $\mathcal{O}(f(n))$ is the class of functions whose asymptotic growth is bounded by $c \times f(n)$ for some constant c. Let X be a class of maps $\mathbb{N} \to \mathbb{R}$. **NTIME**$(X)$ is the class of problems accepted by non-deterministic Turing machines which accept within time $f(n)$ for some $f \in X$. Similarly, **DTIME**(X) [resp. **DSPACE**(X)] is the class of problems accepted by deterministic Turing machines which accept within time [resp. space] $f(n)$ for some $f \in X$. We write $Poly(n)$ [resp. $Lin(n)$] to denote the class of polynomial [resp. linear] functions with domain $\mathbb{N}$. The complexity classes of particular interest in this book are the following:

* **LIN** $\overset{\text{def}}{=}$ **DTIME**$(\bigcup_{f \in Lin(n)} \mathcal{O}(f(n)))$;
* **LOGPSACE** $\overset{\text{def}}{=}$ **DTIME**$(\mathcal{O}(log\ n))$;

* $\mathbf{P} \stackrel{\text{def}}{=} \mathbf{DTIME}(\bigcup_{f \in Poly(n)} \mathcal{O}(f(n)))$;
* $\mathbf{NP} \stackrel{\text{def}}{=} \mathbf{NTIME}(\bigcup_{f \in Poly(n)} \mathcal{O}(f(n)))$;
* $\mathbf{PSPACE} \stackrel{\text{def}}{=} \mathbf{DSPACE}(\bigcup_{f \in Poly(n)} \mathcal{O}(f(n)))$;
* $\mathbf{EXPTIME} \stackrel{\text{def}}{=} \mathbf{DTIME}(\bigcup_{f \in Poly(n)} \mathcal{O}(2^{f(n)}))$;
* $\mathbf{NEXPTIME} \stackrel{\text{def}}{=} \mathbf{NTIME}(\bigcup_{f \in Poly(n)} \mathcal{O}(2^{f(n)}))$.

It is known that $\mathbf{LIN} \subseteq \mathbf{P} \subseteq \mathbf{NP} \subseteq \mathbf{PSPACE} \subseteq \mathbf{EXPTIME} \subseteq \mathbf{NEX\text{-}}$
$\mathbf{PTIME}$, $\mathbf{P} \neq \mathbf{EXPTIME}$, and $\mathbf{NP} \neq \mathbf{NEXPTIME}$. Given a problem,
its complexity depends on the encoding of its instances as strings. For the
problems whose complexity is investigated in this book, there will always
be an obvious and natural encoding that guarantees the stated results. For
instance, a binary relation R on a finite set W of cardinality $n \geq 1$ can be
encoded as an $n \times n$ adjacency matrix such that each element $m_{i,j}$ of the
matrix has the value 0 or 1 according to whether $\langle x_i, x_j \rangle \in R$ or not. In
this example, we arbitrarily order the elements of W. Then the matrix itself
can be easily encoded as a string. Furthermore the length of a formula is
computed taking into account the binary representation of the indices for
propositional variables and for the modal constants, etc. By way of example,
$|p_{100} \vee [c_{10}]p_{11111}| = 16$. Consequently, the length of an integer is not equal
to its value but rather to the number of bits in its binary representation. For
the sake of simplicity, we shall keep the decimal representation for indices,
but their length will always be computed from the binary representation.

Until now, we have considered decision problems, that is sets of words
over a finite alphabet. Now we describe a function computation. In order to
perform a function computation, a deterministic Turing machine has an additional tape, called the *output tape*, which is visited by a head that can only
move from left to right and can print symbols from some output alphabet,
say Σ'. If a machine is in an accepting state and a word $x \in \Sigma'^*$ is on the
output tape, then we say that the machine *returns* x. The transition function δ is extended and either specifies at each step the symbol from Σ' to
be printed (which is followed by a move of the head one cell to the right)
or declares that the output head neither prints nor moves. The space of a
function computation is the space used on the working tapes only. We include
neither the space used on the input tape nor that used on the output tape.
In that way, functions computed within a space smaller than the length of
the output and input can be considered. Let $f : \Sigma^* \to \Sigma'^*$ be a map. Let M
be a deterministic Turing machine. M *computes f within time* [resp. *space*]
$g(n)$ $\stackrel{\text{def}}{\Leftrightarrow}$ the following conditions are satisfied:

* M accepts within time [resp. space] $g(n)$;
* M accepts every element of Σ^* (this guarantees that f is not a partial
  function);

⋆ for every $x \in \Sigma^*$, if $\langle C_1, \ldots, C_n \rangle$ is the (unique) accepting computation of M on input x, then $f(x)$ is the word written on the output tape in the configuration C_n.

The complexity classes for functions that are of particular interest in this book are the following:

⋆ **FP** is the class of functions computable by deterministic Turing machines within polynomial time;
⋆ **FLOGSPACE** is the class of functions computable by deterministic Turing machines within logarithmic space.

Let $\mathcal{P} \subseteq \Sigma^*$ and let $\mathcal{P}' \subseteq \Sigma'^*$. $\mathcal{P}$ is polynomial-time-reducible [resp. logarithmic-space-reducible] to $\mathcal{P}' \overset{\text{def}}{\Leftrightarrow}$ there is $f : \Sigma^* \to \Sigma'^*$ such that $f \in$ **FP** [resp. $f \in$ **FLOGSPACE**] and for every $x \in \Sigma^*$, $x \in \mathcal{P}$ iff $f(x) \in \mathcal{P}'$. f is said to be a *many–one reduction*, or a *transformation*. This notion is a tool to express that a problem is at least as hard as another problem.

Decidability. A set is *decidable* whenever there is an effective algorithm for deciding, given any object, whether it is a member of that set or not. For instance, the truth-table test is an effective procedure for deciding membership of a formula in the set of propositional tautologies. A problem $\mathcal{P} \subseteq \Sigma^*$ is *decidable* $\overset{\text{def}}{\Leftrightarrow}$ there is a DTM M such that given $x \in \Sigma^*$, M returns 0 if $x \in \mathcal{P}$ and returns 1 otherwise.

Let $\mathcal{C}$ be a class of problems, let $\mathcal{C}'$ be a class of functions, and let $\mathcal{P}$ be a problem.

$\mathcal{C}$-hardness. $\mathcal{P}$ is said to be $\mathcal{C}$-*hard* with respect to $\mathcal{C}' \overset{\text{def}}{\Leftrightarrow}$ for every problem $\mathcal{P} \in \mathcal{C}$, there is $f : \Sigma^* \to \Sigma'^*$ such that $f \in \mathcal{C}'$ and for every $x \in \Sigma^*$, $x \in \mathcal{P}$ iff $f(x) \in \mathcal{P}'$. So $\mathcal{P}$ is at least as difficult as any problem in the class $\mathcal{C}$ (with respect to $\mathcal{C}'$). In a sense, $\mathcal{P}$ captures the difficulty of a whole complexity class.

$\mathcal{C}$-completeness. $\mathcal{P}$ is said to be $\mathcal{C}$-*complete* with respect to $\mathcal{C}' \overset{\text{def}}{\Leftrightarrow} \mathcal{P}$ is $\mathcal{C}$-hard and $\mathcal{P} \in \mathcal{C}$.

In the sequel, by **NP**-hard [resp. **PSPACE**-hard, **EXPTIME**-hard, **NEXPTIME**-hard] we mean **NP**-hard [resp. **PSPACE**-hard, **EXPTIME**-hard, **NEXPTIME**-hard] with respect to logarithmic space transformations.

The following results are fundamental in the complexity theory of logical systems.

Theorem 6.4.1. *The classical* **NP***-complete logical problems include:*

(I) the satisfiability problem for propositional calculus PC [Coo71, Lev73];
(II) the satisfiability problem for the modal logic S5 [Lad77].

Theorem 6.4.2. *The classical* **PSPACE**-*complete logical problems include:*

(I) the first-order theory of equality without function symbols [Sto77];
(II) the model-checking problem for first-order logic [CM77];
(III) the satisfiability problems for the modal logics K and S4 [Lad77];
(IV) the quantified Boolean formula (QBF) problem [SM73];
(V) the satisfiability problem for intuitionistic logic [Sta79].

PSPACE is the complexity class of most relevance to modal logic.

Theorem 6.4.3. *The classical* **EXPTIME**-*complete logical problems include:*

(I) the satisfiability problem for PDL with converse [FL79, Pra79, Seg82];
(II) the satisfiability problem for the modal logic K augmented with the universal modal connective [Spa93a];
(III) the satisfiability problem for the guarded fragment of classical logic restricted to predicate symbols of arity at most k, for every fixed $k \geq 2$ [Grä99a].

Theorem 6.4.4. *The classical* **NEXPTIME**-*complete logical problems include:*

(I) the satisfiability problem of a fragment of classical logic with two individual variables, equality and no function symbols [Für81, GKV97] (see also [Mor75]);
(II) the satisfiability problem for the Shönfinkel–Bernays class of first-order formulae that are of the form

$$\exists x_1 \ldots \exists x_k \forall y_1 \ldots \forall y_l \phi(x_1, \ldots, x_k, y_1, \ldots, y_l),$$

where $\phi(x_1, \ldots, x_k, y_1, \ldots, y_l)$ is an open formula [Lew80].

Theorem 6.4.5 is a standard result that will be used in the sequel.

Theorem 6.4.5. *Let* L *be a modal language, let ϕ be an* L-*formula, and let $\mathcal{M} = \langle W, (R_a)_{a \in M}, m \rangle$ be a finite* L-*model. Checking whether there is a $w \in W$ such that $\mathcal{M}, w \models \phi$ can be done in time $\mathcal{O}(|\phi| \times \text{card}(W^2))$.*

6.5 Notes

Hilbert-style proof systems. Extensive historical notes on Hilbert-style proof systems can be found in [Chu56, Sect. 29] and in [TS96, page 48].

Techniques for modal logics. The canonical models for modal logics appeared in [Mak66, LS77, Cre67]. First works on filtration can be found in [LS77, Gab72, Seg71]. The restriction construction is directly inherited from the notion of submodel in classical logic (see for example [CK73]). Such a construction is used in [Lad77, HM92] to prove that S5 satisfiability is in the complexity class **NP**. Extensions of this construction can be found in [Cer94, Dem97b, Dem98]. Theorem 5.3.1 and Theorem 6.3.7 are proved in [Sah75] (see also [Ben85, SV89, Rij93, Ven93]). Other works related to the topics of this chapter are [Gol75, Ben84].

Copying. The copying construction is introduced by Vakarelov in [Vak87]. Since then it has been successfully applied to proving completeness of various logics in [GPT87, Vak87, Pen88, Pen89, Vak89, GP90, Vak90, Vak91c, Vak91b, Bal96b, Bal96a, Bal98, BO99, Dem99a]. Copying is an instance of the more general notion of *bisimulation* [HM80, Par81, Ben84]. If COP is a copying from $\mathcal{M}$ into $\mathcal{M}'$, then $\{\langle f(x), x\rangle : f \in \text{COP}, x \in W\}$ is a bisimulation between $\mathcal{M}'$ and $\mathcal{M}$. Copying is useful when we deal with semantic structures such that some properties of the relations from these structures are not definable with formulae of a modal language under consideration. Copying can be viewed as a particular *p-morphism* (also called *pseudo-epimorphism*) [Seg71].

Computational complexity. General introductions to complexity theory can be found in [AHU74, Sto87, Joh90, Pap94, LR96]. Turing machines were introduced in [Tur37]. The analysis of complexity classes is presented in [HS65]. That paper has originated investigation of computational complexity in complexity theory. The model RAM is introduced in [SS63] and in [ER64]. The notion of **NP**-completeness has been introduced in [Coo71] and in [Lev73]. The classical catalogue of **NP**-complete problems can be found in [GJ79]. Results related to Theorem 6.4.5 can be found, for instance, in [Var82, Imm86].

Complexity of PDL-like logics. Satisfiability for PDL + converse and for PDL + intersection are both decidable problems [FL79, Dan84]. By contrast, PDL + complement is undecidable [Har84]. Satisfiability for combinatory PDL is decidable and **EXPTIME**-complete [PT91] (see also [Gia95, ABM00]).

Part III

Proof Systems for Information Logics

7. Reasoning About Similarity

7.1 Introduction and Outline of the Chapter

In this chapter we study information logics designed for reasoning about similarity of objects in information systems. Similarity is understood as the property of sharing some properties.

In Sect. 7.2 we introduce the logic NIL which provides a means of expressing facts about similarity of objects, together with its limit case when the set of properties of one object is a subset of properties of another object. This limit case is reflected by the two relations referred to as forward and backward inclusion of objects. The modal connectives of NIL are the counterparts to generalised approximation operators. We present a Hilbert-style deductive system for the logic and we prove its soundness and completeness. The proof of completeness is presented in an algebraic setting thus providing an illustration of the algebraic logic approach to information logics. In Sect. 7.2.4 we prove that the semantic structures of NIL are precisely the information frames with relations of similarity and informational inclusions derived from an information system. This property of frames is referred to as informational representability. The theme of informational representability is pursued in full generality in Chap. 13. In Sect. 7.3 we consider the logic IL for reasoning about similarity and its two limit cases: the first is expressed by the forward inclusion of objects (as discussed in the logic NIL), while the second corresponds to the equality of the sets of properties of two objects. The latter situation is reflected by an indiscernibility relation. We develop a Hilbert-style deductive system for IL. The proof of its completeness employs the method of copying presented in Chap. 6. In Sect. 7.4 we consider a family of Rare-logics of similarity whose semantic structures have the form of frames with relative relations which are reflexive and symmetric. The deductive systems of the logics are labelled Rasiowa–Sikorski-style systems. The labels of formulae processed by the system consist of constants representing individual objects. The chapter is concluded with a generalisation of this deduction method to a broader class of Rare-logics, where relative relations from the semantic structures satisfy conditions having the form of Horn formulae. In all of the chapters of Part III we keep the traditional names and denotations for the logics presented in this part as they have been given to the logics in the papers of their origin.

7.2 NIL: a Logic for Reasoning About Non-deterministic Information

The logic NIL is intended to provide a tool for reasoning about similarity, forward inclusion and backward inclusion of objects in information systems, defined in Sect. 3.2, taking into account relationships between these relations. The modal connectives of NIL represent generalised approximation operators determined by these relations, respectively. In particular, the connectives determined by the similarity relation represent the approximations of the forms (1) and (2) defined in Sect. 4.8. In the language of NIL we can represent sets of objects of an information system together with their structure determined by the Boolean operators and the approximation operators as well as the properties of the three information relations mentioned above. However, in the language of NIL we do not have an explicit representation of the sets of attributes that determine the corresponding relations.

7.2.1 Language and Semantics

We define NIL within the framework for modal logics developed in Sect. 5.3.3. The set of basic modal expressions of NIL is $M_0 = \{\leq, \geq, \sigma\}$. These modal constants are representations of abstract counterparts of the relations of inclusions and similarity derived from an information system, respectively. The set O_M of modal operators is empty and the set M of modal expressions coincides with M_0. The set FOR_0 of basic formulae is a countably infinite set of propositional variables. The set of propositional connectives is $O_{FOR} = \{\neg, \wedge, [\leq], [\geq], [\sigma]\}$. Hence, NIL is a standard modal logic with three modal connectives. The set FOR(NIL) of NIL-formulae is defined as in Definition 5.3.2. The NIL-models are the LAN(NIL)-models $\langle W, R_{\leq}, R_{\geq}, R_{\sigma}, m \rangle$ satisfying the following conditions:

(N1) $R_{\leq} = (R_{\geq})^{-1}$;
(N2) $R_{\leq}$ is reflexive and transitive;
(N3) R_{σ} is reflexive and symmetric;
(N4) if $\langle x, y \rangle \in R_{\sigma}$, $\langle x, x' \rangle \in R_{\leq}$, and $\langle y, y' \rangle \in R_{\leq}$, then $\langle x', y' \rangle \in R_{\sigma}$ for all $x, x', y, y' \in W$.

7.2.2 Hilbert-style Proof System

The proof system for NIL is an extension of HK(LAN(NIL)) obtained by adding the following axioms:

(Ax1) $\phi \Rightarrow [\leq]\langle \geq \rangle \phi$;
(Ax2) $\phi \Rightarrow [\geq]\langle \leq \rangle \phi$;
(Ax3) $[a]\phi \Rightarrow \phi$, where a $\in \{\leq, \geq, \sigma\}$;
(Ax4) $[a]\phi \Rightarrow [a][a]\phi$, where a $\in \{\leq, \geq\}$;

(Ax5) $\phi \Rightarrow [\sigma]\langle\sigma\rangle\phi$;
(Ax6) $[\sigma]\phi \Rightarrow [\geq][\sigma][\leq]\phi$.

This proof system is referred to as HNIL. It can be observed that the axiomatisation of NIL contains the axiomatic systems of standard modal logics: S4 applied to modal operators $[\leq]$ and $[\geq]$, and B applied to $[\sigma]$. The remaining axioms reflect the relationships between the relations in the NIL-models. The axioms (Ax1) and (Ax2) correspond to condition (N1) and the axioms (Ax1), (Ax2), and (Ax7) jointly correspond to condition (N4). All the axioms (Ax1)–(Ax6) are Sahlqvist's formulae. So Theorem 6.3.7 and Theorem 5.3.1 apply to them. Furthermore, we have the following lemma.

Lemma 7.2.1. *Let* L *be a modal language such that the modal connectives* [a], [b], *and* [d] *belong to* OM_{FOR}, *let* $p \in \text{FOR}_0$, *and let* $F = \langle W, (R_{a'})_{a' \in M} \rangle$ *be an* L*-frame. Then the following assertions hold:*

(I) $p \Rightarrow [a]\langle b\rangle p$ *is true in* F *iff* $(R_a)^{-1} \subseteq R_b$;
(II) if $(R_a)^{-1} = R_b$, *then* $[d]p \Rightarrow [b][d][a]p$ *is true in* F *iff for all* $x, y, x', y' \in W$, *if* $\langle x, y\rangle \in R_d$, $\langle x, x'\rangle \in R_a$, *and* $\langle y, y'\rangle \in R_a$, *then* $\langle x', y'\rangle \in R_d$;
(III) $[a]p \Rightarrow p$ *is true in* F *iff* R_a *is reflexive;*
(IV) $p \Rightarrow [a]\langle a\rangle p$ *is true in* F *iff* R_a *is symmetric.*

Proof. We prove (I) and (II).
(I) ($\rightarrow$) Let $F = \langle W, (R_{a'})_{a' \in M}\rangle$ be an L-frame such that $p \Rightarrow [a]\langle b\rangle p$ is true in F. Suppose $(R_a)^{-1} \not\subseteq R_b$. Hence, there are $x, y \in W$ such that (i) $\langle x, y\rangle \in (R_a)^{-1}$ and (ii) $\langle x, y\rangle \notin R_b$. We define an L-model $\mathcal{M} = \langle W, (R_{a'})_{a' \in M}, m\rangle$ based on F such that $m(p) \stackrel{\text{def}}{=} \{z : \langle x, z\rangle \notin R_b\}$. By the assumption $\mathcal{M}, y \models p \Rightarrow [a]\langle b\rangle p$. By (ii), we have $\mathcal{M}, y \models p$. Hence, $\mathcal{M}, y \models [a]\langle b\rangle p$, that is for every $z \in W$, if $\langle y, z\rangle \in R_a$, then there is a $t \in W$ such that $\langle z, t\rangle \in R_b$ and $\mathcal{M}, t \models p$. In particular, since $\langle y, x\rangle \in R_a$, we conclude that for some $t \in W$, $\langle x, t\rangle \in R_b$ and $\langle x, t\rangle \notin R_b$, a contradiction.
(I) ($\leftarrow$) Let $F = \langle W, (R_{a'})_{a' \in M}\rangle$ be an L-frame such that $(R_a)^{-1} \subseteq R_b$, let $\mathcal{M} = \langle W, (R_{a'})_{a' \in M}, m\rangle$ be an L-model based on F, and let $x \in W$. Assume that $\mathcal{M}, x \models p$. We have to show that for every $y \in W$, if $\langle x, y\rangle \in R_a$, then there is a $z \in W$ such that $\langle y, z\rangle \in R_b$ and $\mathcal{M}, z \models p$. Let $\langle x, y\rangle \in R_a$. By the assumption $\langle y, x\rangle \in R_b$. By taking x for z above, we can see that the required conditions are satisfied.
(II) ($\rightarrow$) Let $F = \langle W, (R_{a'})_{a' \in M}\rangle$ be an L-frame such that $[d]p \Rightarrow [b][d][a]p$ is true in F and $(R_a)^{-1} = R_b$. Suppose that there are $x, y, x', y' \in W$ such that $\langle x, y\rangle \in R_d$, $\langle x, x'\rangle \in R_a$, $\langle y, y'\rangle \in R_a$, and $\langle x', y'\rangle \notin R_d$. Observe that $\langle x', y'\rangle \in R_b; R_d; R_a$. We define an L-model $\mathcal{M} = \langle W, (R_{a'})_{a' \in M}, m\rangle$ based on F such that $m(p) \stackrel{\text{def}}{=} \{z : \langle x', z\rangle \in R_d\}$. According to the assumption it must be $\mathcal{M}, x' \models [d]p \Rightarrow [b][d][a]p$. We clearly have $\mathcal{M}, x' \models [d]p$. Hence, $\mathcal{M}, x' \models [b][d][a]p$. It means that for every $w \in W$, if $\langle x', w\rangle \in R_b; R_d; R_a$, then $\mathcal{M}, w \models p$. In particular, $\mathcal{M}, y' \models p$, which leads to a contradiction by the definition of $m(p)$.

(II) ($\leftarrow$) Let $F = \langle W, (R_{a'})_{a' \in M} \rangle$ be an L-frame such that for all $x, y, x', y' \in W$, if $\langle x, y \rangle \in R_d$, $\langle x, x' \rangle \in R_a$, and $\langle y, y' \rangle \in R_a$, then $\langle x', y' \rangle \in R_d$ and $(R_a)^{-1} = R_b$. Let $\mathcal{M} = \langle W, (R_{a'})_{a' \in M}, m \rangle$ be an L-model based on F and let $x \in W$. Assume that $\mathcal{M}, x \models [d]p$. That is, (i) for every $y \in W$, if $\langle x, y \rangle \in R_d$, then $\mathcal{M}, y \models p$. Suppose that not $\mathcal{M}, x \models [b][d][a]p$. It follows that there is a $y \in W$ such that $\langle x, y \rangle \in R_b$, there is a $z \in W$ such that $\langle y, z \rangle \in R_d$, there is a $t \in W$ such that $\langle z, t \rangle \in R_a$, and not $\mathcal{M}, t \models p$. Since $\langle x, y \rangle \in R_b$ iff $\langle y, x \rangle \in R_a$, by the assumption we can conclude that $\langle x, t \rangle \in R_d$. Then by (i), we have $\mathcal{M}, t \models p$, a contradiction.   Q.E.D.

Consequently, we can show the following result.

Theorem 7.2.1. *(Soundness Theorem)* THM(HNIL) $\subseteq$ VAL(NIL).

Proof. The proof consists in showing that, first, all the axioms of HNIL are NIL-valid and, second, the inference rules preserve NIL-validity. The latter means that for every inference rule of HNIL, if all the premises are NIL-valid, then the conclusion is NIL-valid. For the first part, Lemma 7.2.1 is used. The second part follows from Lemma 6.3.8(III) for the necessitation rule and for the modus ponens rule it can be easily verified.   Q.E.D.

7.2.3 Completeness

We present an algebraic proof of the completeness theorem. Let T be a HNIL-consistent set of formulae. We define the relation $\sim \subseteq$ FOR(NIL) $\times$ FOR(NIL) such that for all $\phi, \psi \in$ FOR(NIL), $\phi \sim \psi \overset{\text{def}}{\Leftrightarrow} T \vdash \phi \Leftrightarrow \psi$.

Lemma 7.2.2. *The relation $\sim$ satisfies the following properties:*

(I) $\sim$ is an equivalence relation;
(II) $\sim$ is a congruence with respect to $\neg, \wedge$;
(III) if $\phi \sim \psi$, then $[a]\phi \sim [a]\psi$ for every $a \in \{\leq, \geq, \sigma\}$.

Proof. By way of example, we sketch the proof of the statement (III). Assume $T \vdash \phi \Leftrightarrow \psi$. So $T \vdash \phi \Rightarrow \psi$ and $T \vdash \psi \Rightarrow \phi$. Applying a variant of Lemma 6.3.6, $T \vdash [a]\phi \Rightarrow [a]\psi$ and $T \vdash [a]\psi \Rightarrow [a]\phi$.   Q.E.D.

We construct the quotient algebra $\mathcal{A} = \langle \text{FOR}/ \sim, -, \cup, \cap, 1, 0 \rangle$, where FOR/ $\sim$ is the set of equivalence classes of $\sim$, and the operations are defined as follows:

$\star$ $-|\phi| \overset{\text{def}}{=} |\neg \phi|$;
$\star$ $|\phi| \cap |\psi| \overset{\text{def}}{=} |\phi \wedge \psi|$;
$\star$ $|\phi| \cup |\psi| \overset{\text{def}}{=} |\phi \vee \psi|$;
$\star$ $1 \overset{\text{def}}{=} |\phi \vee \neg \phi|$;
$\star$ $0 \overset{\text{def}}{=} |\phi \wedge \neg \phi|$.

By Lemma 7.2.2 these definitions are correct.

Lemma 7.2.3.

(I) The algebra $\mathcal{A}$ is a non-degenerate Boolean algebra;
(II) $|\phi| \leq |\psi|$ iff $T \vdash_{\mathrm{HNIL}} \phi \Rightarrow \psi$, where $\leq$ is the lattice ordering of $\mathcal{A}$;
(III) $T \vdash \phi$ iff $|\phi| = 1$;
(IV) $|\neg\phi| \neq 0$ iff not $T \vdash \phi$.

Proof. The proof is standard and uses basic properties of provability and the corresponding definitions.
(I) It is easy to verify that the axioms of Boolean algebras are satisfied by the operations of FOR(NIL)/ $\sim$. Suppose that the algebra is degenerate. It follows that for every formula ψ, $\psi \in |\phi \vee \neg\phi|$. This is equivalent to $T \vdash_{\mathrm{HNIL}} \psi \Leftrightarrow (\phi \vee \neg\phi)$, which implies that $T \vdash_{\mathrm{HNIL}} (\phi \vee \neg\phi) \Rightarrow \psi$, and hence $T \vdash_{\mathrm{HNIL}} \psi$, a contradiction because T is HNIL-consistent.
(II) Since $\leq$ is the lattice ordering in FOR(NIL)/ $\sim$, we have $|\phi| \leq |\psi|$ iff $|\phi| \cup |\psi| = |\psi|$. Due to the corresponding definitions, the following statements are equivalent:

$\star$ $|\phi| \cup |\psi| = |\psi|$;
$\star$ $|\phi \vee \psi| = |\psi|$;
$\star$ $\phi \vee \psi \sim \psi$;
$\star$ $T \vdash_{\mathrm{HNIL}} \phi \vee \psi \Leftrightarrow \psi$.

Due to the respective theorems of PC, the following statements are equivalent:

$\star$ $T \vdash_{\mathrm{HNIL}} \phi \vee \psi \Leftrightarrow \psi$;
$\star$ $T \vdash_{\mathrm{HNIL}} ((\phi \vee \psi) \Rightarrow \psi) \wedge (\psi \Rightarrow (\phi \vee \psi))$;
$\star$ $T \vdash_{\mathrm{HNIL}} \phi \vee \psi \Rightarrow \psi$;
$\star$ $T \vdash_{\mathrm{HNIL}} \phi \Rightarrow \psi$.

(III) ($\rightarrow$) Let $T \vdash_{\mathrm{HNIL}} \phi$. Since $T \vdash_{\mathrm{HNIL}} \phi \Rightarrow ((\phi \Rightarrow \phi) \Rightarrow \phi)$, by applying modus ponens, we get $T \vdash_{\mathrm{HNIL}} (\phi \Rightarrow \phi) \Rightarrow \phi$. So by the definition of $\leq$, $|\phi \Rightarrow \phi| \leq |\phi|$, which means $|\phi| = 1$.
($\leftarrow$) Let $|\phi| = 1$. This means that $|\phi| = |\phi \Rightarrow \phi|$, in particular, $|\phi| \leq |\phi \Rightarrow \phi|$. It follows that $T \vdash_{\mathrm{HNIL}} (\phi \Rightarrow \phi) \Rightarrow \phi$. Since we have $T \vdash_{\mathrm{HNIL}} \phi \Rightarrow \phi$, by applying modus ponens we get $T \vdash_{\mathrm{HNIL}} \phi$.
(IV) By (III), not $T \vdash_{\mathrm{HNIL}} \phi$ is equivalent to $|\phi| \neq 1$. Since FOR(NIL)/ $\sim$ is a Boolean algebra, $|\phi| \neq 1$ is equivalent to $-|\phi| \neq 0$, that is $|\neg\phi| \neq 0$. *Q.E.D.*

Let $U_{\mathcal{A}}$ be the family of all maximal filters of $\mathcal{A}$. The set $U_{\mathcal{A}}$ is non-empty because the algebra $\mathcal{A}$ is non-degenerate. We define the canonical relations $R_{\leq}^c$, $R_{\geq}^c$, and R_{σ}^c on the set $U_{\mathcal{A}}$ as follows:

$\star$ $\langle \mathrm{F}, \mathrm{G} \rangle \in R_{\mathrm{a}}^c \overset{\mathrm{def}}{\Leftrightarrow}$ for every formula ϕ of LAN(NIL), if $|[a]\phi| \in \mathrm{F}$, then $|\phi| \in \mathrm{G}$, for every a $\in \{\leq, \geq, \sigma\}$.

In the following lemma we state that the relations $R^c_{\leq}$, $R^c_{\geq}$, and R^c_{σ} satisfy the conditions (N1), (N2), (N3), and (N4).

Lemma 7.2.4. *For all* $F, G, F', G' \in U_A$, *the following conditions are satisfied:*

(I) $\langle F, G \rangle \in R^c_{\leq}$ *iff* $\langle G, F \rangle \in R^c_{\geq}$;
(II) the relations $R^c_{\leq}$ *and* $R^c_{\geq}$ *are reflexive and transitive;*
(III) the relation R^c_{σ} *is reflexive and symmetric;*
(IV) if $\langle F, G \rangle \in R^c_{\sigma}$, $\langle F, F' \rangle \in R^c_{\leq}$, *and* $\langle G, G' \rangle \in R^c_{\leq}$, *then* $\langle F', G' \rangle \in R^c_{\sigma}$.

Proof. (I) ($\to$) Assume that (i) for every formula ϕ, if $|[\leq]\phi| \in F$, then $|\phi| \in G$. We have to show that for every formula ϕ, if $|[\geq]\phi| \in G$, then $|\phi| \in F$. Suppose that (ii) $|[\geq]\phi| \in G$ and (iii) $|\phi| \notin F$. Thus from (iii) and by Lemma 1.7.1(IV), $-|\phi| \in F$, hence $|\neg\phi| \in F$. By Lemma 7.2.3(II) and $T \vdash \neg\phi \Rightarrow [\leq]\langle\geq\rangle\neg\phi$ (axiom (Ax1)), we get $|\neg\phi| \leq |[\leq]\langle\geq\rangle\neg\phi|$. Since F is a filter, $|[\leq]\langle\geq\rangle\neg\phi| \in F$. From (i) we obtain $|\langle\geq\rangle\neg\phi| \in G$, which means $|\neg[\geq]\phi| \in G$, a contradiction with (ii).
(I) ($\leftarrow$) Assume that (i) for every formula ϕ, if $|[\geq]\phi| \in G$, then $|\phi| \in F$. We have to show that for every formula ϕ, if $|[\leq]\phi| \in F$, then $|\phi| \in G$. Suppose that (ii) $|[\leq]\phi| \in F$ and (iii) $|\phi| \notin G$. Thus from (iii) we have $|\neg\phi| \in G$ and from the axiom (Ax2), we get $|[\geq]\langle\leq\rangle\neg\phi| \in G$. From (i) we obtain $|\langle\leq\rangle\neg\phi| \in F$, which means $|\neg[\leq]\phi| \in F$, a contradiction with (ii).
The statements (II) and (III) can be easily proved using the respective definitions and axioms (Ax3), (Ax4), and (Ax5).
(IV) Suppose that (i) $|[\sigma]\phi| \in F'$ and (ii) $|\phi| \notin G'$. $\langle G, G' \rangle \in R^c_{\leq}$ is equivalent to: for every formula ϕ, if $|\phi| \notin G'$, then $|[\leq]\phi| \notin G$. Hence, from (ii) we get $|[\leq]\phi| \notin G$. $\langle F, G \rangle \in R^c_{\sigma}$ is equivalent to: for every formula ϕ, if $|\phi| \notin G$, then $|[\sigma]\phi| \notin F$. Hence, we obtain $|[\sigma][\leq]\phi| \notin F$. From (I), we have that $\langle F, F' \rangle \in R^c_{\leq}$ is equivalent to $\langle F', F \rangle \in R^c_{\geq}$, which means that for every formula ϕ, if $|\phi| \notin F$, then $|[\geq]\phi| \notin F'$. Thus $|[\geq][\sigma][\leq]\phi| \notin F'$. From (i) and the axiom (Ax6), we get $|[\geq][\sigma][\leq]\phi| \in F'$, a contradiction.   *Q.E.D.*

The following lemma states that the set U_A contains enough witnesses for the conditions of the form $|\langle a \rangle \phi| \in F$.

Lemma 7.2.5. *Let* $a \in \{\leq, \geq, \sigma\}$ *and let* $F \in U_A$. *Then for every formula* ϕ, *if* $|\langle a \rangle \phi| \in F$, *then there exists a maximal filter* $G \in U_A$ *such that* $\langle F, G \rangle \in R^c_a$ *and* $|\phi| \in G$.

Proof. By way of example we show the lemma for $a = \geq$. Let $|\langle\geq\rangle\phi| \in F$. Consider the set

$$Z_F \stackrel{\text{def}}{=} \{|\psi| : |[\geq]\psi| \in F\}.$$

The set Z_F is non-empty since $1 \in Z_F$. Consider the filter G generated by the set $Z_F \cup \{|\phi|\}$. We have $|\psi| \in G$ iff there exist $|\phi_1|, \ldots, |\phi_n| \in Z_F \cup \{|\phi|\}$, $n \geq 1$, such that $|\phi_1| \cap \ldots \cap |\phi_n| \cap |\phi| \leq |\psi|$ (see Sect. 1.6). We will show that for all $|\phi_1|, \ldots, |\phi_n| \in Z_F$, $|\phi_1| \cap \ldots \cap |\phi_n| \cap |\phi| \neq 0$. For suppose conversely; then $|\phi_1 \wedge \ldots \wedge \phi_n \Rightarrow \neg\phi| = 1$. By Lemma 7.2.3(III), $T \vdash \phi_1 \wedge \ldots \wedge \phi_n \Rightarrow \neg\phi$. Applying the regular rule (see Sect. 6.3.3), we get $T \vdash [\geq](\phi_1 \wedge \ldots \wedge \phi_n) \Rightarrow [\geq]\neg\phi$ (see Lemma 6.3.6). By the definition of Z_F, $\{|[\geq]\phi_1|, \ldots, |[\geq]\phi_n|\} \subseteq F$, so we have $|[\geq]\phi_1 \wedge \ldots \wedge [\geq]\phi_n| \in F$. It follows that $|[\geq](\phi_1 \wedge \ldots \wedge \phi_n)| \in F$. Hence, $|[\geq]\neg\phi| \in F$, which means that $|\neg\langle\geq\rangle\phi| \in F$, a contradiction with the assumption. Thus $0 \notin G$, so the filter G is proper. By Lemma 1.6.2(I), there is a maximal filter G' that contains G. We clearly have $|\phi| \in G'$. We also have $\langle F, G' \rangle \in R_\geq^c$, because for every formula ψ, if $|[\geq]\psi| \in F$, then $|\psi| \in Z_F$, and hence $|\psi| \in G'$. This completes the proof.   Q.E.D.

We define an algebraic canonical structure $\mathcal{M}^c = \langle U_A, R_\leq^c, R_\geq^c, R_\sigma^c, m^c \rangle$ by putting $m^c(p) \stackrel{\text{def}}{=} \{F \in U_A : |p| \in F\}$ for every $p \in FOR_0$.

Lemma 7.2.6. $\mathcal{M}^c$ *is a NIL-model.*

The following lemma is an algebraic counterpart of Theorem 6.3.6.

Lemma 7.2.7. *For every formula ϕ and for every $F \in U_A$, the following statements are equivalent:*

(I) $\mathcal{M}^c, F \models \phi$;
(II) $|\phi| \in F$.

Proof. The proof is by induction on the structure of ϕ. If ϕ is a propositional variable, then the equivalence holds by the definition of m^c. If ϕ is of the form $\neg\psi$ or $\psi_1 \wedge \psi_2$, then since the filter F is maximal and prime, we obtain the required conditions. Now consider ϕ of the form $[a]\psi$ for some $a \in \{\leq, \geq, \sigma\}$.
(I) → (II) Assume that $\mathcal{M}^c, F \models \phi$ and suppose that $|\phi| \notin F$. So, $|\neg[a]\psi| \in F$ and by Lemma 7.2.5, there is a $G \in U_A$ such that $\langle F, G \rangle \in R_a^c$ and $|\psi| \notin G$. By the induction hypothesis, $\mathcal{M}^c, G \not\models \psi$, which leads to a contradiction, since $\langle F, G \rangle \in R_a^c$ and $\mathcal{M}^c, F \models \phi$.
(II) → (I) Assume $|\phi| \in F$ and suppose $\mathcal{M}^c, F \not\models \phi$. So there is a $G \in U_A$ such that $\langle F, G \rangle \in R_a^c$ and $\mathcal{M}^c, G \not\models \psi$. By the induction hypothesis, $|\psi| \notin G$. Since $|\phi| \in F$ and $|\psi| \notin G$, by the definition of R_a^c, we get $\langle F, G \rangle \notin R_a^c$, a contradiction.   Q.E.D.

Theorem 7.2.2. *(Strong Completeness Theorem) For every set T of formulae and for every formula ϕ, if $T \models \phi$, then $T \vdash_{HNIL} \phi$.*

Proof. Suppose that not $T \vdash_{HNIL} \phi$. By Lemma 7.2.3(IV), $|\neg\phi| \neq 0$. Thus there is a maximal filter $F \in U_A$ such that $|\neg\phi| \in F$. By Lemma 7.2.3(III) we have that for every formula $\psi \in T$, $|\psi| \in F$. From Lemma 7.2.7 we obtain that for every formula $\psi \in T$, $\mathcal{M}^c, F \models \psi$ and not $\mathcal{M}^c, F \models \phi$, a contradiction. Q.E.D.

As a corollary, we obtain the following theorem.

Theorem 7.2.3. *(Completeness Theorem)* VAL(NIL) $\subseteq$ THM(HNIL).

7.2.4 Informational Representability of NIL-models

The models of NIL are based on abstract frames whose relations satisfy the conditions (N1), (N2), (N3), and (N4). However, to reason about information relations derived from an information system within the framework of NIL, it should be guaranteed that the abstract NIL-models represent in an adequate way the models based on the frames derived from an information system. In this section we present a result in this direction. Namely, we show that for every NIL-frame $F = \langle W, R_<, R_>, R_\sigma \rangle$, there is a total information system S such that the relations of forward inclusion, backward inclusion, and similarity derived from S coincide with $R_<$, $R_>$, and R_σ, respectively.

Let $F = \langle W, R_<, R_>, R_\sigma \rangle$ be a NIL-frame. We say that $\mathcal{X} \subseteq \mathcal{P}(W)$ is a *nice family of sets* $\overset{\text{def}}{\Leftrightarrow}$ for all $x, y \in W$, the following conditions are satisfied:

(NIL-rep1) if $\langle x, y \rangle \in R_\sigma$, then there is an $X \in \mathcal{X}$ such that $x \in X$ and $y \in X$;

(NIL-rep2) if $\langle x, y \rangle \in R_<$, then for every $X \in \mathcal{X}$, if $x \in X$, then $y \in X$.

Let $\mathcal{N}$ be the collection of all the nice families of members of $\mathcal{P}(W)$. For each $\mathcal{X} \in \mathcal{N}$, we define the mapping $f_\mathcal{X} : W \to \mathcal{P}(\mathcal{X})$ as follows: for every $x \in W$,

$$f_\mathcal{X}(x) \overset{\text{def}}{=} \{X \in \mathcal{X} : x \in X\}.$$

We construct an information system $S_F = \langle OB, AT \rangle$ as follows: $OB \overset{\text{def}}{=} W$ and $AT \overset{\text{def}}{=} \{f_\mathcal{X} : \mathcal{X} \in \mathcal{N}\}$. S_F is obviously a set-theoretical information system. We show that S_F is an information system, and moreover, for every $\mathcal{X} \in \mathcal{N}$ and for every $x \in W$, $f_\mathcal{X}(x) \neq \emptyset$. This will guarantee that S_F is total and therefore the similarity relations derived from S_F will be reflexive.

Lemma 7.2.8. *The information system S_F and the family $\mathcal{N}$ defined above satisfy the following conditions:*

(I) $AT \neq \emptyset$;
(II) for every $\mathcal{X} \in \mathcal{N}$, $\mathcal{X} \neq \emptyset$;
(III) for every $\mathcal{X} \in \mathcal{N}$ and $x \in W$, $f_\mathcal{X}(x) \neq \emptyset$.

Proof. (I) We show that $\mathcal{X}_0 = \{R_<(x) \cup R_<(y) : \langle x, y \rangle \in R_\sigma\} \in \mathcal{N}$. We have to show that $\mathcal{X}_0$ satisfies conditions (NIL-rep1) and (NIL-rep2).
Proof of (NIL-rep1): let $\langle x', y' \rangle \in R_\sigma$ and $X = R_<(x') \cup R_<(y') \in \mathcal{X}_0$. Since $R_<$ is reflexive, $x' \in R_<(x')$ and $y' \in R_<(y')$. Hence, $\mathcal{X}_0$ satisfies condition (NIL-rep1).
Proof of (NIL-rep2): let $\langle x', y' \rangle \in R_<$ and let $X \in \mathcal{X}_0$ be such that $x' \in X$. Then either $x' \in R_<(x)$ or $x' \in R_<(y)$ for some $\langle x, y \rangle \in R_\sigma$. By transitivity of $R_<$, $\langle x, y' \rangle \in R_<$ or $\langle y, y' \rangle \in R_<$. So $y' \in R_<(x) \cup R_<(y)$.
(II) Let $\mathcal{X} \in \mathcal{N}$ and $x \in W$. Since $\langle x, x \rangle \in R_\sigma$ (R_σ is reflexive) and by (NIL-rep1), there is an $X \in \mathcal{X}$ such that $x \in X$. So $\mathcal{X} \neq \emptyset$.

(III) Let $\mathcal{X} \in \mathcal{N}$ and $x \in W$. By (NIL-rep1) there is an $X \in \mathcal{X}$ such that $x \in X$. So $X \in f_{\mathcal{X}}(x)$.   Q.E.D.

Lemma 7.2.9. *Let $F = \langle W, R_\le, R_\ge, R_\sigma \rangle$ be a NIL-frame and let S_F be the information system determined by F. Then the following conditions are satisfied:*

(I) $\langle x, y \rangle \in R_\le$ iff $f_{\mathcal{X}}(x) \subseteq f_{\mathcal{X}}(y)$ for every $\mathcal{X} \in \mathcal{N}$;
(II) $\langle x, y \rangle \in R_\ge$ iff $f_{\mathcal{X}}(y) \subseteq f_{\mathcal{X}}(x)$ for every $\mathcal{X} \in \mathcal{N}$;
(III) $\langle x, y \rangle \in R_\sigma$ iff $f_{\mathcal{X}}(x) \cap f_{\mathcal{X}}(y) \ne \emptyset$ for every $\mathcal{X} \in \mathcal{N}$.

Proof. (I) ($\rightarrow$) Let $\langle x, y \rangle \in R_\le$ and let $X \in f_{\mathcal{X}}(x)$. Then by definition, $x \in X$. Since $\mathcal{X}$ is a nice family, by (NIL-rep2) we have $y \in X$, and hence $X \in f_{\mathcal{X}}(y)$.
(I) ($\leftarrow$) Assume that for every $\mathcal{X} \in \mathcal{N}$, $f_{\mathcal{X}}(x) \subseteq f_{\mathcal{X}}(y)$. Consider $\mathcal{X} = \{R_\le(x)\} \cup \{R_\le(u) \cup R_\le(v) : \langle u, v \rangle \in R_\sigma\}$. We show that $\mathcal{X} \in \mathcal{N}$. To prove (NIL-rep1), take $\langle z, t \rangle \in R_\sigma$. We have to show that there is an $X \in \mathcal{X}$ such that $z \in X$ and $t \in X$. Take $X = R_\le(z) \cup R_\le(t)$. It has been shown in the proof of Lemma 7.2.8(I) that in this case $\mathcal{X}$ satisfies (NIL-rep1). Now we prove that $\mathcal{X}$ satisfies (NIL-rep2). Let $\langle z, t \rangle \in R_\le$. We have to show that for every $X \in \mathcal{X}$, if $z \in X$, then $t \in X$. Consider $X = R_\le(x)$ and let $z \in R_\le(x)$. Then $\langle x, z \rangle \in R_\le$ and, by transitivity, $\langle x, t \rangle \in R_\le$. Hence, $t \in R_\le(x)$ and $t \in X$. Now consider $X = R_\le(u) \cup R_\le(v)$, where $\langle u, v \rangle \in R_\sigma$. It has been shown in the proof of Lemma 7.2.8(I) that in this case $\mathcal{X}$ satisfies (NIL-rep2). So $R_\le(x) \in f_{\mathcal{X}}(x)$, since $x \in R_\le(x)$ and by the assumption $R_\le(x) \in f_{\mathcal{X}}(y)$. This means that $y \in R_\le(x)$ by the definition of $f_{\mathcal{X}}$, that is $\langle x, y \rangle \in R_\le$.
(II) The proof of (II) is similar to the proof of (I). It can be obtained by replacing $\le$ [resp. x, y] by $\ge$ [resp. y, x].
(III) ($\rightarrow$) Let $\langle x, y \rangle \in R_\sigma$ and let $\mathcal{X} \in \mathcal{N}$. By (NIL-rep1) there is an $X \in \mathcal{X}$ such that $x \in X$ and $y \in X$. Hence, $X \in f_{\mathcal{X}}(x)$ and $X \in f_{\mathcal{X}}(y)$, so $f_{\mathcal{X}}(x) \cap f_{\mathcal{X}}(y) \ne \emptyset$.
(III) ($\leftarrow$) Assume that for every $\mathcal{X} \in \mathcal{N}$, $f_{\mathcal{X}}(x) \cap f_{\mathcal{X}}(y) \ne \emptyset$. Consider $\mathcal{X} = \{R_\le(u) \cup R_\le(v) : \langle u, v \rangle \in R_\sigma\}$. In the proof of (I) we have shown that $\mathcal{X}$ is a nice family of sets, and hence $f_{\mathcal{X}} \in AT$. Since by the assumption $f_{\mathcal{X}}(x) \cap f_{\mathcal{X}}(y) \ne \emptyset$, there is an $X \in \mathcal{X}$ such that $X \in f_{\mathcal{X}}(x)$ and $X \in f_{\mathcal{X}}(y)$. By the definition of $\mathcal{X}$, $X = R_\le(u) \cup R_\le(v)$ for some $u, v \in W$ such that $\langle u, v \rangle \in R_\sigma$. We consider four cases:
Case 1: $x \in R_\le(u)$ and $y \in R_\le(u)$.
Hence, $\langle u, x \rangle \in R_\le$ and $\langle u, y \rangle \in R_\le$. Since we also have $\langle u, u \rangle \in R_\sigma$, we get by (N4) that $\langle x, y \rangle \in R_\sigma$.
Case 2: $x \in R_\le(v)$ and $y \in R_\le(u)$.
Hence, $\langle v, x \rangle \in R_\le$ and $\langle u, y \rangle \in R_\le$. Since $\langle u, v \rangle \in R_\sigma$ by the definition of X, by (N4) we get $\langle x, y \rangle \in R_\sigma$.
The cases ($x \in R_\le(v)$ and $y \in R_\le(v)$) and ($x \in R_\le(u)$ and $y \in R_\le(v)$) are analogous to the cases 1 and 2, respectively.   Q.E.D.

The above lemmas lead to the following theorem.

Theorem 7.2.4. *For every NIL-frame $F = \langle W, R_\leq, R_\geq, R_\sigma \rangle$, there is a total information system S such that the relations of forward inclusion, backward inclusion, and similarity derived from S coincide with $R_\leq$, $R_\geq$, and R_σ, respectively.*

This theorem has been an inspiration for introducing a general concept of informational representability of models of information logics. This is the subject of Chap. 13.

7.3 IL: an Information Logic

The logic IL is intended to be a tool for reasoning about indiscernibility, similarity, and forward inclusion, and about relationships between them. Moreover, the language of IL includes a propositional constant interpreted as a set of deterministic objects in an information system, so that we can express in IL various constraints on information relations that hold for deterministic objects only.

7.3.1 Language and Semantics

The set of basic modal expressions of IL is $M_0 = \{\equiv, \leq, \sigma\}$. These modal constants represent abstract counterparts of indiscernibility, forward inclusion, and similarity, respectively. The set O_M of modal operators is empty and the set M of modal expressions coincides with M_0. The set FOR_0 of basic formulae is a countably infinite set of propositional variables augmented with the propositional constant D. The set of propositional connectives is $O_{FOR} = \{\neg, \wedge, [\equiv], [\leq], [\sigma]\}$. The set $FOR(IL)$ is defined as usual. The IL-models are the structures of the form $\langle W, R_\equiv, R_\leq, R_\sigma, D, m \rangle$ such that W is a non-empty set, $R_\equiv, R_\leq, R_\sigma$ are binary relations on W, and D is a subset of W. The meaning function m satisfies $m(p) \subseteq W$ for every propositional variable p and $m(D) = D$. Moreover, for all $x, y, z \in W$, the following conditions are satisfied:

(I1) $R_\equiv$ is an equivalence relation;
(I2) $R_\leq$ is reflexive and transitive;
(I3) R_σ is weakly reflexive and symmetric;
(I4) $\langle x, y \rangle \in R_\sigma$ and $\langle x, z \rangle \in R_\leq$ imply $\langle z, y \rangle \in R_\sigma$;
(I5) $y \in D$ and $\langle x, y \rangle \in R_\leq$ imply $x \in D$;
(I6) $x \in D$ and $\langle x, y \rangle \in R_\sigma$ imply $\langle x, y \rangle \in R_\leq$;
(I7) $\langle x, y \rangle \in R_\equiv$ implies $\langle x, y \rangle \in R_\leq$;
(I8) $x \in D$, $y \in D$, and $\langle x, y \rangle \in R_\sigma$ imply $\langle x, y \rangle \in R_\equiv$;
(I9) $\langle x, y \rangle \in R_\leq$ and $\langle y, x \rangle \in R_\leq$ imply $\langle x, y \rangle \in R_\equiv$;
(I10) $x \notin D$ implies there is a $y \in W$ such that $\langle x, y \rangle \notin R_\leq$.

Conditions (I1)–(I10) are motivated by the following observation. For every information system $S = \langle OB, AT \rangle$, replacing $R_\equiv$ [resp. $R_\leq$, R_σ, D] by $ind(AT)$ [resp. $fin(AT)$, $sim(AT)$, $D(AT)$] in (I1)–(I10) leads to the true statements.

7.3.2 A Hilbert-style Proof System

The proof system for IL is an extension of HK(LAN(IL)) obtained by adding the following axioms:

(Ax1) $[\equiv]\phi \Rightarrow \phi$;
(Ax2) $\phi \Rightarrow [\equiv]\langle\equiv\rangle\phi$;
(Ax3) $[\equiv]\phi \Rightarrow [\equiv][\equiv]\phi$;
(Ax4) $[\leq]\phi \Rightarrow \phi$;
(Ax5) $[\leq]\phi \Rightarrow [\leq][\leq]\phi$;
(Ax6) $\langle\sigma\rangle\top \wedge [\sigma]\phi \Rightarrow \phi$;
(Ax7) $\phi \Rightarrow [\sigma]\langle\sigma\rangle\phi$;
(Ax8) $\langle\leq\rangle[\sigma]\phi \Rightarrow [\sigma]\phi$;
(Ax9) $\langle\leq\rangle D \Rightarrow D$;
(Ax10) $D \wedge [\leq]\phi \Rightarrow [\sigma]\phi$;
(Ax11) $[\leq]\phi \Rightarrow [\equiv]\phi$;
(Ax12) $D \wedge [\equiv]\phi \Rightarrow [\sigma](D \Rightarrow \phi)$.

This proof system is referred to as HIL. The axioms (Ax1), (Ax2), and (Ax3) correspond to reflexivity, symmetry and transitivity of $R_\equiv$, respectively. The axioms (Ax4) and (Ax5) correspond to the reflexivity and transitivity of $R_\leq$. The axiom (Ax6) reflects weak reflexivity of R_σ, and (Ax7) its symmetry. The axioms (Ax8)–(Ax12) correspond to conditions (I4)–(I8), respectively. The proofs of these correspondences can be obtained in the way similar to that presented in Lemma 7.2.1. Conditions (I9) and (I10) are not definable in the language of IL. Nevertheless, we show that the given proof system is IL-complete.

7.3.3 Completeness

We define a logic IL′ whose language coincides with the language of IL, but the class of IL′-models is broader than the class of IL-models, namely the IL′-models are the structures $\langle W, R_\equiv, R_\leq, R_\sigma, D, m \rangle$ such that only the conditions (I1)–(I8) are satisfied. This should not come as a surprise since the conditions (I9) and (I10) are not definable in IL. We show that for every IL′-model $\mathcal{M}$, there is an IL-model $\mathcal{M}'$ and a copying from $\mathcal{M}$ into $\mathcal{M}'$. By Theorem 6.2.3, IL and IL′ have the same set of valid formulae. Next, we show that the proof system HIL is IL′-complete. From these two facts, we will conclude that HIL is IL-complete.

The following correspondence results are used to prove soundness of HIL with respect to IL′-validity.

Lemma 7.3.1. *Let* L *be a modal language such that the modal connectives* [a] *and* [b] *belong to* OM_{FOR}, *let* $\{p, D\} \subseteq FOR_0$, *and let* $F = \langle W, (R_{a'})_{a' \in M} \rangle$ *be an* L-*frame. Then the following assertions hold:*

(I) $\langle a \rangle [b]p \Rightarrow [b]p$ *is true in* F *iff for all* $x, y, z \in W$, $\langle x, y \rangle \in R_b$ *and* $\langle x, z \rangle \in R_a$ *imply* $\langle z, y \rangle \in R_b$;

(II) For every model $\mathcal{M} = \langle W, (R_{a'})_{a' \in M}, m \rangle$ *based on* F, $\langle a \rangle D \Rightarrow D$ *is true in* $\mathcal{M}$ *iff for all* $x, y \in W$, $y \in m(D)$ *and* $\langle x, y \rangle \in R_a$ *imply* $x \in m(D)$;

(III) For every model $\mathcal{M} = \langle W, (R_{a'})_{a' \in M}, m \rangle$ *based on* F *such that for all* $x, y \in W$, $x \in m(D)$, *and* $\langle x, y \rangle \in R_b$ *imply* $\langle x, y \rangle \in R_a$, *we have* $D \wedge [a]p \Rightarrow [b]p$ *is true in* $\mathcal{M}$;

(IV) For every model $\mathcal{M} = \langle W, (R_{a'})_{a' \in M}, m \rangle$ *based on* F *such that for all* $x, y \in W$, $x \in m(D)$, $y \in m(D)$, *and* $\langle x, y \rangle \in R_b$ *imply* $\langle x, y \rangle \in R_a$, *we have* $D \wedge [a]p \Rightarrow [b](D \Rightarrow p)$ *is true in* $\mathcal{M}$.

Proof. (I) ($\rightarrow$) Assume $\langle a \rangle [b]p \Rightarrow [b]p$ is true in F and suppose there exist $x_0, y_0, z_0 \in W$ such that $\langle x_0, y_0 \rangle \in R_b$, $\langle x_0, z_0 \rangle \in R_a$, and $\langle z_0, y_0 \rangle \in R_b$. Let $\mathcal{M}_0 = \langle W, (R_{a'})_{a' \in M}, m_0 \rangle$ be a model based on F such that $m_0(p) = R_b(z_0)$. By the definition of $m_0(p)$, $\mathcal{M}_0, z_0 \models [b]p$ and since $\langle x_0, z_0 \rangle \in R_a$, $\mathcal{M}_0, x_0 \models \langle a \rangle [b]p$. By the assumption, $\mathcal{M}_0 \models \langle a \rangle [b]p \Rightarrow [b]p$, so $\mathcal{M}_0, x_0 \models [b]p$. However, $\mathcal{M}_0, y_0 \not\models p$ ($y_0 \notin R_b(z_0)$) and therefore $\mathcal{M}_0, x_0 \not\models [b]p$, a contradiction.

(I) ($\leftarrow$) Let $\mathcal{M} = \langle W, (R_{a'})_{a' \in M}, m \rangle$ be an L-model such that for all $x, y, z \in W$, $\langle x, y \rangle \in R_b$ and $\langle x, z \rangle \in R_a$ imply $\langle z, y \rangle \in R_b$. Let $x \in W$, assume $\mathcal{M}, x \models \langle a \rangle [b]p$ and suppose $\mathcal{M}, x \not\models [b]p$. So there is an $x' \in R_b(x)$ such that $\mathcal{M}, x' \not\models p$. By the assumption there is a $y \in R_a(x)$ such that $\mathcal{M}, y \models [b]p$. So $\langle x, x' \rangle \in R_b$, $\langle x, y \rangle \in R_a$, and by the assumption this implies that $\langle y, x' \rangle \in R_b$. Since $\mathcal{M}, y \models [b]p$, we get $\mathcal{M}, x' \models p$, a contradiction.

(II) ($\rightarrow$) Assume $\langle a \rangle D \Rightarrow D$ is true in $\mathcal{M} = \langle W, (R_{a'})_{a' \in M}, m \rangle$ and suppose that for some $x_0, y_0 \in W$, $y_0 \in m(D)$, $\langle x_0, y_0 \rangle \in R_a$, and $x_0 \in m(D)$. So $\mathcal{M}, x_0 \models \langle a \rangle D$ and by truth of $\langle a \rangle D \Rightarrow D$ in $\mathcal{M}$, we get $\mathcal{M}, x_0 \models D$, a contradiction.

(II) ($\leftarrow$) The proof is by an easy verification.

The proofs of (III) and (IV) are similar.   *Q.E.D.*

The soundness of HIL can be proved in a similar way as Theorem 7.2.1.

Theorem 7.3.1. *(Soundness Theorem)* THM(HIL) $\subseteq$ VAL(IL').

The following lemma and a copying construction on the canonical structure $\mathcal{M}^c$ will enable us to establish a completeness result.

Lemma 7.3.2. *The canonical structure* $\mathcal{M}^c = \langle W^c, (R_a^c)_{a \in M}, m^c \rangle$ *for* HIL *is an* IL'-*model.*

Proof. By Lemma 6.3.11 $\mathcal{M}^c$ satisfies the conditions (I1), (I2), (I3), and (I7). We show that $\mathcal{M}$ satisfies (I4), (I5), (I6), and (I8).

(I4) Suppose $\mathcal{M}^c$ does not satisfy (I4). So there exist $X, Y, Z \in W^c$ such that

$\langle X, Y \rangle \in R^c_\sigma$, $\langle X, Z \rangle \in R^c_\le$, and $\langle Z, Y \rangle \notin R^c_\sigma$. It follows that there is a formula $[\sigma]\phi$ such that $[\sigma]\phi \in Z$ and $\phi \notin Y$. Since $\langle X, Y \rangle \in R^c_\sigma$, we have $[\sigma]\phi \notin X$. Now since THM(HIL) $\subseteq X$ (by Lemma 6.3.5(IV)) $\langle \le \rangle [\sigma]\phi \Rightarrow [\sigma]\phi \in X$ and therefore $\langle \le \rangle [\sigma]\phi \notin X$. Since $\langle X, Z \rangle \in R^c_\le$, we have $\neg [\sigma]\phi \in Z$, which leads to a contradiction.

(I5) Suppose $\mathcal{M}^c$ does not satisfy (I5). So there exist $X, Y \in W^c$ such that $D \in Y$, $\langle X, Y \rangle \in R^c_\le$, and $D \notin X$. By Lemma 6.3.5(IV), we have $\langle \le \rangle D \Rightarrow D \in X$. Since $D \notin X$, we deduce that $\langle \le \rangle D \notin X$, that is $\neg \langle \le \rangle D \in X$. However, by $\langle X, Y \rangle \in R^c_\le$, we obtain $\neg D \in Y$, a contradiction.

(I6) Suppose $\mathcal{M}^c$ does not satisfy (I6). So there exist $X, Y \in W^c$ such that $D \in X$, $\langle X, Y \rangle \in R^c_\sigma$, and $\langle X, Y \rangle \notin R^c_\le$. It follows that there is a formula $[\le]\phi \in X$ such that $\phi \notin Y$. Since $\langle X, Y \rangle \in R^c_\sigma$, $[\sigma]\phi \notin X$. Since $D \wedge [\le]\phi \Rightarrow [\sigma]\phi \in X$ and $D \in X$, this implies $[\le]\phi \notin X$, a contradiction.

(I8) Suppose $\mathcal{M}^c$ does not satisfy (I8). So there exist $X, Y \in W^c$ such that $D \in X$, $D \in Y$, $\langle X, Y \rangle \in R^c_\sigma$, and $\langle X, Y \rangle \notin R^c_\equiv$. There is $[\equiv]\phi \in X$ such that $\phi \notin Y$. Since $D \in Y$, we have $D \Rightarrow \phi \notin Y$. Since $\langle X, Y \rangle \in R^c_\sigma$, we obtain $[\sigma](D \Rightarrow \phi) \notin X$. By Lemma 6.3.5(IV), $D \wedge [\equiv]\phi \Rightarrow [\sigma](D \Rightarrow \phi) \in X$, and since $D \in X$, we have $[\equiv]\phi \notin X$, a contradiction.   Q.E.D.

Lemma 7.3.2 enables us to prove that HIL is IL'-complete.

Theorem 7.3.2. *(Completeness Theorem)* VAL(IL') $\subseteq$ THM(HIL).

It remains to show that HIL is IL-complete. We prove the forthcoming Theorem 7.3.3 by applying a copying construction. Let

$$\mathcal{M} = \langle W, R_\equiv, R_\le, R_\sigma, D, m \rangle$$

be an IL'-model. Let $\bowtie$ be an equivalence relation on W defined as follows: for all $x, y \in W$,

$$\langle x, y \rangle \in \bowtie \overset{\text{def}}{\Leftrightarrow} \langle x, y \rangle \in R_\le \text{ and } \langle y, x \rangle \in R_\le.$$

By (I1) and (I7), $R_\equiv \subseteq \bowtie$. The relation $\bowtie$ can be viewed as an approximation of $R_\equiv$. An equivalence class X of $\bowtie$ is said to be *normal* $\overset{\text{def}}{\Leftrightarrow} X$ is also an equivalence class of $R_\equiv$. Equivalently, an equivalence class X of $\bowtie$ is normal iff for all $x, y \in X$, $\langle x, y \rangle \in R_\equiv$. Let $NC(\mathcal{M})$ be the set of normal equivalence classes of $\bowtie$. Let $\rhd$ be a well-ordering of all the equivalence classes of $R_\equiv$. Such a relation exists by the well-ordering principle.

Lemma 7.3.3. *For every $x \in W$, if $x \in D$ and $\langle x, x \rangle \in R_\sigma$, then $|x|_\bowtie \in NC(\mathcal{M})$.*

Proof. Let $y \in W$ and $\langle x, y \rangle \in \bowtie$. By the satisfaction of (I5) in $\mathcal{M}$, we have $y \in D$. Since $\langle x, x \rangle \in R_\sigma$ and $\langle x, y \rangle \in R_\le$, by (I4) we get $\langle y, x \rangle \in R_\sigma$. By (I3), $\langle x, y \rangle \in R_\sigma$. Now by the satisfaction of (I8) in $\mathcal{M}$, we get $\langle x, y \rangle \in R_\equiv$. So $|x|_\bowtie$ is normal.   Q.E.D.

Let $\mathcal{M}' = \langle W', R'_{\equiv}, R'_{\leq}, R'_{\sigma}, D', m' \rangle$ be the structure defined as follows:

* $W' \stackrel{\text{def}}{=} \{x \in W : |x|_{\bowtie} \in NC(\mathcal{M})\} \cup \{\langle x, i \rangle : |x|_{\bowtie} \notin NC(\mathcal{M}), i \in \mathbb{N}\}$;
* COP is the set of maps $\{f_i : W \to W' : i \in \mathbb{N}\}$ such that for every $i \in \mathbb{N}$ and for every $x \in W$, if $|x|_{\bowtie} \in NC(\mathcal{M})$, then $f_i(x) \stackrel{\text{def}}{=} x$, otherwise $f_i(x) \stackrel{\text{def}}{=} \langle x, i \rangle$;
* $R'_{\sigma'} \stackrel{\text{def}}{=} \{\langle f_i(x), f_j(y) \rangle : \langle x, y \rangle \in R_{\sigma}, i, j \in \mathbb{N}\}$;
* $R'_{\leq,ok} \stackrel{\text{def}}{=} \{\langle f_i(x), f_j(y) \rangle : \langle x, y \rangle \in R_{\leq}, (|x|_{\bowtie} \in NC(\mathcal{M}) \text{ or } \langle x, y \rangle \notin \bowtie), i, j \in \mathbb{N}\}$;
* $R'_{\leq,defect} \stackrel{\text{def}}{=} \{\langle f_i(x), f_j(y) \rangle : |x|_{\bowtie} \notin NC(\mathcal{M}), \langle x, y \rangle \in \bowtie, i < j \text{ or } (i = j \text{ and } |x|_{R_{\equiv}} \rhd |y|_{R_{\equiv}}), i, j \in \mathbb{N}\}$;
* $R'_{\leq} \stackrel{\text{def}}{=} R'_{\leq,ok} \cup R'_{\leq,defect}$;
* $R'_{\equiv} \stackrel{\text{def}}{=} R'_{\leq} \cap (R'_{\leq})^{-1}$;
* $D' \stackrel{\text{def}}{=} \{f_i(x) : x \in D, i \in \mathbb{N}\}$;
* for every $\mathrm{p} \in FOR_0$, $m'(\mathrm{p}) \stackrel{\text{def}}{=} \{f_i(x) : x \in m(\mathrm{p}), i \in \mathbb{N}\}$.

Observe that the set COP is countably infinite by construction. For every $i \in \mathbb{N}$, the restriction of $\mathcal{M}'$ to $\{f_i(x) : x \in W\}$ is called the ith copy of $\mathcal{M}$. However, if (I9) is not satisfied for some $x, y \in W$, this defect is repaired by considering the next copies or possibly the same copy but with a "limited degree of freedom" (see the definition of $R'_{\leq,defect}$) depending on the well-ordering $\rhd$. Namely, if for some $x, y \in W$, $\langle x, y \rangle \in R_{\equiv}$ iff ($\langle x, y \rangle \in R_{\leq}$ and $\langle x, y \rangle \in R_{\geq}$) and $|x|_{\bowtie}$ is normal ($|x|_{\bowtie}$ is also an equivalence class of $R_{\equiv}$), then $\langle f_i(x), f_j(y) \rangle \in R'_{\leq,ok}$ for all $i, j \in \mathbb{N}$. In this case no defects are to be repaired and therefore there is no constraint on the number of copies. Otherwise, we hope to repair the defect by adding to the corresponding relations the pairs of objects such that one object is from the ith copy and the other from a jth copy of $\mathcal{M}$ for some $j \geq i$. A similar idea is presented in Example 6.2.4, where the lack of irreflexivity has to be repaired.

It is easy to see that $W' = \{f(x) : x \in W, f \in COP\}$ and for every $f \in COP$ and for all $x, y \in W$, $f(x) = f(y)$ implies $x = y$. So conditions (Cop1), (Cop2), and (Cop5) in Definition 6.2.5 are satisfied by COP. The following lemmas state that the remaining conditions (Cop3) and (Cop4) also hold.

Lemma 7.3.4. *For all $x, y \in W$, $i, j \in \mathbb{N}$, $f_i, f_j \in COP$, the following conditions are satisfied:*

(I) (I.1) $\langle f_i(x), f_j(y) \rangle \in R'_{\equiv}$ implies $\langle x, y \rangle \in R_{\equiv}$;
(I.2) $\langle x, y \rangle \in R_{\equiv}$ implies there is an $f \in COP$ such that $\langle f_i(x), f(y) \rangle \in R'_{\equiv}$;
(II) (II.1) $\langle f_i(x), f_j(y) \rangle \in R'_{\leq}$ implies $\langle x, y \rangle \in R_{\leq}$;
(II.2) $\langle x, y \rangle \in R_{\leq}$ implies there is an $f \in I$ such that $\langle f_i(x), f(y) \rangle \in R'_{\leq}$;
(II.3) $\langle f_i(x), f_i(x) \rangle \in R'_{\leq}$;
(III) (III.1) $\langle f_i(x), f_j(y) \rangle \in R'_{\sigma}$ implies $\langle x, y \rangle \in R_{\sigma}$;

(III.2) $\langle x, y \rangle \in R_\sigma$ *implies* $\langle f_i(x), f_j(y) \rangle \in R'_\sigma$;
(IV) for every $a \in \{\equiv, \leq, \geq\}$,
    (IV.1) $\langle f_i(x), f_j(y) \rangle \in R'_a$ *implies* $\langle x, y \rangle \in R_a$;
    (IV.2) $\langle x, y \rangle \in R_a$ *implies there is an* $f \in I$ *such that* $\langle f_i(x), f(y) \rangle \in R'_a$.

Proof. The conditions (II.1), (II.3), (III.1), and (III.2) follow from the respective definitions.

(I.1) Assume $\langle f_i(x), f_j(y) \rangle \in R'_\equiv$. So $\langle f_i(x), f_j(y) \rangle \in R'_\leq$ and $\langle f_j(y), f_i(x) \rangle \in R'_\leq$. By (II.1), $\langle x, y \rangle \in R_\leq$ and $\langle y, x \rangle \in R_\leq$. So $|x|_\bowtie = |y|_\bowtie$ and $\langle x, y \rangle \in \bowtie$. If $\rceil x|_\bowtie \in NC(\mathcal{M})$, then $\langle x, y \rangle \in R_\equiv$, since we have $|x|_\bowtie = |x|_{R_\equiv}$. Otherwise, $(i < j$ or $(i = j$ and $|x|_{R_\equiv} \triangleright |y|_{R_\equiv}))$ and $(j < i$ or $(i = j$ and $|y|_{R_\equiv} \triangleright |x|_{R_\equiv}))$. Hence, $i = j$ and $|x|_{R_\equiv} = |y|_{R_\equiv}$ since $\triangleright$ is antisymmetric, which entails $\langle x, y \rangle \in R_\equiv$.

(I.2) Assume $\langle x, y \rangle \in R_\equiv$. By (I1) and (I7), $\langle x, y \rangle \in \bowtie$. If $|x|_\bowtie$ is normal (and therefore $|y|_\bowtie$ is normal as well), then for every $j \in \mathbb{N}$, $\langle f_i(x), f_j(y) \rangle \in R'_{\leq,ok}$ and $\langle f_j(y), f_i(x) \rangle \in R'_{\leq,ok}$. So $\langle f_i(x), f_j(y) \rangle \in R'_\equiv$ for every $j \in \mathbb{N}$. Otherwise, if $|x|_\bowtie$ is not normal, then $|x|_{R_\equiv} = |y|_{R_\equiv}$ and therefore $|x|_{R_\equiv} \triangleright |y|_{R_\equiv}$ and $|y|_{R_\equiv} \triangleright |x|_{R_\equiv}$. So $\langle f_i(x), f_i(y) \rangle \in R'_{\leq,defect}$ and $\langle f_i(y), f_i(x) \rangle \in R'_{\leq,defect}$. Hence, $\langle f_i(x), f_i(y) \rangle \in R'_\equiv$.

(II.2) Assume $\langle x, y \rangle \in R_\leq$. If $|x|_\bowtie \in NC(\mathcal{M})$ or $\langle x, y \rangle \notin \bowtie$, then for every $j \in \mathbb{N}$, $\langle f_i(x), f_j(y) \rangle \in R'_{\leq,ok}$ and therefore $\langle f_i(x), f_j(y) \rangle \in R'_\leq$. Otherwise, $\langle f_i(x), f_j(y) \rangle \in R'_{\leq,defect}$ for some $j > i$. For instance, take $j = i + 1$. Then $\langle f_i(x), f_{i+1}(y) \rangle \in R'_{\leq,defect}$ and therefore $\langle f_i(x), f_{i+1}(y) \rangle \in R'_\leq$.
Condition (IV) is a consequence of conditions (I), (II), and (III).   *Q.E.D.*

Consequently, COP is a copying from $\mathcal{M}$ into $\mathcal{M}'$. In order to prove completeness, it remains to show that $\mathcal{M}'$ is an IL-model. Actually, as stated in Lemma 7.3.5, $\mathcal{M}'$ is almost an IL-model except that condition (I10) does not hold. However, this can be easily repaired by considering a disjoint union of two isomorphic copies of $\mathcal{M}'$.

Lemma 7.3.5. $\mathcal{M}'$ *satisfies the conditions (I1)–(I9).*

Proof. The conditions (I3), (I7), (I9) and reflexivity of $R'_\leq$ can be easily checked.

(I2) We show that $R'_\leq$ is transitive. So assume $\langle f_i(x), f_j(y) \rangle \in R'_\leq$ and $\langle f_j(y), f_k(z) \rangle \in R'_\leq$.
Case I2.1: $\langle f_i(x), f_j(y) \rangle \in R'_{\leq,ok}$ and $\langle f_j(y), f_k(z) \rangle \in R'_{\leq,ok}$.
Case I2.1.1: $|x|_\bowtie \in NC(\mathcal{M})$.
By definition of $R'_{\leq,ok}$, we have $\langle x, y \rangle \in R_\leq$ and $\langle y, z \rangle \in R_\leq$. By transitivity of $R_\leq$, $\langle x, z \rangle \in R_\leq$. So, $\langle f_i(x), f_k(z) \rangle \in R'_{\leq,ok}$.
Case I2.1.2: $|x|_\bowtie \notin NC(\mathcal{M})$ and $\langle x, y \rangle \notin \bowtie$.
We show that $\langle x, z \rangle \notin \bowtie$ so that $\langle f_i(x), f_k(x) \rangle \in R'_{\leq,ok}$. Suppose $\langle x, z \rangle \in \bowtie$. Hence $\langle z, x \rangle \in R_\leq$. By transitivity of $R_\leq$, $\langle z, y \rangle \in R_\leq$. Since $\langle f_j(y), f_k(z) \rangle \in R'_{\leq,ok}$, $\langle y, z \rangle \in R_\leq$. By transitivity of $R_\leq$, we get $\langle y, x \rangle \in R_\leq$, a contradiction.

Case 12.2: $\langle f_i(x), f_j(y)\rangle \in R'_{\leq,ok}$ and $\langle f_j(y), f_k(z)\rangle \in R'_{\leq,defect}$.

By Lemma 7.3.4(II.1), $\langle x, y\rangle \in R_{\leq}$ and $\langle y, z\rangle \in R_{\leq}$. By transitivity of $R_{\leq}$, $\langle x, z\rangle \in R_{\leq}$. If $|x|_{\bowtie} \in NC(\mathcal{M})$, then $\langle f_i(x), f_k(z)\rangle \in R'_{\leq,ok}$. Otherwise, $\langle x, y\rangle \notin \bowtie$ and therefore $\langle y, x\rangle \notin R_{\leq}$. Since $\langle f_j(y), f_k(z)\rangle \in \bar{R}'_{\leq,defect}$, $|y|_{\bowtie} \notin NC(\mathcal{M})$ and $\langle y, z\rangle \in \bowtie$. So $\langle x, z\rangle \notin \bowtie$, otherwise $\langle y, x\rangle \in R_{\leq}$ by transitivity of $R_{\leq}$, which would lead to a contradiction. So again $\langle f_i(x), f_k(z)\rangle \in R'_{\leq,ok}$.

Case 12.3: $\langle f_i(x), f_j(y)\rangle \in R'_{\leq,defect}$ and $\langle f_j(y), f_k(z)\rangle \in R'_{\leq,ok}$.

Again, $\langle x, z\rangle \in R_{\leq}$. We show that $\langle z, x\rangle \notin R_{\leq}$. Suppose $\langle z, x\rangle \in R_{\leq}$. So $\langle x, z\rangle \in \bowtie$. Now we have to consider the following cases.

Case 12.3.1: $\langle y, z\rangle \notin \bowtie$.

By transitivity of $\bowtie$, $\langle x, z\rangle \notin \bowtie$, a contradiction.

Case 12.3.2: $\langle y, z\rangle \in \bowtie$ and $|y|_{\bowtie} \in NC(\mathcal{M})$.

So $|y|_{\bowtie} = |z|_{\bowtie} \in NC(\mathcal{M})$ and $|x|_{\bowtie} \in NC(\mathcal{M})$, which leads to a contradiction, since $\langle f_i(x), f_j(y)\rangle \in R'_{\leq,defect}$.

Case 12.4: $\langle f_i(x), f_j(y)\rangle \in R'_{\leq,defect}$ and $\langle f_j(y), f_k(z)\rangle \in R'_{\leq,defect}$.

One can easily show that $\langle f_i(x), f_k(z)\rangle \in R'_{\leq,defect}$ by using the transitivity of $\bowtie$ and $\triangleright$.

(I1) is a consequence of (I2) and of the definition of $R'_{\equiv}$.

(I4) Assume $\langle f_i(x), f_j(y)\rangle \in R'_{\sigma}$ and $\langle f_i(x), f_k(z)\rangle \in R'_{\leq}$. We deduce that $\langle x, y\rangle \in R_{\sigma}$ and $\langle x, z\rangle \in R_{\leq}$ by Lemma 7.3.4(IV.1). By (I4) in $\mathcal{M}$, we get $\langle z, y\rangle \in R_{\sigma}$. By the definition of R'_{σ}, we obtain $\langle f_i(z), f_j(y)\rangle \in R'_{\sigma}$.

(I5) Assume $f_j(y) \in D'$ and $\langle f_i(x), f_j(y)\rangle \in R'_{\leq}$. So $y \in D$ (by the definition of D') and $\langle x, y\rangle \in R_{\leq}$ by Lemma 7.3.4(IV.1). By (I5), $x \in D$. So $f_i(x) \in D'$.

(I6) Assume $f_i(x) \in D'$ and $\langle f_i(x), f_j(y)\rangle \in R'_{\sigma}$. By (I3) in $\mathcal{M}'$, $\langle f_i(x), f_i(x)\rangle \in R'_{\sigma}$ and therefore $\langle x, x\rangle \in R_{\sigma}$. By Lemma 7.3.3, $|x|_{\bowtie} \in NC(\mathcal{M})$. By Lemma 7.3.4(IV.1), we get $\langle x, y\rangle \in R_{\sigma}$ and $x \in D$. By (I6) in $\mathcal{M}$, $\langle x, y\rangle \in R_{\leq}$. So $\langle f_i(x), f_j(y)\rangle \in R'_{\leq,ok}$.

(I8) Assume $f_i(x) \in D'$, $f_j(y) \in D'$, and $\langle f_i(x), f_j(y)\rangle \in R'_{\sigma}$. By symmetry of R'_{σ}, $\langle f_j(y), f_i(x)\rangle \in R'_{\sigma}$. From the proof of (I6), we get that $\langle f_i(x), f_j(y)\rangle \in R'_{\leq,ok}$ and $\langle f_j(y), f_i(x)\rangle \in R'_{\leq,ok}$ which implies the following: $\langle f_i(x), f_j(y)\rangle \in R'_{\leq}$, $\langle f_j(y), f_i(x)\rangle \in R'_{\leq}$, and $\langle f_i(x), f_j(y)\rangle \in R'_{\equiv}$.   Q.E.D.

$\mathcal{M}'$ is almost an IL-model with the exception that (I10) does not necessarily hold. By taking a disjoint union of two isomorphic copies of $\mathcal{M}'$, say $\mathcal{M}''$, one can easily show that $\mathcal{M}''$ satisfies the conditions (I1)–(I10) and there is a copying of $\mathcal{M}$ into $\mathcal{M}''$. Consequently, we have the following theorem:

Theorem 7.3.3. Let $\mathcal{M} = \langle W, R_{\equiv}, R_{\leq}, R_{\sigma}, D, m\rangle$ be an IL'-model. Then there is an IL-model $\mathcal{M}'' = \langle W'', R''_{\equiv}, R''_{\leq}, R''_{\sigma}, D'', m''\rangle$ and a copying of $\mathcal{M}$ into $\mathcal{M}''$.

As a corollary, we obtain the following theorem.

Theorem 7.3.4. VAL(IL) = VAL(IL') *and* HIL *is a proof system for* IL.

7.4 SIM: a Logic for Reasoning About Relative Similarity

The logic SIM is a Rare-logic with both object and parameter nominals. Consequently, in its language we can explicitly represent individual objects and individual attributes of an information system. Sets of attributes and their Boolean combinations are represented by the standard parameter expressions. As usual, formulae represent sets of objects. The modal connectives of the logic are based on relative similarity relations determined by sets of attributes. These connectives represent the approximation operations of the forms (1) and (2) defined in Sect. 4.8.

7.4.1 Language and Semantics

The logic SIM is a standard Rare-logic (see Sect. 5.4.2) satisfying the following conditions.

⋆ The set of basic parameter expressions is $P_0 = \text{VARP} \cup \text{VARSP} \cup \{\bot\}$ where VARP is a countable (either finite or infinite) set of parameter nominals interpreted as singleton sets, VARSP is a countably infinite set of variables representing sets of parameters, and $\bot$ is a constant interpreted as the empty set.

⋆ The set O_M of modal operators is empty and the set M of modal expressions coincides with M_0.

⋆ The set of basic formulae is $\text{FOR}_0 = \text{VARE} \cup \text{VARSE}$ where VARE is a countable set of object nominals representing individual objects (entity variables) and VARSE is a countable set of variables representing sets of objects (sets of entity variables).

⋆ The set of logical connectives is $O_{\text{FOR}} = \{\neg, \wedge\} \cup \{[a] : a \in M\}$.

For the sake of simplicity, for every $A \in P$, the modal connectives are written [A] instead of [r(A)]. A formula ϕ is said to be *non-degenerate* $\overset{\text{def}}{\Leftrightarrow}$ either $\text{VARP}(\phi) \neq \emptyset$ or $\text{VARSP}(\phi) \neq \emptyset$. Otherwise, ϕ is said to be *degenerate*.

Definition 7.4.1. *A P-meaning function for SIM is a map* $m : P \rightarrow \mathcal{P}(PAR)$ *such that m is a standard P-meaning function (see Sect. 5.4.1) that satisfies the additional conditions:*

⋆ *for all* $A_1, A_2 \in \text{VARP}$, *if* $A_1 \neq A_2$, *then* $m(A_1) \neq m(A_2)$;
⋆ *if* $A \in \text{VARP}$, *then* $m(A) = \{p\}$ *for some* $p \in PAR$;
⋆ $m(\bot) = \emptyset$.

Let PAR be a non-empty set whose cardinality is the same as the cardinality of VARP. PAR is assumed to be a common set of parameters for all the SIM-models.

The SIM-models are the structures of the form $\langle W, (\sigma_P)_{P \subseteq PAR}, m \rangle$, where

$\star$ W is a non-empty set;
$\star$ $(\sigma_P)_{P \subseteq PAR}$ is a family of binary relations on W such that:
  $*$ σ_P is reflexive and symmetric for every $\emptyset \neq P \subseteq PAR$;
  $*$ $\sigma_{P \cup Q} = \sigma_P \cap \sigma_Q$ for all $P, Q \subseteq PAR$ (condition (C_1));
  $*$ $\sigma_\emptyset = W \times W$ (condition (C'_1));
$\star$ $m : \mathrm{FOR}_0 \cup \mathrm{P} \cup \mathrm{M} \to \mathcal{P}(W) \cup \mathcal{P}(PAR) \cup \mathcal{P}(W \times W)$ is a map such that
  $*$ $m(\mathrm{x})$ is a singleton set in $\mathcal{P}(W)$ for every $\mathrm{x} \in \mathrm{VARE}$;
  $*$ $m(\mathrm{p}) \subseteq W$ for every $\mathrm{p} \in \mathrm{VARSE}$;
  $*$ m restricted to P is a P-meaning function for SIM whose range is $\mathcal{P}(PAR)$;
  $*$ $m(\{A\}) = \sigma_{m(A)}$ for every $A \in \mathrm{P}$.

Since the set of parameter nominals is countably infinite, and any two different parameter nominals are interpreted as different parameters, each model has a countably infinite set of parameters. The relations in the SIM-models are strong tolerance relations. As usual, for all $A, B \in \mathrm{P}$, we write $A \sim \perp$ [resp. $A \sim B$] if for every P-meaning function m, $m(A) = \emptyset$ [resp. $m(A) = m(B)$]. The relation $\sim$ on the set $\mathrm{P} \times \mathrm{P}$ is decidable.

Let SIM$'$ be a logic that differs from SIM in the following:

$\star$ the set of parameters is not necessarily the same in every model;
$\star$ VARP is countably infinite.

The logic SIM$'$ is an auxiliary logic which will be used in the decidability proof of SIM (see Sect. 11.3.2)

Lemma 7.4.1. *For every $\phi \in \mathrm{FOR}$, ϕ is SIM-valid iff $\mathrm{x} \Rightarrow \phi$ is SIM-valid for every $\mathrm{x} \in \mathrm{VARE} \setminus \mathrm{VARE}(\phi)$. The same result holds for SIM$'$.*

Proof. ($\to$) Assume that ϕ is SIM-valid and suppose that for some $\mathrm{x} \in \mathrm{VARE} \setminus \mathrm{VARE}(\phi)$, $\mathrm{x} \Rightarrow \phi$ is not SIM-valid. So there is a SIM-model $\mathcal{M} = \langle W, (\sigma_P)_{P \subseteq PAR}, m \rangle$ and an $e \in W$ such that $\mathcal{M}, e \models \mathrm{x} \wedge \neg \phi$. In particular, $\mathcal{M}, e \models \neg\phi$ and therefore ϕ is not SIM-valid, a contradiction.
($\leftarrow$) Assume that $\mathrm{x} \Rightarrow \phi$ is SIM-valid for every $\mathrm{x} \in \mathrm{VARE} \setminus \mathrm{VARE}(\phi)$ and suppose that ϕ is not SIM-valid. So there is a SIM-model

$$\mathcal{M} = \langle W, (\sigma_P)_{P \subseteq PAR}, m \rangle$$

and an $e \in W$ such that $\mathcal{M}, e \models \neg\phi$. Let $\mathcal{M}'$ be obtained from $\mathcal{M}$ by assuming that $m(\mathrm{x}) = e$ for some $\mathrm{x} \in \mathrm{VARE} \setminus \mathrm{VARE}(\phi)$. It is not difficult to check that $\mathcal{M}'$ is a SIM-model. We have $\mathcal{M}', e \models \mathrm{x}$ and since x does not occur in ϕ, $\mathcal{M}', e \models \neg\phi$. Hence $\mathcal{M}', e \models \mathrm{x} \wedge \neg\phi$ and therefore $\mathrm{x} \Rightarrow \phi$ is not SIM-valid, a contradiction. $\hspace{2em}$ Q.E.D.

Example 7.4.1. Consider a SIM-formula

$$[E_2 \cap -E_2]\mathrm{x} \Rightarrow [E_1 \cup C_1](\mathrm{x} \vee \mathrm{p}),$$

where E_1, E_2 are parameter nominals and x is an object nominal. The modal connective $[E_2 \cap -E_2]$ is a universal modal connective in SIM.

7.4.2 Normal Forms of SIM-formulae

Now we present a normal form of SIM-formulae that is used in the forthcoming proof system for SIM. Let $X = \{C_1, \ldots, C_n\}$, $n \geq 0$, be a set of parameter constants and $Y = \{E_1, \ldots, E_l\}$, $l \geq 0$, be a set of parameter nominals. The set $\text{Comp}(X, Y)$ of $\langle X, Y \rangle$-*components* is defined as in Sect. 5.4 except that if $l = n = 0$, then $\text{Comp}(X, Y) \stackrel{\text{def}}{=} \{\bot, -\bot\}$. Let A be a parameter expression built from $X \cup Y \cup \{\bot\}$ with the operations from O_P. The normal form of A, $N_{X,Y}(A)$, is defined as follows:

$$N_{X,Y}(A) \stackrel{\text{def}}{=} \begin{cases} \bot \text{ if } A \sim \bot; \\ A_{k_1,k_1'} \cup \ldots \cup A_{k_u,k_u'} \text{ if } n, l \geq 1 \text{ and} \\ \quad A \sim A_{k_1,k_1'} \cup \ldots \cup A_{k_u,k_u'}; \\ B_{k_1} \cup \ldots \cup B_{k_u} \text{ if } A \sim B_{k_1} \cup \ldots \cup B_{k_u}, n \geq 1, \text{ and } l = 0; \\ D_{k_1} \cup \ldots \cup D_{k_u} \text{ if } A \sim D_{k_1} \cup \ldots \cup D_{k_u}, l \geq 1, \text{ and } n = 0; \\ -\bot \text{ if } P_0(A) = \{\bot\} \text{ and } A \sim \bot. \end{cases}$$

Observe that this definition captures all the forms of A. $N_{X,Y}(A)$ is often written $N(A)$. If $n \geq 1$ and $l = 0$, by abusing the notation we may write $A_{k,k'}$ instead of B_k. If $l \geq 1$ and $n = 0$, we may write $A_{k,k'}$ instead of $B_{k'}$.

Let ϕ be a SIM-formula. The normal form of ϕ, $N(\phi)$, is obtained from ϕ by replacing every occurrence of A by $N_{P_0(\phi),\text{VARP}(\phi)}(A)$. We shall write $\text{Comp}(\phi)$ instead of $\text{Comp}(\text{VARP}(\phi), P_0(\phi))$.

Lemma 7.4.2. *For every SIM-formula* ϕ, $\phi \Leftrightarrow N(\phi)$ *is SIM-valid.*

Clearly, the definition of $\sim$ guarantees that $\phi \Leftrightarrow N(\phi)$ is SIM-valid.

Example 7.4.2. Let $\phi = [E_1]p \Rightarrow [E_1 \cup E_2 \cup C_1]p$. We have $\text{VARSP}(\phi) = \{C_1\}$ and $\text{VARP}(\phi) = \{E_1, E_2\}$. The set $\text{Comp}(\phi)$ of components consists of the following expressions:

* $A_{0,0} = C_1 \cap -E_1 \cap -E_2$;
* $A_{1,0} = -C_1 \cap -E_1 \cap -E_2$;
* $A_{0,1} = C_1 \cap E_1$;
* $A_{1,1} = -C_1 \cap E_1$;
* $A_{0,2} = C_1 \cap E_2$;
* $A_{1,2} = -C_1 \cap E_2$.

Moreover, $N(E_1) = A_{0,1} \cup A_{1,1}$ and

$$N(E_1 \cup E_2 \cup C_1) = A_{0,0} \cup A_{0,1} \cup A_{1,1} \cup A_{0,2} \cup A_{1,2}.$$

7.4.3 A Rasiowa–Sikorski-style Proof System for SIM

In the rest of this section, let SIM be a similarity logic for some countable set PAR. If the cardinality of PAR is finite, say N, then without any loss of generality we may assume that $PAR = \{1, \ldots, N\}$ and $\text{VARP} = \{E_1, \ldots, E_N\}$.

In this section we define a Rasiowa–Sikorski proof system RS(SIM) for the logic SIM. This type of system is usually known as "dual tableaux". The basic objects of the system are sequences of formulae interpreted as disjunctions of their elements at the metalevel. The rules are applied to construct a decomposition tree for a formula by breaking it down into sequences of simpler formulae. However, unlike in standard tableaux-style calculi, the formula to be proved is not negated at the beginning of the construction of a proof. For every sequence Γ of formulae, we write $\phi \in \Gamma$ if the formula ϕ occurs in the sequence Γ.

Definition 7.4.2. *A sequence of formulae* $\Gamma = \phi_1, \ldots, \phi_k$, $k \geq 1$, *is said to be true in a SIM-model* $\mathcal{M}$ *(in symbols* $\mathcal{M} \models \Gamma$*)* $\overset{\text{def}}{\Leftrightarrow}$ $\mathcal{M} \models \phi_i$ *for some* $i \in \{1, \ldots, k\}$. *The sequence* Γ *is valid (in symbols* $\models \Gamma$*)* $\overset{\text{def}}{\Leftrightarrow}$ $\mathcal{M} \models \Gamma$ *for every SIM-model* $\mathcal{M}$. *A model* $\mathcal{M}$ *falsifies* Γ $\overset{\text{def}}{\Leftrightarrow}$ Γ *is not true in* $\mathcal{M}$.

In the proof system, the role of axioms is played by the fundamental sequences. A sequence Γ of formulae is said to be *fundamental* $\overset{\text{def}}{\Leftrightarrow}$ Γ contains either the formula:

$\star$ $x \Rightarrow x$;

or one of the following pairs of formulae:

$\star$ $x \Rightarrow \phi$, $x \Rightarrow \neg\phi$;
$\star$ $x \Rightarrow [A_{k_1,k'}]\neg y, x' \Rightarrow [A_{k_2,k'}]\neg y'$, $k_1 \neq k_2$,

where $x, y, x', y' \in$ VARE, $\phi \in$ FOR, $A_{k_1,k'}$, and $A_{k_2,k'}$ are $\langle X, Y \rangle$-components for some set X of parameter constants, and, for some set Y of parameter nominals, $k_1, k_2 \in \{0, \ldots, 2^{\text{card}(X)} - 1\}$, $k' \in \{0, \ldots, \text{card}(Y)\}$.

Lemma 7.4.3. *Every fundamental sequence is valid.*

Proof. The proof is by an easy verification. By way of example we show that $x \Rightarrow [A_{k_1,k'}]\neg y, x' \Rightarrow [A_{k_2,k'}]\neg y'$ $(k_1 \neq k_2)$ is valid.

Let $\mathcal{M} = \langle W, (\sigma_P)_{P \subseteq PAR}, m \rangle$ be a SIM-model. Either $m(A_{k_1,k'}) = \emptyset$ or $m(A_{k_2,k'}) = \emptyset$, since $k_1 \neq k_2$. So either $\sigma_{m(A_{k_1,k'})} = W \times W$ or $\sigma_{m(A_{k_2,k'})} = W \times W$. Therefore either $\mathcal{M} \models x \Rightarrow [A_{k_1,k'}]\neg y$ or $\mathcal{M} \models x \Rightarrow [A_{k_2,k'}]\neg y$. Q.E.D.

Definition 7.4.3. *A formula* ϕ *is indecomposable* $\overset{\text{def}}{\Leftrightarrow}$ ϕ *has one of the following forms:*

$\star$ $x \Rightarrow y$, $x \Rightarrow \neg y$, $x \Rightarrow p$, $x \Rightarrow \neg p$ *for some* $x, y \in$ VARE *and* $p \in$ VARSE;
$\star$ $x \Rightarrow [A]\neg y$, $x \Rightarrow \neg[A]\neg y$, *where* $x, y \in$ VARE *and* A *is either* $\perp$, *or* $-\perp$, *or a component of the form:*
  $\ast$ $A_{k,k'}$ *if* PAR *is infinite;*
  $\ast$ $A_{k,k'}$, $k' > 0$ *if* PAR *is finite.*

Otherwise, the formula ϕ is said to be decomposable. A sequence of formulae is said to be indecomposable $\overset{\text{def}}{\Leftrightarrow}$ all of its elements are indecomposable.

The decomposition rules of the Rasiowa–Sikorski calculus for SIM are given in Table 7.1. If PAR is finite, we add the rules from Table 7.2. In Table 7.1 and in Table 7.2, Γ' is a sequence of *indecomposable* formulae. Actually this assumption about Γ' is not needed for completeness but it will be useful for defining a fair systematic procedure for showing completeness. Fairness is the property that whenever a rule can be applied in an essential way, then after a finite amount of steps, the rule is eventually applied.

The rules $(sym_=)$, (sub), (sym_A), $(refl_A)$, and $(univ_\perp)$ are called *expansion rules*. Indeed, if an expansion rule applied to a sequence Γ leads to Γ', then every formula occurring in Γ occurs in Γ' as well. A sequence Γ is said to be *closed under expansion rules* $\overset{\text{def}}{\Leftrightarrow}$ if an expansion rule is applied to a sequence Γ leading to a sequence Γ', then every formula occurring in Γ' occurs in Γ as well. All the other rules are called *replacement rules*. The following observations enable us to interpret the presented Rasiowa–Sikorski proof system as a tableaux-like system. First, every formula $x \Rightarrow \phi$ can be viewed as a prefixed formula $x : \mathbf{F}\phi$ which states that the object x falsifies the formula ϕ. Second, a comma in a sequence of formulae should be interpreted as a conjunction at the metalevel. In the Rasiowa–Sikorski system there are no counterparts to the formulae signed with $\mathbf{T}$ (truth); therefore there is a rule for each connective and for the negation of the connective. Lemma 7.4.4 provides more insight in this direction.

Lemma 7.4.4. *Let $\mathcal{M} = \langle W, (\sigma_P)_{P \subseteq PAR}, m \rangle$ be a SIM-model. Then:*

(I) $x \Rightarrow \phi$ is true in $\mathcal{M}$ iff $m(x) \in \{e \in W : \mathcal{M}, e \models \phi\}$;
(II) $x \Rightarrow \neg\phi$ is true in $\mathcal{M}$ iff $m(x) \notin \{e \in W : \mathcal{M}, e \models \phi\}$;
(III) $x \Rightarrow \neg[A]\neg y$ is true in $\mathcal{M}$ iff $\langle m(x), m(y) \rangle \in \sigma_{m(A)}$;
(IV) $x \Rightarrow [A]\neg y$ is true in $\mathcal{M}$ iff $\langle m(x), m(y) \rangle \notin \sigma_{m(A)}$.

The rules $(refl_A)$ and (sym_A) guarantee reflexivity and symmetry of the relations, respectively. The $(sym_=)$-rule encodes the symmetry of equality. The rule (sub) can be read as follows: if x and y are interpreted by a meaning function m as the same object and ϕ is not satisfied by $m(y)$, then ϕ is not satisfied by $m(x)$. Moreover, (sub) captures transitivity of equality by taking ϕ of the form $\neg z$ for $z \in$ VARE. There is no need to introduce a rule for reflexivity of equality since it is reflected by the fundamental sequence $x \Rightarrow x$.

Observe that expansion rules can be also applied to indecomposable sequences.

Lemma 7.4.5. *For every decomposition rule, the upper sequence is valid iff all the lower sequences are valid.*

$$\frac{\Gamma', x \Rightarrow \phi \wedge \psi, \Gamma''}{\Gamma', x \Rightarrow \phi, \Gamma'' \mid \Gamma', x \Rightarrow \psi, \Gamma''} \ (\wedge) \qquad \frac{\Gamma', x \Rightarrow \neg(\phi \wedge \psi), \Gamma''}{\Gamma', x \Rightarrow \neg\phi, x \Rightarrow \neg\psi, \Gamma''} \ (\neg\wedge)$$

$$\frac{\Gamma', x \Rightarrow \neg\neg\phi, \Gamma''}{\Gamma', x \Rightarrow \phi, \Gamma''} \ (\neg\neg)$$

$$\frac{\Gamma', x \Rightarrow \neg[A]\phi, \Gamma''}{\Gamma', x \Rightarrow \neg[A]\phi, y \Rightarrow \neg\phi, \Gamma''} \ (\neg[A])$$

where $x \Rightarrow [A]\neg y \in \Gamma', \Gamma''$.

$$\frac{\Gamma', x \Rightarrow [A]\phi, \Gamma''}{\Gamma', x \Rightarrow [A]\neg y, y \Rightarrow \phi, \Gamma''} \ ([A])$$

where $y \in$ VARE does not occur in the upper sequence and ϕ is not of the form $\neg z$ with $z \in$ VARE

$$\frac{\Gamma', x \Rightarrow \neg[A \cup B]\neg y, \Gamma''}{\Gamma', x \Rightarrow \neg[A]\neg y, \Gamma'' \mid \Gamma', x \Rightarrow \neg[B]\neg y, \Gamma''} \ (\neg\cup)$$

$$\frac{\Gamma', x \Rightarrow [A \cup B]\neg y, \Gamma''}{\Gamma', x \Rightarrow [A]\neg y, x \Rightarrow [B]\neg y, \Gamma''} \ (\cup)$$

$$\frac{\Gamma', x \Rightarrow \neg y, \Gamma''}{\Gamma', \Gamma'', x \Rightarrow \neg y, y \Rightarrow \neg x} \ (sym_=) \qquad \frac{\Gamma', x \Rightarrow \neg y, \Gamma'', y \Rightarrow \phi, \Gamma'''}{\Gamma', \Gamma'', \Gamma''', x \Rightarrow \neg y, y \Rightarrow \phi, x \Rightarrow \phi} \ (sub)$$

$$\frac{\Gamma', x \Rightarrow [A]\neg y, \Gamma''}{\Gamma', \Gamma'', x \Rightarrow [A]\neg y, y \Rightarrow [A]\neg x} \ (sym_A)$$

$$\frac{\Gamma}{x \Rightarrow [A]\neg x, \Gamma} \ (refl_A) \qquad \frac{\Gamma}{x \Rightarrow [\bot]\neg y, \Gamma} \ (univ_\bot)$$

where $x \in \Gamma \cap$ VARE, A occurs in Γ, $x \Rightarrow [A]\neg x \notin \Gamma$

Table 7.1. Decomposition rules for RS(SIM)

Proof. By way of example, consider the $(\neg[A])$-rule. Assume (i) $\Gamma', x \Rightarrow \neg[A]\phi, \Gamma''$ is valid, that is for every SIM-model $\mathcal{M} = \langle W, (\sigma_P)_{P \subseteq PAR}, m \rangle$, there is a $\psi \in \Gamma', x \Rightarrow \neg[A]\phi, \Gamma''$ such that $\mathcal{M} \models \psi$. If $x \Rightarrow [A]\neg y$ belongs to Γ', Γ'' and ϕ is not of the form $\neg z$ for some $z \in$ VARE, we show that (ii) for every SIM-model $\mathcal{M} = \langle W, (\sigma_P)_{P \subseteq PAR}, m \rangle$, there is a $\psi \in \Gamma', x \Rightarrow \neg[A]\phi, \Gamma'', y \Rightarrow \neg\phi$ such that $\mathcal{M} \models \psi$. This is immediate, since $\Gamma', x \Rightarrow \neg[A]\phi, \Gamma''$ is a subsequence of $\Gamma', x \Rightarrow \neg[A]\phi, \Gamma'', y \Rightarrow \neg\phi$. Now assume (ii) and we show (i). Let $\mathcal{M} = \langle W, (\sigma_P)_{P \subseteq PAR}, m \rangle$ be a SIM-

If *PAR* is finite, then we add the following rules:

$$\frac{\varGamma', x \Rightarrow \neg[A_{k,0}]\neg y, \varGamma''}{\varGamma', x \Rightarrow \neg[\bigcup_{E \in \text{VARP} \setminus \{E_1, \ldots, E_l\}} B_k \cap E]\neg y, \varGamma''}$$

$$\frac{\varGamma', x \Rightarrow [A_{k,0}]\neg y, \varGamma''}{\varGamma', x \Rightarrow [\bigcup_{E \in \text{VARP} \setminus \{E_1, \ldots, E_l\}} B_k \cap E]\neg y, \varGamma''}$$

where the components $A_{k,0}$ and B_k are defined from some set $X = \{C_1, \ldots, C_n\}$ of parameter constants and from some set $Y = \{E_1, \ldots, E_l\}$ of parameter nominals and $k \in \{0, \ldots, 2^n - 1\}$

Table 7.2. Additional rules for RS(SIM) with *PAR* finite

model. If there is a $\psi \in \varGamma', x \Rightarrow \neg[A]\phi, \varGamma''$ such that $\mathcal{M} \models \psi$, then (i) follows. Otherwise, assume $\mathcal{M} \models y \Rightarrow \neg\phi$ and $\mathcal{M} \not\models x \Rightarrow [A]\phi$. So for every $w \in \sigma_{m(A)}(m(x))$, $\mathcal{M}, w \models \phi$. Since $\mathcal{M} \not\models x \Rightarrow [A]\neg y$ and $x \Rightarrow [A]\neg y \in \varGamma', \varGamma''$, we have $m(y) \in \sigma_{m(A)}(m(x))$. So $\mathcal{M}, m(y) \models \phi$, that is $\mathcal{M} \models y \Rightarrow \phi$, a contradiction.   *Q.E.D.*

The *decomposition tree* of a formula ϕ has at its root the formula $x \Rightarrow N(\phi)$, where x is any member of VARE \ VARE(ϕ) and $N(\phi)$ is the normal form of ϕ as described in Sect. 7.4.2. We define a strategy which enables us to identify the unique rule that has to be applied in a current step of construction of a decomposition tree. In this way, we transform a non-deterministic procedure of applying the rules with no specific order, into a deterministic procedure.

Definition 7.4.4. *Let $\varGamma$ be a sequence of formulae. By the rule selected for application to $\varGamma$, we mean a decomposition rule r from Table 7.1 such that at least one of the following conditions is satisfied:*

⋆ *r is a replacement rule applicable to $\varGamma$;*
⋆ *only expansion rules are applicable to $\varGamma$, and r is an expansion rule such that:*
  * *the application of r yields some new formula that does not occur in $\varGamma$;*
  * *there is no expansion rule with the above property which can be applied to a formula or a pair of formulae in $\varGamma$ occurring to the left of the formula or formulae to which r can be applied.*

In the sequel, we assume that VARE is a well-ordered set. If new elements of VARE are to be introduced during the process of application of the rules, then we respect this ordering in selecting the variables.

Definition 7.4.5. *The decomposition tree of a formula $\phi \in$ FOR, denoted $DT(\phi)$, is a FOR*-labelled tree with the nodes labelled by sequences of formulae. $DT(\phi)$ is defined inductively as follows:*

⋆ *The root of $DT(\phi)$ is labelled by* x $\Rightarrow$ N(ϕ), *where* x *is the first variable in* VARE *which does not occur in* ϕ, *and* N(ϕ) *is the normal form of* ϕ;

⋆ *Let* w *be a leaf of the part of $DT(\phi)$ constructed up to now, and suppose that* w *occurs on a branch* BR *of this tree. Let a sequence* Γ *of formulae be the label of* w. *Then:*

* *we terminate the branch* BR *at the node* w *if one of the following conditions is satisfied:*

  · Γ *is a fundamental sequence of formulae;*
  · Γ *is an indecomposable sequence of formulae, and no expansion rule is applicable to* Γ;
  · Γ *is an indecomposable sequence of formulae, and each expansion rule applicable to* Γ *adds no new formula to* Γ;

* *otherwise, we expand the branch* BR *by attaching to* w:

  · *a single child labelled by* Γ_1, *if the unique rule applicable to* Γ *is of the form* $\frac{\Gamma}{\Gamma_1}$;
  · *two children labelled by* Γ_1 *and* Γ_2, *respectively, if the unique rule applicable to* Γ *is of the form* $\frac{\Gamma}{\Gamma_1|\Gamma_2}$.

A sequence Γ is *terminal* in $DT(\phi)$ $\overset{\text{def}}{\Leftrightarrow}$ it is a label of a leaf.

The decomposition tree of ϕ is analogous to a proof obtained by a systematic procedure for tableaux-style or sequent-style calculi. Indeed, the decomposition tree is related to the proof search and it can be seen as a strategy to get a saturated structure. It is easy to see that a node w of $DT(\phi)$ labelled by Γ is a leaf iff Γ is either fundamental or indecomposable and closed under all the expansion rules. A formula $\phi \in$ FOR is said to be *provable* in RS(SIM) $\overset{\text{def}}{\Leftrightarrow}$ $DT(\phi)$ is finite and all of its terminal sequences are fundamental, that is $DT(\phi)$ is a proof of ϕ. The set of provable formulae is denoted by THM(RS(SIM)).

Theorem 7.4.1. *(Soundness Theorem)* THM(RS(SIM)) $\subseteq$ VAL(SIM).

Proof. The proof follows from Lemma 7.4.3 and Lemma 7.4.5.   *Q.E.D.*

The following lemma is a cornerstone of the completeness proof of the proof system RS(SIM).

Lemma 7.4.6. *For every formula ϕ, if a terminal sequence of $DT(\phi)$ is valid, then it is fundamental.*

Proof. Suppose Γ is a terminal sequence which is not fundamental. Since Γ is terminal, Γ is indecomposable and closed under all expansion rules. Each element of Γ has one of the following forms:

$$\text{x} \Rightarrow \neg\text{y}, \quad \text{x} \Rightarrow \text{y}, \quad \text{x} \Rightarrow \neg\text{p}, \quad \text{x} \Rightarrow \text{p}, \quad \text{x} \Rightarrow \neg[\text{A}]\neg\text{y}, \quad \text{x} \Rightarrow \neg[\text{A}]\text{y},$$

where x, y $\in$ VARE, p $\in$ VARSE, and A $\in$ Comp$(\phi) \cup \{\bot, -\bot\}$.
Let VARP$(\phi) = \{E_1, \ldots, E_l\}$, $l \geq 1$ and VARSP$(\phi) = \{C_1, \ldots, C_n\}$, $n \geq 1$. Each term A occurring in Γ has one of the following forms:

⋆ $-\perp$ if ϕ is a degenerate formula such that $\perp$ occurs in ϕ but no element of VARP ∪ VARSP occurs in ϕ;
⋆ $A_{k,k'} \in \text{Comp}(\phi)$ if PAR is infinite and ϕ is non-degenerate;
⋆ $A_{k,k'}$ with $k' > 0$ if PAR is finite and ϕ is non-degenerate.

We construct a model $\mathcal{M}$ such that Γ is not true in $\mathcal{M}$. Let $R \subseteq \text{VARE} \times \text{VARE}$ be a binary relation defined as follows

$$\langle x, y \rangle \in R \overset{\text{def}}{\Leftrightarrow} x \Rightarrow \neg y \text{ belongs to } \Gamma.$$

Since Γ is closed under $(sym_=)$ and (sub), R is symmetric and transitive. So

$$R^* \overset{\text{def}}{=} R \cup \{\langle x, x \rangle : x \in \text{VARE}\}$$

is an equivalence relation.

The structure $\mathcal{M} = \langle W, (\sigma_P)_{P \subseteq PAR}, m \rangle$ is defined as follows:

⋆ W is the set of equivalence classes of R^*;
⋆ for every $x \in \text{VARE}$, $m(x) \overset{\text{def}}{=} \{y : xR^*y\}$;
⋆ for every $p \in \text{VARSE}$, $m(p) \overset{\text{def}}{=} \{m(x) : x \Rightarrow \neg p \in \Gamma\}$;
⋆ $m(\perp) \overset{\text{def}}{=} \emptyset$;
⋆ m restricted to VARP is any 1–1 mapping $\text{VARP} \to PAR$ (VARP and PAR have the same cardinality).

Observe that by definition, for all $x, y \in \text{VARE}$ such that x and y are different, $m(x) = m(y)$ iff $x \Rightarrow \neg y$ belongs to Γ.

If $\text{VARSP}(\phi) = \emptyset$, then for every $C \in \text{VARSP}$, $m(C) \overset{\text{def}}{=} \emptyset$. Now assume that $\text{VARSP}(\phi) \neq \emptyset$. The rest of the definition of the meaning of the elements of VARSP depends on the cardinality of PAR.

First, consider the case of an infinite PAR. Let $PAR' = \{a_0, \ldots, a_{2^n-1}\}$ be a finite subset of $PAR \setminus \{m(E_i) : 1 \leq i \leq l\}$. PAR' can always be defined since PAR is infinite. Since Γ is not a fundamental sequence, for every $k' \in \{1, \ldots, l\}$, there is at most one $k \in \{0, \ldots, 2^n - 1\}$ such that for some $x, y \in \text{VARE}$, the formula $x \Rightarrow [A_{k,k'}]\neg y$ belongs to Γ. Such a k, if it exists, is denoted by $\alpha(k')$ and in that case k' is said to be *positive* in Γ.

⋆ For every $C \in \text{VARSP} \setminus \{C_1, \ldots, C_n\}$, $m(C) \overset{\text{def}}{=} \emptyset$.
⋆ For every $i \in \{1, \ldots, n\}$, $m(C_i) \overset{\text{def}}{=} \{a_k : 0 \leq k \leq 2^n - 1, \; bit_i(k) = 0\} \cup \{m(E_{k'}) : k' \text{ is positive in } \Gamma, \; \alpha(k') = i\}$.

It follows from the above definition that for every $k \in \{0, \ldots, 2^n - 1\}$ and for every $k' \in \{1, \ldots, l\}$, $m(A_{k,k'}) = m(E_{k'})$ if k' is positive in Γ and $k = \alpha(k')$, otherwise $m(A_{k,k'}) = \emptyset$. Moreover, $m(A_{k,0}) = \{a_k\}$.

Second, consider the case of a finite PAR. Let $PAR = \{1, \ldots, N\}$. As in the previous case, for every $k' \in \{1, \ldots, l\}$, there is at most one $k \in \{0, \ldots, 2^n - 1\}$ such that for some $x, y \in \text{VARE}$, the formula $x \Rightarrow [A_{k,k'}]\neg y$ belongs to Γ. If such a k exists, then it is denoted by $\beta(k')$ and k' is again said to be *positive* in Γ. Let us conclude the definition of m.

⋆ For every $C \in$ VARSP $\setminus$ VARSP (ϕ), $m(C) \overset{\text{def}}{=} \emptyset$.

⋆ For every $i \in \{1, \ldots, n\}$, $m(C_i) \overset{\text{def}}{=} \{m(E_{k'}) : k'$ is positive in $\Gamma, \beta(k') = i\}$.

Now we define the family $(\sigma_P)_{P \subseteq PAR}$. The definition depends on the form of the formulae in the sequence Γ. However, in all the cases $\sigma_\emptyset \overset{\text{def}}{=} W \times W$.

If neither a formula of the form $x \Rightarrow \neg[A]\neg y$ nor $x \Rightarrow [A]\neg y$ occurs in Γ, then $\sigma_{\{a\}} \overset{\text{def}}{=} W \times W$ for every $a \in PAR$.

If Γ contains a formula of the form $x \Rightarrow \neg[-\perp]\neg y$ or $x \Rightarrow [-\perp]\neg y$ for some $x, y \in$ VARE, then for every $a \in PAR$,

$$\sigma_{\{a\}} \overset{\text{def}}{=} \{\langle m(x), m(y) \rangle : x \Rightarrow [-\perp]\neg y \in \Gamma\}.$$

In the remaining cases, we again distinguish subcases according to the cardinality of PAR. If PAR is infinite, then for every $a \in PAR$,

$$\sigma_{\{a\}} \overset{\text{def}}{=} \begin{cases} \{\langle m(x), m(y) \rangle : x \Rightarrow [A_{\beta(k'),k'}]\neg y \in \Gamma\} \text{ if } m(E_{k'}) = \{a\} \\ \quad \text{for some } k' \in \{1, \ldots, n\} \text{ such that } k' \text{ is positive in } \Gamma; \\ \{\langle m(x), m(y) \rangle : x \Rightarrow [A_{k,0}]\neg y \in \Gamma\} \text{ if } a = a_k; \\ W \times W \text{ in the remaining cases.} \end{cases}$$

If PAR is finite, then for every $k' \in \{1, \ldots, n\}$,

$$\sigma_{\{m(E_{k'})\}} \overset{\text{def}}{=} \begin{cases} \{\langle m(x), m(y) \rangle : x \Rightarrow [A_{\beta(k'),k'}]\neg y \in \Gamma\} \\ \quad\quad \text{if } k' \text{ is positive in } \Gamma; \\ W \times W \text{ otherwise.} \end{cases}$$

Finally, for every $P \subseteq PAR$, we define $\sigma_P \overset{\text{def}}{=} \bigcap_{a \in P} \sigma_{\{a\}}$. One can easily show that $\mathcal{M}$ is a SIM-model. It remains to show that Γ is not true in $\mathcal{M}$, that is for every $\psi \in \Gamma$, ψ is not true in $\mathcal{M}$. We shall distinguish several forms of ψ.

Case 1: ψ is of the form $x \Rightarrow \neg y$.
So by definition $m(x) = m(y)$ and therefore ψ is not true in $\mathcal{M}$.

Case 2: ψ is of the form $x \Rightarrow y$.
Then x and y are different, since Γ is not fundamental. Suppose $m(x) = m(y)$. This means $x \Rightarrow \neg y \in \Gamma$ and therefore Γ is fundamental, which leads to a contradiction. Hence, $m(x) \neq m(y)$ and ψ is not true in $\mathcal{M}$.

Case 3: ψ is of the form $x \Rightarrow \neg p$ with $p \in$ FOR$_0$.
By definition, $m(x) \in m(p)$ and therefore ψ is not true in $\mathcal{M}$.

Case 4: ψ is of the form $x \Rightarrow p$.
Suppose $m(x) \in m(p)$. So there is a $y \in$ VARE such that $y \Rightarrow \neg p$ occurs in Γ and $m(x) = m(y)$. Since Γ is not fundamental, x and y are different and therefore $x \Rightarrow \neg y$ is in Γ. Since Γ is closed under the (*sub*)-rule, $x \Rightarrow \neg p$ is in Γ and therefore Γ is fundamental, which leads to a contradiction. So $m(x) \notin m(p)$ and ψ is not true in $\mathcal{M}$.

Case 5: ψ is of the form $x \Rightarrow \neg[A]\neg y$, where $A \in$ Comp$(\phi) \cup \{-\perp\}$.

A is different from $\perp$ since Γ is not fundamental. Three subcases are distinguished.

Case 5.1: $A = -\perp$.

Since $m(-\perp) = PAR$, by the definition of the similarity relation $\sigma_{\{a\}}$, we have $\langle m(x), m(y) \rangle \notin \sigma_{\{a\}}$ for every $a \in PAR$, for otherwise Γ is fundamental. So, $\langle m(x), m(y) \rangle \notin \sigma_{PAR}$ and therefore ψ is not true in $\mathcal{M}$.

Case 5.2: A is of the form $A_{k,k'}$, $k' \geq 1$, $k \in \{0, \dots, 2^n - 1\}$.

By definition, k' is positive in Γ and therefore $m(A) = \{m(E_{k'})\}$. By definition, $\langle m(x), m(y) \rangle \notin \sigma_{\{m(E_{k'})\}}$, for otherwise Γ is fundamental. Thus we have $\langle m(x), m(y) \rangle \notin \sigma_{\{m(A)\}}$ and therefore ψ is not true in $\mathcal{M}$.

Case 5.3: PAR is infinite and $A = A_{k,0}$ for some $k \in \{0, \dots, 2^n - 1\}$.

So $m(A) = \{a_k\}$ and hence we have $\langle m(x), m(y) \rangle \notin \sigma_{\{m(A)\}}$ and therefore ψ is not true in $\mathcal{M}$.

Case 6: ψ is of the form $x \Rightarrow [A] \neg y$, where $A \in \mathrm{Comp}(\phi) \cup \{\perp, -\perp\}$.

Three subcases are distinguished.

Case 6.1: if $m(A) = \emptyset$, then $\sigma_{m(A)} = W \times W$ and $\langle m(x), m(y) \rangle \in \sigma_{m(A)}$. So ψ is not true in $\mathcal{M}$.

Case 6.2: $m(A) = \{a\}$ for some $a \in PAR$.

Suppose $\langle m(x), m(y) \rangle \notin \sigma_{\{a\}}$. So there exist x', y' such that $x' \Rightarrow \neg[A]\neg y'$ is in Γ, $m(x) = m(x')$, and $m(y) = m(y')$. Obviously, x and x' are different or y and y' are different, since Γ is not fundamental, for otherwise $x \Rightarrow [A]\neg y$ and $x \Rightarrow \neg[A]\neg y$ belong to Γ. The following cases are possible: (1) $x = x'$ and $y \neq y'$, (2) $x \neq x'$ and $y = y'$, (3) $x \neq x'$ and $y \neq y'$. We consider the most general case (3). Since $m(x) = m(x')$ and $m(y) = m(y')$, we have $x \Rightarrow \neg x'$ and $y \Rightarrow \neg y'$ are in Γ. By closure under (sub), $x \Rightarrow \neg[A]\neg y'$ is in Γ. By closure under $(sym_=)$, $y' \Rightarrow \neg[A]\neg x$ is in Γ. By closure under (sub) and (sym_A), $x \Rightarrow \neg[A]\neg y$ is in Γ, which leads to a contradiction, since Γ is not fundamental. So $\langle m(x), m(y) \rangle \in \sigma_{\{a\}}$ and ψ is not true in $\mathcal{M}$.

Case 6.3: $m(A) = PAR$, i.e. A is $-\perp$.

By definition, for every $a \in PAR$, $(m(x), m(y)) \in \sigma_{\{a\}}$. So $\langle m(x), m(y) \rangle \in \sigma_{PAR}$ and ψ is not true in $\mathcal{M}$.

Hence, Γ is not true in $\mathcal{M}$, which contradicts our assumption about validity of Γ. $\hspace{2cm}$ Q.E.D.

Theorem 7.4.2. *(Completeness Theorem)* $\mathrm{VAL(SIM)} \subseteq \mathrm{THM(RS(SIM))}$.

Proof. Suppose ϕ is SIM-valid. If $DT(\phi)$ is finite, then by Lemma 7.4.5 ϕ is valid iff all the terminal sequences of $DT(\phi)$ are valid. By Lemma 7.4.6, all the terminal sequences of $DT(\phi)$ are fundamental. Now we prove that if $DT(\phi)$ is infinite, then ϕ is not valid. Suppose that $DT(\phi)$ is infinite. By König's lemma which says that every infinite tree with finitary branching has an infinite branch, there is an infinite branch BR in $DT(\phi)$. Let Δ be the set of all indecomposable formulae labelling the vertices of BR. Δ cannot be fundamental since $DT(\phi)$ inherits all the indecomposable formulae from the labels of its ancestors (otherwise BR would be finite). Let $\mathcal{M}$ be the model built from Δ as described in Lemma 7.4.6. The arguments in Lemma 7.4.6

can be easily adapted to the infinite case. The root of $DT(\phi)$ is of the form $z \Rightarrow N(\phi)$, where $z \in \text{VARE} \setminus \text{VARE}(\phi)$. By induction on the well-founded ordering defined below, we show that $z \Rightarrow N(\phi)$ is not true in $\mathcal{M}$.

For every term A and for every formula ψ we define a rank $r(A)$ of A and a rank $r(\psi)$ of ψ as follows:

$\star$ if $A = A_1 \cup \ldots \cup A_k$ where for every $i \in \{1, \ldots, k\}$, $k \geq 1$, $A_i \in \text{Comp}(\phi) \cup \{\perp, -\perp\}$, $\text{rank}(A) \stackrel{\text{def}}{=} k$;

$\star$ if ψ is indecomposable, then $r(\psi) \stackrel{\text{def}}{=} 1$;

$\star$ otherwise, ψ is of the form $x \Rightarrow \varphi$ and $r(\psi) \stackrel{\text{def}}{=} 1 + r'(\varphi)$, where r' is defined as follows:

  $*$ for every $p \in \text{VARSE}$, $r'(p) \stackrel{\text{def}}{=} 1$;

  $*$ for every $x \in \text{VARE}$, $r'(x) \stackrel{\text{def}}{=} 1$;

  $*$ $r'(\neg\varphi) \stackrel{\text{def}}{=} 1 + r'(\varphi)$;

  $*$ $r'(\varphi_1 \wedge \varphi_2) \stackrel{\text{def}}{=} 1 + r'(\varphi_1) + r'(\varphi_2)$;

  $*$ $r'([A]\varphi) \stackrel{\text{def}}{=} 1 + \text{rank}(A) + r'(\varphi)$.

Suppose $z \Rightarrow N(\phi)$ is true in $\mathcal{M}$. For every node w of $DT(\phi)$, let $l(w)$ be the sequence Γ of formulae which is the label of w and let $\Lambda \stackrel{\text{def}}{=} \{\psi : \psi \in l(w), w \in \text{BR}\}$. Suppose $\mathcal{M} \models z \Rightarrow \phi$. Let ψ_0 be a formula in $\Sigma \stackrel{\text{def}}{=} \{\phi : \psi \in \Lambda, \mathcal{M} \models \psi\}$ such that for every $\psi \in \Sigma$, $r(\psi_0) \leq r(\psi)$. Σ is non-empty since $z \Rightarrow N(\phi) \in \Sigma$. Then, there is a node w_0 of BR such that $l(w_0) = \Gamma', \psi_0, \Gamma''$ and Γ' is indecomposable. ψ_0 cannot be of the form $x \Rightarrow \varphi \wedge \varphi'$, for otherwise, either $x \Rightarrow \varphi \in \Sigma$ and $r(x \Rightarrow \varphi) < r(\psi_0)$ or $x \Rightarrow \varphi' \in \Sigma$ and $r(x \Rightarrow \varphi') < r(\psi_0)$. By a similar analysis, ψ_0 cannot be of the following forms:

$$x \Rightarrow \neg\neg\varphi, \quad x \Rightarrow \neg(\varphi \wedge \varphi'), \quad x \Rightarrow \neg[A \cup B]\neg\varphi,$$

$$x \Rightarrow [A \cup B]\neg\varphi, \quad x \Rightarrow [A]\varphi, \quad x \Rightarrow \neg[A]\varphi,$$

with φ different from a negated element of VARE. Thus the only admissible form of ψ_0 is either of $x \Rightarrow y$, $x \Rightarrow \neg y$ $x \Rightarrow p$, $x \Rightarrow \neg p$, $x \Rightarrow [A]\neg y$, $x \Rightarrow \neg[A]\neg y$ with $A \in \text{Comp}(\phi) \cup \{\perp, -\perp\}$. However, this contradicts the fact that for every $\psi \in \Delta$, ψ is not true in $\mathcal{M}$.   Q.E.D.

Let $f : \text{VARP} \to PAR$ be a 1–1 mapping. A P^f-meaning function is a P-meaning function $m : P \to \mathcal{P}(PAR)$ for SIM such that the restriction of m to VARP is f. Let SIM^f be the logic obtained from SIM by replacing the P-meaning functions for SIM by P^f-meaning functions in the corresponding models.

Corollary 7.4.1. $\text{VAL}(\text{SIM}) = \text{VAL}(\text{SIM}^f)$ *for every* f *as above.*

Proof. We have $\text{MOD}(\text{SIM}^f) \subseteq \text{MOD}(\text{SIM})$ and therefore

$$\text{VAL}(\text{SIM}) \subseteq \text{VAL}(\text{SIM}^f).$$

The key observation that enables us to show the converse inclusion, is the following.

Let $\mathcal{M} = \langle W, (\sigma_P)_{P \subseteq PAR}, m \rangle$ be a SIM-model, let $x \in W$, and let ϕ be a formula. Let g be a 1–1 mapping $PAR \to PAR$ and let $\mathcal{M}'$ be a SIM-model $\langle W, (\sigma'_P)_{P \subseteq PAR}, m' \rangle$ defined as follows:

⋆ for every $A \in P$, $m'(A) = \{g(p) : p \in m(A)\}$;
⋆ for every $P \subseteq PAR$, $\sigma'_P = \sigma_{\{g^{-1}(p) : p \in P\}}$.

So for every $A \in P$, we have the following equalities

$$\sigma'_{m'(A)} = \sigma'_{\{g(p) : p \in m(A)\}} = \sigma_{m(A)}.$$

Hence, $\mathcal{M}, x \models \phi$ iff $\mathcal{M}', x \models \phi$. Assume that $\phi \in \mathrm{VAL}(\mathrm{SIM}^f_X)$ and suppose that $\phi \notin \mathrm{VAL}(\mathrm{SIM})$. So there exist a SIM-model $\mathcal{M}$ and an x in $\mathcal{M}$ such that $\mathcal{M}, x \not\models \phi$. Consider the SIM-model $\mathcal{M}'$ built from $\mathcal{M}$ and f as above. $\mathcal{M}'$ is a SIM^f-model and $\mathcal{M}', x \not\models \phi$, a contradiction.   Q.E.D.

Example 7.4.3. We consider a SIM-formula:

$$\phi = ([C_1 \cap C_2]p_1 \wedge [C_1 \cap -C_2]p_2) \Rightarrow [C_1 \cup C_2](p_1 \wedge p_2).$$

The normal form of ϕ is

$$([B_0]p_1 \wedge [B_1]p_2) \Rightarrow [B_0 \cup B_1 \cup B_2 \cup B_3](p_1 \wedge p_2).$$

In Table 7.4.3 a proof of the SIM-validity of ϕ is presented. In this proof, Γ denotes the following sequence

$$\Gamma = x \Rightarrow \neg[B_0]p_1, x \Rightarrow \neg[B_1]p_2, x \Rightarrow \neg[B_0]\neg y,$$

$$x \Rightarrow \neg[B_1]\neg y, x \Rightarrow \neg[B_2]\neg y, x \Rightarrow \neg[B_3]\neg y,$$

and r_1 [resp. r_2, r_3, r_4] denotes "$(4 \times (\cup))$" [resp. "$([B_0 \cup \ldots \cup B_3])$", "$(\neg \wedge)$", "$((\neg\neg))$"].

7.4.4 Extensions

The developments of Sect. 7.4.3 can be adapted to the case when the relations in the models are not only reflexive and symmetric but also transitive. This is a consequence of the fact that the object nominals enable us to express that a pair of objects belongs to a relation. In that sense, the expressive power of the language is quite close to that of classical logic (however not completely, since SIM is decidable, see Theorem 11.3.4). In this section we show how to uniformly extend the results of Sect. 7.4.3 to a broader class of logics.

A *Horn formula* ϕ of FOL-M is a formula of the form $\forall x_1 \ldots \forall x_n \, (\phi_1 \Rightarrow \phi_2)$, where

$$\frac{\frac{\frac{\frac{\frac{x \Rightarrow \neg(([B_0]p_1 \wedge [B_1]p_2)) \wedge \neg[B_0 \cup \ldots \cup B_3](p_1 \wedge p_2))}{x \Rightarrow \neg([B_0]p_1 \wedge [B_1]p_2), x \Rightarrow \neg\neg[B_0 \cup \ldots \cup B_3](p_1 \wedge p_2)} \; r_3}{x \Rightarrow \neg([B_0]p_1 \wedge [B_1]p_2), x \Rightarrow [B_0 \cup \ldots \cup B_3](p_1 \wedge p_2)} \; r_4}{x \Rightarrow \neg[B_0]p_1, x \Rightarrow \neg[B_1]p_2, x \Rightarrow [B_0 \cup \ldots \cup B_3](p_1 \wedge p_2)} \; r_3}{x \Rightarrow \neg[B_0]p_1, x \Rightarrow \neg[B_1]p_2, x \Rightarrow [B_0 \cup \ldots \cup B_3]\neg y, y \Rightarrow (p_1 \wedge p_2)} \; r_2}{\Gamma, y \Rightarrow (p_1 \wedge p_2)} \; r_1$$

$$\frac{\Gamma, y \Rightarrow p_1 \qquad \qquad \Gamma, y \Rightarrow p_2}{\qquad \qquad (\wedge)}$$

$$\frac{\Gamma, y \Rightarrow p_1}{\Gamma, y \Rightarrow \neg p_1, y \Rightarrow p_1} \; (\neg[B_0]) \qquad \frac{\Gamma, y \Rightarrow p_2}{\Gamma, y \Rightarrow \neg p_2, y \Rightarrow p_2} \; (\neg[B_1])$$

Table 7.3. A proof in RS(SIM)

* $n \geq 1$;
* ϕ_1 and ϕ_2 are quantifier-free formulae built from the binary predicate symbol R, from the logical constant $\top$ (true), and from the individual variables $\{x_1, \ldots, x_n\}$;
* ϕ_1 is either $\top$ or a finite conjunction of atomic formulae;
* ϕ_2 is an atomic formula.

Let C be a class of relations defined by means of Horn formulae. We clearly have the following fact.

Lemma 7.4.7. C is closed under intersection, that is if $R_1 \subseteq W_1 \times W_1$ and $R_2 \subseteq W_2 \times W_2$ are in C, then $R_1 \cap R_2$ understood as a relation on $W_1 \cap W_2$ is in C.

For example, reflexivity, symmetry and transitivity can be expressed by Horn formulae. For every countable set PAR, let SIM_C be the logic obtained from SIM by assuming that for every $P \subseteq PAR$, the relations σ_P from models of SIM belong to the class C. We briefly describe how to extend the Rasiowa–Sikorski system of SIM to the system for SIM_C.

Let ψ be a Horn formula of the form

$$\forall x_1, \ldots, x_n \; R(z_1^1, z_2^1) \wedge \ldots \wedge R(z_1^k, z_2^k) \Rightarrow R(z_1^{k+1}, z_2^{k+1}),$$

where

* $k \geq 0$ and if $k = 0$, then the left part of $\Rightarrow$ is $\top$;
* $z_\alpha^\beta \in \text{VARE}$, for all $\alpha \in \{1,2\}$ and $\beta \in \{1, \ldots, k+1\}$.

For all $x, y \in \text{VARE}$, and for every parameter expression A, we define the formula $\varphi(A, x, y)$ as follows:

$$\varphi(A, x, y) \stackrel{\text{def}}{=} x \Rightarrow [A]\neg y.$$

The following rule is associated to ψ:

$$\frac{\Gamma_1, \varphi(\mathrm{A}, \mathrm{x}_1^1, \mathrm{x}_2^1), \Gamma_2, \ldots, \varphi(\mathrm{A}, \mathrm{x}_1^k, \mathrm{x}_2^k), \Gamma_{k+1}}{\varphi(\mathrm{A}, \mathrm{x}_1^{k+1}, \mathrm{x}_2^{k+1}), \varphi(\mathrm{A}, \mathrm{x}_1^1, \mathrm{x}_2^1), \ldots, \varphi(\mathrm{A}, \mathrm{x}_1^k, \mathrm{x}_2^k), \Gamma_1, \ldots, \Gamma_{k+1}} \quad (\psi)\text{-rule.}$$

If $k = 0$, then the upper sequence of the rule is Γ_1 and the lower sequence is $\varphi(\mathrm{A}, \mathrm{x}_1^1, \mathrm{x}_2^1), \Gamma_1$. Moreover, we require that for all $\alpha, \alpha' \in \{1,2\}$ and $\beta, \beta' \in \{1, \ldots, k+1\}$, $z_\alpha^\beta = z_{\alpha'}^{\beta'}$ iff $\mathrm{x}_\alpha^\beta = \mathrm{x}_{\alpha'}^{\beta'}$. So in order to obtain a proof system for $\mathrm{SIM}_\mathcal{C}$, we add the (ψ)-rule to the Rasiowa–Sikorski proof system for SIM for every formula ψ in the set of Horn formulae defining the class $\mathcal{C}$ and we delete the $(refl_\mathrm{A})$-rule and (sym_A)-rule.

Theorem 7.4.3. *A formula ϕ is $SIM_\mathcal{C}$-valid iff it is provable in the Rasiowa–Sikorski proof system described above.*

The proof is analogous to the completeness proof for SIM. Indeed, it is easy to show that the model $\mathcal{M}$ built as in Lemma 7.4.6 is a $\mathrm{SIM}_\mathcal{C}$-model.

7.5 Notes

Logics NIL and IL. The logic NIL is introduced in [OP84, Vak87]. The logic IL is introduced in [Vak89]. The developments on the information logic IL presented in this chapter are from [Vak91c, Vak96]. The copying construction used for IL is not the one from the paper [Vak91c] but it uses the ideas from Vakarelov's works and from his private communications.

Rare-logics of similarity. The logic SIM is defined in [Kon97]. The Rare-logic SIM' is its variant such that the set of parameters in the models is not fixed.

Normal forms. The normal forms introduced in Sect. 7.4.2 are from [Kon97]. They generalise the canonical disjunctive normal form for the formulae of classical propositional calculus to a language with parameter nominals (see for example [Lem65]). The technique of components has been applied to information logics in [Kon97] in order to define Rasiowa–Sikorski-style and Gentzen-style proof systems for relative similarity logics.

Rasiowa–Sikorski proof systems. The Rasiowa–Sikorski-style systems have been introduced in [RS63] (see a tutorial in [Kon00]). These calculi are dual to Smullyan's tableaux [Smu68]. Their computational behaviour is similar to that of tableaux. Proof systems of that kind can be found in [Was71, Sal72, Orło74, Cie80, Orło88c, Orło91, Orło92, Orło93a, BK95, DOR94, FO95, DO96, Kon97, Kon98, Mac97, KMO98, Mac98a, Mac98b, DO00]. A proof editor for Rasiowa–Sikorski-style systems for information logics is described in [HO95]. The calculus defined in Sect. 7.4.3 is a slight variant of those defined in [Kon97, Kon98]. Unlike in [Kon97, Kon98], $\mathrm{x}_1 \Rightarrow \neg[A]\neg \mathrm{x}_1$ is not a fundamental sequence. Instead, we prefer to introduce the $(refl_\mathrm{A})$-rule (see Table 7.1). Actually, our calculus is simpler and can be easily extended as shown in Sect. 7.4.4. One can also deal with irreflexive relations in a similar fashion.

Object nominals. The presence of object nominals in the language of SIM has greatly simplified the definition of RS(SIM). By contrast, no Hilbert-style axiomatisation is known for SIM but it is expectable that techniques from [PT91] could provide a solution of this open problem. The analytic calculi for logics with nominals have been also presented in [Dem99b, Tza99, Bla00a], where the nominals are used implicitly as labels.

Other similarity logics. Logics of similarity can be found in [Vak91b, Bal98, Vak96, AT97, Vak98]. The logics of fuzzy similarity relations are discussed in [DEG+95, EGGR97, EGG99, EGG00].

8. Reasoning About Indiscernibility

8.1 Introduction and Outline of the Chapter

Semantic structures of the logics presented in this chapter contain relations that are the counterparts to indiscernibility relations derived from information systems. The modal operators of the logics represent approximation operators. In Sect. 8.2 we introduce the logic DALLA and we present its Hilbert-style deductive system. A specific property of the semantic structures of DALLA is that any two relations in these structures satisfy a condition referred to as local agreement of the relations. This condition is equivalent to the property that the union of equivalence relations is also an equivalence relation. The language of DALLA includes operators acting on indiscernibility relations, namely intersection and transitive closure of relations. Consequently, we can represent in this logic the corresponding approximation operators and relationships among them. In Sect. 8.3 we study a family of logics for reasoning about relative indiscernibility relations. In Sect. 8.4 we introduce the class of LA-logics that generalises DALLA-style logics by assuming various classes of local agreements in the semantic structures of these logics. We present a Hilbert-style deductive system for LA-logics equipped with a finite amount of constraints on local agreement of relations. In Sect. 8.5 we show that the class of LA-logics is broad enough to capture some fuzzy logics also. Namely, we present a fuzzy logic of graded modalities within the LA-framework and we develop a deductive system for it employing the general results relevant for LA-logics.

8.2 DALLA: Data Analysis Logic with Local Agreement

The data analysis logic DAL (see Example 5.3.4) is the paradigm logic for reasoning about indiscernibility relations. Unfortunately, very few results have been obtained for DAL. Its decidability status is an open problem and no Hilbert-style axiomatisation exists. An axiomatisation of DAL augmented with object nominals is known but a proof of completeness has never been fully published. It is a reason why variants of DAL have been introduced for which more results have been established (often by introducing new original constructions) while preserving properties of DAL. One of such logics is the logic DALLA. It is the subject of this section.

The modal connectives of the logic DALLA represent the approximation operators defined in Sect. 4.2. Each of these connectives is determined by an indiscernibility relation. The family of the indiscernibility relations is endowed with an algebraic structure, namely, we admit in the language of DALLA the operations of intersection, and reflexive and transitive closure of relations. Consequently, DALLA enables us to represent properties of objects which are formed from some other properties as discussed in Sect. 3.4. However, in the language of DALLA we do not have an explicit access to the sets of attributes that determine the corresponding properties. The formulae of DALLA represent sets of objects of an information system. It follows that in the logic DALLA we can reason about various types of definability and/or undefinability of sets of objects, as discussed in Sect. 4.4.

Definition 8.2.1. *Let R and R' be two binary relations on a set W. R and R' are said to be in local agreement $\stackrel{\text{def}}{\Leftrightarrow}$ for every $x \in W$, either $R(x) \subseteq R'(x)$ or $R'(x) \subseteq R(x)$.*

In particular, if $R \subseteq R'$, then R and R' are in local agreement. The converse does not always hold. The following lemma shows an interesting property of the local agreement condition.

Lemma 8.2.1. *For all equivalence relations R and R' on a set W, the following conditions are equivalent:*

(I) R and R' are in local agreement;
(II) $R \cup R'$ is transitive.

Proof. (I) $\rightarrow$ (II). Assume $\langle x, y \rangle \in R$ and $\langle y, z \rangle \in R'$. If $R(x) \subseteq R'(x)$, then by transitivity of R', we get $\langle x, z \rangle \in R'$. Now assume $R'(x) \subseteq R(x)$. If $R'(y) \subseteq R(y)$, then by transitivity of R, $\langle x, z \rangle \in R$. Now assume $R(y) \subseteq R'(y)$. Since R and R' are equivalence relations, $R(x) = R(y)$, $R'(y) = R'(z)$, and therefore $R'(x) \subseteq R(x) = R(y) \subseteq R'(y) = R'(z)$. So $\langle x, z \rangle \in R'$. The case $\langle x, y \rangle \in R'$ and $\langle y, z \rangle \in R$ is analogous. Since R and R' are transitive, $R \cup R'$ is transitive.
The converse can be proved in a similar way. *Q.E.D.*

The language of the logic DALLA is the same as the language of the logic DAL (see Example 5.3.4):

⋆ the set M_0 of basic modal expressions is a countably infinite set of modal constants;
⋆ the set of modal operators is $O_M = \{\cup^*, \cap\}$; they are interpreted as the transitive closure of the union and intersection of relations, respectively;
⋆ the set M of modal expressions is the smallest set including M_0 and closed with respect to the operators from O_M;

* the set FOR_0 of basic formulae is a countably infinite set of propositional variables;
* the set of propositional connectives is $O_{FOR} = \{\neg, \wedge\} \cup \{[a] : a \in M\}$.

A DALLA-model is a LAN(DALLA)-model $\langle W, (R_a)_{a \in M}, m \rangle$ such that

* for every $a \in M$, R_a is an equivalence relation on W;
* for all $a, b \in M$, $R_{a \cup^* b} = R_a \cup R_b$ and $R_{a \cap b} = R_a \cap R_b$.

In view of Lemma 8.2.1, in every DALLA-model any two relations are in local agreement. The class of DALLA-models is a subclass of DAL-models. The Hilbert-style proof system HDALLA is an extension of HK(LAN(DALLA)) obtained by adding the following axioms:

(Ax1) $[a]\phi \Rightarrow \phi$;
(Ax2) $\phi \Rightarrow [a]\langle a \rangle \phi$;
(Ax3) $[a]\phi \Rightarrow [a][a]\phi$;
(Ax4) $[a \cup^* b]\phi \Leftrightarrow [a]\phi \wedge [b]\phi$;
(Ax5) $[a \cap b]\phi \Leftrightarrow [a]\phi \vee [b]\phi$.

Obviously, HDALLA is an extension of HS5(LAN(DALLA)). The first correspondence result concerning local agreement is given below.

Lemma 8.2.2. *For every LAN(DALLA)-frame $F = \langle W, (R_{a'})_{a' \in M} \rangle$ and for all $a, b \in M$, if $R_{a \cap b} = R_a \cap R_b$, then $[a \cap b]p \Rightarrow [a]p \vee [b]p$ is true in F iff R_a and R_b are in local agreement.*

Proof. ($\rightarrow$) Suppose that there exist $x, y_1, y_2 \in W$ such that (i) $\langle x, y_1 \rangle \in R_a$, (ii) $\langle x, y_1 \rangle \notin R_b$, (iii) $\langle x, y_2 \rangle \notin R_a$, and (iv) $\langle x, y_2 \rangle \in R_b$. Consider a model $\langle W, (R_{a'})_{a' \in M}, m \rangle$ based on F such that

$$m(p) \stackrel{\text{def}}{=} (R_a \cap R_b)(x).$$

By assumption, $\mathcal{M}, x \models [a \cap b]p \Rightarrow [a]p \vee [b]p$. By the construction of m we have $\mathcal{M}, x \models [a \cap b]p$. Hence, $\mathcal{M}, x \models [a]p \vee [b]p$. Since neither $y_1 \in (R_a \cap R_b)(x)$ (by (ii)), nor $y_2 \in (R_a \cap R_b)(x)$ (by (iii)), we have $\mathcal{M}, y_1 \not\models p$ and $\mathcal{M}, y_2 \not\models p$. Moreover, we also have either $\mathcal{M}, x \models [a]p$ or $\mathcal{M}, x \models [b]p$. In both cases we obtain a contradiction due to (i) and (iv).
($\leftarrow$) Let $\mathcal{M} = \langle W, (R_{a'})_{a' \in M}, m \rangle$ be a LAN(DALLA)-model such that for some $a, b \in M$, $R_{a \cap b} = R_a \cap R_b$, and R_a and R_b are in local agreement. Let an $x \in W$ be such that $\mathcal{M}, x \models [a \cap b]p$. Hence, for every $y \in W$, if $\langle x, y \rangle \in R_{a \cap b} = R_a \cap R_b$, then $\mathcal{M}, y \models p$. By the local agreement condition, either $(R_a \cap R_b)(x) = R_a(x)$ or $(R_a \cap R_b)(x) = R_b(x)$. It follows that $\mathcal{M}, x \models [a]p \vee [b]p$.   Q.E.D.

The following lemma implies that the formulae of the form $([a][b]\phi \wedge [b][a]\phi) \Leftrightarrow ([a]\phi \wedge [b]\phi)$ are derivable in HDALLA.

Lemma 8.2.3.

THM(HDALLA) = THM(HDALLA + ([a][b]ϕ ∧ [b][a]ϕ) ⇔ ([a]ϕ ∧ [b]ϕ)).

Proof. We show that ([a][b]ϕ ∧ [b][a]ϕ) ⇔ ([a]ϕ ∧ [b]ϕ) ∈ THM(HDALLA) for every LAN(DALLA)-formula ϕ and for all a, b ∈ M. By the axiom (Ax1), [a][b]ϕ ⇒ [b]ϕ ∈ THM(HDALLA).

Similarly, we have [b][a]ϕ ⇒ [a]ϕ ∈ THM(HDALLA). By simple propositional reasoning we obtain

$$([a][b]\phi \wedge [b][a]\phi) \Rightarrow ([a]\phi \wedge [b]\phi) \in \text{THM(HDALLA)}.$$

Now we show that the converse implication is a theorem. By the axiom (Ax4), (i) [a]ϕ ∧ [b]ϕ ⇒ [a ∪* b]ϕ ∈ THM(HDALLA). By the axiom (Ax3), (ii) [a ∪* b]ϕ ⇒ [a ∪* b][a ∪* b]ϕ ∈ THM(HDALLA). By the axiom (Ax4), (iii) [a ∪* b]ϕ ⇒ [a]ϕ ∧ [b]ϕ ∈ THM(HDALLA). Applying the regular rule to (iii), we get

(iv) [a ∪* b][a ∪* b]ϕ ⇒ [a ∪* b]([a]ϕ ∧ [b]ϕ) ∈ THM(HDALLA).

Using the axioms (Ax3) and (Ax4),

(v) [a ∪* b]([a]ϕ ∧ [b]ϕ) ⇒ ([a]ϕ ∧ [a][b]ϕ ∧ [b][a]ϕ ∧ [b]ϕ) ∈ THM(HDALLA).

From (i)–(v), we get

$$([a]\phi \wedge [b]\phi) \Rightarrow ([a][b]\phi \wedge [b][a]\phi) \in \text{THM(HDALLA)}.$$

Q.E.D.

The second correspondence for local agreement uses the specific formulae from Lemma 8.2.3, so it can be expressed without intersection of relations.

Lemma 8.2.4. *For every LAN(DALLA)-frame $F = \langle W, (R_{a'})_{a' \in M} \rangle$ and for all a, b ∈ M, if $R_{a \cap b}$, R_a, and R_b are equivalence relations, then ([a][b]p ∧ [b][a]p) ⇔ ([a]p ∧ [b]p) is true in F iff R_a and R_b are in local agreement.*

Proof. (→) Assume ([a][b]p ∧ [b][a]p) ⇔ ([a]p ∧ [b]p) is true in F and suppose R_a and R_b are not in local agreement. By Lemma 8.2.1, $R_a \cup R_b$ is not transitive. So, there are $x_1, x_2, x_3 \in W$ such that $\langle x_1, x_2 \rangle \in R_a \cup R_b$, $\langle x_2, x_3 \rangle \in R_a \cup R_b$, and $\langle x_1, x_3 \rangle \notin R_a \cup R_b$. Consider a model $\mathcal{M} = \langle W, (R_{a'})_{a' \in M}, m \rangle$ based on F such that

$$m(\text{p}) \overset{\text{def}}{=} (R_a \cup R_b)(x).$$

By the assumption, $\mathcal{M}, x_1 \models [a]\text{p} \wedge [b]\text{p} \Rightarrow [a][b]\text{p} \wedge [b][a]\text{p}$. By the definition of m we have $\mathcal{M}, x_1 \models [a]\text{p} \wedge [b]\text{p}$. So, $\mathcal{M}, x_1 \models [a][b]\text{p} \wedge [b][a]\text{p} \wedge [a][a]\text{p} \wedge [b][b]\text{p}$. Since R_a and R_b are transitive (see Lemma 6.3.9), both [a]p ⇒ [a][a]p and [b]p ⇒ [b][b]p are valid in F. So for every $y \in (R_a; R_b \cup R_b; R_a \cup R_a; R_a \cup R_b; R_b)(x_1)$, $\mathcal{M}, y \models \text{p}$. Since $\langle x_1, x_3 \rangle \in (R_a; R_b \cup R_b; R_a \cup R_a; R_b; R_b)$, $\mathcal{M}, x_3 \models \text{p}$, which leads to a contradiction.
(←) This part is by an easy verification.   *Q.E.D.*

Theorem 8.2.1. *(Soundness Theorem)* THM(HDALLA) $\subseteq$ VAL(DALLA).

The proof of Theorem 8.2.1 is by induction on the length of the derivation. Now, we establish completeness.

Lemma 8.2.5. *The canonical model $\mathcal{M}^c$ for HDALLA is a DALLA-model.*

Proof. Let $\mathcal{M}^c = \langle W^c, (R_a^c)_{a \in M}, m^c \rangle$ be the canonical structure for HDALLA defined as in Sect. 6.3.4. By Lemma 6.3.11, for every a $\in$ M, R_a^c is an equivalence relation on W^c. We show that for all a, b $\in$ M, R_a^c and R_b^c are in local agreement. For suppose otherwise, then $R_a^c \cup R_b^c$ is not transitive by Lemma 8.2.1. Hence, there are $X_1, X_2, X_3 \in W^c$ such that $\langle X_1, X_2 \rangle \in R_a^c \cup R_b^c$, $\langle X_2, X_3 \rangle \in R_a^c \cup R_b^c$, and $\langle X_1, X_3 \rangle \notin R_a^c \cup R_b^c$. So, there exist $[a]\psi_1 \in X_1$ and $[b]\psi_2 \in X_1$ such that $\{\psi_1, \psi_2\} \cap X_3 = \emptyset$. Thus $\{\psi_1 \Rightarrow \psi_1 \vee \psi_2, \psi_2 \Rightarrow \psi_1 \vee \psi_2\} \subseteq$ THM(HDALLA) and by Lemma 6.3.6, $\{[a]\psi_1 \Rightarrow [a](\psi_1 \vee \psi_2), [b]\psi_2 \Rightarrow [b](\psi_1 \vee \psi_2)\} \subseteq$ THM(HDALLA). Since X_1 is a maximal HDALLA-consistent set, by Lemma 6.3.5(IV), $\{[a]\psi_1 \Rightarrow [a](\psi_1 \vee \psi_2), [b]\psi_2 \Rightarrow [b](\psi_1 \vee \psi_2)\} \subseteq X_1$. By Lemma 6.3.5(V), $\{[a](\psi_1 \vee \psi_2), [b](\psi_1 \vee \psi_2)\} \subseteq X_1$. Moreover, by Lemma 6.3.5(IV),

$$([a](\psi_1 \vee \psi_2) \wedge [b](\psi_1 \vee \psi_2)) \Rightarrow ([a][b](\psi_1 \vee \psi_2) \wedge [b][a](\psi_1 \vee \psi_2)) \in X_1.$$

We obtain $\{[a][b](\psi_1 \vee \psi_2), [b][a](\psi_1 \vee \psi_2)\} \subseteq X_1$. Assume $\langle X_1, X_2 \rangle \in R_a^c$ and $\langle X_2, X_3 \rangle \in R_b^c$. That is, $[a]X_1 \subseteq X_2$ and $[b]X_2 \subseteq X_3$. So $\psi_1 \vee \psi_2 \in X_3$. By Lemma 6.3.5(II), either $\psi_1 \in X_3$ or $\psi_2 \in X_3$, a contradiction. The three remaining cases are similar. *Q.E.D.*

Theorem 8.2.2. *(Completeness Theorem)*
VAL(DALLA) $\subseteq$ THM(HDALLA).

Proof. Suppose that $\phi \notin$ THM(HDALLA). The set $\{\neg\phi\}$ is HDALLA-consistent and hence it can be extended to a maximal HDALLA-consistent set X such that $\phi \notin X$. By Theorem 6.3.6, not $\mathcal{M}^c, X \models \phi$, a contradiction. *Q.E.D.*

Let DALLA' be the restriction of DALLA to the language without the operators $\cup^*$ and $\cap$, that is the set of modal expressions of DALLA' is M_0. A Hilbert-style proof system HDALLA' is obtained from the system HDALLA through replacement of the axioms (Ax4) and (Ax5) by

(Ax6) $([c][d]p \wedge [d][c]p) \Leftrightarrow ([c]p \wedge [d]p)$.

Theorem 8.2.3. THM(HDALLA') = VAL(DALLA').

The proof is similar to the proof of the corresponding theorem for DALLA.

8.3 IND: a Logic of Relative Indiscernibility

The importance of the logics DALLA and DALLA$'$ is due to their relation-ships with information systems. Indeed, the binary relations of their semantic structures represent indiscernibility relations. The syntax and semantics of the logics defined in this section are closely related to finite information systems.

The language of IND includes finitely many parameter nominals repre-senting individual attributes and finitely many object nominals representing individual objects. The modal connectives represent approximation operators determined by indiscernibility relations which in turn are defined in terms of Boolean combinations of subsets of attributes. It follows that in the language of IND we can express approximation operators determined by every subset of attributes of an information system. Basic formulae of IND include the formulae which express a fact that a pair of objects belongs to an indiscerni-bility relation determined by an attribute. Models of the language of IND are finite; that is they are based on finite sets of objects. An interesting feature of the logic IND is its very special Hilbert-style proof system.

8.3.1 Language and Semantics

Let $M, N \geq 1$ be two natural numbers fixed for the rest of this section. They determine the cardinality of the set of objects and the cardinality of the set of parameters admitted in the semantic structures. Since N and M are parameters of the logic IND, to be more precise, the present section studies a countable family of indiscernibility logics. The logic IND is a standard Rare-logic defined as follows:

⋆ the set P_0 of basic parameter expressions is $VARP \cup \{\bot\}$, where $VARP = \{E_1, \ldots, E_M\}$ is a finite set of parameter nominals representing individual parameters and $\bot$ is a constant interpreted as the empty set;
⋆ the set of parameter operators is $O_P = \{-, \cap, \cup\}$ and the set P of parameter expressions is the smallest set including P_0 and closed with respect to the operators from O_P;
⋆ the set of relation types is a singleton $\{r\}$;
⋆ the set of basic modal expressions is $M_0 = \{r(A) : A \in P\}$;
⋆ the set O_M of modal operators is empty and the set M of modal expressions is M_0;
⋆ the set FOR_0 of basic formulae is $VARE \cup FOR_{\triangle\triangledown}$, where $VARE = \{x_1, \ldots, x_N\}$ is a finite set of object nominals representing individual ob-jects from the universes of models and

$$FOR_{\triangle\triangledown} \overset{\text{def}}{=} \{\triangle_E(x, x'), \triangledown_E(x, x') : E \in VARP, x, x' \in VARE\};$$

⋆ the set of logical connectives is $O_{FOR} = \{\neg, \wedge\} \cup \{[a] : a \in M\}$.

As usual, for the sake of simplicity, for every $A \in P$, the modal connectives are written $[A]$ instead of $[r(A)]$. We write $\top$ [resp. $\bot$] to denote $\neg(\neg \triangle_{E_1} (x_1, x_1) \wedge \triangle_{E_1}(x_1, x_1))$ [resp. $\neg\top$].

Definition 8.3.1. *A* P-*meaning function for IND is a map* $m : P \to \mathcal{P}(PAR)$ *such that* m *is a standard* P-*meaning function that satisfies the additional conditions:*

* *PAR is a set of cardinality* M;
* *for every* $i \in \{1, \dots, M\}$, $m(E_i)$ *is a singleton;*
* $\bigcup_{i=1}^{M} m(E_i) = PAR$;
* $m(\bot) = \emptyset$.

The constraints on the P-meaning functions for IND induce a very simple normal form of parameter expressions as shown in Lemma 8.3.1.

Lemma 8.3.1. *Let* A *be a parameter expression in* P. *Then, either* $A \sim \bot$ *or there exists a unique sequence* $i_1, \dots, i_k$, $k \geq 1$, *of natural numbers such that* $1 \leq i_1 < \dots < i_k \leq M$ *and* $A \sim E_{i_1} \cup \dots \cup E_{i_k}$.

Proof. We recall that $\sim$ is defined in Sect. 5.3.3. The proof is by induction on the structure of A. The base cases $A = \bot$ and $A = E_j$ are immediate. By way of example, in the induction step, assume $A = -A'$. By the induction hypothesis, either $A' \sim \bot$ or $A' \sim E_{i_1} \cup \dots \cup E_{i_k}$. If $A' \sim \bot$, then $A \sim E_1 \cup \dots \cup E_M$. If $A' \sim E_1 \cup \dots \cup E_M$, then $A \sim \bot$. Finally, in the remaining case, if $A' \sim E_{i_1} \cup \dots \cup E_{i_k}$, where $k < M$, then $A \sim E_{j_1} \cup \dots \cup E_{j_{k'}}$, where

* $1 \leq k' < M$, $1 \leq j_1 < \dots < j_{k'} \leq M$;
* $\{\{i_1, \dots, i_k\}, \{j_1, \dots, j_{k'}\}\}$ is a partition of $\{1, \dots, M\}$.

In the remaining cases, where A is either of the form $A_1 \cup A_2$ or $A_1 \cap A_2$, the proofs are similar.   *Q.E.D.*

The class of IND-models consists of the structures of the form

$$\langle W, (\equiv_P)_{P \subseteq PAR}, m \rangle,$$

where

* W is a non-empty set of cardinality N;
* PAR is a non-empty set of cardinality M;
* $(\equiv_P)_{P \subseteq PAR}$ is a (finite) family of binary relations on W such that
  * $\equiv_P$ is an equivalence relation on W for every $\emptyset \neq P \subseteq PAR$;
  * $\equiv_{P \cup Q} = \equiv_P \cap \equiv_Q$ for all $P, Q \subseteq PAR$ (condition (C_1));
  * $\equiv_\emptyset = W \times W$ (condition (C_1'));
* $m : FOR_0 \cup P \cup M \to \mathcal{P}(W) \cup \mathcal{P}(PAR) \cup \mathcal{P}(W \times W)$ is a map such that
  * for every $i \in \{1, \dots, N\}$, $m(x_i)$ is a singleton set in $\mathcal{P}(W)$;
  * $\bigcup_{i=1}^{N} m(x_i) = W$;

* $m(\nabla_{E_k}(x_i, x_j)) = W$ if $\langle m(x_i), m(x_j) \rangle \notin \equiv_{m(E_k)}$, otherwise
  $m(\nabla_{E_k}(x_i, x_j)) = \emptyset$;
* $m(\triangle_{E_k}(x_i, x_j)) = W \setminus m(\nabla_{E_k}(x_i, x_j))$;
* m restricted to P is a P-meaning function for IND whose range is
  $\mathcal{P}(PAR)$;
* $m(r(A)) = \equiv_{m(A)}$ for every $A \in P$.

Observe that $m(\triangle_{E_k}(x_i, x_j))$ can be viewed as a characteristic function of the
relation $\equiv_{m(E_k)}$. Observe also that since the cardinality of the IND-models is
very constrained, it is expected that the IND-satisfiability problem may be decidable with a low worst-case computational complexity. Although forthcoming Theorem 12.2.1 states that IND-satisfiability requires only linear-time, it
is not immediate that this problem is tractable.

8.3.2 A Hilbert-style Proof System

The Hilbert-style proof system HIND is an extension of HK(LAN(IND)) with
the following axioms:

(Ax1) $[A]\phi \Leftrightarrow [B]\phi$ for all A, B such that $A \sim B$;
(Ax2) $[\bot]\neg x_i \Leftrightarrow \bot$;
(Ax3) $\neg x_i \Leftrightarrow \bigvee_{j \in \{1,\ldots,N\} \setminus \{i\}} x_j$;
(Ax4) $[A \cup B]\neg x_i \Leftrightarrow [A]\neg x_i \vee [B]\neg x_i$;
(Ax5) $[E_k]\neg x_i \Leftrightarrow \bigwedge_{j=1}^{N}(x_j \Rightarrow \nabla_{E_k}(x_j, x_i))$;
(Ax6) $\nabla_{E_k}(x_j, x_i) \Leftrightarrow \neg \triangle_{E_k}(x_j, x_i)$;
(Ax7) $\triangle_{E_k}(x_i, x_i)$;
(Ax8) $\triangle_{E_k}(x_i, x_j) \Leftrightarrow \triangle_{E_k}(x_j, x_i)$;
(Ax9) $\triangle_{E_k}(x_i, x_j) \wedge \triangle_{E_k}(x_j, x_k) \Rightarrow \triangle_{E_k}(x_i, x_k)$;
(Ax10) $[A](\psi \vee \phi) \Leftrightarrow \psi \vee [A]\phi$ for every $\psi \in FOR_{\triangle\nabla}$;

for every $k \in \{1, \ldots, M\}$ and for all $i, j \in \{1, \ldots, N\}$. The axioms (Ax7),
(Ax8), and (Ax9) encode the fact that the relations in the IND-models are
equivalence relations, that is we have the following correspondences.

Lemma 8.3.2. *Let $\mathcal{M}$ be an LAN(IND)-model $\langle W, (\mathcal{R}_P)_{P \subseteq PAR}, m \rangle$ such
that $\mathcal{M}$ satisfies all the conditions of IND-models except that the relations
$\mathcal{R}_P, P \subseteq PAR$, are not necessarily equivalence relations. Then we have:*

(I) $\mathcal{M} \models \bigwedge_{k=1}^{M} \bigwedge_{i=1}^{N} \triangle_{E_k}(x_i, x_i)$ iff for every $p \in PAR$, $\mathcal{R}_{\{p\}}$ is reflexive;
*(II) $\mathcal{M} \models \bigwedge_{k=1}^{M} \bigwedge_{i=1}^{N} \bigwedge_{j=1}^{N}(\triangle_{E_k}(x_i, x_j) \Leftrightarrow \triangle_{E_k}(x_j, x_i))$ iff for every $p \in$
PAR, $\mathcal{R}_{\{p\}}$ is symmetric;*
*(III) $\mathcal{M} \models \bigwedge_{k=1}^{M} \bigwedge_{i=1}^{N} \bigwedge_{j=1}^{N} \bigwedge_{l=1}^{N}(\triangle_{E_k}(x_i, x_j) \wedge \triangle_{E_k}(x_j, x_l) \Rightarrow \triangle_{E_k}(x_i, x_l))$
iff for every $p \in PAR$, $\mathcal{R}_{\{p\}}$ is transitive.*

The proof is by an easy verification.

The axiom (Ax6) can be viewed as a definition of the formula $\nabla_{E_k}(x_j, x_i)$ in terms of the formula $\triangle_{E_k}(x_j, x_i)$. Similarly, the axiom (Ax5) can be viewed as a definition of $[E_k]\neg x_i$. Furthermore, the axioms (Ax2) and (Ax3) assure that for every $i \in \{1, \ldots, N\}$, x_i is a strong nominal (see Sect. 5.3.2). Observe that in HIND there are no axioms enforcing explicitly that $[\bot]$ behaves like an S5 modal connective.

Theorem 8.3.1. *(Soundness Theorem)* THM(HIND) $\subseteq$ VAL(IND).

Proof. The proof is by induction on the length of a derivation in HIND. By way of example, we show that every instance of $[A](\psi \vee \phi) \Leftrightarrow \psi \vee [A]\phi$ for $\psi \in \text{FOR}_{\triangle\nabla}$, $A \in P$, and $\phi \in \text{FOR}$ belongs to VAL(IND).

Let $\mathcal{M} = \langle W, (\equiv_P)_{P \subseteq PAR}, m \rangle$ be an IND-model, $x \in W$ and $\triangle_{E_k}(x_i, x_j) \in \text{FOR}_{\triangle\nabla}$.

($\rightarrow$) Assume $\mathcal{M}, x \models [A](\triangle_{E_k}(x_i, x_j) \vee \phi)$. So for every $y \in \equiv_{m(A)}(x)$, either (i) $\mathcal{M}, y \models \triangle_{E_k}(x_i, x_j)$ or (ii) $\mathcal{M}, y \models \phi$. Take some $y \in \equiv_{m(A)}(x)$ (clearly $\equiv_{m(A)}(x)$ is non-empty). If (i) holds, then for every $z \in W$, we have $\mathcal{M}, z \models \triangle_{p_k}(x_i, x_j)$. Hence, $\mathcal{M}, x \models \triangle_{E_k}(x_i, x_j)$. If (i) does not hold, then for every $z \in W$, we have $\mathcal{M}, z \not\models \triangle_{p_k}(x_i, x_j)$. So for every $z \in \equiv_{m(A)}(x)$, $\mathcal{M}, z \models \phi$. Hence, $\mathcal{M}, x \models [A]\phi$. We conclude that $\mathcal{M}, x \models \triangle_{E_k}(x_i, x_j) \vee [A]\phi$. The proof of ($\leftarrow$) is similar.

The case $\nabla_{E_k}(x_i, x_j) \in \text{FOR}_{\triangle\nabla}$ is similar.   *Q.E.D.*

8.3.3 Completeness

Every IND-formula can be presented in a normal form. The following definition introduces the notion of a strong characteristic formula that is used for defining the normal forms.

Definition 8.3.2. *A strong characteristic formula is a formula of the form $\psi \wedge x_k$, where $x_k \in \text{VARE}$ and ψ is a conjunction (possibly empty) of members of $\text{FOR}_{\triangle\nabla}$.*

An obvious consequence of Definition 8.3.2 is that every member of VARE is a strong characteristic formula.

Lemma 8.3.3. *Let ϕ be a formula having no subformulae of the form $[A]\psi$. Then there exists a finite set $\{\phi_1, \ldots, \phi_l\}$, $l \geq 1$, of strong characteristic formulae such that $\phi \Leftrightarrow \bigvee_{i=1}^{l} \phi_i \in \text{THM(HIND)}$.*

Proof. The proof is by induction on the structure of ϕ.
Base cases.
If $\phi = x_k$, then ϕ is already in the required form. If $\phi = \top$, then we get $\vdash \top \Leftrightarrow x_1 \vee \neg x_1$. Using the axiom (Ax3), $\vdash \top \Leftrightarrow \bigvee_{i=1}^{N} x_i$. If $\phi = \bot$, then using the axioms (Ax3) and (Ax6), we get $\vdash \bot \Leftrightarrow \bigvee_{i=1}^{N}(\triangle_{E_1}(x_1, x_1) \wedge \nabla_{E_1}(x_1, x_1) \wedge x_i)$. If either $\phi = \triangle_{E_k}(x_i, x_j)$ or $\phi = \nabla_{E_k}(x_i, x_j)$, then $\vdash \phi \Leftrightarrow \bigvee_{i=1}^{N}(\phi \wedge x_i)$.

Induction step.

Case 1: $\phi = \phi_1 \vee \phi_2$.

By the induction hypothesis, $\vdash \phi_1 \Leftrightarrow \bigvee_{i=1}^{l_1} \phi_1^i$ and $\vdash \phi_2 \Leftrightarrow \bigvee_{i=1}^{l_2} \phi_2^i$ for some $l_1, l_2 \geq 1$. Hence, we get $\vdash \phi \Leftrightarrow (\bigvee_{i=1}^{l_1} \phi_1^i \vee \bigvee_{i=1}^{l_2} \phi_2^i)$.

Case 2: $\phi = \phi_1 \wedge \phi_2$.

By the induction hypothesis, $\vdash \phi_1 \Leftrightarrow \bigvee_{i=1}^{l_1} \phi_1^i$ and $\vdash \phi_2 \Leftrightarrow \bigvee_{i=1}^{l_2} \phi_2^i$. Thus $\vdash \phi \Leftrightarrow (\bigvee_{i=1}^{l_1} \phi_1^i \wedge \bigvee_{i=1}^{l_2} \phi_2^i)$, and

$$\vdash (\bigvee_{i=1}^{l_1} \phi_1^i \wedge \bigvee_{i=1}^{l_2} \phi_2^i) \Leftrightarrow \bigvee_{\langle i,j \rangle \in \{1,\dots,l_1\} \times \{1,\dots,l_2\}} (\phi_1^i \wedge \phi_2^j).$$

If ϕ_1^i and ϕ_2^j do not share any variable from VARE, then using the axiom (Ax3) one can show that $\vdash (\phi_1^i \wedge \phi_2^j) \Leftrightarrow \bot$. If ϕ_1^i and ϕ_2^j share a variable from VARE, then $\phi_1^i \wedge \phi_2^j$ is a strong characteristic formula. If for some pair $\langle i,j \rangle \in \{1,\dots,l_1\} \times \{1,\dots,l_2\}$, ϕ_1^i and ϕ_2^j share a variable from VARE, then we get a disjunction of strong characteristic formulae as in the previous cases. Otherwise, $\vdash \phi \Leftrightarrow \bot$ and we use the base case for $\bot$.

Case 3: $\phi = \neg\phi_1$.

By the induction hypothesis, $\vdash \phi_1 \Leftrightarrow \bigvee_{i=1}^{l} \phi_1^i$ and therefore $\vdash \phi \Leftrightarrow \bigwedge_{i=1}^{l} \neg\phi_1^i$. Using the axioms (Ax3) and (Ax6), one can show that for every $i \in \{1,\dots,l\}$, we have $\vdash \neg\phi_1^i \Leftrightarrow (\psi_i \vee \bigvee_{k \in \{1,\dots,N\} \setminus \{j(i)\}} x_k)$, where ψ_i is a (possibly empty) disjunction of elements from $\mathrm{FOR}_{\triangle\triangledown}$ and $j(i) \in \{1,\dots,N\}$. By distributing $\wedge$ over $\vee$ in $\bigwedge_{i=1}^{l} (\psi_i \vee \bigvee_{k \in \{1,\dots,N\} \setminus \{j(i)\}} x_k)$, we get a formula ϕ' such that $\vdash \phi \Leftrightarrow \phi'$ and ϕ' is a disjunction of conjunctions. Each conjunction has one of the following forms:

(1) a conjunction of members of $\mathrm{FOR}_{\triangle\triangledown}$. Then using $\vdash \top \Leftrightarrow \bigvee_{i=1}^{N} x_i$, we have $\vdash \psi \Leftrightarrow \bigvee_{i=1}^{N} (\psi \wedge x_i)$ and we obtain that $(\psi \wedge x_i)$ is a strong characteristic formula;

(2) a conjunction containing two different members of VARE. We already know that $\vdash \psi \Leftrightarrow \bigvee_{i=1}^{N} (\triangle_{\mathrm{E}_1}(x_1, x_1) \wedge \triangledown_{\mathrm{E}_1}(x_1, x_1) \wedge x_i)$;

(3) a strong characteristic formula.

So ϕ' is equivalent to a disjunction of strong characteristic formulae and therefore ϕ is equivalent to such a disjunction.   *Q.E.D.*

Lemma 8.3.4. *Let $[A]\phi$ be a formula such that ϕ has no subformulae of the form $[A']\psi$. Then there is a non-empty finite set $\{\phi_1, \dots, \phi_l\}$, $l \geq 1$, of strong characteristic formulae such that $\vdash [A]\phi \Leftrightarrow \bigvee_{i=1}^{l} \phi_i$.*

Proof. Let $[A]\phi$ be a formula such that ϕ has no subformulae of the form $[A']\psi$. By Lemma 6.3.7, and applying the necessitation rule, we get $\vdash [A]\phi \Leftrightarrow [A]\phi_1' \wedge \dots \wedge [A]\phi_l'$, where for every $i \in \{1,\dots,l\}$, ϕ_i' is a disjunction of literals. Using the axioms (Ax6) and (Ax3), we obtain $\vdash [A]\phi \Leftrightarrow [A]\phi_1 \wedge \dots \wedge [A]\phi_l$, where each ϕ_i is a disjunction of members of $\mathrm{FOR}_{\triangle\triangledown} \cup \mathrm{VARE}$. By Lemma

8.3.3, it is sufficient to show that for every $i \in \{1, \ldots, l\}$, there is a finite set $\{\psi_1^i, \ldots, \psi_{j(i)}^i\}$ of strong characteristic formulae such that $\vdash [A]\phi_i \Leftrightarrow \bigvee_{k=1}^{j(i)} \psi_j^i$.
Let us consider the following forms of ϕ_i.

Case 1: ϕ_i is a disjunction of members of $FOR_{\triangle\triangledown}$.
So $\vdash \phi_i \Leftrightarrow (\phi_i \vee \top)$. Using the axiom (Ax10), we get $\vdash [A]\phi_i \Leftrightarrow (\phi_i \vee [A]\top)$.
Applying the necessitation rule, $\vdash \top \Leftrightarrow [A]\top$ and therefore $\vdash [A]\phi_i \Leftrightarrow \phi_i \vee \top$.
By Lemma 8.3.3, $\phi_i \vee \top$ is equivalent to a disjunction of strong characteristic formulae.

Case 2: ϕ_i is a disjunction of all the members of VARE.
So, $\vdash \phi_i \Leftrightarrow \top$ and $\vdash \phi_i \Leftrightarrow (\phi_i \vee \top)$. Using the axiom (Ax10), we get $\vdash [A]\phi_i \Leftrightarrow (\phi_i \vee [A]\top)$. Applying the necessitation rule, we have $\vdash \top \Leftrightarrow [A]\top$ and therefore $\vdash [A]\phi_i \Leftrightarrow \phi_i \vee \top$. By Lemma 8.3.3, $\phi_i \vee \top$ is equivalent to a disjunction of strong characteristic formulae.

Case 3: ϕ_i is a disjunction of (not necessarily all) members of VARE.
Assume that $\phi_i = x_{i_1} \vee \ldots \vee x_{i_k}$, $\{i_1, \ldots, i_k\} \subseteq \{1, \ldots, N\}$, $k \geq 1$.
Using the axiom (Ax3) we have $\vdash \phi_i \Leftrightarrow (\neg x_{j_1} \wedge \ldots \wedge \neg x_{j_{k'}})$, where $\{\{i_1, \ldots, i_k\}, \{j_1, \ldots, j_{k'}\}\}$ is a partition of the set $\{1, \ldots, N\}$. We get $\vdash [A]\phi_i \Leftrightarrow ([A]\neg x_{j_1} \wedge \ldots \wedge [A]\neg x_{j_{k'}})$ by Lemma 6.3.7. Now we distinguish the cases depending on the form of A.

Case 3.1: A $\sim \bot$.
Using the axioms (Ax1) and (Ax2) one can show that $\vdash [A]\phi_i \Leftrightarrow \bot$. By Lemma 8.3.3, $\bot$ is equivalent to a disjunction of strong characteristic formulae.

Case 3.2: A $\sim E_{l_1} \cup \ldots \cup E_{l_m}$, $\{l_1, \ldots, l_m\} \subseteq \{1, \ldots, M\}$.
Using the axioms (Ax1) and (Ax5), we conclude that there is a formula ϕ' such $\vdash [A]\phi_i \Leftrightarrow \phi'$ and ϕ' has no subformulae of the form $[A']\psi$. By Lemma 8.3.3, ϕ' is equivalent to a disjunction of strong characteristic formulae.

Case 4: ϕ_i is a formula of the form $\psi \vee \psi_i$, where ψ is a disjunction of elements from $FOR_{\triangle\triangledown}$ and ψ_i is a disjunction of elements from VARE.
Using the axiom (Ax10) we obtain $\vdash [A]\phi_i \Leftrightarrow \psi \vee [A]\psi_i$. From the previous cases 2 and 3 we get that $[A]\psi_i$ is equivalent to a disjunction of strong characteristic formulae and therefore $\psi \vee [A]\psi_i$ is equivalent to a disjunction of strong characteristic formulae.   Q.E.D.

Theorem 8.3.2. *For every formula ϕ, there is a finite set $\{\phi_1, \ldots, \phi_l\}$ of strong characteristic formulae such that $\vdash \phi \Leftrightarrow \bigvee_{i=1}^{l} \phi_i$.*

Proof. Let ϕ be an IND-formula. We sketch an algorithm that computes a finite set of strong characteristic formulae. Let ψ be a formula variable (at the metalevel). Initialise ψ to ϕ. If ψ contains a subformula of the form $[A]\varphi$ such that $md(\varphi) = 0$, then replace it by its normal form described in Lemma 8.3.4. Repeat the latter step as many times as possible.

After at most $|\phi|$ iterations, ψ is an IND-formula that is equivalent in HIND to ϕ and no formula of the form $[A]\varphi$ occurs in ψ. By Lemma 8.3.3, ψ

has a normal form $\bigvee_{i=1}^{l} \phi_i$, $l \geq 1$, that is equivalent in HIND to ψ, and for every $i \in \{1, \ldots, l\}$, ϕ_i is a strong characteristic formula.   Q.E.D.

Lemma 8.3.5. *Every HIND-consistent formula is IND-satisfiable.*

Proof. If a formula ϕ is HIND-consistent, then by definition not $\vdash \neg\phi$. Equivalently, not $\vdash \phi \Leftrightarrow \bot$. By Theorem 8.3.2, $\vdash \phi \Leftrightarrow \phi'$ for some formula ϕ' being a disjunction of strong characteristic formulae. At least one of the disjuncts of ϕ' is not equivalent to $\bot$, say $\psi \wedge x_k$ for some $k \in \{1, \ldots, N\}$ and for some ψ which is a conjunction of members of $\text{FOR}_{\triangle\triangledown}$. For every $i \in \{1, \ldots, M\}$, we define an equivalence relation $\approx_i^*$. For all $j_1, j_2 \in \{1, \ldots, N\}$, $j_1 \approx_i j_2$ $\overset{\text{def}}{\Leftrightarrow}$ $\triangle_{E_i}(x_{j_1}, x_{j_2})$ occurs in ψ. Then $\approx_i^*$ is defined as the smallest equivalence relation on $\{1, \ldots, N\}$ containing $\approx_i$. By propositional reasoning and by using the axioms (Ax7), (Ax8), and (Ax9), we infer that if $\triangledown_{E_i}(x_{j_1}, x_{j_2})$ occurs in ψ, then not $j_1 \approx_i j_2$. We conclude that not $\vdash \psi \Leftrightarrow \bot$. Let $\mathcal{M} = \langle W, (\equiv_P)_{P \subseteq PAR}, m \rangle$ be the IND-model defined as follows:

⋆ $W \overset{\text{def}}{=} \{1, \ldots, N\}$; $PAR \overset{\text{def}}{=} \{1, \ldots, M\}$;
⋆ for every $i \in \{1, \ldots, N\}$, $m(x_i) \overset{\text{def}}{=} \{i\}$;
⋆ for every $i \in \{1, \ldots, M\}$, $m(E_i) \overset{\text{def}}{=} \{i\}$;
⋆ $\equiv_\emptyset \overset{\text{def}}{=} \{1, \ldots, N\} \times \{1, \ldots, N\}$;
⋆ for every $i \in \{1, \ldots, M\}$, $\equiv_{\{i\}} \overset{\text{def}}{=} \approx_i^*$;
⋆ for every $\emptyset \neq P \subseteq PAR$, $\equiv_P \overset{\text{def}}{=} \bigcap_{i \in P} \equiv_{\{i\}}$.

It is now a routine task to check that $\mathcal{M}, k \models \psi \wedge x_k$ and therefore $\mathcal{M}, k \models \phi$.
Q.E.D.

Theorem 8.3.3. *(Completeness Theorem)* VAL(IND) $\subseteq$ THM(HIND).

Proof. Let ϕ be an IND-valid formula. Suppose $\phi \notin$ THM(HIND). So $\neg\phi$ is HIND-consistent and therefore $\neg\phi$ is IND-satisfiable by Lemma 8.3.5. But this is in contradiction with the IND-validity of ϕ.   Q.E.D.

The developments of this section can be adapted to the case when the relations in the IND-models are not necessarily equivalence relations but are first-order definable with a set of Horn formulae (as in Sect. 7.4.4 for the extensions of the logic SIM). Since the class of relations definable by a set of Horn formulae is closed under intersection, the models still contain a strong family of binary relations. Other first-order definable classes of relations (not necessarily closed under intersection) can also be expressed in the language of IND. For instance, the axiom corresponding to seriality is

$$\bigwedge_{k=1}^{M} \bigwedge_{i=1}^{N} \bigvee_{j=1}^{N} \triangle_{E_k}(x_i, x_j).$$

Since W has a fixed finite cardinality, each existential quantifier is encoded by a disjunction containing exactly N disjuncts. Actually, one can generalise the above observation. Since there is a finite amount of binary relations on a set of cardinality N (modulo the isomorphic copies) and since any binary relation of such a kind can be expressed by a conjunction of conjuncts of the form $\triangle_{E_k}(x_i, x_j)$, any property of a binary relation on a set of cardinality N can be expressed in the language of IND.

8.4 LA-logics

LA-logics are intended to be generalisations of the logic DALLA. Let $\mathcal{M} = \langle W, (R_a)_{a \in M_0}, m \rangle$ be a DALLA'-model. For every $x \in W$, we define a reflexive and transitive relation $\leq_x$ on M_0 as follows: $c \leq_x d \overset{\text{def}}{\Leftrightarrow} R_c(x) \subseteq R_d(x)$ for all $c, d \in M_0$. Observe that the relation $\leq_x$ is totally connected since any two relations in $\mathcal{M}$ are in local agreement. In this section we introduce the class of *LA-logics* $\mathcal{L}$ ("logics with local agreement") such that in every model $\mathcal{M} \in \text{MOD}(\mathcal{L})$ any two relations are in local agreement. Furthermore, each LA-logic is characterised by a class $\text{lin}(\mathcal{L})$ of linear orders such that for every $\mathcal{M} \in \text{MOD}(\mathcal{L})$ and for every $x \in \mathcal{M}$, there is a linear order in $\text{lin}(\mathcal{L})$ which is a subset of $\leq_x$. The elements of $\text{lin}(\mathcal{L})$ are linear orders and therefore antisymmetry is required although $\leq_x$ is not necessarily antisymmetric. However, such a twist is harmless as the following lemma shows.

Lemma 8.4.1. *Let R be a reflexive, transitive, and totally connected binary relation on W. Then there is a linear order R' on W such that $R' \subseteq R$.*

Proof. Let $\mathcal{X}$ be the class of sets $X \subseteq W$ such that $R_{|X} = X \times X$ and for every Y, if $X \subset Y$, then $R_{|Y} \neq Y \times Y$. One can show that $\mathcal{X}$ is a partition of W. Let R' be the relation defined as follows. By the well-ordering principle, for every $X \in \mathcal{X}$, there is a well-ordering $\leq_X$ on X. In particular $\leq_X$ is a linear order. Then:

$$R' \overset{\text{def}}{=} (\bigcup_{X \in \mathcal{X}} \leq_X) \cup \{\langle x, y \rangle : X, Y \in \mathcal{X},\ X \neq Y,\ x \in X, y \in Y,\ \langle x, y \rangle \in R\}.$$

One can check that R' is a linear order on W and $R' \subseteq R$. By way of example, we show that R' is antisymmetric. Assume that $\langle x, y \rangle \in R'$ and $\langle y, x \rangle \in R'$. If x and y belong to the same set X of $\mathcal{X}$, we have $x \leq_X y$ and $y \leq_X x$. Since $\leq_X$ is a linear order on X, we obtain $x = y$. If x and y belong to different classes of $\mathcal{X}$, say X and Y, respectively, then we have $\langle x, y \rangle \in R$ and $\langle y, x \rangle \in R$. So $X = Y$, which leads to a contradiction.   *Q.E.D.*

8.4.1 Language and Semantics

A *modal language* L *for LA-logics* is defined as follows:

⋆ the set M_0 of basic modal expressions is a countable set of modal constants (not necessarily infinite);

* the set O_M is empty and the set M of modal expressions is M_0;
* the set FOR_0 of basic formulae is a countably infinite set of propositional variables and the set O_{FOR} of logical connectives is $\{\neg, \wedge\} \cup \{[a] : a \in M\}$.

Definition 8.4.1. *A logic* $\mathcal{L} = \langle L, S \rangle$ *is said to be an LA-logic* $\overset{\text{def}}{\Leftrightarrow}$ *L is a modal language for LA-logics and there is a non-empty set* $\lin(\mathcal{L})$ *of linear orders on* M_0 *such that for every model* $\mathcal{M} = \langle W, (R_a)_{a \in M}, m \rangle$, $\mathcal{M} \in S$ $\overset{\text{def}}{\Leftrightarrow}$

(1) for every $a \in M$, R_a *is an equivalence relation;*
(2) for every $w \in W$, *there is* $\preceq \in \lin(\mathcal{L})$ *such that for all* $c, d \in M_0$, *if* $c \preceq d$, *then* $R_c(w) \subseteq R_d(w)$.

The set $\lin(\mathcal{L})$ *is said to be the set of local agreements of* $\mathcal{L}$.

Condition (2) in Definition 8.4.1 states that locally the relations in the family $(R_c)_{c \in M_0}$ (or, equivalently in the family $(R_c)_{c \in M}$ since $M_0 = M$) are linearly ordered with respect to the set inclusion. However, several different orderings may be given for each LA-logic. Consequently, every non-empty set Z of linear orders on M_0 determines a unique LA-logic $\mathcal{L}$ such that $\lin(\mathcal{L}) = Z$. It is easy to show that for every LA-logic $\mathcal{L}$ and for every $\mathcal{L}$-model $\mathcal{M} = \langle W, (R_a)_{a \in M}, m \rangle$, for all $c, d \in M_0$, R_c and R_d satisfy the local agreement condition presented in Definition 8.2.1.

Example 8.4.1. Let $\mathcal{L}$ be the LA-logic such that $M_0 = \{1, 2\}$ and for every model $\mathcal{M} = \langle W, R_1, R_2, m \rangle$, $\mathcal{M} \in MOD(\mathcal{L})$ $\overset{\text{def}}{\Leftrightarrow}$ R_1 and R_2 are equivalence relations and $R_1 \subseteq R_2$. $\mathcal{L}$ is an LA-logic such that $\lin(\mathcal{L})$ is the singleton set $\{\leq\}$ with $1 < 2$.

Lemma 8.4.2. DALLA' *is an LA-logic.*

Proof. We show that DALLA' is the LA-logic such that $\lin(\text{DALLA}')$ is the class of all the linear orders on M_0.
First, take a $LAN(\text{DALLA}')$-model $\mathcal{M} = \langle W, (R_a)_{a \in M}, m \rangle$ such that for every $a \in M$, R_a is an equivalence relation and for every $x \in W$, there is a linear order $\preceq$ on $M = M_0$ such that for all $c, d \in M_0$, if $c \preceq d$, then $R_c(x) \subseteq R_d(x)$. Consequently, for every $x \in W$ and for all $c, d \in M_0$, either $R_c(x) \subseteq R_d(x)$ or $R_d(x) \subseteq R_c(x)$, since $\preceq$ is totally connected. So $\mathcal{M}$ is a DALLA'-model. Second, let $\mathcal{M}$ be a DALLA'-model. For every $x \in W$, let $\leq_x$ be the binary relation on M_0 such that $c \leq_x d$ $\overset{\text{def}}{\Leftrightarrow}$ $R_c(x) \subseteq R_d(x)$ for all $c, d \in M_0$. Since $\leq_x$ is reflexive, transitive, and totally connected, by Lemma 8.4.1 there is a linear order $\preceq$ on M_0 such that $\preceq \subseteq \leq_x$. So if $c \preceq d$, then $c \leq_x d$ and therefore $R_c(x) \subseteq R_d(x)$.   *Q.E.D.*

The following lemma states that every LA-logic is closed under restriction (see Sect. 6.2.2).

Lemma 8.4.3. *Let* $\mathcal{L}$ *be an LA-logic and let* $\mathcal{M} = \langle W, (R_a)_{a \in M}, m \rangle \in MOD(\mathcal{L})$. *Then for every* $\emptyset \neq W' \subseteq W$, $\mathcal{M}_{|W'} \in MOD(\mathcal{L})$.

8.4.2 Hilbert-style Proof Systems

In this section we consider the LA-logics with a finite set $\operatorname{lin}(\mathcal{L})$ of linear orders, including the case when M_0 itself is finite. Unless stated otherwise, in the rest of the section $\mathcal{L}$ denotes such an LA-logic.

By Definition 8.4.1, $\operatorname{TFOR}(\operatorname{FR}(\mathcal{L})) = \operatorname{VAL}(\mathcal{L})$. Although it is clear that $\operatorname{FR}(\mathcal{L})$ is closed under restriction (see Lemma 8.4.3), we shall show that, moreover, $\operatorname{TFR}(\operatorname{VAL}(\mathcal{L}))$ is closed under subframes. Now, we can only state the following property.

Lemma 8.4.4. $\operatorname{FR}(\mathcal{L}) \subseteq \operatorname{TFR}(\operatorname{VAL}(\mathcal{L}))$.

Proof. Let $F = \langle W, (R_a)_{a \in M} \rangle$ be in $\operatorname{FR}(\mathcal{L})$. Every model based on F belongs to $\operatorname{MOD}(\mathcal{L})$. Hence, for every $\psi \in \operatorname{VAL}(\mathcal{L})$, $F \models \psi$. So $F \in \operatorname{TFR}(\operatorname{VAL}(\mathcal{L}))$. Q.E.D.

Let $\preceq$ be a linear order on a finite subset $\{c_1, \ldots, c_n\}$, $n \geq 1$, of modal constants. Let σ be the permutation of $\{1, \ldots, n\}$ such that for every $j \in \{1, \ldots, n-1\}$, $c_{\sigma(j)} \preceq c_{\sigma(j+1)}$. σ is said to be a permutation associated to $\preceq$.

The axioms of the deduction system $H\mathcal{L}$ are of the following form. Let X be a finite set of linear orders on a finite set Y of modal constants with at least two elements. Let $\operatorname{fla}(X)$ be the formula

$$\operatorname{fla}(X) \stackrel{\text{def}}{=} \bigvee_{\preceq \in X} \left(\bigwedge_{j \in \{2, \ldots, \operatorname{card}(Y)\}} ([c_{\sigma_\preceq(j)}]p_\preceq \Rightarrow [c_{\sigma_\preceq(j-1)}]p_\preceq) \right),$$

where $\sigma_\preceq$ is a permutation associated to $\preceq$, $Y = \{c_{\sigma_\preceq(1)}, \ldots, c_{\sigma_\preceq(\operatorname{card}(Y))}\}$, and each $p_\preceq$ is a propositional variable such that if $\preceq \neq \preceq'$, then the propositional variables $p_\preceq$ and $p_{\preceq'}$ are different.

Let X be a set of linear orders on M_0. We write $X \uparrow Y$ to denote the restrictions of the linear orders in X to the set $Y \subseteq M_0$. Hence, $X \uparrow Y = \{\preceq_{|Y}: \preceq \in X\}$. Theorem 8.4.1 roughly states that the condition of local agreement with respect to a finite $\operatorname{lin}(\mathcal{L})$ is modally definable.

Theorem 8.4.1. *Let* L *be a language for LA-logics and let* $F = \langle W, (R_a)_{a \in M} \rangle$ *be an* L*-frame. For every LA-logic* $\mathcal{L}$ *with language* L *such that* $\operatorname{lin}(\mathcal{L})$ *is finite, the following statements are equivalent:*

(I) $F \models \{\operatorname{fla}(\operatorname{lin}(\mathcal{L}) \uparrow Y) : Y \subseteq M_0, 2 \leq \operatorname{card}(Y) \leq 2 \times \operatorname{card}(\operatorname{lin}(\mathcal{L}))\}$;
(II) for every $w \in W$ *there exists* $\preceq \in \operatorname{lin}(\mathcal{L})$ *such that for all* $c, d \in M_0$, $c \preceq d$ *implies* $R_c(w) \subseteq R_d(w)$.

Proof. (I) $\rightarrow$ (II) Suppose there is an $x_0 \in W$ such that for every $\preceq \in \operatorname{lin}(\mathcal{L})$, there are $c_\preceq$ and $d_\preceq$ such that $c_\preceq \preceq d_\preceq$ and $R_{c_\preceq}(x_0) \not\subseteq R_{d_\preceq}(x_0)$. Hence, for every $\preceq \in \operatorname{lin}(\mathcal{L})$, there is a $y_\preceq \in W$ such that $\langle x_0, y_\preceq \rangle \in R_{c_\preceq}$ and $\langle x_0, y_\preceq \rangle \notin$

$R_{d_{\prec}}$. Let $Z = \text{lin}(\mathcal{L}) \uparrow Y_0$ where $Y_0 = \bigcup\{\{c_{\prec}, d_{\prec}\} : \preceq \in \text{lin}(\mathcal{L})\}$. We observe that $2 \leq \text{card}(Y_0) \leq 2 \times \text{card}(\text{lin}(\mathcal{L}))$. Consequently, we have

$$\text{fla}(Z) \in \{\text{fla}(\text{lin}(\mathcal{L}) \uparrow Y) : Y \subseteq M_0, 2 \leq \text{card}(Y) \leq 2 \times \text{card}(\text{lin}(\mathcal{L}))\}.$$

By the definition of Z, for every $\rho \in Z$, there is a linear order $\preceq_\rho \in \text{lin}(\mathcal{L})$ such that $(\preceq_\rho)_{|Y_0} = \rho$.

Let $\mathcal{M} = \langle W, (R_a)_{a \in M}, m \rangle$ be a model based on F such that for every $\rho \in Z$, $m(p_\rho) \overset{\text{def}}{=} R_{d_{\preceq_\rho}}(x)$. Since by the assumption $F \models \text{fla}(Z)$, we have $\mathcal{M}, x_0 \models \text{fla}(Z)$ and hence there is a linear order $\rho_0 \in Z$ such that

$$\mathcal{M}, x_0 \models \bigwedge_{j \in \{2, \ldots, \text{card}(Y_0)\}} [c_{\sigma_{\rho_0}(j)}]p_{\rho_0} \Rightarrow [c_{\sigma_{\rho_0}(j-1)}]p_{\rho_0}.$$

Since $\{c_{\preceq_{\rho_0}}, d_{\preceq_{\rho_0}}\} \subseteq Y_0$ and $\langle c_{\preceq_{\rho_0}}, d_{\preceq_{\rho_0}} \rangle \in \rho_0 = (\preceq_{\rho_0})_{|Y_0}$, we get $\mathcal{M}, x \models [d_{\preceq_{\rho_0}}]p_{\rho_0} \Rightarrow [c_{\preceq_{\rho_0}}]p_{\rho_0}$ by transitivity of $\Rightarrow$. By the construction of m, we have $\mathcal{M}, x_0 \models [d_{\preceq_{\rho_0}}]p_{\rho_0}$. Therefore $\mathcal{M}, x_0 \models [c_{\preceq_{\rho_0}}]p_{\rho_0}$ and $\mathcal{M}, y_{\preceq_{\rho_0}} \models p_{\rho_0}$, since we have $\langle x_0, y_{\preceq_{\rho_0}} \rangle \in R_{c_{\preceq_{\rho_0}}}$. However, $\langle x_0, y_{\preceq_{\rho_0}} \rangle \notin R_{d_{\preceq_{\rho_0}}}$ implies $y_{\preceq_{\rho_0}} \notin m(p_{\rho_0})$ by the definition of m, which leads to a contradiction.

(II) $\to$ (I) Let $\mathcal{M} = \langle W, (R_a)_{a \in M}, m \rangle$ be a model based on F. Let $Y \subseteq M_0$ be such that $2 \leq \text{card}(Y) \leq 2 \times M$ and let $Z = \text{lin}(\mathcal{L}) \uparrow Y$. For every $w \in W$, there is a linear order $\preceq \in Z$, such that $R_{c_{\sigma_{\prec}(1)}}(w) \subseteq \ldots \subseteq R_{c_{\sigma_{\prec}(\text{card}(Y))}}(w)$. For every $k \in \{1, \ldots, \text{card}(Y)\}$, for every $k' \in \{1, \ldots, k\}$, and for every propositional variable p, $\mathcal{M}, w \models [c_{\sigma_{\prec}(k)}]p \Rightarrow [c_{\sigma_{\prec}(k')}]p$. Hence $\mathcal{M}, w \models \text{fla}(Z)$, since $\mathcal{M}, w \models \bigwedge_{j \in \{2, \ldots, \text{card}(Y)\}} [c_{\sigma_{\prec}(j)}]p_{\preceq} \Rightarrow [c_{\sigma_{\prec}(j-1)}]p_{\preceq}$.   Q.E.D.

For a finite M_0, Theorem 8.4.1 can be simplified in the following way.

Theorem 8.4.2. *Let L be a language for LA-logics and $F = \langle W, (R_a)_{a \in M} \rangle$ be an L-frame. For every LA-logic $\mathcal{L}$ with language L, if M_0 is finite, then the following statements are equivalent:*

(I) $F \models \text{fla}(\text{lin}(\mathcal{L}))$;
(II) for every $w \in W$ there exists a linear order $\preceq \in \text{lin}(\mathcal{L})$ such that for all c, d $\in M_0$, c $\preceq$ d implies $R_c(w) \subseteq R_d(w)$.

Theorem 8.4.1 and Theorem 8.4.2 provide correspondence results for the generalised local agreement condition. It should be observed that in Theorem 8.4.1, the set $\{\text{fla}(\text{lin}(\mathcal{L}) \uparrow Y) : Y \subseteq M_0, 2 \leq \text{card}(Y) \leq 2 \times \text{card}(\text{lin}(\mathcal{L}))\}$ in (I) is infinite if M_0 is infinite. Moreover, the following holds.

Lemma 8.4.5. *For all finite subsets Y and Y' of M_0, if $Y \subseteq Y'$, then $F \models \text{fla}(\text{lin}(\mathcal{L}) \uparrow Y') \Rightarrow \text{fla}(\text{lin}(\mathcal{L}) \uparrow Y)$ for every L-frame F.*

Proof. Let $\mathcal{M} = \langle W, (R_a)_{a \in M}, m \rangle$ be an L-model and let $x \in W$. Assume that $\mathcal{M}, x \models \text{fla}(\text{lin}(\mathcal{L}) \uparrow Y')$. Since $Y \subseteq Y'$, for every $\preceq \in \text{lin}(\mathcal{L}) \uparrow Y$, there is a linear order $\preceq' \in \text{lin}(\mathcal{L}) \uparrow Y'$ such that $\preceq \subseteq \preceq'$, which leads to $\mathcal{M}, x \models \text{fla}(\text{lin}(\mathcal{L}) \uparrow Y)$.   Q.E.D.

Thus, in Theorem 8.4.1, the set of formulae in (I) can be replaced by

$$\{\mathrm{fla}(\mathrm{lin}(\mathcal{L}) \uparrow Y) : Y \subseteq M_0, \mathrm{card}(Y) = 2 \times \mathrm{card}(\mathrm{lin}(\mathcal{L}))\}.$$

Corollary 8.4.1. *Let* H *be an extension of the system* $\mathrm{HK}(\mathrm{LAN}(\mathcal{L}))$. *If*

$$\{\mathrm{fla}(\mathrm{lin}(\mathcal{L}) \uparrow Y) : Y \subseteq M_0, 2 \leq \mathrm{card}(Y) \leq 2 \times \mathrm{card}(\mathrm{lin}(\mathcal{L}))\} \subseteq \mathrm{THM}(H),$$

then for every $F = \langle W, (R_a)_{a \in M} \rangle \in \mathrm{TFR}(\mathrm{THM}(H))$ *and for every* $w \in W$, *there is a linear order* $\preceq \in lo(\mathcal{L})$ *such that for all* $c, d \in M_0$, $c \preceq d$ *implies* $R_c(w) \subseteq R_d(w)$.

Let H$\mathcal{L}$ be an extension of HS5(L) obtained by adding the axiom:

(Ax1) $\mathrm{fla}(\mathrm{lin}(\mathcal{L}) \uparrow Y)$ for all finite $Y \subseteq M_0$ such that $2 \leq \mathrm{card}(Y) \leq 2 \times \mathrm{card}(\mathrm{lin}(\mathcal{L}))$.

For effectivity reasons, it is desirable that (Ax1) generates a countable set of formulae, which is related to the following $\mathcal{L}$-*ordering problem*:

input: a finite subset Y of M and a linear order $\preceq$ on Y;
question: $\preceq \in \mathrm{lin}(\mathcal{L}) \uparrow Y$?

We assume that $\preceq$ has a finite representation in a succinct encoding. If the $\mathcal{L}$-ordering problem is decidable, then (Ax1) generates a countable set of formulae. If $\mathrm{lin}(\mathcal{L})$ is finite, and if for given $a, b \in M$ and $\preceq \in \mathrm{lin}(\mathcal{L})$) the problem of checking whether $\langle a, b \rangle \in \preceq$ is decidable, then the $\mathcal{L}$-ordering problem is decidable.

Theorem 8.4.3. *(Soundness Theorem)* $\mathrm{THM}(H\mathcal{L}) \subseteq \mathrm{VAL}(\mathcal{L})$.

The proof is based on Corollary 8.4.1.

Let $\mathcal{M}^c$ be the canonical structure for H$\mathcal{L}$ defined as in Sect. 6.3.4.

Lemma 8.4.6. $\mathcal{M}^c \in \mathrm{MOD}(\mathcal{L})$.

Proof. By Lemma 6.3.11, the relations in $\mathcal{M}^c$ are equivalence relations. We prove that for every $X \in W^c$, there is a linear order $\preceq \in \mathrm{lin}(\mathcal{L})$ such that for all $c, d \in M_0$, $c \preceq d$ implies $R_c^c(X) \subseteq R_d^c(X)$. Suppose there is an $X_0 \in W^c$ such that for every $\preceq \in \mathrm{lin}(\mathcal{L})$, there are $c_{\preceq}$ and $d_{\preceq}$ in M_0 such that $c_{\preceq} \preceq d_{\preceq}$ and $R_{c_{\preceq}}^c(X_0) \not\subseteq R_{d_{\preceq}}^c(X_0)$. Hence, for every $\preceq \in \mathrm{lin}(\mathcal{L})$, there is a $Y_{\preceq} \in W^c$ such that $\langle X_0, Y_{\preceq} \rangle \in R_{c_{\preceq}}^c$, and there is a formula $\phi_{\preceq}$ such that $[d_{\preceq}]\phi_{\preceq} \in X_0$ and $\phi_{\preceq} \notin Y_{\preceq}$. Let $Z = \mathrm{lin}(\mathcal{L}) \uparrow Y_0$, where $Y_0 = \bigcup\{\{c_{\preceq}, d_{\preceq}\} : \preceq \in \mathrm{lin}(\mathcal{L})\}$. By the definition of Z, for every $\rho \in Z$, there is a linear order $\preceq_{\rho} \in \mathrm{lin}(\mathcal{L})$ such that $(\preceq_{\rho})_{|Y_0} = \rho$. Let ϕ be the formula obtained from $\mathrm{fla}(Z)$ by simultaneously replacing each p_{ρ} by $\phi_{\preceq_{\rho}}$ for every $\rho \in Z$. The formula ϕ belongs to $\mathrm{THM}(H\mathcal{L})$, $\phi \in X_0$ (by Lemma 6.3.5(IV)), and by Lemma 6.3.5(II) there is a $\rho_0 \in Z$ such that

$$\bigwedge_{j\in\{2,\dots,\mathrm{card}(Y_0)\}} [c_{\sigma_{\rho_0}(j)}]\phi_{\preceq\rho_0} \Rightarrow [c_{\sigma_{\rho_0}(j-1)}]\phi_{\preceq\rho_0}.$$

Since $\langle c_{\preceq\rho_0}, d_{\preceq\rho_0}\rangle \in \rho_0$ and $[d_{\preceq\rho_0}]\phi_{\preceq\rho_0} \in X_0$, we have $[c_{\preceq\rho_0}]\phi_{\preceq\rho_0} \in X_0$, Thus $\phi_{\preceq\rho_0} \in Y_{\preceq\rho_0}$, since $\langle X_0, Y_{\preceq\rho_0}\rangle \in R^c_{c_{\preceq\rho}}$, which leads to a contradiction. $Q.E.D.$

Theorem 8.4.4. $\mathrm{TFOR}(\mathrm{FR}(\mathcal{L})) \subseteq \mathrm{THM}(\mathrm{H}\mathcal{L})$.

Proof. Assume that $\phi \in \mathrm{TFOR}(\mathrm{FR}(\mathcal{L}))$ and suppose $\phi \notin \mathrm{THM}(\mathrm{H}\mathcal{L})$. So $\{\phi\}$ is a H$\mathcal{L}$-consistent set and by Theorem 6.3.4 there is a maximal H$\mathcal{L}$-consistent set, say X, such that $\neg\phi \in X$. Then $\mathcal{M}^c \not\models \phi$ by Theorem 6.3.6. Since $\mathcal{M}^c \in \mathrm{MOD}(\mathcal{L})$, we have $\langle W^c, (R^c_a)_{a\in M}\rangle \in \mathrm{FR}(\mathcal{L})$. This yields $\phi \notin \mathrm{TFOR}(\mathrm{FR}(\mathcal{L}))$, which leads to a contradiction. $\hspace{2cm} Q.E.D.$

Theorem 8.4.5. *(Completeness Theorem)* $\mathrm{VAL}(\mathcal{L}) \subseteq \mathrm{THM}(\mathrm{H}\mathcal{L})$.

Proof. By Theorem 8.4.3 and Theorem 8.4.4, $\mathrm{TFOR}(\mathrm{FR}(\mathcal{L})) = \mathrm{THM}(\mathrm{H}\mathcal{L})$. Hence, $\mathrm{VAL}(\mathcal{L}) = \mathrm{THM}(\mathrm{H}\mathcal{L})$, and therefore H$\mathcal{L}$ is a proof system for $\mathcal{L}$. $Q.E.D.$

If M_0 is finite, then the axiom (Ax1) in the definition of H$\mathcal{L}$ can be replaced by $\mathrm{fla}(\mathrm{lin}(\mathcal{L}))$ and Theorem 8.4.5 still holds true.

One can also observe that the formula fla from the definition of (Ax1) is equivalent in HK(L) to the following conjunction of Sahlqvist formulae:

$$\bigwedge_{f:\mathrm{lin}(\mathcal{L})\to\{2,\dots,\mathrm{card}(Y)\}} \left(\bigwedge_{\preceq\in\mathrm{lin}(\mathcal{L})} [c_{\sigma_{\preceq}(f(\preceq))}]p_{\preceq}\right) \Rightarrow \left(\bigvee_{\preceq\in\mathrm{lin}(\mathcal{L})} [c_{\sigma_{\preceq}(f(\preceq)-1)}]p_{\preceq}\right).$$

Considering the correspondence result of Theorem 8.4.1 and the correspondences for reflexivity, symmetry, and transitivity stated in Sect. 7.2 we get $\mathrm{THM}(\mathrm{H}\mathcal{L}) = \mathrm{TFOR}(\mathrm{FR}(\mathcal{L}))$.

8.5 A Fuzzy Logic of Graded Modalities

The logic LLOM of linearly ordered modalities is intended to provide a means for reasoning about graded equivalence relations. The language of LLOM is defined as follows:

⋆ the set M_0 of basic modal expressions is the set of rational numbers in $[0, 1]_\mathbb{Q}$;
⋆ M equals M_0;
⋆ the set FOR$_0$ of basic formulae is a countably infinite set of propositional variables;
⋆ the set O$_{\mathrm{FOR}}$ of logical connectives is $\{\neg, \wedge\} \cup \{[a] : a \in M\}$.

Let LLOM be the LA-logic such that for every LAN(LLOM)-model $\mathcal{M} = \langle W, (R_\lambda)_{\lambda \in [0,1]_\mathbb{Q}}, m \rangle$, $\mathcal{M} \in \text{MOD(LLOM)} \overset{\text{def}}{\Leftrightarrow}$ for all rational numbers $\lambda, \lambda' \in [0,1]_\mathbb{Q}$, R_λ is an equivalence relation and if $\lambda < \lambda'$, then $R_{\lambda'} \subseteq R_\lambda$. So lin(LLOM) is a singleton set consisting of the natural linear order $\geq$ on $[0,1]_\mathbb{Q}$. Axiomatisation of LLOM can be defined using the results from the previous section since lin(LLOM) is finite. We shall show that the logic LLOM shares many properties with the logic LGM of graded modalities which is a familiar fuzzy logic. Our main result is the equality: VAL(LGM) = VAL(LLOM).

LGM is the logic whose language is the same as the language of LLOM. Semantics of LGM is defined as follows.
An LAN(LGM)-model $\mathcal{M} = \langle W, (R_\lambda)_{\lambda \in [0,1]_\mathbb{Q}}, m \rangle$ is an LGM-model $\overset{\text{def}}{\Leftrightarrow}$ there is a map $\mu : W \times W \to [0,1]$ such that:

(1) $\mu(x,x) = 1$ for every $x \in W$;
(2) $\mu(x,y) = \mu(y,x)$ for all $x, y \in W$;
(3) $\mu(x,z) \geq sup(\{min(\mu(x,y), \mu(y,z)) : y \in W\})$ for all $x, z \in W$;
(4) $R_\lambda = \{\langle x,y \rangle \in W \times W : \mu(x,y) \geq \lambda\}$ for every $\lambda \in [0,1]_\mathbb{Q}$.

Conditions (1)–(3) state that μ is an L_0-fuzzy relation on W, where L_0 is the lattice of real numbers from the unit interval $[0,1]$ (see for example Sect. 2.7) such that μ is reflexive, symmetric, and strongly transitive in the the sense defined in Sect. 3.11. Observe that in the presence of (1), condition (3) is equivalent to

(3′) for all $x, z \in W$, $\mu(x,z) = sup(\{min(\mu(x,y), \mu(y,z)) : y \in W\})$.

One can check that the binary relations R_λ in an LGM-model are equivalence relations. Lemma 8.5.1 is by an easy verification.

Lemma 8.5.1. MOD(LGM) $\subseteq$ MOD(LLOM).

The following lemma states a kind of a converse result.

Lemma 8.5.2. *Let* $\mathcal{M} = \langle W, (R_\lambda)_{\lambda \in [0,1]_\mathbb{Q}}, m \rangle \in \text{MOD(LLOM)}$, *let* $w \in W$, *and let* ϕ *be an LAN(LGM)-formula. Let* $\lambda_1, \ldots, \lambda_n$, $n \geq 1$, *be rational numbers which are the indices of the modal connectives occurring in* ϕ *such that* $\lambda_1 < \ldots < \lambda_n$. *Let* $\mathcal{M}' = \mathcal{M}_{|R_{\lambda_1}(w)} = \langle R_{\lambda_1}(w), (R'_\lambda)_{\lambda \in [0,1]_\mathbb{Q}}, m' \rangle$, *and let* $\mathcal{M}'' = \langle R_{\lambda_1}(w), (R''_\lambda)_{\lambda \in [0,1]_\mathbb{Q}}, m' \rangle$ *be a structure such that:*

⋆ *for every* $\lambda \in [0, \lambda_1]_\mathbb{Q}$, $R''_\lambda \overset{\text{def}}{=} R'_{\lambda_1}$;
⋆ *for every* $i \in \{1, \ldots, n-1\}$ *and for every* $\lambda \in (\lambda_i, \lambda_{i+1}]_\mathbb{Q}$, $R''_\lambda \overset{\text{def}}{=} R'_{\lambda_{i+1}}$;
⋆ *for every* $\lambda \in (\lambda_n, 1]_\mathbb{Q}$, $R''_\lambda \overset{\text{def}}{=} R'_1$.

Then

(I) for every $w' \in R_{\lambda_1}(w)$, *the following conditions are equivalent:*
    (I.1) $\mathcal{M}, w' \models \phi$;

(I.2) $\mathcal{M}', w' \models \phi$;
(I.3) $\mathcal{M}'', w' \models \phi$.
(II) $\mathcal{M}'' \in \text{MOD(LGM)}$.

Proof. (I) Observe that $\mathcal{M}' \in \text{MOD(LLOM)}$ and $R_{\lambda_1} = (R_{\lambda_1} \cup \ldots \cup R_{\lambda_n})^*$ which guarantees that (I.1) iff (I.2). Moreover, for every $\lambda \in \{\lambda_1, \ldots, \lambda_n\}$, $R'_\lambda = R''_\lambda$, so for every $w' \in R_{\lambda_1}(w)$, $\mathcal{M}', w' \models \phi$ iff $\mathcal{M}'', w' \models \phi$, which means (I.2) iff (I.3).
(II) We define the map $\mu : R_{\lambda_1}(w) \times R_{\lambda_1}(w) \to [0,1]$ such that for every pair $\langle x, y \rangle \in R_{\lambda_1}(w) \times R_{\lambda_1}(w)$,

$$\mu(x,y) \stackrel{\text{def}}{=} sup(\{\lambda \in [0,1] : \langle x, y \rangle \in R''_\lambda\}).$$

This definition is correct since the latter set is non-empty (it contains λ_1) and $sup(\{\lambda \in [0,1] : (x,y) \in R''_\lambda\})$ always exists. The number $sup(\{\lambda \in [0,1]_{\mathbb{Q}} : \langle x, y \rangle \in R''_\lambda\})$ is an element of the set $\{\lambda_1, \ldots, \lambda_n, 1\}$. Hence, by construction of μ, for every pair $\langle x, y \rangle \in R_{\lambda_1}(w) \times R_{\lambda_1}(w)$, $\mu(x,y) = sup(\{\lambda \in [0,1]_{\mathbb{Q}} : \langle x, y \rangle \in R''_\lambda\})$.

Now we prove that the conditions (1)–(4) from the definition of LGM-models are satisfied.
Proof of (1): since R''_1 is reflexive, then for every $x \in R_{\lambda_1}(w)$, $\mu(x,x) = 1$.
Proof of (2): for all $x, y \in R_{\lambda_1}(w)$, $\mu(x,y) = max\{\lambda : \langle x, y \rangle \in R''_\lambda\} = max\{\lambda : \langle y, x \rangle \in R''_\lambda\}$ (by symmetry of the relations R''_λ), whence $\mu(x,y) = \mu(y,x)$.
Proof of (3): take $x, y, z \in R_{\lambda_1}(w)$. Let $\kappa = min(\mu(x,y), \mu(y,z))$. By definition of μ, $\kappa = min(sup(\{\lambda : \langle x, y \rangle \in R''_\lambda\}), sup(\{\lambda : \langle y, z \rangle \in R''_\lambda\}))$. It follows that $sup(\{\lambda : \langle x, y \rangle \in R''_\lambda\}) \geq \kappa$. There is a $\kappa' \geq \kappa$ such that $\langle x, y \rangle \in R''_{\kappa'}$ and hence $\langle x, y \rangle \in R''_\kappa$ since $R''_{\kappa'} \subseteq R''_\kappa$. In a similar way it can be shown that $\langle y, z \rangle \in R''_\kappa$. By transitivity, $\langle x, z \rangle \in R''_\kappa$, whence $\mu(x,z) \geq \kappa$ by definition of μ. Thus for all $x, y, z \in R_{\lambda_1}(w)$, $\mu(x,z) \geq min(\mu(x,y), \mu(y,z))$. Consequently, for all $x, z \in R_{\lambda_1}(w)$, $\mu(x,z) \geq sup(\{min(\mu(x,y), \mu(y,z)) : y \in R_{\lambda_1}(w)\})$.
Proof of (4): by construction of $\mathcal{M}''$, $\langle x, y \rangle \in R''_{\lambda'}$ iff $\lambda' \in \{\lambda : \langle x, y \rangle \in R''_\lambda\}$ iff $\lambda' \leq max\{\lambda : \langle x, y \rangle \in R''_\lambda\}$ iff $\lambda' \leq \mu(x,y)$. Hence, for all $x, y \in R_{\lambda_1}(w)$ and for every $\lambda \in [0,1]_{\mathbb{Q}}$, $R''_\lambda = \{\langle x, y \rangle : \mu(x,y) \geq \lambda\}$. This completes the proof. *Q.E.D.*

Theorem 8.5.1. VAL(LGM) = VAL(LLOM).

Proof. ($\to$) Assume $\phi \in$ VAL(LGM) and suppose $\phi \notin$ VAL(LLOM). So there is an $\mathcal{M} \in \text{MOD(LLOM)}$ such that $\mathcal{M} \not\models \phi$. By Lemma 8.5.2, there is an $\mathcal{M}'' \in \text{MOD(LGM)}$ such that $\mathcal{M}'' \not\models \phi$, a contradiction.
($\leftarrow$) Assume $\phi \in$ VAL(LLOM) and suppose $\phi \notin$ VAL(LGM). So there is $\mathcal{M} \in \text{MOD(LLOM)}$ such that $\mathcal{M} \not\models \phi$. By Lemma 8.5.1, there is $\mathcal{M}' \in \text{MOD(LLOM)}$ such that $\mathcal{M}' \not\models \phi$, a contradiction. *Q.E.D.*

Let HLGM be the extension of the Hilbert-style system HS5(LAN(LGM)) obtained by adding the axiom:

.

(Ax1) $[\lambda_1]\phi \Rightarrow [\lambda_2]\phi$ for all $\lambda_1, \lambda_2 \in \mathbb{Q}$ such that $\lambda_1 \le \lambda_2$;

Lemma 8.5.3. *Let* $F = \langle W, (R_\lambda)_{\lambda \in [0,1]_\mathbb{Q}} \rangle$ *be an* LAN(LGM)-*frame. For all* $\lambda_1, \lambda_2 \in [0,1]_\mathbb{Q}$, $[\lambda_1]\mathrm{p} \Rightarrow [\lambda_2]\mathrm{p}$ *is true in* F *iff* $R_{\lambda_2} \subseteq R_{\lambda_1}$.

Proof. See Lemma 6.3.11(V).   Q.E.D.

By applying the canonical model construction, it is easy to show that THM(HLGM) = VAL(LLOM). Consequently, HLGM is a proof system for the logic LGM. Moreover, since lin(LLOM) is a singleton, the axiomatisation of LLOM turns out to be a particular case of the construction presented in Sect. 8.4.2.

Observe that the logics LLOM and DALLA' correspond to the two extreme cases of LA-logics: lin(LLOM) is a singleton, whereas lin(DALLA') contains all the linear orders on the set of modal expressions.

8.6 Notes

Logic IND. The logics studied in Sect. 8.3 have been introduced in [Kon87]. HIND slightly differs from the system defined in [Kon87]. In particular, the necessitation rule is not present in [Kon87], whereas our system does not contain the standard modal axiom for reflexivity. The proof of Theorem 8.3.2 is different from the one in [Kon87]. Lemmas 8.3.3 and 8.3.4 are proved here by induction and then Theorem 8.3.2 is proved using an effective procedure. In [Kon87], a recursive procedure is proposed. In [Rau84], a logic similar to IND has been axiomatised.

Logics with the local agreement condition. The data analysis logic with local agreement (DALLA) has been introduced in [Gar86] as a variant of DAL, where the indiscernibility relations of the models are in local agreement (see Definition 8.2.1). DALLA and DAL have a common language. Completeness of HDALLA has been proved in [Gar86]. The class of LA-logics is introduced in [Dem96a]. If R and R' are equivalence relations in local agreement, then $(R; R')^n = (R'; R)^n$ for every $n \ge 1$. Bimodal logics characterised by frames satisfying properties of that kind are studied in [Gol97a, Gol97b].

Fuzzy logic of graded modalities. The term "graded" should not be confused with its use in, for instance, [HM91, Cer94, MMN95, Mik95]. Its present use is similar to that in [Cha94]. The logic LGM of graded modalities introduced in [Nak93] (see also [Nak92]) is based on the graded equivalence relations, i.e. the graded similarity in Zadeh's meaning [Zad71]. Our version of LGM differs from the one in [Nak93] in that our language is countable. LGM is a fuzzy logic such that fuzziness is only attributed to binary relations determining modal connectives and not to the formulae. Other fuzzy modal logics can be found, for instance in [Yin88, HHE+94, EGGR97]. A general scheme of fuzzy modal logics is presented in Sect. 5.5.

Other logics of indiscerniblity. Logics of indiscernibility relations can be found in [Orło84a, Rau84, Orło85b, Orło88d, AT89, Vak91c, NG91, Rau92, AT97]. Observe also that the logics IL and NIL studied in Chap. 7 contain a modal connective determined by an indiscernibility relation. First-order logics of indiscernibility are studied in [Szc87a, Szc87b, KT91, KS98]. The logics of indiscernibility and complementarity relations are discussed in [DOV99, BV01].

Open questions. The main open question is the axiomatisation of DAL (without nominals). Numerous attempts can be found in the literature but it happens that the logics axiomatised there are not exactly DAL. The axiomatisation of LA-logics with infinite lin($\mathcal{L}$) would also be worth investigating.

9. Reasoning About Knowledge

9.1 Introduction and Outline of the Chapter

The logics presented in this chapter provide a means of representing imperfect knowledge of agents and reasoning with such a knowledge. The modal propositional connectives in these logics are the abstract counterparts of knowledge operators derived from information systems (Sect. 4.6). The underlying knowledge is determined up to indiscernibility relations associated with agents. Consequently, their knowledge depends on a degree of certainty with which they perceive objects from a given domain.

The semantic structures of the logics are based on an ontology that differs from the usual Kripke-style ontology. The worlds in a model are interpreted not as knowledge states but as objects from an information system. Similarly, the relations associated with sets of agents are interpreted not as compatibility relations but as indiscernibility relations between objects.

Our definition of knowledge operators is based on an idea that knowledge about a set of objects is reflected by the ability of an agent to classify objects as members or non-members of this set. This intuition fits well the traditional understanding of knowledge. If the set represents instances of a predicate, say P, then the knowledge of an agent about P is manifested in his ability of exhibiting the instances or non-instances of P among the objects. Since each agent recognises the objects relative to his indiscernibility relation, the objects which he claims to be the instances of P do not necessarily coincide with the actual instances of P. Similarly, if the set represents the states, where some sentence ϕ is true, the knowledge of an agent about ϕ is manifested in his ability of classifying the states into those where ϕ is true or those where ϕ is false.

In Sect. 9.2 we investigate the logic BLKO, a logic with a single knowledge operator. Although the semantic structures of BLKO are based on indiscernibility relations (which are equivalence relations), its deductive system is not an extension of any standard modal deductive system. Consequently, the proofs of properties of this system require their own methods and techniques. In Sect. 9.4 we present an extension LKO of the logic BLKO with a family of knowledge operators based on relative indiscernibility relations. However, an interpretation of parameters determining those relations is related to knowledge agent intuition rather than to intuition of an attribute.

To prove completeness of a deductive system for LKO it is not sufficient to apply the results from Sect. 9.2. For that purpose in Sect. 9.3 we introduce an auxiliary standard modal logic S5' and we develop a Hilbert-style deductive system for it. The respective completeness proof requires application of the copying method. Then, in order to show completeness of the deductive system of LKO, first, we define a satisfiability-preserving translation from formulae of LKO to formulae of S5' and, second, we show how the axioms and inference rules of the LKO deductive system can simulate the axioms and rules of the S5' system. Since the logic S5' is related to many existing epistemic logics, we may consider LKO as an alternative system for reasoning about knowledge in general.

9.2 BLKO: a Basic Logic with Knowledge Operators

BLKO is a modal logic with a single knowledge connective representing the knowledge operator K defined in Sect. 4.6. The operator expresses knowledge of an agent who recognises the objects of an information system in terms of properties determined by a set of attributes. However, this set of attributes does not have any explicit representation in the language of BLKO. In the logic we can express knowledge of an agent about varying sets of objects and their Boolean structure, and the types of knowledge considered in Sect. 4.6, but we cannot express how his knowledge depends on varying sets of attributes.

9.2.1 Language and Semantics

The logic BLKO is defined as follows. The set M_0 of basic modal expressions is the singleton set $\{a\}$, the set O_M of modal operators is empty, and the set M of modal expressions is M_0. The set FOR_0 of basic formulae is a countably infinite set of propositional variables and the set of propositional connectives is $O_{FOR} = \{\wedge, \neg, K(a)\}$. The set of BLKO-models coincides with the set of S5-models (see Example 5.3.3).

9.2.2 A Hilbert-style Proof System

The proof system HBLKO is an extension of HPC obtained by adding the following axioms:

(Ax1) $\phi \wedge K\phi \wedge K(\phi \Rightarrow \psi) \Rightarrow K\psi$;
(Ax2) $K(K\phi \Rightarrow \phi)$;
(Ax3) $K\phi \Leftrightarrow K\neg\phi$;

and the inference rule

$$\frac{\phi}{K\phi} \text{ (K-rule)}.$$

Observe that HBLKO is not an extension of HK. If the connective K is replaced by $\Box$ in the axioms and rules of HBLKO, then the resulting proof system is also not an extension of HK. Axiom (Ax3) corresponds to the equation $K(X) = K(OB \setminus X)$ in Lemma 4.6.2(V). The following lemma states that axiom (Ax2) corresponds to the property of being an equivalence relation.

Lemma 9.2.1. *Let* $F = \langle W, R \rangle$ *be an* LAN(BLKO)*-frame such that* R *is reflexive on* W. *Then,* $F \in \text{TFR}(\{K(Kp \Rightarrow p)\})$ *iff* R *is an equivalence relation on* W.

Proof. ($\leftarrow$) Assume $F = \langle W, R \rangle \in \text{TFR}(\{K(Kp \Rightarrow p)\})$ and R is reflexive. So for every model $\mathcal{M} = \langle W, R, m \rangle$ based on F, we have (i) $\mathcal{M} \models K(Kp \Rightarrow p)$. According to the semantics of the connective K (see Sect. 5.3.2), for every formula ϕ, for every model $\mathcal{M}' = \langle W', R', m' \rangle$, and for every $x \in W'$, we have $\mathcal{M}', x \models K\phi$ iff $\mathcal{M}', x \models \Box\phi \vee \Box\neg\phi$. Then (i) is equivalent to

$$\mathcal{M} \models \Box((\Box p \vee \Box\neg p) \Rightarrow p) \vee \Box((\Box p \vee \Box\neg p) \wedge \neg p).$$

Furthermore, since R is reflexive, we can infer that

$$\mathcal{M} \models \Box((\Box p \vee \Box\neg p) \Rightarrow p) \vee \Box\Box\neg p.$$

For the purpose of the proof, we consider an extended language with the modal connectives K and $\Box$. We show that (ii) R is symmetric and (iii) R is transitive.

Proof of (ii): suppose R is not symmetric. Then there exist $x_0, y_0 \in W$ such that $\langle x_0, y_0 \rangle \in R$, $\langle y_0, x_0 \rangle \notin R$, and $x_0 \neq y_0$. Let $\mathcal{M}_0 = \langle W, R, m_0 \rangle$ be a model based on F such that $m_0(p) \stackrel{\text{def}}{=} \{x_0\}$. By the definition of m_0 and reflexivity of R, we obtain $\mathcal{M}_0, x_0 \not\models \Box\Box\neg p$. Moreover, $\mathcal{M}_0, y_0 \not\models p$ and for every $z \in R(y_0)$, $\mathcal{M}_0, z \not\models p$. So, we have $\mathcal{M}_0, y_0 \models \Box\neg p$ and therefore $\mathcal{M}_0, y_0 \not\models (\Box p \vee \Box\neg p) \Rightarrow p$ and $\mathcal{M}_0, x_0 \not\models \Box((\Box p \vee \Box\neg p) \Rightarrow p)$, since $\langle x_0, y_0 \rangle \in R$, a contradiction.

Proof of (iii): suppose that R is not transitive. Hence, there exist $x_0, y_0, z_0 \in W$ such that $\langle x_0, y_0 \rangle \in R$, $\langle y_0, z_0 \rangle \in R$, $\langle x_0, z_0 \rangle \notin R$, and $x_0 \neq z_0$. Let $\mathcal{M}_0 = \langle W, R, m_0 \rangle$ be a model based on F such that $m_0(p) \stackrel{\text{def}}{=} \{z_0\}$. It follows that $\mathcal{M}_0, x_0 \not\models \Box\Box\neg p$, since $\langle x_0, z_0 \rangle \in R; R$. Moreover, $\mathcal{M}, x_0 \not\models p$ and for every $x' \in R(x_0)$, $\mathcal{M}_0, x' \not\models p$. So $\mathcal{M}_0, x_0 \models \Box\neg p$ and therefore $\mathcal{M}_0, x_0 \not\models (\Box p \vee \Box\neg p) \Rightarrow p$. Since R is reflexive, $\mathcal{M}_0, x_0 \not\models \Box((\Box p \vee \Box\neg p) \Rightarrow p)$, a contradiction.

($\rightarrow$) Now assume $\mathcal{M} = \langle W, R, m \rangle$ is a model such that R is an equivalence relation on W. Let $x \in W$. We show that $\mathcal{M}, x \models K(Kp \Rightarrow p)$ or equivalently that $\mathcal{M}, x \models \Box((\Box p \vee \Box\neg p) \Rightarrow p) \vee \Box\Box\neg p$.
Case 1: $\mathcal{M}, x \models \Box p$.

Consequently, $\mathcal{M}, x \models \Box((\Box p \lor \Box \neg p) \Rightarrow p)$.
Case 2: $\mathcal{M}, x \models \Box \neg p$.
Since $R; R = R$, $\mathcal{M}, x \models \Box \Box \neg p$.
Case 3: $\mathcal{M}, x \models \Diamond p \land \Diamond \neg p$.
So there exist $x_1, x_2 \in R(x)$ such that $\mathcal{M}, x_1 \models p$ and $\mathcal{M}, x_2 \models \neg p$. Let $y \in R(x)$. Since R is an equivalence relation, $x_1, x_2 \in R(y)$ and therefore $\mathcal{M}, y \models \Diamond p \land \Diamond \neg p$, that is $\mathcal{M}, y \not\models (\Box p \lor \Box \neg p)$. This implies $\mathcal{M}, y \models (\Box p \lor \Box \neg p) \Rightarrow p$. So $\mathcal{M}, x \models \Box((\Box p \lor \Box \neg p) \Rightarrow p)$.   *Q.E.D.*

Lemmas 9.2.2, 9.2.3, and 9.2.4, and Corollary 9.2.1, establish the principle of substitution of equivalents in HBLKO.

Lemma 9.2.2. *If* $\vdash \phi \Leftrightarrow \phi'$, *then* $\vdash \psi \Leftrightarrow \psi'$, *where* ψ' *is obtained from* ψ *by replacing an occurrence of* ϕ *which is not in the scope of K by* ϕ'.

Lemma 9.2.2 is a corollary of Lemma 6.3.1 on the substitution of equivalents in PC. As usual, in the rest of the chapter, $\vdash \phi$ stands for $\phi \in$ THM(HBLK0).

Lemma 9.2.3. *For all BLKO-formulae* ϕ *and* ψ, *if* $\vdash \phi \Rightarrow \psi$, *then* $\vdash K\phi \land \phi \Rightarrow K\psi$.

Proof. By applying the K-rule to $\phi \Rightarrow \psi$, we get $\vdash K(\phi \Rightarrow \psi)$. With the axiom (Ax1) we obtain $\vdash \phi \land K\phi \land K(\phi \Rightarrow \psi) \Rightarrow K\psi$. By an easy propositional reasoning, we get $\vdash K(\phi \Rightarrow \psi) \Rightarrow \neg \phi \lor \neg K\phi \lor K\psi$. Applying modus ponens, $\vdash \neg \phi \lor \neg K\phi \lor K\psi$ is obtained and therefore $\vdash \phi \land K\phi \Rightarrow K\psi$.   *Q.E.D.*

It is important to notice that a regular rule of the form:

$$\frac{\phi \Rightarrow \psi}{K\phi \Rightarrow K\psi}$$

is not admissible in HBLKO, unlike in numerous systems of modal logics. This is a consequence of Theorem 9.2.2. For example, $p \land q \Rightarrow p$ is BLKO-valid but $K(p \land q) \Rightarrow Kp$ is not.

Lemma 9.2.4. *For all BLKO-formulae* ϕ *and* ψ, *if* $\vdash \phi \Leftrightarrow \psi$, *then* $\vdash K\phi \Leftrightarrow K\psi$.

Proof. Assume $\vdash \phi \Leftrightarrow \psi$. It follows that $\vdash \phi \Rightarrow \psi$, $\vdash \psi \Rightarrow \phi$, $\vdash \neg \phi \Rightarrow \neg \psi$, and $\vdash \neg \psi \Rightarrow \neg \phi$. Using Lemma 9.2.3 we obtain $\vdash \phi \land K\phi \Rightarrow K\psi$, and therefore $\vdash \phi \Rightarrow (K\phi \Rightarrow K\psi)$. In a similar way, using the axiom (Ax3) and Lemma 9.2.2, we can prove that $\vdash \neg \phi \Rightarrow (K\phi \Rightarrow K\psi)$, $\vdash \psi \Rightarrow (K\psi \Rightarrow K\phi)$, and $\vdash \neg \psi \Rightarrow (K\psi \Rightarrow K\phi)$. By Lemma 6.3.2(III), we obtain $\vdash \phi \land \psi \Rightarrow (K\phi \Rightarrow K\psi)$, $\vdash \phi \land \psi \Rightarrow (K\psi \Rightarrow K\phi)$, $\vdash \neg \phi \land \neg \psi \Rightarrow (K\phi \Rightarrow K\psi)$, and $\vdash \neg \phi \land \neg \psi \Rightarrow (K\psi \Rightarrow K\phi)$. By Lemma 6.3.2(II), we obtain $\vdash \phi \land \psi \Rightarrow (K\phi \Leftrightarrow K\psi)$ and $\vdash \neg \phi \land \neg \psi \Rightarrow (K\phi \Leftrightarrow K\psi)$. Using Lemmas 9.2.2 and 6.3.2(I), we have $\vdash K\phi \Leftrightarrow K\psi$ ($\vdash (\phi \Leftrightarrow \psi) \Leftrightarrow ((\phi \land \psi) \lor (\neg \phi \land \neg \psi)))$.   *Q.E.D.*

Corollary 9.2.1. *If $\vdash \phi \Leftrightarrow \phi'$, then $\vdash \psi \Leftrightarrow \psi'$, where ψ' is obtained from ψ by replacing an occurrence of ϕ by ϕ'.*

Unlike in Lemma 9.2.2, here there is no restriction on the position of the replaced formula. The following lemma is used in the proof of Lemma 9.2.6.

Lemma 9.2.5. *For all BLKO-formulae ϕ and ψ, $\vdash K\phi \wedge K\psi \wedge \phi \wedge \psi \Rightarrow K(\phi \wedge \psi)$.*

Proof. A derivation of the required formula is as follows:

(1) $\vdash K(\psi \Rightarrow (\phi \Rightarrow \psi))$ (K-rule applied to the tautology $\psi \Rightarrow (\phi \Rightarrow \psi)$);
(2) $\vdash \psi \wedge K\psi \wedge K(\psi \Rightarrow (\phi \Rightarrow \psi)) \Rightarrow K(\phi \Rightarrow \psi)$ (Ax1);
(3) $\vdash \psi \wedge K\psi \Rightarrow K(\phi \Rightarrow \psi)$ (modus ponens);
(4) $\vdash \phi \wedge K\phi \wedge K(\phi \Rightarrow \phi \wedge \psi) \Rightarrow K(\phi \wedge \psi)$ (Ax1);
(5) $\vdash (\phi \Rightarrow \phi \wedge \psi) \Leftrightarrow (\phi \Rightarrow \psi)$ (tautology);
(6) $\vdash K(\phi \Rightarrow \phi \wedge \psi) \Leftrightarrow K(\phi \Rightarrow \psi)$ (Lemma 9.2.4 applied to (5));
(7) $\vdash \phi \wedge K\phi \wedge K(\phi \Rightarrow \psi) \Rightarrow K(\phi \wedge \psi)$ (Lemma 9.2.2 applied to (4));
(8) $\vdash K\phi \wedge K\psi \wedge \phi \wedge \psi \Rightarrow K(\phi \wedge \psi)$ (Lemma 6.3.2(IV) applied to (3) and (7)).

$Q.E.D.$

Observe that $K(\mathrm{p} \wedge \mathrm{q}) \Leftrightarrow K\mathrm{p} \wedge K\mathrm{q}$ is not BLKO-valid and therefore the BLKO-formula in Lemma 9.2.5 cannot be significantly shortened.

Theorem 9.2.1. *(Soundness Theorem)* THM(HBLKO) $\subseteq$ VAL(BLKO).

Proof. The proof is by induction on the length of a derivation. As usual, it consists in showing that the axioms are BLKO-valid and the rules preserve BLKO-validity. $\qquad Q.E.D.$

Let X be a set of BLKO-formulae. We define:

$$KX \stackrel{\mathrm{def}}{=} \{\phi : \{\phi, K\phi\} \subseteq X\}.$$

The following lemma is a counterpart of Lemma 6.3.10.

Lemma 9.2.6. *For every set X of BLKO-formulae and for every BLKO-formula ϕ, if $X \cup \{\neg K\phi\}$ is HBLKO-consistent, then both $KX \cup \{\phi\}$ and $KX \cup \{\neg\phi\}$ are HBLKO-consistent.*

Proof. Suppose that $KX \cup \{\phi\}$ is not HBLKO-consistent [resp. $KX \cup \{\neg\phi\}$ is not HBLKO-consistent]. There is a finite set $\{\phi_1, \ldots, \phi_n\} \subseteq KX$, $n \geq 1$, such that $\vdash \neg(\phi_1 \wedge \ldots \phi_n \wedge \phi)$ [resp. $\vdash \neg(\phi_1 \wedge \ldots \phi_n \wedge \neg\phi)$], which leads to $\vdash \phi_1 \wedge \ldots \wedge \phi_n \Rightarrow \neg\phi$ [resp. $\vdash \phi_1 \wedge \ldots \wedge \phi_n \Rightarrow \phi$]. From Lemma 9.2.3 we have $\vdash K(\phi_1 \wedge \ldots \wedge \phi_n) \wedge \phi_1 \wedge \ldots \wedge \phi_n \Rightarrow K\neg\phi$ [resp. $\vdash K(\phi_1 \wedge \ldots \wedge \phi_n) \wedge \phi_1 \wedge \ldots \wedge \phi_n \Rightarrow K\phi$]. Since $\vdash K\phi \Leftrightarrow K\neg\phi$, and using Lemma 9.2.2, in both cases we obtain $\vdash K(\phi_1 \wedge \ldots \wedge \phi_n) \wedge \phi_1 \wedge \ldots \wedge \phi_n \Rightarrow K\phi$. From Lemma 9.2.5,

$K\phi_1 \wedge K\phi_2 \ldots \wedge K\phi_n \wedge \phi_1 \ldots \wedge \phi_n \Rightarrow K(\phi_1 \wedge \ldots \wedge \phi_n) \in$ THM(HBLKO). By propositional transformations we get $\vdash \neg(K\phi_1 \wedge \ldots \wedge K\phi_n \wedge \phi_1 \wedge \ldots \wedge \phi_n \wedge \neg K\phi)$. So $X \cup \{\neg K\phi\}$ is not HBLKO-consistent, which leads to a contradiction. Q.E.D.

In the following definition we provide a notion of canonical model that is similar to that notion for the extensions of HK.

Definition 9.2.1. *The canonical structure for* HBLKO *is the triple* $\mathcal{M}^c \overset{\text{def}}{=} \langle W^c, R^c, m^c \rangle$, *where:*

$\star$ W^c *is the family of all the maximal* HBLKO-*consistent sets of formulae;*
$\star$ *for all* $X, Y \in W^c$, $\langle X, Y \rangle \in R^c \overset{\text{def}}{\Leftrightarrow} KX \subseteq Y$;
$\star$ $m^c(p) \overset{\text{def}}{=} \{X \in W^c \mid p \in X\}$ *for every* $p \in$ FOR$_0$.

We show that the canonical structure for HBLKO is a BLKO-model.

Lemma 9.2.7. R^c *is an equivalence relation.*

Proof. (Reflexivity) It is obvious that if $\{K\phi, \phi\} \subseteq X$, then $\phi \in X$, which leads to $KX \subseteq X$.
(Symmetry) Assume $KX \subseteq Y$ and $\phi \notin X$. We show that either $\phi \notin Y$ or $K\phi \notin Y$. From the axiom (Ax2), Corollary 9.2.1, and Lemma 6.3.5, we have $K(K\phi \Rightarrow \neg\phi) \in X$. By the assumption, $\neg\phi \in X$ (see Lemma 6.3.5), so $\neg K\phi \vee \neg\phi \in X$. It follows that $K\phi \Rightarrow \neg\phi \in Y$. So we have either $\neg K\phi \in Y$ or $\neg\phi \in Y$. Then we get either $K\phi \notin Y$ or $\phi \notin Y$ (Y is a maximal HBLKO-consistent set).
(Transitivity) Let $X_1, X_2, X_3 \in W^c$ be such that $KX_1 \subseteq X_2$ and $KX_2 \subseteq X_3$. Assume $\{K\phi, \phi\} \subseteq X_1$. From the axiom (Ax2) we have $\vdash K(K\neg\phi \Rightarrow \neg\phi)$, and from the axiom (Ax3), we get $\vdash K(K\neg\phi \wedge \phi)$ and, therefore, using Lemma 9.2.1, we obtain $\vdash K(K\phi \wedge \phi)$. So $K(K\phi \wedge \phi) \in X_1$ and therefore $K\phi \wedge \phi \in X_2$, since $K\phi \wedge \phi \in X_1$. This yields $\phi \in X_3$, since $\phi \in KX_2 \subseteq X_3$. Q.E.D.

It remains to show the BLKO counterpart of Theorem 6.3.6.

Lemma 9.2.8. *For every BLKO-formula* ϕ *and for every* $X \in W^c$, *we have* $\phi \in X$ *iff* $\mathcal{M}^c, X \models \phi$.

Proof. The proof is by induction on the structure of ϕ. Only the case $\phi = K\psi$ is presented in detail; the other cases are standard (see Theorem 6.3.6).
($\rightarrow$) Assume that $K\psi \in X$. It follows that $K\neg\psi \in X$.
Case 1: $\psi \notin X$.
Let $Y \in W^c$ be such that $\langle X, Y \rangle \in R^c$. Since $\{K\neg\psi, \neg\psi\} \subseteq X$, then $\neg\psi \in Y$ and therefore $\psi \notin Y$. By the induction hypothesis, for every $Y \in W^c$ such that $\langle X, Y \rangle \in R^c$, we have $\mathcal{M}^c, Y \not\models \psi$. So $\mathcal{M}^c, X \models K\psi$.
Case 2: $\psi \in X$.

Let $Y \in W^c$ be such that $\langle X, Y \rangle \in R^c$. Since $\{K\psi, \psi\} \subseteq X$, we get $\psi \in Y$. By the induction hypothesis, for every $Y \in W^c$ such that $\langle X, Y \rangle \in R^c$, we have $\mathcal{M}^c, Y \models \psi$. So $\mathcal{M}^c, X \models K\psi$.

($\leftarrow$) Now assume that $K\psi \notin X$ and hence $\neg K\psi \in X$. From Lemma 9.2.6, it follows that $KX \cup \{\psi\}$ and $KX \cup \{\neg\psi\}$ are HBLKO-consistent. Hence, there exist $X_1, X_2 \in W^c$ (see Theorem 6.3.4) such that $KX \cup \{\psi\} \subseteq X_1$ and $KX \cup \{\neg\psi\} \subseteq X_2$. Note that $\langle X, X_1 \rangle \in R^c$, $\langle X, X_2 \rangle \in R^c$, and $X_1 \neq X_2$. By the induction hypothesis we have $\mathcal{M}^c, X_1 \models \psi$ and $\mathcal{M}^c, X_2 \not\models \psi$. It follows that $\mathcal{M}^c, X \not\models K\psi$.   Q.E.D.

As a corollary, we obtain the following theorem.

Theorem 9.2.2. *(Completeness Theorem)* VAL(BLKO) $\subseteq$ THM(HBLKO).

9.2.3 Relationship with S5

We define the translation map f from BLKO-formulae into S5-formulae in the following way:

* $f(\mathrm{p}) \stackrel{\text{def}}{=} \mathrm{p}$ for every $\mathrm{p} \in \mathrm{FOR}_0$;
* f is homomorphic with respect to the Boolean connectives;
* $f(K\phi) \stackrel{\text{def}}{=} \Box f(\phi) \vee \Box\neg f(\phi)$.

Observe that for every $n \geq 1$, the modal weight $mw(f(K^n\mathrm{p}))$ is greater than 2^n and $mw(K^n\mathrm{p}) = n$. Similarly, the translation g from S5-formulae into BLKO-formulae is defined as follows:

* $g(\mathrm{p}) \stackrel{\text{def}}{=} \mathrm{p}$ for every $\mathrm{p} \in \mathrm{FOR}_0$;
* g is homomorphic with respect to the Boolean connectives;
* $g(\Box\phi) \stackrel{\text{def}}{=} g(\phi) \wedge Kg(\phi)$.

Lemma 9.2.9. *Let $\mathcal{M} = \langle W, R, m \rangle$ be a LAN(S5)-model and let $w \in W$. Then:*

(I) for every BLKO-formula ϕ, we have $\mathcal{M}, w \models \phi$ iff $\mathcal{M}, w \models f(\phi)$;
(II) if R is reflexive, then for every S5-formula ϕ, we have $\mathcal{M}, w \models \phi$ iff $\mathcal{M}, w \models g(\phi)$.

Proof. (I) The proof is by induction of the structure of ϕ. The only non-trivial case is when ϕ has the form $K\psi$.

($\rightarrow$) Assume that $\mathcal{M}, w \models K\psi$. We have either (i) for every $v \in R(w)$, $\mathcal{M}, v \models \psi$ or (ii) for every $v \in R(w)$, $\mathcal{M}, v \not\models \psi$. If (i) holds, then by the induction hypothesis for every $v \in R(w)$ we have $\mathcal{M}, v \models f(\psi)$. Hence, $\mathcal{M}, u \models \Box f(\psi)$. If (ii) holds, then by the induction hypothesis for every $v \in R(w)$ we have $\mathcal{M}, v \not\models f(\psi)$ and $\mathcal{M}, w \models \Box\neg f(\psi)$. Hence, we get $\mathcal{M}, w \models \Box f(\psi) \vee \Box\neg f(\psi)$. By the definition of f, we have $\mathcal{M}, w \models f(K\psi)$.

($\leftarrow$) Now assume that $\mathcal{M}, w \not\models K\psi$. Then there exist $u_1, u_2 \in W$ such that $\langle u, u_1 \rangle \in R, \langle u, u_2 \rangle \in R$, $\mathcal{M}, u_1 \models \psi$, and $\mathcal{M}, u_2 \not\models \psi$. By the induction hypothesis, $\mathcal{M}, u_1 \models f(\psi)$ and $\mathcal{M}, u_2 \not\models f(\psi)$. Thus we obtain $\mathcal{M}, w \models \neg\Box\neg f(\psi)$ and $\mathcal{M}, w \models \neg\Box f(\psi)$. Hence, $\mathcal{M}, w \not\models \Box f(\psi) \vee \Box\neg f(\psi)$ and therefore by the definition of f, $\mathcal{M}, w \not\models f(K\psi)$.

(II) The proof is by induction on the structure of ϕ. The only non-trivial case is when ϕ has the form $\Box\psi$.

($\rightarrow$) Assume that $\mathcal{M}, w \models \Box\psi$. For every $v \in R(w)$ we have $\mathcal{M}, v \models \psi$. By the induction hypothesis, for every $v \in R(w)$ we have $\mathcal{M}, v \models g(\psi)$ and, in particular, $\mathcal{M}, w \models g(\psi)$ since the relation R is reflexive. Hence, we obtain $\mathcal{M}, w \models g(\psi) \wedge Kg(\psi)$. By the definition of g, we get $\mathcal{M}, w \models g(\Box\psi)$.

($\leftarrow$) Now assume $\mathcal{M}, w \not\models \Box\psi$. There is a $v \in R(w)$ such that $\mathcal{M}, v \not\models \psi$ and either (i) $\mathcal{M}, w \models \psi$ or (ii) $\mathcal{M}, w \not\models \psi$. If (i) holds, then by the induction hypothesis, we have $\mathcal{M}, w \models g(\psi)$ and $\mathcal{M}, v \not\models g(\psi)$. It follows that $\mathcal{M}, w \models \neg Kg(\psi)$ (we get $\{u, w\} \subseteq R(w)$). If (ii) holds, then by the induction hypothesis, $\mathcal{M}, w \not\models g(\psi)$. It follows that $\mathcal{M}, w \models \neg g(\psi) \vee \neg Kg(\psi)$ and therefore $\mathcal{M}, w \not\models g(\psi) \wedge Kg(\psi)$. By the definition of g, we get $\mathcal{M}, w \not\models g(\Box\psi)$. Q.E.D.

As a consequence, we obtain a sufficient condition for f and g to be validity-preserving maps. It follows that f and g are many–one reductions from VAL($\mathcal{L}_1$) into VAL($\mathcal{L}_2$).

Theorem 9.2.3. *Let $\mathcal{L}_1 = \langle \text{LAN(BLKO)}, \mathcal{S} \rangle$ and $\mathcal{L}_2 = \langle \text{LAN(S5)}, \mathcal{S} \rangle$ be two logics sharing the set of models. Then:*

(I) for every BLKO-formula ϕ, we have $\phi \in$ VAL($\mathcal{L}_1$) iff $f(\phi) \in$ VAL($\mathcal{L}_2$);
(II) if $\mathcal{S}$ consists of models whose relations are reflexive, then for every LAN(S5)-formula ϕ, we have $\phi \in$ VAL($\mathcal{L}_2$) iff $g(\phi) \in$ VAL($\mathcal{L}_1$).

By decidability of the modal logic S5 (see Example 6.2.2), we obtain the following result.

Theorem 9.2.4. SAT(BLKO) *is decidable.*

9.3 The Logic S5′

In this section we present the logic S5′ which can be viewed as an extension of the modal logic S5 with modal connectives determined by equivalence relations and their intersections. We present a complete Hilbert-style proof system for S5′. In Sect. 9.4.2 we use S5′ to study the logic LKO with relative knowledge operators.

9.3.1 Language and Semantics

Although S5′ has the status of an auxiliary logic (our goal is to study the knowledge operators derived from information systems), the results for S5′

are crucial for understanding LKO. We show that S5' and LKO are very similar. This will be clarified in Sect. 9.4.

The logic S5' is defined as follows. The set M_0 of basic modal expressions is a countably infinite set of modal constants augmented with the distinguished modal constant U. The set of modal operators is $O_M = \{\cap\}$. The set M of modal expressions includes M_0 and for all $a, b \in M$, if U does not occur in $a \cap b$, then $a \cap b \in M$. The set FOR_0 of basic formulae is a countably infinite set of propositional variables and the set O_{FOR} of logical connectives is $\{\wedge, \neg\} \cup \{[a] : a \in M\}$. The S5'-models are the structures of the form $\mathcal{M} = \langle W, (R_a)_{a \in M}, m \rangle$ such that:

(1) $R_U = W \times W$;
(2) R_a is an equivalence relation for every $a \in M$;
(3) $R_{a \cap b} = R_a \cap R_b$ for every $a \cap b \in M$.

Obviously [U] is a universal modal connective in S5' (see Definition 5.3.10). The models defined above are said to be *standard*.

A *non-standard* S5'-model $\mathcal{M} = \langle W, (R_a)_{a \in M}, m \rangle$ is an LAN(S5')-model which satisfies the conditions (1) and (2) above and the following ones:

(4) $R_{a \cap b} \subseteq R_a \cap R_b$ for every $a \cap b \in M$;
(5) $R_a = R_b$ for all $a, b \in M$ such that $M_0(a) = M_0(b)$.

We recall that according to our notational convention (see Sect. 5.3.1), for every modal expression $a \in M$, $M_0(a)$ denotes the set of basic modal expressions occurring in a.

Let $\mathcal{S}_{ns}$ be the class of non-standard LAN(S5')-models. We shall show that

$$VAL(S5') = VAL(\langle LAN(S5'), \mathcal{S}_{ns} \rangle).$$

Observe that $MOD(S5') \subset \mathcal{S}_{ns}$. So we already have:

$$VAL(\langle LAN(S5'), \mathcal{S}_{ns} \rangle) \subseteq VAL(S5').$$

In the following we introduce the notion of a partial S5'-model. We intend to express the idea that although a non-standard S5'-model $\mathcal{M}$ may not always have a finite representation (M and FOR_0 are infinite sets), in order to show satisfiability of a given formula, we can confine ourselves to a finite part of $\mathcal{M}$.

Definition 9.3.1. *Let* $X \subseteq M$, $\emptyset \neq Y \subseteq FOR_0$ *and* $L = X \cup \{U\}$. *An* $\langle X, Y \rangle$*-partial S5'-model is a structure* $\mathcal{M} = \langle W, (R_a)_{a \in L}, m \rangle$ *such that W is a non-empty set, m is a map* $m : Y \to \mathcal{P}(W)$ *and* $(R_a)_{a \in L}$ *is a family of equivalence relations on W such that for all* $a, b \in L$, *if* $M_0(b) \subseteq M_0(a)$, *then* $R_a \subseteq R_b$.

As a consequence, in every partial S5'-model, we have $R_a \subseteq R_U$ for every $a \in X$. The satisfiability relation $\models$ can be easily defined for partial S5'-models. In order to prove decidability (see Sect. 11.3.2), instead of using finite S5′-models we consider finite $\langle X, Y \rangle$-partial S5′-models. Given a $\langle X, Y \rangle$-partial S5′-model $\mathcal{M}$, the relation $\mathcal{M}, x \models \phi$ is well-defined if $\mathrm{FOR}_0(\phi) \subseteq Y$ and $\mathrm{M}_0(\phi) \subseteq X$.

Lemma 9.3.1. *For every S5′-formula ϕ, the following statements are equivalent:*

(I) ϕ is satisfiable in a non-standard S5′-model;
(II) ϕ is satisfiable in a $\langle \mathrm{M}(\phi), \mathrm{FOR}_0(\phi) \rangle$-partial S5′-model.

Proof. (I) $\to$ (II) Let $\mathcal{M} = \langle W, (R_a)_{a \in M}, m \rangle$ be a non-standard S5′-model and let a $w \in W$ be such that $\mathcal{M}, w \models \phi$. Let $L = \mathrm{M}(\phi) \cup \{U\}$. Let $\mathcal{M}' = \langle W, (R_a)_{a \in L}, m' \rangle$ be a $\langle \mathrm{M}(\phi), \mathrm{FOR}_0(\phi) \rangle$-partial S5′-model such that m' is the restriction of m to $\mathrm{FOR}_0(\phi)$. It is easy to show that $\mathcal{M}', w \models \phi$.

(II) $\to$ (I) Now assume that $\mathcal{M}' = \langle W, (R'_a)_{a \in L}, m' \rangle$ is a $\langle \mathrm{M}(\phi), \mathrm{FOR}_0(\phi) \rangle$-partial S5′-model such that for some $w \in W$, $\mathcal{M}', w \models \phi$. Without any loss of generality we may assume that $R'_U = W \times W$, since $\mathcal{M}'_{|R'_U(x)}, x \models \phi$. We define the following partition $\{M_I, M_{II}, M_{III}, M_{IV}\}$ of M:

$\star$ $M_I \overset{\mathrm{def}}{=} L$;
$\star$ $M_{II} \overset{\mathrm{def}}{=} \{a \in M \setminus \{U\} : \mathrm{M}_0(a) \cap \mathrm{M}_0(\phi) = \emptyset\}$;
$\star$ $M_{III} \overset{\mathrm{def}}{=} \{a \in M \setminus (M_I \cup M_{II}) : \mathrm{M}_0(a) \subseteq \mathrm{M}_0(\phi)\}$;
$\star$ $M_{IV} \overset{\mathrm{def}}{=} M \setminus (M_I \cup M_{II} \cup M_{III})$.

Let $\mathcal{M}$ be a non-standard S5′-model $\langle W, (R_a)_{a \in M}, m \rangle$ defined as follows:

$\star$ for every $a \in M_I$, $R_a \overset{\mathrm{def}}{=} R'_a$;
$\star$ for every $p \in \mathrm{FOR}_0(\phi)$, $m(p) \overset{\mathrm{def}}{=} m'(p)$.

So obviously $\mathcal{M}, w \models \phi$ is guaranteed. We complete the definition of $\mathcal{M}$:

$\star$ for every $p \in \mathrm{FOR}_0 \setminus \mathrm{FOR}_0(\phi)$, $m(p) \overset{\mathrm{def}}{=} W$;
$\star$ for every $a \in M_{II}$, $R_a \overset{\mathrm{def}}{=} W \times W$;
$\star$ for every $a \in M_{III}$,

$$R_a \overset{\mathrm{def}}{=} \bigcap \{R'_b : b \in \mathrm{M}(\phi), \ \mathrm{M}_0(b) \subseteq \mathrm{M}_0(a)\};$$

$\star$ for every $a \in M_{IV}$ such that $\mathrm{M}_0(a) \cap \mathrm{M}_0(\phi) = \{c_1, \ldots, c_n\}$, $n \geq 1$,
$R_a \overset{\mathrm{def}}{=} R_{c_1 \cap \ldots \cap c_n}$ $(c_1 \cap \ldots \cap c_n \in M_{III})$.

For every $\langle a, b \rangle \in \mathrm{M}(\phi) \times M$, if $\mathrm{M}_0(a) = \mathrm{M}_0(b)$, then we have $R_b = R'_a$. Moreover, for every $a \in \mathrm{M}(\phi)$, $R_a = \bigcap \{R'_b : b \in \mathrm{M}(\phi), \ \mathrm{M}_0(b) \subseteq \mathrm{M}_0(a)\}$. This allows us to reduce the number of cases in the following proof. We shall check that for all $a, b \in M$, $\mathrm{M}_0(b) \subseteq \mathrm{M}_0(a)$ implies $R_a \subseteq R_b$. This will prove that $\mathcal{M}$ is a non-standard S5′-model. In particular, the intersection of reflexive [resp. symmetric, transitive] relations is a reflexive [resp. symmetric, transitive] relation. Now assume $\mathrm{M}_0(b) \subseteq \mathrm{M}_0(a)$ for some $a, b \in M$. The following cases have to be considered.

Case 1: $a \in M_I \cup M_{III}, b \in M_I \cup M_{III}$.
Since $M_0(b) \subseteq M_0(a)$, we have

$$\{b' \in M(\phi) : M_0(b') \subseteq M_0(b) \subseteq M_0(a)\} \subseteq \{b' \in M(\phi) : M_0(b') \subseteq M_0(a)\}.$$

Hence $R_a \subseteq R_b$.
Case 2: $b \in M_{II}$.
Since $R_b = W \times W$, we have $R_a \subseteq R_b$.
Case 3: $a \in M_I \cup M_{III}, b \in M_{IV}$.
Assume that $M_0(b) \cap M_0(\phi) = \{c_1, \ldots, c_n\}$, $n \geq 1$. Since $M_0(c_1 \cap \ldots \cap c_n) \subseteq M_0(a)$ and $c_1 \cap \ldots \cap c_n \in M_I \cup M_{III}$, the Case 1 implies $R_a \subseteq R_b = R_{c_1 \cap \ldots \cap c_n}$.
Case 4: $a \in M_{II}, b \in M_I \cup M_{III} \cup M_{IV}$.
This is impossible.
Case 5: $a \in M_{IV}, b \in M_I \cup M_{III}$.
Assume that $M_0(a) \cap M_0(\phi) = \{c_1, \ldots, c_n\}$, $n \geq 1$. Since $M_0(b) \subseteq M_0(c_1 \cap \ldots \cap c_n)$ and $c_1 \cap \ldots \cap c_n \in M_I \cup M_{III}$, the Case 1 implies $R_a = R_{c_1 \cap \ldots \cap c_n} \subseteq R_b$.
Case 6: $a \in M_{IV}, b \in M_{IV}$.
Assume $M_0(a) \cap M_0(\phi) = \{c_1, \ldots, c_n\}$ and $M_0(b) \cap M_0(\phi) = \{d_1, \ldots, d_m\}$, $n, m \geq 1$. Since $M_0(d_1 \cap \ldots \cap d_m) \subseteq M_0(c_1 \cap \ldots \cap c_n)$ and $d_1 \cap \ldots \cap d_m, c_1 \cap \ldots \cap c_n \in M_I \cup M_{III}$, the Case 1 implies $R_a = R_{c_1 \cap \ldots \cap c_n} \subseteq R_{d_1 \cap \ldots \cap d_m} = R_b$.
Q.E.D.

In the forthcoming constructions, partial S5'-models are built instead of non-standard S5'-models.

9.3.2 A Hilbert-style Proof System

The system HS5' is an extension of the proof system HS5(LAN(S5')) obtained by adding the following axioms:

(Ax1) $[a]\phi \vee [b]\phi \Rightarrow [a \cap b]\phi$ for all $a, b \in M \setminus \{U\}$;
(Ax2) $[U]\phi \Rightarrow [a]\phi$ for every $a \in M$;
(Ax3) $[a]\phi \Leftrightarrow [b]\phi$ for all a, b such that $M_0(a) = M_0(b)$.

Observe that the axioms (Ax1) and (Ax3) can be replaced by $[a]\phi \Rightarrow [b]\phi$ for all a, b satisfying $M_0(a) \subseteq M_0(b)$, while preserving the set of theorems.

Theorem 9.3.1. $\mathrm{THM}(HS5') \subseteq \mathrm{VAL}(\langle \mathrm{LAN}(S5'), \mathcal{S}_{ns} \rangle)$.

Moreover, using the canonical model construction, one can show the following.

Theorem 9.3.2. $\mathrm{VAL}(\langle \mathrm{LAN}(S5'), \mathcal{S}_{ns} \rangle) \subseteq \mathrm{THM}(HS5')$.

Theorems 9.3.1 and 9.3.2 together state that HS5' is a proof system for $\langle \mathrm{LAN}(S5'), \mathcal{S}_{ns} \rangle$. It remains to prove a similar proposition for the logic S5'.

Theorem 9.3.3. *(Soundness Theorem)* $\mathrm{THM}(HS5') \subseteq \mathrm{VAL}(S5')$.

The proof of Theorem 9.3.3 is by an easy verification. Now we prepare the completeness proof by introducing a copying construction. Assume that $\phi \notin$ THM(HS5') for some LAN(S5')-formula ϕ. We show that ϕ is not S5'-satisfiable. Let $\mathcal{M}^c \stackrel{\text{def}}{=} \langle W^c, (R_a^c)_{a\in M}, m^c \rangle$ be the canonical model for HS5'. Using Theorems 6.3.6 and 6.3.4, there is an $x_\phi \in W^c$ such that $\mathcal{M}^c, x_\phi \not\models \phi$. We consider the restriction $\mathcal{M}^\phi = \langle W^\phi, (R_a^\phi)_{a\in M}, m^\phi \rangle$ of the model $\mathcal{M}^c$ to the set $R_U^c(x_\phi)$. It is a routine task to check that $\mathcal{M}^\phi$ is a non-standard S5'-model and $\mathcal{M}^\phi, x_\phi \not\models \phi$. Moreover, for every a $\in$ M, for all $X, Y \in W^c$, we have:

$\star$ $\langle X, Y \rangle \in R_a^c$ implies $[a]X = [a]Y$;
$\star$ $\langle X, Y \rangle \in R_a^c$ implies (for every b $\in$ M, $M_0(b) \subseteq M_0(a)$ implies $\langle X, Y \rangle \in R_b^c$).

We recall that $[a]X = \{\psi : [a]\psi \in X\}$. We shall build a standard S5'-model $\mathcal{M} = \langle W, (R_a)_{a\in M}, m \rangle$ verifying the following properties:

$\star$ there is a copying COP from $\mathcal{M}^\phi$ into $\mathcal{M}$;
$\star$ there is a $x'_\phi \in W$ such that $\mathcal{M}, x'_\phi \not\models \phi$.

Here the copying construction is intended to repair the main defect of $\mathcal{M}^\phi$ where $\cap$ is not interpreted exactly as intersection. Consequently, for every $f \in$ COP, $\mathcal{M}, f(x_\phi) \not\models \phi$. So $\phi \in$ THM(HS5') iff ϕ is S5'-valid iff ϕ is valid in every non-standard S5'-model (see Theorem 9.3.4).

In the rest of this section we write $X + Y$ to denote $(X \setminus Y) \cup (Y \setminus X)$ for all $X, Y \in \mathcal{P}(W^\phi)$.

Lemma 9.3.2. *The operation $+$ is commutative, associative, and for every $X \in \mathcal{P}(W^\phi)$, $X + X = \emptyset$.*

Consequently, for every finite family $(X_i)_{i\in\{1,\dots,n\}}$, $n \geq 1$, of elements of $\mathcal{P}(W^\phi)$, let

$$\Sigma_{i\in\{1,\dots,n\}} X_i \stackrel{\text{def}}{=} X_1 + (X_2 + (\dots(X_{n-1} + X_n)\dots)).$$

For every permutation σ of $\{1,\dots,n\}$, $\Sigma_{i\in\{1,\dots,n\}} X_i = \Sigma_{i\in\{1,\dots,n\}} X_{\sigma(i)}$ (by Lemma 9.3.2). A characterisation of the operation $+$ is the following: an element x belongs to $\Sigma_{i\in\{1,\dots,n\}} X_i$ iff the cardinality of the set $\{i \in \{1,\dots,n\} : x \in X_i\}$ is an odd number.

Let COP$_0$ be the set of all the maps $f : M \times M_0 \to \mathcal{P}(W^\phi)$. We also define a variant of COP$_0$. Namely, let COP be the set of maps $f : W^\phi \to (W^\phi \times \text{COP}_0)$ such that there is $f' \in$ COP$_0$ satisfying $f(x) = \langle x, f' \rangle$ for every $x \in W^\phi$. Since f' is unique, in the sequel we write $|f|$ instead of f'. Actually, the sets COP and COP$_0$ are isomorphic, since we also have for every $f' \in$ COP$_0$ there is a unique $f \in$ COP such that $|f| = f'$.

For all $x, y \in W^\phi$ and for every a $\in$ M, we define $\sigma(a, x, y) \subseteq W^\phi$ as follows: $\sigma(a, x, y) \stackrel{\text{def}}{=} R_a^\phi(x) + R_a^\phi(y)$. Observe that $\sigma(a, x, y) = \emptyset$ iff $\langle x, y \rangle \in R_a^\phi$. Let $\mathcal{M} = \langle W, (R_a)_{a\in M}, m \rangle$ be the structure such that:

⋆ $W \overset{\text{def}}{=} W^\phi \times \text{COP}_0$;

⋆ for every $p \in \text{FOR}_0$, $m(p) \overset{\text{def}}{=} \{\langle x, f' \rangle : f' \in \text{COP}_0, x \in m^\phi(p)\}$;

⋆ $R_U \overset{\text{def}}{=} W \times W$;

⋆ for every $a \in M \setminus \{U\}$, $\langle \langle x, f \rangle, \langle y, f' \rangle \rangle \in R_a \overset{\text{def}}{\Leftrightarrow}$

    (1) $\langle x, y \rangle \in R_a^\phi$;

    (2) for every $b \in M \setminus \{U\}$ and for every $c \in M_0(a) \cap M_0(b)$, $f(b,c) = f'(b,c)$;

    (3) for every $b \in M \setminus \{U\}$, $\Sigma_{c \in M_0(b)}(f(b,c) + f'(b,c)) = \sigma(b,x,y)$.

We shall show that $\mathcal{M}$ is a standard S5'-model and COP is a copying from $\mathcal{M}^\phi$ into $\mathcal{M}$, which imply that ϕ is satisfied in $\mathcal{M}$. This is the subject of the two following lemmas.

Lemma 9.3.3. COP *is a copying from $\mathcal{M}^\phi$ into $\mathcal{M}$.*

Proof. The conditions (Cop1), (Cop2), and (Cop5) of Definition 6.2.5 can be checked easily. Now we check (Cop3) and (Cop4).
Proof of (Cop3): we prove that

for all $a \in M$, $x, y \in W^\phi$, and $f \in \text{COP}$, if $\langle x, y \rangle \in R_a^\phi$, then there is some $g \in \text{COP}$ such that $\langle f(x), g(y) \rangle \in R_a$.

Let $a \in M$, $x, y \in W^\phi$, and let $f \in \text{COP}$ be such that $\langle x, y \rangle \in R_a^\phi$. If $a = U$, take $g = f$. If $a \neq U$, we define g and $|g|$ as follows. It is sufficient to define $|g|$ since then g is uniquely determined by $|g|$. For every $b \in M$, we define:

⋆ for every $c \in M_0(a) \cap M_0(b)$, $|g|(b,c) \overset{\text{def}}{=} |f|(b,c)$;

⋆ for every $c \in M_0 \setminus M_0(b)$, $|g|(b,c) \overset{\text{def}}{=} \emptyset$;

⋆ let $\mathcal{X}$ be a "choice function" $\mathcal{X} : M \times M \to M_0$ such that $\mathcal{X}(a,b) \in M_0(b) \setminus M_0(a)$ iff $M_0(b) \setminus M_0(a) \neq \emptyset$. For every $c \in M_0(b) \setminus M_0(a)$,

$$|g|(b,c) \overset{\text{def}}{=} \begin{cases} \Sigma_{d \in M_0(b) \setminus M_0(a)} |f|(b,d) + \sigma(b,x,y) & \text{if } \mathcal{X}(a,b) = c; \\ \emptyset & \text{otherwise.} \end{cases}$$

We check that the three conditions (1)–(3) in the definition of R_a hold.

(1) By hypothesis, $\langle x, y \rangle \in R_a^\phi$.

(2) By definition, for every $c \in M_0(a) \cap M_0(b)$, $|g|(b,c) = |f|(b,c)$.

(3) Let $b \in M \setminus \{U\}$. If $M_0(b) \setminus M_0(a) = \emptyset$, then $\langle x, y \rangle \in R_b^\phi$ because $\mathcal{M}^\phi$ is a non-standard S5'-model and $R_a^\phi \subseteq R_b^\phi$. Consequently, we have $\sigma(b,x,y) = \emptyset$ and

$$\Sigma_{c \in M_0(b)}(|f|(b,c) + |g|(b,c)) = \Sigma_{c \in M_0(a) \cap M_0(b)} |f|(b,c) + |g|(b,c) = \emptyset.$$

Now consider the case $M_0(b) \setminus M_0(a) \neq \emptyset$. Let $X_1 = M_0(a) \cap M_0(b)$ and $X_2 = M_0(b) \setminus M_0(a)$. By definition, we have:

$$\Sigma_{c \in M_0(b)}(|f|(b,c) + |g|(b,c)) = \Sigma_{c \in X_1}(|f|(b,c) + |g|(b,c))$$
$$+ \Sigma_{c \in X_2}(|f|(b,c) + |g|(b,c))$$
$$= \emptyset + (\Sigma_{c \in X_2}|f|(b,c)) + |g|(b, \mathcal{X}(a,b))$$
$$= \Sigma_{c \in X_2}|f|(b,c) + \Sigma_{c \in X_2}|f|(b,c) + \sigma(b,x,y)$$
$$= \sigma(b,x,y).$$

Proof of (Cop4): we prove that

for all $a \in M$, $x \in W^\phi$, $y \in W$, and $g \in COP$, if $\langle \langle x, |g| \rangle, y \rangle \in R_a$, then there exist an $f \in COP$ and an $x' \in W^\phi$ such that $f(x') = y$ and $\langle x, x' \rangle \in R_a^\phi$.

Let $x \in W^\phi$, $y \in W$, and let $g \in COP$ be such that $\langle \langle x, |g| \rangle, y \rangle \in R_a$. By condition (Cop1) of Definition 6.2.5, there exist an $f \in COP$ and an $x' \in W^\phi$ such that $f(x') = y = \langle x', |f| \rangle$. By the definition of R_a, $\langle x, x' \rangle \in R_a^\phi$. Q.E.D.

It remains to show that the structure $\mathcal{M}$ is indeed a model for the logic S5'.

Lemma 9.3.4. $\mathcal{M}$ *is a standard S5'-model.*

Proof. We prove that conditions (1)–(3) in the definition of S5'-models are satisfied by the LAN(S5')-model $\mathcal{M}$.
(1) $R_U = W \times W$ by definition.
(2) We show that for every $a \in M$, R_a is an equivalence relation.
(Reflexivity) Let $\langle x, |f| \rangle \in W$. We prove that $\langle \langle x, |f| \rangle, \langle x, |f| \rangle \rangle \in R_a$. To do so, we have to check three conditions from the definition of relations in $\mathcal{M}$. We have:

⋆ $\langle x, x \rangle \in R_a^\phi$ (because R_a^ϕ is reflexive);
⋆ for every $b \in M \setminus \{U\}$ and for every $c \in M_0(a) \cap M_0(b)$, $f(b,c) = f(b,c)$;
⋆ for every $b \in M \setminus \{U\}$, $\Sigma_{c \in M_0(b)}(f(b,c) + f(b,c)) = \emptyset = \sigma(b,x,x)$, since $\langle x, x \rangle \in R_b^\phi$.

So, $\langle \langle x, |f| \rangle, \langle x, |f| \rangle \rangle \in R_a$.
(Symmetry) Assume that (i) $\langle \langle x, |f| \rangle, \langle y, |f'| \rangle \rangle \in R_a$. We prove that the relation R_a contains the pair $\langle \langle y, |f'| \rangle, \langle x, |f| \rangle \rangle$. To do so, we have to check three conditions from the definition of relations in $\mathcal{M}$. We have:

⋆ $\langle y, x \rangle \in R_a^\phi$ since by (i) $\langle x, y \rangle \in R_a^\phi$ and R_a^ϕ is symmetric;
⋆ for every $b \in M \setminus \{U\}$ and for every $c \in M_0(a) \cap M_0(b)$, $f'(b,c) = f(b,c)$;
⋆ for every $b \in M \setminus \{U\}$, $\Sigma_{c \in M_0(b)}(f'(b,c) + f(b,c)) = \sigma(b,x,y)$ since by (i) $\Sigma_{c \in M_0(b)}(f(b,c) + f'(b,c)) = \sigma(b,x,y)$ and $+$ is commutative.

Consequently, $\langle \langle y, |f'| \rangle, \langle x, |f| \rangle \rangle \in R_a$.
(Transitivity) Assume that:

(ii) $\langle \langle x_1, |f_1| \rangle, \langle x_2, |f_2| \rangle \rangle \in R_a$;
(iii) $\langle \langle x_2, |f_2| \rangle, \langle x_3, |f_3| \rangle \rangle \in R_a$.

We prove that $\langle\langle x_1, |f_1|\rangle, \langle x_3, |f_3|\rangle\rangle \in R_a$. To do so, we have to check three conditions from the definition of relations in $\mathcal{M}$.

$\star$ By (ii) and (iii), $\langle x_1, x_2\rangle \in R_a^\phi$ and $\langle x_2, x_3\rangle \in R_a^\phi$. By transitivity of R_a^ϕ, $\langle x_1, x_3\rangle \in R_a^\phi$.

$\star$ By (ii) and (iii), for every $b \in M \setminus \{U\}$ and for every $c \in M_0(a) \cap M_0(b)$, $f_1(b,c) = f_2(b,c)$ and $f_2(b,c) = f_3(b,c)$. So for every $b \in M \setminus \{U\}$ and for every $c \in M_0(a) \cap M_0(b)$, $f_1(b,c) = f_3(b,c)$.

$\star$ By (ii) and (iii), for every $b \in M \setminus \{U\}$, we have $\Sigma_{c \in M_0(b)}(f_1(b,c) + f_2(b,c)) = \sigma(b, x_1, x_2)$ and $\Sigma_{c \in M_0(b)}(f_2(b,c) + f_3(b,c)) = \sigma(b, x_2, x_3)$. Since $\Sigma_{c \in M_0(b)}(f_2(b,c) + f_2(b,c)) = \emptyset$, for every $b \in M \setminus \{U\}$,

$$\Sigma_{c \in M_0(b)}(f_1(b,c) + f_3(b,c)) = \sigma(b, x_1, x_2) + \sigma(b, x_2, x_3).$$

Moreover, $\sigma(b, x_1, x_2) + \sigma(b, x_2, x_3) = (R_b^\phi(x_1) + R_b^\phi(x_2)) + (R_b^\phi(x_2) + R_b^\phi(x_3)) = R_b^\phi(x_1) + R_b^\phi(x_3)$.

Consequently, $\langle\langle x_1, |f_1|\rangle, \langle x_3, |f_3|\rangle\rangle \in R_a$.

(3) We show that for all $a, b \in M$, $M_0(a) = M_0(b)$ implies $R_a = R_b$. Assume $M_0(b) \subseteq M_0(a)$ and $\langle\langle x, |f_1|\rangle, \langle y, |f_2|\rangle\rangle \in R_a$. We show that the relation R_b contains the pair $\langle\langle x, |f_1|\rangle, \langle y, |f_2|\rangle\rangle$ and therefore $R_a \subseteq R_b$. We check that the three conditions leading to $\langle\langle x, |f_1|\rangle, \langle y, |f_2|\rangle\rangle \in R_b$ are satisfied.

$\star$ Since $\langle x, y\rangle \in R_a^\phi$ and $\mathcal{M}^\phi$ is a non-standard S5'-model, we get $\langle x, y\rangle \in R_b^\phi$.

$\star$ For every $b' \in M \setminus \{U\}$, for every $c \in M_0(a) \cap M_0(b')$, $|f_1|(b',c) = |f_2|(b',c)$ and therefore for every $c \in M_0(b) \cap M_0(b')$, $|f_1|(b',c) = |f_2|(b',c)$.

$\star$ For every $b' \in M \setminus \{U\}$, $\Sigma_{c \in M_0(b')} f_1(b',c) + f_2(b',c) = \sigma(b', x, y)$, which is independent of a and b. Hence $\langle\langle x, |f_1|\rangle, \langle y, |f_2|\rangle\rangle \in R_b$.

(4) We show that for all $a, b \in M \setminus \{U\}$, $R_{a \cap b} = R_a \cap R_b$.

($\subseteq$) Assume that $\langle\langle x, |f|\rangle, \langle y, |g|\rangle\rangle \in R_{a_1 \cap a_2}$. We check that the three conditions leading to $\langle\langle x, |f|\rangle, \langle y, |g|\rangle\rangle \in R_{a_1} \cap R_{a_2}$ are satisfied.

$\star$ Since $\mathcal{M}^\phi$ is a non-standard S5'-model, $\langle x, y\rangle \in R_{a_1 \cap a_2}^\phi \subseteq R_{a_1}^\phi \cap R_{a_2}^\phi$.

$\star$ For every $b \in M$ and for every $c \in M_0(a_1 \cap a_2) \cap M_0(b)$, we have $|f|(b,c) = |g|(b,c)$, which is equivalent to $|f|(b,c) = |g|(b,c)$ for every $b \in M$ and for every $c \in M_0(a_i) \cap M_0(b)$, where $i \in \{1, 2\}$.

$\star$ For every $b \in M$, $\Sigma_{c \in M_0(b)} |f|(b,c) + |g|(b,c) = \sigma(b, x, y)$, which is independent of a_1, a_2, and $a_1 \cap a_2$.

($\supseteq$) Now assume $\langle\langle x, |f_1|\rangle, \langle y, |f_2|\rangle\rangle \in R_{a_1} \cap R_{a_2}$ are satisfied. We check the three conditions leading to $\langle\langle x, |f|\rangle, \langle y, |g|\rangle\rangle \in R_{a_1 \cap a_2}$.

$\star$ We show that $\sigma(a_1 \cap a_2, x, y) = \emptyset$, which is equivalent to $\langle x, y\rangle \in R_{a_1 \cap a_2}^\phi$. We know that $\Sigma_{c \in M_0(a_1 \cap a_2)} |f|(a_1 \cap a_2, c) + |g|(a_1 \cap a_2, c) = \sigma(a_1 \cap a_2, x, y)$. Moreover, for every $i \in \{1, 2\}$, for every $c \in M_0(a_i) \cap M_0(a_1 \cap a_2) = M_0(a_i)$, $|f|(a_1 \cap a_2, c) = |g|(a_1 \cap a_2, c)$. So $\Sigma_{c \in M_0(a_1 \cap a_2)} |f|(a_1 \cap a_2, c) + |g|(a_1 \cap a_2, c) = \emptyset = \sigma(a_1 \cap a_2, x, y)$ and therefore $\langle x, y\rangle \in R_{a_1 \cap a_2}^\phi$.

★ Similar to the second point in ($\subseteq$).
★ Similar to the third point in ($\subseteq$).

$Q.E.D.$

Theorem 9.3.4. *(Completeness Theorem)* VAL(S5$'$) $\subseteq$ THM(HS5$'$).

Proof. Assume $\phi \in$ VAL(S5$'$) and $\phi \notin$ THM(HS5$'$). Let $\mathcal{M}^\phi$ be the model defined earlier in this section. Since $\mathcal{M}^\phi, x_\phi \not\models \phi$ and $\mathcal{M}^\phi$ is an S5$'$-model, we get a contradiction. $Q.E.D.$

9.4 LKO: a Logic with Relative Knowledge Operators

The logic LKO is an extension of the logic BLKO to a Rare-logic. In the language of LKO we have a means for representing varying sets of attributes and a Boolean structure of the family of the sets of attributes. For each set of attributes there is a knowledge connective that represents knowledge of an agent who has an access to the corresponding attributes of an information system and recognises the objects of the system in terms of these attributes. The logic LKO enables us to reason about knowledge of multiple agents and to compare their knowledge according to a hierarchy of degrees of knowledge presented in Sect. 4.6.

9.4.1 Language and Semantics

The logic LKO is a standard Rare-logic in the sense of Definition 5.4.11:

★ the set P of parameter expressions (here referred to as "agent expressions") is the smallest set containing the countably infinite set $P_0 = \{C_i : i \geq 1\}$ of parameter constants ("agent constants") and closed under the operators $-, \cap, \cup$;
★ the set M_0 of basic modal expressions is built from the singleton set $T = \{ind\}$ such that $M_0 \stackrel{\text{def}}{=} \{ind(A) : A \in P\}$;
★ the set O_M of modal connectives is empty and $M = M_0$;
★ the set FOR$_0$ of basic formulae is a countably infinite set of propositional variables;
★ the set O_{FOR} of logical connectives is $\{\neg, \wedge\} \cup \{K(ind(A)) : A \in P\}$.

For the sake of simplicity, $K(ind(A))$ is abbreviated by $K(A)$. The LKO-models are the structures of the form $\langle OB, (\mathcal{R}_P)_{P \subseteq AG}, m \rangle$, where

★ OB and AG are non-empty sets;
★ $(\mathcal{R}_P)_{P \subseteq AG}$ is a family of equivalence relations on OB such that
  (1) $\mathcal{R}_\emptyset = OB \times OB$ (condition (C_1'));
  (2) $\mathcal{R}_{P \cup Q} = \mathcal{R}_P \cap \mathcal{R}_Q$ for all $P, Q \subseteq AG$ (condition (C_1));
★ $m :$ FOR$_0 \cup$ P $\cup$ M $\rightarrow \mathcal{P}(OB) \cup \mathcal{P}(AG) \cup \mathcal{P}(OB)$ is a map such that:

* for every $p \in FOR_0$, $m(p) \subseteq OB$;
* the restriction of m to P is a standard P-meaning function (see Sect. 5.4);
* $\mathcal{R}_{m(A)} = m(ind(A))$ for every $A \in P$.

The elements of OB are interpreted as objects whose characterisation is provided by some agents, AG is a set of agents and $(\mathcal{R}_P)_{P \subseteq AG}$ is a family of binary relations on OB such that $\langle x, x' \rangle \in \mathcal{R}_P$ iff x and x' cannot be distinguished by the set P of agents. Thus $\mathcal{R}_P(x)$ is the set of objects which cannot be distinguished from x by the members of P. In that context, condition (C_1) means that two sets of agents can distinguish more objects than each one can individually, and condition (C_1') means that the empty set of agents cannot distinguish any objects.

By definition of the semantics of LKO, we have:

$$\{x \in OB : \mathcal{M}, x \models K(A)\phi\} = K_{m(A)}(\{x \in OB : \mathcal{M}, x \models \phi\}),$$

where the operator K on the right-hand side of the equality is the knowledge operator defined in Sect. 4.6.

9.4.2 A Transformation from SAT(LKO) into SAT(S5′)

Let ϕ be an LKO-formula. Without any loss of generality, one can assume that if $card(P_0(\phi)) = n$, then $P_0(\phi) = \{C_1, \ldots, C_n\}$, that is $P_0(\phi)$ contains the first n constants in the enumeration of the countably infinite set P_0. Indeed LKO-satisfiability and LKO-validity are not sensitive to the renaming of constants. If ϕ does not contain any constants from P_0, then ϕ is LKO-valid iff ϕ is S5′-valid iff ϕ is valid in the propositional calculus. In the sequel, we assume that $n \geq 1$ unless stated otherwise.

In order to translate LKO into S5′, we consider LKO-formulae in normal form. This normal form is an obvious extension of the normal forms for parameter expressions defined in Sect. 5.4. The normal form of an LKO-formula ϕ is the LKO-formula $N(\phi)$ obtained from ϕ by replacing every occurrence of an agent expression A by $N_{P_0(\phi)}(A)$. The definition of $N_{P_0(\phi)}(A)$ can be found in Sect. 5.4. Then the following result can be easily shown.

Lemma 9.4.1. *For every LKO-formula ϕ, $\phi \Leftrightarrow N(\phi) \in VAL(LKO)$.*

In the rest of the chapter, we shall use the maps f and h defined as follows.

Definition 9.4.1. *Let $f : FOR(LKO) \rightarrow FOR(S5')$ be the map such that $f(\phi) = h(N(\phi))$, where $h : FOR(LKO) \rightarrow FOR(S5')$ is a map defined as follows:*

* *for every $p \in FOR_0$, $h(p) \stackrel{\text{def}}{=} p$;*
* *h is homomorphic with respect to the Boolean connectives;*
* *$h(K(B_{i_1} \cup \ldots \cup B_{i_l})\psi) \stackrel{\text{def}}{=} [c_{i_1} \cap \ldots \cap c_{i_l}]h(\psi) \vee [c_{i_1} \cap \ldots \cap c_{i_l}]\neg h(\psi)$, where $l \geq 1$, $B_{i_1}, \ldots, B_{i_l}$ are components in $Comp(P_0(\phi))$, and $c_{i_1}, \ldots, c_{i_l}$ are S5′ modal constants;*

⋆ $h(K(C_1 \cap -C_1)\psi) \stackrel{\text{def}}{=} [U]h(\psi) \vee [U]\neg h(\psi)$.

The map h defined in Definition 9.4.1 implicitly depends on the agent expressions occurring in ϕ. The first feature of the map h is the translation of a component B_k (an agent expression) into a modal constant c_k. The expression $C_1 \cap -C_1$ is translated into U (see condition (C_1)). The second feature of h is the use of the semantic equivalence between $K\psi$ and $\Box\psi \vee \Box\neg\psi$. The components B_k depend on the agent expressions occurring in ϕ. The following is an example of the translation:

$$f(K(C_2 \cap C_1)p \wedge K(C_2 \cap -C_2)q) = ([c_0]p \vee [c_0]\neg p) \wedge ([U]q \vee [U]\neg q).$$

Lemma 9.4.2. *For every LKO-formula ϕ, the following statements are equivalent:*

(I) $\phi \in$ SAT(LKO);
(II) $f(\phi) \in$ SAT(S5').

Proof. (I) → (II) Assume that ϕ is LKO-satisfiable. There exist an LKO-model $\mathcal{M} = \langle OB, (\mathcal{R}_P)_{P \subseteq AG}, m \rangle$ and an $x \in OB$ such that $\mathcal{M}, x \models N(\phi)$. Let $\mathcal{M}'$ be the standard S5'-model $\langle OB, (R'_a)_{a \in M}, m' \rangle$ such that:

⋆ for every $k \in \{0, \ldots, 2^n - 1\}$, $R'_{c_k} \stackrel{\text{def}}{=} R_{m(B_k)}$, where n is the number of agent constants in ϕ;
⋆ for every $c \in M_0 \setminus \{c_0, \ldots, c_{2^n-1}\}$, $R'_c \stackrel{\text{def}}{=} R'_{c_0}$;
⋆ for every $a \in M \setminus \{U\}$, $R'_a \stackrel{\text{def}}{=} \bigcap_{c \in M_0(a)} R'_c$;
⋆ $R'_U \stackrel{\text{def}}{=} OB \times OB$;
⋆ for every $p \in$ FOR$_0$, $m'(p) \stackrel{\text{def}}{=} m(p)$.

It is a routine task to check that $\mathcal{M}', x \models f(\phi)$ holds.
(II) → (I) Assume that $f(\phi)$ is S5'-satisfiable. There exist a standard S5'-model $\mathcal{M}' = \langle W', (R'_a)_{a \in M}, m' \rangle$ and a $w \in W'$ such that $\mathcal{M}', w \models f(\phi)$. Let $\mathcal{M} = \langle W', (\mathcal{R}_P)_{P \subseteq AG}, m \rangle$ be an LKO-model such that:

⋆ $AG \stackrel{\text{def}}{=} \{0, \ldots, 2^n - 1\}$;
⋆ the restriction of m to FOR$_0$ is m';
⋆ for every $i \in \{1, \ldots, n\}$, $m(C_i) \stackrel{\text{def}}{=} \{k \in AG : bit_i(k) = 0\}$. The interpretation of the other constants is not constrained. We only require that the restriction of m to P is a P-meaning function; such an extension always exists;
⋆ $R_\emptyset \stackrel{\text{def}}{=} W' \times W'$;
⋆ for every $P \subseteq AG$ such that card$(P) \geq 1$, $R_P \stackrel{\text{def}}{=} \bigcap_{x \in P} R_{\{x\}}$.

One can check that the definition of $\mathcal{M}$ is correct and $\mathcal{M}$ is an LKO-model. In particular, for every $k \in \{0, \ldots, 2^n - 1\}$, we have $R_{m(B_k)} = R'_{c_k}$. One can show that $\mathcal{M}, w \models N(\phi)$ by induction on the structure of ϕ.   Q.E.D.

Since $f(\neg\phi) \Leftrightarrow \neg f(\phi)$ is S5′-valid, Lemma 9.4.2 entails that ϕ is LKO-valid iff $f(\phi)$ is S5′-valid.

Theorem 9.4.1.

(I) SAT(LKO) is decidable iff SAT(S5′) is decidable;
(II) every formula ϕ in SAT(LKO) is satisfiable in some LKO-model of the form $\langle OB, (\mathcal{R}_P)_{P \subseteq AG}, m \rangle$ with $\mathrm{card}(AG) \leq 2^{\mathrm{card}(\mathrm{P}_0(\phi))}$.

Proof. (I) Lemma 9.4.2 entails that SAT(S5′) is decidable only if SAT(LKO) is decidable. Now we define a computable map from the problem SAT(S5′) into the problem SAT(LKO). Let ϕ be an S5′-formula such that $M_0(\phi) = \{c_0, \ldots, c_N\}$, $N \geq 1$. Without any loss of generality one can assume that if the cardinality of $M_0(\phi)$ is $N+1$, then $M_0(\phi) = \{c_0, \ldots, c_N\}$, that is $M_0(\phi)$ contains the first $N+1$ constants in the enumeration of the countably infinite set M_0. S5′-satisfiability and S5′-validity are not sensitive to the renaming of modal constants. Let n be the smallest natural number such that $2^n - 1 \geq N$. Take n agent constants from P_0, say $Y \overset{\mathrm{def}}{=} \{C_1, \ldots, C_n\}$. If $M_0(\phi) = \emptyset$, then we just consider $Y \overset{\mathrm{def}}{=} \{C_1\}$. We define the mapping $h^\leftarrow : M \cup \mathrm{FOR}(S5') \to P \cup \mathrm{FOR}(LKO)$ in the following way:

⋆ for every $k \in \{0, \ldots, 2^n - 1\}$, $h^\leftarrow(c_k) \overset{\mathrm{def}}{=} B_k$, where $B_k \in \mathrm{Comp}(Y)$;
⋆ for every $c \in M_0 \setminus \{c_0, \ldots, c_{2^n-1}\}$, $h^\leftarrow(c) \overset{\mathrm{def}}{=} C_1$;
⋆ $h^\leftarrow(a \cap b) \overset{\mathrm{def}}{=} h^\leftarrow(a) \cup h^\leftarrow(b)$;
⋆ $h^\leftarrow(U) \overset{\mathrm{def}}{=} C_1 \cap -C_1$;
⋆ for every $p \in \mathrm{FOR}_0$, $h^\leftarrow(p) \overset{\mathrm{def}}{=} p$;
⋆ $h^\leftarrow$ is homomorphic with respect to the Boolean connectives;
⋆ $h^\leftarrow([a]\psi) \overset{\mathrm{def}}{=} h^\leftarrow(\psi) \wedge K(h^\leftarrow(a))h^\leftarrow(\psi)$.

By the definition of $h^\leftarrow$, we have $N(h^\leftarrow(\phi)) = h^\leftarrow(\phi)$ for every S5′-formula ϕ. Furthermore, since $h(N(h^\leftarrow([a]p))) = p \wedge ([a]p \vee [a]\neg p)$ and $p \wedge ([a]p \vee [a]\neg p) \Leftrightarrow [a]p$ is an S5′-valid formula, the following statements are equivalent:

⋆ $h(N(h^\leftarrow(\phi)))$ is S5′-satisfiable;
⋆ ϕ is S5′-satisfiable.

Hence, ϕ is S5′-satisfiable iff $h(N(h^\leftarrow(\phi)))$ is S5′-satisfiable iff $h^\leftarrow(\phi)$ is LKO-satisfiable (by Lemma 9.4.2).
(II) The proof is based on the proof of Lemma 9.4.2.   *Q.E.D.*

As far as LKO-satisfiability is concerned, we can confine ourselves to the set of LKO-models having a finite set of agents.

9.4.3 A Hilbert-style Proof System

We define the Hilbert-style proof system HLKO for LKO and we show its completeness with respect to the class of LKO-models. The proof system HLKO is an extension of HPC obtained by adding the axioms:

(Ax1) $\phi \wedge K(A)\phi \wedge K(A)(\phi \Rightarrow \psi) \Rightarrow K(A)\psi$;
(Ax2) $K(A)(K(A)\phi \Rightarrow \phi)$;
(Ax3) $K(A)\phi \Leftrightarrow K(A)\neg\phi$;
(Ax4) $K(A)\phi \Rightarrow K(A')\phi$, where $A \sqsubseteq A'$;
(Ax5) $\phi \wedge K(A_1)\phi \Rightarrow K(A_2)\phi$, where $A_1 \sim \perp$;

and the inference rule

$$\frac{\phi}{K(A)\phi} \text{ (K-rule)}.$$

HLKO can be viewed as a multi-modal generalisation of HBLKO, where the knowledge operators are relative to subsets of a set of agents.

Lemma 9.4.3. *Let $\phi \in \text{THM(HLKO)}$. Then $\phi[p \leftarrow \psi] \in \text{THM(HLKO)}$ for every $p \in \text{FOR}_0$ and every $\psi \in \text{FOR(LKO)}$.*

Lemma 9.4.3 states that HLKO is closed under the uniform substitution of propositional variables. Moreover, deleting the axiom (Ax5) does not restrict the set of theorems. We introduce this axiom to emphasize the correspondence with the proof system HS5'.

In order to show that HLKO is LKO-sound, we can use the BLKO-soundness of HBLKO. However, we also need to check that the axioms related to agent expressions behave properly.

Lemma 9.4.4. *Let $\mathcal{M} = \langle OB, (\mathcal{R}_P)_{P \subseteq AG}, m \rangle \in \text{MOD(LKO)}$ and let $A, A' \in P$. If $A \sim A'$, then $\mathcal{M} \models K(A)\phi \Rightarrow K(A')\phi$ for every $\phi \in \text{FOR(LKO)}$.*

The proof of Lemma 9.4.4 is by an easy verification and it allows us to conclude the following result.

Theorem 9.4.2. *(Soundness Theorem)* $\text{THM(HLKO)} \subseteq \text{VAL(LKO)}$.

The following lemma can be shown by using arguments from Sect. 9.2.2.

Lemma 9.4.5. *For all LKO-formulae ϕ and ϕ' the following assertions hold:*

(I) if $\phi \Leftrightarrow \phi' \in \text{THM(HLKO)}$, then $\psi \Leftrightarrow \psi' \in \text{THM(HLKO)}$, where ψ' is obtained from ψ by simultaneously replacing some occurrences of ϕ by ϕ';
(II) for every $A \in P$, $K(A)(\phi \wedge K(A)\phi) \in \text{THM(HLKO)}$.

Another useful result is stated in the following lemma.

Lemma 9.4.6. *Let ϕ be an LKO-formula such that $\text{card}(P_0(\phi)) = n$, $n \geq 1$, and let $h^{\leftarrow}$ be the mapping defined in the proof of Theorem 9.4.1. Then:*

(I) $h^{\leftarrow}(h(N(\phi))) \Leftrightarrow \phi \in \text{THM(HLKO)}$;
(II) for all S5'-formulae ψ, φ and for every propositional variable p, we have

$$h^{\leftarrow}(\psi[p \leftarrow \varphi]) = h^{\leftarrow}(\psi)[p \leftarrow h^{\leftarrow}(\varphi)].$$

Proof. (I) By Lemma 9.4.5(I) and by the axiom (Ax4), $\phi \Leftrightarrow N(\phi) \in$ THM(HLKO). However, $h^{\leftarrow}(h(N(\phi))) = \alpha(N(\phi))$, where α is the following map:

⋆ for every $p \in FOR_0$, $\alpha(p) \stackrel{\text{def}}{=} p$;
⋆ α is homomorphic with respect to the Boolean connectives;
⋆ $\alpha(K(A)\psi) \stackrel{\text{def}}{=} (K(A)\neg\alpha(\psi) \wedge \neg\alpha(\psi)) \vee (K(A)\alpha(\psi) \wedge \alpha(\psi))$.

Since the formula $(K(A)\neg p \wedge \neg p) \vee (K(A)p \wedge p) \Leftrightarrow K(A)p \in$ THM(HLKO), it can be shown by induction on the structure of ϕ and by Lemma 9.4.5(I) that $\alpha(N(\phi)) \Leftrightarrow N(\phi) \in$ THM(HLKO). Hence $\vdash h^{\leftarrow}(h(N(\phi))) \Leftrightarrow \phi$.
(II) The proof is by induction on the structure of ψ.   *Q.E.D.*

The following lemma is the cornerstone of the proof of the LKO-completeness of HLKO.

Lemma 9.4.7. *For every LKO-formula ϕ, if $f(\phi) \in$ THM(HS5'), then $\phi \in$* THM(HLKO).

Proof. We recall that the mapping f is introduced in Definition 9.4.1. Let $\langle \psi_1, \ldots, \psi_N \rangle$, $N \geq 1$, be a derivation of $f(\phi)$ in HS5', that is $\psi_N = f(\phi)$. We show that for every $i \in \{1, \ldots, N\}$, $h^{\leftarrow}(\psi_i) \in$ THM(HLKO), where the number of agent constants involved in the definition of $h^{\leftarrow}$ is $n = max(1, card(P_0(\phi)))$. In such a way, since

$$h^{\leftarrow}(f(\phi)) \Leftrightarrow \phi \in \text{THM(HLKO)},$$

by propositional reasoning, we can prove that $\phi \in$ THM(HLKO). The proof is by induction on the length of the derivation.
Base case: ψ_1 is an axiom of HS5'.
We distinguish cases according to the form of ψ_1.
Base case 1: ψ_1 is a tautology of PC.
We have $\psi_1 \in$ THM(HLKO) and $h^{\leftarrow}(\psi_1) = \psi_1$.
Base case 2: ψ_1 is of the form $([a](\psi_2 \Rightarrow \psi_3) \wedge [a]\psi_2) \Rightarrow [a]\psi_3$.
The formula $h^{\leftarrow}(\psi_1)$ is equal to

$$\overbrace{(h^{\leftarrow}(\psi_2) \Rightarrow h^{\leftarrow}(\psi_3)) \wedge K(h^{\leftarrow}(a))(h^{\leftarrow}(\psi_2) \Rightarrow h^{\leftarrow}(\psi_3))}^{h^{\leftarrow}([a](\psi_2 \Rightarrow \psi_3))} \wedge$$

$$\overbrace{h^{\leftarrow}(\psi_2) \wedge K(h^{\leftarrow}(a))(h^{\leftarrow}(\psi_2))}^{h^{\leftarrow}([a](\psi_2))} \Rightarrow \overbrace{h^{\leftarrow}(\psi_3) \wedge K(h^{\leftarrow}(a))(h^{\leftarrow}(\psi_3))}^{h^{\leftarrow}([a](\psi_3))}.$$

By the axiom (Ax1) (in HLKO), $K(h^{\leftarrow}(a))(h^{\leftarrow}(\psi_2) \Rightarrow h^{\leftarrow}(\psi_3)) \wedge h^{\leftarrow}(\psi_2) \wedge K(h^{\leftarrow}(a))(h^{\leftarrow}(\psi_2)) \Rightarrow K(h^{\leftarrow}(a))(h^{\leftarrow}(\psi_3)) \in$ THM(HLKO) and

$$(h^{\leftarrow}(\psi_2) \Rightarrow h^{\leftarrow}(\psi_3)) \wedge h^{\leftarrow}(\psi_2) \Rightarrow h^{\leftarrow}(\psi_3) \in \text{THM(HLKO)}.$$

Hence we get $h^{\leftarrow}(\psi_1) \in$ THM(HLKO).
Base case 3: ψ_1 is of the form $[a]\psi_2 \Rightarrow \psi_2$.

We have $h^{\leftarrow}(\psi_1) = K(h^{\leftarrow}(\mathrm{a}))h^{\leftarrow}(\psi_2) \wedge h^{\leftarrow}(\psi_2) \Rightarrow h^{\leftarrow}(\psi_2)$, which can be derived in HLKO by an easy propositional reasoning.

Base case 4: ψ_1 is of the form $\langle \mathrm{a}\rangle\psi_2 \Rightarrow [\mathrm{a}]\langle \mathrm{a}\rangle\psi_2$.
We have

$$h^{\leftarrow}(\psi_1) = \neg\psi \Rightarrow \neg\psi \wedge K(h^{\leftarrow}(\mathrm{a}))(\neg\psi),$$

where

$$\psi = (\neg h^{\leftarrow}(\psi_2) \wedge K(h^{\leftarrow}(\mathrm{a}))\neg h^{\leftarrow}(\psi_2)).$$

By Lemma 9.4.5(II), we get

$$K(h^{\leftarrow}(\mathrm{a}))(h^{\leftarrow}(\psi_2) \wedge K(h^{\leftarrow}(\mathrm{a}))h^{\leftarrow}(\psi_2)) \in \mathrm{THM(HLKO)}.$$

By Lemma 9.4.3, we obtain

$$K(h^{\leftarrow}(\mathrm{a}))(\neg h^{\leftarrow}(\psi_2) \wedge K(h^{\leftarrow}(\mathrm{a}))\neg h^{\leftarrow}(\psi_2)) \in \mathrm{THM(HLKO)}.$$

By the axiom (Ax3), $K(h^{\leftarrow}(\mathrm{a}))(\neg\psi) \in \mathrm{THM(HLKO)}$.
So, obviously, $h^{\leftarrow}(\psi_1) \in \mathrm{THM(HLKO)}$.

Base case 5: We omit the details of the cases when ψ_1 is an instance of the axioms (Ax4), (Ax1), or (Ax2) in HS5', since they present no extra difficulties.

Induction step.
If ψ_{i+1} is an instance of an axiom, see the treatment of the base case. Now assume that ψ_{i+1} is computed with an inference rule of HS5'.

Case 1: there exist $j, j' < i+1$ such that $\psi'_j = \psi_j \Rightarrow \psi_{i+1}$.
By the induction hypothesis, $h^{\leftarrow}(\psi_j) \in \mathrm{THM(HLKO)}$ and

$$h^{\leftarrow}(\psi_j \Rightarrow \psi_{i+1}) = h^{\leftarrow}(\psi_j) \Rightarrow h^{\leftarrow}(\psi_{i+1}) \in \mathrm{THM(HLKO)}.$$

By applying modus ponens to the above formulae we get $h^{\leftarrow}(\psi_{i+1}) \in \mathrm{THM(HLKO)}$.

Case 2: there is a $j < i+1$ such that $\psi_{i+1} = [\mathrm{a}]\psi_j$.
By the induction hypothesis, $h^{\leftarrow}(\psi_j) \in \mathrm{THM(HLKO)}$. By applying the necessitation rule to $h^{\leftarrow}(\psi_j)$ with $h^{\leftarrow}(\mathrm{a})$, we can deduce that $K(h^{\leftarrow}(\mathrm{a}))h^{\leftarrow}(\psi_j)$ belongs to THM(HLKO). So, $h^{\leftarrow}(\psi_j) \wedge K(h^{\leftarrow}(\mathrm{a}))h^{\leftarrow}(\psi_j) \in \mathrm{THM(HLKO)}$, equivalently $h^{\leftarrow}(\psi_{i+1}) \in \mathrm{THM(HLKO)}$.   *Q.E.D.*

Theorem 9.4.3. *(Completeness Theorem)* VAL(LKO) $\subseteq$ THM(HLKO).

Proof. Assume that ϕ is LKO-valid. Hence, $f(\phi)$ is S5'-valid, which implies $f(\phi) \in \mathrm{THM(HS5')}$ by Theorem 9.3.4. By Lemma 9.4.7, $\phi \in \mathrm{THM(HLKO)}$. *Q.E.D.*

As a conclusion, VAL(LKO) = THM(HLKO).

9.5 Notes

Knowledge. Techniques and theories of knowledge representation focus on construction of procedures that allow intelligent manipulation of data. The epistemological problem of which facts about the world are available to an agent with given opportunities to perceive, and which rules permit plausible inferences from these facts, plays an important role in many AI problems. A formal analysis of reasoning about knowledge has been a subject of investigation of many authors (see e.g. [Wri51, Hin62, Len78, CM86]), and several epistemic systems have been proposed to formalise the operator "an agent knows". The logics considered in this chapter are based on semantic analysis of knowledge presented in [Orło89].

Knowledge operator K. The operator K considered in this chapter appears in [Hin62], where Kp is intuitively interpreted as "an agent knows whether the proposition p holds". A formalism with the operator K based on a rough set-style semantic treatment of knowledge is presented in [Orło89]. It is also discussed in the survey of logics providing foundations for reasoning with incomplete information [Orło93b]. HBLKO is the original system from [Val88] as has been presented in [Orło89] with a single knowledge operator. The proof system HBLKO has been known since 1966 (see [MR66]). Actually, in [MR66] it is shown that the axiom (Ax2) in HBLKO can be replaced by one of the following axioms while preserving the set of theorems:

$$KK\phi, \quad K(\phi \land K\phi), \quad K(\phi \lor \neg K\phi).$$

Rare-logics with knowledge operators. The possible worlds semantics for knowledge logics initiated by Hintikka [Hin62] has been very fruitful for reasoning about knowledge (see for example [FHMV95]). This approach has also been successfully used for reasoning about protocols in distributed systems (see e.g. [Hal87]). The modal connective $K(A)$ is similar to Aumann's knowledge operator in the event-based approach of knowledge [Aum76, RdS95], where it is defined as: $K(P)(X) \stackrel{\text{def}}{=} \{x \in OB : \mathcal{R}_P(x) \subseteq X\} \cup \{x \in OB : \mathcal{R}_P(x) \subseteq (OB \setminus X)\}$, where P is a set of agents. $K(P)$ also corresponds to the modal operator $\triangle$ in logics of non-contingency. Modal logics of non-contingency have been developed in [Hin62, MR66, MR68, BH83, Cre88, Hum95, Kuh95]. There are many logics based on the approach to knowledge presented in this chapter, see for instance [FdCO85, Orło88b, MR89, Orło89, Vak91c, Orło93b, Rau93, Bal98, Kon97].

Logic S5'. At first glance, it may seem surprising that S5' is considered as a knowledge logic, since it has been introduced as an auxiliary logic in order to study LKO. However, the intersection operator $\cap$ is used for capturing implicit knowledge of a group of agents (see [HM85, FV86a, HM92]). A group of agents has implicit knowledge of a fact if the knowledge of that fact is distributed over the members of that group. S5' is an extension of various epistemic logics defined in [HM85, FV86a, HM92] that contain an implicit knowledge operator.

Axiomatisation of S5'. HS5' is a minor extension of the Hilbert-style system for $S5_n^D$ (see e.g. [Bal98]), where some axioms have been added in order to take into account the universal modal connective [U] and a countably infinite set M of modal constants. HS5' is an extension of the system for the knowledge logic $S5_n^D$ (see e.g. [HM92]). The completeness proof is obtained by adapting the copying construction used in the completeness proof in [Bal98] (see also [Vak91c]).

Axiomatisation of LKO. LKO was introduced in [Orło89]. An axiomatisation of fragments of LKO can be found in [MR68, Val88, Dem97a]. The system HLKO is defined in [Dem99a]. Decidability and complexity issues are also discussed there. In [DG00c], display calculi for logics with relative knowledge operators including LKO are defined.

Normal forms. The operator N presented in Sect. 5.4.1 computes the canonical disjunctive normal form for the formulae of the classical propositional calculus (see for example [Lem65]). The translation from LKO into S5' takes advantage of the existence of these normal forms for Boolean terms following developments from [Lem65, Kon97]. Although the translation may exponentially increase the length of formulae, we will show that the satisfiability problem for LKO is in **EXPTIME** by observing that the translation increases linearly the number of subformulae. The full arguments are given in Sect. 12.7.

Boolean modal logic BML. The Boolean modal logic BML defined in [GP90] admits Boolean terms as modal indices in its language. However, in BML these terms are interpreted as binary relations, unlike in LKO. In the definition of HLKO, (Ax4) corresponds to an axiom from the axiomatisation of BML defined in [GP90] (see also [Gor90a]).

Part IV

Computational Aspects of Information Logics

10. Information Logics Versus Standard Modal Logics

10.1 Introduction and Outline of the Chapter

In this chapter we investigate relationships between the Rare-logics introduced in Sect. 5.4 and standard modal logics defined in Sect. 5.3.3. For the sake of simplicity, we confine ourselves to Rare-logics with a unique relation type, that is, the models of the logics contain a single family of relative relations. The focus is on studying the conditions which enable us to reduce the level of the powerset hierarchy of parameters in the semantic structures of the logics without changing the set of valid formulae. In Sect. 10.2 we introduce several classes of Rare-logics by postulating that the relations from semantic structures satisfy various global conditions, in particular the conditions listed in Sect. 3.9. In Sect. 10.3 and in Sect. 10.4 we show how formulae of some Rare-logics can be translated into formulae of certain standard modal logics with preservation of validity. The standard modal logics associated in this way with Rare-logics must be sufficiently expressive; in particular, often they must include the universal modal connective. In Sect. 10.5 we address the issue of whether the universal modal connective can be eliminated from the language without violating the properties of the translation. Sect. 10.6 and Sect. 10.7 extend the results and techniques from Sect. 10.3 and Sect. 10.4 to the Rare-logics whose languages include constants representing individual objects and individual parameters. In the second part of the chapter we study Rare-logics whose level of the powerset hierarchy of parameters is, in a sense, inessential as far as the set of valid formulae is concerned. These logics are referred to as reducible Rare-logics. They are presented in Sect. 10.8. In Sect. 10.9 we prove sufficient conditions for a Rare-logic to be reducible. As an illustration of this method we show in Sect. 10.10 that the logic DALLA presented in Sect. 8.2 is closely related to Rare-logics of level 2. The results of this chapter provide foundations for the methods of studying decidability and complexity issues of information logics. They are the subject of the remaining two chapters of this part.

10.2 Classes of Rare-logics

As usual, the family of relations from the semantic structures of the logics may satisfy some local and/or global conditions. Typically, the local conditions are some of those listed in Sect. 1.2, and the global conditions are among those listed in Sect. 3.9. Let Y be a set of global conditions. In this section by class(Y) we mean a family of standard Rare-logics whose global conditions are those of Y. Hence, for every $\mathcal{L} \in$ class(Y), the family of relations in the $\mathcal{L}$-models satisfies the global conditions from Y and possibly some local conditions.

For every Rare-logic $\mathcal{L}$ in class($\{C_1, C_1'\}$), if $\langle W, (\mathcal{R}_P)_{P \subseteq PAR}, m \rangle$ is an $\mathcal{L}$-model, then $W \times W$ satisfies the local conditions of $\mathcal{L}$. Similarly, for every Rare-logic $\mathcal{L}$ in class($\{C_5, C_2'\}$), the relations $\mathcal{R}_P$ of the $\mathcal{L}$-models are reflexive and transitive, since for every $P \subseteq PAR$, $\mathcal{R}_P = \mathcal{R}_P \cup^* \mathcal{R}_P$.

Definition 10.2.1. Let $\mathcal{L}_k = \langle L_k, \mathcal{I}_k, \mathcal{S}_k \rangle \in$ class(Y) for some set Y of global conditions, $k = 1, 2$. $\mathcal{L}_1$ and $\mathcal{L}_2$ are similar $\overset{\text{def}}{\Leftrightarrow}$ $L_1 = L_2$, $\mathcal{I}_1 = \mathcal{I}_2$ and $\mathcal{L}_1$ and $\mathcal{L}_2$ have the same local conditions.

This means that similar logics may differ in global conditions. Hence, $\mathcal{S}_1$ and $\mathcal{S}_2$ may be different since each of them is uniquely determined by the local conditions, the global conditions, and the operator interpretation function of the respective logic.

Example 10.2.1. Consider the Rare-logic $\mathcal{L} = \langle L, \mathcal{I}, \mathcal{S} \rangle$ in class($\{C_1, C_1'\}$) such that $O_M = \{\cup, ; , ^* \}$. M is the set of modal expressions built from M_0 with $\{\cup, ; , ^* \}$ and $O_{FOR} \overset{\text{def}}{=} \{\wedge, \neg\} \cup \{[a] : a \in M\}$. The local condition of $\mathcal{L}$ is "true". The $\mathcal{L}$-language coincides with the language of a fragment of PDL, where the program constants have been replaced by basic modal expressions of the form $r(A)$.

The families class($\{C_1, C_1'\}$) [resp. class($\{C_3, C_2'\}$)] and class($\{C_6, C_3'\}$) [resp. class($\{C_7, C_4'\}$)] are dual as Lemma 10.2.1 suggests. These classes are central in this chapter since they contain various information logics from the literature (see Sect. 10.11 for useful references).

Lemma 10.2.1. Let $\mathcal{L}_1 \in$ class($\{C_1, C_1'\}$) [resp. class($\{C_3, C_2'\}$)] and $\mathcal{L}_2 \in$ class($\{C_6, C_3'\}$) [resp. class($\{C_7, C_4'\}$)] be similar logics. Then there is a mapping f_{dual} from FOR($\mathcal{L}_1$) into FOR($\mathcal{L}_2$) such that:

(I) for every L-formula ϕ, $\phi \in$ SAT($\mathcal{L}_1$) [resp. $\phi \in$ SAT($\mathcal{L}_2$)] iff $f_{dual}(\phi) \in$ SAT($\mathcal{L}_2$) [resp. $f_{dual}(\phi) \in$ SAT($\mathcal{L}_1$)];

(II) $\mathcal{L}_1$ has the finite model property [resp. finite parameter sets property] iff $\mathcal{L}_2$ has the finite model property [resp. finite parameter sets property] .

Proof. The map f_{dual} is defined as follows. The formula $f_{dual}(\phi)$ is obtained from ϕ by substituting every occurrence of r(A) by r(−A). By way of example we show that if ϕ is $\mathcal{L}_1$-satisfiable, where $\mathcal{L}_1$ is in class($\{C_1, C_1'\}$), then $f_{dual}(\phi)$ is $\mathcal{L}_2$-satisfiable, where $\mathcal{L}_2$ is in class($\{C_6, C_3'\}$). Let $\mathcal{M}_1 = \langle W, (\mathcal{R}_P)_{P \subseteq PAR}, m \rangle$ be an $\mathcal{L}_1$-model and let $w \in W$ be such that $\mathcal{M}_1, w \models \phi$. Let

$$\mathcal{M}_2 = \langle W, (\mathcal{R}_P')_{P \subseteq PAR}, m' \rangle$$

be the structure such that for every $P \subseteq PAR$, $\mathcal{R}_P' \stackrel{\text{def}}{=} \mathcal{R}_{PAR \setminus P}$ and m' coincides with m on $\mathrm{FOR}_0 \cup P_0$. For all $P, P' \subseteq PAR$, we have

$$
\begin{aligned}
\mathcal{R}_{P \cap P'}' &= \mathcal{R}_{PAR \setminus (P \cap P')} \text{ (by definition of } \mathcal{M}_2)\\
&= \mathcal{R}_{(PAR \setminus P) \cup (PAR \setminus P')}\\
&= \mathcal{R}_{PAR \setminus P} \cap \mathcal{R}_{PAR \setminus P'} \text{ ($\mathcal{L}_1$ in class($\{C_1, C_1'\}$))}\\
&= \mathcal{R}_P' \cap \mathcal{R}_{P'}' \text{ (by definition of } \mathcal{M}_2).
\end{aligned}
$$

Moreover, $\mathcal{R}_{PAR}' = \mathcal{R}_\emptyset = W^2$. Hence, $\mathcal{M}_2$ is an $\mathcal{L}_2$-model and for every parameter expression A $\in P(\phi)$, $\mathcal{R}_{m'(-A)}' = \mathcal{R}_{m(A)}$, which entails $\mathcal{M}_2, w \models f_{dual}(\phi)$.   *Q.E.D.*

Clearly, since Lemma 10.2.1 involves only transformation of families of binary relations, it can be easily adapted to the case that object nominals are a part of the modal languages of the logics in question (see Sect. 10.6).

Sometimes a standard modal logic can be associated with a Rare-logic in such a way that the logics share several properties, e.g. decidability, finite model property, etc.

Definition 10.2.2. *Let Γ consist of $(C_1), \ldots, (C_9), (C_1'), \ldots, (C_4')$, and the conditions $(C_{[f_1, f_2]})$, where f_1 is a set operation of arity n and f_2 is a relation operation of profile $\langle 2, \ldots, 2 \rangle$ and of arity n for some $n \geq 1$. Let $\mathcal{L} = \langle L, \mathcal{I}, \mathcal{S} \rangle$ be a Rare-logic in class(Y) for some finite subset $Y \subseteq \Gamma$. The standard modal logic SM($\mathcal{L}$) associated to $\mathcal{L}$ is the structure $\langle L', \mathcal{I}', \mathcal{S}' \rangle$ defined as follows:*

⋆ *L' is obtained from L by replacing the set $\{r(A) : A \in P\}$ of basic modal expressions from L by a countably infinite set of modal constants;*
⋆ *$\mathcal{I}'$ equals $\mathcal{I}$ restricted to the set of modal operators;*
⋆ *for every L'-model $\mathcal{M} = \langle W, (R_a)_{a \in M_d}, m \rangle$, $\mathcal{M} \in \mathcal{S}' \stackrel{\text{def}}{\Leftrightarrow}$*
  ∗ *$\mathcal{M}$ respects $\mathcal{I}'$;*
  ∗ *for every $c \in M_0$, R_c satisfies the local conditions of $\mathcal{L}$;*
  ∗ *if the global conditions $C_{[f_1^1, f_2^1]}, \ldots, C_{[f_1^s, f_2^s]}$ are in Y, $s \geq 1$, then the relations generated from $\{R_c : c \in M_0\}$ with $f_2^1, \ldots, f_2^s$ satisfy the local conditions of $\mathcal{L}$.*

The above definition applies also to the case that object nominals are a part of the languages (see Sect. 10.6). The standard modal logic associated to the Rare-logic defined in Example 10.2.1 is a fragment of the logic PDL.

Two standard modal logics are said to be *similar* $\overset{\text{def}}{\Leftrightarrow}$ there exist two similar Rare-logics for which they are the respective associated standard modal logics. They share the language and the operator interpretation.

Example 10.2.2. Let $\mathcal{L}_1$ be the Rare-logic $\langle L, \mathcal{I}, \mathcal{S}_1 \rangle$ in class($\{C_1, C_1'\}$) and $\mathcal{L}_2$ be the Rare-logic $\langle L, \mathcal{I}, \mathcal{S}_2 \rangle$ in class($\{C_3, C_2'\}$) with $O_M = \{\cap, \cup^*\}$. The local condition of both $\mathcal{L}_1$ and $\mathcal{L}_2$ is that the relations in the models are equivalence relations. M is the set of modal expressions built from M_0 with $\{\cap, \cup^*\}$ and $O_{FOR} \overset{\text{def}}{=} \{\wedge, \neg\} \cup \{[a] : a \in M\}$. The standard modal logic SM($\mathcal{L}_1$) is the logic DAL (see Example 5.3.4) whereas the standard modal logic SM($\mathcal{L}_2$) is the logic DALLA (see Sect. 8.2). Hence DAL and DALLA are similar standard modal logics.

10.3 Normal Forms of Formulae of Rare-languages

In this section and in Sect. 10.4, unless stated otherwise, $\mathcal{L}$ is a Rare-logic in class($\{C_{[\cup, f_2]}, C_{i_{\mathcal{L}}}'\}$) such that

(H1) $i_{\mathcal{L}} \in \{1, 2\}$ and $\cup$ is the set union;
(H2) f_2 is a binary relation operation of profile $\langle 2, 2, 2 \rangle$ such that for every set W, $\langle \mathcal{P}(W^2), f_2, e_{\mathcal{L}} \rangle$ is a semilattice with zero element and $e_{\mathcal{L}} = \emptyset$ if $i_{\mathcal{L}} = 2$, otherwise $e_{\mathcal{L}} = W \times W$;
(H3) there is a modal operator $\oplus_{\mathcal{L}} \in O_M$ of arity 2 such that $\mathcal{I}(\oplus_{\mathcal{L}}) = f_2$.

Condition $(C_{[\cup, f_2]})$ captures conditions (C_1), (C_3), and (C_5). For instance, we get condition (C_1) taking for f_2 set intersection, $e_{\mathcal{L}} = W \times W$ and $i_{\mathcal{L}} = 1$. Condition (H3) roughly states that a modal operator of the language of $\mathcal{L}$ is interpreted by f_2.

Let $N_1 : FOR(\mathcal{L}) \to FOR(\mathcal{L})$ be the map such that for every $\mathcal{L}$-formula ϕ, the formula $N_1(\phi)$ is obtained from ϕ by replacing every occurrence of any parameter expression A by $N_{P_0(\phi)}(A)$ (see Sect. 5.4). If $P_0(\phi) = \emptyset$, then $N_1(\phi) \overset{\text{def}}{=} \phi$. $N_1(\phi)$ is called the *first normal form* of ϕ.

Lemma 10.3.1. *For every $\mathcal{L}$-formula ϕ, $\phi \Leftrightarrow N_1(\phi) \in VAL(\mathcal{L})$.*

The proof follows easily from the fact that the P-meaning functions of the $\mathcal{L}$-models are standard. The second normal form of an $\mathcal{L}$-formula is obtained by using the global condition $(C_{[\cup, f_2]})$. Let $N_2 : FOR(\mathcal{L}) \to FOR(\mathcal{L})$ be the map such that for every $\mathcal{L}$-formula ϕ, $N_2(\phi)$ is obtained from $N_1(\phi)$ by replacing each occurrence of any basic modal expression $r(N_{P_0(\phi)}(A)) = r(B_{i_1} \cup \ldots \cup B_{i_l})$ by $r(B_{i_1}) \oplus_{\mathcal{L}} \ldots \oplus_{\mathcal{L}} r(B_{i_l})$, where $B_{i_1}, \ldots, B_{i_l}$, $l \geq 1$, are components from Comp($P_0(\phi)$) and the operator $\oplus_{\mathcal{L}}$ satisfies the hypothesis (H3).

Lemma 10.3.2. *For every $\mathcal{L}$-formula ϕ, $\phi \Leftrightarrow N_2(\phi) \in VAL(\mathcal{L})$.*

The proof is immediate because

$$r(B_{i_1} \cup \ldots \cup B_{i_l}) \sim_{\mathcal{L}} r(B_{i_1}) \oplus_{\mathcal{L}} \ldots \oplus_{\mathcal{L}} r(B_{i_l}).$$

The second normal form N_2 depends on condition $(C_{[\cup, f_2]})$, which provides an interpretation of the operator $\oplus_{\mathcal{L}}$.

Definition 10.3.1. *Let* $SM^*(\mathcal{L})$ *be the standard modal logic associated to* $\mathcal{L}$ *and augmented with either the universal modal connective* $[U]$ *if* $i_{\mathcal{L}} = 1$, *or with* $[0]$ *if* $i_{\mathcal{L}} = 2$. *Let* M_0 *be the set of basic modal expressions of* $SM^*(\mathcal{L})$. *We define* $M_0^\star \stackrel{\text{def}}{=} M_0 \setminus \{U\}$ *if* $i_{\mathcal{L}} = 1$ *and* $M_0^\star \stackrel{\text{def}}{=} M_0 \setminus \{0\}$ *if* $i_{\mathcal{L}} = 2$.

10.4 Translation of Rare-logics into Standard Modal Logics

In this section we present a translation from $\mathcal{L}$ into $SM^*(\mathcal{L})$. Let $t :$ $FOR(\mathcal{L}) \to FOR(SM^*(\mathcal{L}))$ be the map defined as follows. For every $\mathcal{L}$-formula ϕ, $t(\phi)$ is obtained from $N_2(\phi)$ by the following replacements of basic modal expressions:

* $r(C_1 \cap -C_1)$ is replaced by U if $i_{\mathcal{L}} = 1$ and by 0 if $i_{\mathcal{L}} = 2$;
* $r(B_k)$ is replaced by the modal constant c_k
  for every $k \in \{0, \ldots, 2^{\text{card}(P_0(\phi))} - 1\}$.

$t(\phi)$ can be computed by an effective procedure in exponential-time in the size of ϕ, because the map N_1 requires exponential-time.

Example 10.4.1. Let $\mathcal{L}$ be a Rare-logic in class$(\{C_1, C_1'\})$ such that $O_M = \{\cap, \cup\}$. Let ϕ be the following $\mathcal{L}$-formula:

$$\phi = [r(C_0)]p \wedge [r(C_0 \cap C_1)]q \wedge [r(C_0 \cap C_1 \cap -C_0) \cup r(C_1)]p.$$

The normal forms of ϕ are as follows:

* $N_1(\phi) = [r((C_0 \cap C_1) \cup (C_0 \cap -C_1))]p \wedge [r(C_0 \cap C_1)]q \wedge [r(C_0 \cap -C_0) \cup r((C_0 \cap C_1) \cup (-C_0 \cap C_1))]p$;
* $N_2(\phi) = [r(C_0 \cap C_1) \cap r(C_0 \cap -C_1)]p \wedge [r(C_0 \cap C_1)]q \wedge [r(C_0 \cap -C_0) \cup (r(C_0 \cap C_1) \cap r(-C_0 \cap C_1))]p$;
* $t(\phi) = [c_0 \cap c_1]p \wedge [c_0]q \wedge [U \cup (c_0 \cap c_2)]p$.

Example 10.4.1 should not mislead the reader about the complexity of the normalisation process. The normal form mapping may increase exponentially the size of the formulae although the number of subformulae does not change.

The following Theorem 10.4.1 is one of the main results of the chapter. It states that t is a satisfiability-preserving transformation from $\mathcal{L}$-satisfiability into $SM^*(\mathcal{L})$-satisfiability. It will be extended to a larger language (see Sect. 10.6) and it has various consequences related to finite model property, complexity upper bounds, and the design of proof systems.

Theorem 10.4.1. *For every $\mathcal{L}$-formula ϕ, the following statements are equivalent:*

(I) $\phi \in \mathrm{SAT}(\mathcal{L})$;
(II) $t(\phi) \in \mathrm{SAT}(\mathrm{SM}^*(\mathcal{L}))$.

Proof. If no parameter expression occurs in ϕ, the proof is by an easy verification. In the sequel, let us assume that $\mathrm{P}(\phi)$ is non-empty.
(I) $\rightarrow$ (II) Assume that ϕ is $\mathcal{L}$-satisfiable.
There exist an $\mathcal{L}$-model $\langle W, (\mathcal{R}_P)_{P \subseteq PAR}, m \rangle$ and a $w \in W$ such that $\mathcal{M}, w \models \phi$. Let $C_1, \ldots, C_n$, $n \geq 1$, be the parameter constants occurring in ϕ. Let $\mathcal{M}'$ be the $\mathrm{SAT}(\mathrm{SM}^*(\mathcal{L}))$-model $\langle W, (R_a)_{a \in \mathrm{M}}, m' \rangle$ such that

★ for every $\mathrm{p} \in \mathrm{FOR}_0$, $m'(\mathrm{p}) \overset{\mathrm{def}}{=} m(\mathrm{p})$;
★ for every $k \in \{0, \ldots, 2^n - 1\}$, $R_{\mathrm{c}_k} \overset{\mathrm{def}}{=} \mathcal{R}_{m(\mathrm{B}_k)}$;
★ for every $\mathrm{c} \in \mathrm{M}_0^* \setminus \{\mathrm{c}_0, \ldots, \mathrm{c}_{2^n - 1}\}$, $R_{\mathrm{c}} \overset{\mathrm{def}}{=} R_{\mathrm{c}_0}$.
★ for every $\oplus(\mathrm{a}_1, \ldots, \mathrm{a}_{\mathrm{ar}(\oplus)}) \in \mathrm{M}$ (of $\mathrm{SM}^*(\mathcal{L})$),

$$R_{\oplus(\mathrm{a}_1, \ldots, \mathrm{a}_{\mathrm{ar}(\oplus)})} \overset{\mathrm{def}}{=} \mathcal{I}(\oplus)(R_{\mathrm{a}_1}, \ldots, R_{\mathrm{a}_{\mathrm{ar}(\oplus)}}).$$

Observe that every relation R generated from $\{R_{\mathrm{c}} : \mathrm{c} \in \mathrm{M}_0\}$ with f_2 is equal to some $\mathcal{R}_P$ for a subset $P \subseteq PAR$. Hence, R satisfies the local conditions of $\mathcal{L}$ and therefore $\mathcal{M}'$ is an $\mathrm{SM}^*(\mathcal{L})$-model. Furthermore, for every $A \in P$ occurring in ϕ such that $\mathrm{N}_{\mathrm{P}_0(\phi)}(A) = \mathrm{B}_{i_1} \cup \ldots \cup \mathrm{B}_{i_l}$, we have $\mathcal{R}_{m(A)} = R_{\mathrm{c}_{i_1} \oplus_{\mathcal{L}} \ldots \oplus_{\mathcal{L}} \mathrm{c}_{i_l}}$ where $\oplus_{\mathcal{L}}$ is as in the hypothesis (H3). Similary, for every $A \in P$ such that $A \sim \perp$, we have $\mathcal{R}_{m(A)} = R_{\mathrm{U}} = W \times W$ if $i_{\mathcal{L}} = 1$ and $\mathcal{R}_{m(A)} = R_0 = \emptyset$ if $i_{\mathcal{L}} = 0$. So $\mathcal{M}', w \models t(\phi)$.
(II) $\rightarrow$ (I) Now assume that $t(\phi)$ is $\mathrm{SM}^*(\mathcal{L})$-satisfiable. So there exist an $\mathrm{SM}^*(\mathcal{L})$-model $\mathcal{M} = \langle W, (R_a)_{a \in \mathrm{M}}, m \rangle$ and a $w \in W$ such that $\mathcal{M}, w \models t(\phi)$. Let $\mathcal{M}' \overset{\mathrm{def}}{=} \langle W, (\mathcal{R}_P)_{P \subseteq PAR}, m' \rangle$ be the $\mathcal{L}$-model such that

★ $PAR \overset{\mathrm{def}}{=} \{0, \ldots, 2^n - 1\}$;
★ $\mathcal{R}_{\emptyset} \overset{\mathrm{def}}{=} W \times W$ and for every $\emptyset \neq P \subseteq PAR$, $\mathcal{R}_P \overset{\mathrm{def}}{=} f_2\{\mathcal{R}_{\{p\}} : p \in P\}$;
★ for every $s \in \{1, \ldots, n\}$, $m(\mathrm{C}_s) \overset{\mathrm{def}}{=} \{k \in PAR : bit_s(k) = 0\}$;
★ for the remaining parameter constants, the restriction of m' to P is not constrained, the only requirement is that it is a standard P-meaning function (such an interpretation always exists);
★ for every $\mathrm{p} \in \mathrm{FOR}_0$, $m'(\mathrm{p}) \overset{\mathrm{def}}{=} m(\mathrm{p})$;
★ for every $\oplus(\mathrm{a}_1, \ldots, \mathrm{a}_{\mathrm{ar}(\oplus)}) \in \mathrm{M}$ (of $\mathcal{L}$),

$$m'(\oplus(\mathrm{a}_1, \ldots, \mathrm{a}_{\mathrm{ar}(\oplus)})) \overset{\mathrm{def}}{=} \mathcal{I}(\oplus)(m'(\mathrm{a}_1), \ldots, m'(\mathrm{a}_{\mathrm{ar}(\oplus)})).$$

It is easy to check that $\mathcal{M}'$ is an $\mathcal{L}$-model. Moreover, for every $A \in P$ occurring in ϕ such that $\mathrm{N}_{\mathrm{P}_0(\phi)}(A) = \mathrm{B}_{i_1} \cup \ldots \cup \mathrm{B}_{i_l}$, we have $\mathcal{R}_{m(A)} = R_{\mathrm{c}_{i_1} \oplus_{\mathcal{L}} \ldots \oplus_{\mathcal{L}} \mathrm{c}_{i_l}}$. Similarly, for every $A \in P$ such that $A \sim \perp$, we have $\mathcal{R}_{m(A)} = R_{\mathrm{U}}$ if $i_{\mathcal{L}} = 1$ and $\mathcal{R}_{m(A)} = R_0$ if $i_{\mathcal{L}} = 2$. So $\mathcal{M}', w \models \phi$.   *Q.E.D.*

Theorem 10.4.1 entails that $SM^*(\mathcal{L})$ is decidable only if $\mathcal{L}$ is decidable. Lemma 10.4.1 will enable us to state the converse.

Lemma 10.4.1. *There is a polynomial-time transformation from the problem* $SAT(SM^*(\mathcal{L}))$ *into the problem* $SAT(\mathcal{L})$.

Proof. We define a map $t^{\leftarrow}$ from the set of $SM^*(\mathcal{L})$-formulae into the set of $\mathcal{L}$-formulae such that ϕ is $SM^*(\mathcal{L})$-satisfiable iff $t^{\leftarrow}(\phi)$ is $\mathcal{L}$-satisfiable. Let ϕ be an $SM^*(\mathcal{L})$-formula such that $M_0(\phi) = \{c_0, \ldots, c_N\}$, $N \geq 1$. Let n be the smallest natural number such that $2^n - 1 \geq N$. Take n parameter constants from the language of $\mathcal{L}$, say $C_1, \ldots, C_n$. If $M_0(\phi) = \emptyset$ we just consider C_1. $t'(\phi)$ is obtained from ϕ by substituting each occurrence of c_k by $r(B_k)$ and each occurrence of 0 [resp. U] by $\{C_1 \cap -C_1\}$ if $i_{\mathcal{L}} = 0$ [resp. $i_{\mathcal{L}} = 1$]. It is easy to see that $N_2(t^{\leftarrow}(\phi)) = t^{\leftarrow}(\phi)$ and $t(t^{\leftarrow}(\phi))$ is $SM^*(\mathcal{L})$-satisfiable iff ϕ is $SM^*(\mathcal{L})$-satisfiable, since ϕ and $t(t^{\leftarrow}(\phi))$ are equal modulo the renaming of modal constants. Hence $t(t^{\leftarrow}(\phi))$ is $SM^*(\mathcal{L})$-satisfiable iff $t^{\leftarrow}(\phi)$ is $\mathcal{L}$-satisfiable (by Theorem 10.4.1) iff ϕ is $SM^*(\mathcal{L})$-satisfiable. *Q.E.D.*

Using the construction from the proof of Theorem 10.4.1, one can establish the following theorem.

Theorem 10.4.2. *Let* $\mathcal{L}$ *be a Rare-logic in* $\text{class}(\{C_{[\cup, f_2]}, C'_{i_{\mathcal{L}}}\})$ *such that*

⋆ $i_{\mathcal{L}} \in \{1, 2\}$ *and* $\cup$ *is the set union;*
⋆ f_2 *is a binary relation operation of profile* $\langle 2, 2, 2 \rangle$ *such that for every set* W, $\langle \mathcal{P}(W^2), f_2, e_{\mathcal{L}} \rangle$ *is a semilattice with zero element* $e_{\mathcal{L}} \overset{\text{def}}{=} \emptyset$ *if* $i_{\mathcal{L}} = 2$, *otherwise* $e_{\mathcal{L}} \overset{\text{def}}{=} W \times W$;
⋆ *there is a modal operator* $\oplus_{\mathcal{L}} \in O_M$ *such that* $\mathcal{I}(\oplus_{\mathcal{L}}) = f_2$.

Then:

(I) $SAT(\mathcal{L})$ *is decidable iff* $SAT(SM^*(\mathcal{L}))$ *is decidable;*
(II) $\mathcal{L}$ *has the finite model property iff* $SM^*(\mathcal{L})$ *has the finite model property;*
(III) *every* $\mathcal{L}$-*satisfiable formula* ϕ *has an* $\mathcal{L}$-*model such that* PAR *is finite and* $\text{card}(PAR) \leq 2^{|\phi|}$;
(IV) *if* $i_{\mathcal{L}} = 1$ *[resp.* $i_{\mathcal{L}} = 0$] *and* $SM^*(\mathcal{L})$ *is* U-*simplifiable [resp.* 0-*simplifiable], then* $SAT(\mathcal{L})$ *is decidable iff* $SAT(\mathcal{L}_d^{\cup -})$ *[resp.* $SAT(\mathcal{L}_d^{0 -})$] *is decidable and* $\mathcal{L}$ *has the finite model property iff* $\mathcal{L}_d^{\cup -}$ *[resp.* $\mathcal{L}_d^{0 -}$] *has the finite model property.*

Generalising the condition $\mathcal{R}_{P \cup Q} = f_2(\mathcal{R}_P, \mathcal{R}_Q)$, where f_2 is either set union or set intersection, to $\mathcal{R}_{\cup\{P : P \in \mathcal{X}\}} = f_2\{\mathcal{R}_P : P \in \mathcal{X}\}$, where $\mathcal{X} \subseteq \mathcal{P}(PAR)$, does not change the set of satisfiable [resp. valid] formulae, since PAR can be assumed to be finite without any loss of generality.

Corollary 10.4.1. *Let* $\mathcal{L} \in \text{class}(\{C_1, C'_1\})$ *[resp.* $\text{class}(\{C_3, C'_2\})$] *be a logic satisfying the assumption of Theorem 10.4.2 and let* $\mathcal{L}' \in \text{class}(\{C_2, C'_1\})$ *[resp.* $\text{class}(\{C_4, C'_2\})$] *be similar to* $\mathcal{L}$. *Then* $SAT(\mathcal{L}) = SAT(\mathcal{L}')$.

By Lemma 10.2.1, the following results for Rare-logics in class($\{C_6, C_3'\}$) $\cup$ class($\{C_7, C_4'\}$) can be easily derived.

Corollary 10.4.2. *Let $\mathcal{L} \in$ class($\{C_6, C_3'\}$) $\cup$ class($\{C_7, C_4'\}$) be a logic having a modal operator $\oplus_{\mathcal{L}} \in O_M$ in its language such that if $\mathcal{L} \in$ class($\{C_6, C_3'\}$), then $\mathcal{I}(\oplus_{\mathcal{L}})$ is the intersection and if $\mathcal{L} \in$ class($\{C_7, C_4'\}$), then $\mathcal{I}(\oplus_{\mathcal{L}})$ is the union. Then the statements (I)–(IV) from Theorem 10.4.2 are satisfied.*

Example 10.4.2. Let $\mathcal{L}$ be the Rare-logic $\langle L, \mathcal{I}, \mathcal{S} \rangle$ in class($\{C_1, C_1'\}$) such that $O_M = \{\cap, ; , ^*, \cup, ^{-1}\}$. The local condition of $\mathcal{L}$ is "true". PDL with converse and intersection (see Example 5.3.5) is a fragment of $SM^*(\mathcal{L})$. Since such an extension of PDL does not have the finite model property, by Theorem 10.4.2(II) $\mathcal{L}$ does not have the finite model property. Indeed, the following formula is satisfiable only in infinite models: $[c^*](\langle c \rangle \top \wedge \neg \langle (c; c^*) \cap (c^{-1}; (c^{-1})^*) \rangle \top)$.

By way of example, we present some logics $\mathcal{L}$ such that $SM^*(\mathcal{L})$ is U-simplifiable.

Lemma 10.4.2. *Let $\mathcal{L} = \langle L, \mathcal{I}, \mathcal{S} \rangle$ be a standard modal logic such that $O_M \subseteq \{\cap, \cup, \cup^*, ; , -, ^{-1}\}$. Then:*

(I) if $; \notin O_M$, then $\mathcal{L}^U$ is U-simplifiable;
(II) if for every $\mathcal{L}$-model $\langle W, (R_a)_{a \in M}, m \rangle$ and for every $a \in M$, R_a and R_a^{-1} are serial, then $\mathcal{L}^U$ is U-simplifiable;
(III) if $- \notin O_M$, then $\mathcal{L}^0$ is 0-simplifiable.

Proof. If a logic $\mathcal{L}$ is U-simplifiable [resp. 0-simplifiable], then for every formula ϕ there is a formula ϕ' (that can be effectively computed) such that the only occurrences of U [resp. of 0] in ϕ' are of the form [U] [resp. [0]]. However, this does not exclude the possibility of having in ϕ' the occurrences of some modal expression $a \neq U$ [resp. $a \neq 0$] such that $a \sim_{\mathcal{L}} U$ [resp. $a \sim_{\mathcal{L}} 0$]. If this happens then, roughly speaking, the addition of U [resp. of 0] to the language of the initial logic does not increase its expressive power.
(I) The fact that $\mathcal{L}^U$ is U-simplifiable is a consequence of the following equivalences:

(i) for every $a \in M \cup \{U\}$, $U \cap b \sim_{\mathcal{L}^U} b$, $U \cup b \sim_{\mathcal{L}^U} U$, $U \cup^* b \sim_{\mathcal{L}^U} U$, $(U)^{-1} \sim_{\mathcal{L}^U} U$;
(ii) for every $a \in M \cup \{U\}$, $-U \cap b \sim_{\mathcal{L}^U} -U$, $-U \cup b \sim_{\mathcal{L}^U} b$, $-U \cup^* b \sim_{\mathcal{L}^U} b \cup^* b$, $(-U)^{-1} \sim_{\mathcal{L}^U} -U$, $-(-U) \sim_{\mathcal{L}^U} U$.

We do not write explicitly the symmetric replacements for $\cup$, $\cap$, and $\cup^*$, since $\mathcal{I}(\cup)$, $\mathcal{I}(\cap)$, and $\mathcal{I}(\cup^*)$ are commutative. Using (i) and (ii), one can show that for every modal expression a, $[a]\phi$ is equivalent to a formula $[a']\phi$ such that either $a' = U$, or $a' = -U$, or a' does not contain any occurrence of U. Now, since $[-U]\varphi \Leftrightarrow \top$ is $\mathcal{L}$-valid, we can easily prove that $\mathcal{L}^U$ is U-simplifiable. The proofs of (II) and (III) are similar.   *Q.E.D.*

Observe that if $- \in O_M$, then one can effectively get rid of every occurrence of 0. Indeed, $[0]\phi \Leftrightarrow \top$ is $\mathcal{L}^0$-valid.

Example 10.4.3. Let $\mathcal{L} = \langle L, \mathcal{I}, \mathcal{S} \rangle$ be the Rare-logic in $\mathrm{class}(\{C_3, C_2'\})$ with $O_M = \{\cup, ;, ^*, -\}$ and with the local condition "true". By application of Theorem 10.4.2(I) and as a consequence of the undecidability of PDL with complement (see Sect. 6.5), we conclude that this logic is undecidable.

In the next theorem, we state that the logics in $\mathrm{class}(\{C_0\})$ can be translated into standard modal logics.

Theorem 10.4.3. *Let $\mathcal{L}$ be a Rare-logic in* $\mathrm{class}(\{C_0\})$. *Then:*

(I) $\mathrm{SAT}(\mathcal{L})$ is decidable iff $\mathrm{SAT}(\mathrm{SM}(\mathcal{L}))$ is decidable;
(II) $\mathcal{L}$ has the finite model property iff $\mathrm{SM}(\mathcal{L})$ has the finite model property;
(III) every $\mathcal{L}$-satisfiable formula ϕ has an $\mathcal{L}$-model such that PAR is finite and $\mathrm{card}(PAR) \leq 2^{|\phi|}$.

The proof rests on the translation from $\mathcal{L}$ into $\mathrm{SM}(\mathcal{L})$ that consists in applying N_1 and then associating a modal constant to every parameter expression in the normal form in such a way that different parameter expressions have associated distinct constants.

10.5 Standard Modal Logics and the Universal Modal Connective

In this section we focus on the elimination of the universal modal connective [U] from formulae of modal logics. We show that such an elimination is harmless as far as decidability of satisfiability in standard modal logics is concerned. Instead of proving $\mathrm{SAT}(\mathrm{SM}(\mathcal{L}))$ is decidable iff $\mathrm{SAT}(\mathrm{SM}^*(\mathcal{L}))$ is decidable, we identify cases when we can prove that $\mathrm{SAT}(\mathcal{L})$ is decidable iff $\mathrm{SAT}(\mathrm{SM}(\mathcal{L}))$ is decidable. In that way, we can take advantage of the decidability of standard modal logics (without the universal modal connective) to deduce decidability of Rare-logics.

Let $\mathcal{L}$ be a standard modal logic. An *elementary disjunction* is an $\mathcal{L}^{U-}$-formula of the form

$$\kappa = \phi_{-1} \vee \langle U \rangle \phi_0 \vee [U]\phi_1 \vee \ldots \vee [U]\phi_n,$$

where $n \geq 1$, $\phi_{-1}, \phi_0, \phi_1, \ldots, \phi_n$ are U-free formulae.

Let $\psi = \kappa_1 \wedge \ldots \wedge \kappa_N$, $N \geq 1$, be a conjunction of elementary disjunctions. For every $\mathcal{L}^{U-}$-formula ϕ, if $\phi \Leftrightarrow \psi$ is $\mathcal{L}^{U-}$-valid, then we say that ψ is a *conjunctive form* of ϕ.

Lemma 10.5.1. *Let $\mathcal{L}$ be a standard modal logic. For every $\mathcal{L}^{U-}$-formula ϕ there exists a conjunctive form.*

Proof. We show that there exists an effective procedure to compute a conjunctive form. Let $a \in M$ and φ, φ' be $\mathcal{L}^{U^-}$-formulae such that φ' is a Boolean combination of formulae prefixed by $[U]$ or $\langle U \rangle$. The following $\mathcal{L}^{U^-}$-formulae are $\mathcal{L}^{U^-}$-valid:

(i) $[a](\varphi \vee \varphi') \Leftrightarrow [a]\varphi \vee \varphi'$;
(ii) $[U](\varphi \vee \varphi') \Leftrightarrow [U]\varphi \vee \varphi'$.

By induction on the structure of ϕ one can show that ϕ is equivalent to a conjunction of elementary disjunctions.

The base case when ϕ is a propositional variable and the cases in the induction step when the outermost connective of ϕ is Boolean are standard and they are omitted here.

Let $\phi = [a]\phi_1$. By the induction hypothesis, there is a finite set $\{\kappa_1, \ldots, \kappa_m\}$, $m \geq 1$, of elementary disjunctions such that $\kappa_1 \wedge \ldots \wedge \kappa_m$ is a conjunctive form of ϕ_1. Hence $[a]\phi_1 \Leftrightarrow [a]\kappa_1 \wedge \ldots \wedge [a]\kappa_m$ is $\mathcal{L}^{U^-}$-valid. (i) guarantees that each $[a]\kappa_j$, $1 \leq j \leq m$, has a conjunctive form. So ϕ has an equivalent conjunctive form. For $\phi = [U]\phi_1$ the proof is similar except that (ii) is used instead of (i).   *Q.E.D.*

Theorem 10.5.1. *Let $\mathcal{L}$ be a standard modal logic closed under disjoint unions and isomorphic copies. The following statements are equivalent:*

(I) the logical $\mathcal{L}$-consequence problem is decidable;
(II) VAL($\mathcal{L}^{U^-}$) is decidable (or equivalently SAT($\mathcal{L}^{U^-}$) is decidable).

Proof. (II) $\rightarrow$ (I) Let ϕ and ψ be $\mathcal{L}$-formulae. It is easy to see that $\phi \models_{\mathcal{L}} \psi$ iff $[U]\phi \Rightarrow [U]\psi$ is $\mathcal{L}^{U^-}$-valid. Hence, the $\mathcal{L}^{U^-}$-validity problem is decidable only if the logical $\mathcal{L}$-consequence problem is decidable.
(I) $\rightarrow$ (II) Let $\kappa = \phi_{-1} \vee \langle U \rangle \phi_0 \vee [U]\phi_1 \vee \ldots \vee [U]\phi_n$, $n \geq 1$, be an elementary disjunction. For every $\mathcal{L}^{U^-}$-model $\mathcal{M}$, $\mathcal{M} \models [U]\kappa$ iff $\mathcal{M} \models \kappa$. Using (ii) from the proof of Lemma 10.5.1, $\mathcal{M} \models [U]\kappa$ iff $\mathcal{M} \models [U]\phi_{-1} \vee \langle U \rangle \phi_0 \vee [U]\phi_1 \vee \ldots \vee [U]\phi_n$. By an easy propositional reasoning, $\mathcal{M} \models \kappa$ iff (iii) $\mathcal{M} \models [U]\neg\phi_0 \Rightarrow ([U]\phi_{-1} \vee [U]\phi_1 \vee \ldots \vee [U]\phi_n)$. Moreover, (iii) holds iff for some $i \in \{-1, 1, \ldots, n\}$, $\mathcal{M} \models [U]\neg\phi_0 \Rightarrow [U]\phi_i$. So, κ is $\mathcal{L}^{U^-}$-valid iff (iv) for every $\mathcal{L}^{U^-}$-model $\mathcal{M}$, there is an $i \in \{-1, 1, \ldots, n\}$ such that $\mathcal{M} \models [U]\neg\phi_0 \Rightarrow [U]\phi_i$. We show that (iv) holds iff (v) there is an $i \in \{-1, 1, \ldots, n\}$ such that for every $\mathcal{L}^{U^-}$-model $\mathcal{M}$, $\mathcal{M} \models [U]\neg\phi_0 \Rightarrow [U]\phi_i$ (or, equivalently, $\neg\phi_0 \models_{\mathcal{L}} \phi_i$). The equivalence between (iv) and (v) corresponds to the permutation of two quantifiers.
(v) implies (iv) is obvious. Now assume (iv) and suppose (v) does not hold. By the definition of $\mathcal{L}^{U^-}$, (v) holds iff there is an $i \in \{-1, 1, \ldots, n\}$ such that for every $\mathcal{L}$-model $\mathcal{M}$, $\mathcal{M} \models \neg\phi_0$ implies $\mathcal{M} \models \phi_i$. It is worth mentioning that $\mathcal{M}$ is an $\mathcal{L}$-model (not an $\mathcal{L}^{U^-}$-model), which is correct, since $\phi_{-1}, \phi_0, \phi_1, \ldots, \phi_n$ are $\mathcal{L}$-formulae. Since (v) is supposed not to hold, for every $i \in \{-1, 1, \ldots, n\}$, there exists an $\mathcal{L}$-model $\mathcal{M}^i = \langle W^i, (R_a^i)_{a \in M}, m^i \rangle$ such that $\mathcal{M}^i \models \phi_0$, and there is an $y_i \in W^i$ such that $\mathcal{M}^i, y_i \not\models \phi_i$. Let $\mathcal{M}'^{-1} = \langle W'^{-1}, (R_a'^{-1})_{a \in M}, m'^{-1} \rangle, \ldots, \mathcal{M}'^n = \langle W'^n, (R_a'^n)_{a \in M}, m'^n \rangle$ be isomorphic

copies of $\mathcal{M}^{-1}, \ldots, \mathcal{M}^n$, respectively, such that for all $i, i' \in \{-1, 1, \ldots, n\}$, $i \neq i'$ implies $W'^i \cap W'^{i'} = \emptyset$. By assumption, $\mathcal{L}$ is closed under isomorphic copies. So $\mathcal{M}'^{-1}, \ldots, \mathcal{M}'^n$ are $\mathcal{L}$-models. Let $\mathcal{M}' = \langle W', (R'_a)_{a \in M}, m' \rangle$ be the structure such that:

$\star$ $W' \stackrel{\text{def}}{=} W'^{-1} \cup W'^1 \cup \ldots \cup W^n$;

$\star$ for every $p \in FOR_0$, $m'(p) = m'^{-1}(p) \cup m'^1(p) \cup \ldots \cup m'^n(p)$;

$\star$ for every $a \in M$, $R'_a \stackrel{\text{def}}{=} R'^{-1}_a \cup R'^1_a \cup \ldots \cup R'^n_a$.

By assumption, $\mathcal{L}$ is closed under disjoint unions, so $\mathcal{M}'$ is an $\mathcal{L}$-model. By induction on the structure of the $\mathcal{L}$-formula ψ, one can show that for every $i \in \{-1, 1, \ldots, n\}$ and for every $x \in W'^i$, $\mathcal{M}'^i, x \models \psi$ iff $\mathcal{M}', x \models \psi$. Consequently, $\mathcal{M}' \models \neg \phi_0$ and for every $i \in \{-1, 1, \ldots, n\}$, $\mathcal{M}' \not\models \phi_i$. By the definition of $\mathcal{L}^{U-}$, (iv) holds iff for every $\mathcal{L}$-model $\mathcal{M}$, there is an $i \in \{-1, 1, \ldots, n\}$ such that $\mathcal{M} \models \neg \phi_0$ implies $\mathcal{M} \models \phi_i$, a contradiction.

We are now in position to conclude the proof. Let ϕ be an $\mathcal{L}^{U-}$-formula such that $\kappa_1 \wedge \ldots \wedge \kappa_N$ is a conjunctive form of ϕ (see Lemma 10.5.1). Let us assume that for every $i \in \{1, \ldots, N\}$, κ_i is of the form

$$\phi^i_{-1} \vee \langle U \rangle \phi^i_0 \vee [U] \phi^i_1 \vee \ldots \vee [U] \phi^i_{n_i}, \; n_i \geq 1.$$

It is easy to see that (vi) ϕ is $\mathcal{L}^{U-}$-valid iff for every $i \in \{1, \ldots, N\}$, κ_i is $\mathcal{L}^{U-}_d$-valid. That is, (vi) holds iff there is a $\langle j_1, \ldots, j_N \rangle \in \{-1, 1, \ldots, n_1\} \times \ldots \times \{-1, 1, \ldots, n_N\}$ such that for every $l \in \{1, \ldots, N\}, \neg \phi^l_0 \models_{\mathcal{L}} \phi^l_{j_l}$. By assumption, the $\mathcal{L}$-consequence problem is decidable and there is an effective procedure for constructing the conjunctive forms, so the $\mathcal{L}^{U-}$-validity problem is decidable. $Q.E.D.$

Although Theorem 10.5.1 is interesting for its own sake, it has also natural consequences for some classes of Rare-logics.

Corollary 10.5.1. *Let $\mathcal{L}$ be a Rare-logic satisfying the assumptions of Theorem 10.4.2. Moreover, assume that $i_\mathcal{L} = 1$, $SM(\mathcal{L})$ is closed under disjoint unions and isomorphic copies, and $SM^*(\mathcal{L})$ is U-simplifiable. Then the following statements are equivalent:*

(I) VAL($\mathcal{L}$) is decidable (or equivalently SAT($\mathcal{L}$) is decidable);
(II) the logical $SM(\mathcal{L})$-consequence problem is decidable.

The following lemma describes logics which satisfy condition (II) in Corollary 10.5.1.

Lemma 10.5.2. *Let $\mathcal{L} = \langle L, \mathcal{I}, \mathcal{S} \rangle$ be a standard modal logic closed under restrictions such that either $\cup^* \in O_M$ or $\{\cup, ^*\} \subseteq O_M$ with $O_M \subseteq \{\cap, \cup, \cup^*, ^*, ^{-1}, ; \}$. Then the following statements are equivalent:*

(I) the logical $\mathcal{L}$-consequence problem is decidable;
(II) VAL($\mathcal{L}$) is decidable.

Proof. (I) → (II) This part of the proof is immediate.

(II) → (I) We prove that (i) $\phi \models_{\mathcal{L}} \psi$ iff (ii) $[a]\phi \Rightarrow \psi$ is $\mathcal{L}$-valid. Let $c_1, \ldots, c_n$, $n \geq 1$, be the modal constants occurring in the formulae ϕ and ψ. Let a be the modal expression defined as follows:

$$a \stackrel{\text{def}}{=} \begin{cases} (c_1 \cup \ldots \cup c_n)^* & \text{if } ^{-1} \notin O_M \text{ and } \{\cup,^*\} \subseteq O_M; \\ c_1 \cup^* \ldots \cup^* c_n & \text{if } ^{-1} \notin O_M, \cup^* \in O_M, \text{ and } \{\cup,^*\} \not\subseteq O_M; \\ (c_1 \cup \ldots \cup c_n \cup c_1^{-1} \cup \ldots \cup c_n^{-1})^* & \text{if } ^{-1} \in O_M \text{ and } \{\cup,^*\} \subseteq O_M; \\ (c_1 \cup^* \ldots \cup^* c_n \cup^* c_1^{-1} \cup^* \ldots \cup^* c_n^{-1} & \text{if } ^{-1} \in O_M, \cup^* \in O_M, \text{ and } \\ \quad \{\cup,^*\} \not\subseteq O_M. \end{cases}$$

(ii) → (i) Assume $[a]\phi \Rightarrow \psi$ is $\mathcal{L}$-valid and $\mathcal{M} \models \phi$ for some $\mathcal{L}$-model $\mathcal{M}$. So $\mathcal{M} \models [a]\phi$ and $\mathcal{M} \models \psi$.

(i) → (ii) Assume $\phi \models_{\mathcal{L}} \psi$. Let $\mathcal{M} = \langle W, (R_a)_{a \in M}, m \rangle$ be an $\mathcal{L}$-model and let $x \in W$ be such that $\mathcal{M}, x \models [a]\phi$. We show that $\mathcal{M}, x \models \psi$. It is easy to see that

$$\bigcup_{b \in M([a]\phi \Rightarrow \psi)} R_b^*(x) \subseteq R_a(x)$$

and (iii) for every $y \in R_a(x)$ and for every $\phi' \in \text{sub}([a]\phi \Rightarrow \psi)$, the following statements are equivalent:

* $\mathcal{M}_{|R_a(x)}, y \models \phi'$;
* $\mathcal{M}, y \models \phi'$.

So $\mathcal{M}_{|R_a(x)} \models [a]\phi$ and $\mathcal{M}_{|R_a(x)} \models \phi$. Since $\mathcal{L}$ is closed under restrictions, $\mathcal{M}_{|R_a(x)}$ is an $\mathcal{L}$-model and therefore $\mathcal{M}_{|R_a(x)} \models \psi$. In particular, $\mathcal{M}_{|R_a(x)}, x \models \psi$ and by (iii) $\mathcal{M}, x \models \psi$ (note that $x \in R_a(x)$ since R_a is reflexive).   *Q.E.D.*

In the following example, we show how the above results enable us to establish decidability of standard modal logics by translation into PDL-like logics.

Example 10.5.1. Let $\mathcal{L} \in \text{class}(C_1, C_1')$ be such that $O_M = \{\cup^*, \cap\}$ and the local condition of $\mathcal{L}$ is "true". $\text{SAT}(\mathcal{L})$ is decidable iff $\text{SAT}(\text{SM}^*(\mathcal{L})^-)$ is decidable by Theorem 10.4.2(IV). Since $\text{SM}(\mathcal{L})$ is closed under isomorphic copies, disjoint unions, and restrictions, by Theorem 10.5.1 and Lemma 10.5.2, $\text{SAT}(\text{SM}(\mathcal{L}))$ is decidable iff $\text{SAT}(\text{SM}^*(\mathcal{L})^-)$ is decidable. Since $\text{SM}(\mathcal{L})$ is a fragment of PDL + intersection (see Example 5.3.5), which is decidable (see Sect. 6.5), $\text{SAT}(\mathcal{L})$ is decidable.

10.6 Normal Forms of Formulae of Rare-languages with Nominals

In this section we consider standard Rare-logics which include nominals in their languages. Let FOR_0^N be a countably infinite set of object nominals and P_0^N be a countably infinite set of parameter nominals. Let $\mathcal{L}$ be a standard Rare-logic such that the set FOR_0 of its basic formulae is disjoint with FOR_0^N and the set P_0 of its basic parameter expressions is disjoint with P_0^N. By $\mathcal{L}(FOR_0^N)$ we denote the logic obtained from $\mathcal{L}$ by including in its language the object nominals of FOR_0^N. Similarly, by $\mathcal{L}(P_0^N)$ we denote the logic obtained from $\mathcal{L}$ by including in its language the parameter nominals of P_0^N. By $\mathcal{L}(FOR_0^N, P_0^N)$ we mean the logic obtained from $\mathcal{L}$ by including both object nominals of FOR_0^N and parameter nominals of P_0^N in its language.

The results from Sect. 5.4.1 cannot be easily applied to the Rare-logics $\mathcal{L}(FOR_0^N, P_0^N)$. Indeed, the notion of normal form has to be revised. This section is devoted to defining satisfiability-preserving maps between Rare-logics $\mathcal{L}(FOR_0^N, P_0^N)$ and the corresponding standard modal logics $SM^*(\mathcal{L})(FOR_0^N)$. In $SM^*(\mathcal{L})(FOR_0^N)$, the only nominals are object nominals. In the rest of the section we assume that the Rare-logics satisfy the assumptions (H1)–(H3) from Sect. 10.3. A proposition similar to Lemma 10.2.1 holds true for the Rare-logics $\mathcal{L}(FOR_0^N, P_0^N)$.

Let L be a modal language of some Rare-logic $\mathcal{L}(FOR_0^N, P_0^N)$ and let $Z = \{c_{i,j} : i,j \in \mathbb{N}\}$ be a countable set of modal constants. Since the validity problem of the combinatory PDL is decidable, one can prove that the following problems are decidable:

(1) for every $A \in P$, does $A \sim A \cap -A$ hold?
(2) for every $A \in P$, does $A \sim A \cup -A$ hold?

Let $E_1, \ldots, E_l$, $l \geq 0$, be parameter nominals from P_0^N and $C_1, \ldots, C_n$, $n \geq 0$, be parameter constants from P_0. If $l = 0$, then the developments from Sect. 10.3 apply. Let X be a set of parameter expressions built from $X' = \{C_1, \ldots, C_n\}$ and $Y' = \{E_1, \ldots, E_l\}$ with the operations $\cup$, $\cap$, and $-$. For every $A \in X$, the *normal form* of A with respect to X' and Y', written $N_{X',Y'}(A)$, is defined as follows:

$$N_{X',Y'}(A) \stackrel{\text{def}}{=} \begin{cases} C_1 \cap -C_1 & \text{if } A \sim C_1 \cap -C_1; \\ A_{k_1,k_1'} \cup \ldots \cup A_{k_u,k_u'} & \text{if } A \sim A_{k_1,k_1'} \cup \ldots \cup A_{k_u,k_u'}, \end{cases}$$

where the $A_{k,k'}$ are $\langle X',Y'\rangle$-components from $Comp(X',Y')$ (defined in Sect. 5.4.1). For every $k' \in \{1, \ldots, l\}$, we define the sets:

$$occ_{k'}^X \stackrel{\text{def}}{=} \{k \in \{0, \ldots, 2^n - 1\} : A \in X, N_{X',Y'}(A) = \ldots \cup A_{k,k'} \cup \ldots\};$$

$$setocc_{k'}^X \stackrel{\text{def}}{=} \{Y \subseteq occ_{k'}^X : \text{card}(occ_{k'}^X) - 1 \leq \text{card}(Y) \leq 2^n - 1\}.$$

Informally, $occ_{k'}^X$ is the set of indices $k \in \{0, \ldots, 2^n - 1\}$ such that $A_{k,k'}$ occurs in the normal form of some element of X. The definition of $setocc_{k'}^X$ is motivated by the fact that for every standard P-meaning function m, there is a unique $k \in \{0, \ldots, 2^n - 1\}$ such that $m(A_{k,k'}) \neq \emptyset$ and $m(A_{k,k'}) = m(E_{k'})$. In the forthcoming constructions we shall enforce $m(A_{k,k'}) = \emptyset$, for every $Y \in setocc_{k'}^X$ and for every $k \in Y$.

Unless stated otherwise, $\mathcal{L}$ is a Rare-logic in class($\{C_{[\cup,f_2]}, C'_{i_\mathcal{L}}\}$) satisfying the hypotheses (H1)–(H3) from Sect. 10.3. We will study the logic $\mathcal{L}(\text{FOR}_0^N, \text{P}_0^N)$ with nominals. First, we present normal forms for formulae with nominals. Let $\text{N}_1 : \text{FOR}(\mathcal{L}(\text{FOR}_0^N, \text{P}_0^N)) \to \text{FOR}(\mathcal{L}(\text{FOR}_0^N, \text{P}_0^N))$ be the map such that for every $\mathcal{L}(\text{FOR}_0^N, \text{P}_0^N)$-formula ϕ, $\text{N}_1(\phi)$ is obtained from ϕ by replacing every occurrence of any parameter expression A by $\text{N}_{\text{P}_0(\phi), \text{P}_0^N(\phi)}(\text{A})$. If $\text{P}_0(\phi) = \text{P}_0^N(\phi) = \emptyset$, then we define $\text{N}_1(\phi) \overset{\text{def}}{=} \phi$, whereas if $\text{P}_0^N(\phi) = \emptyset$ and $\text{P}_0(\phi) \neq \emptyset$, $\text{N}_1(\phi)$ is obtained from ϕ by replacing every occurrence of any parameter expression A by $\text{N}_{\text{P}_0(\phi)}(\text{A})$. In the rest of this section and in Sect. 10.7 we assume that $\text{P}_0(\phi) \neq \emptyset$ and $\text{P}_0^N(\phi) \neq \emptyset$; the remaining cases can be obtained in a similar way. The following lemma can be easily shown.

Lemma 10.6.1. *For every $\mathcal{L}(\text{FOR}_0^N, \text{P}_0^N)$-formula ϕ,*
$\text{N}_1(\phi) \Leftrightarrow \phi \in \text{VAL}(\mathcal{L}(\text{FOR}_0^N, \text{P}_0^N))$.

The second normal form is obtained by using the global condition $(C_{[\cup,f_2]})$ as was done for a language without parameter nominals.
Let $\text{N}_2 : \text{FOR}(\mathcal{L}(\text{FOR}_0^N, \text{P}_0^N)) \to \text{FOR}(\mathcal{L}(\text{FOR}_0^N, \text{P}_0^N))$ be the map such that for every $\mathcal{L}(\text{FOR}_0^N, \text{P}_0^N)$-formula ϕ, $\text{N}_2(\phi)$ is obtained from $\text{N}_1(\phi)$ by replacing every occurrence of a basic modal expression $\text{r}(\text{A}_{k_1,k'_1} \cup \ldots \cup \text{A}_{k_u,k'_u})$ by $\text{r}(\text{A}_{k_1,k'_1}) \oplus_\mathcal{L} \ldots \oplus_\mathcal{L} \text{r}(\text{A}_{k_u,k'_u})$, $u \geq 1$, where for every $i \in \{1,\ldots,u\}$, $\text{A}_{k_i,k'_i} \in \langle \text{P}_0(\phi), \text{P}_0^N(\phi) \rangle$.

Lemma 10.6.2. *For every $\mathcal{L}(\text{FOR}_0^N, \text{P}_0^N)$-formula ϕ,*
$\text{N}_2(\phi) \Leftrightarrow \phi \in \text{VAL}(\mathcal{L}(\text{FOR}_0^N, \text{P}_0^N))$.

The proof is by an easy verification.

10.7 Translation of Rare-logics with Nominals

In this section we show how the results from Sect. 10.4 can be extended to the Rare-logics with nominals. Let

$$t : \text{FOR}(\mathcal{L}(\text{FOR}_0^N, \text{P}_0^N)) \to \text{FOR}(\text{SM}^*(\mathcal{L})(\text{FOR}_0^N))$$

be the map defined as follows. For every $\mathcal{L}(\text{FOR}_0^N, \text{P}_0^N)$-formula ϕ, $t(\phi)$ is obtained from $\text{N}_2(\phi)$ by replacing each occurrence of the basic modal expression

* $\text{r}(\text{C}_1 \cap -\text{C}_1)$ by U if $i_\mathcal{L} = 1$ and by 0 if $i_\mathcal{L} = 2$;
* $\text{r}(\text{A}_{k,k'})$ by the modal constant $c_{k,k'}$ for every $\text{A}_{k,k'} \in \text{Comp}(\phi)$.

$t(\phi)$ can be computed by an effective procedure in exponential-time in the size of ϕ. The translation process is not finished yet. At least one of the components $\text{E}_1 \cap \text{A}_1$ or $\text{E}_1 \cap -\text{A}_1$ (in the case $n = 1$) is interpreted as the empty set. However, this fact is not taken into account in the current definition of t. The following developments provide a solution to this problem.

Let ψ be an $SM^*(\mathcal{L})(FOR_0^N)$-formula with $n \geq 1$ parameter constants and $l \geq 1$ parameter nominals. For every $k' \in \{1, \ldots, l\}$ and for every $Y \in setocc_{k'}^{P(\phi)}$ let $\psi[k', Y]$ be the formula obtained from ψ by substituting U [resp. 0] for $c_{k,k'}$ with $k \in Y$, in the case when $i_\mathcal{L} = 1$ [resp. in the case when $i_\mathcal{L} = 2$].

Let $SETOCC = setocc_1^{P(\phi)} \times \cdots \times setocc_l^{P(\phi)}$. For every $\sigma = \langle O_1, \ldots, O_l \rangle \in SETOCC$, we define the formula $\psi[\sigma]$ as follows:

$$\psi[\sigma] \overset{\text{def}}{=} ((\psi[1, O_1]) \cdots [l, O_l]).$$

Theorem 10.7.1. *For every $\mathcal{L}(FOR_0^N, P_0^N)$-formula ϕ, the following statements are equivalent:*

(I) $\phi \in SAT(\mathcal{L}(FOR_0^N, P_0^N))$;
(II) $\bigvee \{t(\phi)[\sigma] : \sigma \in SETOCC\} \in SAT(SM^*(\mathcal{L})(FOR_0^N))$.

Proof. Let $C_1, \ldots, C_n$, $n \geq 1$, be the parameter constants occurring in ϕ and $E_1, \ldots, E_l$, $l \geq 1$, be the parameter nominals occurring in ϕ.

(II) $\to$ (I). Assume there exist a formula $\phi' = t(\phi)[\sigma]$ with $\sigma = \langle O_1, \ldots, O_l \rangle$, an $SM^*(\mathcal{L})(FOR_0^N)$-model $\mathcal{M} = \langle W, (R_a)_{a \in M}, m \rangle$, and a $w \in W$ such that $\mathcal{M}, w \models \phi'$. We define the auxiliary family $(R'_c)_{c \in M_0}$ as follows:

$$R'_c \overset{\text{def}}{=} \begin{cases} e_\mathcal{L} \text{ if } c = c_{k,k'} \text{ with } k' \in \{1, \ldots, l\} \text{ and } k \in (\sigma)_{k'}, \\ R_c \text{ otherwise.} \end{cases}$$

For every $k' \in \{1, \ldots, l\}$, we choose $u_{k'} \in \{0, \ldots, 2^n - 1\} \setminus O_{k'}$ such that if $occ_{k'}^X \neq O_{k'}$, then $\{u_{k'}\} = occ_{k'}^X \setminus O_{k'}$. Let PAR be the set of natural numbers. We define a P-meaning function m' such that for every $s \in \{1, \ldots, n\}$,

$$m'(C_s) \overset{\text{def}}{=} \{k \in \{0, \ldots, 2^n - 1\} : bits_s(k) = 0\} \cup$$

$$\{2^n - 1 + k' : k' \in \{1, \ldots, l\}, bits_s(u_{k'}) = 0\}.$$

For the remaining parameter constants, the map m' is not constrained except that m' is the restriction of a standard P-meaning function. For every $s \in \mathbb{N}$, $m'(E_s) \overset{\text{def}}{=} \{2^n - 1 + s\}$. By construction, for every $k \in \{0, \ldots, 2^n - 1\}$, we have $\{k\} \subseteq m'(B_k)$ and for every $\langle k, k' \rangle \in \{0, \ldots, 2^n - 1\} \times \{1, \ldots, l\}$, $2^n - 1 + k' \in m'(B_k)$ iff $u_{k'} = k$. Let $(\mathcal{R}_P)_{P \subseteq PAR}$ be defined as follows:

★ $\mathcal{R}_\emptyset \overset{\text{def}}{=} e_\mathcal{L}$;
★ for every $k \in \{0, \ldots, 2^n - 1\}$, $\mathcal{R}_{\{k\}} \overset{\text{def}}{=} R'_{c_{k,0}}$;
★ for every $k' \in \{1, \ldots, l\}$, $\mathcal{R}_{\{2^n-1+k'\}} \overset{\text{def}}{=} R'_{c_{u_{k'},k'}}$;
★ for the remaining $P \subseteq PAR$, $\mathcal{R}_P \overset{\text{def}}{=} \mathcal{R}_{P \cap \{0, \ldots, 2^n-1+l\}}$.

Consequently,

⋆ $\mathcal{R}_\emptyset = e_\mathcal{L}$ and for all $P, Q \subseteq PAR$, $\mathcal{R}_{P \cup Q} = f_2(\mathcal{R}_P, \mathcal{R}_Q)$;
⋆ for every parameter expression $A \in P(\phi)$ such that $N_{P_0(\phi), P_0^N(\phi)}(A) = A_{k_1, k_1'} \cup \ldots \cup A_{k_u, k_u'}$ with $A_{k_1, k_1'}, \ldots, A_{k_u, k_u'} \in \text{Comp}(\phi)$, $u \geq 1$, we have

$$\mathcal{R}_{m(A)} \overset{\text{def}}{=} \mathcal{R}_{c_{k_1, k_1'}} f_2 \ldots f_2 \mathcal{R}_{c_{k_u, k_u'}};$$

⋆ for every $k' \in \{1, \ldots, l\}$ and for every $k \in (\sigma)_{k'}$, $m(A_{k, k'}) \overset{\text{def}}{=} \emptyset$.

Let $\mathcal{M}' = \langle W, (\mathcal{R}_P)_{P \subseteq PAR}, m' \rangle$ be the $\mathcal{L}(\text{FOR}_0^N, P_0^N)$-model defined as in the second part of the proof of Theorem 10.4.1 except that we add: for every $E \in \text{FOR}_0^N$, $m'(E) = m(E)$. It is easy to verify that $\mathcal{M}'$ is an $\mathcal{L}$-model and $\mathcal{M}, w \models \phi'$ iff $\mathcal{M}', w \models \phi''$ iff $\mathcal{M}', w \models \phi$.
(I) $\rightarrow$ (II). Similar to the first part of the proof of Theorem 10.4.1.   Q.E.D.

The construction presented in the proof of Theorem 10.7.1 can be seen as a generalisation of the proof of Theorem 10.4.1. Lemma 10.4.1 can be also extended in a natural way to showing a reduction from $\text{SAT}(\text{SM}^*(\mathcal{L})(\text{FOR}_0^N))$ into $\text{SAT}(\mathcal{L}(\text{FOR}_0^N, P_0^N))$.

Lemma 10.7.1. *There is a polynomial-time transformation from the problem* $\text{SAT}(\text{SM}^*(\mathcal{L})(\text{FOR}_0^N))$ *into the problem* $\text{SAT}(\mathcal{L}(\text{FOR}_0^N, P_0^N))$.

The proof of Lemma 10.7.1 is analogous to the proof of Lemma 10.4.1. We only have to deal with more complex components of parameter expressions.
The following notion of a relevant part of a model is inspired by the construction of a model in the proof of Theorem 10.7.3.
Let $\mathcal{M} = \langle W, (\mathcal{R}_P)_{P \subseteq PAR}, m \rangle$ be an $\mathcal{L}(\text{FOR}_0^N, P_0^N)$-model. A set $X \subseteq PAR$ is said to be *relevant for* $\mathcal{M}$ $\overset{\text{def}}{\Leftrightarrow}$ X is non-empty and finite, and for every $P \subseteq PAR$, $\mathcal{R}_{P \cap X} = \mathcal{R}_P$. In other words, the value of $\mathcal{R}_P$ is determined by a finite subset of P which is fixed for the model $\mathcal{M}$.

Theorem 10.7.2. *If* $\phi \in \text{SAT}(\mathcal{L}(\text{FOR}_0^N, P_0^N))$, *then there is a model for* $\mathcal{L}(\text{FOR}_0^N, P_0^N)$ *with a relevant part of cardinality at most* $2^{\text{card}(P_0(\phi))} + \text{card}(P_0^N(\phi))$ *that satisfies* ϕ.

Hence, we obtain the following correspondences between decidability and finite model property of a Rare-logic with nominals and the respective properties of the associated standard modal logics.

Theorem 10.7.3. *Let* $\mathcal{L}$ *be a Rare-logic satisfying the assumptions of Theorem 10.4.2 and let* $\mathcal{L}(\text{FOR}_0^N)$, $\mathcal{L}(P_0^N)$, $\mathcal{L}(\text{FOR}_0^N, P_0^N)$ *be extensions of* $\mathcal{L}$ *with object nominals, parameter nominals, and both object and parameter nominals, respectively. Then the following conditions are satisfied:*

(I) $\text{SAT}(\mathcal{L}(\text{FOR}_0^N, P_0^N))$ *[resp.* $\text{SAT}(\mathcal{L}(P_0^N))$, $\text{SAT}(\mathcal{L}(\text{FOR}_0^N))$*] is decidable iff* $\text{SAT}(\text{SM}^*(\mathcal{L})(\text{FOR}_0^N))$ *[resp.* $\text{SAT}(\text{SM}^*(\mathcal{L}))$, $\text{SAT}(\text{SM}^*(\mathcal{L})(\text{FOR}_0^N))$*] is decidable;*

(II) $\mathcal{L}(\text{FOR}_0^N, \text{P}_0^N)$ *[resp.* $\mathcal{L}(\text{P}_0^N)$, $\mathcal{L}(\text{FOR}_0^N)$*] has the finite model property iff* $\text{SM}^*(\mathcal{L})(\text{FOR}_0^N)$ *[resp.* $\text{SM}^*(\mathcal{L})$, $\text{SM}^*(\mathcal{L})(\text{FOR}_0^N)$*] has the finite model property;*

(III) *if the logic* $\text{SM}^*(\mathcal{L})$ *is U-simplifiable, then* $\text{SAT}(\mathcal{L}(\text{FOR}_0^N, \text{P}_0^N))$ *[resp.* $\text{SAT}(\mathcal{L}(\text{P}_0^N))$, $\text{SAT}(\mathcal{L}(\text{FOR}_0^N))$*] is decidable iff* $\text{SAT}(\text{SM}^*(\mathcal{L})^-(\text{FOR}_0^N))$ *[resp.* $\text{SAT}(\text{SM}^*(\mathcal{L})^-)$, $\text{SAT}(\text{SM}^*(\mathcal{L})^-(\text{FOR}_0^N))$*] is decidable.*

Example 10.7.1. Let $\mathcal{L}(\text{FOR}_0^N, \text{P}_0^N) \in \text{class}(\{C_7, C_4'\})$ be such that the local condition of $\mathcal{L}$ is "true" and $O_M = \{\cup, ; , {}^*\}$. For every $\mathcal{L}(\text{FOR}_0^N, \text{P}_0^N)$-model $\mathcal{M} = \langle W, (\mathcal{R}_P)_{P \subseteq PAR}, m \rangle$ and for all $P, Q \subseteq PAR$, $\mathcal{R}_{P \cap Q} = \mathcal{R}_P \cup \mathcal{R}_Q$ and $\mathcal{R}_{PAR} = \emptyset$. The problem $\text{SAT}(\mathcal{L}(\text{FOR}_0^N, \text{P}_0^N))$ is decidable. Indeed, by Theorem 10.7.3(III), $\text{SAT}(\mathcal{L}'(\text{FOR}_0^N, \text{P}_0^N))$ is decidable iff $\text{SAT}(\text{SM}^*(\mathcal{L}')(\text{FOR}_0^N))$ is decidable, where $\mathcal{L}'$ is the logic in $\text{class}(\{C_1, C_1'\})$ similar to $\mathcal{L}$. Since $\text{SM}^*(\mathcal{L}')(\text{FOR}_0^N)$ is a fragment of the combinatory PDL (see Example 5.3.5), and combinatory PDL is decidable (see Sect. 6.5), we have $\text{SAT}(\mathcal{L}'(\text{FOR}_0^N, \text{P}_0^N))$ is decidable. Hence, $\text{SAT}(\mathcal{L}(\text{FOR}_0^N, \text{P}_0^N))$ is decidable by using Lemma 10.2.1 extended to logics with nominals.

The other results from Sect. 10.3 can also be extended to the languages with nominals.

10.8 Reducible Rare-logics

In the subsequent sections, we study a class of Rare-logics for which the distinction between parameter expressions and modal expressions is immaterial as far as satisfiability is concerned. Unlike in the previous sections, elimination of parameter expressions is not necessarily due to a Boolean reasoning.

Now we define two specific global conditions for a family $(\mathcal{R}_P)_{P \subseteq PAR}$ of relative relations.

Definition 10.8.1. *Let* f, g, ρ *be a set operation, a relation operation, and a relation predicate in* $\{=, \subseteq, \supseteq\}$*, respectively.* f *and* g *are assumed to be of the same finite arity. Let* ϕ_1, ϕ_2, ϕ_3 *be closed first-order formulae from FOL-M such that the only predicate symbols occurring in them are a binary predicate symbol* R *and* $=$*. Let* W *and* PAR *be non-empty sets and let* $(\mathcal{R}_P)_{P \in \mathcal{P}^n(PAR)}$*,* $n \geq 1$*, be a family of binary relations on* W*. We say that* $(\mathcal{R}_P)_{P \in \mathcal{P}^n(PAR)}$ *satisfies the global conditions* $(C_{\phi_1, \phi_2, \phi_3})$ *and* $(C_{\langle \rho, f, g \rangle})$ $\overset{\text{def}}{\Leftrightarrow}$

$(C_{\phi_1, \phi_2, \phi_3})$*:* $\langle W, \mathcal{R}_\emptyset \rangle \models \phi_1$*,* $\langle W, \mathcal{R}_{\mathcal{P}^{n-1}(PAR)} \rangle \models \phi_2$*, and for the remaining* $P \in \mathcal{P}^n(PAR)$*,* $\langle W, \mathcal{R}_P \rangle \models \phi_3$*;*

$(C_{\langle \rho, f, g \rangle})$*: for all* $P_1, \ldots, P_{\text{ar}(f)} \in \mathcal{P}^n(PAR)$*,*

$$\rho(\mathcal{R}_{f(P_1, \ldots, P_{\text{ar}(f)})}, g(\mathcal{R}_{P_1}, \ldots, \mathcal{R}_{P_{\text{ar}(f)}})) \text{ holds.}$$

Definition 10.8.2. *A Rare-logic $\mathcal{L} = \langle L, \mathcal{I}, \mathcal{S} \rangle$ of level $n \geq 1$ is a reducible Rare-logic for some set operations $f_1, \ldots, f_k$ and relation operations $g_1, \ldots, g_k$, $k \geq 1$, $\overset{\text{def}}{\Leftrightarrow}$*

(1) the set M_0 of basic modal expressions is of the form $\{r(A) : A \in P\}$ for some set P of parameter expressions determined by P_0 and O_P, and the set of relational types is a singleton;

(2) $O_M = \emptyset$ and $M = M_0$;

(3) for every $\oplus \in O_P$, there is a unique $j \in \{1, \ldots, k\}$ such that $\oplus$ and f_j are of the same arity and $\mathcal{I}(\oplus) = f_j$;

(4) the $\mathcal{L}$-models are the $\mathrm{LAN}(\mathcal{L})$-models $\mathcal{M} = \langle W, (\mathcal{R}_P)_{P \in \mathcal{P}^n(PAR)}, m \rangle$ respecting $\mathcal{I}$ such that $(\mathcal{R}_P)_{P \in \mathcal{P}^n(PAR)}$ satisfies $(C_{\phi_1, \phi_2, \phi_3})$ and $(C_{\langle =, f_1, g_1 \rangle})$, $\ldots, (C_{\langle =, f_k, g_k \rangle})$.

The class of such reducible Rare-logics is denoted by

$$\mathrm{class}^{\mathrm{red}}(\{C_{\phi_1, \phi_2, \phi_3}, C_{\langle =, f_1, g_1 \rangle}, \ldots, C_{\langle =, f_k, g_k \rangle}, \ldots\}).$$

Intuitively, a Rare-logic is reducible if the interpretation of the operators used for building parameter expressions can be encoded by the global conditions.

Example 10.8.1. We define the reducible Rare-logic $S5_{L1}^S$ of level 1 as follows. The set P of parameter expressions contains a set P_0 of basic parameter expressions and is closed under the binary operator $\cap$ from $O_P = \{\cap\}$. So, $M_0 = M = \{r(A) : A \in P\}$. The set FOR_0 of basic formulae is a countably infinite set of propositional variables and the set of logical connectives is $\{\neg, \wedge\} \cup \{[r(A)] : A \in P\}$. The $S5_{L1}^S$-models are the structures of the form $\langle W, (\mathcal{R}_P)_{P \in \mathcal{P}(PAR)}, m \rangle$, where W and PAR are non-empty sets, m satisfies the usual conditions, and the restriction of m to P is a P-interpretation respecting an $\mathcal{I}$ whose range is $\mathcal{P}(PAR)$ and $\mathcal{I}(\cap) = \cup$, and each $\mathcal{R}_P$ is an equivalence relation. The global conditions are $\mathcal{R}_{P \cup Q} = \mathcal{R}_P \cap \mathcal{R}_Q$ for all $P, Q \in \mathcal{P}(PAR)$ (condition (C_1)) and $\mathcal{R}_\emptyset = W \times W$ (condition (C_1')). So, $S5_{L1}^S$ is a reducible Rare-logic of level 1. Moreover, for every $S5_{L1}^S$-model $\mathcal{M} = \langle W, (\mathcal{R}_P)_{P \in \mathcal{P}(PAR)}, m \rangle$ and for all $A, B \in P$, $m(r(A \cap B)) = m(r(A)) \cap m(r(B))$.

Lemma 10.8.1. *Let $\mathcal{L}$ be a reducible Rare-logic of level $n \geq 1$. For every $\mathcal{L}$-model $\mathcal{M} = \langle W, (\mathcal{R}_P)_{P \in \mathcal{P}^n(PAR)}, m \rangle$, and for every parameter expression $\oplus(A_1, \ldots, A_{\mathrm{ar}(\oplus)}) \in P$,*

$$\mathcal{R}_{m(\oplus(A_1, \ldots, A_{\mathrm{ar}(\oplus)}))} = g(\mathcal{R}_{m(A_1)}, \ldots, \mathcal{R}_{m(A_{\mathrm{ar}(\oplus)})}),$$

where g is the unique relation operation associated to $\oplus$.

The proof is by an easy verification.

10.9 Reducing the Level of Rare-logics

In this section, we present sufficient conditions for collapsing the levels of the hierarchy of the reducible Rare-logics. We translate the reducible Rare-logics into standard modal logics in a similar way to that developed for the logics from Sect. 10.2. Let $\mathcal{L}$ be a reducible Rare-logic $\mathcal{L}$ of level $n \geq 1$. A *standard modal logic* $\mathrm{SM}(\mathcal{L})$ *associated to* $\mathcal{L}$ is defined as follows:

* the set M_0 of basic modal expressions is P_0 (or equivalently replace P_0 by some set of modal constants isomorphic to P_0);
* the set O_M of modal operators is O_P;
* the set M of modal expressions is P;
* $\mathcal{L}$ and $\mathrm{SM}(\mathcal{L})$ have the same sets of basic formulae and logical connectives (modulo the fact that in $\mathcal{L}$ the modal expressions are of the form $r(A)$ for $A \in P$);
* the $\mathrm{SM}(\mathcal{L})$-models are the structures of the form $\langle W, (R_A)_{A \in P}, m \rangle$ such that W is a non-empty set, for every $p \in \mathrm{FOR}_0$, $m(p) \subseteq W$, and $(R_A)_{A \in P}$ is a family of binary relations on W satisfying the following conditions:
    * for every $\oplus(A_1, \ldots, A_{ar(\oplus)}) \in P$, $R_{\oplus(A_1,\ldots,A_{ar(\oplus)})} = g(R_{A_1}, \ldots, R_{A_{ar(\oplus)}})$, where g is the unique relation operation associated to $\oplus$ in $\mathcal{L}$;
    * for every $A \in P$, if in every $\mathrm{SM}(\mathcal{L})$-model $m(A) = \emptyset$, then $\langle W, R_A \rangle \models \phi_1$;
    * for every $A \in P$, if in every $\mathrm{SM}(\mathcal{L})$-model $m(A) = PAR$, then $\langle W, R_A \rangle \models \phi_2$;
    * for the remaining $A \in P$, $\langle W, R_A \rangle \models \phi_3$.

For every such a logic $\mathcal{L}$, $\mathrm{SM}(\mathcal{L})$ is a standard modal logic that uses the parameter expressions from $\mathcal{L}$ as modal expressions. Although the $\mathcal{L}$-models and $\mathrm{SM}(\mathcal{L})$-models are structures of different form, our intention is to find conditions so that $\mathcal{L}$-satisfiability and $\mathrm{SM}(\mathcal{L})$-satisfiability are similar problems.

Definition 10.9.1. *Let $\mathcal{L}$ be a reducible Rare-logic of level $n \geq 1$. $\mathcal{L}$ is said to be finitely generated $\overset{\mathrm{def}}{\Leftrightarrow}$ for every $\mathrm{SM}(\mathcal{L})$-model $\mathcal{M}' = \langle W, (R_A)_{A \in P}, m' \rangle$ and for every non-empty finite set $\{C_1, \ldots, C_k\}$ of parameter constants, $k \geq 1$, there exists an $\mathcal{L}$-model $\mathcal{M} = \langle W, (\mathcal{R}_P)_{P \in \mathcal{P}^n(PAR)}, m \rangle$ such that:*

(1) for every $i \in \{1, \ldots, k\}$, $\mathcal{R}_{m(C_i)} = R_{C_i}$;
(2) the restrictions of m and m' to FOR_0 coincide.

The logic $\mathrm{S5}_{\mathrm{L1}}^S$ is finitely generated. Indeed, take some $\mathrm{SM}(\mathrm{S5}_{\mathrm{L1}}^S)$-model $\mathcal{M}' = \langle W, (R_A)_{A \in P}, m' \rangle$ and some $k \geq 1$. We build the $\mathrm{S5}_{\mathrm{L1}}^S$-model $\mathcal{M} = \langle W, (\mathcal{R}_P)_{P \in \mathcal{P}(PAR)}, m \rangle$ such that:

* $PAR \overset{\mathrm{def}}{=} \{C_1, \ldots, C_k\}$, $k \geq 1$, where for every $i \in \{1, \ldots, k\}$, C_i is a parameter constant of $\mathrm{S5}_{\mathrm{L1}}^S$;
* for every $A \in P$, $m(A) = PAR(A)$, that is $m(A)$ is the set of basic parameter expressions from PAR occurring in A;

⋆ for every $i \in \{1, \ldots, k\}$, $\mathcal{R}_{\{C_i\}} = R_{C_i}$;
⋆ $\mathcal{R}_\emptyset = W^2$ and for every $P \subseteq PAR$ such that $\mathrm{card}(P) \geq 2$, $\mathcal{R}_P = \bigcap_{p \in P} \mathcal{R}_{\{p\}}$;
⋆ the restriction of m to FOR_0 is m'.

One can easily check that $\mathcal{M}$ is an $\mathrm{S5}_{\mathrm{L1}}^S$-model satisfying the conditions (1) and (2) of Definition 10.9.1. Intuitively, $\mathrm{S5}_{\mathrm{L1}}^S$ is finitely generated since every parameter expression $C_1 \cap \ldots \cap C_n$ can be encoded by the set of parameters $\{C_1, \ldots, C_n\}$.

Theorem 10.9.1. *For every finitely generated reducible Rare-logic $\mathcal{L}$ of level $n \geq 1$, we have* $\mathrm{VAL}(\mathcal{L}) = \mathrm{VAL}(\mathrm{SM}(\mathcal{L}))$.

Proof. ($\leftarrow$) Let $\phi \in \mathrm{VAL}(\mathrm{SM}(\mathcal{L}))$ and suppose $\phi \notin \mathrm{VAL}(\mathcal{L})$. So, there is an $\mathcal{L}$-model $\mathcal{M} = \langle W, (\mathcal{R}_P)_{P \in \mathcal{P}^n(PAR)}, m \rangle$ and an $x \in W$ such that $\mathcal{M}, x \not\models \phi$. Let $\mathcal{M}'$ be the $\mathrm{LAN}(\mathrm{SM}(\mathcal{L}))$-model $\langle W, (R_A)_{A \in P}, m' \rangle$ such that m' is the restriction of m to FOR_0 and for every $A \in P$, $R_A \stackrel{\mathrm{def}}{=} \mathcal{R}_{m(A)}$. $\mathcal{M}'$ is indeed an $\mathrm{SM}(\mathcal{L})$-model. Using Lemma 10.8.1 and the definition of $(R_A)_{A \in P}$ one can show that for every $\oplus(A_1, \ldots, A_{\mathrm{ar}(\oplus)}) \in P$, $R_{\oplus(A_1, \ldots, A_{\mathrm{ar}(\oplus)})} = g(R_{A_1}, \ldots, R_{A_{\mathrm{ar}(\oplus)}})$, where g is the unique relation operation associated to $\oplus$. Hence, $\mathcal{M}', x \not\models \phi$. Indeed, for every $\mathrm{p} \in \mathrm{FOR}_0$, $m'(\mathrm{p}) = m(\mathrm{p})$ and for every $A \in P$, $R_a = m(\mathrm{r}(a))$. So ϕ is not $\mathrm{SM}(\mathcal{L})$-valid, a contradiction.
($\rightarrow$) Now let $\phi \in \mathrm{VAL}(\mathcal{L})$ and suppose $\phi \notin \mathrm{VAL}(\mathrm{SM}(\mathcal{L}))$. So, there is a $\mathrm{SM}(\mathcal{L})$-model $\mathcal{M} = \langle W, (R_A)_{A \in P}, m \rangle$ and an $x \in W$ such that $\mathcal{M}, x \not\models \phi$. Let X be a finite set of basic parameter expressions defined as follows. If $\mathrm{P}_0(\phi) \neq \emptyset$, then $X = \mathrm{P}_0(\phi) = \{C_1, \ldots, C_k\}$ for some $k \geq 1$. Otherwise, ϕ is Boolean and let X be the singleton $\{C_1\}$. Since $\mathcal{L}$ is finitely generated, there exists an $\mathcal{L}$-model $\langle W, (\mathcal{R}_P)_{P \in \mathcal{P}^n(PAR)}, m' \rangle$ such that:

(1) for every $i \in \{1, \ldots, k\}$, $\mathcal{R}_{m'(C_i)} = R_{C_i}$;
(2) the restriction of m' to FOR_0 is m.

In order to conclude the proof, we observe that, for every $A \in \mathrm{P}(\phi)$, we have $m'(\mathrm{r}(A)) = R_A$. The proof is by induction on the structure of the parameter expressions. The base case is immediate from (1) above, whereas the induction step is by an easy verification using Lemma 10.8.1. Then we have $\mathcal{M}', x \not\models \phi$, which leads to a contradiction.   Q.E.D.

The proof of Theorem 10.9.1 is not difficult; it uses the definitions appropriately. What requires more ingenuity is to prove that a particular reducible Rare-logic is finitely generated. Theorem 10.9.1 enables us to provide an axiomatisation of $\mathrm{S5}_{\mathrm{L1}}^S$, since $\mathrm{VAL}(\mathrm{S5}_{\mathrm{L1}}^S) = \mathrm{VAL}(\mathrm{SM}(\mathrm{S5}_{\mathrm{L1}}^S))$ and $\mathrm{SM}(\mathrm{S5}_{\mathrm{L1}}^S)$ is a fragment of $\mathrm{S5}'$. Let $\mathrm{HS5}_{\mathrm{L1}}^S$ be the extension of the proof system $\mathrm{HS5}(\mathrm{LAN}(\mathrm{S5}_{\mathrm{L1}}^S))$ obtained by adding the following axioms:

(Ax1) $[\mathrm{r}(A)]\phi \vee [\mathrm{r}(B)]\phi \Rightarrow [\mathrm{r}(A \cap B)]\phi$;
(Ax2) $[\mathrm{r}(A)]\phi \Leftrightarrow [\mathrm{r}(B)]\phi$ for all A and B such that $\mathrm{P}_0(A) = \mathrm{P}_0(B)$.

By Theorem 10.9.1 we get the following result.

Theorem 10.9.2. VAL(S5$_{L1}^S$) = THM(HS5$_{L1}^S$).

10.10 S5$_{L2}$: a Rare-logic of Level 2

In this section we show a reduction from the Rare-logic S5$_{L2}$ defined in Example 5.4.4 into DALLA. It is easy to show that S5$_{L2}$ is a reducible Rare-logic of level 2. We define the logic SM(S5$_{L2}$) as follows:

* the set M$_0$ of basic modal expressions is P$_0$;
* the set O$_M$ of modal operators is $\{\text{ⓜ}, \text{ⓤ}\}$ and both operators are binary;
* the set M of modal expressions is P;
* the set FOR$_0$ of basic formulae is a countably infinite set of propositional variables and the set of logical connectives is $\{\neg, \wedge\} \cup \{[A] : A \in P\}$;
* the SM($\mathcal{L}$)-models are the LAN(SM($\mathcal{L}$))-models $\langle W, (R_A)_{A \in P}, m \rangle$ such that $(R_A)_{A \in P}$ is a family of equivalence relations satisfying for all $A_1, A_2 \in$ P, $R_{A_1 \text{ⓤ} A_2} = R_{A_1} \cup R_{A_2}$ and $R_{A_1 \text{ⓜ} A_2} = R_{A_1} \cap R_{A_2}$.

By Lemma 8.2.1, two equivalence relations are in local agreement iff their union is transitive. So, for all $A_1, A_2 \in$ P, the relations R_{A_1} and R_{A_2} are in local agreement. Actually, DALLA is exactly SM(S5$_{L2}$) modulo the following simple syntactic differences:

(1) the modal operator $\cup^*$ [resp. $\cap$] in DALLA corresponds to ⓤ [resp. ⓜ] in SM(S5$_{L2}$);
(2) every modal constant in DALLA corresponds to a parameter constant in SM(S5$_{L2}$).

In view of these observations, DALLA and SM(S5$_{L2}$) are identified in the sequel.

One can observe that for every $A \in$ P, there is an A' of the form $(C_{i_{1,1}} \text{ⓤ} \ldots \text{ⓤ} C_{i_{1,k_1}}) \text{ⓜ} \ldots \text{ⓜ} (C_{i_{l,1}} \text{ⓤ} \ldots \text{ⓤ} C_{i_{l,k_l}})$ such that P$_0$(A) = P$_0$(A') and for every P-meaning function m respecting an $\mathcal{I}$ such that $\mathcal{I}(\text{ⓤ})$ is the set union and $\mathcal{I}(\text{ⓜ})$ is the set intersection, we have $m(A) = m(A')$ where $l \geq 1$, $k_l \geq 1$, and each $i_{p,q} \geq 1$ for $p = 1, \ldots, l$, $q = k_1, \ldots, k_l$. A' is not necessarily unique. We refer to A' as a *flat form* of A.

Theorem 10.10.1. VAL(S5$_{L2}$) = VAL(DALLA).

Proof. It is sufficient to show that S5$_{L2}$ is finitely generated, since Theorem 10.9.1 implies VAL(S5$_{L2}$) = VAL(DALLA). Let $\mathcal{M}' = \langle W, (R_A)_{A \in P}, m' \rangle$ be a SM(S5$_{L2}$)-model. The model $\mathcal{M} = \langle W, (\mathcal{R}_P)_{P \in \mathcal{P}^2(PAR)}, m \rangle$ is built as follows:

* $PAR \overset{\text{def}}{=} \{C_1, \ldots, C_k\}$, $k \geq 1$;
* for every $i \in \{1, \ldots, k\}$, $m(C_i) \overset{\text{def}}{=} \{\{C_i\}\}$;

* for every $C \in P_0 \setminus \{C_1, \ldots, C_k\}$, $m(C_i) \stackrel{\text{def}}{=} \{\{C_1\}\}$;
* for every $A \in P$ such that $P_0(A) \cap \{C_1, \ldots, C_k\} = \emptyset$, $m(A) \stackrel{\text{def}}{=} \emptyset$;
* let $A \in P$ be such that $P_0(A) \cap \{C_1, \ldots, C_k\} \neq \emptyset$ and A' be a flat form of A. Let A'' be the element of P obtained from A' by replacing every occurrence of $C \in P_0 \setminus \{C_1, \ldots, C_k\}$ by C_1. Assume that A'' has the form:

$$(C_{i_{1,1}} \uplus \ldots \uplus C_{i_{1,k_1}}) \sqcap \ldots \sqcap (C_{i_{l,1}} \uplus \ldots \uplus C_{i_{l,k_l}}).$$

Then,

$$m(A) \stackrel{\text{def}}{=} \{\{C_{i_{1,1}} \ldots, C_{i_{1,k_1}}\}, \ldots, \{C_{i_{l,1}}, \ldots, C_{i_{l,k_l}}\}\}.$$

One can check that m is indeed a P-meaning function of $S5_{L2}$. We complete the definition of $\mathcal{M}$:

* for every $i \in \{1, \ldots, k\}$, $\mathcal{R}_{\{\{C_i\}\}} \stackrel{\text{def}}{=} R_{C_i}$;
* $\mathcal{R}_\emptyset \stackrel{\text{def}}{=} W^2$;
* for every $P \subseteq \mathcal{P}(PAR)$ such that $\emptyset \in P$, $\mathcal{R}_P \stackrel{\text{def}}{=} \emptyset$;
* for the remaining $P \subseteq \mathcal{P}(PAR)$,

$$\mathcal{R}_P \stackrel{\text{def}}{=} \bigcap_{X \in P} \bigcup_{C \in X} \mathcal{R}_{\{\{C\}\}};$$

* the restriction of m to FOR_0 is m'.

One can easily check that $\mathcal{M}$ is a model satisfying the conditions (1) and (2) of Definition 10.9.1. One can also show that $\mathcal{M}$ is an $S5_{L2}$-model.   Q.E.D.

Intuitively, $S5_{L2}$ is finitely generated since every parameter expression $(C_{1,1} \uplus \ldots \uplus C_{1,k_1}) \sqcap \ldots \sqcap (C_{l,1} \uplus \ldots \uplus C_{l,k_l})$ can be encoded by

$$\{\{C_{1,1} \ldots, C_{1,k_1}\}, \ldots, \{C_{l,1}, \ldots, C_{l,k_l}\}\}.$$

The proofs of Theorems 10.9.1 and 10.10.1 allow us to deduce the following cardinality result.

Corollary 10.10.1. *For every formula $\phi \in \text{SAT}(S5_{L2})$, there exist an $S5_{L2}$-model $\mathcal{M} = \langle W, (\mathcal{R}_P)_{P \in \mathcal{P}^2(PAR)}, m \rangle$ and an $x \in W$ such that $\mathcal{M}, x \models \phi$, PAR is finite, and $\text{card}(PAR) \leq \text{card}(P_0(\phi))$.*

The Hilbert-style proof system $HS5_{L2}$ is an extension of $HK(\text{LAN}(S5_{L2}))$ obtained by adding the following axioms:

(Ax1) $[r(A)]\phi \Rightarrow \phi$;
(Ax2) $\phi \Rightarrow [r(A)]\langle r(A) \rangle \phi$;
(Ax3) $[r(A)]\phi \Rightarrow [r(A)][r(A)]\phi$;
(Ax4) $[r(A \uplus B)]\phi \Leftrightarrow [r(A)]\phi \wedge [r(B)]\phi$;
(Ax5) $[r(A \sqcap B)]\phi \Leftrightarrow [r(A)]\phi \vee [r(B)]\phi$.

Theorem 10.10.2. $\text{THM}(HS5_{L2}) = \text{VAL}(S5_{L2})$.

Theorem 10.10.2 is a corollary of Theorems 8.2.1, 8.2.2, and 10.10.1.

10.11 Notes

Translation between logics. A method of interpretation of a logic in some other logic is presented in [Tar53], where several decidability/undecidability results for first-order theories are established with the method. An interpretation is obtained by a translation of the formulae of a logic under consideration into the formulae of a target logic with the requirement that the translation preserves validity. More recently, translations are discussed in [Wój88, Eps90]. A study of properties of modal logics preserved under translations can be found in [FS92]. The method of translation is extensively applied in the field of computer science logics (see e.g. [Ohl91, Sch91, Var97, ANB98, Grä99b, ONdRG01]). In general, the method of translation enables us to study relationships between logics. In the case of mutual interpretability of two logics, we may infer properties of one logic from the properties of the other.

Rare-logics. Many Rare-logics can be found in [Orło88a, Orło89, Orło90, Orło93b, Bal96b, Bal96a, Bal98, BO99, Dem99a], whereas Rare-logics treated in this chapter have been studied in [Orło88b, Orło88a, Orło93b, Orło95, Kon98]. In [Bal98], some logics from class($\{C_{[f_1, f_2]}\}$) are considered. Logics having global conditions in the form of inclusion (for instance, $\mathcal{R}_{P \cup Q} \subseteq \mathcal{R}_P \cap \mathcal{R}_Q$) are also considered in [Bal98]. The study of translation between Rare-logics and standard modal logics can be found in [DG00a, DG00b]. In [DG00a], logics without nominals are treated whereas in [DG00b] the logics with nominals are dealt with. Furthermore, in [DG00b], a method of defining Hilbert-style proof systems for Rare-logics is presented.

Elimination of the universal modal connective. Theorem 10.5.1 is a reformulation of the results from [GP92]. The notion of elementary disjunction is from [GP92]. However, while in [GP92] the focus is on proof systems, we provide here a semantic proof whose consequences have not been explored in the literature until now. A result similar to Lemma 10.5.2 has been proved in [KT90] for some dynamic logics.

Reducible Rare-logics. Reducible Rare-logics considered in this chapter and their deductive systems are from [BO99]. The minor differences are: in [BO99] the levels of Rare-logics are defined for the natural numbers without 0; in [BO99] the models of logic S5$_{L2}$ involve only finite elements of $\mathcal{P}^2(PAR)$. Corollary 10.10.1 shows that the latter difference is immaterial as far as validity and satisfiability are concerned.

11. Decidability of Information Logics

11.1 Introduction and Outline of the Chapter

In this chapter we study the decidability of the satisfiability problem of information logics presented in Part III. Some of the decidability results of this chapter are general enough to apply to larger classes of logics. We use two standard proof methods to establish decidability:

* the method of finite structures;
* the method of translation.

The principle of the method of translation is very simple. Let $\mathcal{L}$ and $\mathcal{L}'$ be logics for which there is a computable map $f : \text{FOR}(\mathcal{L}) \to \text{FOR}(\mathcal{L}')$ such that for every $\phi \in \text{FOR}(\mathcal{L})$, $\phi \in \text{SAT}(\mathcal{L})$ iff $f(\phi) \in \text{SAT}(\mathcal{L}')$. If $\text{SAT}(\mathcal{L}')$ is known to be decidable, then decidability of $\text{SAT}(\mathcal{L})$ immediately follows. This approach can be generalised to arbitrary mathematical theories. The essential and difficult steps of such a method are to find the target logic $\mathcal{L}'$, to define the map f, and to prove its correctness.

The method of finite structures is a bit more subtle in the general case but it provides a direct means for showing that $\text{SAT}(\mathcal{L})$ is decidable. Assume that there are computable maps $f, g : \text{FOR}(\mathcal{L}) \to \mathbb{N}$ such that for every $\mathcal{L}$-formula ϕ, there is a finite set $\{\mathcal{M}_1, \ldots, \mathcal{M}_n\}$ of finite structures satisfying:

(1) $n \le f(\phi)$;
(2) for every $i \in \{1, \ldots, n\}$, the size of $\mathcal{M}_i$ is less than $g(\phi)$;
(3) $\{\mathcal{M}_1, \ldots, \mathcal{M}_n\}$ can be effectively computed from ϕ;
(4) $\phi \in \text{SAT}(\mathcal{L})$ iff $\{\mathcal{M}_1, \ldots, \mathcal{M}_n\}$ and ϕ satisfy a decidable property.

Then, $\text{SAT}(\mathcal{L})$ is decidable. Most often, $\mathcal{M}_1, \ldots, \mathcal{M}_n$ are finite $\mathcal{L}$-models and the decidable property in (4) above states that for some $i \in \{1, \ldots, n\}$, there is a $w \in \mathcal{M}_i$ such that $\mathcal{M}_i, w \models \phi$. However, the situation is not always that favourable, since the domains of the $\mathcal{L}$-models (for instance, the set W of objects or the set PAR of parameters) and the set M of modal expressions may be infinite. In that case, the structures $\mathcal{M}_1, \ldots, \mathcal{M}_n$ are finite approximations of $\mathcal{L}$-models relative to the formula ϕ. This method reflects the intuition that decidability is related to the possibility of bounding the proof search of the problem with respect to the size of the input. It is worth mentioning that due to condition (4), the method of finite structures can be viewed as a particular case of the method of translation.

Sect. 11.2 employs the method of finite structures, whereas Sect. 11.3 presents decidability results obtained by translation between languages of the logics. Sect. 11.2.1 presents a proof of the decidability of the logic NIL obtained by a filtration construction. In Sect. 11.2.2 decidability of the logic IL is shown by appropriately extending the proof given in Sect. 11.2.1. In Sect. 11.2.3 we prove the decidability of the logic S5' by using filtration. This leads to the decidability of the logic LKO. The proof applies the translation from formulae of LKO to formulae of S5' presented in Sect. 9.4.2. In Sect. 11.2.4 we present sufficient conditions for decidability of LA-logics. As a consequence we obtain decidability of the logics DALLA and LGM.

One of the important open problems in the field of information logics is the decidability status of the logic DAL (see Example 5.3.4). In Sect. 11.3.1 we show that the decidability of the logic DAL is equivalent to the decidability of the Rare-logic LIR. The proof is based on the results of Chap. 10. In Sect. 11.3.2 we establish the decidability of some of the similarity logics discussed in Sect. 7.4.

11.2 Decidability by Finite Models

11.2.1 The Information Logic NIL

We shall show that the logic NIL introduced in Sect. 7.2 is decidable by using a filtration method. Then, in Sect. 11.2.2 the decidability of IL' will be shown by appropriately extending the construction presented in this section.

Definition 11.2.1. *For every NIL-formula ϕ, $\mathrm{cl_{NIL}}(\phi)$ is the smallest set of NIL-formulae satisfying the following conditions:*

* $\mathrm{cl_{NIL}}(\phi)$ *is closed under subformulae;*
* $\phi \in \mathrm{cl_{IL}}(\phi)$;
* $[\sigma]\psi \in \mathrm{cl_{NIL}}(\phi)$ *implies* $[\leq]\psi \in \mathrm{cl_{NIL}}(\phi)$;
* $[\leq]\psi \in \mathrm{cl_{NIL}}(\phi)$ *implies* $[\sigma]\psi \in \mathrm{cl_{NIL}}(\phi)$;
* *for every* $\psi \in \mathrm{sub}(\phi)$, $\neg\psi \Rightarrow [\leq]\neg[\geq]\psi \in \mathrm{cl_{NIL}}(\phi)$.

To prove decidability of NIL with a filtration construction based on $\mathrm{cl_{NIL}}(\phi)$, one has to check the finiteness of $\mathrm{cl_{NIL}}(\phi)$.

Lemma 11.2.1. *For every NIL-formula ϕ, $\mathrm{card}(\mathrm{cl_{NIL}}(\phi)) \leq 11 \times |\phi|$.*

Proof. Observe that $\mathrm{sub}(\phi) \subseteq \mathrm{cl_{NIL}}(\phi)$. Actually, $\mathrm{cl_{NIL}}(\phi)$ is the union of the following sets:

* $\mathrm{sub}(\phi)$;
* $\{\neg\psi : \psi \in \mathrm{sub}(\phi)\}$;

* $\{[\geq]\psi : \psi \in \mathrm{sub}(\phi)\}$;
* $\{\neg[\geq]\psi : \psi \in \mathrm{sub}(\phi)\}$;
* $\{[\leq]\neg[\geq]\psi : \psi \in \mathrm{sub}(\phi)\}$;
* $\{[\sigma]\neg[\geq]\psi : \psi \in \mathrm{sub}(\phi)\}$;
* $\{\neg\psi \Rightarrow [\leq]\neg[\geq]\psi : \psi \in \mathrm{sub}(\phi)\}$;
* $\{(\neg\psi \wedge \neg[\leq]\neg[\geq]\psi : \psi \in \mathrm{sub}(\phi)\}$;
* $\{\neg[\leq]\neg[\geq]\psi : \psi \in \mathrm{sub}(\phi)\}$;
* $\{[\sigma]\psi : [\leq]\psi \in \mathrm{sub}(\phi)\}$;
* $\{[\leq]\psi : [\sigma]\psi \in \mathrm{sub}(\phi)\}$.

Each set from the above list is of cardinality at most $\mathrm{card}(\mathrm{sub}(\phi))$. Since $\mathrm{card}(\mathrm{sub}(\phi)) < |\phi|$, we have $\mathrm{card}(\mathrm{cl}_{\mathrm{NIL}}(\phi)) \leq 11 \times |\phi|$ (by using that $\varphi \Rightarrow \varphi'$ is an abbreviation for $\neg(\varphi \wedge \neg\varphi')$).   Q.E.D.

Let $\mathcal{M} = \langle W, R_\leq, R_\geq, R_\sigma, m \rangle$ be a NIL-model and let ϕ be a NIL-formula. For every $x \in W$, we write $|x|$ to denote the equivalence class $|x|_{\mathrm{cl}_{\mathrm{NIL}}(\phi),\mathcal{M}}$ (see Sect. 6.2.3). Let $\mathcal{M}' = \langle W', R'_\leq, R'_\geq, R'_\sigma, m' \rangle$ be the structure defined as follows:

* $W' \stackrel{\mathrm{def}}{=} \{|x| : x \in W\}$;
* for every $\mathrm{p} \in \mathrm{FOR}_0$, $m'(\mathrm{p}) \stackrel{\mathrm{def}}{=} \{|x| : x \in m(\mathrm{p})\}$;
* $\langle |x|, |y| \rangle \in R'_\sigma \stackrel{\mathrm{def}}{\Leftrightarrow}$ for every $[\sigma]\psi \in \mathrm{cl}_{\mathrm{NIL}}(\phi)$, the following conditions hold:
  (1) $\mathcal{M}, x \models [\sigma]\psi$ implies $\mathcal{M}, y \models [\leq]\psi$;
  (2) $\mathcal{M}, y \models [\sigma]\psi$ implies $\mathcal{M}, x \models [\leq]\psi$;
* $\langle |x|, |y| \rangle \in R'_\leq \stackrel{\mathrm{def}}{\Leftrightarrow}$ the following conditions hold:
  (3) for every $[\leq]\psi \in \mathrm{cl}_{\mathrm{NIL}}(\phi)$, $\mathcal{M}, x \models [\leq]\psi$ implies $\mathcal{M}, y \models [\leq]\psi$;
  (4) for every $|z| \in W'$, $\langle |x|, |z| \rangle R'_\sigma$ implies $\langle |y|, |z| \rangle \in R'_\sigma$;
* $\langle |x|, |y| \rangle \in R'_\geq \stackrel{\mathrm{def}}{\Leftrightarrow} \langle |y|, |x| \rangle \in R'_\leq$.

The rest of this section is mainly devoted to showing that $\mathcal{M}'$ is a NIL-model and $\mathcal{M}'$ is a $\mathrm{cl}_{\mathrm{NIL}}(\phi)$-filtration of $\mathcal{M}$. The following lemma states that the definition of $\mathcal{M}'$ is correct.

Lemma 11.2.2. *For every* $\mathrm{a} \in \{\leq, \geq, \sigma\}$, *for all* $x, x', y, y' \in W'$, *if* $|x| = |x'|$ *and* $|y| = |y'|$, *then* $\langle |x|, |y| \rangle \in R'_\mathrm{a}$ *implies* $\langle |x'|, |y'| \rangle \in R'_\mathrm{a}$.

Proof. Suppose $|x| = |x'|$ and $|y| = |y'|$. By way of example, let $\mathrm{a} = \sigma$. Suppose $\langle |x|, |y| \rangle \in R'_\mathrm{a}$ and $\mathcal{M}, x' \models [\sigma]\psi$ for some $[\sigma]\psi \in \mathrm{cl}_{\mathrm{IL}}(\phi)$. We show that $\mathcal{M}, y' \models [\leq]\psi$. Since $|x| = |x'|$, $\mathcal{M}, x \models [\sigma]\psi$ and since $\langle |x|, |y| \rangle \in R'_\sigma$, $\mathcal{M}, y \models [\leq]\psi$. Since $|y| = |y'|$, $\mathcal{M}, y' \models [\leq]\psi$. The second implication, namely $\mathcal{M}, y' \models [\sigma]\psi$ implies $\mathcal{M}, x' \models [\leq]\psi$, can be shown in a similar way.   Q.E.D.

Now we check the conditions that guarantee that $\mathcal{M}'$ is a $\mathrm{cl}_{\mathrm{NIL}}(\phi)$-filtration of $\mathcal{M}$. The following lemma states the satisfaction of condition (Fil3).

Lemma 11.2.3. *For all $x, y \in W$, the following conditions are satisfied:*

(I) $\langle x, y \rangle \in R_\sigma$ *implies* $\langle |x|, |y| \rangle \in R_\sigma'$;
(II) $\langle x, y \rangle \in R_\leq$ *implies* $\langle |x|, |y| \rangle \in R_\leq'$;
(III) $\langle x, y \rangle \in R_\geq$ *implies* $\langle |x|, |y| \rangle \in R_\geq'$.

Proof. (I) By definition, we have to show:

(i) $\langle x, y \rangle \in R_\sigma$ implies for every $[\sigma]\psi \in \mathrm{cl}_{\mathrm{NIL}}(\phi)$, $\mathcal{M}, x \models [\sigma]\psi$ implies $\mathcal{M}, y \models [\leq]\psi$;
(ii) $\langle x, y \rangle \in R_\sigma$ implies for every $[\sigma]\psi \in \mathrm{cl}_{\mathrm{NIL}}(\phi)$, $\mathcal{M}, y \models [\sigma]\psi$ implies $\mathcal{M}, x \models [\leq]\psi$.

Proof of (i): assume $\langle x, y \rangle \in R_\sigma$, $\mathcal{M}, x \models [\sigma]\psi$, and $\langle y, z \rangle \in R_\leq$. By symmetry of R_σ and (N4), $\langle x, z \rangle \in R_\sigma$ and therefore $\mathcal{M}, z \models \psi$. So $\mathcal{M}, y \models [\leq]\psi$.
Proof of (ii): assume $\langle x, y \rangle \in R_\sigma$, $\mathcal{M}, y \models [\sigma]\psi$, and $\langle x, z \rangle \in R_\leq$. By symmetry of R_σ and (N4), $\langle y, z \rangle \in R_\sigma$ and therefore $\mathcal{M}, z \models \psi$. So, $\mathcal{M}, x \models [\leq]\psi$.
(II) By definition, we have to show

(iii) $\langle x, y \rangle \in R_\leq$ implies for every $[\leq]\psi \in \mathrm{cl}_{\mathrm{NIL}}(\phi)$, $\mathcal{M}, x \models [\leq]\psi$ implies $\mathcal{M}, y \models [\leq]\psi$;
(iv) $\langle x, y \rangle \in R_\leq$ implies for all $|z| \in W'$, $\langle |x|, |z| \rangle \in R_\sigma'$ implies $\langle |y|, |z| \rangle \in R_\sigma'$.

Proof of (iii): assume $\langle x, y \rangle \in R_\leq$, $\mathcal{M}, x \models [\leq]\psi$, and $\langle y, z \rangle \in R_\leq$. By transitivity of $R_\leq$, $\langle x, z \rangle \in R_\leq$ and therefore $\mathcal{M}, z \models \psi$. So $\mathcal{M}, y \models [\leq]\psi$.
Proof of (iv): by definition, we have to show

(v) $\langle x, y \rangle \in R_\leq$ and $\langle |x|, |z| \rangle \in R_\sigma'$ implies for every $[\sigma]\psi \in \mathrm{cl}_{\mathrm{NIL}}(\phi)$, $\mathcal{M}, y \models [\sigma]\psi$ implies $\mathcal{M}, z \models [\leq]\psi$;
(vi) $\langle x, y \rangle \in R_\leq$ and $\langle |x|, |z| \rangle \in R_\sigma'$ implies for every $[\sigma]\psi \in \mathrm{cl}_{\mathrm{NIL}}(\phi)$, $\mathcal{M}, z \models [\sigma]\psi$ implies $\mathcal{M}, y \models [\leq]\psi$.

Proof of (v): assume $\langle x, y \rangle \in R_\leq$, $\langle |x|, |z| \rangle \in R_\sigma'$, and $\mathcal{M}, y \models [\sigma]\psi$. Suppose that $\mathcal{M}, z \not\models [\leq]\psi$. By definition of R_σ', $\mathcal{M}, x \not\models [\sigma]\psi$. So there is a $t \in R_\sigma(x)$ such that $\mathcal{M}, t \not\models \psi$. By symmetry of R_σ and (N4), we have $\langle y, t \rangle \in R_\sigma$. Since $\mathcal{M}, y \models [\sigma]\psi$, $\mathcal{M}, t \models \psi$, which leads to a contradiction.
Proof of (vi): assume $\langle x, y \rangle \in R_\leq$, $\langle |x|, |z| \rangle \in R_\sigma'$, and $\mathcal{M}, z \models [\sigma]\psi$. Suppose that $\mathcal{M}, y \not\models [\leq]\psi$. So there is a $t \in R_\leq(y)$ such that $\mathcal{M}, t \not\models \psi$. By definition of R_σ', since $\langle |x|, |z| \rangle \in R_\sigma'$, we get $\mathcal{M}, x \models [\leq]\psi$. By transitivity of $R_\leq$, $\langle x, t \rangle \in R_\leq$ and therefore $\mathcal{M}, t \models \psi$, which leads to a contradiction.
(III) Direct consequence of (II) and (N1).   *Q.E.D.*

The following lemma states the satisfaction of condition (Fil4).

Lemma 11.2.4. *Let* a $\in \{\leq, \geq, \sigma\}$. *Then for all* $x, y \in W$, $\langle |x|, |y| \rangle \in R_a'$ *implies that for every* $[a]\psi \in \mathrm{cl}_{\mathrm{NIL}}(\phi)$, $\mathcal{M}, x \models [a]\psi$ *implies* $\mathcal{M}, y \models \psi$.

Proof. The proof for a $\in \{\leq, \sigma\}$ is by an easy verification. Now assume that $\langle |x|, |y| \rangle \in R_\geq'$ and $\mathcal{M}, x \models [\geq]\psi$ for some $[\geq]\psi \in \mathrm{cl}_{\mathrm{NIL}}(\phi)$. Suppose $\mathcal{M}, y \not\models$

ψ. So $\psi \in \text{sub}(\phi)$ (see the proof of Lemma 11.2.1) and $\mathcal{M}, y \models \neg\psi$. Therefore $\mathcal{M}, y \models [\leq]\neg[\geq]\psi$ and $[\leq]\neg[\geq]\psi \in \text{cl}_{\text{NIL}}(\phi)$. Since $\langle |y|, |x| \rangle \in R'_\leq$, we have $\mathcal{M}, x \models [\leq]\neg[\geq]\psi$. By reflexivity of $R_\leq$, $\mathcal{M}, x \models \neg[\geq]\psi$, a contradiction. Q.E.D.

Lemma 11.2.5. $\mathcal{M}'$ *is a* $\text{cl}_{\text{NIL}}(\phi)$-*filtration of* $\mathcal{M}$.

Proof. By construction, conditions (Fil1) and (Fil2) in Definition 6.2.4 are satisfied in $\mathcal{M}'$. By Lemma 11.2.3, condition (Fil3) is satisfied in $\mathcal{M}'$, whereas by Lemma 11.2.4 condition (Fil4) is satisfied in $\mathcal{M}'$.   Q.E.D.

It remains to show that the structure $\mathcal{M}'$ is in MOD(NIL).

Lemma 11.2.6. $\mathcal{M}'$ *is a NIL-model.*

Proof. (N1), (N2) and the symmetry of R'_σ can be checked easily.
(N3) We show that R'_σ is reflexive. Since the relations in $\mathcal{M}$ satisfy (N1)–(N4), we have $R_\leq \subseteq R_\sigma$. So it is immediate that R'_σ is reflexive, since $[\sigma]\psi \Rightarrow [\leq]\psi$ is true in every NIL-model.
(N4) Assume $\langle |x|, |y| \rangle \in R'_\sigma$, $\langle |x|, |x'| \rangle \in R'_\leq$, and $\langle |y|, |y'| \rangle \in R'_\leq$. We show that $\langle |x'|, |y'| \rangle \in R'_\sigma$. By the definition of $R'_\leq$ and since we have $\langle |x|, |y| \rangle \in R'_\sigma$ and $\langle |x|, |x'| \rangle \in R'_\leq$, we get $\langle |x'|, |y| \rangle \in R'_\sigma$. By symmetry of R'_σ, we get $\langle |y|, |x'| \rangle \in R'_\sigma$. By the definition of $R'_\leq$, we get $\langle |y'|, |x'| \rangle \in R'_\sigma$. By symmetry of R'_σ, $\langle |x'|, |y'| \rangle \in R'_\sigma$.   Q.E.D.

As a corollary, we obtain the following theorem.

Theorem 11.2.1. *For every* $\phi \in \text{FOR(NIL)}$, $\phi \in \text{SAT(NIL)}$ *iff there exist* $\mathcal{M} = \langle W, R_\leq, R_\geq, R_\sigma, m \rangle \in \text{MOD(NIL)}$ *and a* $w \in W$ *such that* $\mathcal{M}, w \models \phi$ *and* $\text{card}(W) \leq 2^{11 \times |\phi|}$.

The proof is immediate from the filtration construction. Since the number of non-isomorphic NIL-models of cardinality at most n, $n \geq 1$, is finite and those structures can be easily computed, we have the following result.

Theorem 11.2.2. SAT(NIL) *is decidable.*

Consequently, SAT(NIL) $\in$ **NEXPTIME**. Indeed, given a NIL-formula ϕ, in order to check whether $\phi \in \text{SAT(NIL)}$, we guess a NIL-model $\mathcal{M} = \langle W, R_\leq, R_\geq, R_\sigma, m \rangle$ of size $2^{\mathcal{O}(|\phi|)}$ and we check whether there is a $w \in W$ such that $\mathcal{M}, w \models \phi$, which can be done in time $2^{\mathcal{O}(|\phi|^2)}$ (see Theorem 6.4.5). In Sect. 12.5 we show that SAT(NIL) is **PSPACE**-complete.

11.2.2 The Information Logic IL

In this section we shall use a filtration construction to establish the decidability of SAT(IL) (see Sect. 7.3.1 for the definition of the logic IL). However, the proof is more involved than in the previous section because the IL-models satisfy many constraints. By Theorem 7.3.4, SAT(IL) is decidable iff SAT(IL′) is decidable. In this section we show that IL′ has the finite model property and hence its decidability will be established. Moreover, a bound on the size of the IL′-models will be given.

Definition 11.2.2. *For every IL-formula ϕ, $\mathrm{cl}_{IL}(\phi)$ is the smallest set of IL-formulae satisfying the following conditions:*

$\star$ $\mathrm{cl}_{IL}(\phi)$ *is closed under subformulae;*
$\star$ $\phi \in \mathrm{cl}_{IL}(\phi)$;
$\star$ $\neg[\sigma]\neg\top \in \mathrm{cl}_{IL}(\phi)$;
$\star$ $[\leq]\neg D \in \mathrm{cl}_{IL}(\phi)$;
$\star$ $[\sigma]\psi \in \mathrm{cl}_{IL}(\phi)$ *implies* $[\leq]\psi \in \mathrm{cl}_{IL}(\phi)$;
$\star$ $[\leq]\psi \in \mathrm{cl}_{IL}(\phi)$ *implies* $[\sigma]\psi \in \mathrm{cl}_{IL}(\phi)$;
$\star$ $[\equiv]\psi \in \mathrm{cl}_{IL}(\phi)$ *implies* $[\sigma](D \Rightarrow [\equiv]\psi) \in \mathrm{cl}_{IL}(\phi)$.

As with $\mathrm{cl}_{NIL}(\phi)$, we show the finiteness of $\mathrm{cl}_{IL}(\phi)$.

Lemma 11.2.7. *For every IL-formula ϕ, $\mathrm{cl}_{IL}(\phi)$ is finite and* $\mathrm{card}(\mathrm{cl}_{IL}(\phi)) \leq 4 \times |\phi| + 12$.

Proof. Obviously, $\mathrm{sub}(\phi) \subseteq \mathrm{cl}_{IL}(\phi)$. Moreover, $\mathrm{cl}_{IL}(\phi)$ is the union of the following sets:

$\star$ $\mathrm{sub}(\phi)$;
$\star$ $\{[\leq]\neg D, \neg D, D, [\sigma]\neg D, \neg[\sigma]\neg\top, [\sigma]\neg\top, \neg\top, \top, [\leq]\neg\top, p \wedge \neg p, \neg p, p\}$
   (where $\top$ is an abbreviation for $\neg(p \wedge \neg p)$);
$\star$ $\{[\leq]\psi : [\sigma]\psi \in \mathrm{sub}(\phi)\}$;
$\star$ $\{[\sigma]\psi : [\leq]\psi \in \mathrm{sub}(\phi)\}$;
$\star$ $\{[\sigma](D \Rightarrow [\equiv]\psi) : [\equiv]\psi \in \mathrm{sub}(\phi)\}$;
$\star$ $\{D \Rightarrow [\equiv]\psi : [\equiv]\psi \in \mathrm{sub}(\phi)\}$;
$\star$ $\{[\leq](D \Rightarrow [\equiv]\psi) : [\equiv]\psi \in \mathrm{sub}(\phi)\}$.

The latter five sets are of cardinality at most $\mathrm{card}(\mathrm{sub}(\phi))$. Moreover, for all $a, b \in \{\sigma, \leq, \equiv\}$, if $a \neq b$, then

$$\{[a]\psi : [a]\psi \in \mathrm{sub}(\phi)\} \cap \{[b]\psi : [b]\psi \in \mathrm{sub}(\phi)\} = \emptyset.$$

So, $\mathrm{card}(\mathrm{cl}_{IL}(\phi)) \leq 4 \times |\phi| + 12$, since $\mathrm{card}(\mathrm{sub}(\phi)) < |\phi|$.   *Q.E.D.*

Let $\mathcal{M} = \langle W, R_{\equiv}, R_{\leq}, R_{\sigma}, D, m \rangle$ be an IL′-model (satisfying the conditions (I1)–(I8) from Sect. 7.3.1) and ϕ be an IL-formula. For every $x \in W$, we write $|x|$ to denote the equivalence class $|x|_{\mathrm{cl}_{IL}(\phi),\mathcal{M}}$ (see Sect. 6.2.3). Let $\mathcal{M}' = \langle W', R'_{\equiv}, R'_{\leq}, R'_{\sigma}, D', m' \rangle$ be the structure defined as follows:

$\star$ $W' \overset{\text{def}}{=} \{|x| : x \in W\}$;

$\star$ for every p $\in$ FOR$_0$, $m'(\text{p}) \overset{\text{def}}{=} \{|x| : x \in m(\text{p})\}$, in particular

$$D' = m'(D) \overset{\text{def}}{=} \{|x| : x \in m(D)\};$$

$\star$ $\langle |x|, |y| \rangle \in R'_\sigma \overset{\text{def}}{\Leftrightarrow}$ for every $[\sigma]\psi \in \text{cl}_{\text{IL}}(\phi)$, the following conditions hold:
 (1) $\mathcal{M}, x \models [\sigma]\psi$ implies $\mathcal{M}, y \models [\leq]\psi$;
 (2) $\mathcal{M}, y \models [\sigma]\psi$ implies $\mathcal{M}, x \models [\leq]\psi$;
 (3) $\mathcal{M}, x \models \neg[\sigma]\neg\top$;
 (4) $\mathcal{M}, y \models \neg[\sigma]\neg\top$;

$\star$ $\langle |x|, |y| \rangle \in R'_\leq \overset{\text{def}}{\Leftrightarrow}$ the following conditions hold:
 (5) for every $[\leq]\psi \in \text{cl}_{\text{IL}}(\phi)$, $\mathcal{M}, x \models [\leq]\psi$ implies $\mathcal{M}, y \models [\leq]\psi$;
 (6) for every $|z| \in W'$, $\langle |x|, |z| \rangle R'_\sigma$ implies $\langle |y|, |z| \rangle \in R'_\sigma$;

$\star$ $\langle |x|, |y| \rangle \in R'_\equiv \overset{\text{def}}{\Leftrightarrow}$ the following conditions hold:
 (7) for every $[\equiv]\psi \in \text{cl}_{\text{IL}}(\phi)$, $\mathcal{M}, x \models [\equiv]\psi$ iff $\mathcal{M}, y \models [\equiv]\psi$;
 (8) $\langle |x|, |y| \rangle \in R'_\leq$;
 (9) $\langle |y|, |x| \rangle \in R'_\leq$.

The rest of this section is devoted to showing that $\mathcal{M}'$ is an IL$'$-model and $\mathcal{M}'$ is a $\text{cl}_{\text{IL}}(\phi)$-filtration of $\mathcal{M}$. The following lemma states the correctness of the definition of $\mathcal{M}'$.

Lemma 11.2.8. *For every* a $\in \{\equiv, \leq, \sigma\}$, *for all* $x, x', y, y' \in W'$, *if* $|x| = |x'|$ *and* $|y| = |y'|$, *then* $\langle |x|, |y| \rangle \in R'_a$ *implies* $\langle |x'|, |y'| \rangle \in R'_a$.

Proof. Suppose $|x| = |x'|$ and $|y| = |y'|$. Let a $= \sigma$. Suppose $\langle |x|, |y| \rangle \in R'_a$ and $\mathcal{M}, x' \models [\sigma]\psi$ for some $[\sigma]\psi \in \text{cl}_{\text{IL}}(\phi)$. We show that $\mathcal{M}, y' \models [\leq]\psi$. Since $|x| = |x'|$, $\mathcal{M}, x \models [\sigma]\psi$ and since $\langle |x|, |y| \rangle \in R'_\sigma$, we get $\mathcal{M}, y \models [\leq]\psi$. Since $|y| = |y'|$, $\mathcal{M}, y' \models [\leq]\psi$. The second implication, namely $\mathcal{M}, y' \models [\sigma]\psi$ implies $\mathcal{M}, x' \models [\leq]\psi$, can be shown in a similar way. Finally, we show that $\mathcal{M}, x' \models \neg[\sigma]\neg\top$ and $\mathcal{M}, y' \models \neg[\sigma]\neg\top$. By Definition 11.2.2, $\neg[\sigma]\neg\top \in \text{cl}_{\text{IL}}(\phi)$ and therefore $\mathcal{M}, x' \models \neg[\sigma]\neg\top$. Since $|x| = |x'|$ and $|y| = |y'|$, $\mathcal{M}, y' \models \neg[\sigma]\neg\top$. The case a $=\leq$ makes use of the case a $= \sigma$, whereas the case a $=\equiv$ makes use of the case a $=\leq$.   *Q.E.D.*

Now we check the conditions which guarantee that $\mathcal{M}'$ is a $\text{cl}_{\text{IL}}(\phi)$-filtration of $\mathcal{M}$. The following lemma states the satisfaction of condition (Fil3).

Lemma 11.2.9. *For all* $x, y \in W$, *the following conditions are satisfied:*

(I) $\langle x, y \rangle \in R_\sigma$ *implies* $\langle |x|, |y| \rangle \in R'_\sigma$;
(II) $\langle x, y \rangle \in R_\leq$ *implies* $\langle |x|, |y| \rangle \in R'_\leq$;
(III) $\langle x, y \rangle \in R_\equiv$ *implies* $\langle |x|, |y| \rangle \in R'_\equiv$.

Proof. (I) By definition, we have to show:

(i) $\langle x, y \rangle \in R_\sigma$ implies for every $[\sigma]\psi \in \text{cl}_{\text{IL}}(\phi)$, $\mathcal{M}, x \models [\sigma]\psi$ implies $\mathcal{M}, y \models [\leq]\psi$;

(ii) $\langle x, y \rangle \in R_\sigma$ implies for every $[\sigma]\psi \in \mathrm{cl}_{\mathrm{IL}}(\phi)$, $\mathcal{M}, y \models [\sigma]\psi$ implies $\mathcal{M}, x \models [\leq]\psi$;

(iii) $\langle x, y \rangle \in R_\sigma$ implies $\mathcal{M}, x \models \neg[\sigma]\neg\top$;

(iv) $\langle x, y \rangle \in R_\sigma$ implies $\mathcal{M}, y \models \neg[\sigma]\neg\top$.

Proof of (i): assume $\langle x, y \rangle \in R_\sigma$, $\mathcal{M}, x \models [\sigma]\psi$, and $\langle y, z \rangle \in R_\leq$. By symmetry of R_σ and (I4), $\langle x, z \rangle \in R_\sigma$ and therefore $\mathcal{M}, z \models \psi$. So, $\mathcal{M}, y \models [\leq]\psi$.

Proof of (ii): assume $\langle x, y \rangle \in R_\sigma$, $\mathcal{M}, y \models [\sigma]\psi$, and $\langle x, z \rangle \in R_\leq$. By symmetry of R_σ and (I4), $\langle y, z \rangle \in R_\sigma$ and therefore $\mathcal{M}, z \models \psi$. So, $\mathcal{M}, x \models [\leq]\psi$.

Proof of (iii): assume $\langle x, y \rangle \in R_\sigma$. So $\mathcal{M}, x \models \neg[\sigma]\neg\top$.

Proof of (iv): by symmetry of R_σ, $\langle y, x \rangle \in R_\sigma$ and therefore $\mathcal{M}, y \models \neg[\sigma]\neg\top$.

(II) By definition, we have to show:

(v) $\langle x, y \rangle \in R_\leq$ implies for every $[\leq]\psi \in \mathrm{cl}_{\mathrm{IL}}(\phi)$, $\mathcal{M}, x \models [\leq]\psi$ implies $\mathcal{M}, y \models [\leq]\psi$;

(vi) $\langle x, y \rangle \in R_\leq$ implies for every $|z| \in W'$, $\langle |x|, |z| \rangle \in R'_\sigma$ implies $\langle |y|, |z| \rangle \in R'_\sigma$.

Proof of (v): assume $\langle x, y \rangle \in R_\leq$, $\mathcal{M}, x \models [\leq]\psi$, and $\langle y, z \rangle \in R_\leq$. By transitivity of $R_\leq$, $\langle x, z \rangle \in R_\leq$ and therefore $\mathcal{M}, z \models \psi$. So $\mathcal{M}, y \models [\leq]\psi$.

Proof of (vi): by definition, we have to show

(vii) $\langle x, y \rangle \in R_\leq$ and $\langle |x|, |z| \rangle \in R'_\sigma$ imply for every $[\sigma]\psi \in \mathrm{cl}_{\mathrm{IL}}(\phi)$, $\mathcal{M}, y \models [\sigma]\psi$ imply $\mathcal{M}, z \models [\leq]\psi$;

(viii) $\langle x, y \rangle \in R_\leq$ and $\langle |x|, |z| \rangle \in R'_\sigma$ imply for every $[\sigma]\psi \in \mathrm{cl}_{\mathrm{IL}}(\phi)$, $\mathcal{M}, z \models [\sigma]\psi$ imply $\mathcal{M}, y \models [\leq]\psi$;

(ix) $\langle x, y \rangle \in R_\leq$ and $\langle |x|, |z| \rangle \in R'_\sigma$ imply $\mathcal{M}, z \models \neg[\sigma]\neg\top$;

(x) $\langle x, y \rangle \in R_\leq$ and $\langle |x|, |z| \rangle \in R'_\sigma$ imply $\mathcal{M}, y \models \neg[\sigma]\neg\top$.

Proof of (vii): assume $\langle x, y \rangle \in R_\leq$, $\langle |x|, |z| \rangle \in R'_\sigma$, and $\mathcal{M}, y \models [\sigma]\psi$. Suppose that $\mathcal{M}, z \not\models [\leq]\psi$. By the definition of R'_σ, $\mathcal{M}, x \not\models [\sigma]\psi$. So there is a $t \in R_\sigma(x)$ such that $\mathcal{M}, t \not\models \psi$. By symmetry of R_σ and (I4) we have $\langle y, t \rangle \in R_\sigma$. Since $\mathcal{M}, y \models [\sigma]\psi$, $\mathcal{M}, t \models \psi$, which leads to a contradiction.

Proof of (viii): assume $\langle x, y \rangle \in R_\leq$, $\langle |x|, |z| \rangle \in R'_\sigma$, and $\mathcal{M}, z \models [\sigma]\psi$. Suppose that $\mathcal{M}, y \not\models [\leq]\psi$. So there is a $t \in R_\leq(y)$ such that $\mathcal{M}, t \not\models \psi$. By the definition of R'_σ, $\mathcal{M}, x \models [\leq]\psi$. By transitivity of $R_\leq$, $\langle x, t \rangle \in R_\leq$ and therefore $\mathcal{M}, t \models \psi$, which leads to a contradiction.

Proof of (ix): assume $\langle x, y \rangle \in R_\leq$ and $\langle |x|, |z| \rangle \in R'_\sigma$. By the definition of R'_σ, $\mathcal{M}, z \models \neg[\sigma]\neg\top$ and $\mathcal{M}, x \models \neg[\sigma]\neg\top$.

Proof of (x): assume $\langle x, y \rangle \in R_\leq$ and $\langle |x|, |z| \rangle \in R'_\sigma$. By the definition of R'_σ, $\mathcal{M}, x \models \neg[\sigma]\neg\top$ and therefore there is a $t \in R_\sigma(x)$. By (I4), $\langle y, t \rangle \in R_\sigma$ and therefore $\mathcal{M}, y \models \neg[\sigma]\neg\top$.

The proof of (III) is similar. $\hspace{2cm}$ *Q.E.D.*

The following lemma states the satisfaction of condition (Fil4).

Lemma 11.2.10. *Let* $\mathrm{a} \in \{\equiv, \leq, \sigma\}$. *Then for all* $x, y \in W$, $\langle |x|, |y| \rangle \in R'_\mathrm{a}$ *implies that for every* $[\mathrm{a}]\psi \in \mathrm{cl}_{\mathrm{IL}}(\phi)$, $\mathcal{M}, x \models [\mathrm{a}]\psi$ *implies* $\mathcal{M}, y \models \psi$.

The proof is by an easy verification.

Lemma 11.2.11. $\mathcal{M}'$ *is a* $\mathrm{cl}_{\mathrm{IL}}(\phi)$*-filtration of* $\mathcal{M}$.

Proof. By construction, conditions (Fil1) and (Fil2) in Definition 6.2.4 are satisfied in $\mathcal{M}'$. By Lemma 11.2.9, condition (Fil3) is satisfied in $\mathcal{M}'$, whereas by Lemma 11.2.10 condition (Fil4) is satisfied by $\mathcal{M}'$.   Q.E.D.

It remains to show the following result.

Lemma 11.2.12. $\mathcal{M}'$ *is an* IL'*-model.*

Proof. We shall show that $\mathcal{M}'$ satisfies the conditions (I1)–(I8) listed in Sect. 7.3.1. The conditions of reflexivity and transitivity of $R'_\leq$, symmetry of R'_σ, reflexivity, symmetry, and transitivity of $R'_\equiv$ and (I7) can be shown easily.

(I3) We show that R'_σ is weakly reflexive, that is for all $x, y \in W'$, $\langle |x|, |y| \rangle \in R'_\sigma$ implies $\langle |x|, |x| \rangle \in R'_\sigma$. First, we show:

(i) $\langle |x|, |y| \rangle \in R'_\sigma$ implies for every $[\sigma]\psi \in \mathrm{cl}_{\mathrm{IL}}(\phi)$, $\mathcal{M}, x \models [\sigma]\psi$ implies
   $\mathcal{M}, x \models [\leq]\psi$;

(ii) $\langle |x|, |y| \rangle \in R'_\sigma$ implies $\mathcal{M}, x \models \neg[\sigma]\neg\top$.

Proof of (i) and (ii): assume $\langle |x|, |y| \rangle \in R'_\sigma$, $\mathcal{M}, x \models [\sigma]\psi$, and $\langle x, z \rangle \in R_\leq$. By the definition of R'_σ, $\mathcal{M}, x \models \neg[\sigma]\neg\top$. So there is a $t \in R_\sigma(x)$ and hence (ii) holds. By weak reflexivity of R_σ, $\langle x, x \rangle \in R_\sigma$. By (I4) and by symmetry of R_σ, $\langle x, z \rangle \in R_\sigma$. So, $\mathcal{M}, z \models \psi$ and therefore $\mathcal{M}, x \models [\leq]\psi$.

(I4) We show that $\langle |x|, |y| \rangle \in R'_\sigma$ and $\langle |x|, |z| \rangle \in R'_\leq$ imply $\langle |z|, |y| \rangle \in R'_\sigma$. By the definition of $R'_\leq$, for every $|u| \in W'$, $\langle |x|, |u| \rangle \in R'_\sigma$ implies $\langle |z|, |u| \rangle \in R'_\sigma$. Since $\langle |x|, |y| \rangle \in R'_\sigma$, we get $\langle |z|, |y| \rangle \in R'_\sigma$.

(I5) We show that $|y| \in D'$ and $\langle |x|, |y| \rangle \in R'_\leq$ imply $|x| \in D'$. Assume $|y| \in D'$ and $\langle |x|, |y| \rangle \in R'_\leq$. Suppose that $|x| \notin D'$. So $y \in D$ and $x \notin D$. By IL-completeness of HIL (proved in Sect. 7.3.2), $\mathcal{M}, x \models \langle\leq\rangle D \Rightarrow D$ and, moreover, since $x \notin D$, $\mathcal{M}, x \not\models D$. So $\mathcal{M}, x \models [\leq]\neg D$. By Definition 11.2.2, $[\leq]\neg D \in \mathrm{cl}_{\mathrm{IL}}(\phi)$ and since $\langle |x|, |y| \rangle \in R'_\leq$, we get $\mathcal{M}, y \models \neg D$, which leads to a contradiction.

(I6) We show that $|x| \in D'$ and $\langle |x|, |y| \rangle \in R'_\sigma$ imply $\langle |x|, |y| \rangle \in R'_\leq$. We show the following implications:

(iii) $|x| \in D'$ and $\langle |x|, |y| \rangle \in R'_\sigma$ imply for all $[\leq]\psi \in \mathrm{cl}_{\mathrm{IL}}(\phi)$, $\mathcal{M}, x \models [\leq]\psi$
   implies $\mathcal{M}, y \models [\leq]\psi$;

(iv) $|x| \in D'$ and $\langle |x|, |y| \rangle \in R'_\sigma$ imply for all $|z| \in W'$, $\langle |x|, |z| \rangle \in R'_\sigma$ implies
   $\langle |y|, |z| \rangle \in R'_\sigma$.

Proof of (iii): assume $|x| \in D'$, $\langle |x|, |y| \rangle \in R'_\sigma$, and $\mathcal{M}, x \models [\leq]\psi$. Suppose that $\mathcal{M}, y \not\models [\leq]\psi$. By Definition 11.2.2, $[\sigma]\psi \in \mathrm{cl}_{\mathrm{IL}}(\phi)$ and by the definition of R'_σ, $\mathcal{M}, x \not\models [\sigma]\psi$. So there is a $t \in R_\sigma(x)$ such that $\mathcal{M}, t \not\models \psi$. By (I6), $\langle x, t \rangle \in R_\leq$ and therefore $\mathcal{M}, t \models \psi$, which leads to a contradiction.
Proof of (iv): we show the following implications:

(v) $|x| \in D'$, $\langle |x|, |y| \rangle \in R'_\sigma$, and $\langle |x|, |z| \rangle \in R'_\sigma$ imply for all $[\sigma]\psi \in \text{cl}_{\text{IL}}(\phi)$, $\mathcal{M}, y \models [\sigma]\psi$ implies $\mathcal{M}, z \models [\leq]\psi$;

(vi) $|x| \in D'$, $\langle |x|, |y| \rangle \in R'_\sigma$, and $\langle |x|, |z| \rangle \in R'_\sigma$ imply for all $[\sigma]\psi \in \text{cl}_{\text{IL}}(\phi)$, $\mathcal{M}, z \models [\sigma]\psi$ implies $\mathcal{M}, y \models [\leq]\psi$;

(vii) $|x| \in D'$, $\langle |x|, |y| \rangle \in R'_\sigma$, and $\langle |x|, |z| \rangle \in R'_\sigma$ imply $\mathcal{M}, y \models \neg[\sigma]\neg\top$;

(viii) $|x| \in D'$, $\langle |x|, |y| \rangle \in R'_\sigma$, and $\langle |x|, |z| \rangle \in R'_\sigma$ imply $\mathcal{M}, z \models \neg[\sigma]\neg\top$.

Proof of (v): assume $|x| \in D'$, $\langle |x|, |y| \rangle \in R'_\sigma$, $\langle |x|, |z| \rangle \in R'_\sigma$, and $\mathcal{M}, y \models [\sigma]\psi$. Suppose that $\mathcal{M}, z \not\models [\leq]\psi$. Since $\langle |x|, |z| \rangle \in R'_\sigma$ and $[\leq]\psi \in \text{cl}_{\text{IL}}(\phi)$, we get $\mathcal{M}, x \not\models [\sigma]\psi$. So there is a $t \in R_\sigma(x)$ such that $\mathcal{M}, t \not\models \psi$. By (I6), $\langle x, t \rangle \in R_\leq$. So $\mathcal{M}, x \not\models [\leq]\psi$ and by the definition of R'_σ, $\mathcal{M}, y \not\models [\sigma]\psi$, which leads to a contradiction.

Proof of (vi): suppose $|x| \in D'$, $\langle |x|, |y| \rangle \in R'_\sigma$, $\langle |x|, |z| \rangle \in R'_\sigma$, and $\mathcal{M}, z \models [\sigma]\psi$. Suppose that $\mathcal{M}, y \not\models [\leq]\psi$. Since $\langle |x|, |y| \rangle \in R'_\sigma$ and $[\leq]\psi \in \text{cl}_{\text{IL}}(\phi)$, $\mathcal{M}, x \not\models [\sigma]\psi$. So there is a $t \in R_\sigma(x)$ such that $\mathcal{M}, t \not\models \psi$. By (I6), $\langle x, t \rangle \in R_\leq$. So $\mathcal{M}, x \not\models [\leq]\psi$ and by the definition of $\langle |x|, |z| \rangle \in R'_\sigma$, $\mathcal{M}, z \not\models [\sigma]\psi$, which leads to a contradiction.

(vii) and (viii) follow directly from the definition of R'_σ.

(I8) We show that $|x| \in D'$, $|y| \in D'$, and $\langle |x|, |y| \rangle \in R'_\sigma$ imply $\langle |x|, |y| \rangle \in R'_\equiv$. First we prove the following implications:

(ix) $|x| \in D'$, $|y| \in D'$, and $\langle |x|, |y| \rangle \in R'_\sigma$ imply for every $[\equiv]\psi \in \text{cl}_{\text{IL}}(\phi)$, $\mathcal{M}, x \models [\equiv]\psi$ implies $\mathcal{M}, y \models [\equiv]\psi$;

(x) $|x| \in D'$, $|y| \in D'$, and $\langle |x|, |y| \rangle \in R'_\sigma$ imply for every $[\equiv]\psi \in \text{cl}_{\text{IL}}(\phi)$, $\mathcal{M}, y \models [\equiv]\psi$ implies $\mathcal{M}, x \models [\equiv]\psi$;

(xi) $|x| \in D'$, $|y| \in D'$, and $\langle |x|, |y| \rangle \in R'_\sigma$ imply $\langle |x|, |y| \rangle \in R'_\leq$ and $\langle |y|, |x| \rangle \in R'_\leq$.

Proof of (ix): assume $|x| \in D'$, $|y| \in D'$, $\langle |x|, |y| \rangle \in R'_\sigma$, and $\mathcal{M}, x \models [\equiv]\psi$. Suppose that $\mathcal{M}, x \not\models [\sigma](\text{D} \Rightarrow [\equiv]\psi)$. So there is a $z \in R_\sigma(x)$ such that $z \in D$ (or equivalently $|z| \in D'$ or $\mathcal{M}, z \models \text{D}$) and $\mathcal{M}, z \not\models [\equiv]\psi$. Hence, there is a $t \in R_\equiv(z)$ such that $\mathcal{M}, t \not\models \psi$. By (I8), $\langle x, z \rangle \in R_\equiv$ and therefore $\langle x, t \rangle \in R_\equiv$. So $\mathcal{M}, t \models \psi$, which leads to a contradiction. Hence, $\mathcal{M}, x \models [\sigma](\text{D} \Rightarrow [\equiv]\psi)$. By Definition 11.2.2, $[\sigma](\text{D} \Rightarrow [\equiv]\psi) \in \text{cl}_{\text{IL}}(\phi)$. Since $\langle |x|, |y| \rangle \in R'_\sigma$, by Lemma 11.2.10, we get $\mathcal{M}, y \models \text{D} \Rightarrow [\equiv]\psi$. But since $\mathcal{M}, y \models \text{D}$ ($|y| \in D'$), we have $\mathcal{M}, y \models [\equiv]\psi$.

Proof of (x): it is easy to see that x and y can be interchanged in (ix) and (x) since R'_σ is symmetric.

Proof of (xi): suppose $|x| \in D'$, $|y| \in D'$, and $\langle |x|, |y| \rangle \in R'_\sigma$. By (I6), we have $\langle |x|, |y| \rangle \in R'_\leq$. By symmetry of R'_σ, we obtain $\langle |y|, |x| \rangle \in R'_\sigma$. By (I6), we get $\langle |y|, |x| \rangle \in R'_\leq$.   Q.E.D.

As a corollary, we obtain the following theorem.

Theorem 11.2.3. *For every formula $\phi \in \text{SAT}(\text{IL}')$, there exist an IL′-model $\mathcal{M} = \langle W, R_\equiv, R_<, R_\sigma, D, m \rangle$ and a $w \in W$ such that $\mathcal{M}, w \models \phi$ and the cardinality of W is at most $2^{4 \times |\phi| + 12}$.*

Theorem 11.2.3 is a direct consequence of Lemmas 11.2.11 and 11.2.12 by applying a $\mathrm{cl_{IL}}(\phi)$-filtration of some IL'-model of ϕ.

Theorem 11.2.4. SAT(IL) *and* SAT(IL') *are decidable.*

By Theorem 7.3.4, SAT(IL) = SAT(IL'). A decision procedure for the problem SAT(IL') is roughly the following. Let ϕ be a formula; to check whether $\phi \in$ SAT(IL') we proceed as follows. We enumerate all the IL'-models which are non-isomorphic modulo ϕ such that $W \subseteq \{1,\ldots,2^{4\times|\phi|+12}\}$ and then we check whether ϕ is satisfied in some of them (see also Theorem 6.4.5).

11.2.3 The Logics LKO and S5'

We show that the logic LKO defined in Sect. 9.4.1 is decidable. Lemma 9.4.2 states that there exists a computable map from the problem SAT(LKO) into the problem SAT(S5') (S5' is defined in Sect. 9.3). In this section we show that SAT(S5') is decidable and therefore SAT(LKO) is decidable. We use a filtration-like construction. Let ϕ be an S5'-satisfiable formula. Let

$$\mathrm{sub}^+(\phi) \stackrel{\mathrm{def}}{=} \mathrm{sub}(\phi) \cup \{\neg\psi : \psi \in \mathrm{sub}(\phi)\}.$$

The cardinality of $\mathrm{sub}^+(\phi)$ is at most $2 \times \mathrm{card}(\mathrm{sub}(\phi)) \leq 2 \times |\phi|$. Let $\mathcal{M}^c = \langle W^c, (R^c_a)_{a\in M}, m^c \rangle$ be the canonical model for HS5'. There is an $x_\phi \in W^c$ such that $\mathcal{M}^c, x_\phi \models \phi$. It is a routine task to check that $\mathcal{M}^c_{|R^c_U(x_\phi)}$ is a non-standard S5'-model. As a consequence,

(1) for every a $\in$ M and for all $X, Y \in W^c$, $\langle X, Y \rangle \in R^c_a$ implies $[a]X = [a]Y$;
(2) for every a $\in$ M $\setminus \{U\}$, and for all $X, Y \in W^c$, $\langle X, Y \rangle \in R^c_a$ implies for every b $\in$ M, $M_0(b) \subseteq M_0(a)$ implies $\langle X, Y \rangle \in R^c_b$.

For every $X \in W^c$, we define

$$|X| \stackrel{\mathrm{def}}{=} X \cap \mathrm{sub}^+(\phi),$$

where X is a maximal HS5'-consistent set of S5'-formulae. Let $\mathcal{M}^{fc}_\phi$ be the structure $\langle W^{fc}, (R^{fc}_a)_{a\in M(\phi)\cup\{U\}}, m^{fc} \rangle$ such that

★ $W^{fc} \stackrel{\mathrm{def}}{=} \{|X| : X \in W^c\}$;
★ for all $|X|, |Y| \in W^{fc}$, $\langle|X|,|Y|\rangle \in R^{fc}_U \stackrel{\mathrm{def}}{\Leftrightarrow}$ for every $[U]\psi \in \mathrm{sub}(\phi)$, $\mathcal{M}^c, X \models [U]\psi$ iff $\mathcal{M}^c, Y \models [U]\psi$;
★ for all $|X|, |Y| \in W^{fc}$, for every a $\in$ M$(\phi) \setminus \{U\}$, $\langle|X|,|Y|\rangle \in R^{fc}_a \stackrel{\mathrm{def}}{\Leftrightarrow}$ $\langle|X|,|Y|\rangle \in R^{fc}_U$ and for every b $\in$ M$(\mathrm{sub}(\phi)) \setminus \{U\}$ such that $M_0(b) \subseteq M_0(a)$ and for every $[b]\psi \in \mathrm{sub}(\phi)$, we have $\mathcal{M}^c, X \models [b]\psi$ iff $\mathcal{M}^c, Y \models [b]\psi$;
★ $m^{fc} : \mathrm{FOR}_0(\phi) \to \mathcal{P}(W^{fc})$ is defined as $m^{fc}(\mathrm{p}) \stackrel{\mathrm{def}}{=} \{|X| : X \in m^c(\mathrm{p}), \mathrm{p} \in \mathrm{sub}(\phi)\}$ for every $\mathrm{p} \in \mathrm{FOR}_0(\phi)$.

Observe that $\mathrm{card}(W^{fc}) \leq 2^{\mathrm{card}(\mathrm{sub}^+(\phi))}$.

Lemma 11.2.13. $\mathcal{M}_\phi^{fc}$ *is a* $\langle \mathrm{M}(\phi), \mathrm{FOR}_0(\phi) \rangle$*-partial S5'-model.*

Proof. We recall that partial S5'-models are defined in Definition 9.3.1. We have to show that for every a $\in$ M(ϕ) $\cup$ {U},

(i) R_a^{fc} is an equivalence relation;
(ii) for every b $\in$ M(ϕ) $\cup$ {U}, if $\mathrm{M}_0(\mathrm{b}) \subseteq \mathrm{M}_0(\mathrm{a})$, then $R_\mathrm{a}^{fc} \subseteq R_\mathrm{b}^{fc}$.

Proof of (i): by definition, $\langle |X|, |Y| \rangle \in R_\mathrm{U}^{fc}$ iff $[\mathrm{U}]|X| = [\mathrm{U}]|Y|$. So, obviously, R_U^{fc} is an equivalence relation.
By definition, for every a $\in$ M(ϕ) \ {U}, $\langle |X|, |Y| \rangle \in R_\mathrm{a}^{fc}$ iff $\langle |X|, |Y| \rangle \in R_\mathrm{U}^{fc}$ and for every b $\in$ M(sub(ϕ)) \ {U} such that $\mathrm{M}_0(\mathrm{b}) \subseteq \mathrm{M}_0(\mathrm{a})$, $[\mathrm{b}]|X| = [\mathrm{b}]|Y|$. Since R_U^{fc} is an equivalence relation and the intersection of equivalence relations is an equivalence relation, R_a^{fc} is an equivalence relation.
Proof of (ii): assume b $\in$ M(ϕ) $\cup$ {U} and $\mathrm{M}_0(\mathrm{b}) \subseteq \mathrm{M}_0(\mathrm{a})$. If b = U, it is obvious that $R_\mathrm{a}^{fc} \subseteq R_\mathrm{U}^{fc}$. Now assume that b $\neq$ U. The modal expression a is different from U, for otherwise $\mathrm{M}_0(\mathrm{b}) \not\subseteq \mathrm{M}_0(\mathrm{a})$. By definition, $\langle |X|, |Y| \rangle \in R_\mathrm{a}^{fc}$ iff $\langle |X|, |Y| \rangle \in R_\mathrm{U}^{fc}$ and for every b' $\in$ M(sub(ϕ)) \ {U} such that $\mathrm{M}_0(\mathrm{b'}) \subseteq \mathrm{M}_0(\mathrm{a})$, $[\mathrm{b'}]|X| = [\mathrm{b'}]|Y|$. Equivalently, $\langle |X|, |Y| \rangle \in R_\mathrm{a}^{fc}$ iff

$\star$ $\langle |X|, |Y| \rangle \in R_\mathrm{U}^{fc}$ and
$\star$ for every b' $\in$ M(sub(ϕ)) \ {U}, if $\mathrm{M}_0(\mathrm{b'}) \subseteq \mathrm{M}_0(\mathrm{b})$, then we have $[\mathrm{b'}]|X| = [\mathrm{b'}]|Y|$) and
$\star$ for every b' $\in$ M(sub(ϕ)) \ {U} if $\mathrm{M}_0(\mathrm{b'}) \not\subseteq \mathrm{M}_0(\mathrm{b})$ and $\mathrm{M}_0(\mathrm{b'}) \subseteq \mathrm{M}_0(\mathrm{a})$, then $[\mathrm{b'}]|X| = [\mathrm{b'}]|Y|$.

We have just splitted $\mathrm{M}_0(\mathrm{b}) \subseteq \mathrm{M}_0(\mathrm{a})$ into two subcases. So, $\langle |X|, |Y| \rangle \in R_\mathrm{a}^{fc}$ iff

$\star$ $\langle |X|, |Y| \rangle \in R_\mathrm{b}^{fc}$ and,
$\star$ for every b' $\in$ M(sub(ϕ)) \ {U} if $\mathrm{M}_0(\mathrm{b'}) \not\subseteq \mathrm{M}_0(\mathrm{b})$ and $\mathrm{M}_0(\mathrm{b'}) \subseteq \mathrm{M}_0(\mathrm{a})$, then we have $[\mathrm{b'}]|X| = [\mathrm{b'}]|Y|$.

So $R_\mathrm{a}^{fc} \subseteq R_\mathrm{b}^{fc}$.   Q.E.D.

Furthermore, for every $\psi \in \mathrm{sub}^+(\phi)$ and for every $X \in W^c$, $\psi \in X$ iff $\mathcal{M}^c, X \models \psi$ (see Theorem 6.3.6) iff $\mathcal{M}_\phi^{fc}, |X| \models \psi$ iff $\psi \in |X|$. Observe that $\mathcal{M}_\phi^c$ is actually a sub$^+(\phi)$-filtration of $\mathcal{M}^c$. Indeed, one can easily show the following lemmas.

Lemma 11.2.14. *For every modal expression* a $\in$ M(ϕ) $\cup$ {U}, *if* $\langle X, Y \rangle \in R_\mathrm{a}^c$, *then* $\langle |X|, |Y| \rangle \in R_\mathrm{a}^{fc}$.

Lemma 11.2.15. *For all* $|X|, |Y| \in W^{fc}$, *if* $\mathcal{M}^c, X \models [\mathrm{a}]\psi$ *for some* $[\mathrm{a}]\psi \in$ sub(ϕ) *and* $\langle |X|, |Y| \rangle \in R_\mathrm{a}^{fc}$, *then* $\mathcal{M}^c, Y \models \psi$.

Theorem 6.2.1 enables us to state the following lemma.

Lemma 11.2.16. *For every $\psi \in \text{sub}^+(\phi)$ and for every $X \in W^c$, we have $\mathcal{M}^c, X \models \psi$ iff $\mathcal{M}_\phi^{fc}, |X| \models \psi$.*

For every formula ϕ, $\phi \in \text{SAT}(\text{S5}')$ iff ϕ is satisfiable in a $\langle M(\phi), \text{FOR}_0(\phi) \rangle$-partial S5'-model (by Lemma 9.3.1) iff ϕ is satisfiable in $\mathcal{M}_\phi^c$. Since W^{fc} is finite and $\text{card}(W^{fc}) \leq 2^{2 \times \text{card}(\text{sub}(\phi))}$, we get the following theorem.

Theorem 11.2.5. $\text{SAT}(\text{S5}')$ *is decidable.*

Consequently, by applying the map f that transforms LKO-formulae into S5'-formulae as defined in Sect. 9.4.2, we have the following result.

As a corollary we obtain the following theorem.

Theorem 11.2.6. $\text{SAT}(\text{LKO})$ *is decidable.*

11.2.4 LA-logics

Finite models by restriction

Although the modal connectives of the LA-logics behave as S5 modal connectives, the usual filtration construction for the multi-modal logics S5_k (with k independent S5 modal operators) cannot be used straightforwardly for the LA-logics. Instead of employing equivalence classes of objects, restrictions of models are used here.

First, we need to present basic facts about LA-logics. Let $\mathcal{L}$ be an LA-logic whose language is $\langle M_0, O_M, M, \text{FOR}_0, O_{\text{FOR}} \rangle$. The following lemma states that in every $\mathcal{L}$-model $\langle W, (R_a)_{a \in M}, m \rangle$, if $R_a(x) = R_a(y)$, then the linear orders associated to x and y are not independent.

Lemma 11.2.17. *Let $\{a_1, \ldots, a_n\} \subseteq M$, $n \geq 1$, and $\mathcal{M} = \langle W, (R_a)_{a \in M}, m \rangle \in \text{MOD}(\mathcal{L})$. For all $x, y \in W$, if $R_{a_1}(x) \subseteq \ldots \subseteq R_{a_n}(x)$ and $\langle x, y \rangle \in R_{a_k}$ for some $k \in \{1, \ldots, n\}$, then:*

(I) for every $l \in \{k, \ldots, n\}$, $R_{a_k}(y) = R_{a_l}(x)$;
(II) for every $l \in \{1, \ldots, k-1\}$, $R_{a_l}(y) \subseteq R_{a_k}(y)$.

The proof is by an easy verification. Observe also that for every $\mathcal{M} = \langle W, (R_a)_{a \in M}, m \rangle \in \text{MOD}(\mathcal{L})$, for every $\text{LAN}(\mathcal{L})$-formula ϕ, and for every $w \in W$, if for some $a \in M_0(\phi)$ and for every $b \in M_0(\phi)$, $R_b(w) \subseteq R_a(w)$, then $\mathcal{M}, w \models \phi$ iff $\mathcal{M}_{|R_a(w)}, w \models \phi$. It is easy to check that in that case $(\bigcup_{b \in M_0(\phi)} R_b)^*(w) = R_a(w)$.

The rest of this section is aimed at showing that every $\mathcal{L}$-satisfiable formula has a finite model. Let ϕ be a formula, let $\mathcal{M} = \langle W, (R_a)_{a \in M}, m \rangle \in \text{MOD}(\mathcal{L})$, and let a $w \in W$ be such that $\mathcal{M}, w \models \phi$. We show that ϕ

has a finite $\mathcal{L}$-model that can be defined from $\mathcal{M}$. Assume that $M_0(\phi) = \{a_1, \ldots, a_n\}$, $n \geq 1$, with $R_{a_1}(w) \subseteq \ldots \subseteq R_{a_n}(w)$. Such an ordering always exists because $\mathcal{L}$ is an LA-logic. If $M_0(\phi) = \emptyset$ and $\phi \in \mathrm{SAT}(\mathcal{L})$, then ϕ is satisfiable in a model of cardinality 1.

We shall construct a set $W' \subseteq W$ such that

* $w \in W'$;
* W' is finite and $\mathrm{card}(W') \leq 1 + n \times \mathrm{mw}(\phi)^n$;
* $\mathcal{M}_{|W'}, w \models \phi$.

The set W' is defined as the union $\bigcup_{i=0}^{\alpha} W'_i$ for some $\alpha \in \{0, \ldots, n\}$ and for every $i \in \{0, \ldots, \alpha\}$, W'_i is a finite subset of W. Each set W'_{i+1} is defined recursively from W'_i for every $i \in \{0, \ldots, \alpha - 1\}$ and $W'_0 = \{w\}$.

In order to define W', we need to introduce a few notions. The set Nec is defined as follows:

$$\mathrm{Nec} \overset{\mathrm{def}}{=} \{[b]\psi : [a]\psi \in \mathrm{sub}(\phi), b \in M_0(\phi)\}.$$

Nec is the set of formulae of the form $[a]\psi$ occurring in ϕ with their copies $[b]\psi$ for every modal expression b occurring in ϕ. The basic idea behind the definition of W'_{i+1} from W'_i can be stated as follows. If $\mathcal{M}, u \not\models [a]\psi$ for some $[a]\psi \in \mathrm{Nec}$ and $u \in W'_i$, then there is a witness $u' \in W$ of this fact, that is $\langle u, u' \rangle \in R_a$ and $\mathcal{M}, u' \not\models \psi$. So we add u' to W'_{i+1}. Moreover, if $\mathcal{M}, u \not\models [a_{j'}]\psi$, $\mathcal{M}, u \not\models [a_j]\psi$, and $R_{a_{j'}}(u) \subseteq R_{a_j}(u)$ for some $j, j' \in \{1, \ldots, n\}$, then a single witness u' needs to be considered satisfying $\langle u, u' \rangle \in R_{a_{j'}}$ and $\mathcal{M}, u' \not\models \psi$.

With such an inductive process, termination is not guaranteed. We refine further our construction so that we shall also be able to enforce α to be less than n. Assume that for some $u \in W'_i$ and for some $j, j' \in \{1, \ldots, n\}$, $\mathcal{M}, u \not\models [a_{j'}]\psi$ requires a witness and $R_{a_{j'}}(u) \subseteq R_{a_j}(u)$. There exists an $u' \in W'_{i+1}$ such that $\mathcal{M}, u' \not\models \psi$ and $\langle u, u' \rangle \in R_{a_{j'}}$. We can show that if $\mathcal{M}, u' \not\models [a_j]\varphi$ for some $[a_j]\varphi \in \mathrm{Nec}$, then there is no need to consider a new witness. Indeed, there exists an $u'' \in W'_0 \cup \ldots \cup W'_i$ such that $\langle u', u'' \rangle \in R_{a_j}$ and $\mathcal{M}, u'' \not\models \varphi$. Since R_{a_j} is an equivalence relation and $\langle u, u'' \rangle \in R_{a_j}$, we have $\mathcal{M}, u \not\models [a_j]\varphi$. If the set W'_{i+1} is properly built (this should become clear in the formal definition presented in the sequel), there exists a $v \in W'_{i+1}$ such that $\langle u, v \rangle \in R_{a_j}$ and $\mathcal{M}, v \not\models \varphi$. Since $\langle u', v \rangle \in R_{a_j}$, v is already a witness for $\mathcal{M}, u' \not\models [a_j]\varphi$. This observation enables us to find an $\alpha \in \{0, \ldots, n\}$ such that no witness is needed for the elements of W'_α.

Now, we give the formal definition of W'. Let $\sigma = \langle j_1, \ldots, j_k \rangle$, $k \geq 1$, be a sequence of natural numbers from $\{1, \ldots, n\}$ (without repetition) and let an $x \in W$ be such that $R_{a_{j_1}}(x) \subseteq \ldots \subseteq R_{a_{j_k}}(x)$. The set Nec_x^σ is defined as follows:

$$\mathrm{Nec}_x^\sigma \overset{\mathrm{def}}{=} \{[a_{j_{k'}}]\psi \in \mathrm{Nec} : k' \in \{1, \ldots, k\}, \mathcal{M}, x \models \neg[a_{j_{k'}}]\psi, \text{ and}$$
$$\text{if } k' \geq 2, \text{ then } \mathcal{M}, x \models [a_{j_{k'-1}}]\psi\}.$$

Observe that $\text{card}(\text{Nec}) \leq n \times \text{mw}(\phi)$, $\text{card}(\text{Nec}_x^\sigma) \leq \text{mw}(\phi)$, and $\text{Nec}_x^\sigma = \emptyset$ if $\sigma = \lambda$. The set Nec_x^σ contains the elements $[a]\psi$ of Nec such that there is an $u \in W$ with $\mathcal{M}, u \not\models \psi$ and $\langle x, u \rangle \in R_a$. Moreover, there is an $i \in set(\sigma)$ such that $a_i = a$ and no i' preceding i in σ satisfies this property. Therefore, if $a, b \in M$, $\mathcal{M}, x \not\models [a]\psi$, and $\mathcal{M}, x \not\models [b]\psi$, then at most one witness is needed which entails that $\text{card}(\text{Nec}_x^\sigma \cap \{[a]\psi, [b]\psi\}) \leq 1$. In particular, if $\{[a]\psi, [b]\psi\} \cap \text{Nec} = \emptyset$, then $\text{card}(\text{Nec}_x^\sigma \cap \{[a]\psi, [b]\psi\}) = 0$.

We shall introduce an auxiliary family $(W_i)_{i \in \{0,\ldots,\alpha\}}$ of sets for some $\alpha \leq n$. For every $i \in \{1,\ldots,n\}$ the elements of W_i are triples of the form $\langle w', \sigma, tag \rangle$, where

$\star$ $w' \in W$;
$\star$ σ is a sequence of elements of $\{1,\ldots,n\}$ without repetitions, so $|\sigma| = \text{card}(set(\sigma))$;
$\star$ tag is either λ or some $[a_k]\psi \in \text{Nec}$ with $k \notin set(\sigma)$.

Then, for every $i \in \{0,\ldots,\alpha\}$, the set W_i' is defined as

$$W_i' \overset{\text{def}}{=} \{w' : \langle w', \sigma, tag \rangle \in W_i\},$$

where W_i is defined as follows:

$\star$ $W_0 \overset{\text{def}}{=} \{\langle w, \langle 1,\ldots,n \rangle, \lambda \rangle\}$. In the triple $\langle w, \langle 1,\ldots,n \rangle, \lambda \rangle$, λ carries an information that w has not been introduced as a witness and $\langle 1,\ldots,n \rangle$ is an encoding of the inclusions $R_{a_1}(w) \subseteq \ldots \subseteq R_{a_n}(w)$.
$\star$ Let W_i be defined. For every $\langle w', \sigma, tag \rangle \in W_i$, for every $[a_j]\psi \in \text{Nec}_{w'}^\sigma$, there is a witness $u = u(\langle w', \sigma, tag \rangle, [a_j]\psi) \in W$ such that $\langle w', u \rangle \in R_{a_j}$ and $\mathcal{M}, u \models \neg\psi$. If $\sigma = \langle j_1,\ldots,j_k \rangle$, then let k' be the element of $\{1,\ldots,k\}$ such that $j_{k'} = j$. The existence of k' is guaranteed by the definition of $\text{Nec}_{w'}^\sigma$. Let

$$\langle u, \langle j_1',\ldots,j_{k'-1}' \rangle, [a_j]\psi \rangle$$

be the triple such that
$*$ $set(\langle j_1',\ldots,j_{k'-1}' \rangle) = set(\langle j_1,\ldots,j_{k'-1} \rangle)$;
$*$ $R_{a_{j_1'}}(u) \subseteq \ldots \subseteq R_{a_{j_{k'-1}'}}(u)$ if $k' > 1$.
The set $V_{\langle w', \sigma, tag \rangle}$ is defined as follows:

$$V_{\langle w', \sigma, tag \rangle} \overset{\text{def}}{=}$$

$$\{\langle u(\langle w', \sigma, tag \rangle, [a_j]\psi), \langle j_1',\ldots,j_{k'-1}' \rangle, [a_j]\psi \rangle : [a_j]\psi \in \text{Nec}_{w'}^\sigma\}.$$

Finally,

$$W_{i+1} \overset{\text{def}}{=} \bigcup \{V_{\langle w', \sigma, tag \rangle} : \langle w', \sigma, tag \rangle \in W_i\}.$$

Observe that if $\langle w', \sigma, tag \rangle \in W_i$, then $|\sigma| \leq n - i$. Consequently, there exists an $\alpha \in \{0,\ldots,n\}$ such that $W_\alpha \neq \emptyset$ and $W_{\alpha+1} = \emptyset$. Let

$$W' = \bigcup_{i=0}^{\alpha} W_i'.$$

The following lemma states the main properties of the construction.

Lemma 11.2.18. *For every $i \in \{0, \ldots, \alpha\}$ and for every $k \geq 1$, if $\langle w_i, \langle j_1, \ldots, j_k \rangle, tag \rangle \in W_i$, then:*

(I) $R_{a_{j_1}}(w_i) \subseteq \ldots \subseteq R_{a_{j_k}}(w_i)$;
(II) if $tag = [a]\psi$, then $R_{a_{j_k}}(w_i) \subseteq R_a(w_i)$ and $\mathcal{M}, w_i \models \neg\psi$;
(III) for every $j \in \{1, \ldots, n\} \setminus set(\langle j_1, \ldots, j_k \rangle)$, $R_{a_{j_k}}(w_i) \subseteq R_{a_j}(w_i)$.

Proof. (I) and (II) are immediate by construction of W_i.
(III) The proof is by induction on i.
Base case: $i = 0$.
Necessarily $\langle j_1, \ldots, j_k \rangle = \langle 1, \ldots, n \rangle$ and therefore the universal quantification in (III) is over an empty domain.
Induction step.
Let $\langle w_i, \sigma.\langle j_{k'}, \ldots, j_k \rangle, tag \rangle \in W_i$ and $\langle w_{i+1}, \langle j_1, \ldots, j_{k'-1} \rangle, [a_{j_{k'}}]\phi' \rangle \in W_{i+1}$ such that:

$\star$ $\{j_1, \ldots, j_k\} \subseteq \{1, \ldots, n\}$;
$\star$ $set(\sigma) = \{j_1, \ldots, j_{k'-1}\}$ and $0 \leq k' < k \leq n$;
$\star$ w_{i+1} is the witness for $\mathcal{M}, w_i \not\models [a_{j_{k'}}]\psi$ which implies that $\langle w_i, w_{i+1} \rangle \in R_{a_{j_{k'}}}$ and $\mathcal{M}, w_{i+1} \not\models \psi$.

By the induction hypothesis, for every $j \in \{1, \ldots, n\} \setminus set(\sigma.\langle j_1, \ldots, j_k \rangle)$, $R_{a_{j_k}}(w_i) \subseteq R_{a_j}(w_i)$. By the satisfaction of (I), we have $R_{a_{j_{k'}}}(w_i) \subseteq \ldots \subseteq R_{a_{j_k}}(w_i)$. So for every $j \in (\{1, \ldots, n\} \setminus set(\langle j_1, \ldots, j_k \rangle)) \cup \{j_{k'+1}, \ldots, j_k\}$, we have $R_{a_{j_{k'}}}(w_i) \subseteq R_{a_j}(w_i)$. By Lemma 11.2.17, for every $j \in \{1, \ldots, n\} \setminus set(\langle j_1, \ldots, j_{k'-1} \rangle)$, $R_{a_j}(w_{i+1}) = R_{a_j}(w_i)$. Since $R_{a_{j_{k'-1}}}(w_{i+1}) \subseteq R_{a_{j_{k'}}}(w_{i+1})$, by the satisfaction of (II) for every $j \in \{1, \ldots, n\} \setminus set(\langle j_1, \ldots, j_{k'-1} \rangle)$, we have $R_{a_{j_{k'-1}}}(w_{i+1}) \subseteq R_{a_j}(w_{i+1})$.   *Q.E.D.*

For every $i \in \{0, \ldots, \alpha-1\}$, $card(W_{i+1}) \leq card(W_i) \times mw(\phi)$ and therefore $card(W') \leq 1 + n \times mw(\phi)^n$. The rest of the section is devoted to showing that $\mathcal{M}, w \models \phi$ iff $\mathcal{M}_{|W'}, w \models \phi$. The following lemma states that the set W' contains sufficiently many objects.

Lemma 11.2.19. *For every $w' \in W$ and for every $j \in \{1, \ldots, n\}$, if $[a_j]\psi \in$ Nec and $\mathcal{M}, w' \models \neg[a_j]\psi$, then there is a $w'' \in W'$ such that $\langle w', w'' \rangle \in R_{a_j}$ and $\mathcal{M}, w'' \not\models \psi$.*

Proof. We recall that $W' = \bigcup_{i=0}^{\alpha} W_i'$ and for every $i \in \{0, \ldots, \alpha\}$, $W_i' = \{w' : \langle w', \sigma, tag \rangle \in W_i\}$. The proof is by induction on i.
Base case: $i = 0$.
By the assumption $w' = w$. Assume that $\mathcal{M}, w \models \neg[a_j]\psi$ for some $j \in \{1, \ldots, n\}$. There exist $[a_k]\psi \in Nec_w^{\langle 1, \ldots, n \rangle}$ and $\langle u_1, \langle j_1, \ldots, j_{k-1} \rangle, [a_k]\psi \rangle \in W_1$ for some $k \in \{1, \ldots, n\}$ such that $\langle w, u_1 \rangle \in R_{a_k}$ and $\mathcal{M}, u_1 \not\models \psi$. Since $R_{a_k}(w) \subseteq R_{a_j}(w)$, by the definition of $Nec_w^{\langle 1, \ldots, n \rangle}$ we have $\langle w, u_1 \rangle \in R_{a_j}$.

Induction step.

Let $\langle w_{i+1}, \langle j_1, \ldots, j_{k'-1} \rangle, [\mathsf{a}_{j_k}]\psi \rangle \in W_{i+1}$ and $\mathcal{M}, w_{i+1} \models \neg[\mathsf{a}_j]\psi$ for some $j, k' \in \{1, \ldots, n\}$.

If $j \in set(\langle j_1, \ldots, j_{k'-1} \rangle)$, then a new object in W_{i+2} is built. There exist $[\mathsf{a}_k]\psi \in \mathrm{Nec}_{w_{i+1}}^{\langle j_1, \ldots, j_{k'-1} \rangle}$ and $\langle u_{i+2}, \langle j_1', \ldots, j_{k''-1}' \rangle, [\mathsf{a}_k]\psi \rangle \in W_{i+2}$ for some $k'' < k'$ such that $\langle w_{i+1}, u_{i+2} \rangle \in R_{\mathsf{a}_k}$ and $\mathcal{M}, u_{i+2} \models \neg\psi$. By the definition of $\mathrm{Nec}_{w_{i+1}}^{\langle j_1, \ldots, j_{k'-1} \rangle}$ and by Lemma 11.2.18(I), we have $R_{\mathsf{a}_k}(w_{i+1}) \subseteq R_{\mathsf{a}_j}(w_{i+1})$ and therefore $\langle w_{i+1}, u_{i+2} \rangle \in R_{\mathsf{a}_j}$. Otherwise, assume $j \notin set(\langle j_1, \ldots, j_{k'-1} \rangle)$, whence $w_{i+1} \neq w$. There exists $\langle u_i, \sigma'.\langle j_{k'}, \ldots, j_k \rangle, tag \rangle \in W_i$ such that $\langle u_i, w_{i+1} \rangle \in R_{\mathsf{a}_{j_k}}$, $set(\sigma') = \{j_1, \ldots, j_{k'-1}\}$, and $|\sigma'| = k' - 1$. We get $R_{\mathsf{a}_{j_k}}(u_i) \subseteq R_{\mathsf{a}_j}(u_i)$ by Lemma 11.2.18(III). Hence, $\langle u_i, w_{i+1} \rangle \in R_{\mathsf{a}_j}$ and therefore $\mathcal{M}, u_i \models \neg[\mathsf{a}_j]\psi$, since R_{a_j} is transitive. By the induction hypothesis, there is an $u \in W'$ such that $\langle u_i, u \rangle \in R_{\mathsf{a}_j}$ and $\mathcal{M}, u \not\models \psi$. Hence, $\langle w_{i+1}, u \rangle \in R_{\mathsf{a}_j}$, since R_{a_j} is an equivalence relation.   *Q.E.D.*

The following theorem provides a bound for the size of the models.

Theorem 11.2.7. *For every LA-logic $\mathcal{L}$, for every formula $\phi \in \mathrm{SAT}(\mathcal{L})$, there exist an $\mathcal{L}$-model $\mathcal{M}$ and a $w \in W$ such that $\mathcal{M}, w \models \phi$ and $\mathrm{card}(W) \leq 1 + n \times \mathrm{mw}(\phi)^n$, where $n = \mathrm{card}(\mathrm{M}_0(\phi))$.*

Proof. (sketch) Assume that there exist $\mathcal{M} = \langle W, (R_\mathsf{a})_{\mathsf{a} \in \mathrm{M}}, m \rangle \in \mathrm{MOD}(\mathcal{L})$ and an object $w \in W$ such that $\mathcal{M}, w \models \phi$. Let $\mathcal{M}'$ be the restriction of $\mathcal{M}$ to W'. We recall that a construction of W' from $\mathcal{M}$ is described at the beginning of Sect. 11.2.4. Since the set of $\mathcal{L}$-models is closed under restriction, $\mathcal{M}'$ is also an $\mathcal{L}$-model. One can show that for every object $u' \in W'$ and for every $\psi \in \mathrm{sub}(\phi)$, $\mathcal{M}, u' \models \psi$ iff $\mathcal{M}', u' \models \psi$. So $\mathcal{M}', u \models \phi$. The proof is by induction on the structure of ψ and if ψ is of the form $[\mathsf{a}]\psi'$, then Lemma 11.2.19 is used in the induction step.   *Q.E.D.*

As a corollary we obtain the following theorem.

Theorem 11.2.8. *Every LA-logic has the finite model property.*

Sufficient conditions for decidability

In the sequel we provide sufficient conditions for proving the decidability of LA-logics. Although every LA-logic has the finite model property and the size of the models can be bounded (see Theorem 11.2.7), this does not imply decidability. The question that needs to be examined is whether a finite structure $\langle W, (R_\mathsf{a})_{\mathsf{a} \in \mathrm{M}}, m \rangle$ is a member of $\mathrm{MOD}(\mathcal{L})$ or at least whether it is a relevant part of a member of $\mathrm{MOD}(\mathcal{L})$ as stated in the following problem.

The *$\mathcal{L}$-completion problem* is defined as follows:

input: a finite subset Y of the set M of modal expressions of the language of $\mathcal{L}$, a structure $\langle W, (R_a)_{a \in Y} \rangle$ such that $W \neq \emptyset$ is finite and for every $a \in Y$, R_a is an equivalence relation on W;

question: is there an $\mathcal{L}$-model $\langle W, (R'_a)_{a \in M}, m \rangle$ such that for every $a \in Y$, $R_a = R'_a$?

Theorem 11.2.9 provides sufficient conditions for the decidability of LA-logics.

Theorem 11.2.9. *For every LA-logic $\mathcal{L}$, if the $\mathcal{L}$-ordering problem and the $\mathcal{L}$-completion problem are decidable, then* $\mathrm{SAT}(\mathcal{L})$ *is decidable.*

Proof. We recall that the $\mathcal{L}$-ordering problem is defined in Sect. 8.4.2. In order to check whether a formula ϕ is $\mathcal{L}$-satisfiable we proceed as follows. By Theorem 11.2.7, $\phi \in \mathrm{SAT}(\mathcal{L})$ iff there exist an $\mathcal{L}$-model $\mathcal{M} = \langle W, (R_a)_{a \in M}, m \rangle$ and a $w \in W$ such that $\mathcal{M}, w \models \phi$ and $\mathrm{card}(W) \leq 1 + n \times \mathrm{mw}(\phi)^n$, where $n = \mathrm{card}(\mathrm{M}_0(\phi))$. We enumerate all the structures $\mathcal{M}' = \langle W, (R_a)_{a \in \mathrm{M}_0(\phi)}, m \rangle$ modulo the isomorphic copies with respect to ϕ (see Definition 6.2.2), where

* $W = \{w_1, \ldots, w_l\}$ is a finite non-empty set such that $l \leq 1 + n \times \mathrm{mw}(\phi)^n$;
* $(R_a)_{a \in \mathrm{M}_0(\phi)}$ is a family of binary relations on W;
* m is a meaning function of $\mathcal{M}$;

and we check whether

(i) $\mathcal{M}', w \models \phi$ for some $w \in W$;
(ii) for all $a, b \in \mathrm{M}_0(\phi)$, R_a and R_b are equivalence relations in local agreement;
(iii) for every $i \in \{1, \ldots, l\}$, there is a linear order $\preceq$ on $\mathrm{M}_0(\phi)$ such that for all $a, b \in \mathrm{M}_0(\phi)$ if $a \preceq b$, then $R_a(w_i) \subseteq R_b(w_i)$ and $\preceq \in \mathrm{lin}(\mathcal{L}) \uparrow \mathrm{M}_0(\phi)$;
(iv) there is an $\mathcal{L}$-model $\mathcal{M} = \langle W, (R'_a)_{a \in M}, m' \rangle$ such that for every $a \in \mathrm{M}_0(\phi)$, $R'_a = R_a$ and the restriction of m' to $\mathrm{FOR}_0(\phi)$ is m.

If (i)–(iv) hold, then the formula $\phi \in \mathrm{SAT}(\mathcal{L})$. It can be observed that the condition (i) can be checked in polynomial-time in $l + |\phi|$ (see Theorem 6.4.5). Condition (ii) can be checked in $\mathcal{O}(n! \times l^5)$ and conditions (iii) and (iv) are instances of decidable problems by the assumption. Since the set of structures $\langle W, (R_a)_{a \in \mathrm{M}_0(\phi)}, m \rangle$ (modulo the isomorphic copies) such that $\mathrm{card}(W) \leq 1 + n \times \mathrm{mw}(\phi)^n$ is finite, the decidability of $\mathrm{SAT}(\mathcal{L})$ follows.   *Q.E.D.*

One can expect that there are LA-logics with a countably infinite set of modal constants that are not decidable. A simple cardinality argument is used. Indeed, there is an uncountable set of linear orders on M_0. So, there is an uncountable set of LA-logics of such a kind. But, there is only a countable set of Turing machines and therefore there is a countable set of decision problems that are decidable. Hence, there is an uncountable set of LA-logics that are undecidable unless the validity problem of any LA-logic is equal to the validity of some decidable LA-logic, which is unlikely.

Example 11.2.1. Let $\mathcal{L}$ be an LA-logic such that $\lin(\mathcal{L})$ is the set of all the linear orders on M. It can be shown that both the $\mathcal{L}$-ordering problem and the $\mathcal{L}$-completion problem are decidable. Then SAT($\mathcal{L}$) is decidable. DALLA' defined in Sect. 8.2 belongs to this class of LA-logics.

Similarly, let $\mathcal{L}'$ be an LA-logic such that $\lin(\mathcal{L}') = \{\preceq\}$ is a singleton and it is decidable whether $\langle a, b \rangle \in \preceq$ for all $a, b \in M$. It can be shown that both the $\mathcal{L}'$-ordering problem and the $\mathcal{L}'$-completion problem are decidable. Then SAT($\mathcal{L}'$) is decidable. LLOM defined in Sect. 8.5 belongs to this class of LA-logics.

Theorem 11.2.10. SAT(DALLA') *is decidable.*

Data analysis logic DALLA

Although DALLA (see Sect. 8.2) is not exactly an LA-logic, there exists a simple transformation from SAT(DALLA) into SAT(DALLA'), where DALLA' is the LA-logic defined in Sect. 8.2.

Lemma 11.2.20. *There is a polynomial-time transformation from the problem* SAT(DALLA) *into the problem* SAT(DALLA').

Proof. Let $g : \mathrm{FOR}(\mathrm{DALLA}) \to \mathrm{FOR}(\mathrm{DALLA})$ be the map such that $g(\phi) \stackrel{\mathrm{def}}{=} \phi$ if no modal operators occur in ϕ, otherwise

$$g(\phi) \stackrel{\mathrm{def}}{=} \phi' \wedge \bigwedge_{\alpha=1}^{l} \bigwedge_{i=1}^{\beta} [c_\alpha](\mathrm{p}_{new}^i \Leftrightarrow \psi^i),$$

where

* $\{\phi^1, \ldots, \phi^\beta\}$ are elements of $\mathrm{sub}(\phi)$ such that for every $i \in \{1, \ldots, \beta\}$, ϕ^i is of the form $[a \oplus b]\psi^i$ for some $\oplus \in \{\cap, \cup^*\}$ and $a, b \in M$, and neither $\cap$ nor $\cup^*$ occurs in ψ^i;
* $M_0(\phi) = \{c_1, \ldots c_l\}$, $l \geq 1$;
* $\mathrm{p}_{new}^1, \ldots, \mathrm{p}_{new}^\beta$ are distinct propositional variables that do not occur in ϕ, $\beta \geq 1$;
* ϕ' is obtained from ϕ by substituting every occurrence of $[a \oplus b]\psi^i$ by $[a]\mathrm{p}_{new}^i \wedge [b]\mathrm{p}_{new}^i$ if $\oplus = \cup^*$ and by $[a]\mathrm{p}_{new}^i \vee [b]\mathrm{p}_{new}^i$ if $\oplus = \cap$.

$g(\phi)$ can be computed in polynomial-time in $|\phi|$ and $\phi \in \mathrm{SAT}(\mathrm{DALLA})$ iff $g(\phi) \in \mathrm{SAT}(\mathrm{DALLA})$. Hence, $\phi \in \mathrm{SAT}(\mathrm{DALLA})$ iff $g^{|\phi|}(\phi) \in \mathrm{SAT}(\mathrm{DALLA})$. $g^{|\phi|}(\phi)$ can be computed in polynomial-time in $|\phi|$ and it is a DALLA'-formula. *Q.E.D.*

As a corollary, we have the following theorem.

Theorem 11.2.11. SAT(DALLA) *is decidable.*

Fuzzy logic of graded modalities

By Theorem 8.5.1, SAT(LGM) = SAT(LLOM). Hence, by Example 11.2.1, we have the following result.

Theorem 11.2.12. SAT(LGM) *and* SAT(LLOM) *are decidable.*

Observe that for all the modal indices λ_1 and λ_2 occurring in $\phi \in$ FOR(LGM), it is decidable whether $\lambda_1 \leq \lambda_2$. We recall that λ_1 and λ_2 are rational numbers represented as pairs of natural numbers in the binary representation.

Although LGM is not an LA-logic (see Theorem 11.2.7), one can prove the following result.

Theorem 11.2.13. *For every* $\phi \in$ SAT(LGM), *there exist an LGM-model and a* $w \in W$ *such that* $\mathcal{M}, w \models \phi$ *and* card$(W) \leq 1 + n \times$ mw$(\phi)^n$, *where* n *is the number of the rational numbers that occur in* ϕ.

11.3 Decidability by Translation

In this section we show how the results of the previous sections enable us to state new decidability results and equivalence between decidability problems for information logics. Actually, this was the original motivation for most of the results of Sect. 10.3 and Sect. 10.6.

11.3.1 Logic LIR of Indiscernibility Relations

The logic LIR is presented in Example 5.4.3. It is a standard Rare-logic in class($\{C_1, C_1'\}$) such that its set of modal operations is $O_M = \{\cap, \cup^*\}$. The local condition for the relations of the LIR-models is being an equivalence relation. The following theorem states a reduction of decidability of SAT(LIR).

Theorem 11.3.1. SAT(LIR) *is decidable iff* SAT(DAL) *is decidable.*

Proof. Since SM*(LIR) is U-simplifiable then, by Theorem 10.4.2(II), the problem SAT(LIR) is decidable iff the problem SAT(SM*(LIR)$^-$) is decidable. By Theorem 10.5.1, VAL(SM*(LIR)) is decidable iff SAT(SM*(LIR)$^-$) is decidable iff the SM(LIR)-consequence problem is decidable. Observe that SM(LIR) is closed under isomorphic copies, disjoint unions, and restrictions. By Lemma 10.5.2, the SM*(LIR)-consequence problem is decidable iff the VAL(SM(LIR)) is decidable iff SAT(SM(LIR)) is decidable. Hence SAT(LIR) is decidable iff SAT(SM(LIR)) is decidable. Moreover, SM(LIR) coincides with the logic DAL.   *Q.E.D.*

Decidability of SAT(DAL) is open, although various attempts to prove such a result can be found in the literature. This fact is rather surprising considering that DAL is similar to various other polymodal logics, among them PDL. It is not difficult to show that if PDL with converse and intersection is decidable, which is commonly conjectured in the literature, then SAT(DAL) is also decidable. By contrast, the logic LIR$'$ obtained from LIR by removing the modal operator $\cup^*$ from its language is decidable. Indeed, SAT(LIR$'$) is decidable iff SAT(SM*(LIR$'$)$^-$) is decidable. However, SAT(SM*(LIR$'$)$^-$) is decidable, since S5$'$ = SM*(LIR$'$)$^-$ and SAT(S5$'$) is decidable, which is shown in Sect. 11.2.3.

Theorem 11.3.2.

(I) SAT(LIR(P$_0^N$)) *is decidable iff* SAT(DAL) *is decidable;*
(II) LIR *has the finite parameter set property.*

Proof. (I) is a consequence of Theorem 10.7.3(I) and Theorem 11.3.1.
(II) is a corollary of Theorem 10.4.2(III).   *Q.E.D.*

11.3.2 Logics for Reasoning about Similarity

Let SIM$'$ be the standard Rare-logic in class($\{C_1, C_1'\}$) that admits both parameter nominals (from a set P$_0^N$) and object nominals (from a set FOR$_0^N$), $O_M = \emptyset$ and the local conditions for the models of SIM$'$ are that their relations are reflexive and symmetric. SIM$'$ has been defined in Sect. 7.4.1.

Theorem 11.3.3. SAT(SIM$'$) *is decidable.*

Proof. Let SIM$''$ be the extension of SIM$'$ obtained by adding $\cap$ to the modal operators and by assuming that it is interpreted as the set intersection.

By Theorem 10.4.2(I), the decidability of SAT(SIM$'$) is equivalent to the decidability of SAT(SM*(SIM$''$)$^-$(FOR$_0^N$)). The modal connectives of SM*(SIM$''$)$^-$ are the universal modal connective [U] and the modal connectives of the form $[c_1 \cap \ldots \cap c_n]$, $n \geq 1$, where for every $i \in \{1, \ldots, n\}$, c_i is a modal constant. Each modal constant c_i is interpreted by a reflexive and symmetric relation. Let ST be the map from SM*(SIM$''$)$^-$(FOR$_0^N$)-formulae into FOL-formulae defined as follows. For every $i \in \{0, 1\}$,

* $ST(\mathrm{p}_j, x_i) \stackrel{\text{def}}{=} P_{2 \times j}(x_i)$ for every propositional variable p_j, $j \geq 0$;
* $ST(\mathrm{x}_j, x_i) \stackrel{\text{def}}{=} P_{2 \times j + 1}(x_i)$ for every object nominal x_j, $j \geq 1$;
* ST is homomorphic with respect to the Boolean connectives;
* $ST([\mathrm{U}]\phi, x_i) \stackrel{\text{def}}{=} \forall x_0\ ST(\phi, x_0)$;
* $ST([c_{i_1} \cap \ldots \cap c_{i_n}]\phi, x_i) \stackrel{\text{def}}{=} \forall x_{1-i}\ (R_{i_1}(x_i, x_{1-i}) \wedge \ldots \wedge R_{i_n}(x_i, x_{1-i})) \Rightarrow ST(\phi, x_{1-i})$, $i_1, \ldots, i_n \geq 0$.

For every $SM^*(SIM')^-(FOR_0^N)$-formula ϕ, $ST(\phi, x_i)$ belongs to FOL_2, the fragment of classical logic with two individual variables, identity and no function symbols.

Let ϕ be a $SM^*(SIM'')^-(FOR_0^N)$-formula with $FOR_0^N(\phi) = \{x_1, \ldots, x_l\}$, $l \geq 1$, and $M_0(\phi) = \{c_1, \ldots, c_m\}$, $m \geq 1$. Let ϕ_0 be the FOL_2-formula expressing that for every $k \in \{1, \ldots, m\}$, R_k is interpreted as a reflexive and symmetric binary relation. Let ϕ_1 be the FOL_2-formula expressing that for every $k \in \{1, \ldots, l\}$, the unary predicate symbol $P_{2 \times k+1}$ is interpreted as a singleton, for instance

$$\bigwedge_{k=1}^{l} \exists x_0 \ (P_{2 \times k+1}(x_0) \wedge (\forall x_1 \neg(x_0 = x_1) \Rightarrow \neg P_{2 \times k+1}(x_1))).$$

If $l = 0$ [resp. $m = 0$], then $\phi_0 \stackrel{\text{def}}{=} \top$ [resp. $\phi_1 \stackrel{\text{def}}{=} \top$]. One can show that $\phi \in SAT(SM^*(SIM'')^-(FOR_0^N))$ iff $\phi_0 \wedge \phi_1 \wedge \exists x_0 \ ST(\phi, x_0)$ is FOL_2-satisfiable. Since FOL_2-satisfiability is decidable (see Theorem 6.4.4(I)), $SAT(SIM')$ is decidable.   Q.E.D.

Let us consider the decidability status of $SAT(SIM)$.

Theorem 11.3.4. $SAT(SIM)$ *is decidable.*

Proof. In the proof we distinguish two cases (I) PAR finite and (II) PAR countably infinite.
(I) Assume that PAR is finite. Without any loss of generality we may assume that $PAR = \{1, \ldots, \alpha\}$ for some $\alpha \geq 1$ and $VARP = \{E_1, \ldots, E_\alpha\}$. Let ϕ be a SIM-formula such that:

* $VARP(\phi) = \{E_{i_1}, \ldots, E_{i_l}\}$ with $i_1, \ldots, i_l \in \{1, \ldots, \alpha\}$, $l \geq 1$;
* $VARSP(\phi) = \{C_{j_1}, \ldots, C_{j_n}\}$ with $j_1, \ldots, j_n \in \mathbb{N}$, $n \geq 1$.

For every P-meaning function m of a SIM-model, we define a parameter expression $N(m, A)$ for every $A \in P(\phi)$, and a formula $N(m, \phi)$ as follows:

* if $m(A) = \{k_1, \ldots, k_s\} \subseteq PAR$, then $N(m, A) \stackrel{\text{def}}{=} E_{k_1} \cup \ldots \cup E_{k_s}$, $s \geq 1$;
* if $m(A) = \emptyset$, then $N(m, A) \stackrel{\text{def}}{=} \bot$;
* $N(m, \phi)$ is the formula obtained from ϕ by replacing every occurrence of A by $N(m, A)$.

We define a finite set

$$X_\phi \stackrel{\text{def}}{=} \{m_{|P(\phi)} : m \text{ is a meaning function from some SIM -model}\}.$$

$N(f, \phi)$ is defined in the natural way for every $f \in X_\phi$. We show that for every SIM-formula ϕ, the following conditions are equivalent:

(i) ϕ is SIM-satisfiable;
(ii) $\bigvee_{f \in X_\phi} N(f, \phi)$ is SIM'-satisfiable.

(i) $\rightarrow$ (ii) Assume there exist a SIM-model $\mathcal{M} = \langle W, (\sigma_P)_{P \subseteq PAR}, m \rangle$ and a $w_0 \in W$ such that $\mathcal{M}, w_0 \models \phi$. Let $\mathcal{M}' = \langle W, (\sigma_P)_{P \subseteq PAR}, m' \rangle$ be the SIM'-model such that for every $i \in \{1, \ldots, \alpha\}$, $m'(E_i) \stackrel{\text{def}}{=} \{i\}$, for every $p \in FOR_0$, $m'(p) \stackrel{\text{def}}{=} m(p)$ and for every $C \in P_0$, $m'(C) \stackrel{\text{def}}{=} m(C)$. It is easy to check that $\mathcal{M}', w_0 \models N(m, \phi)$. Let $\mathcal{M}'' = \langle W, (\sigma_P'')_{P \subseteq \mathbb{N}}, m'' \rangle$ be a SIM'-model such that

* m' and m'' coincide on the common sublanguage of SIM' and SIM (LAN(SIM') is LAN(SIM) augmented with $\{E_i : i > \alpha\}$);
* for every $i > \alpha$, $m''(E_i) \stackrel{\text{def}}{=} \{i\}$;
* for every $P \subseteq \mathbb{N}$, $\sigma_P'' \stackrel{\text{def}}{=} \sigma_{P \cap PAR}$.

It is a routine task to check that $\mathcal{M}'', w_0 \models N(m, \phi)$ and therefore $\mathcal{M}'', w_0 \models \bigvee_{f \in X_\phi} N(f, \phi)$. Indeed, for every $A \in P(\phi)$, we have $\sigma_{m(A)} = \sigma_{m''(N(f,A))}''$.

(ii) $\rightarrow$ (i) Assume $\bigvee_{f \in X_\phi} N(f, \phi)$ is SIM'-satisfiable. There exist a SIM'-model $\mathcal{M}' = \langle W', (\sigma_P')_{P \subseteq PAR'}, m' \rangle$, a $w_0 \in W'$, and an $f_0 \in X_\phi$ such that $\mathcal{M}', w_0 \models N(f_0, \phi)$.

By the proof of Theorem 10.7.1, we can assume that $\{u_1, \ldots, u_\alpha\}$ is relevant for $\mathcal{M}'$ and for every $i \in \{1, \ldots, \alpha\}$, $m'(E_i) = u_i$. Indeed, PAR' is at least countable, $VARSP(\bigvee_{f \in X_\phi} N(f, \phi)) = \emptyset$, and the cardinality of $VARP(\bigvee_{f \in X_\phi} N(f, \phi))$ is at most α, since $VARP(\bigvee_{f \in X_\phi} N(f, \phi))$ is a subset of $\{E_1, \ldots, E_\alpha\}$. Let $\mathcal{M} = \langle W', PAR, (\sigma_P)_{P \subseteq PAR}, m \rangle$ be the SIM-model such that:

* m and f_0 coincide on P_0 and FOR_0, and for every $i \in \{1, \ldots, \alpha\}$, $m(E_i) \stackrel{\text{def}}{=} f_0(E_i)$;
* for every $P \subseteq PAR$, $\sigma_P \stackrel{\text{def}}{=} \sigma_{\{u_i : i \in P\}}'$.

It is a routine task to check that $\mathcal{M}, w_0 \models \phi$, since for every $A \in P(\phi)$, $\sigma_{m(A)} = \sigma_{m'(N(f_0,A))}'$.

(II) Assume PAR is countably infinite, that is there is a bijection f from $\mathbb{N}$ into PAR. Without any loss of generality we may assume that $PAR = \mathbb{N}$. The proof of Theorem 10.7.1 allows to conclude that the following statements are equivalent:

* ϕ is SIM-satisfiable;
* ϕ is SIM'-satisfiable.

$Q.E.D.$

A nice corollary of the above proof is the following.

Corollary 11.3.1. *The Rasiowa–Sikorski-style proof system RS(SIM), in the case of PAR infinite, is complete for the logic SIM'.*

11.4 Notes

Decidability of NIL. In this chapter we presented a self-contained proof of decidability of NIL by the method of finite models based on [Vak96]. A simpler decidability proof is obtained by translation into PDL with converse. Let f be the logarithmic space map from NIL-satisfiability into PDL-satisfiability defined as follows:

* $f(\mathrm{p}) = \mathrm{p}$ for every propositional variable p;
* f is homomorphic with respect to the Boolean connectives;
* $f([\sigma]\phi) \stackrel{\text{def}}{=} [(c_2^{-1})^*; (c_1 \cup c_1^{-1} \cup id); c_2^*]f(\phi);$
* $f([\leq]\phi) \stackrel{\text{def}}{=} [c_2^*]f(\phi);$
* $f([\geq]\phi) \stackrel{\text{def}}{=} [(c_2^{-1})^*]f(\phi).$

One can show that ϕ is NIL-satisfiable iff $f(\phi)$ is PDL-satisfiable. Hence, NIL-satisfiability is in **EXPTIME**, since PDL with converse is in **EXPTIME** (Theorem 6.4.3(I)). To be precise, we use a version of PDL with converse and test that is known to be **EXPTIME**-complete [FL79, Pra79].

Decidability of IL. The filtration construction for IL is due to [Vak96].

Restriction construction. The restriction construction for LA-logics is introduced in [Dem96b, Dem98]. It generalises the construction defined in [Lad77] (see also [HM92]) for the modal logic S5. The proof of Theorem 11.2.7 follows the lines of the proof of [Lad77, Lemma 6.1].

Decidability of SIM. A proof similar to that presented in Sect. 11.3.2 is described in [DK98]. It uses a direct translation from SIM' into FOL_2 obtained from the standard relational translation [Ben85] by extending it to a language with nominals [GG93].

Open problems. Although both PDL with intersection and PDL with converse have a decidable validity problem (see Sect. 6.5), as far as we know, it is an open problem whether PDL with intersection and converse is decidable. Decidability of PDL with intersection and converse would entail that SAT(DAL) is decidable. However, satisfiability of DAL without $\cup^*$ is decidable by decidability of S5' and DAL without $\cap$ is decidable by decidability of PDL with converse. Indeed, every equivalence relation can be represented by the program expression of the form $(c \cup c^{-1})^*$ (see [FL79, Sect. 5]). A way to prove decidability of DAL would be to translate it into a decidable guarded fragment of FOL_2 augmented with operators which are not first-order definable. The form of that hypothetical fragment has still to be defined. However, in [GO99] it is already shown that the guarded fragment of classical logic with only two individual variables, no function symbols, and four equivalence relations is undecidable. An attempt to prove the decidability of DAL can be found in [AT89]. Unfortunately, the logic which is shown to be decidable there is different from DAL.

12. Complexity of Information Logics

12.1 Introduction and Outline of the Chapter

In this chapter we study the computational complexity of logics presented in the previous chapters. Most of the results concern the complexity upper bounds. For each complexity analysis we present a different proof technique, thus providing a useful toolkit for investigating the complexity of other information logics. Although the general principles of the techniques in complexity theory for modal logics are standard, the peculiarity of the information logics under consideration leads to substantial modifications of known techniques. In order to be able to deal with more involved logics, we have to develop various extensions of the known methods.

In Sect. 12.2 we show that the satisfiability of the logic IND requires only linear time. The proof employs a natural model-checking algorithm. Sect. 12.3 presents sufficient conditions for **NP**-completeness of some LA-logics. In Sect. 12.4 we prove the **NP**-completeness of the BLKO-satisfiability problem. The proof uses a construction of restriction of models presented in Sect. 6.2.2. In Sect. 12.5 we investigate the complexity of the logic NIL. By using a Ladner-like algorithm we prove that the NIL-satisfiability problem is in **PSPACE**, and the **PSPACE** lower bound is established by reducing the NIL-satisfiability problem to the S4-satisfiability problem. In Sect. 12.6 we show that the S5'-satisfiability problem is **EXPTIME**-complete. The complexity upper bound is obtained by adapting the respective proof for propositional dynamic logic. Using the translation from formulae of LKO to formulae of S5' presented in Sect. 9.4.2 we also conclude that the LKO-satisfiability problem is **EXPTIME**-complete. This is the subject of Sect. 12.7. Sect. 12.8 outlines complexity bounds for some other information logics. In particular, we mention that the logics DALLA and LGM are **PSPACE**-complete and IL-satisfiability is **PSPACE**-hard and in **NEXPTIME**.

12.2 IND-satisfiability is in LIN

In this section we consider the logic IND presented in Sect. 8.3 and we show that SAT(IND) can be solved in linear-time. This should not come as a surprise, since the set of IND-models is finite modulo isomorphic copies. The following theorem uses a simple model-checking algorithm involving the finite set of IND-models.

Theorem 12.2.1. SAT(IND) *is in* **LIN**.

Proof. The key property of the logic IND is that it has a finite set of models modulo the isomorphic copies. Two IND-models $\langle W, PAR, (\equiv_P)_{P \subseteq PAR}, m \rangle$ and $\langle W', PAR', (\equiv'_P)_{P \subseteq PAR'}, m' \rangle$ are isomorphic $\overset{\text{def}}{\Leftrightarrow}$ there are 1–1 mappings $f_1 : W \to W'$ and $f_2 : PAR \to PAR'$ such that:

★ for every $P \subseteq PAR$, $\equiv'_P = \{\langle f_1(x), f_1(x') \rangle : \langle x, x' \rangle \in \equiv_P\}$;
★ for every parameter nominal E_i, $i \in \{1, \ldots, M\}$, $m'(\mathrm{E}_i) = f_2(m(\mathrm{E}_i))$;
★ for every object nominal x_i, $i \in \{1, \ldots, N\}$, $m'(\mathrm{x}_i) = f_1(m(\mathrm{x}_i))$.

Let $\mathcal{M}_1, \mathcal{M}_2, \ldots$ be an enumeration of all the IND-models modulo isomorphic copies. Let K be the following natural number:

$$K \overset{\text{def}}{=} (2^{N^2})^{2^M} \times N! \times M!$$

K is a constant of the logic IND and we can show that any enumeration of IND-models contains at most K IND-models. 2^M is the number of binary relations of any IND-model and $2^{N \times N}$ is the number of different binary relations on a set of cardinality N. $N!$ is the number of different assignments for VARE whereas $M!$ is the number of different assignments for VARP. Let ϕ be a formula whose IND-satisfiability is in question. For every $i \in \{1, \ldots, K\}$, checking whether $\mathcal{M}_i$ has an object x such that $\mathcal{M}_i, x \models \phi$ can be done in time $\mathcal{O}(|\phi|)$. Actually it requires time in $\mathcal{O}(N^2 \times |\phi|)$ (see Theorem 6.4.5) but N is a constant of the logic IND. So checking whether ϕ is IND-satisfiable can be done in time $\mathcal{O}(N \times K \times |\phi|)$. *Q.E.D.*

Consequently, VAL(IND) is also in **LIN**. In spite of this low worst-case complexity measure, axiomatising the logic IND is not a trivial task, since it is a Rare-logic with object nominals and the universal modal connective.

12.3 NP-complete LA-logics

In this section we show how the results of Sect. 11.2.4 lead to the characterisation of the complexity of LA-logics. The complexity upper bound **NP** for these logics is proved by using a finite model property argument.

The complexity of LA-logics whose set of modal expressions is finite is characterised in the following theorem.

Theorem 12.3.1. *Let $\mathcal{L}$ be an LA-logic such that its set* M *of modal expressions is finite. Then:*

(I) the $\mathcal{L}$-ordering problem is in **P***;*

(II) for every LAN($\mathcal{L}$)-*model* $\mathcal{M} = \langle W, (R_a)_{a \in M}, m \rangle$ *such that* W *is finite, one can check that* $\mathcal{M} \in \text{MOD}(\mathcal{L})$ *in polynomial-time in* $\text{card}(W)$;
(III) SAT($\mathcal{L}$) *is* **NP**-*complete*.

Proof. (I) Immediate by definition of an $\mathcal{L}$-ordering problem.
(II) Simple calculations lead to the conclusion that $\mathcal{M} \in \text{MOD}(\mathcal{L})$ can be checked in $\mathcal{O}(\text{card}(M)! \times \text{card}(W)^5)$.
(III) A direct consequence of Theorem 11.2.7 and (II).   *Q.E.D.*

For the sake of comparison, it is known that for every $k \geq 2$, the satisfiability problem for the multi-modal logics $S5_k$ is **PSPACE**-complete. It means that adding the local agreement condition to $S5_k$ decreases its complexity, unless **NP** = **PSPACE**.

Corollary 12.3.1. *For* $\mathcal{L} \in \{\text{LGM}, \text{LGM}', \text{DALLA}, \text{DALLA}'\}$ *and for every* $k \geq 1$, SAT($\mathcal{L}$) $\cap \{\phi \in \text{FOR}(\mathcal{L}) : \text{card}(M(\phi)) \leq k\}$ *is* **NP**-*complete*.

12.4 BLKO-satisfiability is NP-complete

In this section we consider the logic BLKO defined in Sect. 9.2 and we show that SAT(BLKO) is **NP**-complete. Unfortunately, it is not possible to use straightforwardly the translation f from Sect. 9.2.3 and the fact that SAT(S5) is **NP**-complete, because the function f may exponentially increase the size of the formulae (in particular the modal weight). A polynomial-time transformation can be easily defined by renaming of subformulae. This leads to the fact that BLKO-satisfiability is in **NP**. We present an alternative proof of the finite model property of BLKO together with a bound on the size of the models. As far as the modal logic S5 is concerned, if $\phi \in \text{SAT}(S5)$, then ϕ has an S5-model with at most $\text{mw}(\phi) + 1$ elements (see Example 6.2.2). We shall prove a similar result for BLKO.

Lemma 12.4.1. *For every BLKO-formula* ϕ, $\phi \in \text{SAT}(\text{BLKO})$ *iff there are an BLKO-model* $\mathcal{M} = \langle W, R, m \rangle$ *and a* $w \in W$ *such that* $\mathcal{M}, w \models \phi$ *and* $\text{card}(W) \leq \text{mw}(\phi) + 1$.

Proof. Assume that there are a BLKO-model $\mathcal{M} = \langle W, R, m \rangle$ and a $w \in W$ such that $\mathcal{M}, w \models \phi$. Without any loss of generality we may assume that $R = W \times W$, since $\mathcal{M}_{|R(w)}$ is also an BLKO-model and $\mathcal{M}_{|R(w)}, w \models \phi$. We define

$$\text{Witnesses} \overset{\text{def}}{=} \{K\psi \mid K\psi \in \text{sub}(\phi), \mathcal{M}, w \not\models K\psi\}.$$

For every $K\psi \in \text{Witnesses}$, there exist w_ψ^1 and w_ψ^2 such that $\mathcal{M}, w_\psi^1 \models \psi$ and $\mathcal{M}, w_\psi^2 \models \neg\psi$. Since either $\mathcal{M}, w \models \psi$ or $\mathcal{M}, w \models \neg\psi$, we have $w \in \{w_\psi^1, w_\psi^2\}$. Let $\mathcal{M}' = \langle W', R', m' \rangle$ be the BLKO-model such that $\mathcal{M}' \overset{\text{def}}{=} \mathcal{M}_{|W'}$ with

$$W' \overset{\text{def}}{=} \{w\} \cup \{w_\psi^1 : K\psi \in \text{Witnesses}\} \cup \{w_\psi^2 : K\psi \in \text{Witnesses}\}.$$

Observe that card$(W') \leq$ mw$(\phi) + 1$. By induction on the structure of ψ, we can easily show that for every $w' \in W'$ and for every $\psi \in$ sub(ϕ), $\mathcal{M}, w' \models \psi$ iff $\mathcal{M}', w' \models \psi$. $Q.E.D.$

Theorem 12.4.1. SAT(BLKO) *is* **NP***-complete.*

As mentioned previously, **NP**-completeness of SAT(BLKO) can be alternatively established by defining a polynomial-time transformation from SAT(BLKO) into SAT(S5) (for the **NP**-easy part), making appropriate renamings. However, the bound on the size of the models cannot be established in that way.

12.5 NIL-satisfiability is PSPACE-complete

12.5.1 Preliminary Results

In this section we consider the logic NIL defined in Sect. 7.2. First, we need to introduce some notation. For every a $\in \{\sigma, \leq, \geq\}$, the formula $[a]^i \phi$ is inductively defined as follows: $[a]^0 \phi = \phi$ and $[a]^{i+1} \phi = [a][a]^i \phi$ for $i \geq 1$. For every $s \in \{[\leq], [\geq], [\sigma]\}^*$, an s-formula is a formula prefixed by s. For instance, $[\sigma][\leq][\geq]p_0$ is a $[\sigma][\leq]$-formula.

Observe also that in every NIL-model, we have $(R_{\leq} \cup R_{\geq}) \subseteq R_{\sigma}$. Condition (N4) is mainly responsible for the difficulty in showing that NIL satisfiability is in **PSPACE**. The conditions (N2) and (N4) from the definition of the NIL-models can be equivalently replaced by the following conditions:

(N2') the relation $R_{\geq}$ is reflexive and transitive;
(N4') if $\langle x, y \rangle \in R_{\sigma}$ and $\langle y, y' \rangle \in R_{\leq}$, then $\langle x, y' \rangle \in R_{\sigma}$.

Condition (N4') can be understood as a pseudo-transitivity condition involving two binary relations. Due to the transitivity of $R_{\leq}$ and $R_{\geq}$, the algorithm for solving NIL-satisfiability requires a mechanism for detecting cycles. Moreover, a complexity lower bound can be easily established, since NIL is an extension of S4.

Theorem 12.5.1. SAT(NIL) *is logarithmic space hard in* **PSPACE***.*

Proof. Let X be the set of NIL-satisfiable formulae ϕ such that neither $[\sigma]$ nor $[\geq]$ occurs in ϕ. We shall show that X is the set of S4-satisfiable formulae modulo the replacement of $[\leq]$ by the standard modal connective $\square$. Since SAT(S4) is logarithmic space hard in **PSPACE** (see Theorem 6.4.2), so is SAT(NIL). If $\phi \in X$, then ϕ is S4-satisfiable, since by removing from a NIL-model the components R_{σ} and $R_{\geq}$ we get an S4-model. Moreover, if ϕ is S4-satisfiable, then there exist an S4-model $\mathcal{M} = \langle W, R, m \rangle$ and a $w \in W$ satisfying $\mathcal{M}, w \models \phi$. Let $\mathcal{M}' = \langle W, R_{\leq}, R_{\geq}, R_{\sigma}, m \rangle$ be a NIL-model such that $R_{\leq} \stackrel{\text{def}}{=} R$, $R_{\geq} \stackrel{\text{def}}{=} R^{-1}$, and $R_{\sigma} \stackrel{\text{def}}{=} W \times W$. Obviously, $\mathcal{M}', w \models \phi$ (modulo the replacement of $[\leq]$ by $\square$) and $\mathcal{M}'$ is indeed a NIL-model. $Q.E.D.$

In the proof of Theorem 12.5.1, we work at the level of Kripke-style structures. However, it can also be interpreted at the level of information systems. Indeed, let $S = \langle OB, AT \rangle$ and $S' = \langle OB, AT' \rangle$ be total information systems such that:

* $AT' \stackrel{\text{def}}{=} \{a' : a \in AT\}$;
* for every $a' \in AT'$, $VAL_{a'} \stackrel{\text{def}}{=} VAL_a \cup \{Dummy\}$ with $Dummy \notin \bigcup\{VAL_a : a \in AT\}$;
* for every $a' \in AT'$ and $x \in OB$, $a'(x) \stackrel{\text{def}}{=} a(x) \cup \{Dummy\}$.

One can check that $fin(AT) = fin(AT')$ and $sim(AT') = OB \times OB$, that is the S4-frame $\langle OB, fin(AT) \rangle$ can be extended to the NIL-frame

$$\langle OB, fin(AT'), bin(AT'), sim(AT') \rangle,$$

where $sim(AT')$ is the universal relation $OB \times OB$.

Results from the literature easily entail the following theorem.

Theorem 12.5.2.

*(I) For every $a \in \{\leq, \geq, \sigma\}$, the fragment of NIL with a single modal connective [a] has a **PSPACE**-complete satisfiability problem.*

*(II) The fragment of NIL without the connective $[\sigma]$ has a **PSPACE**-complete satisfiability problem.*

It remains to show that NIL-satisfiability of formulae with the three modal connectives $[\leq]$, $[\geq]$, and $[\sigma]$ living together and interacting is in **PSPACE**. It is worth mentioning that interactions between modal connectives can lead to an increase of computational complexity. K-satisfiability and S5-satisfiability are in **PSPACE** and in **NP**, respectively (see Theorem 6.4.2(III) and Theorem 6.4.1(I)). However, the bimodal logic with an S5 modal connective [1] and with a K modal connective [2] such that $[1]\phi \Rightarrow [2]\phi$ is an additional axiom has an **EXPTIME**-hard satisfiability problem (see Theorem 6.4.3(II)). It is well known that the axiom $[1]\phi \Rightarrow [2]\phi$ corresponds to the semantic condition $R_2 \subseteq R_1$, where R_i is the accessibility relation associated to the modal connective $[i]$, $i = 1, 2$.

In Definition 12.5.1 we introduce a closure operator for sets of NIL-formulae similar to the one presented in Definition 11.2.1. However, the two operators are incomparable as they serve different purposes.

Definition 12.5.1. *Let X be a set of NIL-formulae. $\mathrm{cl}(X)$ is the smallest set of formulae such that:*

* $X \subseteq \mathrm{cl}(X)$;
* *if $\neg\phi \in \mathrm{cl}(X)$, then $\phi \in \mathrm{cl}(X)$;*
* *if $\phi_1 \wedge \phi_2 \in \mathrm{cl}(X)$, then $\phi_1, \phi_2 \in \mathrm{cl}(X)$;*
* *if $[\leq]\phi \in \mathrm{cl}(X)$, then $\phi \in \mathrm{cl}(X)$;*
* *if $[\geq]\phi \in \mathrm{cl}(X)$, then $\phi \in \mathrm{cl}(X)$;*

⋆ *if* $[\sigma]\phi \in \mathrm{cl}(X)$, *then* $[\geq]\phi \in \mathrm{cl}(X)$;
⋆ *if* $[\sigma]\phi \in \mathrm{cl}(X)$ *and* ϕ *is not a* $[\leq]$-*formula, then* $[\sigma][\leq]\phi \in \mathrm{cl}(X)$;
⋆ *if* $[\sigma][\leq]\phi \in \mathrm{cl}(X)$, *then* $[\sigma]\phi \in \mathrm{cl}(X)$.

Consequently, if $[\sigma]\phi \in \mathrm{cl}(X)$ and ϕ is not a $[\leq]$-formula, then $[\leq]\phi \in \mathrm{cl}(X)$ and if $[\sigma]\phi \in \mathrm{cl}(X)$, then $\phi \in \mathrm{cl}(X)$. A set X of formulae is said to be *closed* $\overset{\text{def}}{\Leftrightarrow}$ $\mathrm{cl}(X) = X$. For every finite set X of formulae, we have $\mathrm{md}(\mathrm{cl}(X)) \leq \mathrm{md}(X) + 1$, where the modal degree md is defined in Sect. 5.3.1. Moreover, for every formula ϕ, $\mathrm{md}([\leq]\phi) = \mathrm{md}([\geq]\phi) = \mathrm{md}(\mathrm{cl}(\{[\leq]\phi\})) = \mathrm{md}(\mathrm{cl}(\{[\geq]\phi\}))$.

Lemma 12.5.1. *For every NIL-formula* ϕ, $\mathrm{card}(\mathrm{cl}(\{\phi\})) < 5 \times |\phi|$.

Proof. Let $\mathrm{sub}(\phi)$ be the set of subformulae of the formula ϕ. Obviously, $\mathrm{sub}(\phi) \subseteq \mathrm{cl}(\{\phi\})$. Moreover, $\mathrm{cl}(\{\phi\})$ is the union of the following sets:

(1) $\mathrm{sub}(\phi)$;
(2) $\{[\geq]\psi : [\sigma]\psi \in \mathrm{sub}(\phi)\}$;
(3) $\{[\geq]\psi : [\sigma][\leq]^n\psi \in \mathrm{sub}(\phi), n \geq 1\}$;
(4) $\{[\geq][\leq]\psi : [\sigma]\psi \in \mathrm{sub}(\phi), \psi \neq [\leq]\psi'\}$;
(5) $\{[\sigma][\leq]\psi : [\sigma]\psi \in \mathrm{sub}(\phi), \psi \neq [\leq]\psi'\}$;
(6) $\{[\sigma]\psi : [\sigma][\leq]^n\psi \in \mathrm{sub}(\phi), n \geq 1\}$;
(7) $\{[\leq]\psi : [\sigma]\psi \in \mathrm{sub}(\phi), \psi \neq [\leq]\psi'\}$.

Each of the above sets is of the cardinality at most $\mathrm{card}(\mathrm{sub}(\phi))$ and every formula in $\mathrm{sub}(\phi)$ can generate at most four formulae in $\mathrm{cl}(\{\phi\})$. So $\mathrm{card}(\mathrm{cl}(\{\phi\})) < 5 \times |\phi|$, since $\mathrm{card}(\mathrm{sub}(\phi)) < |\phi|$.   *Q.E.D.*

In order to determine the NIL-satisfiability of a formula ϕ, we need to handle sets of formulae. All those sets shall be subsets of $\mathrm{cl}(\{\phi\})$. In establishing the **PSPACE** complexity upper bound, the fact that $\mathrm{cl}(\{\phi\})$ is finite and its cardinality is linear in the size of ϕ plays an important role.

In order to check whether $\phi \in \mathrm{SAT}(\mathrm{NIL})$, we build sequences of the form (i) $X_0\ x_0\ X_1\ x_1\ X_2\ x_2 \ldots$, where $\phi \in X_0 \subseteq \mathrm{cl}(\{\phi\})$, for every $i \in \mathbb{N}$, X_i is a subset of $\mathrm{cl}(\{\phi\})$, and $x_i \in \{\sigma, \leq, \geq\}$. We extend a finite sequence $X_0\ x_0\ X_1 x_1 \ldots x_{i-1}X_i$ with $x_i X_{i+1}$ whenever we need a witness of $[x_i]\psi \notin X_i$ for some formula ψ such that $\psi \notin X_{i+1}$. The intention is to build a tree-like skeleton of some NIL-model $\mathcal{M} = \langle W, R_<, R_>, R_\sigma, m \rangle$ such that for every $i \in \mathbb{N}$, there is a $w_i \in W$ such that $\mathcal{M}, w_i \models \psi$ iff $\psi \in X_i$ and $\langle w_i, w_{i+1} \rangle \in R_{x_i}$. This, roughly, corresponds to the exploration of a branch in the depth-first proof search in a tableaux-style calculus.

In order to establish termination of the process of building a sequence of the form (i) which is a necessary step for obtaining the **PSPACE** complexity upper bound, we define subsets $\mathrm{cl}(s, \phi) \subseteq \mathrm{cl}(\{\phi\})$ for $s \in \{\sigma, \leq, \geq\}^*$ such that for every $i \in \mathbb{N}$,

$$X_i \subseteq \mathrm{cl}(x_0 \ldots x_{i-1}, \phi).$$

For every $s \in \{\sigma, \leq, \geq\}^*$ and for every $x \in \{\sigma, \leq, \geq\}$, $\mathrm{cl}(s \cdot x, \phi)$ contains all the formulae $\psi \in \mathrm{cl}(x_0 \ldots x_{i-1}, \phi)$ which could possibly be put into X_{i+1}.

The process will terminate if there is a computable map $f : \mathbb{N} \to \mathbb{N}$ such that if $|s| \geq f(|\phi|)$, then $\mathrm{cl}(s, \phi) = \emptyset$. To establish the **PSPACE** complexity upper bound, f should preferably be bounded by a polynomial in the size of the tested formula ϕ. Those general principles may look quite attractive but in concrete examples of modal logics they are seldom sufficient to show that the satisfiability problem is in **PSPACE**. In NIL, since transitivity of $R_\leq$ is assumed, if $[\leq]\psi \in X_i$, then $\mathcal{M}, w_i \models [\leq]\psi$ and $\mathcal{M}, w_i \models [\leq][\leq]\psi$, and therefore one can expect that $[\leq]\psi \in X_{i+1}$ if $x_i = \leq$. However, this does not guarantee termination. The duplicates can be identified in $X_0 \, x_0 \, X_1 \, x_1 \, X_2 \, x_2 \ldots$ which corresponds to a cycle detection. Since $\mathrm{card}(\mathcal{P}(\mathrm{cl}(\{\phi\})))$ is in $\mathcal{O}(2^{|\phi|})$, a finer analysis is necessary for establishing the **PSPACE** complexity upper bound. Furthermore, by condition (N4), if $[\sigma]\psi \in X_i$, then $\mathcal{M}, w_i \models [\sigma]\psi$ and $\mathcal{M}, w_i \models [\geq]^n[\sigma][\leq]^{n'}\psi$ for all $n, n' \in \mathbb{N}$. One can expect that $[\geq]^{n-1}[\sigma][\leq]^{n'}\psi \in X_{i+1}$ if $x_i = \geq$ and $n \geq 1$. But even this is not sufficient for termination and we shall also provide a technical answer to this problem. We omit at this stage the complications caused by having a symmetric relation in the NIL-models.

In order to conclude this introductory part that motivates the introduction of the sets of the form $\mathrm{cl}(s, \phi)$, we only say that once X_i is built and x_i is chosen, X_{i+1} satisfies:

⋆ X_{i+1} is a consistent subset of $\mathrm{cl}(x_0 \ldots x_i, \phi)$;
⋆ $\langle X_i, X_{i+1} \rangle$ satisfies a certain condition (to be specified in the sequel) that shall guarantee that $\mathcal{M}$ is a NIL-model and $\langle w_i, w_{i+1} \rangle \in R_{x_i}$.

Definition 12.5.2. *For every formula ϕ, and for every $s \in \{\sigma, \leq, \geq\}^*$, $\mathrm{cl}(s, \phi)$ is the smallest set such that:*

(1) $\mathrm{cl}(\lambda, \phi) = \mathrm{cl}(\{\phi\})$;
(2) $\mathrm{cl}(s, \phi)$ is closed;
(3) if $[\sigma][\leq]\psi \in \mathrm{cl}(s, \phi)$, then $[\leq]\psi \in \mathrm{cl}(s \cdot \sigma, \phi)$;
(4) if $[\leq]\psi \in \mathrm{cl}(s, \phi)$, then $[\leq]\psi \in \mathrm{cl}(s \cdot \leq, \phi)$;
(5) if $[\geq]\psi \in \mathrm{cl}(s, \phi)$, then $[\geq]\psi \in \mathrm{cl}(s \cdot \geq, \phi)$;
(6) if $[\sigma][\leq]\psi \in \mathrm{cl}(s, \phi)$, then $[\sigma][\leq]\psi \in \mathrm{cl}(s \cdot \geq, \phi)$.

Example 12.5.1. Let $\phi = [\sigma]p_0$. We have:

⋆ $\mathrm{cl}(\lambda, \phi) = \mathrm{cl}(\{\phi\}) = \{[\sigma]p_0, p_0, [\geq]p_0, [\sigma][\leq]p_0, [\geq][\leq]p_0, [\leq]p_0\}$;
⋆ $\mathrm{cl}(\geq, \phi) = \mathrm{cl}(\{\phi\})$;
⋆ $\mathrm{cl}(\geq \cdot \sigma, \phi) = \{p_0, [\leq]p_0\}$;
⋆ $\mathrm{cl}(\geq \cdot \sigma \cdot \leq, \phi) = \{p_0, [\leq]p_0\}$;
⋆ $\mathrm{cl}(\geq \cdot \sigma \cdot \leq \cdot \geq, \phi) = \emptyset$.

One can check that for every $s \in \{\sigma, \geq, \leq\}^*$ such that $|s| \geq 4$, we have $\mathrm{cl}(s, \phi) = \emptyset$.

Lemma 12.5.2 states some basic properties of the sets $cl(s, \phi)$.

Lemma 12.5.2. *For every NIL-formula ϕ and for all $s, s' \in \{\sigma, \leq, \geq\}^*$, the following hold:*

(I) if s is a prefix of s', then $cl(s', \phi) \subseteq cl(s, \phi)$;
(II) if $[\sigma]\psi \in cl(s, \phi)$, then $\psi \in cl(s \cdot \sigma, \phi)$;
(III) if $[\sigma]\psi \in cl(s, \phi)$, then $[\sigma]\psi \in cl(s \cdot \geq, \phi)$;
(IV) if $[\leq]\psi \in cl(s \cdot \geq, \phi)$, then $md([\leq]\psi) < md(cl(s \cdot \geq, \phi))$.

Proof. (I) This is immediate by Definition 12.5.2, since both $cl(s, \phi)$ and $cl(s', \phi)$ are closed.
(II) Let $[\sigma]\psi \in cl(s, \phi)$. If $\psi = [\leq]\psi'$, then by Definition 12.5.2(3) $\psi \in cl(s \cdot \sigma, \phi)$. If $\psi \neq [\leq]\psi'$, then since $cl(s, \phi)$ is closed and $[\sigma][\leq]\psi \in cl(s, \phi)$, $[\sigma][\leq]\psi \in cl(s, \phi)$. By definition, $[\leq]\psi \in cl(s \cdot \sigma, \phi)$. Since $cl(s \cdot \sigma, \phi)$ is closed, $\psi \in cl(s \cdot \sigma, \phi)$.
(III) Similar to (II).
(IV) Let $[\leq]\psi \in cl(s \cdot \geq, \phi)$. Two cases are considered depending on the way the formula $[\leq]\psi$ can appear in $cl(s \cdot \geq, \phi)$.
Case 1: $[\leq]\psi \in cl(\{[\geq]\psi'\})$ for some $[\geq]\psi' \in cl(s, \phi)$ (see Definition 12.5.2(5)). Again we have two cases corresponding to the reasons why $[\leq]\psi$ occurs in $cl(\{[\geq]\psi'\})$. If $[\leq]\psi$ is a subformula of $[\geq]\psi'$ (see the point (1) in the proof of Lemma 12.5.1), then $md([\leq]\psi) < md([\geq]\psi')$, since $[\leq]\psi \neq [\geq]\psi'$ and $[\geq]\psi' \in cl(s \cdot \geq, \phi)$. So $md([\leq]\psi) < md(cl(s \cdot \geq, \phi))$. If $[\sigma]\psi$ is a subformula of $[\geq]\psi'$ and ψ is not a $[\leq]$-formula (see the point (7) in the proof of Lemma 12.5.1), then $[\sigma][\leq]\psi \in cl(\{[\geq]\psi'\}) \subseteq cl(s \cdot \geq, \phi)$. Hence, $md([\leq]\psi) < md(cl(s \cdot \geq, \phi))$.
Case 2: $[\leq]\psi \in cl(\{[\sigma][\leq]\psi'\})$ for some $[\sigma][\leq]\psi' \in cl(s, \phi)$ (see Definition 12.5.2(6)).
So we have $[\leq]\psi \in cl(\{[\leq]\psi'\})$ and $md([\leq]\psi) \leq md([\leq]\psi') = md(cl(\{[\leq]\psi'\}))$. Hence, $md([\leq]\psi) \leq md([\leq]\psi') < md([\sigma][\leq]\psi') \leq md(cl(s \cdot \geq, \phi))$.   *Q.E.D.*

The following lemma is crucial for the forthcoming Theorem 12.5.3 which is the cornerstone for termination of the procedure NIL-WORLD defined in Sect. 12.5.2. It states sufficient conditions which guarantee that for some s' the modal degree of $cl(s \cdot s', \phi)$ is strictly less than the modal degree of $cl(s, \phi)$.

Lemma 12.5.3. *For every NIL-formula ϕ, for every $s \in \{\sigma, \leq, \geq\}^*$, and for every $s' \in \{\geq \cdot \leq \cdot \geq, \leq \cdot \geq \cdot \leq, \sigma\}$, $md(cl(s \cdot s', \phi)) \leq max(0, md(cl(s, \phi)) - 1)$.*

Proof. Assume that $md(cl(s, \phi)) \geq 1$, otherwise the proof is immediate by Lemma 12.5.2(I). Let $\varphi \in cl(s, \phi)$ be such that $md(\varphi) = md(cl(s, \phi))$. This means that $md(\varphi) = max\{md(\varphi') : \varphi' \in cl(s, \phi)\}$. By Lemma 12.5.2(I), we have to show that $\varphi \notin md(cl(s \cdot s', \phi))$. The proof is by cases depending on the form of s'. By way of example, we consider the case $s' = \leq \cdot \geq \cdot \leq$.
Case 1: the outermost connective of φ is in $\{\wedge, \neg\}$.

By Definition 12.5.2, we have $\varphi \in \text{cl}(s \cdot \leq, \phi)$ iff there is $[\leq]\psi \in \text{cl}(s, \phi)$ such that $\varphi \in \text{cl}(\{[\leq]\psi\})$. Suppose $\varphi \in \text{cl}(s \cdot \leq, \phi)$. φ can only be a proper subformula of $[\leq]\psi$, that is a subformula of ψ. But then $\text{md}(\varphi) < \text{md}([\leq]\psi)$, a contradiction. Thus, $\varphi \notin \text{cl}(s \cdot \leq, \phi)$ and therefore $\varphi \notin \text{cl}(s \cdot s', \phi)$.

Case 2: $\varphi = [\sigma][\leq]\varphi'$.

Suppose $\varphi \in \text{cl}(s \cdot \leq, \phi)$ (otherwise $\varphi \notin \text{cl}(s \cdot s', \phi)$ by Lemma 12.5.2(I)). So there is $[\leq]\psi \in \text{cl}(s, \phi)$ such that $\varphi \in \text{cl}(\{[\leq]\psi\})$. $[\sigma][\leq]\varphi'$ cannot be a subformula of $[\leq]\psi$, for otherwise $\text{md}([\sigma][\leq]\varphi') < \text{md}([\leq]\psi)$. Similarly, $[\sigma][\leq]^{n+1}\varphi'$ with $n \geq 1$ is not a subformula of $[\leq]\psi$ (see the point (3) in the proof of Lemma 12.5.1) by maximality of $\text{md}(\varphi)$. Otherwise, $\text{md}(\varphi) < \text{md}([\leq]\psi)$. The only remaining possibility is that $[\sigma]\varphi'$ is a subformula of some $[\leq]\psi$ in $\text{cl}(s, \phi)$ and φ' is not a $[\leq]$-formula. So $\text{md}([\leq]\psi) = \text{md}(\varphi)$. Now since $\varphi \in \text{cl}(s \cdot \leq \cdot \geq, \phi)$, $\text{md}(\varphi) = \text{md}(\text{cl}(s \cdot \leq \cdot \geq, \phi))$. By Lemma 12.5.2(IV), for every $[\leq]\psi'$ in $\text{cl}(s, \phi)$, if $\text{md}([\leq]\psi') = \text{md}(\text{cl}(s, \phi))$, then we have $[\leq]\psi' \notin \text{cl}(s \cdot \leq \cdot \geq, \phi)$. In particular, $[\leq]\psi \notin \text{cl}(s \cdot \leq \cdot \geq, \phi)$. We are now in a position to conclude the present case. $[\sigma][\leq]\varphi' \in \text{cl}(s \cdot s', \phi)$ iff there is $[\leq]\psi' \in \text{cl}(s \cdot \leq \cdot \geq, \phi)$ such that $[\sigma][\leq]\varphi' \in \text{cl}(\{[\leq]\psi'\})$. Suppose $[\sigma][\leq]\varphi' \in \text{cl}(s \cdot s', \phi)$. Hence, $\text{md}([\sigma][\leq]\varphi') = \text{md}([\leq]\psi')$ and from the above developments, we can conclude that $[\leq]\psi' \notin \text{cl}(s \cdot \leq \cdot \geq, \phi)$, a contradiction.

Case 3: $\varphi = [\leq]\varphi'$.

So $\varphi \in \text{cl}(s \cdot \leq, \phi)$. Now suppose $\varphi \in \text{cl}(s \cdot \leq \cdot \geq, \phi)$. By Lemma 12.5.2(IV), $\text{md}(\varphi) < \text{md}(\text{cl}(s \cdot \leq \cdot \geq, \phi))$. By Lemma 12.5.2(I), $\text{md}(\text{cl}(s \cdot \leq \cdot \geq, \phi)) \leq \text{md}(\text{cl}(s, \phi))$. Hence, $\text{md}(\varphi) < \text{md}(\text{cl}(s, \phi))$, a contradiction.

Case 4: $\varphi = [\geq]\varphi'$.

Assume $\varphi \in \text{cl}(s \cdot \leq, \phi)$ (otherwise $\varphi \notin \text{cl}(s \cdot s', \phi)$ by Lemma 12.5.2(I)). Thus, there is $[\leq]\psi \in \text{cl}(s, \phi)$ such that $\varphi \in \text{cl}(\{[\leq]\psi\})$ (see Definition 12.5.2(2)). So $\text{md}([\leq]\psi) = \text{md}(\varphi)$. Since $\text{md}(\varphi) = \text{md}(\text{cl}(s, \phi))$, φ cannot be a subformula of $[\leq]\psi$ (see the point (1) in the proof of Lemma 12.5.1). Similarly, there is no subformula $[\sigma][\leq^n]\varphi'$ of $[\leq]\psi$ for some $n \geq 1$ (see the point (3) in the proof of Lemma 12.5.1) by maximality of $\text{md}(\varphi)$. φ can only be of the form $[\geq][\leq]\varphi''$ for some subformula $[\sigma]\varphi''$ of $[\leq]\psi$ such that φ'' is not a $[\leq]$-formula (see the point (4) in the proof of Lemma 12.5.1)). Hence, $\varphi \in \text{cl}(s \cdot \leq \cdot \geq, \phi)$. By Lemma 12.5.2(IV), $[\leq]\psi \notin \text{cl}(s \cdot \leq \cdot \geq, \phi)$. Otherwise, we have $\text{md}(\varphi) = \text{md}([\leq]\psi) = \text{md}(\text{cl}(s \cdot \leq \cdot \geq, \phi))$. Actually, for every formula $[\leq]\psi' \in \text{cl}(s, \phi)$ such that $\text{md}([\leq]\psi') = \text{md}(\text{cl}(s, \phi))$, we can conclude that $[\leq]\psi'$ is not in $\text{cl}(s \cdot \leq \cdot \geq, \phi)$.

Now $[\geq]\varphi' \in \text{cl}(s \cdot \leq \cdot \geq \cdot \leq, \phi)$ iff there is $[\leq]\psi' \in \text{cl}(s \cdot \leq \cdot \geq, \phi)$ such that $[\geq]\varphi' \in \text{cl}(\{[\leq]\psi'\})$. Similarly, we can conclude that $[\sigma]\varphi''$ is a subformula of $[\leq]\psi'$. Suppose $[\geq][\leq]\varphi'' \in \text{cl}(s \cdot \leq \cdot \geq \cdot \leq, \phi)$. By Lemma 12.5.2(I), we have $\text{cl}(s \cdot \leq \cdot \geq, \phi) \subseteq \text{cl}(s, \phi)$ and therefore $[\leq]\psi' \in \text{cl}(s, \phi)$ and $\text{md}([\leq]\psi') = \text{md}(\varphi)$, which lead to a contradiction. So $[\geq][\leq]\varphi'' \notin \text{cl}(s \cdot \leq \cdot \geq \cdot \leq, \phi)$. Q.E.D.

Theorem 12.5.3. *For every formula ϕ and for every $s \in \{\sigma, \leq, \geq\}^*$, if neither $\geq \cdot \geq$ nor $\leq \cdot \leq$ is a substring of s and $|s| \geq 3 \times |\phi|$, then $\text{cl}(s, \phi) = \emptyset$.*

Proof. Observe that for every substring s' of length 3 in s, either σ occurs in s' or $s' \in \{\leq \cdot \geq \cdot \leq, \geq \cdot \leq \cdot \geq\}$. Since $\mathrm{md}(\phi) + 1 \leq |\phi|$, let s'' be the prefix of s of length $3 \times \mathrm{md}(\phi)$. By Lemma 12.5.3, $\mathrm{md}(\mathrm{cl}(s'', \phi)) = 0$ and therefore $\mathrm{cl}(s', \phi) = \emptyset$.   *Q.E.D.*

What is really important in Theorem 12.5.3 is that for some $s \in \{\sigma, \leq, \geq\}^*$ of polynomial length in $|\phi|$, $\mathrm{cl}(s, \phi)$ is empty. It is reasonable to assume that the strings $\geq \cdot \geq$ and $\leq \cdot \leq$ do not occur in s, since by the conditions (N1) and (N2) we shall identify any element of $\{\geq\}^+$ [resp. $\{\leq\}^+$] with $\geq$ [resp. $\leq$]. Theorem 12.5.3 can be extended in the following way.

Theorem 12.5.4. *Let $f : \mathbb{N} \to \mathbb{N}$ be a computable map. For every formula ϕ and for every $s \in \{\sigma, \leq, \geq\}^*$, if neither $\geq^{k+1}$ nor $\leq^{k+1}$ is a substring of s for some $k \geq f(|\phi|)$ and $|s| \geq 3 \times |\phi| \times f(|\phi|)$, then $\mathrm{cl}(s, \phi) = \emptyset$.*

Theorem 12.5.3 is a particular case of Theorem 12.5.4, where f is the constant map 1. The proof of Theorem 12.5.4 uses the facts that for every $k \geq 1$, $\mathrm{cl}(s \cdot \geq^k, \phi) = \mathrm{cl}(s \cdot \geq, \phi)$ and $\mathrm{cl}(s \cdot \leq^k, \phi) = \mathrm{cl}(s \cdot \leq, \phi)$.

The question arises whether Theorem 12.5.3 is optimal. We show that we can hardly do better: the factor 3 cannot be replaced by the factor 2.

Lemma 12.5.4. *For every $n \geq 1$ there exist a formula ϕ_n and an $s_n \in \{\sigma, \geq, \leq\}^*$ such that:*

(I) $\mathrm{md}(\phi_n) = n + 1$ and $|\phi_n| = n + 3$;
(II) neither $\geq \cdot \geq$ nor $\leq \cdot \leq$ occurs in s_n;
(III) $|s_n| = 3 \times n + 1$;
(IV) $\mathrm{cl}(s_n, \phi_n) \neq \emptyset$.

Proof. For every $n \geq 1$, we define

$$\phi_n \stackrel{\mathrm{def}}{=} [\leq][\sigma]^n \mathrm{p}, \qquad s_n \stackrel{\mathrm{def}}{=} (\leq \cdot \geq \cdot \sigma)^n \cdot \leq.$$

We show that $\mathrm{cl}(s_n, \phi_n) \neq \emptyset$. To do so, we prove that for every $i \in \{0, \ldots, n\}$, $[\leq][\sigma]^i \mathrm{p} \in \mathrm{cl}((\leq \cdot \geq \cdot \sigma)^{n-i}, \phi_n)$. The proof is by induction.
Base case: $i = n$.
$[\leq][\sigma]^n \mathrm{p_0} \in \mathrm{cl}(\lambda, \phi_n)$.
Induction step.
Assume that $[\leq][\sigma]^{i+1} \mathrm{p_0} \in \mathrm{cl}((\leq \cdot \geq \cdot \sigma)^{n-i-1}, \phi_n)$ for some $i \geq 0$. It follows that:

* $[\leq][\sigma]^{i+1} \mathrm{p_0} \in \mathrm{cl}((\leq \cdot \geq \cdot \sigma)^{n-i-1} \cdot \leq, \phi_n)$;
* $[\sigma]^{i+1} \mathrm{p_0} \in \mathrm{cl}((\leq \cdot \geq \cdot \sigma)^{n-i-1} \cdot \leq, \phi_n)$;
* $[\sigma][\leq][\sigma]^i \mathrm{p_0} \in \mathrm{cl}((\leq \cdot \geq \cdot \sigma)^{n-i-1} \cdot \leq, \phi_n)$;
* $[\sigma][\leq][\sigma]^i \mathrm{p_0} \in \mathrm{cl}((\leq \cdot \geq \cdot \sigma)^{n-i-1} \cdot \leq \cdot \geq, \phi_n)$;
* $[\leq][\sigma]^i \mathrm{p_0} \in \mathrm{cl}((\leq \cdot \geq \cdot \sigma)^{n-i-1} \cdot \leq \cdot \geq \cdot \sigma, \phi_n)$.

Hence,

$\star$ $[\leq]p_0 \in \text{cl}((\leq \cdot \geq \cdot \sigma)^n, \phi_n)$ and
$\star$ $[\leq]p_0 \in \text{cl}((\leq \cdot \geq \cdot \sigma)^n \cdot \leq, \phi_n)$.

$$Q.E.D.$$

Definition 12.5.3. *The binary relations $\approx$ and $\preceq$ on the family of subsets of NIL-formulae are defined as follows. Let X, Y be sets of formulae, then*

$\star$ $X \approx Y \overset{\text{def}}{\Leftrightarrow}$ *for every formula ψ,*
  (1) *if $[\sigma]\psi \in X$, then $\psi \in Y$;*
  (2) *if $[\sigma]\psi \in Y$, then $\psi \in X$.*
$\star$ $X \preceq Y \overset{\text{def}}{\Leftrightarrow}$ *for every formula ψ,*
  (1) *if $[\leq]\psi \in X$, then $[\leq]\psi, \psi \in Y$;*
  (2) *if $[\geq]\psi \in Y$, then $[\geq]\psi, \psi \in X$;*
  (3) *if $[\sigma]\psi \in Y$, then $[\sigma]\psi \in X$.*

Definition 12.5.4. *For every NIL-formula ϕ, we define the set $\text{cl}^{\text{ref}}(\phi)$ of closed subsets of $\text{cl}(\{\phi\})$ with respect to reflexivity as follows:*

$$\text{cl}^{\text{ref}}(\phi) \overset{\text{def}}{=} \{Y \subseteq \text{cl}(\{\phi\}) : [a]\psi \in Y \text{ implies } \psi \in Y \text{ for every } a \in \{\sigma, \geq, \leq\}\}.$$

The relation $\approx$ is reflexive and symmetric on $\text{cl}^{\text{ref}}(\phi)$ and $\preceq$ is reflexive and transitive on $\text{cl}^{\text{ref}}(\phi)$. For every $s \in \{\sigma, \leq, \geq\}^*$, we define the set of *s-consistent* sets, which is a subset of $\text{cl}^{\text{ref}}(\phi)$, as follows.

Definition 12.5.5. *Let X be a subset of $\text{cl}(s, \phi)$ for some $s \in \{\sigma, \geq, \leq\}^*$ and for some formula ϕ. The set X is said to be s-consistent $\overset{\text{def}}{\Leftrightarrow}$ for every $\psi \in \text{cl}(s, \phi)$ the following conditions hold:*

(1) *if $\psi = \neg\varphi$, then $\varphi \in X$ iff $\psi \notin X$;*
(2) *if $\psi = \varphi_1 \wedge \varphi_2$, then $\{\varphi_1, \varphi_2\} \subseteq X$ iff $\psi \in X$;*
(3) *if $\psi = [a]\varphi$ for some $a \in \{\sigma, \leq, \geq\}$ and $\psi \in X$, then $\varphi \in X$;*
(4) *if $\psi = [\sigma]\varphi$, $\varphi \neq [\leq]\varphi'$ and $\psi \in X$, then $[\sigma][\leq]\varphi \in X$;*
(5) *if $\psi = [\sigma][\leq]\varphi$ and $\psi \in X$, then $[\sigma]\varphi \in X$;*
(6) *if $\psi = [\sigma]\varphi$ and $\psi \in X$, then $[\geq]\varphi \in X$.*

Roughly speaking, the s-consistency entails the maximal propositional consistency with respect to the set $\text{cl}(s, \phi)$ of formulae. Furthermore, modal conditions (3)–(6) in Definition 12.5.5 refer to reflexivity of the relations in the NIL-models and to the condition $R_\leq \cup R_\geq \subseteq R_\sigma$. It is worth mentioning that if X is s-consistent and $[\sigma]\psi \in X$, then $\{[\leq]\psi, [\geq]\psi\} \subseteq X$.

Lemma 12.5.5. *For every NIL-model $\mathcal{M} = \langle W, R_\leq, R_\geq, R_\sigma, m \rangle$, for every $w \in W$, for every $s \in \{\sigma, \leq, \geq\}^*$, and for every NIL-formula ϕ, $\{\psi \in \text{cl}(s, \phi) : \mathcal{M}, w \models \psi\}$ is s-consistent.*

The proof of the above lemma is by an easy verification. It uses the fact that $\mathrm{cl}(s, \phi)$ is closed. Lemma 12.5.6(II) roughly states that $\preceq \subseteq \approx$, which is the syntactic version of $R_\leq \subseteq R_\sigma$ in the NIL-models. Similarly, Lemma 12.5.6(I) states a syntactic version of $R_\geq ; R_\sigma ; R_\leq \subseteq R_\sigma$ in the NIL-models.

Lemma 12.5.6. *For every formula ϕ, if for every $i \in \{1, \ldots, 4\}$ X_i is an s_i-consistent subset of $\mathrm{cl}(\{\phi\})$ for some $s_i \in \{\sigma, \leq, \geq\}^*$, and $X_1 \succeq X_2 \approx X_3 \preceq X_4$, then:*

(I) if $[\sigma]\psi \in X_1$, then $\psi \in X_4$;
(II) $X_1 \approx X_2$.

Proof. (I) Let $[\sigma]\psi \in X_1$. Since $X_1 \succeq X_2$, we have $[\sigma]\psi \in X_2$ and $\psi \in X_2$ by Definition 12.5.5(3). If $\psi = [\leq]\varphi$, then by $X_2 \approx X_3$, we get $[\leq]\varphi \in X_3$ and by $X_3 \preceq X_4$, we get $[\leq]\varphi \in X_4$. Otherwise, if $\psi \neq [\leq]\varphi$, then by s_2-consistency of X_2, we have $[\sigma][\leq]\psi \in X_2$. By $X_2 \approx X_3$, we have $[\leq]\psi \in X_3$. By $X_3 \preceq X_4$, we obtain $\psi \in X_4$.
(II) Let $[\sigma]\psi \in X_2$. If $\psi \neq [\leq]\varphi$, then $[\sigma][\leq]\psi \in X_2$ by s_2-consistency. Moreover, by s_2-consistency, $[\leq]\psi \in X_2$. Now, since $X_2 \preceq X_1$, we get $\psi \in X_1$. In the case that $\psi = [\leq]\varphi$, by s_2-consistency, $\psi \in X_2$. Since $X_2 \preceq X_1$, we obtain $[\leq]\varphi \in X_1$.
Let $[\sigma]\psi \in X_1$. If $\psi \neq [\leq]\varphi$, then $[\sigma][\leq]\psi \in X_1$ by s_1-consistency. By s_1-consistency, $[\geq][\leq]\psi \in X_1$. Now since $X_2 \preceq X_1$, $[\leq]\psi \in X_2$. By s_2-consistency of X_2, $\psi \in X_2$. In the case that $\psi = [\leq]\varphi$, by s_1-consistency, $[\geq]\psi \in X_1$. Now, since $X_2 \preceq X_1$, we get $\psi \in X_2$.   *Q.E.D.*

In the forthcoming Lemmas 12.5.7, 12.5.8, 12.5.9, 12.5.10, and 12.5.11 we state some basic facts about the sets of the form $\mathrm{sub}(s, \phi)$.

Lemma 12.5.7. *For every $s \in \{\sigma, \geq, \leq\}^*$ and for all formulae ϕ and ψ, the following conditions hold:*

(I) if $[\sigma]\psi \in \mathrm{cl}(s, \phi)$, then $\psi \in \mathrm{cl}(s \cdot \sigma, \phi)$;
(II) if $[\sigma]\psi \in \mathrm{cl}(s, \phi)$, then $\psi \in \mathrm{cl}(s \cdot \leq, \phi)$;
(III) if $[\sigma]\psi \in \mathrm{cl}(s \cdot \geq, \phi)$, then $\psi \in \mathrm{cl}(s, \phi)$;
(IV) if $[\sigma]\psi \in \mathrm{cl}(s, \phi)$, then $\psi \in \mathrm{cl}(s, \phi)$.

Proof. (I) By Lemma 12.5.2(II).
(II) Assume $[\sigma]\psi \in \mathrm{cl}(s, \phi)$. If $\psi \neq [\leq]\varphi$, then $[\sigma][\leq]\psi \in \mathrm{cl}(s, \phi)$ and $[\leq]\psi \in \mathrm{cl}(s, \phi)$. By the definition of $\mathrm{cl}(s \cdot \leq, \phi)$ we get $[\leq]\psi, \psi \in \mathrm{cl}(s \cdot \leq, \phi)$. If $\psi = [\leq]\varphi$, then $[\leq]\varphi \in \mathrm{cl}(s, \phi)$ and by the definition of $\mathrm{cl}(s \cdot \leq, \phi)$, $[\leq]\varphi \in \mathrm{cl}(s \cdot \leq, \phi)$.
(III) Assume $[\sigma]\psi \in \mathrm{cl}(s \cdot \geq, \phi)$. So $[\sigma]\psi \in \mathrm{cl}(s, \phi)$ by Lemma 12.5.2(I) and therefore $\psi \in \mathrm{cl}(s, \phi)$.
(IV) Immediate since $\mathrm{cl}(s, \phi)$ is closed.   *Q.E.D.*

Lemma 12.5.8. *For every $s \in \{\sigma, \geq, \leq\}^*$ and for all formulae ϕ and ψ, the following conditions hold:*

(I) if $[\sigma]\psi \in \mathrm{cl}(s \cdot \sigma, \phi)$, then $\psi \in \mathrm{cl}(s, \phi)$;
(II) if $[\sigma]\psi \in \mathrm{cl}(s \cdot \leq, \phi)$, then $\psi \in \mathrm{cl}(s, \phi)$;
(III) if $[\sigma]\psi \in \mathrm{cl}(s, \phi)$, then $\psi \in \mathrm{cl}(s \cdot \geq, \phi)$;
(IV) if $[\sigma]\psi \in \mathrm{cl}(s, \phi)$, then $\psi \in \mathrm{cl}(s, \phi)$.

Proof. (I) Since $\mathrm{cl}(s \cdot \sigma, \phi) \subseteq \mathrm{cl}(s, \phi)$ and $\mathrm{cl}(s, \phi)$ is closed, the proof is immediate.
(II) Since $\mathrm{cl}(s \cdot \leq, \phi) \subseteq \mathrm{cl}(s, \phi)$ and $\mathrm{cl}(s, \phi)$ is closed, the condition follows.
(III) Assume $[\sigma]\psi \in \mathrm{cl}(s, \phi)$. If $\psi = [\leq]\psi'$, then $[\sigma]\psi \in \mathrm{cl}(s \cdot \geq, \phi)$ and $\psi \in \mathrm{cl}(s \cdot \geq, \phi)$, since $\mathrm{cl}(s \cdot \geq, \phi)$ is closed. If $\psi \neq [\leq]\psi'$, then $[\sigma][\leq]\psi \in \mathrm{cl}(s, \phi)$, since $\mathrm{cl}(s, \phi)$ is closed. We also have $[\sigma][\leq]\psi, [\leq]\psi, [\sigma]\psi, \psi \in \mathrm{cl}(s \cdot \geq, \phi)$.
(IV) By Lemma 12.5.7(IV).   *Q.E.D.*

Lemma 12.5.9. *For every $s \in \{\sigma, \geq, \leq\}^*$ and for all formulae ϕ and ψ, the following conditions hold:*

(I) if $[\leq]\psi \in \mathrm{cl}(s, \phi)$, then $\psi \in \mathrm{cl}(s \cdot \leq, \phi)$;
(II) if $[\leq]\psi \in \mathrm{cl}(s \cdot \geq, \phi)$, then $\psi \in \mathrm{cl}(s, \phi)$;
(III) if $[\leq]\psi \in \mathrm{cl}(s, \phi)$, then $\psi \in \mathrm{cl}(s, \phi)$;

Proof. (I) By definition, since $\mathrm{cl}(s \cdot \leq, \phi)$ is closed.
(II) Since $\mathrm{cl}(s \cdot \geq, \phi) \subseteq \mathrm{cl}(s, \phi)$ and $\mathrm{cl}(s, \phi)$ is closed, condition (II) follows.
(III) It is immediate since $\mathrm{cl}(s, \phi)$ is closed.   *Q.E.D.*

Lemma 12.5.10. *For every $s \in \{\sigma, \geq, \leq\}^*$ and for all formulae ϕ and ψ, the following conditions hold:*

(I) if $[\geq]\psi \in \mathrm{cl}(s \cdot \leq, \phi)$, then $\psi \in \mathrm{cl}(s, \phi)$;
(II) if $[\geq]\psi \in \mathrm{cl}(s, \phi)$, then $\psi \in \mathrm{cl}(s \cdot \geq, \phi)$;
(III) if $[\geq]\psi \in \mathrm{cl}(s, \phi)$, then $\psi \in \mathrm{cl}(s, \phi)$.

Proof. (I) It is immediate since $\mathrm{cl}(s \cdot \leq, \phi) \subseteq \mathrm{cl}(s, \phi)$ and $\mathrm{cl}(s, \phi)$ is closed.
(II) and (III) follow from the facts that $\mathrm{cl}(s \cdot \leq, \phi)$ and $\mathrm{cl}(s, \phi)$ are closed, respectively.   *Q.E.D.*

Lemma 12.5.11. *For every $s \in \{\sigma, \geq, \leq\}^*$ and for all formulae ϕ and ψ, the following conditions hold:*

(I) if $[\sigma]\psi \in \mathrm{cl}(s \cdot \leq, \phi)$, then $[\sigma]\psi \in \mathrm{cl}(s, \phi)$;
(II) if $[\sigma]\psi \in \mathrm{cl}(s, \phi)$, then $[\sigma]\psi \in \mathrm{cl}(s \cdot \geq, \phi)$;
(III) if $[\sigma]\psi \in \mathrm{cl}(s, \phi)$, then $[\sigma]\psi \in \mathrm{cl}(s, \phi)$.

Proof. (I) It is immediate since $\mathrm{cl}(s \cdot \leq, \phi) \subseteq \mathrm{cl}(s, \phi)$.
(II) See the proof of Lemma 12.5.8(III).
(III) Obvious.   *Q.E.D.*

Before defining the main algorithm of the section, let us conclude by presenting some relationships between the relations $\preceq$, $\approx$, and the relations from NIL-models.

Lemma 12.5.12. *For every* NIL-*model* $\mathcal{M} = \langle W, R_\leq, R_\geq, R_\sigma, m \rangle$, *for every* $w \in W$, *for every* $s \in \{\sigma, \geq, \leq\}^*$, *for every* $t, t' \in \{\lambda, \sigma, \leq, \geq\}$, *and for every formula* ϕ *the following conditions are satisfied:*

(I) $X_{w,s\cdot t} \stackrel{\text{def}}{=} \{\psi \in \text{cl}(s \cdot t, \phi) : \mathcal{M}, w \models \psi\}$ *is* $s \cdot t$-*consistent;*
(II) if $\langle t, t' \rangle \in \{\langle \lambda, \sigma \rangle, \langle \sigma, \lambda \rangle, \langle \lambda, \lambda \rangle\}$ *and* $\langle w, w' \rangle \in R_\sigma$, *then* $X_{w,s\cdot t} \approx X_{w',s\cdot t'}$;
(III) if $\langle t, t' \rangle \in \{\langle \lambda, \leq \rangle, \langle \geq, \lambda \rangle, \langle \lambda, \lambda \rangle\}$ *and* $\langle w, w' \rangle \in R_\leq$, *then* $X_{w,s\cdot t} \preceq X_{w',s\cdot t'}$.

The proof is by an easy verification using the previous lemmas.

12.5.2 The Algorithm in PSPACE

Let Σ be a non-empty finite sequence of subsets of $\text{cl}(\{\phi\})$, $s \in \{\sigma, \leq, \geq\}^*$, and ϕ be a NIL-formula. In Table 12.1, the function $\texttt{NIL-WORLD}(\Sigma, s, \phi)$ returning a Boolean is defined. It has the property that for every $X \subseteq \text{cl}(\{\phi\})$ and for every call of $\texttt{NIL-WORLD}(\Sigma, s, \phi)$ in $\texttt{NIL-WORLD}(X, \lambda, \phi)$ (at any recursion depth), $last(\Sigma) \subseteq \text{cl}(s, \phi)$. In the next section we shall show that

⋆ $|\Sigma| \leq 25 \times |\phi|^2$;
⋆ $|s| \leq 3 \times |\phi|$.

A call of $\texttt{NIL-WORLD}(\Sigma, s, \phi)$ is *successful* if it returns true. We say that $\texttt{NIL-WORLD}(\Sigma, s, \phi)$ *directly calls* $\texttt{NIL-WORLD}(\Sigma', s', \phi)$ if $\texttt{NIL-WORLD}(\Sigma', s', \phi')$ is called at depth one in the computation tree of $\texttt{NIL-WORLD}$ calls from the execution of $\texttt{NIL-WORLD}(\Sigma, s, \phi)$. If the call is made at some depth (not necessarily one) in the computation tree of $\texttt{NIL-WORLD}$ calls from the execution of $\texttt{NIL-WORLD}(\Sigma, s, \phi)$, we say that $\texttt{NIL-WORLD}(\Sigma', s', \phi)$ is called in $\texttt{NIL-WORLD}(\Sigma, s, \phi)$.

The results given in Sect. 12.5.1 will guarantee that $\texttt{NIL-WORLD}$ is correct and terminates. Correctness means that for every formula ϕ, ϕ is NIL-satisfiable iff there is an $X \subseteq \text{cl}(\{\phi\})$ such that $\phi \in X$ and $\texttt{NIL-WORLD}(X, \lambda, \phi)$ returns true.

First, we show termination. Each subset $X \subseteq \text{cl}(\{\phi\})$ can be represented in space $\mathcal{O}(|\phi|)$ by using pointers to a copy of the formula, since $\text{card}(\text{cl}(\phi)) < 5 \times |\phi|$. At each level of the recursion we use space in $\mathcal{O}(|\phi|)$ by implementing Σ as a global stack.

Suppose that in the call of $\texttt{NIL-WORLD}(X, \lambda, \phi)$, at some recursion depth, $\texttt{NIL-WORLD}(\Sigma, s, \phi)$ is called with $\Sigma = X_1 \cdot \ldots \cdot X_n$, $n \geq 2$. We treat the case $s = s' \cdot \leq$; the case $s = s' \cdot \geq$ is similar. Moreover, if $s = s' \cdot \sigma$, then $|\Sigma| = 1$ and hence this case is not relevant, since we assume that $n \geq 2$. For every $i \in \{1, \ldots, n-1\}$, $[\leq]\psi \in X_i$ implies $[\leq]\psi \in X_{i+1}$. So Σ can be written as $\Sigma = \Sigma_1 \cdot \ldots \cdot \Sigma_{n'}$, $n' \geq 1$, where for all $i, i' \in \{1, \ldots, n'\}$

⋆ the elements of Σ_i contain the same $[\leq]$-formulae;
⋆ $i < i'$ implies that the set of $[\leq]$-formulae of Σ_i is a proper subset of the set of $[\leq]$-formulae of $\Sigma_{i'}$.

---

function NIL-WORLD(Σ, s, ϕ)

    if $last(\Sigma)$ is not s-consistent, then return false;
    % ``σ'' **segment**
    for $[\sigma]\psi \in cl(s, \phi) \setminus last(\Sigma)$ do
        for each $X_\psi \subseteq cl(s \cdot \sigma, \phi) \setminus \{\psi\}$ such that $last(\Sigma) \approx X_\psi$, call
        NIL-WORLD$(X_\psi, s \cdot \sigma, \phi)$. If all these calls return false, then return false;
    % ``$\leq$'' **segment**
    for $[\leq]\psi \in cl(s, \phi) \setminus last(\Sigma)$ do
        if there is no $X \in \Sigma$ such that $\psi \notin X$, $last(\Sigma) \preceq X$, and $last(s) =\leq$, then
        for each $X_\psi \subseteq cl(s \cdot \leq, \phi) \setminus \{\psi\}$ such that $last(\Sigma) \preceq X_\psi$, if $last(s) =\leq$,
        then call NIL-WORLD$(\Sigma \cdot X_\psi, s, \phi)$, otherwise call NIL-WORLD$(X_\psi, s \cdot \leq, \phi)$.
        If all these calls return false, then return false;
    % ``$\geq$'' **segment**
    for $[\geq]\psi \in cl(s, \phi) \setminus last(\Sigma)$ do
        if there is no $X \in \Sigma$ such that $\psi \notin X$, $last(\Sigma) \succeq X$, and $last(s) =\geq$, then
        for each $X_\psi \subseteq cl(s \cdot \geq, \phi) \setminus \{\psi\}$ such that $X_\psi \preceq last(\Sigma)$, if $last(s) =\geq$,
        then call NIL-WORLD$(\Sigma \cdot X_\psi, s, \phi)$, otherwise call NIL-WORLD$(X_\psi, s \cdot \geq, \phi)$.
        If all these calls return false, then return false;
    Return true.

Table 12.1.

Since there are less than $5 \times |\phi|$ $[\leq]$-formulae in $cl(\{\phi\})$, we have $n' \leq 5 \times |\phi|$.

Let $i \in \{1, \ldots, n'\}$. Σ_i can be written $\Sigma_i = \Sigma_i^1 \cdot \ldots \cdot \Sigma_i^{l(i)}$, where for all $j, j' \in \{1, \ldots, l(i)\}$, the elements of Σ_i^j contain the same $[\geq]$-formulae and $[\sigma]$-formulae and $j < j'$ implies that the set of $[\geq]$-formulae and $[\sigma]$-formulae of $\Sigma_i^{j'}$ is a proper subset of the set of $[\geq]$-formulae and $[\sigma]$-formulae of Σ_i^j, respectively.
For every $i \in \{1, \ldots, n\}$, let

$\star$ $Z_i^1 \stackrel{\text{def}}{=} \{[\geq]\psi : [\geq]\psi \in X_i\}$ and
$\star$ $Z_i^2 \stackrel{\text{def}}{=} \{[\sigma]\psi : [\sigma]\psi \in X_i\}$.

We have

$$(Z_n^1 \cup Z_n^2) \subseteq \ldots \subseteq (Z_1^1 \cup Z_1^2).$$

One can see that $l(1) + \ldots + l(n')$ is in $\mathcal{O}(|\phi|)$, since the above sequence contains at most $\mathcal{O}(|\phi|)$ proper inclusions. Actually, $l(1) + \cdots + l(n') < 5 \times |\phi|$.

Now we estimate the maximal length $|\Sigma_i^j|$ for all $i \in \{1, \ldots, n'\}$ and $j \in \{1, \ldots, l(i)\}$. Suppose $\Sigma_i^j = Y_1 \cdot \ldots \cdot Y_k$. If $1 \leq u < u' \leq k$, then for every formula ϕ, if $[\leq]\psi \in Y_u$, then $[\leq]\psi \in Y_{u'}$. Since for every α such that $2 \leq \alpha < k$, NIL-WORLD$(\Sigma_1 \ldots \Sigma_{i-1} Y_1 \cdot \ldots \cdot Y_\alpha, s, \phi)$ calls NIL-WORLD$(\Sigma_1 \ldots \Sigma_{i-1} Y_1 \cdot \ldots \cdot Y_{\alpha+1}, s, \phi)$, there are formulae $\psi_2, \ldots, \psi_k$ in $cl(\{\phi\})$ such that $\psi_\alpha \notin Y_\alpha$ and for every α' such that $1 \leq \alpha' < \alpha$, $\psi_\alpha \in Y_{\alpha'}$. Hence, $\psi_2, \ldots, \psi_k$ are $(k-1)$ different formulae in $cl(\{\phi\})$ and k is in $\mathcal{O}(|\phi|)$. More precisely, $k < 5 \times |\phi|$. So the maximal length of Σ is in $\mathcal{O}(|\phi|^2)$. More precisely, $|\Sigma| \leq 25 \times |\phi|^2$. Termination is not yet proved, since there are moments in the computation when the length of Σ strictly decreases. However, the following observations will help finish the proof of termination of NIL-WORLD(X, λ, ϕ):

★ if NIL-WORLD(Σ, s, ϕ) calls directly NIL-WORLD(Σ', s', ϕ), then either $|\Sigma| < |\Sigma'|$ or $|s| < |s'|$;
★ every call of NIL-WORLD(Σ, s, ϕ) from NIL-WORLD(X, λ, ϕ) satisfies that neither $\geq \cdot \geq$ nor $\leq \cdot \leq$ is a substring of s;
★ it follows from Theorem 12.5.3 that for every call of NIL-WORLD(Σ, s, ϕ), if $|s| \geq 3 \times |\phi|$, then no more recursive calls to NIL-WORLD are executed.

Consequently, the depth of the recursion is in $\mathcal{O}(|\phi|^3)$. More precisely, the depth is bounded by $75 \times |\phi|^3$. Since at each step of the recursion we need space in $\mathcal{O}(|\phi|)$, for every $X \subseteq \mathrm{cl}(\{\phi\})$ the total space for computing NIL-WORLD(X, λ, ϕ) is in $\mathcal{O}(|\phi|^4)$.

Theorem 12.5.5. *For every formula ϕ and for every $X \subseteq \mathrm{cl}(\{\phi\})$, the following hold:*

(I) NIL-WORLD(X, λ, ϕ) terminates and requires space in $\mathcal{O}(|\phi|^4)$;
(II) for every NIL-WORLD(Σ, s, ϕ) call in NIL-WORLD(X, λ, ϕ), $|\Sigma| \leq 25 \times |\phi|^2$ and $|s| \leq 3 \times |\phi|$;
(III) for every direct call of NIL-WORLD(Σ', s', ϕ) in NIL-WORLD(Σ, s, ϕ) in the computation of NIL-WORLD(X, λ, ϕ), either $3 \times |\phi| - |s'| < 3 \times |\phi| - |s|$ or $(3 \times |\phi| - |s'| = 3 \times |\phi| - |s|$ and $25 \times |\phi|^2 - |\Sigma'| < 25 \times |\phi|^2 - |\Sigma|)$.

Theorem 12.5.5 is an important step in proving that SAT(NIL) is in **PSPACE** but it is not sufficient. Indeed, up to now we have no guarantee that the function NIL-WORLD is correct. This is shown in the following two lemmas.

Lemma 12.5.13. *For every NIL-formula ϕ and for every $Y \subseteq \mathrm{cl}(\{\phi\})$, if $\phi \in Y$ and NIL-WORLD(Y, λ, ϕ) returns true, then $\phi \in \mathrm{SAT(NIL)}$.*

Proof. Assume that NIL-WORLD(Y, λ, ϕ) returns true. We build a NIL-model $\mathcal{M} = \langle W, R_\leq, R_\geq, R_\sigma, m \rangle$ and a $w \in W$ such that for every $\psi \in \mathrm{cl}(\{\phi\})$, we have $\mathcal{M}, w \models \psi$ iff $\psi \in Y$.

Let STR be the set of strings s over $\{\sigma, \geq, \leq\}$ such that $|s| \leq 3 \times |\phi|$. We define W as the set of pairs $\langle X, s \rangle$ for which there is a finite sequence $\langle \Sigma_1, s_1 \rangle, \ldots, \langle \Sigma_k, s_k \rangle$, $k \geq 1$, such that:

(1) NIL-WORLD(Σ_k, s_k, ϕ) is called in NIL-WORLD(Y, λ, ϕ) (at any depth of the recursion);
(2) $\Sigma_1 = Y$; $s_1 = \lambda$; $last(\Sigma_k) = X$; $s_k = s$;
(3) for every $i \in \{1, \ldots, k\}$, NIL-WORLD(Σ_i, s_i, ϕ) returns true;
(4) for every $i \in \{1, \ldots, k-1\}$, NIL-WORLD(Σ_i, s_i, ϕ) calls directly NIL-WORLD$(\Sigma_{i+1}, s_{i+1}, \phi)$.

Conditions (3) and (4) state that we only want to record those pairs $\langle X, s \rangle \in$ $\mathrm{cl}^{\mathrm{ref}}(\phi) \times \mathrm{STR}$ that contribute to making $\mathrm{NIL\text{-}WORLD}(Y, \lambda, \phi)$ true. By definition, $\langle Y, \lambda \rangle \in W$. Furthermore, for every $\langle X, s \rangle \in W$, we have $X \subseteq \mathrm{cl}(s, \phi)$ and X is s-consistent.

We define an auxiliary binary relation S_σ on W as follows:
$\langle \langle X, s \rangle, \langle X', s' \rangle \rangle \in S_\sigma \overset{\mathrm{def}}{\Leftrightarrow}$ there is a successful call of $\mathrm{NIL\text{-}WORLD}(\Sigma, s, \phi)$ in $\mathrm{NIL\text{-}WORLD}(Y, \lambda, \phi)$ (at any depth of the recursion) such that:

* $last(\Sigma) = X$;
* $\mathrm{NIL\text{-}WORLD}(\Sigma, s, \phi)$ calls $\mathrm{NIL\text{-}WORLD}(\Sigma', s', \phi)$ in the "σ" segment of $\mathrm{NIL\text{-}WORLD}(\Sigma, s, \phi)$ and $\mathrm{NIL\text{-}WORLD}(\Sigma', s', \phi)$ returns true;
* $last(\Sigma') = X'$.

Observe that if $\langle \langle X, s \rangle, \langle X', s' \rangle \rangle \in S_\sigma$, then $s' = s \cdot \sigma$, $\Sigma' = X'$, and $X \approx X'$. In a similar way, we define the binary relation $S_\leq$ [resp. $S_\geq$] on W as follows: $\langle \langle X, s \rangle, \langle X', s' \rangle \rangle \in S_\leq$ [resp. $\langle \langle X, s \rangle, \langle X', s' \rangle \rangle \in S_\geq$] $\overset{\mathrm{def}}{\Leftrightarrow}$ there is a successful call of $\mathrm{NIL\text{-}WORLD}(\Sigma, s, \phi)$ in $\mathrm{NIL\text{-}WORLD}(Y, \lambda, \phi)$ (at any depth of the recursion) such that:

* either
  * $last(\Sigma) = X$;
  * $\mathrm{NIL\text{-}WORLD}(\Sigma, s, \phi)$ calls $\mathrm{NIL\text{-}WORLD}(\Sigma', s', \phi)$ in the "$\leq$" [resp. "$\geq$"] segment of $\mathrm{NIL\text{-}WORLD}(\Sigma, s, \phi)$ and $\mathrm{NIL\text{-}WORLD}(\Sigma', s', \phi)$ returns true;
  * $last(\Sigma') = X'$.
* or there is a finite sequence $\langle \Sigma_1, s_1 \rangle, \ldots, \langle \Sigma_k, s_k \rangle$ such that:
  * $last(\Sigma_k) = X$; $last(\Sigma_1) = X'$;
  * $\Sigma_k = \Sigma$; $s_k = s$; $s_1 = s'$;
  * for every $i \in \{1, \ldots, k\}$, $\langle last(\Sigma_i), s_i \rangle \in W$;
  * for every $i \in \{1, \ldots, k-1\}$, $\mathrm{NIL\text{-}WORLD}(\Sigma_i, s_i, \phi)$ calls $\mathrm{NIL\text{-}WORLD}(\Sigma_{i+1}, s_{i+1}, \phi)$ in the "$\leq$" [resp. "$\geq$"] segment of the function $\mathrm{NIL\text{-}WORLD}$ and both $\mathrm{NIL\text{-}WORLD}(\Sigma_i, s_i, \phi)$ and $\mathrm{NIL\text{-}WORLD}(\Sigma_{i+1}, s_{i+1}, \phi)$ return true;
  * the call of $\mathrm{NIL\text{-}WORLD}(\Sigma_k, s_k, \phi)$ enters in the "'$\leq$" [resp. "$\geq$"] segment of $\mathrm{NIL\text{-}WORLD}$, $last(s_k) = \leq$ [resp. $last(s_k) = \geq$], and for some formula $[\leq]\psi \in \mathrm{cl}(s, \phi) \setminus X$ [resp. $[\geq]\psi \in \mathrm{cl}(s, \phi) \setminus X$], the set X' satisfies $\psi \notin X'$ and $X \preceq X'$ [resp. $X \succeq X'$].

Whereas the first alternative is based on the construction of a new witness, the second one establishes a symbolic link between $\langle X, s \rangle$ and $\langle X', s' \rangle$. Now the definition of $\mathcal{M}$ can be completed:

* $R_\leq \overset{\mathrm{def}}{=} (S_\leq \cup S_\geq^{-1})^*$;
* $R_\geq \overset{\mathrm{def}}{=} (S_\geq \cup S_\leq^{-1})^*$;
* $R_\sigma \overset{\mathrm{def}}{=} R_\geq ; (S_\sigma \cup S_\sigma^{-1} \cup \{\langle \langle X, s \rangle, \langle X, s \rangle \rangle : \langle X, s \rangle \in W\}); R_\leq$;
* for every $\mathrm{p} \in \mathrm{FOR}_0$, $m(\mathrm{p}) \overset{\mathrm{def}}{=} \{\langle X, s \rangle \in W : \mathrm{p} \in X\}$.

It is easy to see that $R_\leq$ and $R_\geq$ are reflexive and transitive and $R_\geq$ is the converse of $R_\leq$. Moreover, it is easy to show that R_σ is reflexive and symmetric and $R_\geq; R_\sigma; R_\leq \subseteq R_\sigma$. So $\mathcal{M}$ is a NIL-model and W is of cardinality $2^{\mathcal{O}(|\phi|)}$. One can show:

(i) $\langle\langle X, s\rangle, \langle X', s'\rangle\rangle \in (S_\leq \cup S_\geq^{-1})$ implies $X \preceq X'$;

(ii) $\langle\langle X, s\rangle, \langle X', s'\rangle\rangle \in (S_\geq \cup S_\leq^{-1})$ implies $X' \preceq X$;

(iii) $\langle\langle X, s\rangle, \langle X', s'\rangle\rangle \in (S_\sigma \cup \bar{S}_\sigma^{-1} \cup \{\langle\langle X, s\rangle, \langle X, s\rangle\rangle : \langle X, s\rangle \in W\})$ implies $X \approx X'$.

So

(iv) $\langle\langle X, s\rangle, \langle X', s'\rangle\rangle \in R_\leq$ implies for every formula ψ, if $[\leq]\psi \in X$, then $\psi \in X'$ (by the definition of $\preceq$);

(v) $\langle\langle X, s\rangle, \langle X', s'\rangle\rangle \in R_\geq$ implies for every formula ψ, if $[\geq]\psi \in X$, then $\psi \in X'$ (by the definition of $\preceq$);

(vi) $\langle\langle X, s\rangle, \langle X', s'\rangle\rangle \in R_\sigma$ implies for every formula ψ, if $[\sigma]\psi \in X$, then $\psi \in X'$ (by the definition of $\approx$ and by Lemma 12.5.6(I)).

By induction on the structure of ψ we show that for every $\langle X, s\rangle \in W$ and for every $\psi \in \mathrm{cl}(s, \phi)$, $\psi \in X$ iff $\mathcal{M}, \langle X, s\rangle \models \psi$. If ψ is a propositional variable, the condition holds by definition of the meaning function m.

Induction hypothesis: for every $\psi \in \mathrm{cl}(\{\phi\})$, for every $\langle X, s\rangle \in W$, if $\psi \in \mathrm{cl}(s, \phi)$ and $|\psi| \leq n$, then $\psi \in X$ iff $\mathcal{M}, \langle X, s\rangle \models \psi$.

Let ψ be a formula in $\mathrm{cl}(\{\phi\})$ such that $|\psi| \leq n + 1$. If the outermost connective of ψ is Boolean, then the induction step can be shown using the s-consistency of X and the induction hypothesis. Let us treat the other cases.

Case 1: $\psi = [\leq]\psi'$.

Let $\langle X, s\rangle \in W$ be such that $\psi \in \mathrm{cl}(s, \phi)$. By the definition of W, there is a sequence Σ such that $last(\Sigma) = X$ and $\texttt{NIL-WORLD}(\Sigma, s, \phi)$ returns true. If $\psi \notin X$ one of the following two cases occurs.

Case 1.1: there is an X' in Σ such that $X \preceq X'$, $\psi' \notin X'$, and $last(s) = \leq$. By the definition of W, there are a subsequence Σ' of Σ and an s' such that $last(\Sigma') = X'$ and $\texttt{NIL-WORLD}(\Sigma', s', \phi)$ returns true (see the conditions (3) and (4) defining W). Thus, $\langle\langle X, s\rangle, \langle X', s'\rangle\rangle \in S_\leq$ by definition and therefore we have $\langle\langle X, s\rangle, \langle X', s'\rangle\rangle \in R_\leq$. Observe that either $s' = s$ or $s = s' \cdot \leq$. By Lemma 12.5.9, $\psi' \in \mathrm{cl}(s', \phi)$. By the induction hypothesis, we have $\mathcal{M}, \langle X', s'\rangle \not\models \psi'$ and therefore $\mathcal{M}, \langle X, s\rangle \not\models \psi$.

Case 1.2: the assumption of Case 1.1 does not hold.

Hence, $\texttt{NIL-WORLD}(\Sigma, s, \phi)$ calls successfully $\texttt{NIL-WORLD}(\Sigma', s', \phi)$ in the "$\leq$" segment of $\texttt{NIL-WORLD}$, $last(\Sigma') = X'$, $\psi' \notin last(\Sigma')$, $X \preceq X'$, and $X' \subseteq \mathrm{cl}(s', \phi)$. We have either $s' = s$ or $s' = s \cdot \leq$, since the call $\texttt{NIL-WORLD}(\Sigma, s, \phi)$ returns true. By the definition of $S_\leq$, we have $\langle\langle X, s\rangle, \langle X', s'\rangle\rangle \in S_\leq$. Furthermore, $\psi' \in \mathrm{cl}(s', \phi)$ by Lemma 12.5.9. By the induction hypothesis, we have $\mathcal{M}, \langle X', s'\rangle \not\models \psi'$ and therefore $\mathcal{M}, \langle X, s\rangle \not\models \psi$.

If $\psi \in X$, then by (iv), for every $\langle X', s'\rangle \in R_\leq(\langle X, s\rangle)$, we have $\psi' \in X'$

(and $\psi' \in cl(s', \phi)$ by Lemma 12.5.9). By the induction hypothesis, we obtain $\mathcal{M}, \langle X', s' \rangle \models \psi'$ and therefore $\mathcal{M}, \langle X, s \rangle \models \psi$.

Case 2: $\psi = [\geq]\psi'$.

This is analogous to the Case 1 and can be proved by using (v) above and Lemma 12.5.10.

Case 3: $\psi = [\sigma]\psi'$.

By the definition of W, there is a sequence Σ such that $last(\Sigma) = X$ and NIL-WORLD(Σ, s, ϕ) returns true. If $\psi \notin X$, then NIL-WORLD(Σ, s, ϕ) calls NIL-WORLD$(X', s \cdot \sigma, \phi)$ in its "σ" segment, $\psi' \notin last(X')$, $X \approx X'$, and $X' \subseteq cl(s', \phi)$. This is so since NIL-WORLD(Σ, s, ϕ) returns true. By the definition of S_σ, $\langle\langle X, s \rangle, \langle X', s \cdot \sigma \rangle\rangle \in S_\sigma$. By Lemma 12.5.7, $\psi' \in cl(s \cdot \sigma, \phi)$. By the induction hypothesis, we have $\mathcal{M}, \langle X', s \cdot \sigma \rangle \not\models \psi'$ and therefore $\mathcal{M}, \langle X, s \rangle \not\models \psi$.

If $\psi \in X$, then by (vi) for every $\langle X', s' \rangle \in R_\sigma(\langle X, s \rangle)$, we have $\psi' \in X'$ (and $\psi' \in cl(s', \phi)$ by Lemmas 12.5.7 and 12.5.8). By the induction hypothesis, we have $\mathcal{M}, \langle X', s' \rangle \models \psi'$ and therefore $\mathcal{M}, \langle X, s \rangle \models \psi$.

As a conclusion, since $\phi \in Y$ and NIL-WORLD(Y, λ, ϕ) returns true, we get $\mathcal{M}, \langle Y, \lambda \rangle \models \phi$ and therefore ϕ is NIL-satisfiable.   Q.E.D.

Lemma 12.5.14. *For every NIL-formula ϕ, if $\phi \in$ SAT(NIL), then there is a $Y \subseteq cl(\{\phi\})$ such that $\phi \in Y$ and NIL-WORLD(Y, λ, ϕ) returns true.*

Proof. Assume that ϕ is NIL-satisfiable. Hence, there are a NIL-model $\mathcal{M}^0 = \langle W^0, R^0_\leq, R^0_\geq, R^0_\sigma, m^0 \rangle$ and $w^0 \in W^0$ such that $\mathcal{M}^0, w^0 \models \phi$. We shall show that

(i) for every $s \in \{\sigma, \leq, \geq\}^*$ such that neither $\geq \cdot \geq$ nor $\leq \cdot \leq$ occurs in s, if Σ is a finite non-empty sequence of subsets of $cl(s, \phi)$ without repetitions with $last(\Sigma) = X \neq \emptyset$, and there are a NIL-model $\mathcal{M} = \langle W, R_\leq, R_\geq, R_\sigma, m \rangle$ and a $w \in W$ satisfying for every $\psi \in cl(s, \phi)$, $\mathcal{M}, w \models \psi$ iff $\psi \in X$, then NIL-WORLD(Σ, s, ϕ) returns true.

Consequently, by taking $s = \lambda$, $X = \{\psi \in cl(\{\phi\}) : \mathcal{M}^0, w^0 \models \psi\}$, and $\Sigma = X$, we get that NIL-WORLD(X, λ, ϕ) returns true.

The proof of (i) is by double induction on the length of s and on the length of Σ.

Base case 1: $|s| > 3 \times |\phi|$.

Then $cl(s, \phi) = \emptyset$ and therefore (i) holds.

Induction hypothesis 1: for every $s' \in \{\sigma, \leq, \geq\}^*$ if neither $\geq \cdot \geq$ nor $\leq \cdot \leq$ occurs in s', $|s'| \geq n$ for some $n \geq 1$, Σ is a finite non-empty sequence of subsets of $cl(s, \phi)$ without repetitions with $last(\Sigma) = X \neq \emptyset$, and there are a NIL-model $\mathcal{M} = \langle W, R_\leq, R_\geq, R_\sigma, m \rangle$ and a $w \in W$ satisfying for every $\psi \in cl(s', \phi)$, $\mathcal{M}, w \models \psi$ iff $\psi \in X$, then NIL-WORLD(Σ, s', ϕ) returns true.

Let $s \in \{\sigma, \leq, \geq\}^*$ and neither $\geq \cdot \geq$ nor $\leq \cdot \leq$ occurs in s, $|s| = n - 1$. Let Σ be a finite non-empty sequence of subsets of $cl(s, \phi)$ without repetitions with $last(\Sigma) = X \neq \emptyset$ such that there are a NIL-model $\mathcal{M} = \langle W, R_\leq, R_\geq, R_\sigma, m \rangle$

and a $w \in W$ satisfying for every $\psi \in \mathrm{cl}(s, \phi)$, $\mathcal{M}, w \models \psi$ iff $\psi \in X$. Now we apply a second induction on the length of Σ.

Base case 2: $|\Sigma| > 2^{\mathrm{card}(\mathrm{cl}(s,\phi))}$.

Σ contains duplicates and (i) holds.

Induction hypothesis 2: for every finite non-empty sequence Σ of subsets of $\mathrm{cl}(s, \phi)$ that contains no duplicates, $last(\Sigma) = X$, $|\Sigma| \geq n'$ for some $n' \geq 1$, and there are a NIL-model $\mathcal{M} = \langle W, R_<, R_>, R_\sigma, m \rangle$ and a $w \in W$ satisfying for every $\psi \in \mathrm{cl}(s, \phi)$, $\mathcal{M}, w \models \psi$ iff $\psi \in X$, then NIL-WORLD(Σ, s, ϕ) returns true.

Assume that Σ is a sequence of subsets of $\mathrm{cl}(s, \phi)$ that contains no duplicates, $last(\Sigma) = X$, $|\Sigma| = n' - 1$, and there are a NIL-model $\mathcal{M} = \langle W, R_<, R_>, R_\sigma, m \rangle$ and a $w \in W$ satisfying for every $\psi \in \mathrm{cl}(s, \phi)$, $\mathcal{M}, w \models \psi$ iff $\psi \in X$. X is s-consistent by Lemma 12.5.5 and NIL-WORLD(Σ, s, ϕ) returns false only because either the segment "σ", or the segment "$\geq$", or the segment "$\leq$" returns false.

Case 1: for every $[\leq]\psi \in \mathrm{cl}(s, \phi) \setminus X$, $\mathcal{M}, w \not\models [\leq]\psi$.

So there is a $w' \in W$ such that $\langle w, w' \rangle \in R_<$ and $\mathcal{M}, w' \not\models \psi$. Let Y be a subset of $\mathrm{cl}(s \cdot \leq, \phi)$ such that for every $\varphi \in \mathrm{cl}(s \cdot \leq, \phi)$, $\varphi \in Y \stackrel{\text{def}}{\Leftrightarrow} \mathcal{M}, w' \models \varphi$. So $\psi \notin Y$ and $X \preceq Y$ by Lemma 12.5.12(III).

If $Y \in \Sigma$ and $last(s) = \leq$, then no recursive call to NIL-WORLD is needed by definition of the procedure NIL-WORLD. If $Y \notin \Sigma$ or $last(s) \neq \leq$, then either NIL-WORLD$(\Sigma.Y, s, \phi)$ returns true (by the induction hypothesis 2) or NIL-WORLD$(Y, s \cdot \leq, \phi)$ returns true (by the induction hypothesis 1). Therefore, NIL-WORLD(Σ, s, ϕ) does not return false in the "$\leq$" segment of NIL-WORLD. Similarly, we can show that NIL-WORLD(Σ, s, ϕ) does not return false in the "$\geq$" segment of NIL-WORLD.

Case 2: for every $[\sigma]\psi \in \mathrm{cl}(s, \phi) \setminus X$, $\mathcal{M}, w \not\models [\sigma]\psi$.

So there is a $w' \in W$ such that $\langle w, w' \rangle \in R_\sigma$ and $\mathcal{M}, w' \not\models \psi$. Let Y be the subset of $\mathrm{cl}(s \cdot \sigma, \phi)$ such that for every $\varphi \in \mathrm{cl}(s \cdot \sigma, \phi)$, $\varphi \in Y \stackrel{\text{def}}{\Leftrightarrow} \mathcal{M}, w' \models \varphi$. Hence, $\psi \notin Y$ and $X \approx Y$ by Lemma 12.5.12(II). By the induction hypothesis 1 (remember that $\psi \in \mathrm{cl}(s \cdot \sigma, \phi)$), NIL-WORLD$(Y, s \cdot \sigma, \phi)$ returns true. Therefore, NIL-WORLD(Σ, s, ϕ) does not return false in the "σ" segment of NIL-WORLD. Observe that the induction hypothesis 2 is not used in this case. Indeed, NIL-WORLD$(\Sigma'', s'' \cdot \sigma, \phi) = $ NIL-WORLD$(last(\Sigma''), s'' \cdot \sigma, \phi)$ for every finite non-empty sequence Σ'' of elements of $\mathrm{cl}(s'' \cdot \sigma, \phi)$ and $s'' \in \{\sigma, \leq, \geq\}^*$. In other words, for a "σ" transition, we do not need to keep track of the history of the R_σ-path.

Consequently, since neither the segment "σ", nor the segment "$\geq$", nor the segment "$\leq$" returns false, NIL-WORLD(Σ, s, ϕ) returns true and this completes the proof.   *Q.E.D.*

Since NIL-WORLD is correct, the proof of Lemma 12.5.13 provides the finite model property for NIL and an exponential bound for the size of the models. These results could be also obtained using a filtration construction (see Sect. 11.2.1) but here we get them as a by-product of the complexity result. Finally, we obtain the following theorem.

Theorem 12.5.6. SAT(NIL) *is in* **PSPACE**.

Proof. By Lemmas 12.5.13 and 12.5.14, for every formula ϕ, ϕ is NIL-satisfiable iff there is an $X \subseteq \text{cl}(\{\phi\})$ such that $\text{NIL-WORLD}(X, \lambda, \phi)$ returns true. By Theorem 12.5.5, $\text{NIL-WORLD}(X, \lambda, \phi)$ requires space in $\mathcal{O}(|\phi|^4)$ and the bit-string encoding the subsets of $\text{cl}(\{\phi\})$ is of length $\mathcal{O}(|\phi|)$.   *Q.E.D.*

12.6 S5′-satisfiability is EXPTIME-complete

To show the **EXPTIME**-hardness of SAT(S5′), it is sufficient to observe that the general results can be applied here (see Sect. 12.9 for references). To show that SAT(S5′) is in **EXPTIME**, we use the same method that is applied to proving that PDL-satisfiability is in **EXPTIME**. First, we recall some facts about the canonical structure for HS5′ presented in Sect. 11.2.3. Let ϕ be an S5′-formula and $\text{sub}^+(\phi)$ be the set of S5′-formulae defined in Sect. 11.2.3. Given the canonical structure $\mathcal{M}^c$ for HS5′ and a formula ϕ, one can define a $\langle M(\phi), \text{FOR}_0(\phi) \rangle$-partial S5′-model $\mathcal{M}_\phi^{fc}$. The set W^{fc}, the domain of $\mathcal{M}_\phi^{fc}$, consists of subsets of $\text{sub}^+(\phi)$. More precisely, W^{fc} is the greatest set of maximal HS5′-consistent subsets of $\text{sub}^+(\phi)$, that is for every $X \in W^{fc}$ and for all formulae ψ, ψ_1, and ψ_2, we have:

(1) $X \subset \text{sub}^+(\phi)$;
(2) if $\psi \in \text{sub}(\phi)$, then $\{\psi, \neg\psi\} \not\subseteq X$;
(3) if $\psi \in \text{sub}(\phi)$, then $\{\psi, \neg\psi\} \cap X \neq \emptyset$;
(4) if $\neg\neg\psi \in X$, then $\psi \in X$;
(5) if $\psi_1 \wedge \psi_2 \in X$, then $\{\psi_1, \psi_2\} \subseteq X$;
(6) if $\neg(\psi_1 \wedge \psi_2) \in X$, then $\{\neg\psi_1, \neg\psi_2\} \cap X \neq \emptyset$;
(7) if $\neg[a]\psi \in X$, then there is a $Y \in W^{fc}$ such that
    (7.1) $\neg\psi \in Y$;
    (7.2) $[U]X = [U]Y$;
    (7.3) for every $b \in M(\phi) \setminus \{U\}$ such that $M_0(b) \subseteq M_0(a)$, $[b]X = [b]Y$;
(8) if $[a]\psi \in X$, then $\psi \in X$.

A set X of S5′-formulae is said to be *maximally propositionally consistent with respect to* $\text{sub}^+(\phi) \overset{\text{def}}{\Leftrightarrow} X$ satisfies conditions (1)–(6) above. So $\phi \in$ SAT(S5′) iff ϕ is satisfiable in $\mathcal{M}_\phi^c$ iff there is a maximal HS5′-consistent subset $X \in W^{fc}$ such that $\phi \in X$. Hence, for every set X that is maximally propositionally consistent with respect to $\text{sub}^+(\phi)$, if X does not satisfy any of conditions (7) and (8), then the S5′-formula $\bigwedge_{\psi \in X} \psi$ is not S5′-satisfiable. We are now in a position to show the following result.

Theorem 12.6.1. SAT(S5′) *is in* **EXPTIME**.

Proof. The present proof can be viewed as a partial construction of W^{fc} with ϕ being the input formula. Such a construction requires at most exponential-time in $|\phi|$. Actually, it takes time $p_1(|\phi|) + 2^{p_2(\text{card}(\text{sub}(\phi)))}$ for some polynomials p_1 and p_2. The different occurrences of $|\phi|$ and $\text{card}(\text{sub}(\phi))$ in the complexity function will be of great importance for showing that SAT(LKO) is in **EXPTIME**.

Let ϕ be an S5'-formula. We shall either construct a $\langle M(\phi), \text{FOR}_0(\phi) \rangle$-partial S5'-model satisfying ϕ or prove that none exists.
Let $M(\phi) = \{a_1, \ldots, a_n\}$, $n \geq 1$, and let

$$Mat \overset{\text{def}}{=} (Mat_{\langle i,j \rangle})_{\langle i,j \rangle \in \{1,\ldots,n\} \times \{1,\ldots,n\}}$$

be the Boolean matrix such that for all $i, j \in \{1, \ldots, n\}$, $Mat_{i,j} \overset{\text{def}}{=} 1$ if $M_0(a_i) \subseteq M_0(a_j)$, otherwise $Mat_{i,j} \overset{\text{def}}{=} 0$. The matrix Mat can be built in deterministic polynomial-time in $|\phi|$.

Let $W^1(\phi)$ be the set of all the sets that are maximally proposition-ally consistent with respect to $\text{sub}^+(\phi)$. The set $W^1(\phi)$ contains less than $2^{\text{card}(\text{sub}^+(\phi))}$ sets and $W^{fc} \subseteq W^1(\phi)$. $W^1(\phi)$ can be built in deterministic exponential-time in $\text{card}(\text{sub}(\phi))$. We define a finite sequence of structures

$$\mathcal{M}^j = \langle W^j, (R_a^j)_{a \in M(\phi) \cup \{U\}}, m^j \rangle,$$

where $j \in \{1, \ldots, k+1\}$ for some $k \geq 1$, $W^1 = W^1(\phi)$, $W^{k+1} = W^k$, and for every $j < k$, $W^{j+1} \subset W^j$. Suppose we have defined W^j. We define $(R_a^j)_{a \in M(\phi) \cup \{U\}}$ and m^j as follows:

* for every $p \in \text{FOR}_0(\phi)$, $X \in m^j(p) \overset{\text{def}}{\Leftrightarrow} p \in X$;
* $\langle X, Y \rangle \in R_U^j \overset{\text{def}}{\Leftrightarrow} [U]X = [U]Y$;
* for every $a \in M(\phi) \setminus \{U\}$ $\langle X, Y \rangle \in R_a^j \overset{\text{def}}{\Leftrightarrow} [U]X = [U]Y$ and for every $b \in M(\text{sub}(\phi))$, if $M_0(b) \subseteq M_0(a)$, then $[b]X = [b]Y$.

A set $X \in W^j$ is *locally fine* $\overset{\text{def}}{\Leftrightarrow}$

* if $\neg[a]\psi \in X$, then there is a $Y \in W^j$ such that
  * $\neg\psi \in Y$;
  * $[U]X = [U]Y$;
  * for every $b \in M(\phi) \setminus \{U\}$, if $M_0(b) \subseteq M_0(a)$, then $[b]X = [b]Y$;
* X satisfies condition (8).

If every set in W^j is locally fine and $\phi \in X$ for some $X \in W^j$, then return "yes" (ϕ is S5'-satisfiable). If there is no locally fine state $X \in W^j$ such that $\phi \in X$, then return "no" (ϕ is not S5'-satisfiable). Otherwise, let W^{j+1} be the set of all locally fine sets in W^j and continue the construction.

Since $W^{j+1} \subset W^j$ and W^1 has at most $2^{\text{card}(\text{sub}^+(\phi))}$ elements, this construction terminates after at most exponentially many steps. Computing which sets of W^j are locally fine can be done in deterministic polynomial-time in card(W^j), that is in at most exponential-time in card(sub(ϕ)). Observe that in order to determine what are the locally fine sets of W^j, at each step we only need to compute the relations R_a^j for a $\in$ M(sub(ϕ))$\cup\{U\}$. Moreover, the cardinality of M(sub(ϕ))$\cup\{U\}$ is linear in card(sub(ϕ)). Thus, the whole construction can be done in deterministic exponential-time in card(sub(ϕ)) plus the time to compute the matrix Mat which is polynomial in $|\phi|$. It remains to show:

(i) $\mathcal{M}^j$ is a $\langle M(\phi), FOR_0(\phi)\rangle$-partial S5'-model;
(ii) if all the sets in W^j are locally fine, then $\mathcal{M}^j, X \models \psi$ iff $\psi \in X$ for every $X \in W^j$ and for every $\psi \in$ sub(ϕ).

Proof of (i): let a, b $\in$ M(ϕ) $\cup\{U\}$.
Case 1: b = U.
So $\emptyset = M_0(b) \subseteq M_0(a)$. If a = U, then $R_a^j = R_b^j$. Otherwise, $R_a^j = R_U^j$ by the definition of R_a^j.
Case 2: a = U and b $\neq$ U.
Since $M_0(b) \not\subseteq M_0(a)$, the proof is immediate.
Case 3: $M_0(b) \subseteq M_0(a)$ and U $\notin \{a, b\}$.
By definition, for all $X, Y \in W^j$, $\langle X, Y\rangle \in R_a^j$ iff $\langle X, Y\rangle \in R_U^j$ and for every b' $\in$ M(sub(ϕ)) such that $M_0(b') \subseteq M_0(a)$, we have $[b']X = [b']Y$. So $\langle X, Y\rangle \in R_a^j$ iff

$\star$ $\langle X, Y\rangle \in R_U^j$;
$\star$ for every b' $\in$ M(sub(ϕ)) such that $M_0(b') \subseteq M_0(b)$, we have $[b']X = [b']Y$;
$\star$ for every b' $\in$ M(sub(ϕ)) such that $M_0(b) \not\subseteq M_0(b')$ and $M_0(b') \subseteq M_0(a)$, we have $[b']X = [b']Y$.

So $\langle X, Y\rangle \in R_a^j$ iff $\langle X, Y\rangle \in R_b^j$ and for every b' $\in$ M(sub(ϕ)), if $M_0(b) \not\subseteq M_0(b')$ and $M_0(b') \subseteq M_0(a)$, then we have $[b']X = [b']Y$. Consequently, $R_a^j \subseteq R_b^j$.
The proof of (ii) is by induction on the structure of formulae.
It follows that ϕ is S5'-satisfiable whenever a set W^j (all its elements are locally fine) contains a set X such that $\phi \in X$. Furthermore, if there are no locally fine sets $X \in W^j$ such that $\phi \in X$, then ϕ is not S5'-satisfiable. Indeed, by construction $W^{fc} \subseteq W^j$. Furthermore, ϕ is not S5'-satisfiable iff there is no $X \in W^{fc}$ such that $\phi \in X$. This concludes the correctness of the algorithm.   Q.E.D.

12.7 LKO-satisfiability is EXPTIME-complete

The results presented in Sect. 11.2.3 enable us to prove the following theorem.

Theorem 12.7.1. SAT(LKO) *is* **EXPTIME**-*complete*.

Proof. Let $h^\leftarrow$ be the map defined in the proof of Theorem 9.4.1 for a given S5'-formula ϕ. $h^\leftarrow(\phi)$ cannot be computed in polynomial-time in $|\phi|$, since $h^\leftarrow(\psi)$ occurs twice in the recursive definition of $h^\leftarrow([a]\psi)$. We define a variant of $h^\leftarrow$ by renaming subformulae. Let ϕ be an S5'-formula. With every $\psi \in$ sub(ϕ), we associate a *fresh* (not occurring in ϕ and not used so far by the algorithm) propositional variable p_ψ and a formula φ_ψ defined as follows:

⋆ if ψ is a propositional variable, then $\varphi_\psi \overset{\text{def}}{=} \top$;
⋆ if $\psi = \psi_1 \wedge \psi_2$, then $\varphi_\psi \overset{\text{def}}{=} (p_\psi \Leftrightarrow (p_{\psi_1} \wedge p_{\psi_2}))$;
⋆ if $\psi = [U]\psi_1$, then $\varphi_\psi \overset{\text{def}}{=} (p_\psi \Leftrightarrow (p_{\psi_1} \wedge K(C_1 \cap -C_1)p_{\psi_1}))$;
⋆ if $\psi = [c_{i_1} \cap \ldots \cap c_{i_l}]\psi_1$, then $\varphi_\psi \overset{\text{def}}{=} (p_\psi \Leftrightarrow (p_{\psi_1} \wedge K(B_{i_1} \cap \ldots \cap B_{i_l})p_{\psi_1}))$.

Let $f^\leftarrow(\phi)$ be defined as follows:

$$f^\leftarrow(\phi) \overset{\text{def}}{=} (\bigwedge_{\psi \in \text{sub}(\phi)} \varphi_\psi \wedge K(B_{i_1} \cap \ldots \cap B_{i_l})\varphi_\psi) \wedge p_\phi.$$

We already know that $\phi \in$ SAT(S5') iff $h^\leftarrow(\phi) \in$ SAT(LKO). By using standard methods for the renaming of subformulae, we can establish that $h^\leftarrow(\phi) \in$ SAT(LKO) iff $f^\leftarrow(\phi) \in$ SAT(LKO). So there is a logarithmic space transformation from SAT(S5') into SAT(LKO).

Now we prove the complexity upper bound. For every LKO-formula ϕ, N(ϕ) can be computed in time $\mathcal{O}(2^{p(|\phi|)})$ for some polynomial p. Moreover:

⋆ card(sub(ϕ)) = card(sub(N(ϕ))) and
⋆ card(sub($f(\phi)$)) $\leq 3 \times$ card(sub(ϕ)).

So there is a polynomial $p'(n)$ such that $|f(\phi)|$ is in $\mathcal{O}(2^{p'(|\phi|)})$ where f is defined in Sect. 9.4.2. Hence, deciding whether $f(\phi)$ is S5'-satisfiable can be solved in time $\mathcal{O}(2^{p(|\phi|)} + p_1(2^{p'(|\phi|)}) + 2^{p_2(3 \times \text{card}(\text{sub}(\phi)))})$, which is of the form $\mathcal{O}(2^{q(|\phi|)})$ for some polynomial q (see Sect. 12.6).   *Q.E.D.*

12.8 Other Complexity Bounds

Complexity bounds for many other information logics can be given based on the known results. As far as the satisfiability problem for consistent information logics is concerned, **NP**-hardness is obvious, since SAT(PC) is **NP**-hard.

12.8.1 Sharp Characterisations

SAT(DALLA) is in **NEXPTIME**, since every $\phi \in$ SAT(DALLA) has a finite DALLA-model of the size exponential in $|\phi|$ and the class of DALLA-frames is first-order definable. However, a Ladner-like algorithm leads to the following result.

Theorem 12.8.1. SAT(DALLA) *is* **PSPACE**-*complete.*

The **PSPACE** lower bound can be shown by reducing QBF (see Theorem 6.4.2) into the satisfiability problem SAT(DALLA$'$). One can also prove that SAT(DALLA) is in **PSPACE** by constructing a Ladner-like algorithm that employs the developments of Sect. 12.5. Similarly, one can show the following result.

Lemma 12.8.1. SAT(LGM) *is* **PSPACE**-*complete.*

12.8.2 Loose Characterisations

To show the **EXPTIME**-hardness of SAT(SIM$'$), it is sufficient to observe that known results can be applied here (see Sect. 12.9 for references).

Theorem 12.8.2. SAT(SIM$'$) *is* **EXPTIME**-*hard.*

The **EXPTIME**-hardness of SAT(DAL) can be also obtained applying the known results quoted in Sect. 12.9.

Lemma 12.8.2. SAT(DAL) *is* **EXPTIME**-*hard.*

SAT(IL) is in **NEXPTIME**, since every $\phi \in$ SAT(IL) has a finite IL-model of size exponential in $|\phi|$. Furthermore, the following holds.

Lemma 12.8.3. SAT(IL) *is* **PSPACE**-*hard.*

Proof. Let $X =$ SAT(IL)$\cap \{\phi \in$ FOR(IL)$: M(\phi) \subseteq \{\leq\}\}$. We shall show that X and SAT(S4) are equal modulo the replacement of $[\leq]$ by $\Box$. If $\phi \in X$, it is easy to see that $\phi \in$ SAT($S4$) since by removing R_σ, $R_\equiv$, and D from an IL-model for ϕ, we get an S4-model. Moreover, if $\phi \in$ SAT($S4$), then there is an S4-model $\mathcal{M} = \langle W, R, m \rangle$ such that $\mathcal{M}, w \models \phi$ for some $w \in W$. Let $\mathcal{M}' = \langle W \times \{1, 2\}, R_\equiv, R_\leq, R_\sigma, D, m' \rangle$ be the IL-model such that:

* $R_\leq \overset{\text{def}}{=} \{\langle\langle x, i\rangle, \langle y, j\rangle\rangle \in (W \times \{1, 2\}) \times (W \times \{1, 2\}) : \langle x, y\rangle \in R, i = j\}$;
* $R_\equiv \overset{\text{def}}{=} R_\leq \cap R_\leq^{-1}$;
* $R_\sigma \overset{\text{def}}{=} (W \times \{1, 2\}) \times (W \times \{1, 2\})$;
* $D = \emptyset$;
* for every p $\in$ FOR$_0$, $m'(\mathrm{p}) \overset{\text{def}}{=} \{\langle x, i\rangle : i \in \{1, 2\}, x \in m(\mathrm{p})\}$.

Obviously, $\mathcal{M}', \langle w, 1\rangle \models \phi$ (modulo the replacement of $[\leq]$ by $\Box$).   *Q.E.D.*

We conjecture that IL-satisfiability is in **PSPACE**. The proof could be based on a technique similar to the one presented in Sect. 12.5 for the logic NIL.

12.9 Notes

Complexity of IND. A better complexity upper bound for SAT(IND) can be established. Indeed, a more sophisticated proof based on [Lyn77] can show that SAT(IND) is in **LOGSPACE**.

Complexity of NIL. The procedure designed in Sect. 12.5 has a direct filiation with the results in [Lad77, HM92, Spa93b]. The function NIL-WORLD is actually defined as the function K-WORLD in [Lad77] and it is an extension of the function $S4_t$-WORLD defined in [Spa93b]. The detection of cycles for S4 modal connectives in NIL is similar to the proof-theoretical results from [CCM97] that are related to the techniques from [Lad77, Fit88].

The proof of Lemma 12.5.13 can be viewed as a way to transform a successful call NIL-WORLD(Y, λ, ϕ) into a quasi-NIL-model by analysing the computation tree of NIL-WORLD(Y, λ, ϕ). Then, this quasi-NIL-model is appropriately completed in order to get a NIL-model. The idea to construct a (standard) model from different coherent pieces is very common in establishing decidability and complexity results for modal logics (see for instance [Lad77, Pra79, VW94, Mar97, BS01, BRV01]). A mosaics technique also applies such an approach (see e.g. [Mar97]). The **PSPACE**-completeness of NIL is proved in [Dem00]. This is in agreement with the fact that **PSPACE** is known to be the complexity class for modal logics. However, it is also known that the satisfiability of polymodal logics can be **EXPTIME**-hard if the universal modal connective or the reflexive transitive modal connective is added to their languages [Hem96]. Furthermore, **PSPACE**-hardness for satisfiability is not a systematic feature of polymodal information logics (assuming **NP** $\neq$ **PSPACE**). For instance, the bi-modal information logic containing a modal connective for indiscernibility and a modal connective for complementarity has an **NP**-complete satisfiability problem [DOV99]. Furthermore, the approximation multi-modal logics AML(τ_m) introduced in [Ste98] can be shown to have a **PSPACE** satisfiability problem by adapting our developments for NIL [DS00]. By contrast, in [DS00] it is shown that multi-modal logics with modal connectives based on tolerance relations have **EXPTIME**-complete satisfiability problems. Theorem 12.5.2(I) is a consequence of [Lad77, CL94, Mar97] whereas Theorem 12.5.2(II) is a consequence of [Spa93b].

Complexity of S5'. **EXPTIME**-hardness of the satisfiability problems for the logics S5', SIM', and DAL is a corollary of [Hem96, Theorem 5.1]. The technique we use in Sect. 12.6 is a variant of the one used in [HM92, Theorem 6.20] for showing that the satisfiability problem for the knowledge logic $S5_n^C$ is in **EXPTIME**. This technique has been originally introduced in [Pra79] for showing that the satisfiability problem for PDL is in **EXPTIME**. For the sake of comparison, the satisfiability problems for PDL and for the knowledge logic $S5_n^C$, $n > 1$, are also **EXPTIME**-complete.

Complexity of LKO. Although LKO and Boolean modal logic BML [GP90] have many similarities (their modal connectives are indexed by Boolean terms), BML-satisfiability is **NEXPTIME**-complete [LS00] but LKO-satisfiability is "only" **EXPTIME**-complete.

Nice unbounded LA-logics. The logics DALLA and LGM are nice unbounded LA-logic in the sense of [Dem02]. **PSPACE**-completeness of every nice unbounded LA-logics is shown in [Dem02].

Complexity of SIM'. The **EXPTIME**-completeness of SIM' satisfiability is an open question.

Part V

Representability and Duality

13. Informational Representability

13.1 Introduction and Outline of the Chapter

Any abstract mathematical structure, for example an abstract algebra or an abstract relational system, is intended to serve as a pattern of a class of "concrete" structures. In the concrete structures their components, for instance the operations or the relations, are defined directly, while in the abstract structures they are defined in terms of a set of conditions treated as axioms. As an example consider Boolean algebras. In the algebras of sets the operations of union, intersection, and complement of sets are defined in the well known way. These are the direct definitions saying how the respective compound sets are made out of the component sets. An abstract Boolean algebra is defined in an axiomatic way. Join, meet, and complement of elements of any algebra from the class are assumed to satisfy some conditions.

The adequacy of an abstract structure for providing a general scheme of concrete structures is typically expressed as a representation theorem of the following form: for every abstract structure F from a certain class C of structures there is a concrete structure S that is a member of the class C and F and S are isomorphic in a suitable sense. For example, the Stone representation theorem for Boolean algebras establishes an isomorphism between any abstract Boolean algebra and a Boolean algebra of sets.

In this chapter we put forward an idea of representability for the structures that arise in connection with reasoning about incomplete information. The abstract structures dealt with in this chapter are relational systems that are extensions of relative frames. The concrete structures are frames derived from information systems. The relations in those frames are defined in terms of the informational resources of an information system.

The purpose of this chapter is to elaborate a formal framework for expressing and proving informational representability of abstract information frames. Let a relation $\triangleright$ in a class C of frames be given, for example the relation of "being isomorphic" or "being modally equivalent". Intuitively, a frame F from the class C is informationally $\triangleright$-representable $\overset{\text{def}}{\Leftrightarrow}$ there are an information system S and a frame F' derived from the system S such that F' is in the class C and, moreover, F is $\triangleright$-related to F'. In this chapter, we introduce a general notion of informational representability, we develop a method of proving informational representability, and we give examples of informational representability and non-representability of frames.

In Sect. 13.2 we introduce a general notion of frame that generalises the notion of relative frame introduced in Sect. 3.9. Our intention is to capture all the structures derived from information systems that have been considered in the literature. In Sect. 13.3 we introduce a natural first-order theory of information systems. The formulae of this theory, referred to as specifications, provide a means for defining relations derived from information systems. The concept of informational representability of frames is introduced in Sect. 13.4. In Sects. 13.5 and 13.6 we develop a method of proving informational representability. The method is referred to as the nice set proof technique after the name of an important construction which is a part of it. The method is very general and can be applied to a variety of classes of frames. In Sect. 13.7 we study a number of syntactic transformations of specifications that induce representability-preserving transformations of frames. In Sect. 13.8 we give several examples of informational representability of frames; in particular, we develop representability results for information frames presented in Sect. 3.9. By contrast, in Sect. 13.9 we present frames that are not informationally representable in our framework.

13.2 Frames with Relative Relations

The abstract information structures studied in this chapter are generalisations of the relative frames of level 1 in the sense of Definition 3.9.2. In those relative frames the relations in each family of relations are indexed with all the elements of $\mathcal{P}(PAR)$. In this section, we define frames such that the relations in a family may be indexed with a subfamily of $\mathcal{P}(PAR)$. For that purpose, we consider a *subpowerset map* $f : \mathcal{P}(U) \to \mathcal{P}^2(U)$, for a non-empty set U, such that for all $X, Y \in \mathcal{P}(U)$, $f(X) \subseteq \mathcal{P}(X)$ and for every 1–1 mapping $g : X \to Y$, we have $f(Y) = \{g(x) : x \in f(X)\}$. A *frame signature* Σ is a non-empty sequence $\langle n_1, \ldots, n_k \rangle$, $k \geq 1$, of natural numbers strictly greater than 0. The number k determines the number of (families of) relations and each element of the sequence $\langle n_1, \ldots, n_k \rangle$ represents the arity of the relations from the corresponding family.

Definition 13.2.1. *Let $\Sigma = \langle n_1, \ldots, n_k \rangle$ be a frame signature and let f be a subpowerset map. By a $\langle \Sigma, f \rangle$-frame we mean a structure*

$$\langle W, (\mathcal{R}_P^1)_{P \in f(PAR)}, \ldots, (\mathcal{R}_P^k)_{P \in f(PAR)} \rangle,$$

where W and PAR are non-empty sets and for every $P \in f(PAR)$, for every $l \in \{1, \ldots, k\}$, $\mathcal{R}_P^l$ is a n_l-ary relation on W.

If $f = \mathcal{P}$ (the powerset map), then $\langle W, (\mathcal{R}_P^1)_{P \subseteq PAR}, \ldots, (\mathcal{R}_P^k)_{P \subseteq PAR} \rangle$ is called a *full Σ-frame*. If $f = f_0$ with $f_0(PAR) \overset{\text{def}}{=} \{PAR\}$, then

$$\langle W, (\mathcal{R}_P^1)_{P \in \{PAR\}}, \ldots, (\mathcal{R}_P^k)_{P \in \{PAR\}} \rangle$$

is called a *plain Σ-frame.*

An obvious generalisation consists in introducing a vector $\langle f_1, \ldots, f_k \rangle$, $k \geq 1$, of subpowerset maps and in postulating that each family of relations may have different indices.

Definition 13.2.2. *Let $F_i = \langle W_i, (\mathcal{R}_P^{i,1})_{P \in f(PAR_i)}, \ldots, (\mathcal{R}_P^{i,k})_{P \in f(PAR_i)} \rangle$, $i = 1, 2$ be $\langle \Sigma, f \rangle$-frames. F_1 and F_2 are said to be isomorphic (written $F_1 \simeq F_2$) $\overset{def}{\Leftrightarrow}$ there exist 1-1 mappings $g_1 : W_1 \to W_2$ and $g_2 : PAR_1 \to PAR_2$ such that for every $l \in \{1, \ldots, k\}$, for every $P \in f(PAR_1)$, and for all $w_1, \ldots, w_{n_l} \in W_1$, $\langle w_1, \ldots, w_{n_l} \rangle \in \mathcal{R}_P^{1,l}$ iff $\langle g_1(w_1), \ldots, g_1(w_{n_l}) \rangle \in \mathcal{R}_{g_2(P)}^{2,l}$.*

Example 13.2.1. Any indiscernibility frame in FVS-IND is a full $\langle 2 \rangle$-frame, whereas any modal frame $\langle W, R \rangle$ is a plain $\langle 2 \rangle$-frame.

Definition 13.2.3. *A relative $\langle \Sigma, f \rangle$-frame*

$$\langle W', (\mathcal{R}_P'^1)_{P \in f(PAR)}, \ldots, (\mathcal{R}_P'^k)_{P \in f(PAR)} \rangle$$

is said to be a subframe of the $\langle \Sigma, f \rangle$-frame

$$\langle W, (\mathcal{R}_P^1)_{P \in f(PAR)}, \ldots, (\mathcal{R}_P^k)_{P \in f(PAR)} \rangle$$

$\overset{def}{\Leftrightarrow}$ $W' \subseteq W$ *and for every $l \in \{1, \ldots, k\}$ and for every $P \in f(PAR)$, $\mathcal{R}_P'^l = \mathcal{R}_P^l \cap (W')^{n_l}$.*

13.3 Derivation of Frames from Information Systems

We introduce a natural first-order theory of information systems for which the formulae provide a means for defining relations derived from information systems.

13.3.1 A First-order Theory of Information Systems

In this section we introduce a fragment FOL-IS of FOL referred to as a first-order theory of information systems. FOL-IS is obtained from FOL by restricting the set of predicate symbols. The only predicate symbols of FOL-IS are the following:

⋆ unary predicate symbols OB, AT, VAL;
⋆ a binary predicate symbol IsValueOf;
⋆ a ternary predicate symbol Value;
⋆ the identity =.

Let $S = \langle OB, AT, (VAL_a)_{a \in AT}, f \rangle$ be an information system and $A \subseteq AT$. Let $\mathcal{M}_{S,A} = \langle D, m \rangle$ be the FOL-IS structure such that

⋆ $D \stackrel{\text{def}}{=} OB \cup A \cup \bigcup\{VAL_a : a \in A\}$;
⋆ $m(\text{OB}) \stackrel{\text{def}}{=} OB$; $m(\text{AT}) \stackrel{\text{def}}{=} A$; $m(\text{VAL}) \stackrel{\text{def}}{=} \bigcup\{VAL_a : a \in A\}$;
⋆ $m(\text{IsValueOf}) \stackrel{\text{def}}{=} \{\langle a, u \rangle \in A \times m(\text{VAL}) : u \in VAL_a\}$;
⋆ $m(\text{Value}) \stackrel{\text{def}}{=} \{\langle x, a, u \rangle \in OB \times AT \times m(\text{VAL}) : u \in f(x, a)\}$.

In the sequel, we may write $\mathcal{M}_S$ instead of $\mathcal{M}_{S,AT}$ and $S, v \models \phi$ instead of $\mathcal{M}_S, v \models \phi$ for every valuation v in $\mathcal{M}_S$.

Lemma 13.3.1. *For every information system $S = \langle OB, AT \rangle$, for every $\emptyset \neq A \subseteq AT$, the following formulae are true in $\mathcal{M}_{S,A}$:*

(F1) $\exists x\ \text{OB}(x)$;
(F2) $\exists x\ \text{AT}(x)$;
(F3) $\forall x\ \text{AT}(x) \Rightarrow \exists y\ \text{IsValueOf}(x, y)$;
(F4) $\forall x\ \text{VAL}(x) \Rightarrow \exists y\ \text{IsValueOf}(y, x)$;
(F5) $\forall x\ (\text{OB}(x) \vee \text{AT}(x) \vee \text{VAL}(x))$;
(F6) $\forall x_1, x_2\ (\text{IsValueOf}(x_1, x_2) \Rightarrow \text{AT}(x_1) \wedge \text{VAL}(x_2))$;
(F7) $\forall x_1, x_2, x_3\ (\text{Value}(x_1, x_2, x_3) \Rightarrow \text{OB}(x_1) \wedge \text{IsValueOf}(x_2, x_3))$.

The proof is by an easy verification.

Lemma 13.3.2. *For every FOL-IS structure $\mathcal{M}$ satisfying (F1)–(F7), there is an information system S such that $\mathcal{M}_S = \mathcal{M}$.*

A *pseudo-information system* is a FOL-IS structure satisfying (F1), (F3), (F4), (F5), (F6), (F7), and

(F2') $\neg \exists x\ \text{AT}(x) \wedge \neg \exists x\ \text{VAL}(x)$.

A pseudo-information system is a degenerate information system with the empty set of attributes.

Let $\mathcal{M} = \langle D, m \rangle$ be a FOL-IS structure and ϕ be a formula such that the free variables occurring in ϕ are $x_1, \ldots, x_n$, $n \geq 1$ (in the order of enumeration). The extension of ϕ in $\mathcal{M}$ is defined as follows:

$$ext(\mathcal{M}, \phi) \stackrel{\text{def}}{=} \{\langle v(x_1), \ldots, v(x_n) \rangle : v \text{ is a valuation in } \mathcal{M}, \text{ and } \mathcal{M}, v \models \phi\}.$$

Example 13.3.1. Let ϕ^{ind} be the following FOL-IS-formula:

$$\phi^{ind} \stackrel{\text{def}}{=} (\text{OB}(x_1) \wedge \text{OB}(x_2)) \wedge \forall x_3\ (\text{AT}(x_3) \Rightarrow$$

$$\forall x_4\ (\text{IsValueOf}(x_3, x_4) \Rightarrow (\text{Value}(x_1, x_3, x_4) \Leftrightarrow \text{Value}(x_2, x_3, x_4))))).$$

It is easy to see that $ext(\mathcal{M}_S, \phi^{ind})$ is the indiscernibility relation $ind(AT)$.

13.3.2 Σ-specification

The language FOL-IS can express definitions of relations derived from information systems (see Sect. 3.2). These definitions will be referred to as *specifications*.

Definition 13.3.1. *Let* $\Sigma = \langle n_1, \ldots, n_k \rangle$, $k \geq 1$, *be a frame signature. An atomic Σ-specification is a FOL-IS-formula* ϕ *of the form* $\mathrm{OB}(x_1) \wedge \ldots \wedge \mathrm{OB}(x_n) \wedge \phi'(x_1, \ldots, x_n)$, $n \geq 1$, *such that the only free variables in* ϕ' *are* $x_1, \ldots, x_n$. *An atomic Σ-specification* $\mathrm{OB}(x_1) \wedge \ldots \wedge \mathrm{OB}(x_n) \wedge \phi'(x_1, \ldots, x_n)$ *is said to be*

★ *strong* $\overset{\text{def}}{\Leftrightarrow}$ $\phi'(x_1, \ldots, x_n)$ *is of the form* $\forall x(\mathrm{AT}(x) \Rightarrow \phi''(x, x_1, \ldots, x_n))$;
★ *weak* $\overset{\text{def}}{\Leftrightarrow}$ $\phi'(x_1, \ldots, x_n)$ *is of the form* $\exists x(\mathrm{AT}(x) \wedge \phi''(x, x_1, \ldots, x_n))$.

A Σ-specification S *is a sequence* $\langle \phi_1, \ldots, \phi_k \rangle$ *of* $k \geq 1$ *atomic Σ-specifications such that for every* $i \in \{1, \ldots, k\}$, ϕ_i *is either strong or weak.*

In the sequel q denotes one of the quantifiers $\forall$ or $\exists$ and *op* denotes a propositional connective $\Rightarrow$ or $\wedge$. Let ϕ be an atomic specification of the form

$$\mathrm{OB}(x_1) \wedge \ldots \wedge \mathrm{OB}(x_n) \wedge q\, x\, (\mathrm{AT}(x)\ op\ \phi''),$$

where $\langle q, op \rangle \in \{\langle \forall, \Rightarrow \rangle, \langle \exists, \wedge \rangle\}$.
We define an atomic specification

$$\phi^{\neg} \overset{\text{def}}{=} \mathrm{OB}(x_1) \wedge \ldots \wedge \mathrm{OB}(x_n) \wedge q\, x\, (\mathrm{AT}(x)\ op\ \neg\phi'').$$

The formula ϕ'' is referred to as a matrix of the specification ϕ.

Lemma 13.3.3. *Let* $S = \langle OB, AT \rangle$ *be an information system, let* $A \subseteq AT$, *and let* ϕ *be an atomic specification. Then the following assertions hold:*

(I) if ϕ is strong, then $ext(\mathcal{M}_{S,A}, \phi) = \bigcap_{a \in A} ext(\mathcal{M}_{S,\{a\}}, \phi)$;
(II) if ϕ is weak, then $ext(\mathcal{M}_{S,A}, \phi) = \bigcup_{a \in A} ext(\mathcal{M}_{S,\{a\}}, \phi)$.

The proof of Lemma 13.3.3 is based on the properties of (universal and existential) quantifiers in classical first-order logic, and hence in FOL-IS.

13.4 Representability of Σ-frames

We are now in a position to define a general concept of a frame derived from an information system.

Definition 13.4.1. *Let* $\Sigma = \langle n_1, \ldots, n_k \rangle$, $k \geq 1$, *be a frame signature and* f *be a subpowerset map. By a $\langle \Sigma, f \rangle$-frame derived from an information system* $S = \langle OB, AT \rangle$ *according to a Σ-specification* S $= \langle \phi_1, \ldots, \phi_k \rangle$, *we mean the* $\langle \Sigma, f \rangle$-frame

$$D_{\Sigma,\mathsf{S},f}(S) \overset{\text{def}}{=} \langle OB, (\mathcal{R}_A^1)_{A \in f(AT)}, \ldots, (\mathcal{R}_A^k)_{A \in f(AT)} \rangle$$

such that for every $l \in \{1, \ldots, k\}$, for every $A \in f(AT)$, $\mathcal{R}_A^l \overset{\text{def}}{=} ext(\mathcal{M}_{S,A}, \phi_l)$.

Each $D_{\Sigma,\mathsf{S},f}$ is referred to as a *derivation function*.

Example 13.4.1. In the present setting for every information system S, the frame $D_{ind}(S)$ defined in Sect. 3.9 is represented as $D_{\langle 2 \rangle, \phi^{ind}, \mathcal{P}}(S)$ where ϕ^{ind} is a strong atomic Σ-specification defined in Example 13.3.1.

Now we present a formal notion of informational representability.

Definition 13.4.2. *Let Σ, f, and X be a frame signature, a subpowerset map, and a class of $\langle \Sigma, f \rangle$-frames, respectively. Let S be a Σ-specification. The class X of $\langle \Sigma, f \rangle$-frames is said to be S-inf-representable in a family Y of information systems $\overset{\text{def}}{\Leftrightarrow}$*

(1) for every information system $S \in Y$, the $\langle \Sigma, f \rangle$-frame $D_{\Sigma,\mathsf{S},f}(S)$ belongs to X;

(2) for every $\langle \Sigma, f \rangle$-frame $F \in X$, there exists an information system $S \in Y$ such that $D_{\Sigma,\mathsf{S},f}(S)$ is isomorphic to F.

The notion of representability introduced above depends on the derivation functions $D_{\Sigma,\mathsf{S},f}$. A more general concept of representability can be introduced, but Definition 13.4.2 will be sufficient for the forthcoming developments. Condition (2) in Definition 13.4.2 is very general. It states that for every frame F belonging to a family X of $\langle \Sigma, f \rangle$-frames, there is an information system from which a $\langle \Sigma, f \rangle$-frame isomorphic to F can be derived.

13.5 Nice Set Proof Technique for Full Σ-frames

In this section we focus our attention on full Σ-frames for a given frame signature Σ. The present framework can be adapted to other classes of frames, for instance to plain Σ-frames (see Sect. 13.6). As shown in Sect. 13.7, any representability result for a class of full Σ-frames has a counterpart for plain frames.

Let X be a non-empty set and let $Y \in \mathcal{P}(\mathcal{P}(X))$. We define $at^Y : X \to \mathcal{P}(Y)$ as follows:

$$at^Y(x) \overset{\text{def}}{=} \{Z : x \in Z \in Y\}.$$

Consequently, we have $Z \in at^Y(x)$ iff $x \in Z$. This is similar to the concept of a nice family of sets defined in Sect. 7.2.4.

Example 13.5.1. Let $X = \{Krakow, Lyon, Cachan, Warsaw\}$ and $Y = \{\{Krakow, Warsaw\}, \{Lyon, Cachan\}\}$.

$\star$ $at^Y(Krakow) = \{\{Krakow, Warsaw\}\}$;

$\star$ $at^Y(Lyon) = \{\{Lyon, Cachan\}\}$;

X can be viewed as a set of objects (cities) and Y can be viewed as an attribute assigning a country to each town.

Definition 13.5.1. *Let $F = \langle W, (\mathcal{R}_P^1)_{P \subseteq PAR}, \ldots, (\mathcal{R}_P^k)_{P \subseteq PAR} \rangle$ be a full Σ-frame, and let $S = \langle \phi_1, \ldots, \phi_k \rangle$ be a Σ-specification, $k \geq 1$. A nice family of sets $(Z_p)_{p \in PAR}$ with respect to F and S is a family of subsets of $\mathcal{P}(W)$ such that for every $l \in \{1, \ldots, k\}$ and for every $p \in PAR$, $\mathcal{R}_{\{p\}}^l = ext(\mathcal{M}_{\langle W, \{at^{Z_p}\}\rangle}, \phi_l)$.*

Let $S_{(Z_p)_{p \in PAR}} = \langle W, \{at^{Z_p} : p \in PAR\}\rangle$ be a set-theoretical information system (see Sect. 2.2).

Definition 13.5.2. *Let Σ be a frame signature, let $S = \langle \phi_1, \ldots, \phi_k \rangle$, $k \geq 1$, be a Σ-specification, and let X be a set of full Σ-frames. A nice set function with respect to S and X is a mapping nsf such that for every $F \in X$, $nsf(F)$ is a nice family of sets with respect to S and F.*

Example 13.5.2. (Example 13.3.1 continued) Consider the Σ_0-specification $S^{ind} = \langle \phi^{ind} \rangle$ with $\Sigma_0 = \langle 2 \rangle$. Let $F = \langle W, (\mathcal{R}_P)_{P \subseteq PAR} \rangle$ be a full Σ_0-frame in FVS-IND. For every $p \in PAR$, let $X_p = \{\mathcal{R}_{\{p\}}(w) : w \in W\}$. For all $w, v \in W$, we have:

$$\langle w, v \rangle \in \mathcal{R}_{\{p\}} \text{ iff } \mathcal{R}_{\{p\}}(w) = \mathcal{R}_{\{p\}}(v)$$
$$\text{iff } \{Y : w \in Y \in X_p\} = \{Y : v \in Y \in X_p\}$$
$$\text{iff } at^{X_p}(w) = at^{X_p}(v)$$
$$\text{iff } \langle w, v \rangle \in ext(\mathcal{M}_{\langle W, \{at^{X_p}\}\rangle}, \phi^{ind}).$$

So $(X_p)_{p \in PAR}$ is a nice family of sets with respect to S^{ind} and F.

The following lemma establishes correspondences between full Σ-frames and set-theoretical information systems obtained from a nice family of sets.

Lemma 13.5.1. *Let $F = \langle W, (\mathcal{R}_P^1)_{P \subseteq PAR}, \ldots, (\mathcal{R}_P^k)_{P \subseteq PAR} \rangle$ be a full Σ-frame, let $S = \langle \phi_1, \ldots, \phi_k \rangle$ be a Σ-specification, and let $(Z_p)_{p \in PAR}$ be a nice family of sets with respect to F and S. Assume also that for every $l \in \{1, \ldots, k\}$, if ϕ_l is strong, then $\langle W, (\mathcal{R}_P^l)_{P \subseteq PAR} \rangle \in$ FVS, and if ϕ_l is weak, then $\langle W, (\mathcal{R}_P^l)_{P \subseteq PAR} \rangle \in$ FVW. Then, for every $P \subseteq PAR$ and for every $l \in \{1, \ldots, k\}$, $\mathcal{R}_P^l = ext(\mathcal{M}_{\langle W, \{at^{Z_p} : p \in P\}\rangle}, \phi_l)$.*

Proof. Let $P \subseteq PAR$ and let $l \in \{1, \ldots, k\}$. If $P = \emptyset$ and ϕ_l is strong [resp. weak], then $\mathcal{R}_\emptyset^l = W^{n_l} = ext(\langle W, \emptyset\rangle, \phi_l)$ [resp. $\mathcal{R}_\emptyset^l = \emptyset = ext(\langle W, \emptyset\rangle, \phi_l)$]. If $P = \{p\}$ is a singleton, then $(Z_p)_{p \in PAR}$ is a nice family of sets with respect to F and S and we have $\mathcal{R}_{\{p\}}^l = ext(\langle W, \{at^{Z_p}\}\rangle, \phi_l)$. Finally, assume that $card(P) \geq 2$. By Lemma 13.3.3,

$\star$ if ϕ_l is strong,
  then $ext(\langle W, \{at^{Z_p} : p \in P\}\rangle, \phi_l) = \bigcap_{p \in P} ext(\langle W, \{at^{Z_p}\}\rangle, \phi_l)$;

$\star$ if ϕ_l is weak,

then $ext(\langle W, \{at^{Z_p} : p \in P\}\rangle, \phi_l) = \bigcup_{p \in P} ext(\langle W, \{at^{Z_p}\}\rangle, \phi_l)$.

Consequently, $ext(\langle W, \{at^{Z_p} : p \in P\}\rangle, \phi_l) = \bigcap_{p \in P} \mathcal{R}^l_{\{p\}}$
[resp. $ext(\langle W, \{at^{Z_p} : p \in P\}\rangle, \phi_l) = \bigcup_{p \in P} \mathcal{R}^l_{\{p\}}$].
Since $\langle W, (\mathcal{R}^l_P)_{P \subseteq PAR}\rangle \in$ FVS [resp. $\langle W, (\mathcal{R}^l_P)_{P \subseteq PAR}\rangle \in$ FVW], $\mathcal{R}^l_P = ext(\langle W, \{at^{Z_p} : p \in P\}\rangle, \phi_l)$.   Q.E.D.

The following theorem provides sufficient conditions for informational representability.

Theorem 13.5.1. *Let Σ be a frame signature and let* $S = \langle \phi_1, \ldots, \phi_k \rangle$, $k \geq 1$, *be a Σ-specification. Let X be a set of full Σ-frames. Assume also that for every $l \in \{1, \ldots, k\}$, for every $F = \langle W, (\mathcal{R}^1_P)_{P \subseteq PAR}, \ldots, (\mathcal{R}^k_P)_{P \subseteq PAR}\rangle \in X$, if ϕ_l is strong, then $\langle W, (\mathcal{R}^l_P)_{P \subseteq PAR}\rangle \in$ FVS, otherwise $\langle W, (\mathcal{R}^l_P)_{P \subseteq PAR}\rangle \in$ FVW. Let Y be a family of information systems such that:*

(1) for every system $S \in Y$, there is a frame $F \in X$ such that $D_{\Sigma,S,\mathcal{P}}(S) \simeq F$;

(2) there is a nice set function nsf with respect to S and X such that $\{S_{nsf(F)} : F \in X\} \subseteq Y$.

Then X is S-inf-representable in Y.

The proof of Theorem 13.5.1 is by an easy verification.

Example 13.5.3. (Example 13.5.2 continued) We show that FVS-IND is S^{ind}-inf-representable in the class of information systems. It is easy to check that for every information system S, $D_{\Sigma_0, S^{ind}, \mathcal{P}}(S) \in$ FVS-IND. For every $F \in$ FVS-IND we build the set $nsf(F) = (X_p)_{p \in PAR}$ as in Example 13.5.2. It follows that $nsf(F)$ is a nice family of sets with respect to S and F. By Theorem 13.5.1, FVS-IND is S^{ind}-inf-representable in the class of information systems.

13.6 Nice Set Proof Technique for Plain Σ-frames

In this section we focus our attention on plain Σ-frames, for a given frame signature Σ. Definition 13.5.1 admits the following plain version.

Definition 13.6.1. *Let $F = \langle W, R^1, \ldots, R^k \rangle$, $k \geq 1$, be a plain Σ-frame and let* $S = \langle \phi_1, \ldots, \phi_k \rangle$ *be a Σ-specification. A nice family of sets with respect to F and S is a set $Z \subseteq \mathcal{P}^2(W)$ such that for every $l \in \{1, \ldots, k\}$, $R^l = ext(\langle W, Z\rangle, \phi_l)$.*

Let $S_Z = \langle W, \{at^X : X \in Z\}\rangle$ be a set-theoretical information system. Lemma 13.5.1 admits the following version for plain frames.

Lemma 13.6.1. *Let Σ be a frame signature, let $F = \langle W, R^1, \ldots, R^k \rangle$, $k \geq 1$, be a plain Σ-frame, let $S = \langle \phi_1, \ldots, \phi_k \rangle$ be a Σ-specification, and let Z be a nice family of sets with respect to F and S. Then for every $l \in \{1, \ldots, k\}$, $R^l = ext(\langle W, Z \rangle, \phi_l)$.*

The proof of Lemma 13.6.1 is similar to the proof of Lemma 13.5.1.

Theorem 13.6.1. *Let Σ be a frame signature and let $S = \langle \phi_1, \ldots, \phi_k \rangle$, $k \geq 1$, be a Σ-specification. Let X be a set of plain Σ-frames. Let Y be a family of information systems such that:*

(1) for every system $S \in Y$, there is a frame $F \in X$ such that $D_{\Sigma,S,\mathcal{P}}(S) \simeq F$;

(2) there is a nice set function nsf with respect to S and X such that $\{S_{nsf(F)} : F \in X\} \subseteq Y$.

Then X is S-inf-representable in Y.

The proof of Theorem 13.6.1 is by an easy verification.

13.7 Preservation of Informational Representability

In this section we discuss various ways of obtaining representability results from existing ones by relating adequately the corresponding specifications and the classes of frames. More precisely, the semantics of logical connectives of FOL-IS used in the specifications enables us to establish some preservation properties.

13.7.1 Permutation of Variables in Specifications

Let ϕ be a FOL-IS-formula such that $x_1, \ldots, x_n$, $n \geq 1$, are the only free variables in ϕ. For every permutation σ of the set $\{1, \ldots, n\}$, $\phi\sigma$ is the formula obtained from ϕ by replacing simultaneously x_i by $x_{\sigma(i)}$ in ϕ for every $i \in \{1, \ldots, n\}$. For every n-ary relation R and for every permutation σ of the set $\{1, \ldots, n\}$, we define

$$R\sigma \stackrel{\text{def}}{=} \{\langle x_{\sigma(1)}, \ldots, x_{\sigma(n)} \rangle : \langle x_1, \ldots, x_n \rangle \in R\}.$$

An obvious consequence of the above definition is the following result.

Lemma 13.7.1. *For every information system $S = \langle OB, AT \rangle$, $ext(S, \phi)\sigma = ext(S, \phi\sigma)$.*

Before stating the next lemma we introduce some notation. For every family $(\sigma_l)_{1 \leq l \leq k}$ of permutations of $\{1, \ldots, n\}$, for every full Σ-frame $F = \langle W, (\mathcal{R}_P^1)_{P \subseteq PAR}, \ldots, (\mathcal{R}_P^k)_{P \subseteq PAR} \rangle$ let

$$F\sigma_1 \ldots \sigma_k \stackrel{\text{def}}{=} \langle W, (\mathcal{R}_P^1 \sigma_1)_{P \subseteq PAR}, \ldots, (\mathcal{R}_P^k \sigma_k)_{P \subseteq PAR} \rangle.$$

Lemma 13.7.2. *(Reordering)*
Let Σ be a frame signature, let $S = \langle \phi_1, \ldots, \phi_k \rangle$, $k \geq 1$, be a Σ-specification, let X be a set of full Σ-frames, and let nsf be a nice set function with respect to S and X. Let σ_l be a permutation of the set $\{1, \ldots, n_l\}$ for every $l \in \{1, \ldots, k\}$ and let $nsf'(F\sigma_1 \ldots \sigma_k) \stackrel{\text{def}}{=} nsf(F)$ for every $F \in X$. Then nsf' is a nice set function with respect to $S' = \langle \phi_1\sigma_1, \ldots, \phi_k\sigma_k \rangle$ and $X' = \{F\sigma_1 \ldots \sigma_k : F \in X\}$.

Proof. Let $F = \langle W, (\mathcal{R}_P^1)_{P \subseteq PAR}, \ldots, (\mathcal{R}_P^k)_{P \subseteq PAR} \rangle$ be a full Σ-frame, and let $nsf(F) = (Y_p)_{p \in PAR}$. Let $p \in PAR$, $l \in \{1, \ldots, k\}$, and $x_1, \ldots, x_{n_l} \in W$. We have:

$\langle x_1, \ldots, x_{n_l} \rangle \in \mathcal{R}_{\{p\}}^l \sigma_l$ iff $\langle x_{\sigma_l(1)}, \ldots, x_{\sigma_l(n_l)} \rangle \in \mathcal{R}_{\{p\}}^l$
$\qquad$ (by definition of $F\sigma_1 \ldots \sigma_k$)
$\qquad$ iff $\langle x_{\sigma_l(1)}, \ldots, x_{\sigma_l(n_l)} \rangle \in ext(\langle W, \{at^{Y_p}\} \rangle, \phi_l)$
$\qquad$ (by Lemma 13.5.1)
$\qquad$ iff $\langle x_1, \ldots, x_{n_l} \rangle \in (ext(\langle W, \{at^{Y_p}\} \rangle, \phi_l)\sigma_l)$
$\qquad$ (by definition of $R\sigma$)
$\qquad$ iff $\langle x_1, \ldots, x_{n_l} \rangle \in ext(\langle W, \{at^{Y_p}\} \rangle, \phi_l\sigma_l)$
$\qquad$ (by Lemma 13.7.1).

Hence, nsf' is a nice set function with respect to $S' = \langle \phi_1\sigma_1, \ldots, \phi_k\sigma_k \rangle$ and $X' = \{F\sigma_1 \ldots \sigma_k : F \in X\}$. $\hfill$ *Q.E.D.*

Theorem 13.7.1. *Let $\mathcal{C}$ be a class of full Σ-frames and let $S = \langle \phi_1, \ldots, \phi_k \rangle$, $k \geq 1$, be a Σ-specification such that $\mathcal{C}$ is S-inf-representable in the class of information systems. Let σ_l be a permutation of the set $\{1, \ldots, n_l\}$ for every $l \in \{1, \ldots, k\}$ and let $S' = \langle \phi_1\sigma_1, \ldots, \phi_k\sigma_k \rangle$. Then $\mathcal{C}' = \{F\sigma_1 \ldots \sigma_k : F \in \mathcal{C}\}$ is S'-inf-representable in the class of information systems.*

Proof. Let S be an information system. Since $\mathcal{C}$ is S-inf-representable in the class of information systems, $D_{\Sigma,S,\mathcal{P}}(S) \simeq F$ for some $F \in \mathcal{C}$. Consequently, $D_{\Sigma,S,\mathcal{P}}(S)\sigma_1 \ldots \sigma_k \simeq F\sigma_1 \ldots \sigma_k$. One can check that $D_{\Sigma,S,\mathcal{P}}(S)\sigma_1 \ldots \sigma_k = D_{\Sigma,S',\mathcal{P}}(S)$. So there is a frame $F\sigma_1 \ldots \sigma_k \in \mathcal{C}'$ such that $D_{\Sigma,S',\mathcal{P}}(S) \simeq F\sigma_1 \ldots \sigma_k$. By Lemma 13.7.2, there is a nice set function nsf' with respect to S' and $\mathcal{C}'$. By Theorem 13.5.1, $\mathcal{C}'$ is S'-inf-representable in the class of information systems. $\hfill$ *Q.E.D.*

13.7.2 Complementing Value Predicates in Specifications

Let ϕ be an atomic specification of the form

$$\mathrm{OB}(x_1) \wedge \ldots \wedge \mathrm{OB}(x_n) \wedge$$

$$q\ x\ (\mathrm{AT}(x)\ op\ q'\ x'(\mathrm{IsValueOf}(x, x')\ op'\ \psi(x_1, \ldots, x_n, x, x'))),$$

where $\psi(x_1, \ldots, x_n, x, x')$ is a Boolean combination of formulae of the form $\mathrm{Value}(x_i, x, x')$, $i \in \{1, \ldots, n\}$, and $\langle q, op \rangle, \langle q', op' \rangle \in \{\langle \forall, \Rightarrow \rangle, \langle \exists, \wedge \rangle\}$. Let ϕ^-

be an atomic specification obtained from ϕ by putting a negation $\neg$ in front of each atomic formula $\text{Value}(x_i, x, x')$.

Let $S = \langle \phi_1, \ldots, \phi_k \rangle$, $k \geq 1$, be a Σ-specification made of atomic specifications as above. We write S^- to denote the Σ-specification $\langle \phi_1^-, \ldots, \phi_k^- \rangle$.

Lemma 13.7.3. *Let C be a class of $\langle \Sigma, f \rangle$-frames and let $S = \langle \phi_1, \ldots, \phi_k \rangle$, $k \geq 1$, be a Σ-specification such that C is S-inf-representable in the class of information systems. Then C is also S^--inf-representable in the class of information systems.*

Proof. Let $S = \langle OB, AT, (VAL_a)_{a \in AT}, g \rangle$ be an information system. Let $S^- = \langle OB^-, AT^-, (VAL_a^-)_{a \in AT^-}, g^- \rangle$ be the following information system:

* $OB^- \stackrel{\text{def}}{=} OB$;
* $AT^- \stackrel{\text{def}}{=} AT$;
* for every $a \in AT$, $VAL_a^- \stackrel{\text{def}}{=} VAL_a$, and for every $x \in OB$, $g^-(x, a^-) \stackrel{\text{def}}{=} VAL_a \setminus g(x, a)$.

Clearly, the structures $(S^-)^-$ and S are isomorphic. According to Definition 13.4.2, we have to check that

(i) for every information system S, $D_{\Sigma, S^-, \mathcal{P}}(S) \in C$;
(ii) for every $F \in C$, there is an information system S such that $D_{\Sigma, S^-, \mathcal{P}}(S) \simeq F$.

First, observe that for every information system S, for every $l \in \{1, \ldots, k\}$, and for every $A \subseteq AT$, we have $ext(\mathcal{M}_{S,A}, \phi_l) = ext(\mathcal{M}_{S^-,A}, \phi_l^-)$.
Proof of (i): let S be an information system and

$$D_{\Sigma, S^-, f}(S) = \langle W, (\mathcal{R}_A^1)_{A \in f(AT)}, \ldots, (\mathcal{R}_A^k)_{A \in f(AT)} \rangle.$$

For every $l \in \{1, \ldots, k\}$ and for every $A \in f(AT)$, we have $\mathcal{R}_A^l = ext(\mathcal{M}_{S,A}, \phi_l^-)$. We also have $\mathcal{R}_A^l = ext(\mathcal{M}_{S^-,A}, \phi_l^-)$. Hence, $D_{\Sigma, S^-, f}(S) \in C$.
Proof of (ii): let $F \in C$. Since C is S-inf-representable in the class of information systems, there is an information system S such that $F = D_{\Sigma, S, f}(S)$. Using arguments as above, $D_{\Sigma, S, f}(S) = D_{\Sigma, S^-, f}(S^-)$.   Q.E.D.

13.7.3 Complementing the Matrix in Specifications

Let $S = \langle \phi_1, \ldots, \phi_k \rangle$, $k \geq 1$, be a specification. We write $S^\neg$ to denote the specification $\langle \phi_1^\neg, \ldots, \phi_k^\neg \rangle$. We recall that for every atomic specification ϕ, $\phi^\neg$ is defined in Sect. 13.3.2. Let C be a class of full Σ-frames. Let $C^\neg$ be the class of full Σ-frames such that $F = \langle W, (\mathcal{R}_P^1)_{P \subseteq PAR}, \ldots, (\mathcal{R}_P^k)_{P \subseteq PAR} \rangle \in C^\neg$ iff the following conditions hold:

(1) there is $\langle W, (\mathcal{R}_P'^1)_{P \subseteq PAR}, \ldots, (\mathcal{R}_P'^k)_{P \subseteq PAR} \rangle \in C$ such that
    for every $l \in \{1, \ldots, k\}$, for every $p \in PAR$, $\mathcal{R}_{\{p\}}'^l = W^{n_l} \setminus \mathcal{R}_{\{p\}}^l$;

(2) for every $l \in \{1, \ldots, k\}$, if ϕ_l is strong, then $\langle W, (\mathcal{R}^l_P)_{P \subseteq PAR} \rangle \in$ FVS, otherwise $\langle W, (\mathcal{R}^l_P)_{P \subseteq PAR} \rangle \in$ FVW.

$C^\neg$ is said to be the S-complement of C. The class $C^\neg$ includes the frames defined in Sect. 3.10.

Lemma 13.7.4. *Let C be a class of full Σ-frames and let $S = \langle \phi_1, \ldots, \phi_k \rangle$, $k \geq 1$, be a specification such that C is S-inf-representable in the class of information systems. Then $C^\neg$ is $S^\neg$-inf-representable in the class of information systems.*

Proof. Let S be an information system. Since C is S-inf-representable in the class of information systems, there is a full Σ-frame F' such that $D_{\Sigma, S, \mathcal{P}} \simeq F'$. Now let F be the unique full Σ-frame in $C^\neg$ satisfying the conditions (1) and (2) of the definition of $C^\neg$. It is not difficult to show that $D_{\Sigma, S^\neg, \mathcal{P}} \simeq F$. So condition (1) in Definition 13.4.2 is satisfied. Now we check that condition (2) in Definition 13.4.2 is also satisfied. Let $F \in C^\neg$. By the definition of $C^\neg$, there is $F' \in C$ such that conditions (1) and (2) of the definition of $C^\neg$ hold. Since C is S-inf-representable in the class of information systems, there is an information system S such that $D_{\Sigma, S, \mathcal{P}} \simeq F'$. As previously, one can easily show that $D_{\Sigma, S^\neg, \mathcal{P}} \simeq F$.   *Q.E.D.*

Lemma 13.7.4 is a generalisation of Lemma 3.10.2(III, IV).

13.7.4 Interchanging the Quantifiers in Specifications

Let ϕ be an atomic Σ-specification of the form

$$\mathrm{OB}(x_1) \wedge \ldots \wedge \mathrm{OB}(x_n) \wedge q \; x \; (\mathrm{AT}(x) \; op \; \phi')$$

where $\langle q, op \rangle \in \{\langle \forall, \Rightarrow \rangle, \langle \exists, \wedge \rangle\}$. We define an atomic Σ-specification

$$\phi^{inter} \stackrel{\mathrm{def}}{=} \mathrm{OB}(x_1) \wedge \ldots \wedge \mathrm{OB}(x_n) \wedge q' \; x \; (\mathrm{AT}(x) \; op' \; \phi'),$$

where $\{\langle q, op \rangle, \langle q', op' \rangle\} = \{\langle \forall, \Rightarrow \rangle, \langle \exists, \wedge \rangle\}$. Let $S = \langle \phi_1, \ldots, \phi_k \rangle$, $k \geq 1$, be a specification; we define the specification $S^{inter} \stackrel{\mathrm{def}}{=} \langle \phi_1^{inter}, \ldots, \phi_k^{inter} \rangle$.

Lemma 13.7.5. *Let C be a class of full Σ-frames and let $S = \langle \phi_1, \ldots, \phi_k \rangle$, $k \geq 1$, be a Σ-specification such that C is S-inf-representable in the class of information systems. Let C^{inter} be the class of full Σ-frames such that $F = \langle W, (\mathcal{R}^1_P)_{P \subseteq PAR}, \ldots, (\mathcal{R}^k_P)_{P \subseteq PAR} \rangle \in C^{inter}$ iff the following conditions hold*

$\star$ *there is $\langle W, (\mathcal{R}'^1_P)_{P \subseteq PAR}, \ldots, (\mathcal{R}'^k_P)_{P \subseteq PAR} \rangle \in C$ such that for every $l \in \{1, \ldots, k\}$ and for every $p \in PAR$, $\mathcal{R}'^l_{\{p\}} = \mathcal{R}^l_{\{p\}}$;*

$\star$ *for every $l \in \{1, \ldots, k\}$, if ϕ_l is strong, then $\langle W, (\mathcal{R}^l_P)_{P \subseteq PAR} \rangle \in$ FVW, otherwise $\langle W, (\mathcal{R}^l_P)_{P \subseteq PAR} \rangle \in$ FVS.*

Then, C^{inter} is S^{inter}-inf-representable in the class of information systems.

The proof is similar to the proof of Lemma 13.7.4.

13.7.5 Full Σ-frames are Sufficient

Let $\mathcal{C}$ be a class of full Σ-frames. For every subpowerset map f, let $\mathcal{C}^f$ be the class of $\langle \Sigma, f \rangle$-frames obtained from the Σ-frames in $\mathcal{C}$ by restricting the family of relations to the relations indexed according to f.

Lemma 13.7.6. *Let* S *be a* Σ-*specification and let* $\mathcal{C}$ *be a class of full* Σ-*frames that is* S-*inf-representable in a class* Y *of information systems. Then* $\mathcal{C}^f$ *is* S-*inf-representable in* Y.

Proof. Let S be an information system in Y. Since $\mathcal{C}$ is S-inf-representable in Y, there is a full Σ-frame F such that $D_{\Sigma,S,\mathcal{P}} \simeq F$. Now let F' be the $\langle \Sigma, f \rangle$-frame obtained from F by restricting each family of relations to the family of relations indexed by a family of sets determined by f. By the assumption, $F' \in \mathcal{C}^f$ and it is easy to check that $D_{\Sigma,S,f} \simeq F'$. So condition (1) of Definition 13.4.2 is satisfied. Now we check that condition (2) of Definition 13.4.2 is also satisfied. Let $F' \in \mathcal{C}^f$. By the definition of $\mathcal{C}^f$, there is $F \in \mathcal{C}$ such that F' is the $\langle \Sigma, f \rangle$-frame obtained from F by restricting the family of relations to the family of relations indexed by a family of sets determined by f. Since $\mathcal{C}$ is S-inf-representable in Y, there is an information system $S \in Y$ such that $D_{\Sigma,S,\mathcal{P}} \simeq F$. Consequently, $D_{\Sigma,S,f} \simeq F'$.   Q.E.D.

Observe that the two instances of informational representability in Lemma 13.7.6 are different, since the subpowerset maps are different. Roughly speaking, the lemma states that informational representability for full Σ-frames is the most general one.

13.8 Examples of Informational Representability

We present examples of informational representability of full Σ-frames with information relations presented in Chap. 3. The analogous representability results for many other classes of frames can be obtained using the method developed in this chapter. Throughout this section Σ is assumed to be the signature $\langle 2 \rangle$.

13.8.1 Indiscernibility Frames

Let $S = \langle OB, AT \rangle$ be an information system. In the language of FOL-IS the relation $ind(AT)$ is defined as follows: $ind(AT) = ext(S, \phi^{ind})$, where ϕ^{ind} is defined in Example 13.3.1. Let nsf be the mapping such that for every full Σ-frame $F = \langle W, (\mathcal{R}_P)_{P \subseteq PAR} \rangle$, $nsf(F) = (X_p)_{p \in PAR}$ with

$$X_p \stackrel{\text{def}}{=} \{ \mathcal{R}_{\{p\}}(w) : w \in W \}.$$

Observe that for every $p \in PAR$, we have $\bigcup_{Y \in X_p} Y = W$. Hence, $S_{nsf(F)}$ is a total information system.

Lemma 13.8.1. *Let* $F = \langle W, (\mathcal{R}_P)_{P \subseteq PAR} \rangle$ *be a full* Σ*-frame in* FVS-IND. *For every* $p \in PAR$, *for all* $w, v \in W$, *we have* $\langle w, v \rangle \in \mathcal{R}_{\{p\}}$ *iff (for every* $Y \in X_p$, $w \in Y$ *iff* $v \in Y$ *).*

Proof. The proof follows easily from Example 13.5.2.   *Q.E.D.*

Lemma 13.8.2. *Let* $F = \langle W, (\mathcal{R}_P)_{P \subseteq PAR} \rangle$ *be a full* Σ*-frame in* FVS-IND. *Then* $nsf(F)$ *is a family of nice sets with respect to* S^{ind} *and* F.

Proof. Observe that for every $p \in PAR$ and for all $w, v \in W$, we have

$$\langle w, v \rangle \in ext(\langle W, \{at^{X_p}\}\rangle, \phi^{ind}) \text{ iff for every } Y \in X_p, w \in Y \text{ iff } v \in Y.$$

Hence, $nsf(F)$ satisfies the condition of the lemma.   *Q.E.D.*

As a consequence we have the following theorem.

Theorem 13.8.1. FVS-IND *is* S^{ind}*-inf-representable in the class of information systems.*

13.8.2 Diversity Frames

Let $S = \langle OB, AT \rangle$ be an information system. We recall that two objects x_1 and x_2 are in the relation of *diversity with respect to* $A \subseteq AT \overset{\text{def}}{\Leftrightarrow}$ for every $a \in A$, $a(x_1) \neq a(x_2)$. In the language of FOL-IS the relation $div(AT)$ is defined as follows: $div(AT) = ext(S, \phi^{div})$ with

$$\phi^{div} = (\phi^{ind})^{\neg}.$$

Let S^{div} be the Σ-specification $\langle \phi^{div} \rangle$. By observing that FVS-DIV is the S^{ind}-complement of FVS-IND, by application of Lemma 13.7.4 we get the following representability result.

Theorem 13.8.2. FVS-DIV *is* S^{div}*-inf-representable in the class of information systems.*

13.8.3 Complementarity Frames

Let $S = \langle OB, AT \rangle$ be an information system. We recall that two objects x_1 and x_2 are in the relation of *complementarity with respect to* $A \subseteq AT \overset{\text{def}}{\Leftrightarrow}$ for every $a \in A$, $a(x_1) = VAL_a \setminus a(x_2)$. In the language of FOL-IS the relation $comp(AT)$ is defined as follows: $comp(AT) = ext(S, \phi^{comp})$ with

$$\phi^{comp} = \text{OB}(x_1) \wedge \text{OB}(x_2) \wedge \forall x_3 \, (\text{AT}(x_3) \Rightarrow$$

$$\forall x_4 \, (\text{IsValueOf}(x_3, x_4) \Rightarrow (\text{Value}(x_1, x_3, x_4) \Leftrightarrow \neg\text{Value}(x_2, x_3, x_4)))).$$

If $\langle x_1, x_2 \rangle \in comp(A)$ holds, then for every $a \in A$, VAL_a is uniquely determined by $a(x_1)$ and $a(x_2)$, namely $VAL_a = a(x_1) \cup a(x_2)$.

Let R be a binary relation on a set W. R is said to be a *complementarity relation* $\overset{\text{def}}{\Leftrightarrow}$ R is symmetric, irreflexive, and 3-transitive. Hence, every complementarity relation R does not contain cycles of an odd length.

Let $R' = R \cup R^{-1}$ be the symmetric closure of a relation R on W. For every binary relation R on a set W, for every $w \in W$, let $C_{w,R}$ be the largest subset of W such that $w \in C_{w,R}$ and for every $v \in C_{w,R} \setminus \{w\}$, there is an R'-path between w and v. Observe that $\{C_{w,R} : w \in W\}$ is a partition of W.

For every $w \in W$, let $C^0_{w,R}$ [resp. $C^1_{w,R}$] be the largest subset of $C_{w,R}$ such that for every $v \in C^0_{w,R}$, there is an R'-path of even [resp. odd] length between w and v. Moreover, for every $W' \subseteq W$,

$$D^{W'}_{w,R} \overset{\text{def}}{=} \begin{cases} C^0_{w,R} \text{ if } w \in W'; \\ C^1_{w,R} \text{ otherwise.} \end{cases}$$

Observe that for all $u, v, w \in W$, if $\{v, w\} \subseteq C_{u,R}$, then $\{C^1_{v,R}, C^0_{v,R}\} = \{C^1_{w,R}, C^0_{w,R}\}$ for every complementarity relation R, and $\{C^i_{w,R} : w \in W, i \in \{0,1\}\}$ is a partition of W.

Let $F = \langle W, (\mathcal{R}_P)_{P \subseteq PAR} \rangle \in$ FVS-COM. Let nsf be the mapping such that $nsf(F) = (X_p)_{p \in PAR}$ with

$$X_p \overset{\text{def}}{=} \{ \bigcup_{u \in Y} D^{W'}_{u, \mathcal{R}_{\{p\}}} : W' \subseteq W, \ Y \in W_p \},$$

and $W_p \overset{\text{def}}{=} \{ Y \subseteq W : \forall u, v \in Y, \ C_{u, \mathcal{R}_{\{p\}}} \neq C_{v, \mathcal{R}_{\{p\}}}, \ \bigcup_{u \in Y} C_{u, \mathcal{R}_{\{p\}}} = W \}$. The set W_p contains the subsets of W with exactly one element from each set of the family $\{C_{u, \mathcal{R}_{\{p\}}} : u \in W\}$. Observe that every $Z \in X_p$ is a maximal subset of W such that $\mathcal{R}_{\{p\}} \cap (Z \times Z) = \emptyset$. It is easy to show that for every $p \in PAR$ and for every $Y_0 \in W_p$,

$$X_p = \{ \bigcup_{u \in Y_0} D^{W'}_{u, \mathcal{R}_{\{p\}}} : W' \subseteq W \}.$$

For all $u, v \in W$, we have (for all $Y \in X_p$, either $u \in Y$ and $v \notin Y$ or $u \notin Y$ and $v \in Y$) iff $\langle u, v \rangle \in ext(\langle W, \{^{X_p}\} \rangle, \phi^{comp})$. Furthermore, for every $p \in PAR$, $\bigcup_{Y \in X_p} Y = W$. Hence, $S_{nsf(F)}$ is a total information system.

Lemma 13.8.3. *Let* $F = \langle W, (\mathcal{R}_P)_{P \subseteq PAR} \rangle \in$ *FVS-COM. For every* $p \in PAR$, *for all* $u, v \in W$, $\langle u, v \rangle \in \mathcal{R}_{\{p\}}$ *iff for every* $Y \in X_p$, *either* $(u \in Y$ *and* $v \notin Y)$ *or* $(u \notin Y$ *and* $v \in Y)$.

Proof. ($\rightarrow$) Assume $\langle u, v \rangle \in \mathcal{R}_{\{p\}}$. Since $u \in C^0_{u, \mathcal{R}_{\{p\}}}$ and $v \in C^1_{u, \mathcal{R}_{\{p\}}}$, it follows that for every $W' \subseteq W$, $\{u, v\} \not\subseteq D^{W'}_{u, \mathcal{R}_{\{p\}}}$. Hence, there is no $Y \in X_p$ such that $u \in Y$ and $v \in Y$. Moreover, for every $W' \subseteq W$, for every $Y' \in W_p$,

$$\{u, v\} \cap \bigcup_{u' \in Y'} D^{W'}_{u', \mathcal{R}_{\{p\}}} \neq \emptyset \quad \text{and} \quad \bigcup_{u' \in Y'} D^{W'}_{u', \mathcal{R}_{\{p\}}} \in X_p.$$

So for every $Y \in X_p$, either $(u \in Y$ and $v \notin Y)$ or $(u \notin Y$ and $v \in Y)$.
($\leftarrow$) Now assume that for every $Y \in X_p$, $u \in Y$ iff $v \notin Y$. Suppose that $C_{u,\mathcal{R}_{\{p\}}} \neq C_{v,\mathcal{R}_{\{p\}}}$. By the axiom of choice, for every non-empty set $C_{w,\mathcal{R}_{\{p\}}}$, we may choose an element, say x^w. Let Y_0 be $(\{x^w : w \in W\} \setminus \{x^u, x^v\}) \cup \{u, v\})$. Hence,

$$\{u, v\} \subseteq \bigcup_{u' \in Y_0} D^{\{u,v\}}_{u',\mathcal{R}_{\{p\}}} = X_0.$$

So there is an $X_0 \in X_p$ such that $\{u, v\} \subseteq X_0$, which lead to a contradiction. Hence, $C_{u,\mathcal{R}_{\{p\}}} = C_{v,\mathcal{R}_{\{p\}}}$. Suppose that there is a $\mathcal{R}_{\{p\}}$-path of even length between u and v, say $\langle u_0, \ldots, u_n, \ldots, u_{2 \times n} \rangle$ with $u_0 = u$ and $v = u_{2 \times n}$ (we recall that $\mathcal{R}_{\{p\}}$ is symmetric). There is an $Y_0 \in W_p$ such that $u_n \in Y_0$. Hence,

$$\{u, v\} \subseteq \bigcup_{u' \in Y_0} D^{W'}_{u',\mathcal{R}_{\{p\}}} = X_0,$$

where $W' = W$ if n is even, otherwise $W' = \emptyset$. So $X_0 \in X_p$ and $\{u, v\} \subseteq X_0$, which lead to a contradiction. Hence, there is an $\mathcal{R}_{\{p\}}$-path of odd length between u and v, say $\langle u_0, \ldots, u_{(2 \times n)+1} \rangle$ with $u_0 = u$ and $v = u_{(2 \times n)+1}$. If $n = 0$, then $\langle u, v \rangle \in \mathcal{R}_{\{p\}}$. If $n = 1$, then by the 3-transitivity condition $\langle u, v \rangle \in \mathcal{R}_{\{p\}}$. Now assume $n > 1$. By the 3-transitivity condition, $\langle u_{(2 \times (n-1))}, u_{(2 \times n)+1} \rangle \in R^1_{\{p\}}$. So there is a path of length $(2 \times (n-1)) + 1$ between u and v. By induction on n we can prove that $\langle u, v \rangle \in \mathcal{R}_{\{p\}}$. Q.E.D.

Lemma 13.8.4. *Let $F = \langle W, (\mathcal{R}_P)_{P \subseteq PAR} \rangle \in$ FVS-COM be a full Σ-frame. Then $nsf(F)$ is a family of nice sets with respect to S^{comp} and F.*

Proof. The proof is a direct consequence of Lemma 13.8.3.   Q.E.D.

Theorem 13.8.3. FVS-COM *is S^{comp}-inf-representable in the class of information systems.*

Proof. The proof is a direct consequence of Lemmas 3.10.2(II) and 13.8.4 and Theorem 13.5.1.   Q.E.D.

13.8.4 Incomplementarity Frames

Let $S = \langle OB, AT \rangle$ be an information system. We recall that two objects x_1 and x_2 are in the relation of *incomplementarity with respect to $A \subseteq AT$* $\overset{\text{def}}{\Leftrightarrow}$ for every $a \in A$, $(VAL_a \setminus a(x_1)) \neq a(x_2)$. In the language of FOL-IS, the relation $incomp(AT)$ is defined as follows: $incomp(AT) = ext(S, \phi^{incomp})$ with

$$\phi^{incomp} = (\phi^{comp})^{\neg}.$$

Let S^{incomp} be the Σ-specification $\langle \phi^{incomp} \rangle$. By observing that FVS-ICOM is the S^{comp}-complement of FVS-COM, applying Lemma 13.7.4 we get the following result.

Theorem 13.8.4. FVS-ICOM *is S^{incomp}-inf-representable in the class of information systems.*

13.8.5 Similarity and Negative Similarity Frames

Let $S = \langle OB, AT \rangle$ be an information system. We recall that two objects x_1 and x_2 are in the relation of *similarity [resp. negative similarity] with respect to* $A \subseteq AT$ $\overset{\text{def}}{\Leftrightarrow}$ for every $a \in A$, $a(x_1) \cap a(x_2) \neq \emptyset$ [resp. $(VAL_a \setminus a(x_1)) \cap (VAL_a \setminus a(x_2)) \neq \emptyset$]. In the language FOL-IS the relations $sim(AT)$ and $nim(AT)$ are defined as follows: $sim(AT) = ext(S, \phi^{sim})$, $nim(AT) = ext(S, \phi^{nim})$, where

$$\phi^{sim} = OB(x_1) \wedge OB(x_2) \wedge \forall x_3 \, (AT(x_3) \Rightarrow$$

$$\exists x_4 \, (\text{IsValueOf}(x_3, x_4) \wedge (\text{Value}(x_1, x_3, x_4) \wedge \text{Value}(x_2, x_3, x_4)))),$$

$$\phi^{nim} = OB(x_1) \wedge OB(x_2) \wedge \forall x_3 \, (AT(x_3) \Rightarrow$$

$$\exists x_4 \, (\text{IsValueOf}(x_3, x_4) \wedge (\neg\text{Value}(x_1, x_3, x_4) \wedge \neg\text{Value}(x_2, x_3, x_4))).$$

Let S^{sim} [resp. S^{nim}] be the specification $\langle \phi^{sim} \rangle$ [resp. $\langle \phi^{nim} \rangle$]. Let $F = \langle W, (\mathcal{R}_P)_{P \subseteq PAR} \rangle$ be a full Σ-frame and nsf be the mapping such that $nsf(F) = (X_p)_{p \in PAR}$ with

$$X_p \overset{\text{def}}{=} \{\{u, v\} : \langle u, v \rangle \in \mathcal{R}_{\{p\}}\}.$$

Lemma 13.8.5. *Let* $F \in$ *FVS-SIM and let* $p \in PAR$. *For all* $u, v \in W$, $\langle u, v \rangle \in \mathcal{R}_{\{p\}}$ *iff there is a* $Y \in X_p$ *such that* $u \in Y$ *and* $v \in Y$.

Proof. First, observe that $\langle u, v \rangle \in ext(\langle W, \{at^{X_p}\}\rangle, \phi^{sim})$ iff there is a $Y \in X_p$ such that $u \in Y$ and $v \in Y$.
$(\rightarrow)$ Assume $\langle u, v \rangle \in \mathcal{R}_{\{p\}}$. So we have $X_p = \{\{x, y\} : \langle x, y \rangle \in \mathcal{R}_{\{p\}}\}$. Take $Y = \{u, v\}$.
$(\leftarrow)$ Now assume that there is a $Y \in X_p$ such that $u \in Y$ and $v \in Y$.
Case 1: $u \neq v$.
Then $\{u, v\} \in X_p$, which means that $\langle u, v \rangle \in \mathcal{R}_{\{p\}}$ by the definition of $nsf(F)$.
Case 2: $u = v$.
Suppose $\langle u, v \rangle \notin \mathcal{R}_{\{p\}}$. Since $\mathcal{R}_{\{p\}}$ is weakly reflexive and symmetric, for every $y \in W$, we have $\langle u, y \rangle \notin \mathcal{R}_{\{p\}}$ and $\langle y, u \rangle \notin \mathcal{R}_{\{p\}}$. Hence, $u \notin Y$, a contradiction.   *Q.E.D.*

We get the following representability result.

Theorem 13.8.5. *FVS-SIM is* S^{sim}-*inf-representable in the class of information systems. FVS-SIM-TOT is* S^{sim}-*inf-representable in the class of total information systems.*

By Theorem 13.8.5 and Lemma 13.7.3 the following theorem holds.

Theorem 13.8.6. *FVS-SIM is* S^{nim}-*inf-representable in the class of information systems.*

13.8.6 Left and Right Orthogonality Frames

Let $S = \langle OB, AT \rangle$ be an information system. We recall that two objects x_1 and x_2 are in the relation of *right orthogonality [resp. left orthogonality] with respect to* $A \subseteq AT \overset{\text{def}}{\Leftrightarrow}$ for every $a \in A$, $a(x_1) \subseteq (VAL_a \backslash a(x_2))$ [resp. $(VAL_a \backslash a(x_1)) \subseteq a(x_2)$]. In the language of FOL-IS the relation $rort(AT)$ [resp. $lort(AT)$] is defined as follows: $rort(AT) = ext(S, \phi^{rort})$ [resp. $lort(AT) = ext(S, \phi^{lort})$] with

$$\phi^{rort} = (\phi^{sim})^{\neg} \quad [\text{resp. } \phi^{lort} = (\phi^{nim})^{\neg}].$$

Let S^{rort} be the Σ-specification $\langle \phi^{rort} \rangle$ and S^{lort} be the Σ-specification $\langle \phi^{lort} \rangle$ By observing that FVS-RORT is the S^{sim}-complement of FVS-SIM and by application of Lemma 13.7.4 we get the following theorem.

Theorem 13.8.7. *FVS-RORT is S^{rort}-inf-representable in the class of information systems and FVS-RORT is S^{lort}-inf-representable in the class of information systems.*

Moreover, one can show the following result.

Theorem 13.8.8. *FVS-RORT-TOT is S^{rort}-inf-representable in the class of total information systems.*

13.8.7 Backward and Forward Inclusion Frames

Let $S = \langle OB, AT \rangle$ be an information system. We recall that two objects x_1 and x_2 are in the relation of *forward inclusion* with respect to $A \subseteq AT$ $\overset{\text{def}}{\Leftrightarrow}$ for every $a \in A$, $a(x_1) \subseteq a(x_2)$. In the language of FOL-IS, the relation $fin(AT)$ is defined as follows: $fin(AT) = ext(S, \phi^{fin})$ with

$$\phi^{fin} = \text{OB}(x_1) \wedge \text{OB}(x_2) \wedge \forall x_3 \, (\text{AT}(x_3) \Rightarrow$$

$$\forall x_4 \, (\text{IsValueOf}(x_3, x_4) \Rightarrow (\text{Value}(x_1, x_3, x_4) \Rightarrow \text{Value}(x_2, x_3, x_4)))).$$

Let nsf be the map such that for every full Σ-frame $F = \langle W, (\mathcal{R}_P)_{P \subseteq PAR} \rangle$, $nsf(F) = (X_p)_{p \in PAR}$ with

$$X_p \overset{\text{def}}{=} \{\mathcal{R}_{\{p\}}(w) : w \in W\}.$$

Following the lines of the previous sections and using the map nsf defined above, we can show the following theorem.

Theorem 13.8.9. *FVS-FIN is S^{fin}-inf-representable in the class of information systems.*

The results about permutation of variables from Sect. 13.7.1 enable us to obtain the following result.

Theorem 13.8.10. $\{F\sigma : F \in$ FVS-FIN $\}$ *is $\langle \phi^{fin} \sigma \rangle$-inf-representable in the class of information systems, where σ is a 1-1 mapping $\{1, 2\} \rightarrow \{1, 2\}$ such that $\sigma(1) = 2$.*

13.8.8 Representability of IL-frames

In this section, we consider a frame signature $\Sigma^{IL} = \langle 2, 2, 2, 1 \rangle$ and the plain Σ^{IL}-frames $F = \langle W, R_\equiv, R_\le, R_\sigma, D \rangle$. We are interested in the plain Σ^{IL}-frames of the form $\langle OB, ind(AT), fin(AT), sim(AT), D(AT) \rangle$ for an information system $S = \langle OB, AT \rangle$. For the sake of simplicity in the rest of this section, these frames will be denoted by $\langle OB, \equiv_S, \le_S, \sigma_S, D_S \rangle$.

We recall that the logic IL' is introduced in Sect. 7.3.1.

Definition 13.8.1. *Let* $F = \langle W, R_\equiv, R_\le, R_\sigma, D \rangle$ *be a plain* Σ^{IL}*-frame. F is an IL-structure* $\overset{\text{def}}{\Leftrightarrow}$ *there exists an IL-model based on F. F is an IL'-structure* $\overset{\text{def}}{\Leftrightarrow}$ *there exists an IL'-model based on F. Let* $S = \langle OB, AT \rangle$ *be an information system. The structure* $\langle OB, \equiv_S, \le_S, \sigma_S, D_S \rangle$ *is a standard IL-structure over S.*

Lemma 13.8.6. *For every information system S, the following assertions hold:*

(I) the standard IL-structure over S is an IL'-structure satisfying (I9) (see Sect. 7.3.1);

(II) if S is separable, then the standard IL-structure over S is an IL-structure.

The proof is by an easy verification. The informational representability proof for IL-frames can be viewed as an extension of the informational representability proof for NIL-frames (see Sect. 7.2.4). We introduce a few more notions.

Definition 13.8.2. *Let* $F = \langle W, \equiv, \le, \sigma, D \rangle$ *be an IL-structure. A subset* $X \subseteq W$ *is* $\le$*-hereditary* $\overset{\text{def}}{\Leftrightarrow}$ *for all* $x, y \in W$, $x \in X$ *and* $\langle x, y \rangle \le$ *imply* $y \in X$. *A set* $X \subseteq W$ *is a* σ*-set* $\overset{\text{def}}{\Leftrightarrow}$ X *is* $\le$*-hereditary and for all* $x, y \in X$, $\langle x, y \rangle \in \sigma$.

The $\le$-hereditary sets and σ-sets satisfy the following properties.

Lemma 13.8.7. *Let* $F = \langle W, \equiv, \le, \sigma, D \rangle$ *be an IL-structure. Then for all* $x, y \in W$ *and for all* $X, Y \subseteq W$, *the following conditions are satisfied:*

(I) $\le (x)$ *is the smallest* $\le$*-hereditary set containing x;*

(II) $\le (x) \cup \le (y)$ *is the smallest* $\le$*-hereditary set containing* $\{x, y\}$;

(III) if $\langle x, y \rangle \in \sigma$, *then* $\le (x) \cup \le (y)$ *is a* σ*-set;*

(IV) if $x \in D \cap X$ *and X is a* σ*-set, then* $X = \le (x)$;

(V) if X is a σ*-set, Y is* $\le$*-hereditary, and* $X \cap Y \cap D \ne \emptyset$, *then* $X \subseteq Y$;

(VI) if X, Y are σ*-sets and* $X \cap Y \cap D \ne \emptyset$, *then* $X = Y$.

Proof. (I) and (II) follow from the definition of $\leq$-hereditarity and reflexivity and transitivity of $\leq$.

(III) By (II), $\leq(x)\cup\leq(y)$ is $\leq$-hereditary. It remains to show that if $\langle x,y\rangle \in \sigma$, then for all $z,t \in \leq(x)\cup\leq(y)$, we have $\langle z,t\rangle \in \sigma$. If $\langle x,t\rangle \in\leq$ and $\langle y,z\rangle \in\leq$, then by (I4), $\langle t,y\rangle \in \sigma$. By symmetry of σ, $\langle y,t\rangle \in \sigma$. By (I4), $\langle t,z\rangle \in \sigma$. By symmetry of σ, $\langle z,t\rangle \in \sigma$. If $\langle x,t\rangle \in\leq$ and $\langle x,z\rangle \in\leq$, then by (I3), we get $\langle x,z\rangle \in \sigma$. By (I4) and symmetry of σ, we obtain $\langle z,t\rangle \in \sigma$. The cases $\langle y,t\rangle \in\leq$, $\langle y,z\rangle \in\leq$ and $\langle x,z\rangle \in\leq$, $\langle y,t\rangle \in\leq$ are treated in a similar way.

(IV) Suppose $x \in D\cap X$ and X is a σ-set. Since X is $\leq$-hereditary and $x \in X$, we get $\leq(x) \subseteq X$. Suppose that there is a $y \in X\setminus \leq(x)$. So $x \in D$, $\langle x,y\rangle \not\in\leq$ (by the assumption), and $\langle x,y\rangle \in \sigma$ (by the definition of the σ-sets). By (I6), $x \in D$ and $\langle x,y\rangle \in \sigma$ imply $\langle x,y\rangle \in\leq$ which leads to a contradiction.

(V) Suppose that X is a σ-set, Y is $\leq$-hereditary and $X \cap Y \cap D \neq \emptyset$. Take an $x \in X$ and a $z \in X\cap Y\cap D$. So, $z \in X\cap D$ and by (IV), $X =\leq(z)$. By the definition of σ-set, $\langle z,x\rangle \in \sigma$ and by (I6), $\langle z,x\rangle \in\leq$. Since Y is $\leq$-hereditary, if $z \in Y$ and $\langle z,x\rangle \in\leq$, then $x \in Y$.

(VI) Direct consequence of (V).   Q.E.D.

Let $F = \langle W,\equiv,\leq,\sigma,D\rangle$ be an IL-structure. Let $S = \langle W,V\rangle$ be a set-theoretical information system defined as follows. For every $X \in \mathcal{P}(\mathcal{P}(W))$, $X \in V \overset{\text{def}}{\Leftrightarrow}$ for all $x,y \in W$, the following conditions hold:

(IL-rep1) $\langle x,y\rangle \in\leq$ implies for every $v \in X$, $x \in v$ implies $y \in v$;

(IL-rep2) $\langle x,y\rangle \in \sigma$ implies there is a $v \in X$ such that $\{x,y\} \subseteq v$;

(IL-rep3) $x \in D$ implies for all $v,v' \in X$, ($x \in v\cap v'$ implies $v = v'$).

We define a nice set function nsf^{IL} as follows: $nsf^{\mathrm{IL}}(F) = V$, where F is a plain Σ^{IL}-frame and V is the set defined above. The following lemmas are the intermediate results needed for proving Theorem 13.8.11.

Lemma 13.8.8. *For all $x,y \in W$, $\langle x,y\rangle \in\leq$ iff for every $X \in V$ and for every $v \in X$, $x \in v$ implies $y \in v$.*

Proof. ($\rightarrow$) Assume $\langle x,y\rangle \in\leq$, $X \in V$, $v \in X$, and $x \in v$. By (IL-rep1), $y \in v$.

($\leftarrow$) Assume that for every $X \in V$ and for every $v \in X$, $x \in v$ implies $y \in v$. Suppose that $\langle x,y\rangle \not\in\leq$. We show that there are an $X_0 \in V$ and a $v_0 \in X_0$ such that $x \in v_0$ and $y \notin v_0$. Take

$$X_0 = \{\leq(x)\}\cup\{\leq(z)\cup\leq(z') : \langle z,z'\rangle \in \sigma, \leq(x)\cap D\cap(\leq(z)\cup\leq(z')) = \emptyset\}$$

and $v_0 =\leq(x)$. Observe that $y \notin v_0$. It remains to show that $X_0 \in V$.

By Lemma 13.8.7(I, II), every $v \in X_0$ is $\leq$-hereditary, and hence X_0 satisfies (IL-rep1). Now suppose $\langle z,z'\rangle \in \sigma$. If $\leq(x)\cap D\cap(\leq(z)\cup\leq(z')) = \emptyset$, then by definition $\leq(z)\cup\leq(z') \in X_0$ and $\{z,z'\} \subseteq (\leq(z)\cup\leq(z'))$. Otherwise, $\langle z,z'\rangle \in \sigma$ implies $\leq(z)\cup\leq(z')$ is a σ-set (by Lemma 13.8.7(III)). Using Lemma 13.8.7(V), since $\leq(z)\cup\leq(z')$ is a σ-set, $\leq(x)$ is $\leq$-hereditary and $(\leq (z)\cup \leq (z'))\cap \leq (x)\cap D \neq \emptyset$. Hence $(\leq (z)\cup \leq (z')) \subseteq \leq (x)$ and therefore $\{z, z'\} \subseteq \leq (x)$. Since $\leq (x) \in X_0$, there is a $v \in X_0$ such that $z \in v$ and $z' \in v$.

To show (IL-rep3) suppose $z \in D$, $v, v' \in X_0$, and $z \in (v \cap v')$. So $D \cap v \cap v' \neq \emptyset$. If $v \neq \leq (x)$ and $v' \neq \leq (x)$, then:

$\star$ there are $z_1', z_1'' \in W$ such that $v =\leq (z_1')\cup \leq (z_1'')$ and $\langle z_1', z_1'' \rangle \in \sigma$;
$\star$ there are $z_2', z_2'' \in W$ such that $v' =\leq (z_2')\cup \leq (z_2'')$ and $\langle z_2', z_2'' \rangle \in \sigma$.

By Lemma 13.8.7(III), v and v' are σ-sets and by Lemma 13.8.7(VI), $v = v'$. If $v =\leq (x)$ and $v' =\leq (x)$, we clearly have $v = v'$. By the definition of X_0, no other cases are possible.   *Q.E.D.*

Lemma 13.8.9. *For all $x, y \in W$, $\langle x, y \rangle \in\equiv$ iff for every $X \in V$ and for every $v \in X$, $x \in v$ iff $y \in v$.*

Proof. ($\rightarrow$) If $\langle x, y \rangle \in\equiv$, then $\langle x, y \rangle \in\leq$ and $\langle y, x \rangle \in\leq$ (by (I1) and (I7)). By Lemma 13.8.8, for every $X \in V$ and for every $v \in X$, $x \in v$ iff $y \in v$.
($\leftarrow$) Assume that for every $X \in V$ and for every $v \in X$, $x \in v$ iff $y \in v$. By Lemma 13.8.8, $\langle x, y \rangle \in\leq$ and $\langle y, x \rangle \in\leq$. So, $\langle x, y \rangle \in\equiv$ by (I9).   *Q.E.D.*

Lemma 13.8.10. *For all $x, y \in W$, $\langle x, y \rangle \in \sigma$ iff for every $X \in V$, there is a $v \in X$ such that $\{x, y\} \subseteq v$.*

Proof. ($\rightarrow$) This is a consequence of (IL-rep2).
($\leftarrow$) Assume that for every $X \in V$, there is a $v \in X$ such that $\{x, y\} \subseteq v$. Suppose $\langle x, y \rangle \notin \sigma$. We show that there is an $X_0 \in V$ such that for every $v \in X_0$, $\{x, y\} \not\subseteq v$. Take

$$X_0 = \{\leq (z)\cup \leq (z') : \langle z, z' \rangle \in \sigma\}.$$

By Lemma 13.8.7(III), all the elements of X_0 are σ-sets. For every $v \in X_0$, $\{x, y\} \not\subseteq v$, otherwise, $\langle x, y \rangle \in \sigma$ (by definition of the σ-sets). We show that $X_0 \in V$, which will lead to a contradiction. (IL-rep1) is satisfied because every σ-set is $\leq$-hereditary. (IL-rep2) follows by construction. To show (IL-rep3), suppose $z \in D$, $v, v' \in X_0$, and $z \in (v \cap v')$. Since v and v' are σ-sets and $z \in (v \cap v' \cap D)$, by Lemma 13.8.7(VI), we get $v = v'$.   *Q.E.D.*

Lemma 13.8.11. *For all $x, y \in W$, $x \in D$ iff for every $X \in V$ and for all $v, v' \in X$, $x \in (v \cap v')$ implies $v = v'$.*

Proof. ($\rightarrow$) This is a consequence of (IL-rep3).
($\leftarrow$) Assume that for every $X \in V$, for all $v, v' \in X$, $x \in (v \cap v')$ implies $v = v'$. Suppose $x \notin D$. We shall show that there are $X_0 \in V$ and $v_0, v_0' \in X_0$ such that $x \in (v_0 \cap v_0')$ and $v_0 \neq v_0'$. By (I10), there is a $y \in W$ such that $\langle x, y \rangle \notin\leq$. Take $v_0 =\leq (x)$, $v_0' =\leq (x)\cup \leq (y)$, and

$$X_0 = \{v_0, v_0'\}\cup\{\leq (z)\cup \leq (z') : \langle z, z' \rangle \in \sigma, \ \leq (y)\cap D\cap(\leq (z)\cup \leq (z')) = \emptyset\}.$$

So $x \in v_0$, $y \notin v_0$, and $\{x, y\} \subseteq v_0'$. Clearly, $v_0 \neq v_0'$. X_0 satisfies (IL-rep1) since all the elements of X_0 are $\leq$-hereditary.

To show (IL-rep2), suppose $\langle z_1, z_2 \rangle \in \sigma$. If $D \cap \leq (y) \cap (\leq (z_1) \cup \leq (z_2)) = \emptyset$, then by definition $\{z_1, z_2\} \subseteq \leq (z_1) \cup \leq (z_2) \in X_0$. Otherwise, since $\leq (y)$ is $\leq$-hereditary and $\leq (z_1) \cup \leq (z_2)$ is a σ-set, by Lemma 13.8.7(V) we get $\leq (z_1) \cup \leq (z_2) \subseteq \leq (y)$. So $\{z_1, z_2\} \subseteq v_0'$.

To show (IL-rep3), suppose $z \in D$, $v, v' \in X_0$, and $z \in v \cap v'$. We can observe that $v \neq v_0$ and $v' \neq v_0$. For otherwise, $x \leq z$ and by (I5) $x \in D$, which leads to a contradiction. Now suppose $v = v_0'$ and $v' \neq v_0'$. So there exist $z_1, z_2 \in W$ such that $D \cap \leq (y) \cap (\leq (z_1) \cup \leq (z_2)) = \emptyset$, $v' = \leq (z_1) \cup \leq (z_2)$, and $\langle z_1, z_2 \rangle \in \sigma$ (remember $v' \neq v_0$). Since $z \in D$ and $z \in \leq (z_1) \cup \leq (z_2)$, we have $z \notin \leq (y)$, for otherwise $D \cap \leq (y) \cap v' \neq \emptyset$. But since $z \in v$, we get $z \in \leq (x)$ and by (I5) $x \in D$, which leads to a contradiction. Now we treat the case $v, v' \notin \{v_0, v_0'\}$. So v and v' are σ-sets by Lemma 13.8.7(III) and, by Lemma 13.8.7(VI), we get $v = v'$.   Q.E.D.

Theorem 13.8.11. *Every IL-structure is a standard IL-structure over a separable information system.*

The proof is a straightforward consequence of the previous lemmas.

Let ϕ^{ind}, ϕ^{fin}, ϕ^{sim} be the formulae defined in Sects. 13.3.1, 13.8.7, and 13.8.5, respectively, and let

$$\phi^D \stackrel{\text{def}}{=} OB(x_1) \wedge \forall\ x_2\ AT(x_2) \Rightarrow$$

$$(\forall\ x_3, x_4\ (\text{Value}(x_1, x_2, x_3) \wedge \text{Value}(x_1, x_2, x_4)) \Rightarrow x_3 = x_4).$$

Let $S^{IL} = \langle \phi^{ind}, \phi^{fin}, \phi^{sim}, \phi^D \rangle$ be the Σ^{IL}-specification.

Lemma 13.8.12. *Let F be a plain Σ^{IL}-frame. Then $nsf^{IL}(F)$ is a family of nice sets with respect to S^{IL} and F.*

Proof. The proof is a direct consequence of Lemmas 13.8.8, 13.8.9, 13.8.10, and 13.8.11.   Q.E.D.

Theorem 13.8.12. *The class of IL-structures is S^{IL}-inf-representable in the class of information systems.*

The proof is a straightforward consequence of the previous results.

13.9 Examples of Non-representability

We present classes of frames that are not informationally representable in our framework.

13.9.1 Classes of Σ-frames Closed Under Subframes

An information system $S' = \langle OB', AT' \rangle$ is said to be a *subsystem* of the information system $S = \langle OB, AT \rangle \overset{\text{def}}{\Leftrightarrow}$

(1) $OB' \subseteq OB$;
(2) $\{a_{|OB'} : a \in AT\} = AT'$ where $a_{|OB'}$ is the restriction of a to OB'.

The following result provides an insight into properties of classes of information systems closed under subsystems and classes of Σ-frames closed under subframes. Although Theorem 13.9.1 might appear quite natural, it has some unexpected consequences (see for instance Corollary 13.9.1).

Theorem 13.9.1. *Let Σ be a frame signature, let S be a Σ-specification, let X be a set of full Σ-frames, and let Y be a family of information systems closed under subsystems. If X is S-inf-representable in Y, then X is closed under subframes.*

Proof. Let $F = \langle W, (\mathcal{R}_P^1)_{P \subseteq PAR}, \ldots, (\mathcal{R}_P^k)_{P \subseteq PAR} \rangle \in X$. There exists an information system $S \in Y$ such that $D_{\Sigma,S}(S) \simeq F$. Let

$$F' = \langle W', (\mathcal{R}_P^{'1})_{P \subseteq PAR}, \ldots, (\mathcal{R}_P^{'k})_{P \subseteq PAR} \rangle$$

be a subframe of F. It can be shown that $D_{\Sigma,S,P}(S') \simeq F'$, where S' is the restriction of S to W'. Since Y is closed under subsystems, we have $S' \in Y$. By Definition 13.4.2(1) we have $F' \in X$.   *Q.E.D.*

Corollary 13.9.1. *Let Σ be a frame signature, let S be a Σ-specification such that all its atomic specifications are strong, and let X be a set of full Σ-frames $\langle W, (\mathcal{R}_P^1)_{P \subseteq PAR}, \ldots, (\mathcal{R}_P^k)_{P \subseteq PAR} \rangle$ such that for every $l \in \{1, \ldots, k\}$, $\langle W, (\mathcal{R}_P^l)_{P \subseteq PAR} \rangle \in$ FVS, and for every $p \in PAR$, $\mathcal{R}_{\{p\}}^l$ is serial [resp. atomic, weakly dense, discrete]. Then X is not S-inf-representable in the class of information systems.*

13.9.2 Non-representability of Local Agreement Frames

Let $\mathcal{C}^{LA}$ be the class of full Σ-frames $\langle W, (\mathcal{R}_P)_{P \subseteq PAR} \rangle \in$ FVS-IND such that for all $P, Q \subseteq PAR$, $\mathcal{R}_P$ and $\mathcal{R}_Q$ are in local agreement. Observe that $\mathcal{C}^{LA}$ is closed under subframes and the class of information systems is closed under subsystems (see Sect. 13.9.1). We show that $\mathcal{C}^{LA}$ is not S^{ind}-inf-representable in the class of information systems.

Lemma 13.9.1. *For every full Σ-frame F in $\mathcal{C}^{LA}$, there is an information system S such that $D_{\Sigma,S^{ind},P}(S) \simeq F$.*

Proof. See the construction of the nice set function nsf in Sect. 13.8.1. *Q.E.D.*

However, we have the following theorem.

Theorem 13.9.2. C^{LA} *is not* S^{ind}-*inf-representable in the class of information systems.*

Proof. Let $S = \langle \{x_1, x_2, x_3, \}, \{a, b\} \rangle$ be the information system such that

$\star$ $a(x_1) = a(x_2) = \{1\}$;
$\star$ $b(x_1) = b(x_3) = \{1\}$;
$\star$ $a(x_3) = b(x_2) = \{2\}$;

with $VAL_a = VAL_b = \{1, 2\}$. It is easy to show that in the full Σ-frame $F = D_{\Sigma, S^{ind}, \mathcal{P}}(S)$, $\mathcal{R}_{\{a\}}$ and $\mathcal{R}_{\{b\}}$ are not in local agreement.   *Q.E.D.*

13.10 Notes

Informational representability. Numerous informational representability results can be found in [Vak87, Vak89, Vak91c, Vak91a, Vak95, Vak98, DO98b, DO98a, DOV99]. The first theorem of this kind has been proved in [Vak87, Vak89]. In [Orło93c] it has been observed that a property of informational representability might be meaningful in investigations of non-classical logics, and a notion of informational representability has been proposed. The informational representability of some classes of Σ-frames with multiple families of binary relations can be found in [Vak87, Vak91a, Vak91b, Vak98]. These classes can be shown to be informationally representable by using the results of the previous sections and [Vak87, Vak91a, Vak91b, Vak98, DOV99]. This chapter is a completed and corrected version of [DO98b], except for Sect. 13.8.8, where the material is from [Vak91c]. The major differences here are that the language for information systems is treated as a fragment of FOL and a class of Σ-frames under consideration may include the frames that have different sets PAR of parameters as indices of their relative relations. Moreover, many technical developments have been simplified and corrected.

Frames with indiscerniblity and complementarity. Informational representability of frames with the relations of indiscernibility and complementarity with respect to the class of information systems is proved in [DOV99].

Nice family of sets. The technique of nice sets has been introduced by Vakarelov for the information logic NIL [Vak87]. In this chapter, we illustrate how this technique can be extended to full Σ-frames.

14. Informational Interpretation of Standard Algebraic Structures

14.1 Introduction and Outline of the Chapter

In this chapter we discuss relationships between some structures with information operators presented in Chap. 4 and various standard algebraic systems of algebraic logic. These relationships are of the two kinds. First, we show that structures with information operators can be equipped with some standard algebraic structures, thus obtaining an informational example of the underlying classes of algebras. Second, in some cases we present an informational representation theorem for a standard class of algebras, namely, a theorem of the following form: every algebra from the given class of algebras is isomorphic to a subalgebra of an algebra determined by a structure with information operators.

The material of this chapter shows, on the one hand, that many usual algebraic structures are useful in an analysis of data in information systems. On the other hand, it also shows that these algebraic structures do not capture all the essential features of information operators. In particular, they are not sufficient for representing the way information about objects depends on the set of attributes. Usually, either one approximation space is fixed and, as a consequence, we deal with a fixed indiscernibility relation, or a family of indiscernibility relations is treated as a plain family of relations, without any information on how the relations depend on sets of attributes.

A solution to these problems is proposed in Chap. 15, where the classes of information algebras are discussed. These algebras are designed for a variety of information operators, not only for the operators determined by the indiscernibility relations. Moreover, they provide a means for expressing an information resulting from the changes of sets of attributes.

In Sect. 14.2 we present a complete lattice of indiscernibility relations derived from an information system. The key point is a construction of a set of attributes that determines the indiscernibility relations obtained by applying the lattice operations. In Sect. 14.3 we show that any family of sets closed under the information operators considered in Sect. 4.6 is a Boolean algebra. In Sects. 14.4 and 14.5 we present representation theorems for three-valued Łukasiewicz algebras and for Stone algebras, respectively. These theorems say that any algebra from each of these two classes is isomorphic to a subalgebra of an algebra from the respective class, derived from an approximation space. In Sect. 14.6 we investigate rough relations. Any approximation space induces in a natural way an approximation space on the product of its universe. The corresponding equivalence relation is defined componentwise from the equivalence relation of the original space. Then rough relations are the pairs consisting of a lower approximation and an upper approximation of a relation in the product approximation space. A class of rough relation algebras is presented that provides an abstract characterisation of rough relations. The main result of this section is a necessary and sufficient condition for representability of rough relation algebras. In Sect. 14.7 we discuss an abstract characterisation of fuzzy relations. We present a class of fuzzy relation algebras and we show that every fuzzy relation algebra is representable, that is it is isomorphic to an algebra of L_0-fuzzy relations such that L_0 is a lattice on the real interval $[0, 1]$. In Sect. 14.8 we mention the representation theorem for a class of Nelson algebras, analogous to the representation theorems in Sects. 14.4 and 14.5.

In Sect. 14.9 we present generalisations of standard algebraic structures obtained by equipping the algebras with generalised approximation operators. In some cases we do not present proofs of the theorems but in Sect. 14.10 we indicate the literature where the proofs can be found.

14.2 A Lattice of Indiscernibility Relations

Let an information system $S = \langle OB, AT \rangle$ be given. We show that the family $(ind(A))_{A \subseteq AT}$ of indiscernibility relations can be given a lattice structure and, moreover, this lattice is complete. We define the operation $C_S : \mathcal{P}(AT) \to \mathcal{P}(AT)$ so that for every $A \subseteq AT$,

$$C_S(A) \overset{\text{def}}{=} \{a \in AT : ind(A) \subseteq ind(\{a\})\}.$$

Theorem 14.2.1. $\langle \{ind(A) : A \subseteq AT\}, \subseteq \rangle$ *is a complete lattice such that for every family* $(B_i)_{i \in I}$ *of subsets of* AT, *the supremum and the infimum are defined as follows:*

(I) $inf(\{ind(B_i) : i \in I\}) = \bigcap_{i \in I} ind(B_i) = ind(\bigcup_{i \in I} B_i)$;
(II) $sup(\{ind(B_i) : i \in I\}) = ind(\bigcap_{i \in I} C_S(B_i))$.

Proof. By Lemma 3.3.7(I, III), the poset $\langle \{ind(A) : A \subseteq AT\}, \subseteq \rangle$ has the top element $ind(\emptyset)$ and the bottom element $ind(AT)$.
(I) If $I = \emptyset$, then $\bigcap_{i \in \emptyset} ind(\{B_i\}) = OB \times OB = ind(\emptyset) = ind(\bigcup_{i \in \emptyset} B_i)$. If $I \neq \emptyset$, then $\langle x, y \rangle \in \bigcap_{i \in I} ind(B_i)$ iff for every $i \in I$, $\langle x, y \rangle \in ind(B_i)$ iff for every $i \in I$, for every $a \in B_i$, $a(x) = a(y)$ iff for every $a \in \bigcup_{i \in I} B_i$, $a(x) = a(y)$ iff $\langle x, y \rangle \in ind(\bigcup_{i \in I} B_i)$.
(II) Since $inf(\{ind(B_i) : i \in I\})$ exists, $sup(\{ind(B_i) : i \in I\})$ equals the infimum of the set of the upper bounds of $\{ind(B_i) : i \in I\}$. Hence, using

(I), we get $sup(\{ind(B_i) : i \in I\}) = \bigcap\{ind(A) : (\bigcup_{i \in I} ind(B_i)) \subseteq ind(A)\} = ind(\bigcup\{A \subseteq AT : (\bigcup_{i \in I} ind(B_i)) \subseteq ind(A)\}$.

We show that $\bigcup\{A \subseteq AT : (\bigcup_{i \in I} ind(B_i)) \subseteq ind(A)\} = \bigcap_{i \in I} C_S(B_i)$. Let $a \in \bigcup\{A \subseteq AT : (\bigcup_{i \in I} ind(B_i)) \subseteq ind(A)\}$. Hence, there exists an $A \subseteq AT$ such that $a \in A$ and $ind(B_i) \subseteq ind(A)$ for every $i \in I$. Then, $a \in C_S(B_i)$ for every $i \in I$. It means that $a \in \bigcap_{i \in I} C_S(B_i)$. Conversely, if $a \in \bigcap_{i \in I} C_S(B_i)$, then $ind(B_i) \subseteq ind(\{a\})$ for every $i \in I$. Hence, $\{a\} \in \{A \subseteq AT : ind(B_i) \subseteq ind(A)$ for every $i \in I\}$. It follows that $a \in \bigcup\{A \subseteq AT : (\bigcup_{i \in I} ind(B_i)) \subseteq ind(A)\}$.

We conclude that condition (II) holds.   Q.E.D.

14.3 A Boolean Algebra of Certainty Regions

Consider the clone of information operators presented in Sect. 4.7:

$$Clo \overset{\text{def}}{=} \{Pos, Neg, Bl, Bu, K, Id, H, H_0, -Pos,$$

$$-Neg, -Bl, -Bu, B, -Id, -H, H_1\}$$

and the set

$$Gen \overset{\text{def}}{=} \{Pos, Neg, Bl, Bu\}.$$

Let an approximation space $\langle W, R \rangle$ be given and let $X \subseteq W$. We define the sets $Clo_R(X)$ and $Gen_R(X)$ as follows:

$$Clo_R(X) \overset{\text{def}}{=} \{f_R(X) : f \in Clo\},$$

$$Gen_R(X) \overset{\text{def}}{=} \{f_R(X) : f \in Gen\}.$$

Lemma 14.3.1. *For every approximation space $\langle W, R \rangle$ and for every $X \subseteq W$, the following assertions hold:*

(I) if X is R-definable, then $Gen_R(X) = \{X, W \setminus X, \emptyset\}$;

(II) if X is internally R-indefinable, then

  (II.1) $Gen_R(X) = \{f_R(X) : f \in \{Neg, Id, Bu\}\}$;

  (II.2) $Clo_R(X) =$

$$\{f(R)(X) : f \in \{Neg, Id, Bu, H_0, -Neg, -Id, -Bu, H_1\}\};$$

(III) if X is externally R-indefinable, then

  (III.1) $Gen_R(X) = \{f_R(X) : f \in \{Pos, -Id, Bl\}\}$;

  (III.2) $Clo_R(X) =$

$$\{f_R(X) : f \in \{Pos, -Id, Bl, H_0, -Pos, Id, -Bl, H_1\}\}.$$

Proof. (I) If X is R-definable, then $Pos_R(X) = X$, $Neg_R(X) = W \setminus X$, and $Bu_R(X) = Bl_R(X) = \emptyset$.
(II) If X is internally R-indefinable, then $Bl_R(X) = X$ and $Pos_R(X) = \emptyset$.
(III) If X is externally R-indefinable, then we have $Bu_R(X) = X$ and $Neg_R(X) = \emptyset$.   *Q.E.D.*

Lemma 14.3.2. *For every approximation space $\langle W, R \rangle$ and for every $X \subseteq W$, the set $Clo_R(X)$ is a Boolean algebra generated by $Gen_R(X)$.*

Proof. By the definition of Clo, $Clo_R(X)$ is closed with respect to the complement operation. By Lemma 4.7.1, $Clo_R(X)$ includes $Gen_R(X)$ and is closed with respect to the union operation. The proof of Lemma 4.7.1 shows that every member of $Clo_R(X)$ is a Boolean combination of elements of $Gen_R(X)$. *Q.E.D.*

Observe that if X is roughly R-definable, then $Clo_R(X)$ is the algebra with 16 elements. By Lemma 14.3.2, if X is externally or internally R-indefinable, then $Clo_R(X)$ has 8 elements. If X is a non-empty set, then if X is R-definable, then $Clo_R(X)$ has 4 elements.

14.4 An Informational Interpretation of Monadic Algebras and Łukasiewicz Algebras

A *monadic algebra* is a structure of the form

$$\langle W, +, \cdot, -, 1, 0, M \rangle,$$

where

* $\langle W, +, \cdot, -, 1, 0 \rangle$ is a Boolean algebra;
* M is a unary operation on W that satisfies
  * $M(0) = 0$;
  * $x \cdot M(x) = x$;
  * $M(x \cdot M(y)) = M(x) \cdot M(y)$.

Let $\langle W, R \rangle$ be an approximation space. It is easy to see that the Boolean algebra of subsets of W with the operation of upper R-approximation is a monadic algebra.

Example 14.4.1. Any structure $\langle W, R \rangle$ such that W is a non-empty set and R is an equivalence relation on W determines a complete Boolean subalgebra of the algebra $\mathcal{P}(W)$ of subsets of W, namely, the algebra whose atoms are the equivalence classes of R and whose elements are the R-definable subsets of W.

Conversely, any atomic complete subalgebra $\mathcal{B}$ of the Boolean algebra of subsets of W determines an approximation space $\langle W, R' \rangle$, where the equivalence relation R' is defined as follows: $\langle x, y \rangle \in R'$ iff x and y are contained in the same atom of $\mathcal{B}$. The atoms of $\mathcal{B}$ are the equivalence classes of R', and hence the elements of $\mathcal{B}$ are $\emptyset$ and the R-definable subsets of W.

Lemma 14.4.1. *For every approximation space $\langle W, R \rangle$, the system*

$$\langle \mathcal{P}(W), \cup, \cap, -, W, \emptyset, U(R) \rangle$$

is a monadic algebra.

Proof. Let $M = U(R)$. By definition of the upper approximation, $M(\emptyset) = \emptyset$ and for every $X \subseteq W$, $X \subseteq M(X)$. Now, let $X, Y \subseteq W$ and $x \in M(X \cap M(Y))$. Then there is a $z \in X \cap M(Y)$ such that $x \in |z|_R$. Furthermore, $z \in X$ and there is a $t \in Y$ such that $z \in |t|_R$. Hence $|z|_R = |t|_R$, and therefore $x \in M(X) \cap M(Y)$. Conversely, let $x \in M(X) \cap M(Y)$. Then there are $z \in X$ and $t \in Y$ such that $x \in |z|_R$ and $x \in |t|_R$. Hence, $|z|_R = |t|_R$. It follows that $z \in X \cap M(Y)$ and $x \in M(X \cap M(Y))$. $\qquad$ *Q.E.D.*

The algebra presented in the above lemma is referred to as a *monadic algebra derived from the approximation space* $\langle W, R \rangle$.

A *three-valued Łukasiewicz algebra* is a structure of the form

$$\langle W, +, \cdot, \sim, \triangledown, 1, 0 \rangle,$$

where

* $\langle W, +, \cdot, 1, 0 \rangle$ is a bounded distributive lattice;
* $\sim$ is a *De Morgan complement*, that is $\sim (x + y) = \sim x \cdot \sim y$ and $\sim\sim x = x$;
* $\triangledown$ is a unary operation on W that satisfies
  * $\sim x + \triangledown x = 1$;
  * $x \cdot \sim x = \sim x \cdot \triangledown x$;
  * $\triangledown(x \cdot y) = \triangledown x \cdot \triangledown y$.

The operator $\triangle$ dual to $\triangledown$ is defined by $\triangle x \stackrel{\text{def}}{=} \sim \triangledown \sim x$. The following lemma presents some properties of the operations of the three-valued Łukasiewicz algebras.

Lemma 14.4.2.
For every three-valued Łukasiewicz algebra $\langle W, +, \cdot, \sim, \triangledown, 1, 0 \rangle$, for all $x, y \in W$, the following conditions are satisfied:

(I) $\triangledown$ *is a closure operator;*
(II) $\triangledown(x + y) = \triangledown x + \triangledown y$;
(III) If $\triangledown x = \triangledown y$ and $\triangle x = \triangle y$, then $x = y$;
(IV) $\triangledown \triangle x = \triangle x$, $\triangle \triangledown x = \triangledown x$;
(V) $\triangle x \leq x$, $x \leq \triangledown x$;
(VI) $x \leq y$ *implies* $\sim y \leq \sim x$;
(VII) $\triangledown x + \sim \triangledown x = 1$, $\triangledown x \cdot \sim \triangledown x = 0$;
(VIII) $x \cdot \sim x \leq y + \sim y$.

Condition (VIII) is referred to as the *Kleene property*. It is equivalent to condition (III).

Definition 14.4.1. *Let $\langle W, R \rangle$ be an approximation space. In the family $\mathcal{P}_r(W, R)$ of the rough subsets of W with respect to R we define the following operations:*

★ $\langle L_R(X), U_R(X) \rangle + \langle L_R(Y), U_R(Y) \rangle \overset{\text{def}}{=}$
  $\langle L_R(X) \cup L_R(Y), U_R(X) \cup U_R(Y) \rangle$;
★ $\langle L_R(X), U_R(X) \rangle \cdot \langle L_R(Y), U_R(Y) \rangle \overset{\text{def}}{=}$
  $\langle L_R(X) \cap L_R(Y), U_R(X) \cap U_R(Y) \rangle$;
★ $\sim \langle L_R(X), U_R(X) \rangle \overset{\text{def}}{=} \langle W \setminus U_R(X), W \setminus L_R(X) \rangle$;
★ $\triangledown \langle L_R(X), U_R(X) \rangle \overset{\text{def}}{=} \langle U_R(X), U_R(X) \rangle$;
★ $0 \overset{\text{def}}{=} \langle \emptyset, \emptyset \rangle$;
★ $1 \overset{\text{def}}{=} \langle W, W \rangle$.

Lemma 14.4.3. *For every approximation space $\langle W, R \rangle$, the system*

$$\langle \mathcal{P}_r(W, R), +, \cdot, \sim, \triangledown, 1, 0 \rangle$$

is a three-valued Łukasiewicz algebra.

The proof is by an easy verification.

Let $\mathcal{A} = \langle Z, +, \cdot, \sim, \triangledown, 1, 0 \rangle$ be a three-valued Łukasiewicz algebra. Let $W_{\mathcal{A}}$ be the set of prime filters of $\mathcal{A}$ and let the mapping $g : W_{\mathcal{A}} \to W_{\mathcal{A}}$ be defined as $g(\mathrm{F}) = Z \setminus \sim \mathrm{F}$, where $\mathrm{F} \in W_{\mathcal{A}}$ and $\sim \mathrm{F} \overset{\text{def}}{=} \{\sim p : p \in \mathrm{F}\}$. Finally, let $R_{\mathcal{A}}$ be the binary relation on $W_{\mathcal{A}}$ defined so that $\langle \mathrm{F}, \mathrm{G} \rangle \in R_{\mathcal{A}} \overset{\text{def}}{\Leftrightarrow}$ either $\mathrm{F} \subseteq \mathrm{G}$ or $\mathrm{G} \subseteq \mathrm{F}$.

The following two lemmas state some properties of $W_{\mathcal{A}}$ and $R_{\mathcal{A}}$.

Lemma 14.4.4. *For all $\mathrm{F}, \mathrm{G} \in W_{\mathcal{A}}$ we have:*

(I) if $\triangle x \in \mathrm{F}$, then $\triangle x \in g(\mathrm{F})$;
(II) if $g(\mathrm{F}) \subseteq \mathrm{F}$ and $\triangledown x \in \mathrm{F}$, then $x \in \mathrm{F}$;
(III) if $g(\mathrm{F}) \subseteq \mathrm{F}$ and $x \in g(\mathrm{F})$, then $\triangle x \in g(\mathrm{F})$;
(IV) if $\mathrm{F} \subseteq \mathrm{G}$, then $g(\mathrm{G}) \subseteq g(\mathrm{F})$.

Proof. By way of example we prove (II) and (III).
(II) If $x \notin \mathrm{F}$, then $\sim x \notin\sim \mathrm{F}$. Hence, $\sim x \in g(\mathrm{F})$ and since $g(\mathrm{F}) \subseteq \mathrm{F}$ we also have $\sim x \in \mathrm{F}$. Since $\triangledown x \in \mathrm{F}$ and $x \cdot \sim x = \sim x \cdot \triangledown x$, we have $x \cdot \sim x \in \mathrm{F}$. Hence $x \in \mathrm{F}$, a contradiction.
(III) Suppose that $\triangle x \notin g(\mathrm{F})$. Since $1 = \triangle x + \sim \triangle x \in g(\mathrm{F})$ and $g(\mathrm{F})$ is prime, we have $\sim \triangle x = \triangledown \sim x \in g(\mathrm{F})$. Since $x \in g(\mathrm{F})$, we get $x \cdot \triangledown \sim x = \sim x \cdot x \in g(\mathrm{F})$. Hence, $\sim x \cdot x \in \mathrm{F}$. Thus $\sim x \in \mathrm{F}$. But since $x \in g(\mathrm{F}) = Z \setminus \sim \mathrm{F}$, we have $x \notin\sim \mathrm{F}$. Thus $\sim x \notin \mathrm{F}$, a contradiction. $\qquad$ Q.E.D.

Lemma 14.4.5.

(I) $\langle W_A, \subseteq \rangle$ *is a disjoint union of chains each consisting of one or two elements;*

(II) R_A *is an equivalence relation;*

For all $F, G \in W_A$,

(III) $\langle F, g(F) \rangle \in R_A$;

(IV) *If* $\langle F, G \rangle \in R_A$, *then* $\langle g(F), g(G) \rangle \in R_A$.

Proof. By way of example we prove (I) and (III).

(I) Let Z be the universe of A. Consider the set $\mathcal{B}(A)$ of complemented elements of A. It is a Boolean algebra and a subalgebra of A. For every prime filter F of A there is a maximal filter F' of $\mathcal{B}(A)$ such that $F = \bigtriangledown^{-1}(F') = \{x \in Z : \bigtriangledown x \in F'\}$ or $F = \bigtriangleup^{-1}(F') = \{x \in Z : \bigtriangleup x \in F'\}$. Due to Lemma 14.4.2(V), we have $\bigtriangleup^{-1}(F') \subseteq \bigtriangledown^{-1}(F')$ for every F'.

(III) Suppose that not $G \subseteq g(G)$. It follows that there is an x such that $x \in G$ and $x \notin g(G)$. The latter means that $\sim x \in G$. Hence, (i) $x \cdot \sim x \in G$. We shall show that $g(G) \subseteq G$. If $y \in g(G)$, then we get $\sim y \notin G$. By Lemma 14.4.2(VIII) and (i), $y \cdot \sim y \in G$. Since G is a prime filter, we infer that $y \in G$.   *Q.E.D.*

Consider the approximation space $\langle W_A, R_A \rangle$ and the monadic Boolean algebra $\langle \mathcal{P}(W_A), \cup, \cap, -, \emptyset, W_A, U_{R_A} \rangle$ derived from it. Let Z be the universe of A and $s : Z \to \mathcal{P}(W_A)$ be a mapping defined as $s(x) \overset{\text{def}}{=} \{F \in W_A : x \in F\}$. It is easy to see that the following lemma holds.

Lemma 14.4.6.

(I) $s(x + y) = s(x) \cup s(y)$;

(II) $s(x \cdot y) = s(x) \cap s(y)$;

(III) $s(0) = \emptyset$, $s(1) = W_A$.

Let $L = L_{R_A}$ and $U = U_{R_A}$ be the operators of lower and upper approximations with respect to the relation R_A, respectively. Let

$$T = \{\langle L(s(x)), U(s(x)) \rangle : x \in Z\}$$

and define the operations $+$, $\cdot$, $\sim$, $\bigtriangledown$, 0, and 1 on T by applying Definition 14.4.1 to the approximation space $\langle W_A, R_A \rangle$. It is easy to check that the system $A^\star = \langle T, +, \cdot, \sim, \bigtriangledown, 0, 1 \rangle$ is a three-valued Lukasiewicz algebra.

The following two lemmas present properties of the approximation operators derived from $\langle W_A, R_A \rangle$. They are a basis for proving forthcoming Theorem 14.4.1.

Lemma 14.4.7. *Let* $A = \langle Z, +, \cdot, \sim, \bigtriangledown, 1, 0 \rangle$ *be a three-valued Lukasiewicz algebra. Then the approximation operators* $L = L_{R_A}$ *and* $U = U_{R_A}$ *satisfy the following conditions for every* $x \in Z$:

(I) $U(s(\nabla x)) = s(\nabla x)$;
(II) $U(s(x)) = s(\nabla x)$;
(III) $L(s(\triangle x)) = s(\triangle x)$;
(IV) $L(s(x)) = s(\triangle x)$.

Proof. By way of example we prove (I) and (IV).
(I) ($\subseteq$) Let F $\in U(s(\nabla x))$. By the definition of U, there is a G $\in W_A$ such that $\langle$F, G$\rangle \in R_A$ and G $\in s(\nabla x)$. Hence, $\nabla x \in$ G. If G $\subseteq$ F, then $\nabla x \in$ F; hence F $\in s(\nabla x)$.
Now let F $\subset$ G and suppose that $\nabla x \notin$ F. Since F is a filter, $1 = \nabla x + \sim \nabla x \in$ F. Since F is prime, $\sim \nabla x \in$ F. Hence $\sim \nabla x \in$ G. It follows that $\nabla x \cdot \sim \nabla x = 0 \in$ G, a contradiction.
($\supseteq$) By the definition of U we have $s(\nabla x) \subseteq U(s(\nabla x))$.
(IV)($\subseteq$) Let F $\in L(s(x))$. Then $|F|_{R_A} \subseteq s(x)$. Hence, $x \in$ F and since $g(F) \in |F|_{R_A}$ by Lemma 14.4.5(III), we have $x \in g(P)$.
If $g(F) \subseteq$ F, then by Lemma 14.4.4(III) we get $\triangle x \in g(F)$. Thus $\triangle x \in$ F and hence F $\in s(\triangle x)$.
If F $\subset g(F)$, then by Lemma 14.4.4(III) we get $\triangle x \in g(F)$. For otherwise, if $\triangle x \notin g(F)$, then either F $\subseteq g(F)$ or $x \notin g(F)$, a contradiction.
($\supseteq$) Since $\triangle x \leq x$, we have $s(\triangle x) \subseteq s(x)$. Hence, $Ls(\triangle x) \subseteq Ls(x)$. By (III), $s(\triangle x) \subseteq Ls(x)$.
Observe that the cases $g(F) \subseteq$ F and F $\subset g(F)$ exhaust all the possibilities due to Lemma 14.4.5(III).   Q.E.D.

Lemma 14.4.8. *Let* $A = \langle Z, +, \cdot, \sim, \nabla, 1, 0 \rangle$ *be a three-valued Lukasiewicz algebra. Then the approximation operators* $L = L_{R_A}$ *and* $U = U_{R_A}$ *satisfy the following conditions for every* $x \in Z$:

(I) $-U(s(x)) = s(\sim \nabla x)$;
(II) $-L(s(x)) = s(\sim \triangle x)$;
(III) $L(s(\sim x)) = s(\sim \nabla x)$;
(IV) $U(s(\sim x)) = s(\sim \triangle x)$.

Proof. (I) Obviously, F $\in s(\sim \nabla x)$ iff $\sim \nabla x \in$ F iff $\nabla x \notin$ F iff F $\notin s(\nabla x)$ iff F $\in -s(\nabla x)$. Hence, F $\in -U(s(x))$ by Lemma 14.4.7(II).
(II) The following statements are equivalent: F $\in s(\sim \triangle x)$ iff $\sim \triangle x \in$ F iff $\triangle x \notin$ F iff F $\notin s(\triangle x)$ iff F $\in -s(\triangle x)$. By Lemma 14.4.7(IV), $p \in -L(s(x))$.
(III) We have F $\in s(\sim \nabla x)$ iff F $\in s(\triangle \sim x)$. By Lemma 14.4.7(IV), F $\in L(s(\sim x))$.
(IV) We have F $\in s(\sim \triangle x)$ iff F $\in s(\nabla \sim x)$. By Lemma 14.4.7(II), we get F $\in U(s(\sim x))$.   Q.E.D.

Now we are in a position to prove the following informational representation theorem.

Theorem 14.4.1. *Every three-valued Lukasiewicz algebra is isomorphic to a three-valued Lukasiewicz algebra derived from an approximation space.*

Proof. Let $\mathcal{A} = \langle Z, +, \cdot, \sim, \bigtriangledown, 1, 0 \rangle$ be a three-valued Lukasiewicz algebra. Consider the approximation space $\langle W_{\mathcal{A}}, R_{\mathcal{A}} \rangle$ constructed above and the algebra $\mathcal{A}^*$. Let $h : Z \to T$ be defined by $h(x) \overset{\text{def}}{=} \langle L(s(x)), U(s(x)) \rangle$. We show that h is an isomorphism from $\mathcal{A}$ onto $\mathcal{A}^*$. Using Lemma 14.4.7 and Lemma 14.4.8 we can easily show that h is a homomorphism. We show that h is injective. Let $\langle L(s(x)), U(s(x)) \rangle = \langle L(s(y)), U(s(y)) \rangle$. Using Lemma 14.4.7(IV, II) we get $\langle s(\triangle x), s(\bigtriangledown x) \rangle = \langle s(\triangle y), s(\bigtriangledown y) \rangle$. Hence, $s(\triangle x) = s(\triangle y)$ and $s(\bigtriangledown x) = s(\bigtriangledown y)$. Since s is injective, we have $\triangle x = \triangle y$ and $\bigtriangledown x = \bigtriangledown y$. By Lemma 14.4.2(III) we have $x = y$. Clearly, h is onto. $\hspace{2cm} Q.E.D.$

14.5 An Informational Interpretation of Stone Algebras

To extend relation algebras to the algebraic structures that represent relations which may be defined approximatively, we need the notion of Stone algebra.

A *double Stone algebra* is a structure of the form

$$\langle W, +, \cdot, ^*, ^+, 1, 0 \rangle,$$

where

(1) $\langle W, +, \cdot, 1, 0 \rangle$ is a bounded distributive lattice;
(2) * is a unary operation such that x^* is the pseudo-complement of x;
(3) $^+$ is a unary operation such that x^+ is the dual pseudo-complement of x;
(4) $x^* + x^{**} = 1$, $x^+ \cdot x^{++} = 0$.

Condition (2) can be replaced by the equations: $x \cdot (x \cdot y)^* = x \cdot y^*$, $x \cdot 0^* = x$, and $0^{**} = 0$. Similarly, condition (3) can be replaced by the following equations: $x + (x + y)^+ = x + y^+$, $x + 1^+ = x$, and $1^{++} = 1$.

A double Stone algebra is *regular* $\overset{\text{def}}{\Leftrightarrow}$ it satisfies the inequality:

(5) $x \cdot x^+ \leq y + y^*$.

Condition (5) is equivalent to

(5') $x^+ = y^+$ and $x^* = y^*$ imply $x = y$.

Let $\langle W, R \rangle$ be an approximation space. In the family $\mathcal{P}_r(W, R)$ of the rough subsets of W with respect to R we define the following operations:

$\star$ $\langle L_R(X), U_R(X) \rangle + \langle L_R(Y), U_R(Y) \rangle \overset{\text{def}}{=}$
$\langle L_R(X) \cup L_R(Y), U_R(X) \cup U_R(Y) \rangle$;
$\star$ $\langle L_R(X), U_R(X) \rangle \cdot \langle L_R(Y), U_R(Y) \rangle \overset{\text{def}}{=}$
$\langle L_R(X) \cap L_R(Y), U_R(X) \cap U_R(Y) \rangle$;
$\star$ $\langle L_R(X), U_R(X) \rangle^* \overset{\text{def}}{=} \langle W \setminus U_R(X), W \setminus U_R(X) \rangle$;
$\star$ $\langle L_R(X), U_R(X) \rangle^+ \overset{\text{def}}{=} \langle W \setminus L_R(X), W \setminus L_R(X) \rangle$;

$\star$ $0 \overset{\text{def}}{=} \langle \emptyset, \emptyset \rangle$;
$\star$ $1 \overset{\text{def}}{=} \langle W, W \rangle$.

Lemma 14.5.1. *For every approximation space $\langle W, R \rangle$, the structure $\langle \mathcal{P}_r(W, R), +, \cdot, ^*, ^+, 1, 0 \rangle$ with the operations defined above is a regular double Stone algebra.*

The proof is by an easy verification. This algebra is referred to as the *regular double Stone algebra derived from the approximation space $\langle W, R \rangle$.*

Let $\mathcal{A} = \langle W, +, \cdot, ^*, ^+, 1, 0 \rangle$ be a double Stone algebra. The *centre* of $\mathcal{A}$ is the set

$$C(\mathcal{A}) \overset{\text{def}}{=} \{x^* : x \in W\}.$$

The *dense set* of $\mathcal{A}$ is the set

$$D(\mathcal{A}) \overset{\text{def}}{=} \{x \in W : x^* = 0\}.$$

For every $X \subseteq W$, we define $X^+ \overset{\text{def}}{=} \{x^+ : x \in X\}$.

Lemma 14.5.2. *For every double Stone algebra $\mathcal{A}$, the following assertions hold:*

(I) $C(\mathcal{A})$ is a subalgebra of $\mathcal{A}$;
(II) $C(\mathcal{A})$ is a Boolean algebra such that * and $^+$ coincide with the Boolean complement;
(III) $D(\mathcal{A})$ is a distributive lattice;
(IV) $D(\mathcal{A})^{++}$ is a filter of $\mathcal{A}$.

The proof is by an easy verification.

Let $2 = \langle \{0, 1\}, \leq \rangle$ be the chain such that $0 < 1$ and let $3 = \langle \{0, a, 1\}, \leq \rangle$ be the chain such that $0 < a < 1$. Let I, J be non-empty sets, and consider the set $2^I \times 3^J$ of pairs $\langle f, g \rangle$ of functions $f : I \to 2$, $g : 3 \to J$. Let $f, f' \in 2^I$ and $g, g' \in 3^J$. We define the following operations on $2^I \times 3^J$:

$\star$ $\langle f, g \rangle + \langle f', g' \rangle \overset{\text{def}}{=} \langle f + f', g + g' \rangle$;
$\star$ $\langle f, g \rangle \cdot \langle f', g' \rangle \overset{\text{def}}{=} \langle f \cdot f', g \cdot g' \rangle$;
   where for $h = f, g$ and $h' = f', g'$,
   $*$ $(h + h')(i) \overset{\text{def}}{=} sup(\{h(i), h'(i)\})$;
   $*$ $(h \cdot h')(i) \overset{\text{def}}{=} inf(\{h(i), h'(i)\})$;
      if $h = f$, then $i \in I$, if $h = g$, then $i \in J$;
$\star$ $\langle f, g \rangle^* \overset{\text{def}}{=} \langle f^*, g^* \rangle$, where $f^*(i) = 1 - i$, $g^*(0) = 1$, $g^*(a) = 0$, and $g^*(1) = 0$;
$\star$ $\langle f, g \rangle^+ \overset{\text{def}}{=} \langle f^+, g^+ \rangle$, where $f^+(i) = 1 - i$, $g^+(0) = 1$, $g^+(a) = 1$, and $g^+(1) = 0$.

We also define an ordering $\leq$ on $2^I \times 3^J$ as follows: $\langle f, g \rangle \leq \langle f', g' \rangle \overset{\text{def}}{\Leftrightarrow} f \leq f'$ and $g \leq g'$, where for $h = f, g$, we have $h \leq h'$ iff for every i, $h(i) \leq h'(i)$, and if $h = f$, then $i \in I$, if $h = g$, then $i \in J$.

Lemma 14.5.3. *For all non-empty sets I and J, the algebra $\mathcal{A}_{I,J} = \langle 2^I \times 3^J, +, \cdot, ^*, ^+, 1, 0 \rangle$ with the operations defined above is a regular double Stone algebra.*

The proof is by an easy verification.

For all non-empty sets I and J, we define:

$$\mathcal{B}_{I,J} = \{\langle f, g \rangle \in 2^I \times 3^J : f(i) \in \{0,1\}, g(j) \in \{0,1\}, \text{for all } i \in I, j \in J\},$$

$$F_{I,J} = \{\langle f, g \rangle \in 2^I \times 3^J : f(i) = 1, \text{for every } i \in I\}.$$

Lemma 14.5.4. *For all non-empty sets I and J the following assertions hold:*

(I) $\mathcal{B}_{I,J}$ is the centre of $\mathcal{A}_{I,J}$;
(II) $\mathcal{B}_{I,J}$ is isomorphic to $2^{I \cup J}$;
(III) $F_{I,J}$ is a filter of $\mathcal{B}_{I,J}$;
(IV) $F_{I,J} = D(\mathcal{A}_{I,J})^{++}$.

Proof. By Lemmas 14.5.3 and 14.5.2(II) we know that $\mathcal{B}_{I,J}$ is a Boolean algebra. By way of example, we prove (III) and (IV).
(III) Let $\langle f, g \rangle \in F_{I,J}$ and $\langle f, g \rangle \leq \langle f', g' \rangle$. Then $f(i) \leq f'(i)$ for every $i \in I$, and hence $f'(i) = 1$ for every $i \in I$. We conclude that $\langle f', g' \rangle \in F_{I,J}$. Now let $\langle f, g \rangle, \langle f', g' \rangle \in F_{I,J}$. Then for every $i \in I$, $f(i) = f'(i) = 1$. Hence $f(i) \cdot f'(i) = 1$, which implies that $\langle f, g \rangle \cdot \langle f', g' \rangle \in F_{I,J}$.
(IV) ($\subseteq$) Let $\langle f, g \rangle \in F_{I,J}$. Define $g'(j) = a$ if $g(0) = 0$, otherwise $g'(j) = g(j)$. Then $\langle f, g' \rangle \in D(\mathcal{A}_{I,J})$ and $\langle f, g' \rangle^{++} = \langle f, g \rangle$.
($\supseteq$) If $\langle f, g \rangle \in D(\mathcal{A}_{I,J})^{++}$, then $f(i) = 1$ for every $i \in I$, because $f(i) \neq 0$. Hence, $f^{++}(i) = 1$ for every $i \in I$. Thus $\langle f, g \rangle^{++} \in F_{I,J}$.   Q.E.D.

Observe that by Lemma 14.5.4(II) the elements of $\mathcal{B}_{I,J}$ can be represented as 0–1 sequences. The atoms of $\mathcal{B}_{I,J}$ are the sequences with exactly one non-zero element. A sequence is a dense element of $\mathcal{A}_{I,J}$ if none of its elements is 0.

Let $\mathcal{B} = \langle W, +, \cdot, -, 1, 0 \rangle$ be a Boolean algebra and let F be a filter of $\mathcal{B}$. Let

$$\langle \mathcal{B}, F \rangle \overset{\text{def}}{=} \{\langle x, y \rangle \in W \times W : x \leq y, x + (-y) \in F\}.$$

We define the following operations on $\langle \mathcal{B}, F \rangle$:

$\star$ $\langle x, y \rangle + \langle x', y' \rangle \overset{\text{def}}{=} \langle x + x', y + y' \rangle$;
$\star$ $\langle x, y \rangle \cdot \langle x', y' \rangle \overset{\text{def}}{=} \langle x \cdot x', y \cdot y' \rangle$;
$\star$ $\langle x, y \rangle^* \overset{\text{def}}{=} \langle -y, -y \rangle$;

* $\langle x, y \rangle^+ \overset{\text{def}}{=} \langle -x, -x \rangle$;
* $0 \overset{\text{def}}{=} \langle 0, 0 \rangle$;
* $1 \overset{\text{def}}{=} \langle 1, 1 \rangle$.

Clearly, on the right-hand side of the above equalities we have the operations of $\mathcal{B}$. Every algebra of the form described above is referred to as a *Katrinak algebra*. If $F = W$, then $\langle \mathcal{B}, F \rangle$ is denoted by $\mathcal{B}^{[2]}$.

Lemma 14.5.5. *For every Boolean algebra $\mathcal{B}$ and every filter F of $\mathcal{B}$ the following conditions are satisfied:*

(I) every Katrinak algebra $\mathcal{A} = \langle \mathcal{B}, F \rangle$ is a regular double Stone algebra;
(II) the centre $C(\mathcal{A})$ is isomorphic to $\mathcal{B}$;
(III) the dense set $D(\mathcal{A})$ is isomorphic to F (as lattices).

Proof. The proof of (I) is by an easy verification. To prove (II) and (III) observe that $C(\mathcal{A}) = \{\langle x, x \rangle : x \in W\}$ and $D(\mathcal{A}) = \{\langle x, 1 \rangle : x \in F\}$.   *Q.E.D.*

Lemma 14.5.6. *Every regular double Stone algebra $\mathcal{A}$ is isomorphic to the Katrinak algebra $\langle C(\mathcal{A}), D(\mathcal{A})^{++} \rangle$.*

Proof. The required isomorphism is the map h defined by $h(x) \overset{\text{def}}{=} \langle x^{++}, x^{**} \rangle$.   *Q.E.D.*

Lemma 14.5.7. *The algebra $\mathcal{A}_{I,J}$ is isomorphic to the Katrinak algebra $\langle \mathcal{B}_{I,J}, F_{I,J} \rangle$.*

Proof. The lemma follows from Lemmas 14.5.4 and 14.5.5.   *Q.E.D.*

For every regular double Stone algebra $\mathcal{A}$, and every prime ideal I, let $\mathcal{A}/\text{I}$ be the quotient algebra determined by the congruence defined by $x \equiv_I y$ iff there is a $z \in \text{I}$ such that $x + z = y + z$.

The following properties of Stone algebras are well known.

Lemma 14.5.8. *For every regular double Stone algebra $\mathcal{A}$, the following assertions hold:*

(I) every chain of prime ideals of $\mathcal{A}$ has at most two elements;
(II) if I is a minimal prime ideal of $\mathcal{A}$, then the ordered set of prime ideals of $\mathcal{A}/\text{I}$ is isomorphic to the set of all prime ideals of $\mathcal{A}$ containing I.

Proof. By way of example we sketch the proof of (II). Let $f : \mathcal{A} \to \mathcal{A}/\text{I}$ be defined by $f(x) = |x|\equiv_I$. Then the required isomorphism h is defined as $h(P) = f^{-1}(P)$ for every prime ideal P of $\mathcal{A}/\text{I}$.   *Q.E.D.*

The following lemma is a step towards the informational representation theorem for Stone algebras.

Lemma 14.5.9. *For every regular double Stone algebra $\mathcal{A}$, the following assertions hold:*

(I) if I *is a prime ideal of* $\mathcal{A}$, *then* $\mathcal{A}/$I *is isomorphic to either* 2 *or* 3.
(II) $\mathcal{A}$ *is isomorphic to a subdirect product of* $\{\mathcal{A}/$I : I *a prime ideal of* $\mathcal{A}\}$.

Proof. (I) follows from Lemma 14.5.8. (II) follows from Theorem 1.5.1. *Q.E.D.*

Let $\mathcal{B}$ be a complete atomic subalgebra of the Boolean algebra of subsets of a set W and let $\langle W, R \rangle$ be the approximation space determined by $\mathcal{B}$, that is the equivalence relation R is defined as $\langle x, y \rangle \in R \overset{\text{def}}{\Leftrightarrow} x$ and y are contained in the same atom of $\mathcal{B}$. Let F be a filter of $\mathcal{B}$ generated by the union of singleton elements of $\mathcal{B}$. Consider the following Katrinak algebra: $\langle \mathcal{P}(W), F \rangle = \{\langle X, Y \rangle : X, Y \subseteq W, X \subseteq Y$ and $X \cup -Y \in F\}$.

Lemma 14.5.10. $\mathcal{P}_r(W, R) \subseteq \langle \mathcal{P}(W), F \rangle$.

Proof. If $X = L_R(Z)$ and $Y = U_R(Z)$ for some $Z \subseteq W$, then clearly $X \subseteq Y$. Furthermore, since the set $U_R(Z) \setminus L_R(Z)$ of R-borderline instances of Z does not contain singleton equivalence classes of R, we have $X \cup -Y \in F$. *Q.E.D.*

Observe that if R is the identity on W, then F $= \{W\}$ and every subset of W is R-definable.

We conclude that every family of rough subsets of an approximation space can be endowed with the algebraic structure of a regular double Stone algebra. It is known that the converse also holds, namely every regular double Stone algebra has a representation as the algebra of rough subsets of an approximation space.

Theorem 14.5.1. *For every regular double Stone algebra* $\mathcal{A}$, *there is an approximation space* $\langle W, R \rangle$ *such that* $\mathcal{A}$ *is isomorphic to a subalgebra of the regular double Stone algebra derived from* $\langle W, R \rangle$.

Proof. By Lemmas 14.5.9 and 14.5.3 it is sufficient to show that an algebra $\mathcal{A}_{I,J} = \langle 2^I \times 3^J, +, \cdot, ^*, ^+, 1, 0 \rangle$ is isomorphic to a regular double Stone algebra derived from an approximation space.

Let $W = I \cup (J \times 2)$ and $R = Id_I \cup \{\langle\langle j_1, n_1 \rangle, \langle j_2, n_2 \rangle\rangle : j_1 = j_2, j_1, j_2 \in J, n_1, n_2 \in 2\}$. R is an equivalence relation on W, and its equivalence classes are the sets of the form $\{i\}$ for every $i \in I$ and $\{\langle j, 0 \rangle, \langle j, 1 \rangle\}$ for every $j \in J$. Let $\mathcal{B}$ be the Boolean algebra generated by the classes of R. Hence, its elements are the R-definable subsets of W. Let G be a filter of $\mathcal{B}$ generated by the union of the singleton classes of R. Consider the Katrinak algebra $\langle \mathcal{B}, G \rangle$. It follows from the construction that (i) $\langle \mathcal{B}, G \rangle$ is isomorphic to $\mathcal{P}_r(W, R)$. Let U be the universe of $\mathcal{B}$. We define a mapping $h : U \to \mathcal{B}_{I,J}$ by its action on the atoms of $\mathcal{B}$. If $x = \{i\}$, then $h(x)(n) = 1$ if $n = i$, otherwise $h(x)(n) = 0$. If $x = \langle\langle j, 0 \rangle, \langle j, 1 \rangle\rangle$, then $h(x)(n) = 1$ if $n = j$, otherwise $h(x)(n) = 0$. In the above definition we use Lemma 14.5.4(II) that allows us to treat $\mathcal{B}_{I,J}$ as a set of bit-strings; more exactly they are functions $b : I \cup J \to \{0, 1\}$. Clearly,

h is bijective, so it can be uniquely extended to an isomorphism from $\mathcal{B}$ to $\mathcal{B}_{I,J}$.

Observe that $h(I) = \{b \in \mathcal{B}_{I,J} : b(n) = 1 \text{ iff } n \in I\}$. It follows that $b \in h(\mathrm{F}_{I,J})$ iff $b(n) = 1$ for every $n \in I$ iff $b \in G$. Hence, $h(\mathrm{F}_{I,J}) = G$. It is easy to verify that h can be extended to an isomorphism from $\langle \mathcal{B}, G \rangle$ onto $\langle \mathcal{B}_{I,J}, \mathrm{F}_{I,J} \rangle$.

We conclude that (ii) $\langle \mathcal{B}, G \rangle$ is isomorphic to $\langle \mathcal{B}_{I,J}, \mathrm{F}_{I,J} \rangle$. We have (iii) $\langle \mathcal{B}_{I,J}, \mathrm{F}_{I,J} \rangle$ is isomorphic to $\mathcal{A}_{I,J}$ by Lemma 14.5.7. From (i), (ii), (iii), and Lemma 14.5.7 we get that $\mathcal{A}_{I,J}$ is isomorphic to $\mathcal{P}_r(W, R)$.   Q.E.D.

14.6 Algebras of Rough Relations

In this section we define rough relations following the developments of Sects. 4.2, 4.4, and 4.10. Along these lines, a relation is rough if it can only be determined by its approximations.

Let an approximation space $\langle W, R \rangle$ be given. We define the binary relation ^2R on $W \times W$ as follows:

$$\langle \langle x, y \rangle, \langle u, v \rangle \rangle \in {}^2R \overset{\mathrm{def}}{\Leftrightarrow} \langle x, y \rangle \in R \text{ and } \langle u, v \rangle \in R.$$

It is easy to see that ^2R is an equivalence relation, and hence $\langle W \times W, ^2R \rangle$ is an approximation space. According to the definition of approximation operations given in Sect. 4.9, the approximations of any relation $Q \subseteq W \times W$ with respect to ^2R are as follows:

* $L_{^2R}(Q) = \{\langle x, y \rangle \in W \times W : |\langle x, y \rangle|_{^2R} \subseteq Q\}$;
* $U_{^2R}(Q) = \{\langle x, y \rangle \in W \times W : |\langle x, y \rangle|_{^2R} \cap Q \neq \emptyset\}$.

In the rest of this section, we shall use a simpler notation, writing Q_l and Q_u for $L_{^2R}(Q)$ and $U_{^2R}(Q)$, respectively.

By a *rough relation*, we mean a rough subset of an approximation space $\langle W \times W, ^2R \rangle$. It is shown in Sect. 14.5 that the family of rough subsets of an approximation space can be endowed with the operations of a regular double Stone algebra. Hence, in the family $\mathcal{P}_r(W \times W, ^2R)$, we can define the Stone operations $+, \cdot, ^*, ^+$ as in Sect. 14.5. We can also define relational operations as follows:

* $\langle Q_l, Q_u \rangle; \langle Q'_l, Q'_u \rangle \overset{\mathrm{def}}{=} \langle Q_l; Q'_l, Q_u; Q'_u \rangle$,
* $\langle Q_l, Q_u \rangle^{-1} \overset{\mathrm{def}}{=} \langle Q_l^{-1}, Q_u^{-1} \rangle$,
* $Id_{W \times W} \overset{\mathrm{def}}{=} \langle R, R \rangle$.

Then, the structure

$$Rel_r(W) \overset{\mathrm{def}}{=} \langle \mathcal{P}_r(W \times W, ^2R), +, \cdot, ^*, ^+, 1, 0, ;, ^{-1}, \langle R, R \rangle \rangle$$

is the *full algebra of rough relations* on W and any subalgebra of $Rel_r(W)$ is referred to as an *algebra of rough relations* on W.

Lemma 14.6.1. *Let* $Rel_r(W) \overset{\text{def}}{=} \langle \mathcal{P}_r(W \times W, {}^2R), +, \cdot, {}^*, {}^+, 1, 0, ;, {}^{-1}, \langle R, R \rangle \rangle$ *be the full algebra of rough relations. Then the following conditions are satisfied:*

(I) the centre of $Rel_r(W)$ *is* $C(Rel_r(W)) = \{\langle Q_l, Q_u \rangle : Q \in Rel_r(W)\}$;

(II) the dense set of $Rel_r(W)$ *is* $D(Rel_r(W)) = \{\langle Q_l, W \times W \rangle : Q \cap (R(x) \times R(y)) \neq \emptyset$ *for all* $x, y \in W\}$;

(III) if $\langle Q_l, Q_u \rangle$, $\langle S_l, S_u \rangle \in Rel_r(W)$, *then for every operation* $\# \in \{;, +, \cdot\}$, *there is a* $T \in Rel_r(W)$ *such that* $\langle Q_l, Q_u \rangle \# \langle S_l, S_u \rangle = \langle T_l, T_u \rangle$.

Proof. We prove condition (III) for $;$. Let $x, y, v, w \in W$. We have $(R(u) \times R(w)); (R(x) \times R(y)) = \emptyset$ if $R(w) \neq R(x)$, otherwise $(R(v) \times R(w)); (R(x) \times R(y)) = R(v) \times R(y)$. Since $;$ in $Rel_r(W)$ is defined componentwise, and composition in algebras of relations distributes over arbitrary joins, it follows that $Q_l; S_l = (Q_l; S_l)_l$ and $Q_u; S_u = (Q_u; S_u)_u$. Suppose that $R(x) \times R(y) \subseteq (Q_u \times S_u) - (Q_l \times S_l)$. Then $R(x) \times R(y)$ is not a singleton, for otherwise $R(x) \times R(y) \subseteq Q_l; S_l$. Thus $(R(x) \times R(y)) - \{\langle x, y \rangle\} \neq \emptyset$. We set $T = (Q_l; S_l) \cup \{\langle x, y \rangle : R(x) \times R(y) \in (Q_u; S_u) - (Q_l; S_l)\}$. Then $T_l = Q_l; S_l$ and $T_u = Q_u; S_u$. $\qquad$ Q.E.D.

In an abstract setting, a rough relation algebra is a structure of the form

$$\langle W, +, \cdot, {}^*, {}^+, 1, 0, ;, {}^{-1}, 1' \rangle,$$

where

⋆ $\langle W, +, \cdot, {}^*, {}^+, 1, 0 \rangle$ is a regular double Stone algebra,

⋆ $;$ is an associative binary operation that distributes over $+$,

⋆ ${}^{-1}$ is a unary operation that distributes over $+$ and satisfies $(x^{-1})^{-1} = x$ and $(x; y)^{-1} = y^{-1}; x^{-1}$,

⋆ $1'; x = x; 1' = x$,

⋆ $(x^*)^{-1} = (x^{-1})^*$, $(x^+)^{-1} = (x^{-1})^+$,

⋆ $(x^{-1}; (x; y)^*) \cdot y = 0$,

⋆ $(x^*; y^*)^{**} = x^*; y^*$,

⋆ $(1')^{**} = 1'$.

Let R_rA be the class of rough relation algebras. It is easy to verify the following result.

Lemma 14.6.2. *Every algebra of rough relations is a member of* R_rA.

A rough relation algebra is said to be *representable* $\overset{\text{def}}{\Leftrightarrow}$ it is isomorphic to an algebra of rough relations.

Let $\mathcal{A}$ be a rough relation algebra. Let $\mathcal{K}(\mathcal{A}) = \langle C(\mathcal{A}), D(\mathcal{A})^{++} \rangle$ be the Katrinak algebra which is the image of $\mathcal{A}$, understood as a regular double Stone algebra, under the isomorphism $h(x) = \langle x^{++}, x^{**} \rangle$ defined in Sect. 14.5.

We define the relational operations $;$ and ${}^{-1}$ and the identity $1'$ on $\mathcal{K}(\mathcal{A})$ as follows:

$\star$ $\langle x^{++}, x^{**}\rangle; \langle y^{++}, y^{**}\rangle \overset{\text{def}}{=} \langle (x;y)^{++}, (x;y)^{**}\rangle,$
$\star$ $\langle x^{++}, x^{**}\rangle^{-1} \overset{\text{def}}{=} \langle (x^{++})^{-1}, (x^{**})^{-1}\rangle,$
$\star$ $1' \overset{\text{def}}{=} \langle 1', 1'\rangle.$

We shall denote this algebra by $\mathcal{K}_r(\mathcal{A})$. We clearly have the following theorem.

Theorem 14.6.1. *Every rough relation algebra $\mathcal{A}$ is isomorphic to $\mathcal{K}_r(\mathcal{A})$.*

Lemma 14.6.3. *Let $\mathcal{A} = \langle W, +, ., ^*, ^+, 1, 0, ', ^{-1}, 1'\rangle$ be a rough relation algebra.*

(I) $C(\mathcal{A})$ is closed under $;$, $^{-1}$, and $1' \in C(\mathcal{A})$;
(II) $C(\mathcal{A})$ is a relation algebra and a subalgebra of $\mathcal{A}$;
(III) $D(\mathcal{A})$ is closed under $;$ and $^{-1}$;
(IV) $(x;y)^{**} = x^{**}; y^{**}$ for all $x, y \in W$.

Proof. We prove (I). Closure under $;$ and membership of $1'$ in $C(\mathcal{A})$ follow from the last two axioms of relation algebras. Now, let $x \in C(\mathcal{A})$. By the definition of the centre, there is a $y \in W$ such that $x = y^*$. By the definition of *, $y^* \cdot y = 0$. This implies that $(y^*)^{-1} \cdot y^{-1} = 0$. Since for all $a, b \in W$, $a \cdot b = 0$ iff $a \leq b^*$, we obtain $(y^*)^{-1} \leq (y^1)^*$. Similarly, since $y^{-1} \cdot (y^{-1})^* = 0$, then $y \cdot ((y^{-1})^*)^{-1} = 0$, and hence $((y^{-1})^*)^{-1} \leq y^*$. It follows that $(y^{-1})^* \leq (y^*)^{-1}$. We conclude that $x^{-1} = (y^{-1})^*$, hence $x^{-1} \in C(\mathcal{A})$.   *Q.E.D.*

Definition 14.6.1. *A rough relation algebra $\mathcal{A}$ is said to be canonical $\overset{\text{def}}{\Leftrightarrow}$ it satisfies $(x;y)^{++} = x^{++}; y^{++}$.*

Lemma 14.6.4. *A rough relation algebra is canonical iff for all $\langle x, y\rangle$, $\langle z, t\rangle \in \mathcal{K}_r(\mathcal{A})$, we have $\langle x, y\rangle; \langle z, t\rangle = \langle x; z, y; t\rangle$.*

Proof. ($\rightarrow$) Let $\mathcal{A}$ be canonical and let $\langle x, y\rangle, \langle z, t\rangle \in \mathcal{K}_r(\mathcal{A})$. Then there are $a, b \in \mathcal{A}$ such that $x = a^{++}$, $y = a^{**}$, $z = b^{++}$, and $t = b^{**}$. Then we have:

$$\langle a^{++}, a^{**}\rangle; \langle b^{++}, b^{**}\rangle = \langle (a;b)^{++}, (a;b)^{**}\rangle \text{ (by definition of $;$ in $\mathcal{K}_r(\mathcal{A})$)}$$
$$= \langle a^{++}; b^{++}, a^{**}; b^{**}\rangle$$
$$\text{(by canonicity of $\mathcal{A}$ and Lemma 14.6.3(IV)).}$$

($\leftarrow$)

$$(\langle x, y\rangle; \langle z, t\rangle)^{++} = \langle x; z, y; t\rangle^{++} \quad \text{(by the assumption)}$$
$$= \langle x; z, x; z\rangle \quad \text{(by definition of $^+$)}$$
$$= \langle x; x\rangle; \langle z; z\rangle \quad \text{(by the assumption)}$$
$$= \langle x, y\rangle^{++}; \langle z, t\rangle^{++} \quad \text{(by definition of $^{++}$).}$$

Q.E.D.

Let $\mathcal{A}$ be a relation algebra. Consider the Katrinak algebra $\mathcal{A}^{[2]}$ obtained from $\mathcal{A}$, understood as a Boolean algebra, and define the operations $;$ and $^{-1}$ on $\mathcal{A}^{[2]}$ componentwise. Let $\mathcal{A}_r^{[2]}$ be the resulting algebra.

Lemma 14.6.5. *For every relation algebra $\mathcal{A}$, the following assertions hold:*

(I) $\mathcal{A}_r^{[2]} = \{\langle a, b\rangle : a \le b\}$ is a rough relation algebra;
(II) $\mathcal{A}_r^{[2]}$ is canonical;
(III) $\mathrm{C}(\mathcal{A}_r^{[2]})$ is isomorphic to $\mathcal{A}$ (as relation algebras);
(IV) $\mathrm{C}(\mathcal{A}_r^{[2]})$ is isomorphic to $\mathrm{D}(\mathcal{A}_r^{[2]})$ (as lattices).

The proofs follow easily from the respective definitions.

Lemma 14.6.6. *For every rough relation algebra $\mathcal{A}$, the following assertions hold:*

(I) $\mathrm{C}(\mathcal{A})_r^{[2]}$ is canonical;
(II) if $\mathcal{A}$ is canonical, then $\mathcal{A}$ is isomorphic to a subalgebra of $\mathrm{C}(\mathcal{A})_r^{[2]}$.

The proof follows from the definition of $\mathrm{C}(\mathcal{A})_r^{[2]}$ and Lemma 14.6.4.

Lemma 14.6.7. *If a relation algebra $\mathcal{A}$ is isomorphic to a full algebra of relations $Rel(U)$ for some set U, then $\mathcal{A}_r^{[2]}$ is isomorphic to a full algebra of rough relations.*

Proof. Let $U' = \{x' : x \in U\}$ be a set such that $U \cap U' = \emptyset$. Let $V = U \cup U'$, and let R be the equivalence relation on V such that the equivalence classes of R are the sets $\{x, x'\}$ for every $x \in U$. Consider the full algebra of rough relations $\mathcal{R}_V = \mathcal{P}_r(V \times V, ^2 R)$. By the assumption we may identify $\mathcal{A}$ with $Rel(U)$. Hence, $\mathcal{A}_r^{[2]} = \{\langle Q, S\rangle : Q, S \subseteq U^2, \ Q \subseteq S\}$. We will show that $\mathcal{A}_r^{[2]}$ is isomorphic to $\mathcal{R}_V$. By Theorem 14.6.1, it is sufficient to show that:

(i) $Rel(U)$ is isomorphic to $\mathrm{C}(\mathcal{R}_V)$ (as relation algebras), and
(ii) $Rel(U)$ is isomorphic to $\mathrm{D}(\mathcal{R}_V)^{++}$ (as lattices).

Proof of (i): it is sufficient to specify the required isomorphism h by its action on the atoms of $Rel(U)$. These are of the form $\{\langle x, y\rangle\}$ for all $x, y \in U$. We define $h(\{x, y\}) = \langle R(x) \times R(y), R(x) \times R(y)\rangle$. Clearly, h is bijective between the sets of atoms. Hence, it can be extended to a Boolean isomorphism. We show that h is also an isomorphism with respect to the relational operations. Since ; distributes over joins, it is sufficient to prove that $h(Q; S) = h(Q); h(S)$ for atoms of the form $Q = \{\langle v, w\rangle\}$, $S = \{\langle x, y\rangle\}$.

We have $Q; S = \emptyset$ if $w \ne x$, otherwise $Q; S = \{\langle v, y\rangle\}$. Then $h(Q; S) = \{\langle \emptyset, \emptyset\rangle\}$ if $w \ne x$, otherwise $h(Q; S) = \{\langle R(v) \times R(y), R(v) \times R(y)\rangle\}$. We also have $h(R) = \{\langle R(v) \times R(w), R(v) \times R(w)\rangle\}$ and $h(S) = \{\langle R(x) \times R(y), R(x) \times R(y)\rangle\}$. Then

$$h(Q); h(R) = \{\langle (R(v) \times R(w)); (R(x) \times R(y)), (R(v) \times R(w)); (R(x) \times R(y))\rangle\}.$$

We have $(R(v) \times R(w)); (R(x) \times R(y)) = \emptyset$ if $w \ne x$, otherwise $(R(v) \times R(w)); (R(x) \times R(y)) = R(v) \times R(y)$. Clearly, $h(R)^{-1} = h(R^{-1})$ and

$h(1') = 1'$, which ends the proof of (i).

Proof of (ii): we show that $C(\mathcal{R}_V) = D(\mathcal{R}_V)^{++}$. Part ($\supseteq$) holds by the respective definitions.

($\subseteq$) Let $\langle Q_l, Q_l \rangle \in C(\mathcal{R}_V)$. If $Q_l = V \times V = 1$, then $\langle 1, 1 \rangle \in D(\mathcal{R}_V)^{++}$. Now let $Q_l \subset V \times V$. Let $T = Q_l \cup \{\langle x, y \rangle : R(x) \times R(y) \subseteq -Q_l\}$. Then $T_l = Q_l$ and $T_u = V \times V$. Hence, $T \in D(\mathcal{R}_V)$, because $\langle T_l, T_u \rangle^* = \langle -T_u, -T_u \rangle = \langle \emptyset, \emptyset \rangle$. Thus $T^{++} = \langle Q_l, Q_l \rangle \in D(\mathcal{R}_V)^{++}$. $Q.E.D.$

Now we are in position to prove a necessary and sufficient condition for the representability of rough relation algebras.

Theorem 14.6.2. *A rough relation algebra $\mathcal{A}$ is representable iff $C(\mathcal{A})$ is a representable relation algebra and $\mathcal{A}$ is canonical.*

Proof. ($\rightarrow$) Since $\mathcal{A}$ is representable, it is sufficient to show the required conditions for a full algebra of rough relations determined by some approximation space, say $\langle W, R \rangle$. Clearly, $C(\mathcal{A})$ is isomorphic to $Rel(W/R)$. Now we prove that $\mathcal{A}$ is canonical.

$$
\begin{aligned}
(\langle Q_l, Q_u \rangle; \langle S_l, S_u \rangle)^{++} &= \langle Q_l; S_l, Q_u; S_u \rangle^{++} && \text{(by definition of ;)}\\
&= \langle Q_l; S_l, Q_l; S_l \rangle && \text{(by definition of } ^{++}\text{)}\\
&= \langle Q_l, Q_l \rangle; \langle S_l, S_l \rangle && \text{(by definition of ;)}\\
&= \langle Q_l, Q_u \rangle^{++}; \langle S_l, S_u \rangle^{++} && \text{(by definition of } ^{++}\text{).}
\end{aligned}
$$

($\leftarrow$) Since $\mathcal{A}$ is canonical, by Lemma 14.6.6 $\mathcal{A}$ is isomorphic to a subalgebra of $C(\mathcal{A})_r^{[2]}$. Since $C(\mathcal{A})$ is a representable relation algebra, it is isomorphic to a subalgebra of $\Pi_i Rel(U_i)$ for some sets U_i. Hence, $C(\mathcal{A})_r^{[2]}$ is isomorphic to a subalgebra of $(\Pi_i Rel(U_i))^{[2]}$. Clearly, $(\Pi_i Rel(U_i))^{[2]}$ is isomorphic to $(\Pi_i Rel(U_i)^{[2]})$. By Lemma 14.6.7 each $Rel(U_i)^{[2]}$ is representable, thus so is $(\Pi_i Rel(U_i)^{[2]})$. $Q.E.D.$

14.7 Algebras of Fuzzy Relations

The classical relation algebras consist of a Boolean part which models the set-theoretical structure of relations and of a purely relational part. In a similar way, fuzzy relation algebras consist of a part relevant to a fuzzy set structure of fuzzy relations and of a part representing a fuzzy relational structure. The fuzzy set structure is modelled by fuzzy algebras. Since with a lattice structure alone there is no way of expressing crispness, there is a need of extending a lattice with an additional operation.

A *fuzzy algebra* is a structure of the form

$$\langle W, +, \cdot, \otimes, \top, \bot \rangle,$$

where

(1) $\langle W, +, \cdot, \top, \bot \rangle$ is a complete distributive lattice with a least element $\bot$ and a greatest element $\top$;

(2) $\otimes : [0,1] \times W \to W$ is a mapping referred to as a *semiscalar product* and satisfying the following conditions for all $k, k' \in [0,1]$ and for all $x, y \in W$:

(2a) $0 \otimes x = \bot$, $1 \otimes x = x$;

(2b) $k \otimes (k' \otimes x) = (k \times k') \otimes x$, where $\times$ is the multiplication of reals;

(2c) $k \otimes \sup_i x_i = \sup_i (k \otimes x_i)$;

(2d) $k \otimes \inf_i x_i = \inf_i (k \otimes x_i)$;

(2e) $(\inf_i k_i) \otimes x = \inf_i (k_i \otimes x)$;

(2f) if $k \otimes x \leq k \otimes y$ and $k > 0$, then $x \leq y$, where $\leq$ is the natural lattice ordering on W;

(3) if $x \cdot (k \otimes \top) = k \otimes x$ for every $k \in [0,1]$, then there is a $y \in W$ such that $x + y = \top$ and $x \cdot y = \bot$.

In this section the elements of $[0,1]$ are referred to as *scalars*. We assume that the fuzzy algebras considered in this section are non-degenerate, that is $\top \neq \bot$.

The following lemma presents some properties of the semiscalar product.

Lemma 14.7.1. *For every fuzzy algebra* $\langle W, +, \cdot, \otimes, \top, \bot \rangle$, *for all* $k, k' \in [0,1]$, *and for all* $x, y \in W$ *we have:*

(I) if $x \leq y$, *then* $k \otimes x \leq k \otimes y$;

(II) if $k \leq k'$, *then* $k \otimes x \leq k' \otimes x$;

(III) $k \otimes x \leq x$ *and* $k \otimes \bot = \bot$;

(IV) $k \otimes x \leq x \cdot (k \otimes \top)$;

(V) $(k \otimes x) + (k' \otimes x) = max(k, k') \otimes x$.

Proof. (I) If $x \leq y$, then $k \otimes x = k \otimes (x \cdot y) = (k \otimes x) \cdot (k \otimes y)$.

(II) If $k \leq k'$, then $k \otimes x = min(k, k') \otimes x$. By the condition (2e) from the definition of fuzzy algebras, $min(k, k') \otimes x = (k \otimes x) \cdot (k' \otimes x) \leq k' \otimes x$.

(III) Since $k \leq 1$, from (II) we get $k \otimes x \leq 1 \otimes x$, and by condition (2a) from the definition of fuzzy algebras, $1 \otimes x = x$. The proof of the second condition is similar.

(IV) Since $x \leq \top$, from (II) we obtain $k \otimes x \leq k \otimes \top$. From (III) we have $k \otimes x \leq x$. Hence, $k \otimes x \leq x \cdot (k \otimes \top)$.

(V) Assume that $k \leq k'$. Then by (II), $k \otimes x + k' \otimes x = k' \otimes x = max(k, k') \otimes x$. If $k' \leq k$, then the proof is analogous.   Q.E.D.

An element x of a fuzzy algebra is said to be *crisp* if $x \cdot (k \otimes \top) = k \otimes x$ for every $k \in [0,1]$.

Lemma 14.7.2. *The set of crisp elements of every fuzzy algebra is a Boolean algebra.*

Proof. Let $\langle W, +, \cdot, \otimes, \top, \bot \rangle$ be a fuzzy algebra and $x, y \in W$. First, we show that if x and y are crisp, then so are $x + y$ and $x \cdot y$. Applying distributivity of $\cdot$ over $+$ and condition (2c) from the definition of fuzzy algebras, we have $(x + y) \cdot (k \otimes \top) = x \cdot (k \otimes \top) + y \cdot (k \otimes \top) = (k \otimes x) + (k \otimes y) = k \otimes (x + y)$. In a similar way one can show that $(x \cdot y) \cdot (k \otimes \top) = k \otimes (x \cdot y)$.

Clearly the elements $\top$ and $\bot$ are crisp. Moreover, condition (3) in the definition of fuzzy algebras guarantees the existence of a complement for every crisp element.   *Q.E.D.*

To define a relational part of fuzzy relation algebras we need a generalised notion of a relation algebra, where the Boolean part is replaced by a complete distributive lattice.

By a *generalised relation algebra* we mean a structure of the form

$$\langle W, +, \cdot, ;, ^{-1}, \top, \bot, 1' \rangle,$$

where

(1) $\langle W, +, \cdot, \top, \bot \rangle$ is a complete distributive lattice,
(2) $\langle W, ;, 1' \rangle$ is a monoid,
(3) $^{-1}$ is a unary operation on W such that $(x^{-1})^{-1} = x$, $(x;y)^{-1} = y^{-1};x^{-1}$, and $x \le y$ implies $x^{-1} \le y^{-1}$,
(4) $x; sup_i\, y_i = sup_i\, (x;y_i)$ and $(sup_i\, x_i); y = sup_i\, (x_i;y)$,
(5) $(x;y) \cdot z \le x; (y \cdot (x^{-1};z))$.

Condition (5) is referred to as the *Dedekind formula*. If the lattice is a Boolean algebra, then we say that the algebra $\langle W, +, \cdot, ;, ^{-1}, \top, \bot, 1' \rangle$ is a Boolean relation algebra. From now on we assume that $\top \ne \bot$.

Let $L_0 = \langle [0, 1], max, min, 0, 1 \rangle$ be a lattice of real numbers from the unit interval $[0, 1]$. It can be viewed as a double residuated lattice in which the product $\odot$ coincides with min and the sum $\oplus$ coincides with max.

Lemma 14.7.3. *For every non-empty set U the following conditions are satisfied:*

(I) $\langle \mathcal{F}_{L_0} Rel(U), \subseteq_{L_0} \rangle$ is a complete and distributive lattice;
(II) $\langle \mathcal{F}_{L_0} Rel(U), \cup_{L_0}, \cap_{L_0}, ;_{L_0}, ^{-1_{L_0}}, 0_{L_0}, 1_{L_0}, 1'_{L_0} \rangle$ is a generalised relation algebra.

Proof. (I) The least upper bound and the greatest lower bound of a family $(R_i)_{i \in I}$ are as follows: $(sup_i\, R_i)(x, y) = sup_i\, (R_i(x, y))$ and $(inf_i\, R_i)(x, y) = inf_i\, (R_i(x, y))$.
(II) By way of example, we show that the Dedekind formula is satisfied by all fuzzy relations R, S, and T:

$((R;_{L_0} S) \cap_{L_0} T)(x, y)$

$$
\begin{aligned}
&= min(sup(\{min(R(x, z), S(z, y)) : z \in U\}), T(x, y)) \\
&= sup(\{min(R(x, z), S(z, y), T(x, y)) : z \in U\}) \\
&= sup(\{min(R(x, z), S(z, y), R^{-1_{L_0}}(z, x), T(x, y)) : z \in U\}) \\
&\leq sup(\{min(R(x, z), S(z, y), (R^{-1_{L_0}};_{L_0} T)(z, y)) : z \in U\}) \\
&= sup(\{min(R(x, z), (S(z, y) \cap_{L_0} (R^{-1_{L_0}};_{L_0} T)(z, y)) : z \in U\}) \\
&= (R;_{L_0} (R^{-1_{L_0}};_{L_0} T))(x, y).
\end{aligned}
$$

$$Q.E.D.$$

A *fuzzy relation algebra* is a structure of the form

$$\langle W, +, \cdot, ;, \otimes, \mathsf{T}, \bot, 1' \rangle,$$

where

(1) $\langle W, +, \cdot, \otimes, \mathsf{T}, \bot \rangle$ is a fuzzy algebra;
(2) $\langle W, +, \cdot, ;, ^{-1}, \mathsf{T}, \bot \rangle$ is a generalised relation algebra;
(3) $k \otimes (x; y) = (k \otimes x); (k \otimes y)$;
(4) $(k \otimes x); y = (k \otimes x); (y \cdot (k \otimes \mathsf{T}))$;
(5) $(k \otimes x)^{-1} = k \otimes x^{-1}$.

For the sake of simplicity, in this section both the elements of a relation algebra and the elements of a fuzzy relation algebra will be referred to as relations.

The family $\mathcal{F}_{L_0} Rel(U)$ can be endowed with the structure of a fuzzy relation algebra as follows. Let the semiscalar product $\otimes_{L_0} : [0, 1] \times \mathcal{F}_{L_0} Rel(U) \to \mathcal{F}_{L_0} Rel(U)$ be defined as follows:

$$(k \otimes_{L_0} R)(x, y) \stackrel{\text{def}}{=} k \times R(x, y).$$

Then it is easy to verify that we have the following lemma.

Lemma 14.7.4. *For every non-empty set U the following conditions are satisfied:*

(I) $\langle \mathcal{F}_{L_0} Rel(U), \cup_{L_0}, \cap_{L_0}, ;_{L_0}, ^{-1_{L_0}}, \otimes_{L_0}, 0_{L_0}, 1_{L_0}, 1'_{L_0} \rangle$ *is a fuzzy relation algebra;*

(II) $R \cap_{L_0} (k \otimes_{L_0} 1_{L_0}) = k \otimes_{L_0} R$ *iff for all $x, y \in U$, $R(x, y) = 1$ or $R(x, y) = 0$.*

Proof. (II) Observe that for all $x, y \in U$, $k \otimes_{L_0} 1_{L_0} = k$. Then the condition follows from the following equivalences: $R \cap_{L_0} (k \otimes_{L_0} 1_{L_0}) = k \otimes_{L_0} R$ iff for every $k \in [0, 1]$, $min(R(x, y), k) = k \times R(x, y)$ iff $R(x, y) = 1$ or $R(x, y) = 0$. *Q.E.D.*

Observe that condition (II) of the above lemma shows that the abstract characterisation of crispness of relations corresponds adequately to its intuitive understanding.

The following lemma is a direct consequence of the definition of fuzzy relation algebras.

Lemma 14.7.5. *For all relations x, y, and z the following hold:*

(I) $\perp^{-1}=\perp$, $\top^{-1} = \top$, $1'^{-1} = 1'$,
(II) $(x + y)^{-1} = x^{-1} + y^{-1}$,
(III) $(x \cdot y)^{-1} = x^{-1} \cdot y^{-1}$,
(IV) *if $x \leq y$, then $z; x \leq z; y$ and $x; z \leq y; z$,*
(V) $z; (x \cdot y) \leq z; x \cdot z; y$.

The following lemma presents some properties of crisp relations.

Lemma 14.7.6. *For all relations x, y and for every scalar k the following hold:*

(I) $(k \otimes x); y \leq k \otimes (x; \top)$,
(II) *if y is crisp, then $(k \otimes x); y = k \otimes (x; y)$,*
(III) $x; (k \otimes y) \leq k \otimes (\top; y)$,
(IV) *if x is crisp, then $x; (k \otimes y) = k \otimes (x; y)$,*
(V) *if x is crisp and $\top; x = x$, then the following are equivalent: $1' \leq x; x^{-1}$,*
    $\top = x; x^{-1}$, $\top = x; \top$, $x; \top = k \otimes \top$ *for every $k > 0$;*
(VI) *if y is crisp and $k \otimes x \leq y$ for every $k > 0$, then $x \leq y$;*
(VII) *if $x + y = \top$ and $x \cdot y = \perp$, then both x and y are crisp.*

Proof. By way of example we prove (I) and (II).

(I) $(k \otimes x); y = (k \otimes x); (y \cdot (k \otimes \top))$
        (by condition (4) in the definition of fuzzy relation algebras)
        $\leq (k \otimes x); (k \otimes \top)$ (since $y \cdot (k \otimes \top) \leq (k \otimes \top)$ and
        by Lemma 14.7.5(IV))
        $= k \otimes (x; \top)$
        (by condition (3) in the definition of fuzzy relation algebras).

(II) $(k \otimes x); y = (k \otimes x); (y \cdot (k \otimes \top))$
        (by condition (4) in the definition of fuzzy relation algebras)
        $= (k \otimes x); (k \otimes \top)$ (since y is crisp)
        $= k \otimes (x; y)$
        (by condition (3) in the definition of fuzzy relation algebras).

$$Q.E.D.$$

Lemma 14.7.7. *The set of crisp relations of any fuzzy relation algebra is a Boolean algebra.*

Proof. Let $\mathcal{A} = \langle W, +, \cdot, ;, \otimes, \top, \perp, 1' \rangle$ be a fuzzy relation algebra. It follows from Lemma 14.7.2 that the family of crisp relations is closed on $+$ and $\cdot$ and includes $\top$ and $\perp$. Now we show that if x and y are crisp, then so are $x; y$ and x^{-1}.

$(x; y) \cdot (k \otimes \top) \leq x; (y \cdot (x^{-1}; (k \otimes \top)))$ (by the Dedekind formula)
$ \leq x; (y \cdot (k \otimes (\top; \top)))$ (by Lemma 14.7.6(III))
$ \leq x; (y \cdot (k \otimes \top))$
$ $ (by Lemma 14.7.1(I) applied to $1' \leq \top$)
$ = x; (k \otimes y)$ (since y is crisp)
$ = k \otimes (x; y)$ (by Lemma 14.7.6(IV)).

By applying Lemma 14.7.1(IV) we conclude that $x; y$ is crisp. Similarly,

$x^{-1} \cdot (k \otimes \top) = (x \cdot (k \otimes \top))^{-1}$ (by Lemma 14.7.5(I, III))
$\phantom{x^{-1} \cdot (k \otimes \top)} = (k \otimes x)^{-1}$ (since x is crisp)
$\phantom{x^{-1} \cdot (k \otimes \top)} = k \otimes x^{-1}$
$\phantom{x^{-1} \cdot (k \otimes \top)} $ (by condition (5) in the definition of fuzzy relation algebras).

Now we show that $1'$ is crisp, that is $1' \cdot (k \otimes \top) = k \otimes 1'$ for every $k \in [0, 1]$. ($\geq$) First, observe that we have (i) $k \otimes 1' \leq 1'$ since $k \otimes 1' \leq 1 \otimes 1'$ (by Lemma 14.7.2(II)) and $1 \otimes 1' = 1'$ (by condition (2a) from the definition of fuzzy algebras). Second, we have (ii) $k \otimes 1' \leq k \otimes \top$, by $1' \leq \top$ and Lemma 14.7.1(I). Hence, from (i) and (ii) we obtain $k \otimes 1' \leq 1' \cdot (k \otimes \top)$.

($\leq$) $1' \cdot (k \otimes \top) = 1' \cdot (k \otimes (1'; \top)) = 1' \cdot ((k \otimes 1'); \top)$
$ $ (by condition (4) in the definition of fuzzy algebras
$ $ and Lemma 14.7.6(II))
$ \leq (k \otimes 1'); (((k \otimes 1')^{-1}; 1') \cdot \top)$
$ $ (by the Dedekind formula)
$ = k \otimes 1'$ (by (i)).

$$\textit{Q.E.D.}$$

A relation x is a *point relation* $\overset{\text{def}}{\Leftrightarrow}$

(1) x is crisp,
(2) $x^{-1}; x \leq 1'$,
(3) $1' \leq x; x^{-1}$,
(4) $\top; x = x$.

Point relations will be denoted by a and b, with indices if necessary.

Lemma 14.7.8. *Let $U \neq \emptyset$ and let $R \in \mathcal{F}_{L_0}Rel(U)$. If for all $x, y \in U$, $R(x, y) = 1$ or $R(x, y) = 0$, $R^{-1}{}_{L_0};_{L_0} R \subseteq 1_{L_0}$, $1'_{L_0} \subseteq R;_{L_0} R^{-1}{}_{L_0}$ and $1_{L_0};_{L_0} R = R$, then there is a $y_0 \in U$ such that for all $x, y \in U$, $R(x, y) = 1$ if $y = y_0$, otherwise $R(x, y) = 0$.*

Proof. In what follows we drop the index L_0 in the operation signs. Observe that since $1' \subseteq R; R^{-1}$, for every $x \in U$ we have $(R; R^{-1})(x, x) = sup(\{min(R(x, y), R^{-1}(y, x)) : y \in U\}) = sup(\{R(x, y) : y \in U\}) = 1$. Hence, (i) $R \neq 0_{L_0}$.

Now, since U is non-empty, there is an $x_0 \in U$. By (i) and since for all $x, y \in U$, $R(x, y) = 1$ or $R(x, y) = 0$, there is a $y_0 \in U$ such that for all

$x, y \in U$, $R(x_0, y_0) = 1$. Since $1_{L_0}; R = R$, we have $R(x, y_0) = 1$ for every $x \in U$.

Now we use the assumption $R^{-1}; R \subseteq 1'$. We have $(R^{-1}; R)(y, y_0) = sup(\{min(R^{-1}(y, z), R(z, y_0)) : z \in U\}) = sup(\{min(R(z, y), R(z, y_0)) : z \in U\}) \leq min(R(x, y), R(x, y_0)) = R(x, y) \leq 1'(y, y_0)$. We conclude that $R(x, x) = 1$ if $y = y_0$, otherwise $R(x, y) = 0$.   Q.E.D.

A *pair relation* is a relation of the form $a^{-1}; b$, where a and b are point relations. The following two lemmas present some properties of point relations.

Lemma 14.7.9. *For all point relations a and b the following conditions hold:*

(I) $a \neq \perp$;
(II) if $a \leq b$, then $a = b$;
(III) if $a \neq b$, then $a \cdot b = \perp$ and $a; b^{-1} = \perp$;
(IV) $a^{-1}; b \neq \perp$.

Proof. (II) Let a and b be point relations. Since by condition (3) from the definition of point relations $1' \leq a; a^{-1}$, we have $b \leq x; (x^{-1}; b)$. Since $b \neq \perp$, the condition follows.

The proof of the remaining conditions is similar.   Q.E.D.

Lemma 14.7.10. *For every relation x and for all point relations a and b the following conditions are satisfied:*

(I) if $a^{-1}; b \leq a'^{-1}; b'$, then $a = a'$ and $b = b'$,
(II) $x \cdot (a^{-1}; b) = k \otimes (a^{-1}; b)$ iff $(a; x) \cdot b = k \otimes b$ for every scalar k.

Proof. (II) First we show:

(i) $(a; x) \cdot b = a; (x \cdot (a^{-1}; b))$ and
(ii) $x \cdot (a^{-1}; b) = a^{-1}((a; x) \cdot b)$.

Proof of (i):

$(a; x) \cdot b \leq a; (x \cdot (a^{-1}; b))$ (by the Dedekind formula)
$\qquad \leq a; a^{-1}; ((a; x) \cdot b)$ (by the Dedekind formula)
$\qquad = \top; ((a; x) \cdot b)$ (by Lemma 14.7.6(V))
$\qquad \leq (a; x) \cdot b$ (by Lemma 14.7.5(V)
$\qquad$ and condition (4) in the definition of point relations).

Proof of (ii):

$x \cdot (a^{-1}; b) \leq a^{-1}; ((a; x) \cdot b)$ (by the Dedekind formula)
$\qquad \leq a^{-1}; a; (x \cdot (a^{-1}; b))$ (by the Dedekind formula)
$\qquad \leq 1'; (x \cdot (a^{-1}; b))$
$\qquad$ (by condition (2) in the definition of point relations
$\qquad$ and Lemma 14.7.5(IV))
$\qquad \leq x \cdot (a^{-1}; b)$.

Now assume that $x \cdot (a^{-1}; b) = k \otimes (a^{-1}; b)$. Then we have:

$$(a; x) \cdot b = a; (x \cdot (a^{-1}; b)) \text{ (by (i))}$$
$$= a; (k \otimes (a^{-1}; b)) \text{ (by the assumption)}$$
$$= k \otimes (a; (a^{-1}; b)) \text{ (by Lemma 14.7.6(IV))}$$
$$= k \otimes (\top; b) \text{ (by Lemma 14.7.6(V))}$$
$$= k \otimes b$$

(by condition (4) in the definition of point relations).

Conversely, assume that $(a; x) \cdot b = k \otimes b$. Then we have:

$$x \cdot (a^{-1}; b) = a^{-1}; ((a; x) \cdot b) \text{ (by (ii))}$$
$$= a^{-1}; (k \otimes b) \text{ (by the assumption)}$$
$$= k \otimes (a^{-1}; b) \text{ (by Lemma 14.7.6(IV))}.$$

$$Q.E.D.$$

We say that a fuzzy relation algebra satisfies a *point axiom* $\overset{\text{def}}{\Leftrightarrow}$ for every relation $x \neq \bot$ there are a scalar $k > 0$ and the point relations a and b such that $x \cdot (a^{-1}; b) = k \otimes (a^{-1}; b)$.

The following two lemmas state some properties of relations in fuzzy relation algebras satisfying the point axiom.

Lemma 14.7.11. *For all relations x, y in a fuzzy relation algebra satisfying the point axiom, the following assertions hold:*

(I) if $\top; x = x$, $x + y = \top$, and $x \cdot y = \bot$, then $\top; y = y$,
(II) if $\top; x = x$ and $x \neq \bot$, then there are a scalar $k > 0$ and a point relation a such that $k \otimes a \leq x$.

Proof. By way of example, we prove (II). By the point axiom there are a $k > 0$ and point relations a and b such that (i) $k \otimes (a^{-1}; b) \leq x$. Hence we have:

$$k \otimes b = k \otimes (\top; b)$$
$$\text{(by condition (4) in the definition of point relations)}$$
$$= k \otimes (a; a^{-1}; b) \text{ (by Lemma 14.7.6(V))}$$
$$= a; (k \otimes (a^{-1}; b)) \text{ (by Lemma 14.7.6(IV))}$$
$$\leq a; x \text{ (by (i))}$$
$$\leq \top; x = x \text{ (by } a \leq \top \text{ and the assumption).}$$

$$Q.E.D.$$

Lemma 14.7.12. *For every relation x and for all point relations a and b of a fuzzy relation algebra satisfying the point axiom the following conditions are satisfied:*

(I) for all scalars k and k', if x is a crisp relation such that $x \neq \bot$ and $k \otimes x \leq k' \otimes x$, then $k \leq k'$;
(II) if $x \leq a^{-1}; b$, then there is a unique scalar k such that $x = k \otimes (a^{-1}; b)$.

Proof. (II) If $x = \perp$, then by condition (2a) in the definition of fuzzy algebras $x = 0 \otimes (a^{-1}; b)$. Now assume that $x \neq \perp$. By the point axiom there are a $k > 0$ and point relations a_0 and b_0 such that (i) $x \cdot (a^{-1}; b) = k \otimes (a_0^{-1}; b_0)$. Hence, $k \otimes (a_0^{-1}; b_0) \leq x \leq a^{-1}; b$. By Lemma 14.7.6(VI) we have $a_0^{-1}; b_0 \leq a^{-1}; b$. By Lemma 14.7.10(I) we get (ii) $a = a_0$ and $b = b_0$. Since $x \leq a^{-1}; b$, we have $x \cdot (a^{-1}; b) = x$. Hence, by (ii) and (i) we conclude that $x = k \otimes (a^{-1}; b)$. Since $a^{-1}; b$ is a crisp relation, the uniqueness of k follows from (I). *Q.E.D.*

It follows from Lemma 14.7.12(II) that for every relation x of a fuzzy relation algebra satisfying the point axiom, there is a unique scalar k such that $x \cdot (a^{-1}; b) = k \otimes (a^{-1}; b)$ for some point relations a and b. Let $\chi(x)(a, b)$ be the unique scalar such that

$$x \cdot (a^{-1}; b) = \chi(x)(a, b) \otimes (a^{-1}; b).$$

$\chi(x)$ defines a fuzzy relation on the set of all point relations of a fuzzy relation algebra.

The following Lemma 14.7.13 and Theorem 14.7.1 are crucial for a representation theorem for fuzzy relation algebras.

Lemma 14.7.13. *Let* $\mathcal{A} = \langle W, +, \cdot, ; , \otimes, \top, \perp, 1' \rangle$ *be a fuzzy relation algebra satisfying the point axiom and let* $X_{\mathcal{A}}$ *be the set of all point relations of* $\mathcal{A}$. *Then we have:*

(I) $\top = sup(\{a : a \in X_{\mathcal{A}}\})$;
(II) $1' = sup(\{a^{-1}; a : a \in X_{\mathcal{A}}\})$.

Proof. (I) Let $x = sup(\{a : a \in X_{\mathcal{A}}\})$. Since point relations are crisp, x is also crisp by Lemma 14.7.7. By condition (3) from the definition of fuzzy algebras there is a $y \in W$ such that $x + y = \top$ and $x \cdot y = \perp$. Then $\top; y = y$ by Lemma 14.7.11(I). Suppose that $y \neq \perp$. By Lemma 14.7.11(II) there is a scalar $k > 0$ and a point relation b such that $k \otimes b \leq y$. Since by Lemma 14.7.6(VII) y is crisp, by Lemma 14.7.6(VI) we have $b \leq y$. Hence, $b \leq x \cdot y = \perp$, which is in contradiction with $y \neq \perp$. We conclude that $y = \perp$, and therefore $x = \top$. The proof of (II) is similar.   *Q.E.D.*

Theorem 14.7.1. *Let* $\mathcal{A}$ *be a fuzzy relation algebra satisfying the point axiom and let* $X_{\mathcal{A}}$ *be the set of all point relations of* $\mathcal{A}$. *Then for every relation* x *of* $\mathcal{A}$, $x = sup(\{\chi(x)(a, b) \otimes (a^{-1}; b) : a, b \in X_{\mathcal{A}}\})$.

Proof. For every relation x and for every point relation a,

$a; x = (a; x) \cdot \top = (a; x) \cdot sup(\{b : b \in X_{\mathcal{A}}\})$
　　(by condition (1) in the definition of generalised relation algebras)
　　$= sup(\{(a; x) \cdot b : b \in X_{\mathcal{A}}\})$ (by Lemma 2.7.4)
　　$= sup(\{\chi(x)(a, b) \otimes b : b \in X_{\mathcal{A}}\})$
　　(by the point axiom and the definition of χ).

Then we have:

$x = 1'; x = sup(\{a^{-1}; a; x : a \in X_A\})$ (by Lemma 14.7.13(II))
$= sup(\{a^{-1}; sup(\{\chi(x)(a, b) \otimes b : b \in X_A\}) : a \in X_A\})$
(by the definition of χ, the point axiom, and Lemma 14.7.10(II))
$= sup(\{sup(\{\chi(x)(a, b) \otimes b : b \in X_A\}) : a \in X_A\})$
(by condition (4) in the definition of generalised relation algebras)
$= sup(\{\chi(x)(a, b) \otimes b : a, b \in X_A\})$ (by Lemma 14.7.6(IV)).

Now we show that the representation of relations postulated in this theorem is unique. Suppose that $x = sup(\{k_{ab} \otimes (a^{-1}; b) : a, b \in X_A\})$. Then for all $a_0, b_0 \in X_A$ we have $a_0; x = sup(\{k_{ab} \otimes (a_0; a^{-1}; b) : a, b \in X_A\})$. If $a_0 \neq a$, then by Lemma 14.7.9(III), $a_0; a^{-1} = \perp$, which leads to a contradiction. By Lemma 14.7.6(V) $a_0; a_0^{-1} = \top$ and $\top; b = b$ by condition (4) of the definition of point relations. Hence, we obtain $a_0; x = sup(\{k_{a_0 b} \otimes b : b \in X_A\})$.
Similarly, $(a_0; x) \cdot b_0 = sup(\{(k_{a_0 b} \otimes b_0) \cdot b : b \in X_A\}) = sup(\{k_{a_0 b} \otimes (b_0 \cdot b) : b \in X_A\})$. If $b \neq b_0$, then by Lemma 14.7.9(III), $b \cdot b_0 = \perp$, which leads to a contradiction. Hence $(a_0; x) \cdot b_0 = k_{a_0 b_0} \otimes b_0$. By Lemma 14.7.12(II), $k_{ab} = \chi(x)(a, b)$.   Q.E.D.

Theorem 14.7.2. *(Representation Theorem) Every fuzzy relation algebra* $\mathcal{A}$ *satisfying the point axiom is isomorphic to the fuzzy relation algebra* $\mathcal{F}_{L_0} Rel(X_A)$.

Proof. We show that $\chi(x)$ is a homomorphism of fuzzy relation algebras.

$\chi(x + y)(a, b) \otimes b = (a; (x + y)) \cdot b$
$= (a; x + a; y) \cdot b$
$= ((a; x) \cdot b) + ((a; y) \cdot b)$
$= \chi(x)(a, b) \otimes b + \chi(y)(a, b) \otimes b$
$= max(\chi(x)(a, b), \chi(y)(a, b)) \otimes b$
$= (\chi(x) + \chi(y))(a, b) \otimes b.$

The proof of the preservation of the remaining operations is similar. It is easy to check that $\chi(x)$ also preserves the constant relations.

Now we show that $\chi(x)$ is a bijection. If $\chi(x) = \chi(y)$, then using the representation from Theorem 14.7.1, we get $x = y$. Hence, χ is injective. Given $R \in \mathcal{F}_{L_0} Rel(X_A)$, let $x_R = sup(\{R(a, b) \otimes (a^{-1}; b) : a, b \in X_A\})$. By the uniqueness of the representation from Theorem 14.7.1 we have $R(a, b) = \chi(x_R)(a, b)$.   Q.E.D.

14.8 Approximation Spaces and Nelson Algebras

A *Nelson algebra* is a structure of the form

$$\langle W, +, \cdot, \rightarrow, \neg, \sim, 1, 0 \rangle,$$

where

(1) $\langle W, +, \cdot, \rightarrow, 1, 0 \rangle$ is a bounded distributive lattice;

(2) $\sim (x + y) = \sim x \cdot \sim y$;

(3) $\sim\sim x = x$;

(4) $x \cdot \sim x \leq y + \sim y$;

(5) $x \cdot z \leq (\sim x + y)$ iff $z \leq x \rightarrow y$;

(6) $x \rightarrow (y \rightarrow z) = (x \cdot y) \rightarrow z$;

(7) $\neg x = x \rightarrow \sim x = x \rightarrow 0$.

Conditions (2) and (3) express that $\sim$ is a De Morgan complement. Condition (5) says that $\rightarrow$ is a pseudo-complement of x relative to $\sim x + y$. Condition (7) says that $\neg x$ is the pseudo-complement of x relative to $\sim x$.

Let $\langle W, R \rangle$ be an approximation space and let

$$K(W, R) = \{\langle Pos_R(X), Neg_R(X) \rangle : X \subseteq W\}$$

be its knowledge structure. Consider the Boolean algebra $\mathcal{P}(W)$ of subsets of W. Let F_R be the filter of $\mathcal{P}(W)$ generated by $\{x \in W : |x|_R = \{x\}\}$. We define a binary relation Q on $\mathcal{P}(W)$:

$$\langle X, Y \rangle \in Q \overset{\text{def}}{\Leftrightarrow} \text{there is a } Z \in \mathrm{F}_R \text{ such that } X \cap Z = Y \cap Z.$$

It follows that $\langle X, W \rangle \in Q$ iff there is a $Z \in \mathrm{F}_R$ such that $Z \subseteq X$. We define

$$N_Q(W, R) \overset{\text{def}}{=} \{\langle X, Y \rangle : X, Y \in \mathcal{P}(W), X \cap Y = \emptyset, \langle X \cup Y, W \rangle \in Q\}.$$

Theorem 14.8.1. *For every approximation space* $\langle W, R \rangle$,

$$N_Q(W, R) = K(W, R).$$

We define the following operations on $N_Q(W, R)$:

$\star$ $1 \overset{\text{def}}{=} \langle W, \emptyset \rangle$;

$\star$ $0 \overset{\text{def}}{=} \langle \emptyset, W \rangle$;

$\star$ $\langle X_1, Y_1 \rangle + \langle X_2, Y_2 \rangle \overset{\text{def}}{=} \langle X_1 \cup X_2, Y_1 \cap Y_2 \rangle$;

$\star$ $\langle X_1, Y_1 \rangle \cdot \langle X_2, Y_2 \rangle \overset{\text{def}}{=} \langle X_1 \cap X_2, Y_1 \cup Y_2 \rangle$;

$\star$ $\langle X_1, Y_1 \rangle \rightarrow \langle X_2, Y_2 \rangle \overset{\text{def}}{=} \langle (W \setminus X_1) \cup X_2, X_1 \cap Y_2 \rangle$;

$\star$ $\sim \langle X, Y \rangle \overset{\text{def}}{=} \langle Y, X \rangle$;

$\star$ $\neg \langle X, Y \rangle \overset{\text{def}}{=} \langle W \setminus X, X \rangle$.

Lemma 14.8.1. *For every approximation space* $\langle W, R \rangle$, *the structure* $\langle N_Q(W, R), +, \cdot, \rightarrow, \neg, \sim, 1, 0 \rangle$ *with the operations defined above is a semisimple Nelson algebra.*

We also have the following informational representation theorem for semisimple Nelson algebras.

Theorem 14.8.2. *For every semisimple Nelson algebra* $\mathcal{A}$, *there is an approximation space* $\langle W, R \rangle$ *such that* $\mathcal{A}$ *is isomorphic to* $N_Q(W, R)$.

14.9 Standard Algebraic Structures with Generalised Approximation Operations

Let $L = \langle W, \leq \rangle$ be a poset.

Definition 14.9.1. *A map* $p : W \to W$ *is a preclosure* $\overset{\text{def}}{\Leftrightarrow}$ p *is idempotent and extensive. If* $p(x) = x$, *then* x *is a* p-*exact element of* W. *A preclosure* p *is an upper approximation operation in* L $\overset{\text{def}}{\Leftrightarrow}$ $p(0) = 0$. *A lower approximation operation* p *in* L *is a preclosure in the dual poset* L^d *that additionally satisfies* $p(1) = 1$.

Observe that $p(1) = 1$ by extensivity of p.

Let $L = \langle W, \leq \rangle$ be a bounded poset and let E be a subset of W such that $1, 0 \in E$. Consider the system $\langle E, \leq_E \rangle$, where $\leq_E$ is the restriction of $\leq$ to E. If $\langle E, \leq_E \rangle$ is a complete lattice, then the triple $Lr = \langle W, E, \leq \rangle$ is said to be a *rough poset*. The elements of E are referred to as the *exact elements* of Lr. If, in addition, L is a lattice, a complete lattice, a Boolean algebra, etc., then the respective structure Lr is referred to as a *rough lattice*, a *rough complete lattice*, a *rough Boolean algebra*, etc.

Example 14.9.1. Let W be a non-empty set and C be a finite partition of W. Let $E_C = \{\emptyset\} \cup \{Z \subseteq W : Z$ is a union of some classes of $C\}$. Clearly, $\langle E_C, \subseteq \rangle$ is a subposet of $L = \langle \mathcal{P}(W), \subseteq \rangle$. Moreover, it is a finite lattice with set union and intersection as join and meet, respectively, and it has the top element $W = sup(C)$ and the bottom element $\emptyset$ of L. Hence, the structure $\langle \mathcal{P}(W), E_C, \subseteq \rangle$ is a rough algebra of sets.

Let $Lr = \langle W, E, \leq \rangle$ be a rough poset. For every element $x \in W$, we consider the set of upper bounds of x that belong to E:

$$M(x) \overset{\text{def}}{=} \{e \in E : x \leq e\}.$$

The set $M(x)$ is non-empty, since $x \leq 1$ and $1 \in E$. Let $Min(M(x))$ be the set of all the minimal elements of $M(x)$.

We say that an element $x \in W$ is *top-recognisable* in Lr $\overset{\text{def}}{\Leftrightarrow}$

(M1) for every $z \in M(x)$, there is a $y \in Min(M(x))$ such that $y \leq z$.

Observe that every element of E is top-recognisable, since if $x \in E$, then $Min(M(x)) = \{x\}$ and, clearly, (M1) holds by taking $y = x$. If E is a finite subset of W, then every element of W is top-recognisable. Let W_t be the set of all top-recognisable elements of Lr. We define the unary operation $U(E)$ on the set W_t as follows:

$$U_E(x) \overset{\text{def}}{=} sup(Min(M(x))).$$

The operation is well defined since $\langle E, \leq_E \rangle$ is a complete lattice. The structure $Lr_t = \langle W_t, E, \leq \rangle$ is a rough poset whose elements are top-recognisable.

A similar construction leads to a notion of bottom-recognisable elements. For every element $x \in W$, we consider the set of lower bounds of x that belong to E:

$$K(x) \stackrel{\text{def}}{=} \{e \in E : e \leq x\}.$$

Let $Max(K(x))$ be the set of all the maximal elements of $K(x)$. We say that an element $x \in W$ is *bottom-recognisable* in Lr $\stackrel{\text{def}}{\Leftrightarrow}$

(K1) for every $z \in K(x)$, there is a $y \in Max(K(x))$ such that $z \leq y$.

It follows that every element of E is bottom-recognisable and if E is finite, then all the elements of W are bottom-recognisable. Let W_b be the set of all the bottom-recognisable elements of Lr. We define the operation L_E on the set W_b:

$$L_E(x) \stackrel{\text{def}}{=} inf(Max(K(x))).$$

The structure $Lr_b = \langle W_b, E, \leq \rangle$ is a rough poset whose elements are bottom-recognisable.

Lemma 14.9.1. *Let $Lr = \langle W, E, \leq \rangle$ be a rough poset, and let Lr_t, Lr_b, U_E, L_E be as defined above. Then:*

(I) the operation U_E is an upper approximation operation in Lr_t and E is the set of all the U_E-exact elements of W_t;

(II) the operation L_E is a lower approximation operation in Lr_b and E is the set of all the L_E-exact elements of W_b.

Proof. (I) If $x \in E$, then $U_E(x) = sup(\{x\}) = x$. In particular, $U_E(0) = 0$. For every $x \in W$, the element $U_E(x)$ belongs to E by definition. It follows that $U_E(U_E(x)) \in E$ and hence the operation U_E is idempotent. If x is a top-recognisable element, then by condition (M1) there exists a $y \in Min(M(x))$ such that $x \leq y \leq U_E(x)$ which implies that U_E is extensive.

If $U_E(x) = x$ holds for some $x \in W$, then $x \in E$ and it follows that E is the set of all the U_E-exact elements.
The proof of (II) is similar.   Q.E.D.

Lemma 14.9.1 explains why the elements of E are called exact elements. Namely, it implies that an element $x \in W$ is exact iff it is U_E-exact iff it is L_E-exact.

Let $Lr = \langle W, E, \leq \rangle$ be a complete rough lattice, that is $L = \langle W, \leq \rangle$ is a complete lattice and $\langle E, \leq_E \rangle$ is a complete sublattice of L with $\leq_E$ being the restriction of $\leq$ to E. Then, the approximation operations in Lr satisfy the conditions: $U_E(x) = sup(M(x))$ and $L_E(x) = inf(K(x))$, where $M(x)$ and $K(x)$ are defined as above.

Lemma 14.9.2. *In a complete rough lattice, the following conditions are satisfied:*

(I) $U_E(x + y) = U_E(x) + U_E(y)$;
(II) $U_E(x \cdot y) \leq U_E(x) \cdot U_E(x)$;
(III) $L_E(x \cdot y) = L_E(x) \cdot L_E(y)$;
(IV) $L_E(x) + L_E(y) \leq L_E(x + y)$.

Proof. By way of example, we prove (III) and (IV).
(III) The operation L_E is a dual closure, so we have $L_E(x) \leq x$ and $L_E(y) \leq y$. It follows that $L_E(x) \cdot L_E(y) \leq x \cdot y$ in Lr. The element $L_E(x) \cdot L_E(y)$ belongs to E, hence $L_E(L_E(x) \cdot L_E(y)) = L_E(x) \cdot L_E(y)$.

Since L_E is isotone, we have $L_E(x) \cdot L_E(y) \leq L_E(x \cdot y)$. By isotonicity, we also have $L_E(x \cdot y) \leq L_E(x)$ and $L_E(x \cdot y) \leq L_E(y)$. Consequently, $L_E(x \cdot y) \leq L_E(x) \cdot L_E(y)$. Hence, (III) is satisfied.
(IV) Since $L_E(x) \leq x$ and $L_E(y) \leq y$, we have $L_E(x) + L_E(y) \leq x + y$. Both $L_E(x)$ and $L_E(y)$ belong to E, so $L_E(x) + L_E(y)$ belongs to E as well, because E is a sublattice of L. Therefore, we have $L_E(x) + L_E(y) = L_E(L_E(x) + L_E(y)) \leq L_E(x + y)$.
The conditions (I) and (II) hold by duality.   Q.E.D.

Example 14.9.2. Let $Lr = \langle \mathcal{P}(W), E_C, \subseteq \rangle$ be the rough algebra defined in Example 14.9.1. We define the following operations in Lr. Let $X \subseteq W$. Then:

★ $U_{E_C}(X) \stackrel{\text{def}}{=} \bigcap \{Z \in C_E : X \subseteq Z\}$;
★ $L_{E_C}(X) \stackrel{\text{def}}{=} \bigcup \{Z \in C_E : Z \subseteq X\}$.

It is easy to see that U_{E_C} and L_{E_C} are the upper approximation operation and the lower approximation operation, respectively. Moreover, they are a closure operator and a dual closure operator, respectively. The family E_C is the set of the exact elements in Lr. If the given partition C is determined by an approximation space $\langle W, R \rangle$, that is C is a family of the equivalence classes of an equivalence relation R, then the operations defined above coincide with the approximation operations presented in Sect. 4.9.

Lemma 14.9.3. *Let $\langle W, E, \leq \rangle$ and $\langle W, G, \leq \rangle$ be complete rough lattices such that $G \subseteq E$. Then, for all $x, y \in W$, the following conditions hold:*

(I) $L_E(L_G(x)) = L_G(L_E(x)) = L_G(x) \leq L_E(x) \leq x$;
(II) $x \leq U_E(x) \leq U_G(x) = U_G(U_E(x)) = U_E(U_G(x))$.

Proof. (I) Observe that for every $X \subseteq G$, we have $inf_E(X) = inf_G(X) = inf_W(X)$ and $sup_E(X) = sup_G(X) = sup_W(X)$. Hence, $\langle G, \leq_G \rangle$ is a complete sublattice of $\langle E, \leq_E \rangle$. If $x \in W$, then $L_G(x) \leq L_E(x)$, since $L_G(x)$ is one of the lower bounds of x in E. Since L_G is isotone, we have $L_G(L(e)(x)) \leq L_G(x)$. The following three statements are equivalent:

★ $y \in G$ and $y \leq x$;
★ $y \in G$, $y \in E$, and $y \leq x$;
★ $y \in G$ and $y \leq L_E(x)$.

It follows that $L_G(x) = L_G(L_E(x))$ for every $x \in W$. Since $L_G(x)$ is E-exact, we have $L_G(x) = L_E(L_G(x))$.
The proof of (II) is similar. $Q.E.D.$

A generalisation of the notion of approximation space can be obtained as follows. Let $L = \langle W, \leq \rangle$ be a complete lattice, let D be a non-empty subset of W, and let $r : D \to \mathcal{P}(W)$ be a function. The structure $\langle L, r \rangle$ is an *approximation system* $\overset{\text{def}}{\Leftrightarrow}$ the following conditions hold:

(1) $\langle D, \leq \rangle$ is a meet-sublattice of L;
(2) $\langle W, r(x), \leq \rangle$ is a complete rough lattice for every $x \in D$;
(3) $x \in r(x)$ for every $x \in D$;
(4) $x \leq y$ implies $r(y) \subseteq r(x)$ for all $x, y \in D$.

Let $\langle L, r \rangle$ be an approximation system and let $e \in D$. Consider the complete rough lattice $\langle W, r(e), \leq \rangle$. In what follows, we shall use the abbreviation L_e for the lower approximation operation $L_{r(e)}$.

Lemma 14.9.4. *For all $e, f \in D$ and for all $x, y \in W$, the following conditions hold:*

(I) $L_e(e) = e$;
(II) $L_e(L_e(x)) = x$;
(III) $L_e(x \cdot y) = L_e(x) \cdot L_e(y)$ and $L_e(x) + L_e(y) \leq L_e(x + y)$;
(IV) if $e \leq f$, then $L_f(x) \leq L_e(x)$;
(V) if $e \leq f$, then $L_e(L_f(x)) = L_f(L_e(x)) = L_f(x)$;
(VI) $L_e(x) + L_f(x) \leq L_{e \cdot f}(x)$;
(VII) if $e + f \in D$, then $L_{e+f}(x) \leq L_e(x) \cdot L_f(x)$.

Proof. (I) is a consequence of condition (3) in the definition of the approximation system. For every $e \in D$, the mapping L_e is a dual closure in $\langle W, \leq \rangle$ and D is the set of all L_e-closed elements of W. Hence (II) holds.
(III) follows from Lemma 14.9.2.
(IV) is implied by condition (4) in the definition of the approximation system.
(V) results from Lemma 14.9.3.
(VI) and (VII) follow from (IV). $Q.E.D.$

14.10 Notes

Algebras of indiscernibility and certainty regions. An algebraic approach to the representation and analysis of data in information systems originated in [Iwi87]. Since then various algebraic structures have been proposed for studying the properties of approximation operations and other information operators. A lattice structure of indiscernibility relations derived from an information system is investigated in [Jär97]. Theorem 14.2.1 is presented there. The material of Sect. 14.3 is based on developments in [Che92].

Monadic and Lukasiewicz algebras. Monadic Boolean algebras are introduced in [Hal62] for studying monadic predicate logic. Lukasiewicz algebras are introduced in [Moi72] in connection with algebraisation of many-valued Lukasiewicz logics [Luka20]. Relationships between those two classes of algebras are studied, among others, in [Mon68]. The construction presented in Definition 14.4.1 is given in [Mon68]. Lemma 14.4.1 is proved in [Itu98]. Lemma 14.4.3 is announced in [Pag95] and the proof is presented in [Pag98]. Lemma 14.4.5 follows from the developments of [BBR58]. Different proofs of Theorem 14.4.1 can be found in [Pag98, Dün97, Itu98], see also [Ban97].

Stone algebras. Stone algebras originated in connection with the problem posed by Grätzer of characterising the most general pseudo-complemented lattice in which $x^* + x^{**} = 1$. The basics of Stone algebras can be found in [CG69]. Katrinak algebras are introduced and investigated in [Kat74b, Kat74a]. Condition (I) of Lemma 14.5.8 is proved in [Var68] and condition (II) in [Dün80]. Lemma 14.5.10 and Theorem 14.5.1 are proved in [Com91, Com93]. The fact that the family of rough subsets of an approximation space is a Stone algebra is proved in [PP88]. In [Com93] this result is extended to regular double Stone algebras (Lemma 14.5.1). In [GW92] a characterisation of the class of Stone algebras derived from approximation spaces in the category of Stone algebras is presented. It is shown that this class is precisely the class of injective Stone algebras with atomic centres.

Rough relation algebras. The notion of rough relation is from [Paw81b]. Rough relations are investigated in [Ste98]. Rough relation algebras are introduced in [Com93]. Theorem 14.6.2 is proved in [Dün94]. In that paper an extensive survey of the properties of the class RrA is presented.

Fuzzy relation algebras. Fuzzy relation algebras are introduced in [Fur98] as an abstract formalisation of fuzzy relations. The material of Sect. 14.7 is from [KF99].

Nelson algebras. Nelson algebras are introduced in [Nel49]. They are semantic structures for a constructive logic developed in [BBR58] in connection with a search for a constructive negation which could replace the intuitionistic negation. Since then the study of constructive logic has been pursued by many authors; see for example [Sen84, Sen90, Vak77]. Theorem 14.8.1 and Lemma 14.8.1 are proved in [Pag96]. Theorem 14.8.2 for finite Nelson algebras is proved in [Pag98], and for infinite Nelson algebras which are complete and completely distributive the result is implicitly contained in the developments in [BC96]. Whether further improvement in the case of any arbitrary Nelson algebra is possible, is still an open question.

Generalised approximation operations. Generalisations of standard algebraic structures presented in Sect. 14.9 are introduced in [Iwi91]. The material of Sect. 14.9 is from that paper.

Other algebras with informational interpretation. Topological Boolean algebras are given an informational interpretation in [WV95, WB95, Was97]. In [Cat97] and [Cat98] informational interpretation in terms of rough sets is given to the orthocomplemented lattices. Some algebraic structures related to rough sets are also presented in [Bon94] and [BC93].

15. Information Algebras

15.1 Introduction and Outline of the Chapter

In this chapter we present the algebraic systems which are the counterparts to the information frames defined in Sect. 3.10. In analogy to the classes of information frames, we present the major classes of algebras, namely the algebras of indistinguishability and distinguishability. All these algebras are Boolean algebras with some additional operators. The operators are intended to be the abstract counterparts to the information operators presented in Chap. 4. However, the standard theory of Boolean algebras with the normal and additive operators does not provide a sufficient framework for characterising the algebraic structures of all information operators. We extend the theory BAO of Boolean algebras with normal and additive operators to several other classes of operators in order to capture the features of the information operators. Similarly to the information relations, an important aspect of information operators is their dependence on varying subsets of attributes. So, in analogy to the relative frames, we introduce Boolean algebras with relative operators. Throughout this chapter the relative frames we refer to are of the form $\langle W, (\mathcal{R}_P)_{P \subseteq PAR} \rangle$.

In the theory of information algebras, there are still many open problems to be solved, in order to get a complete characterisation of all these classes of algebras and their relationships to the respective classes of information frames. Several such problems are indicated in this chapter.

In Sect. 15.2 we present the three classes of algebras to be considered: modal algebras whose operators represent approximation operators, sufficiency algebras whose operators correspond to sufficiency operators derived from an approximation space, and mixed algebras that contain both modal and sufficiency operators. These classes are the basis for information algebras. In Sect. 15.3 we present some major classes of information algebras. Each of these consists of either modal, or sufficiency, or mixed algebras; however their operators are extended to relative operators. This enables us to capture the information operators of the corresponding types determined by given sets of attributes. Algebras with operators derived from information systems are the most typical examples of these algebras. The important methodological problems that are discussed in this chapter concern relationships between information frames and information algebras. In Sect. 15.4 we address this issue in the case of complete information algebras. In Sect. 15.5 we introduce specific classes of information algebras. They are grouped into two major categories: the first one contains algebras whose operators can be applied to an analysis of indistinguishability of objects, the second one applies to an analysis of distinguishability. In Sect. 15.6 we define canonical extensions of information algebras. In Sect. 15.7 we extend the notion of identity to identities of a language of Boolean algebras with relative operators and we present various classes of identities characterised in a syntactic way. In Sect. 15.8 we discuss preservation of identities of information algebras by their canonical extensions and canonicity of the classes of algebras introduced in Sect. 15.5. Next, in Sect. 15.9 we continue the discussion of the relationships between information frames and information algebras in the more general case of possibly incomplete information algebras. In Sect. 15.10 we outline methodological problems concerning relationship between information logics and information algebras.

15.2 Modal, Sufficiency, and Mixed Algebras

Let $\mathcal{B} = \langle W, +, \cdot, -, 1, 0 \rangle$ be a Boolean algebra and let $f : W \to W$ be a unary operation on W. The operator f is said to be:

* *normal* $\overset{\text{def}}{\Leftrightarrow}$ $f(0) = 0$;
* *dual normal* $\overset{\text{def}}{\Leftrightarrow}$ $f(1) = 1$;
* *conormal* $\overset{\text{def}}{\Leftrightarrow}$ $f(0) = 1$;
* *codual normal* $\overset{\text{def}}{\Leftrightarrow}$ $f(1) = 0$;
* *additive* $\overset{\text{def}}{\Leftrightarrow}$ for all $x, y \in W$, $f(x + y) = f(x) + f(y)$;
* *coadditive* $\overset{\text{def}}{\Leftrightarrow}$ for all $x, y \in W$, $f(x + y) = f(x) \cdot f(y)$;
* *multiplicative* $\overset{\text{def}}{\Leftrightarrow}$ for all $x, y \in W$, $f(x \cdot y) = f(x) \cdot f(y)$;
* *comultiplicative* $\overset{\text{def}}{\Leftrightarrow}$ for all $x, y \in W$, $f(x \cdot y) = f(x) + f(y)$.

We recall that $f(X) \overset{\text{def}}{=} \{f(x) : x \in X\}$ for every $X \subseteq W$. We say that the operator f is:

* *completely additive* $\overset{\text{def}}{\Leftrightarrow}$ for every $X \subseteq W$, if $sup(X)$ exists in $\mathcal{B}$, then $sup(f(X))$ exists in $\mathcal{B}$ and $f(sup(X)) = sup(f(X))$;
* *completely multiplicative* $\overset{\text{def}}{\Leftrightarrow}$ for every $X \subseteq W$, if $inf(X)$ exists in $\mathcal{B}$, then $inf(f(X))$ exists in $\mathcal{B}$ and $f(inf(X)) = inf(f(X))$;
* *completely coadditive* $\overset{\text{def}}{\Leftrightarrow}$ for every $X \subseteq W$, if $sup(X)$ exists in $\mathcal{B}$, then $inf(f(X))$ exists in $\mathcal{B}$ and $f(sup(X)) = inf(f(X))$;
* *completely comultiplicative* $\overset{\text{def}}{\Leftrightarrow}$ for every $X \subseteq W$, if $inf(X)$ exists in $\mathcal{B}$, then $sup(f(X))$ exists in $\mathcal{B}$ and $f(inf(X)) = sup(f(X))$.

Let f be an operator on $\mathcal{B} = \langle W, +, \cdot, -, 1, 0 \rangle$. We define $f^{\neg} : W \to W$ as $f^{\neg}(x) \overset{\text{def}}{=} f(-x)$ and $\neg f : W \to W$ as $(\neg f)(x) \overset{\text{def}}{=} -f(x)$. By the operator dual to f we mean the operator $f^d \overset{\text{def}}{=} (\neg f)^{\neg}$. An operator f is said to be:

⋆ a *(complete) modal operator* $\overset{\text{def}}{\Leftrightarrow}$ f is normal and (completely) additive;
⋆ a *(complete) dual modal operator* $\overset{\text{def}}{\Leftrightarrow}$ f is dual normal and (completely) multiplicative;
⋆ a *(complete) sufficiency operator* $\overset{\text{def}}{\Leftrightarrow}$ f is conormal and (completely) coadditive;
⋆ a *(complete) dual sufficiency operator* $\overset{\text{def}}{\Leftrightarrow}$ f is codual normal and (completely) comultiplicative.

Two unary operators f and g on a Boolean algebra $\langle W, +, \cdot, -, 1, 0 \rangle$ are *conjugated* $\overset{\text{def}}{\Leftrightarrow}$ for all $x, y \in W$, $x \cdot f(y) = 0$ iff $g(x) \cdot y = 0$. This condition is equivalent to $x \leq f^d(y)$ iff $g(x) \leq y$ for all $x, y \in W$. Conjugated operators are completely additive.

The following lemmas follow directly from the respective definitions.

Lemma 15.2.1. *For every operator f on a Boolean algebra the following assertions hold:*

(I) f is a modal [resp. dual modal] operator iff $f^{\neg}$ is a dual sufficiency [resp. sufficiency] operator;
(II) f is a modal [resp. dual modal] operator iff $^{\neg}f$ is a sufficiency [resp. dual sufficiency] operator;
(III) $(f^{\neg})^{\neg} = f$;
(IV) $^{\neg}(^{\neg}f) = f$.

Lemma 15.2.2. *For all operators f and g on a Boolean algebra $\mathcal{B} = \langle W, +, \cdot, -, 1, 0 \rangle$ and for every $x \in W$ the following assertions hold:*

(I) f is a modal [resp. sufficiency] operator iff f^d is a dual modal [resp. dual sufficiency] operator;
(II) $(f^d)^d = f$;
(III) if $h(x) = f(x) + g(x)$, then $h^d(x) = f^d(x) \cdot g^d(x)$, $h^{\neg}(x) = f^{\neg}(x) + g^{\neg}(x)$, $(^{\neg}h)(x) = (^{\neg}f)(x) \cdot (^{\neg}g)(x)$.

Lemma 15.2.3.

(I) Any modal or dual modal operator is isotone.
(II) Any sufficiency or dual sufficiency operator is antitone.

For any operators f and g we write fg to denote the composition of these operators, instead of $f; g$.

Lemma 15.2.4. *For all operators f, g, and h on a Boolean algebra the following assertions hold:*

(I) the composition of any number of modal operators is a modal operator;
(II) the composition of an even [resp. odd] number of sufficiency operators is isotone [resp. antitone];

(III) if f, g, h are sufficiency operators, then fg^d is a dual modal operator and $fg^d h$ is a sufficiency operator;

(IV) for every operator f, $(f^{\neg})f = f(^{\neg}f)$.

Lemma 15.2.5. *For every Boolean algebra $\mathcal{B} = \langle W, +, \cdot, -, 1, 0 \rangle$ the following assertions hold:*

(I) if f and g are modal operators on $\mathcal{B}$ and $h(x) = f(x) + g(x)$ for every $x \in W$, then h is a modal operator on $\mathcal{B}$;

(II) if f and g are sufficiency operators on $\mathcal{B}$ and $h(x) = f(x) \cdot g(x)$ for every $x \in W$, then h is a sufficiency operator on $\mathcal{B}$.

Lemma 15.2.6. *For every operator f on a Boolean algebra $\langle W, +, \cdot, -, 1, 0 \rangle$ and for all $x, y \in W$ the following conditions are equivalent:*

(I) $x \leq f^d(f(x))$;
(II) $f(x) \cdot y = 0$ iff $f(y) \cdot x = 0$.

Condition (II) says that f is an autoconjugated operator.

We recall that the operators $\langle \mathcal{R}_P \rangle$, $[\mathcal{R}_P]$, $[[\mathcal{R}_P]]$, $\langle\langle \mathcal{R}_P \rangle\rangle$ are defined in Sect. 4.9.

Lemma 15.2.7. *Let $\langle W, (\mathcal{R}_P)_{P \subseteq PAR} \rangle$ be a relative frame. Then, $\langle \mathcal{R}_P \rangle$ [resp. $[\mathcal{R}_P]$, $[[\mathcal{R}_P]]$, $\langle\langle \mathcal{R}_P \rangle\rangle$] is a complete modal [resp. dual modal, sufficiency, dual sufficiency] operator for every $P \subseteq PAR$.*

The proof is by an easy verification.

A *modal algebra* is a Boolean algebra with an additional modal operator. The class of modal algebras will be denoted by MOA. A *sufficiency algebra* is a Boolean algebra with an additional sufficiency operator. The class of sufficiency algebras will be denoted by SUA. Similarly, the classes DMOA and DSUA are the classes of dual modal algebras and dual sufficiency algebras, respectively. In the rest of this chapter we assume that the underlying Boolean algebras are complete and atomic.

A *mixed algebra* $\langle W, +, \cdot, -, 1, 0, f, g \rangle$ is an algebra such that

$\star$ $\mathcal{B} = \langle W, +, \cdot, -, 1, 0 \rangle$ is a complete and atomic Boolean algebra;
$\star$ f is a modal operator;
$\star$ g is a sufficiency operator;
$\star$ $f(x) = g(x)$ for every atom x of $\mathcal{B}$.

The class of all mixed algebras will be denoted by MIA.

If $\mathcal{B} = \langle W, +, \cdot, -, 1, 0 \rangle$ is a complete Boolean algebra and f is a complete operator, then $\langle W, +, \cdot, -, 1, 0, f \rangle$ is a complete algebra.

15.3 Boolean Algebras with Relative Operators

In this section we define several classes of Boolean algebras with the additional operators which are intended to be abstract counterparts of information operators discussed in Sect. 4.9. However, to capture an essential feature of information operators, that is their dependence on subsets of attributes, we introduce Boolean algebras with relative operators. The algebras are of the form

$$\langle W, +, \cdot, -, 1, 0, (f_P)_{P \subseteq PAR} \rangle$$

or of the form

$$\langle W, +, \cdot, -, 1, 0, (f_P)_{P \subseteq PAR}, (g_P)_{P \subseteq PAR} \rangle$$

where $\mathcal{B} = \langle W, +, \cdot, -, 1, 0 \rangle$ is a complete atomic Boolean algebra with the set $\mathrm{At}(\mathcal{B})$ of atoms. $(f_P)_{P \subseteq PAR}$ and $(g_P)_{P \subseteq PAR}$ are families of unary relative operators on W, where PAR is a non-empty set of parameters. We shall often write $\langle \mathcal{B}, (f_P)_{P \subseteq PAR} \rangle$ and $\langle \mathcal{B}, (f_P)_{P \subseteq PAR}, (g_P)_{P \subseteq PAR} \rangle$, respectively, for such algebras.

We extend the classes defined in Sect. 15.2 to the algebras with multiple operators. We say that an algebra $\varDelta = \langle \mathcal{B}, (f_P)_{P \subseteq PAR} \rangle \in \mathsf{MOA}$ [resp. DMOA, SUA, DSUA] iff f_P is a modal [resp. dual modal, sufficiency, dual sufficiency] operator for every $P \subseteq PAR$. Similarly, $\varDelta = \langle \mathcal{B}, (f_P)_{P \subseteq PAR}, (g_P)_{P \subseteq PAR} \rangle \in \mathsf{MIA}$ iff for every $P \subseteq PAR$, f_P is a modal operator, g_P is a sufficiency operator, and $f_P(x) = g_P(x)$ for every atom x of $\mathcal{B}$.

As with relative relations, relative operators may satisfy some local conditions, e.g. they can be modal or sufficiency operators, but also some global condition that refer to the whole family of operators. The global conditions express relationships between the operators indexed with a compound set of parameters and the operators indexed with its components. They are intended to be the counterparts to the global conditions defined in Sect. 3.10 for the families of relative relations.

We define the following classes of information algebras of the form $\varDelta = \langle W, +, \cdot, -, 1, 0, (f_P)_{P \subseteq PAR} \rangle$.

⋆ SMOA is the class of modal algebras such that for all $P, Q \subseteq PAR$ and for every $x \in W$:
  * f_P is a modal operator;
  * if $x \neq 0$, then $f_\emptyset(x) = 1$;
  * $f_{P \cup Q}(x) = f_P(x) \cdot f_Q(x)$ for every $x \in \mathrm{At}(\mathcal{B})$.
  The members of SMOA are called *strong modal algebras*.

⋆ WMOA is the class of modal algebras such that for all $P, Q \subseteq PAR$ and for every $x \in W$:
  * f_P is a modal operator;

* $f_\emptyset(x) = 0$;
* $f_{P \cup Q}(x) = f_P(x) + f_Q(x)$.

The members of WMOA are called *weak modal algebras*.

⋆ SDMOA is the class of modal algebras such that for all $P, Q \subseteq PAR$ and for every $x \in W$:
* f_P is a dual modal operator;
* if $x \neq 1$, then $f_\emptyset(x) = 0$;
* $f_{P \cup Q}(-x) = f_P(-x) + f_Q(-x)$ for every $x \in At(\mathcal{B})$.

The members of SDMOA are called *strong dual modal algebras*.

⋆ WDMOA is the class of modal algebras such that for all $P, Q \subseteq PAR$ and for every $x \in W$:
* f_P is a dual modal operator;
* $f_\emptyset(x) = 1$;
* $f_{P \cup Q}(x) = f_P(x) \cdot f_Q(x)$.

The members of WDMOA are called *weak dual modal algebras*.

⋆ SSUA is the class of modal algebras such that for all $P, Q \subseteq PAR$ and for every $x \in W$:
* f_P is a sufficiency operator;
* $f_\emptyset(x) = 1$;
* $f_{P \cup Q}(x) = f_P(x) \cdot f_Q(x)$.

The members of SSUA are called *strong sufficiency algebras*.

⋆ WSUA is the class of modal algebras such that for all $P, Q \subseteq PAR$ and for every $x \in W$:
* f_P is a sufficiency operator;
* if $x \neq 0$, then $f_\emptyset(x) = 0$;
* $f_{P \cup Q}(x) = f_P(x) + f_Q(x)$ for every $x \in At(\mathcal{B})$.

The members of WSUA are called *weak sufficiency algebras*.

⋆ SDSUA is the class of modal algebras such that for all $P, Q \subseteq PAR$ and for every $x \in W$:
* f_P is a dual sufficiency operator;
* $f_\emptyset(x) = 0$;
* $f_{P \cup Q}(x) = f_P(x) + f_Q(x)$.

The members of SDSUA are called *strong dual sufficiency algebras*.

⋆ WDSUA is the class of modal algebras such that for all $P, Q \subseteq PAR$ and for every $x \in W$:
* f_P is a dual sufficiency operator;
* If $x \neq 1$, then $f_\emptyset(x) = 1$;
* $f_{P \cup Q}(-x) = f_P(-x) \cdot f_Q(-x)$ for every $x \in At(\mathcal{B})$.

The members of WDSUA are called *weak dual sufficiency algebras*.

We define the following classes of mixed information algebras of the form
$\Delta = \langle W, +, \cdot, -, 1, 0, (f_P)_{P \subseteq PAR}, (g_P)_{P \subseteq PAR} \rangle$.

★ SMIA is the class of mixed information algebras such that
 * $\langle W, +, \cdot, -, 1, 0, (f_P)_{P \subseteq PAR} \rangle \in$ SMOA;
 * $\langle W, +, \cdot, -, 1, 0, (g_P)_{P \subseteq PAR} \rangle \in$ SSUA;
 * for every $P \subseteq PAR$ and for every $x \in \mathrm{At}(\mathcal{B})$, $f_P(x) = g_P(x)$.
 The members of SMIA are called *strong mixed algebras*.

★ WMIA is the class of mixed information algebras such that
 * $\langle W, +, \cdot, -, 1, 0, (f_P)_{P \subseteq PAR} \rangle \in$ WMOA;
 * $\langle W, +, \cdot, -, 1, 0, (g_P)_{P \subseteq PAR} \rangle \in$ WSUA;
 * for every $P \subseteq PAR$ and for every $x \in \mathrm{At}(\mathcal{B})$, $f_P(x) = g_P(x)$.
 The members of WMIA are called *weak mixed algebras*.

By an AS-*algebra* [resp. AW-*algebra*] we mean any algebra from any of
the classes SMOA, SDMOA, SSUA, SDSUA, SMIA [resp. WMOA, WDMOA,
WSUA, WDSUA, WMIA]. By an *information algebra* we mean an algebra from
any of these classes.

The natural examples of algebras from the classes defined above are as
follows. Let $F = \langle W, (\mathcal{R}_P)_{P \subseteq PAR} \rangle$ be a relative frame. We define:

★ $\langle F \rangle \overset{\text{def}}{=} \langle \mathcal{P}(W), (\langle \mathcal{R}_P \rangle)_{P \subseteq PAR} \rangle$;
★ $[F] \overset{\text{def}}{=} \langle \mathcal{P}(W), ([\mathcal{R}_P])_{P \subseteq PAR} \rangle$;
★ $[[F]] \overset{\text{def}}{=} \langle \mathcal{P}(W), ([[\mathcal{R}_P]])_{P \subseteq PAR} \rangle$;
★ $\langle\langle F \rangle\rangle \overset{\text{def}}{=} \langle \mathcal{P}(W), (\langle\langle \mathcal{R}_P \rangle\rangle)_{P \subseteq PAR} \rangle$;
★ $(F) \overset{\text{def}}{=} \langle \mathcal{P}(W), (\langle \mathcal{R}_P \rangle)_{P \subseteq PAR}, ([[\mathcal{R}_P]])_{P \subseteq PAR} \rangle$.

Lemma 15.3.1. *For every relative frame* $F = \langle W, (\mathcal{R}_P)_{P \subseteq PAR} \rangle$, *if* $F \in$ FS
[resp. $F \in$ FW*], then* $\langle F \rangle \in$ SMOA *[resp.* WMOA*],* $[F] \in$ SDMOA *[resp.*
WDMOA*],* $[[F]] \in$ SSUA *[resp.* WSUA*],* $\langle\langle F \rangle\rangle \in$ SDSUA *[resp.* WDSUA*],*
$(F) \in$ SMIA *[resp.* WMIA*].*

The proof is by an easy verification.

15.4 Relationship Between Complex Information Algebras and Information Frames

Let $F = \langle W, (\mathcal{R}_P)_{P \subseteq PAR} \rangle$ be a relative frame. The algebras considered in
Lemma 15.3.1 are referred to as complex algebras of F:

★ $\langle F \rangle$ is the *full modal complex algebra*;
★ $[F]$ is the *full dual modal complex algebra*;

* $[[F]]$ is the *full sufficiency complex algebra*;
* $\langle\langle F\rangle\rangle$ is the *full dual sufficiency complex algebra*;
* (F) is the *full mixed complex algebra*.

By a *complex algebra* of any of the above types we mean a subalgebra of the full complex algebra of that type.

Consider algebras of the form $\Delta = \langle \mathcal{P}(W), (f_P)_{P \subseteq PAR}\rangle$. We define binary relations $|f_P|$ and $|f_P|^d$ on the set W as follows:

* if f_P is a modal or a sufficiency operator, then

$$|f_P| \overset{\text{def}}{=} \{\langle x, y\rangle \in W \times W : x \in f_P(\{y\})\};$$

* if f_P is a dual modal or a dual sufficiency operator, then

$$|f_P|^d \overset{\text{def}}{=} \{\langle x, y\rangle \in W \times W : x \notin f_P(-\{y\})\}.$$

We slightly abuse the notation using the index d both for indicating a dual operator and the above relation, but it should not lead to any confusion. The following two lemmas state some properties of these relations.

Lemma 15.4.1. *Let* $\Delta = \langle \mathcal{P}(W), (f_P)_{P \subseteq PAR}\rangle$ *be an information algebra. Then the following hold:*

(I) if f_P is a modal [resp. sufficiency] operator, then $|{}^{\neg}f_P| = (W \times W)\setminus|f_P|$;
(II) if f_P is a dual modal [resp. dual sufficiency] operator, then
    (II.1) $(W \times W)\setminus|f_P|^d = |f_P^{d\neg}|^d$;
    (II.2) $|f_P^d| = |f_P|^d$;
(III) $|f_P^{d\neg}| = |{}^{\neg}f_P|$.

Proof. By way of example we prove condition (II.1). Let f_P be a dual modal [resp. dual sufficiency] operator. Then, by Lemma 15.2.2(I), f_P^d is a modal [resp. sufficiency] operator; by Lemma 15.2.1(I), $f_P^{d\neg}$ is a dual sufficiency [resp. dual modal] operator. Therefore we have: $\langle x, y\rangle \in |f_P^{d\neg}|^d$ iff $x \notin f_P^{d\neg}(-\{y\})$ iff $x \notin f_P^d(\{y\})$ iff $x \notin -f_P(-\{y\})$ iff $x \in f_P(-\{y\})$ iff $\langle x, y\rangle \notin |f_P|^d$. Q.E.D.

Lemma 15.4.2. *If* $\Delta = \langle \mathcal{P}(W), (f_P)_{P \subseteq PAR}, (g_P)_{P \subseteq PAR}\rangle$ *is a mixed information algebra, then* $|f_P| = |g_P|$ *for every* $P \subseteq PAR$.

The proof follows directly from the corresponding definitions. The following two lemmas present relationships between the relative operators and the respective derived relations.

Lemma 15.4.3. *If* $F = \langle W, (\mathcal{R}_P)_{P \subseteq PAR}\rangle$ *is a relative frame, then we have:*

(I) $\mathcal{R}_P = |\langle \mathcal{R}_P\rangle| = |[[\mathcal{R}_P]]|$;
(II) $\mathcal{R}_P = |[\mathcal{R}_P]|^d = |\langle\langle \mathcal{R}_P\rangle\rangle|^d$.

Proof. By way of example we prove that $\mathcal{R}_P = |\langle\langle\mathcal{R}_P\rangle\rangle|^d$. We have $\langle x, y\rangle \in |\langle\langle\mathcal{R}_P\rangle\rangle|^d$ iff $x \notin \langle\langle\mathcal{R}_P\rangle\rangle(-\{y\})$ iff for every z, $z \in -\{y\}$ or $\langle x, z\rangle \in \mathcal{R}_P$ iff for every z, if $z = y$, then $\langle x, z\rangle \in \mathcal{R}_P$ iff $\langle x, y\rangle \in \mathcal{R}_P$.
In the remaining cases the proofs are similar.   Q.E.D.

Lemma 15.4.4. *Let* $\Delta = \langle \mathcal{P}(W), (f_P)_{P \subseteq PAR}\rangle$ *be a complete information algebra. Then we have:*

(I) if f_P is a modal operator, then $\langle|f_P|\rangle = f_P$;
(II) if f_P is a sufficiency operator, then $[[|f_P|]] = f_P$;
(III) if f_P is a dual modal operator, then $[|f_P|^d] = f_P$;
(IV) if f_P is a dual sufficiency operator, then $\langle\langle|f_P|^d\rangle\rangle = f_P$.

Proof. By way of example we prove (II). Let $X \subseteq W$. We have $x \in [[|f_P|]](X)$ iff for every $y \in W$, if $y \in X$, then $\langle x, y\rangle \in |f_P|$ iff for every y, if $y \in X$, then $x \in f_P(\{y\})$ iff $x \in f_P(X)$.   Q.E.D.

Let $\Delta = \langle \mathcal{P}(W), (f_P)_{P \subseteq PAR}\rangle$ be an information algebra. The relations determined by the relative operators lead to the following relative frames:

$\star$ $|\Delta| \stackrel{\text{def}}{=} \langle W, (|f_P|)_{P \subseteq PAR}\rangle$;
$\star$ $|\Delta|^d \stackrel{\text{def}}{=} \langle W, (|f_P|^d)_{P \subseteq PAR}\rangle$.

These frames are referred to as the *canonical frames of the algebra* Δ. The following theorem shows that in the case of complete information algebras there is an intended correspondence between the classes of these algebras and the respective classes of information frames.

Theorem 15.4.1. *Let* $\Delta = \langle \mathcal{P}(W), (f_P)_{P \subseteq PAR}\rangle$ *be a complete information algebra. Then the following hold:*

(I) if $\Delta \in$ MOA $\cup$ SUA, then
    (I.1) Δ is an AS-algebra iff $|\Delta| \in$ FS;
    (I.1) Δ is an AW-algebra iff $|\Delta| \in$ FW.
(II) if $\Delta \in$ DMOA $\cup$ DSUA, then
    (II.1) Δ is an AS-algebra iff $|\Delta|^d \in$ FS;
    (II.2) Δ is an AW-algebra iff $|\Delta|^d \in$ FW.

Proof. By way of example we prove (II.2) for WDSUA algebras.
$(\rightarrow)$ By the assumption we have:

(i) $f_{P \cup Q}^-(\{x\}) = f_P^-(\{x\}) \cap f_Q^-(\{x\})$ for every $x \in W$;
(ii) if $X \neq W$, then $f_\emptyset(X) = W$.

We have to show:

(iii) $|f_{P \cup Q}|^d = |f_P|^d \cup |f_Q|^d$;
(iv) $|f_\emptyset|^d = \emptyset$.

Proof of (iii): the following equivalent statements follow from the respective definitions and from (i): $\langle x, y \rangle \in |f_{P \cup Q}|^d$ iff $x \notin f_{P \cup Q}(-\{y\})$ iff $x \notin f_P(-\{y\}) \cap f_Q(-\{y\})$ iff $x \notin f_P(-\{y\})$ or $x \notin f_Q(-\{y\})$ iff $\langle x, y \rangle \in |f_P|^d$ or $\langle x, y \rangle \in |f_Q|^d$ iff $\langle x, y \rangle \in |f_P|^d \cup |f_Q|^d$.

Proof of (iv): this part of the proof follows from (ii). We have $\langle x, y \rangle \in |f_\emptyset|^d$ iff $x \notin f_\emptyset(-\{y\})$ iff $x \notin W$, a contradiction. Hence, $|f_\emptyset|^d = \emptyset$.

($\leftarrow$) Now assume that (iii) and (iv) hold and we have to show (i) and (ii).

Proof of (i): the following equivalences follow from (iii) and the respective definitions: $z \notin f_{P \cup Q}(-\{x\})$ iff $z \notin f_P(-\{x\})$ or $z \notin f_Q(-\{x\})$ iff $z \notin f_P(-\{x\}) \cap f_Q(-\{x\})$.

Proof of (ii): let $X \neq W$ and suppose that $f_\emptyset(X) \neq W$. Hence, there are z and x such that $z \notin X$ and $x \notin f_\emptyset(X)$. By (iv) for every $x \in W$, $x \in f_\emptyset(-\{z\})$. So we have $\bigcap \{f_\emptyset(-\{z\}) : z \in W\} = W$. By complete comultiplicativity, for every $X \subset W$ we get $f_\emptyset(X) = W$.   Q.E.D.

15.5 Information Algebras of Indistinguishability and Distinguishability

The algebras of indistinguishability/distinguishability are obtained from the classes of algebras defined in Sect. 15.3 by postulating some specific axioms. These algebras are intended to be the counterparts to the respective classes of information frames. Unless stated otherwise, the algebras are of the form $\Delta = \langle W, +, \cdot, -, 1, 0, (f_P)_{P \subseteq PAR} \rangle$.

15.5.1 AS-algebras of Indistinguishability

We define the following classes of AS-algebras.

⋆ AS-IND is the class of SMOA algebras such that for every $P \subseteq PAR$ and for every $x \in W$:
  * $x \leq f_P(x)$;
  * $x \leq f_P^d(f_P(x))$;
  * $f_P(f_P(x)) \leq f_P(x)$.
  The members of AS-IND are called *strong indiscernibility algebras*.

⋆ AS-SIM-TOT is the class of SMOA algebras such that for every $P \subseteq PAR$ and for every $x \in W$:
  * $x \leq f_P(x)$;
  * $x \leq f_P^d(f_P(x))$.
  The members of AS-SIM-TOT are called *strong total similarity algebras*.

⋆ AS-SIM is the class of SMOA algebras such that for every $P \subseteq PAR$ and for every $x \in W$:

* $x \cdot f_P(1) \leq f_P(x)$;
* $x \leq f_P^d(f_P(x))$.

The members of AS-SIM are called *strong similarity algebras*.

★ AS-ICOM is the class of SMIA algebras

$$\langle W, +, \cdot, -, 1, 0, (f_P)_{P \subseteq PAR}, (g_P)_{P \subseteq PAR} \rangle$$

such that for every $P \subseteq PAR$ and for every $x \in W$:
* $x \leq f_P(x)$ for $P \neq \emptyset$;
* $x \leq g_P(g_P(x))$;
* $g_{\{p\}}(x) \leq g_{\{p\}}(g_{\{p\}}^d(g_{\{p\}}(x)))$ for every $p \in PAR$.

The members of AS-ICOM are called *strong incomplementarity algebras*.

★ AS-IN is the class of algebras

$$\langle W, +, \cdot, -, 1, 0, (f_P)_{P \subseteq PAR}, (g_P)_{P \subseteq PAR} \rangle$$

such that the algebras $\langle W, +, \cdot, -, 1, 0, (f_P)_{P \subseteq PAR} \rangle$ and $\langle W, +, \cdot, -, 1, 0, (g_P)_{P \subseteq PAR} \rangle$ are in SMOA and for every $P \subseteq PAR$ and for every $x \in W$:
* $x \leq f_P(x), \quad x \leq g_P(x)$;
* $f_P(f_P(x)) \leq f_P(x), \quad g_P(g_P(x)) \leq g_P(x)$;
* $f_P(g_P^d(x)) \leq x, \quad g_P(f_P^d(x)) \leq x$.

The members of AS-IN are called *strong inclusion algebras*.

15.5.2 AW-algebras of Indistinguishability

We define the following classes of AW-algebras.

★ AW-IND is the class of WMOA-algebras such that for every $P \subseteq PAR$ and for every $x \in W$:
* $x \leq f_P(x)$;
* $x \leq f_P^d(f_P(x))$;
* $f_{\{p\}}(f_{\{p\}}(x)) \leq f_{\{p\}}(x)$ for every $p \in PAR$.

The members of AW-IND are called *weak indiscernibility algebras*.

★ AW-SIM-TOT is the class of WMOA-algebras such that for every $P \subseteq PAR$ and for every $x \in W$:
* $x \leq f_P(x)$;
* $x \leq f_P^d(f_P(x))$.

The members of AW-SIM-TOT are called *weak total similarity algebras*.

★ AW-SIM is the class of WMOA-algebras such that for every $P \subseteq PAR$ and for every $x \in W$:

* $x \cdot f_P(1) \leq f_P(x)$;
* $x \leq f_P^d(f_P(x))$.

The members of AW-SIM are called *weak similarity algebras*.

⋆ AW-ICOM is the class of WMIA algebras

$$\langle W, +, \cdot, -, 1, 0, (f_P)_{P \subseteq PAR}, (g_P)_{P \subseteq PAR} \rangle$$

such that for every $P \subseteq PAR$ and for every $x \in W$:
* $x \leq f_P(x)$;
* $x \leq g_P(g_P(x))$;
* $g_{\{p\}}(x) \leq g_{\{p\}}(g_{\{p\}}^d(g_{\{p\}}(x)))$ for every $p \in PAR$.

The members of AW-ICOM are called *weak incomplementarity algebras*.

⋆ AW-IN is the class of algebras of the form

$$\langle W, +, \cdot, -, 1, 0, (f_P)_{P \subseteq PAR}, (g_P)_{P \subseteq PAR} \rangle$$

such that the algebras $\langle W, +, \cdot, -, 1, 0, (f_P)_{P \subseteq PAR} \rangle$ and
$\langle W, +, \cdot, -, 1, 0, (g_P)_{P \subseteq PAR} \rangle$ are in WMOA and for every $P \subseteq PAR$ and
for every $x \in W$:
* $x \leq f_P(x), \quad x \leq g_P(x)$;
* $f_{\{p\}}(f_{\{p\}}(x)) \leq f_{\{p\}}(x), \quad g_{\{p\}}(g_{\{p\}}(x)) \leq g_{\{p\}}(x)$ for every $p \in PAR$;
* $f_P(g_P^d(x)) \leq x, \quad g_P(f_P^d(x)) \leq x$.

The members of AW-IN are called *weak inclusion algebras*.

15.5.3 AS-algebras of Distinguishability

We define the following classes of AS-algebras.

⋆ AS-DIV is the class of SSUA algebras such that for every $P \subseteq PAR$ and
for every $x \in W$:
* $f_P(x) \leq -x$ for $P \neq \emptyset$;
* $x \leq f_P(f_P(x))$;
* $f_{\{p\}}(x) \leq f_{\{p\}}(f_{\{p\}}^d(-x))$ for every $p \in PAR$.

The members of AS-DIV are called *strong diversity algebras*.

⋆ AS-RORT is the class of SSUA algebras such that for every $P \subseteq PAR$ and
for every $x \in W$:
* $x \cdot f_P(x) \leq f_P(1)$;
* $x \leq f_P(f_P(x))$.

The members of AS-RORT are called *strong right orthogonality algebras*.

⋆ AS-RLNIM is the class of algebras of the form

$$\langle W, +, \cdot, -, 1, 0, (f_P)_{P \subseteq PAR}, (g_P)_{P \subseteq PAR} \rangle$$

such that the algebras $\langle W, +, \cdot, -, 1, 0, (f_P)_{P \subseteq PAR} \rangle$ and $\langle W, +, \cdot, -, 1, 0, (g_P)_{P \subseteq PAR} \rangle$ are in SSUA and for every $P \subseteq PAR$ and for every $x \in W$:
  * $f_P(x) \le -x, \quad g_P(x) \le -x$;
  * $f_{\{p\}}(x) \le f_{\{p\}}(f_{\{p\}}^d(-x))$ for every $p \in PAR$;
  * $g_{\{p\}}(x) \le g_{\{p\}}(g_{\{p\}}^d(-x))$ for every $p \in PAR$;
  * $x \le f_P(g_P(x)), x \le g_P(f_P(x))$.
The members of AS-RLNIM are called *strong right–left negative similarity algebras*.

⋆ AS-COM is the class of SMIA algebras

$$\langle W, +, \cdot, -, 1, 0, (f_P)_{P \subseteq PAR}, (g_P)_{P \subseteq PAR} \rangle$$

such that for every $P \subseteq PAR$ and for every $x \in W$:
  * $g_P(x) \le -x$ for $P \ne \emptyset$;
  * $x \le g_P(g_P(x))$;
  * $f_P(f_P(f_P(x))) \le f_P(x)$.
The members of AS-COM are called *strong complementarity algebras*.

15.5.4 AW-algebras of Distinguishability

We define the following classes of AW-algebras.

⋆ AW-DIV is the class of WSUA algebras such that for every $P \subseteq PAR$ and for every $x \in W$:
  * $f_P(x) \le -x$;
  * $x \le f_P(f_P(x))$;
  * $f_P(x) \le f_P(f_P^d(f_P(x)))$ for every $x \in At(\mathcal{B})$.
The members of AW-DIV are called *weak diversity algebras*.

⋆ AW-RORT is the class of WSUA algebras such that for every $P \subseteq PAR$ and for every $x \in W$:
  * $x \cdot f_P(x) \le f_P(1)$;
  * $x \le f_P(f_P(x))$.
The members of AW-RORT are called *weak right orthogonality algebras*.

⋆ AW-RLNIM is the class of algebras

$$\langle W, +, \cdot, -, 1, 0, (f_P)_{P \subseteq PAR}, (g_P)_{P \subseteq PAR} \rangle$$

such that both algebras $\langle W, +, \cdot, -, 1, 0, (f_P)_{P \subseteq PAR} \rangle$ and $\langle W, +, \cdot, -, 1, 0, (g_P)_{P \subseteq PAR} \rangle$ are in WSUA and for every $P \subseteq PAR$ and for every $x \in W$:

* $f_P(x) \leq -x, \quad g_P(x) \leq -x;$
* $f_P(x) \leq f_P(f_P^d(-x)), \quad g_P(x) \leq g_P(g_P^d(-x));$
* $x \leq f_P(g_P(x)), \quad x \leq g_P(f_P(x)).$

The members of AW-RLNIM are called *weak right–left negative similarity algebras*.

★ AW-COM is the class of WMIA algebras

$$\langle W, +, \cdot, -, 1, 0, (f_P)_{P \subseteq PAR}, (g_P)_{P \subseteq PAR} \rangle$$

such that for every $P \subseteq PAR$ and for every $x \in W$:
* $g_{\{p\}}(x) \leq -x$ for every $p \in PAR$;
* $x \leq g_P(g_P(x));$
* $f_{\{p\}}(f_{\{p\}}(f_{\{p\}}(x))) \leq f_{\{p\}}(x)$ for every $p \in PAR$.

The members of AW-COM are called *weak complementarity algebras*.

The natural examples of algebras belonging to the classes defined above are the complex algebras of the corresponding frames as the following lemma shows.

Lemma 15.5.1. *Let* type$_1$ = IND, SIM, SIM-TOT, IN, type$_2$ = DIV, RORT, RLNIM, *and* type$_3$ = ICOM, COM.
For every relative frame $F = \langle W, (\mathcal{R}_P)_{P \subseteq PAR} \rangle$ *the following assertions hold:*

(I) if $F \in$ FS-type$_1$ *[resp. FW-type$_1$], then* $\langle F \rangle \in$ AS-type$_1$ *[resp. AW-type$_1$];*
(II) if $F \in$ FS-type$_2$ *[resp. FW-type$_2$], then* $[[F]] \in$ AS-type$_2$ *[resp. AW-type$_2$];*
(III) if $F \in$ FS-type$_3$ *[resp. FW-type$_3$], then* $(F) \in$ AS-type$_3$ *[resp. AW-type$_3$].*

Clearly, the classes of algebras corresponding to the classes of frames FS-FIN, FS-RORT-TOT, and their FW-versions can be easily defined.

15.6 Canonical Extensions of Information Algebras

The relationships between information frames and information algebras presented in Theorem 15.4.1 require that the underlying information operators are complete. However, the operators defined on complete and atomic Boolean algebras are not necessarily complete and hence the algebras presented in Sect. 15.5 may not be complete. In the present section we introduce extensions of information algebras such that their respective relative operators are complete.

Let $\mathcal{B} = \langle W, +, \cdot, -, 1, 0 \rangle$ be a Boolean algebra and let $U_\mathcal{B}$ be the family of maximal filters of $\mathcal{B}$. The canonical extension $\mathcal{B}^c$ of $\mathcal{B}$ is the Boolean algebra of all the subsets of $U_\mathcal{B}$. The following two lemmas are well known in the theory of Boolean algebras.

Lemma 15.6.1. *For every Boolean algebra $\mathcal{B}$ its canonical extension $\mathcal{B}^c$ is a complete atomic Boolean algebra.*

Let $s : W \to \mathcal{P}(U_\mathcal{B})$ be a mapping defined by $s(x) \overset{\text{def}}{=} \{F \in U_\mathcal{B} : x \in F\}$ and let $W^s \overset{\text{def}}{=} \{s(x) : x \in W\}$. Then we have the following lemma.

Lemma 15.6.2. *For every Boolean algebra $\mathcal{B}$ the following assertions hold:*

(I) for every atom x of $\mathcal{B}$, $s(x) = \{\uparrow x\}$ is an atom of $\mathcal{B}^c$;
(II) every atom of $\mathcal{B}^c$ is a meet of elements of W^s;
(III) s is a Boolean homomorphism.

Let $\Delta = \langle \mathcal{B}, (f_P)_{P \subseteq PAR} \rangle$ be an information algebra and let $\mathcal{B}^c$ be the canonical extension of $\mathcal{B}$. To every operator f_P, $P \subseteq PAR$, we assign an operator f_P^c on $\mathcal{P}(U_\mathcal{B})$ referred to as a canonical extension of f_P. The operators f_P^c are defined by cases depending on the type of the operator f_P. For every $X \subseteq U_\mathcal{B}$ we define:

⋆ if f_P is a modal operator, then $f_P^c(X) \overset{\text{def}}{=} sup(\{inf(\{s(f_P(x)) : x \in F\}) : F \in X\})$;
⋆ if f_P is a sufficiency operator, then $f_P^c(X) \overset{\text{def}}{=} inf(\{sup(\{s(f_P(x)) : x \in F\}) : F \in X\})$;
⋆ if f_P is a dual modal operator, then $f_P^c(X) \overset{\text{def}}{=} inf(\{sup(\{s(f_P(x)) : x \notin F\}) : F \notin X\})$;
⋆ if f_P is a dual sufficiency operator, then $f_P^c(X) \overset{\text{def}}{=} sup(\{inf(\{s(f_P(x)) : x \notin F\}) : F \notin X\})$.

The following lemma provides a relationship between relative operators and their canonical extensions.

Lemma 15.6.3. *For every information operator f_P, $P \subseteq PAR$, the following hold:*

(I) if f_P is a modal [resp. dual modal, sufficiency, dual sufficiency] operator, then f_P^c is a complete modal [resp. dual modal, sufficiency, dual sufficiency] operator;
(II) $(\,^\neg f_P)^c = {}^\neg (f_P^c)$;
(III) $(f_P^\neg)^c = (f_P^c)^\neg$;
(IV) $(f_P^d)^c = (f_P^c)^d$.

Proof. By way of example we prove condition (III) for a sufficiency operator. If f_P is a sufficiency operator, then $f_P^\neg$ is a dual modal operator and we have: $(f_P^\neg)^c(X) = inf(\{sup(\{s(f_P^\neg(x)) : x \notin F\}) : F \notin X\}) = inf(\{sup(\{s(f_P(-x)) : x \notin F\}) : F \notin X\}) = inf(\{sup(\{s(f_P(-x)) : x \in -F\}) : F \in -X\}) = inf(\{sup(\{s(f_P(x)) : x \in F\}) : F \in -X\}) = f_P^c(-X) = (f_P^c)^\neg(X)$.   *Q.E.D.*

Lemma 15.6.4. *For every Boolean algebra $\mathcal{B} = \langle W, +, \cdot, -, 1, 0 \rangle$ the following assertions hold:*

(I) if f and g are modal operators on $\mathcal{B}$ and $h(x) = f(x) + g(x)$ for every $x \in W$, then $h^c(x) = f^c(x) + g^c(x)$ for every x of $\mathcal{B}^c$;

(II) if f and g are sufficiency operators on $\mathcal{B}$ and $h(x) = f(x) \cdot g(x)$ for every $x \in W$, then $h^c(x) = f^c(x) \cdot g^c(x)$ for every x of $\mathcal{B}^c$;

(III) if f and g are conjugated modal operators on $\mathcal{B}$, then so are f^c and g^c on $\mathcal{B}^c$.

Let $\Delta = \langle \mathcal{B}, (f_P)_{P \subseteq PAR} \rangle$ be an information algebra. The *canonical extension* of Δ is the algebra $\Delta^c = \langle \mathcal{B}^c, (f_P^c)_{P \subseteq PAR} \rangle$. We have the following representation theorem for the canonical extensions of information algebras.

Theorem 15.6.1. *For every information algebra $\Delta = \langle \mathcal{B}, (f_P)_{P \subseteq PAR} \rangle$, the following assertions hold:*

(I) if $\Delta \in$ MOA, then Δ^c is isomorphic to $\langle |\Delta^c| \rangle$;

(II) if $\Delta \in$ SUA, then Δ^c is isomorphic to $[[|\Delta^c|]]$;

(III) if $\Delta \in$ DMOA, then Δ^c is isomorphic to $[|\Delta^c|^d]$;

(IV) if $\Delta \in$ DSUA, then Δ^c is isomorphic to $\langle \langle |\Delta^c|^d \rangle \rangle$.

The theorem follows from Lemmas 15.6.3(I), 15.4.3, and 15.4.4. The theorem says that the canonical extensions of information algebras are isomorphic to the complex algebras of their canonical frames.

Theorem 15.6.2. *If $\Delta \in$ MOA $\cup$ SUA $\cup$ DMOA $\cup$ DSUA, then Δ is isomorphic to a subalgebra of Δ^c.*

This theorem is a direct consequence of the respective definitions and Lemma 15.6.2. From Theorems 15.6.1 and 15.6.2 we deduce that if $\Delta \in$ MOA $\cup$ SUA $\cup$ DMOA $\cup$ DSUA, then Δ is isomorphic to a complex algebra.

15.7 Identities of Information Algebras

Let P be a set of standard parameter expressions and let $\Sigma = \{+, \cdot, -\} \cup \{f_A : A \in P\}$ be a signature as understood in Sect. 1.5. We define a set T of Σ-information terms as follows. Let T_0 be a set of individual variables and $T_c = \{0, 1\}$. Then T is the smallest set that includes $T_0 \cup T_c$, and if $s, t \in T$ and $A \in P$, then $-t, t + s, t \cdot s, f_A(t) \in T$. Let $\Delta = \langle \mathcal{B}, (f_P)_{P \subseteq PAR} \rangle$ be an information algebra and let $t(x_1, \ldots, x_n)$, $n \geq 0$, be a Σ-information term such that all variables appearing in t are among $x_1, \ldots, x_n$. Let m be a P-meaning function $m : P \to PAR$. We define the mapping $t^{\Delta,m} : W^n \to W$ as follows:

* if $t = x$, then $t^{\Delta,m}(a) \overset{\text{def}}{=} a$;

* if $t \in T_c$, then $t^{\Delta,m} \overset{\text{def}}{=}$ the respective element of $\mathcal{B}$;

$\star$ if $t \in T$ and $f_A \in \Sigma$,

   then $(f_A(t))^{\Delta,m}(a_1, \ldots, a_n) \overset{\text{def}}{=} f_{m(A)}(t^{\Delta,m}(a_1, \ldots, a_n))$;

$\star$ $(t_1 + t_2)^{\Delta,m}(a_1, \ldots, a_n) \overset{\text{def}}{=} t_1^{\Delta,m}(a_1, \ldots, a_n) + t_2^{\Delta,m}(a_1, \ldots, a_n)$;

$\star$ $(t_1 \cdot t_2)^{\Delta,m}(a_1, \ldots, a_n) \overset{\text{def}}{=} t_1^{\Delta,m}(a_1, \ldots, a_n) \cdot t_2^{\Delta,m}(a_1, \ldots, a_n)$;

$\star$ $(-t)^{\Delta,m}(a_1, \ldots, a_n) \overset{\text{def}}{=} -t^{\Delta,m}(a_1, \ldots, a_n)$.

By an *information term* we mean a Σ-information term for some set P of standard parameter expressions. Let t be an information term; by $\neg t$ [resp. $t^\neg$, t^d] we denote the term obtained from t by replacing every occurence of an operator f_A by $\neg f_A$ [resp. $f_A^\neg$, f_A^d]. An identity $t_1(x_1, \ldots, x_n) = t_2(x_1, \ldots, x_n)$, $n \geq 0$, is true in Δ if for every choice of $a_1, \ldots, a_n \in W$ and for every P-meaning function $m : P \to PAR$, we have $t_1^{\Delta,m}(a_1, \ldots, a_n) = t_2^{\Delta,m}(a_1, \ldots, a_n)$. Let C be a class of information algebras. Identities α and β are C-equivalent $\overset{\text{def}}{\Leftrightarrow}$ for every algebra $\Delta \in$ C, α is true in Δ iff β is true in Δ. Clearly, if D $\subseteq$ C and α and β are C-equivalent, then α and β are D-equivalent.

The set T_{spos} of *strictly positive* Σ-*information terms* is the smallest set of information terms such that:

$\star$ $T_0 \cup T_c \subseteq T_{spos}$;

$\star$ if $t, s \in T_{spos}$, $A \in$ P, then $t + s, t \cdot s, f_A(t) \in T_{spos}$.

An identity $t_1 = t_2$ is a *strictly positive* identity if the terms t_1 and t_2 are strictly positive.

The set T_{pos} of *positive information terms* consists of the information terms t such that every occurrence of an individual variable in t is within the scope of an even number of complement symbols.

The set T_s of *special information terms* is defined as follows:

$\star$ $T_0 \subseteq T_s$;

$\star$ if $t \in T_s$, $A \in$ P, then $f_A^d(t) \in T_s$.

Let $t, t_1, \ldots, t_n$, $n \geq 1$, be terms and let all the variables appearing in t be among $x_1, \ldots, x_n$. By $t(t_1, \ldots, t_n)$ we denote a term obtained from t by substituting t_i for x_i for every $i = 1, \ldots, n$. A *Sahlqvist information term* is an information term of the form $t(s_1, \ldots, s_n, -t_1, \ldots, -t_m)$, where $n, m \geq 1$, $t \in T_{spos}$, $s_i \in T_s$ for every $i = 1, \ldots, n$, and $t_j \in T_{pos}$ for every $j = 1, \ldots, m$. An identity of the form $t = 0$, where t is a Sahlqvist information term, is said to be a *Sahlqvist identity*.

Let $\Delta = \langle \mathcal{B}, (f_P)_{P \subseteq PAR} \rangle$ be an information algebra. By $\neg \Delta$ [resp. $\Delta^\neg$, Δ^d] we mean the algebra $\langle \mathcal{B}, (\neg f_P)_{P \subseteq PAR} \rangle$ [resp. $\langle \mathcal{B}, (f_P^\neg)_{P \subseteq PAR} \rangle$, $\langle \mathcal{B}, (f_P^d)_{P \subseteq PAR} \rangle$].

Lemma 15.7.1. *For every information algebra* $\Delta = \langle \mathcal{B}, (f_P)_{P \subseteq PAR} \rangle$, *the following conditions are satisfied:*

(I) $\Delta \in$ MOA *[resp. DMOA] iff* $\Delta^\neg \in$ DSUA *[resp. SUA];*

(II) $\Delta \in$ MOA *[resp.* DMOA*] iff* $\neg\Delta \in$ SUA *[resp.* DSUA*];*
(III) $\Delta \in$ MOA *[resp.* SUA*] iff* $\Delta^d \in$ DMOA *[resp.* DSUA*];*
(IV) $(\Delta^{\neg})^{\neg} = \Delta;$
(V) $\neg(\neg\Delta) = \Delta.$

Proof. The proof follows easily from Lemma 15.2.1.   Q.E.D.

Lemma 15.7.2. *For all information terms t_1 and t_2, and for every information algebra $\Delta = \langle \mathcal{B}, (f_P)_{P \subseteq PAR} \rangle$, the following conditions are equivalent:*

(I) $t_1 = t_2$ *is true in* $\Delta;$
(II) $t_1^{\neg} = t_2^{\neg}$ *is true in* $\Delta^{\neg};$
(III) $\neg t_1 = \neg t_2$ *is true in* $\neg\Delta;$
(IV) $t_1^d = t_2^d$ *is true in* $\Delta^d.$

Proof. By way of example we prove the part (I) implies (II). For every x in the universe of $\mathcal{B}$ and for every $P \subseteq PAR$, we have $-(-f_P(x)) = f_P(x)$ which entails $t^{\Delta,m} =^{\neg} t^{\neg\Delta,m}$ for every meaning function m. The analogous argument proves all the remaining parts.   Q.E.D.

15.8 Closure Under Canonical Extensions

Let C be a class of information algebras. An *identity* α is said to be C-*canonical* if for every algebra $\Delta \in$ C, if α is true in Δ, then α is true in Δ^c. Observe that we have the following fact.

Lemma 15.8.1. *Let* C *and* D *be classes of information algebras such that* D $\subseteq$ C. *Then for every identity α, if α is* C-*canonical, then α is* D-*canonical.*

A *class* C of information algebras is *canonical* if it is closed under the appropriate canonical extension, i.e. for every information algebra Δ, if $\Delta \in$ C, then $\Delta^c \in$ C.

The following theorem is a reformulation of some of the preservation results from the classical theory of Boolean algebras with operators.

Theorem 15.8.1.

(I) Every strictly positive identity is MOA-*canonical.*
(II) Every Sahlqvist identity is MOA-*canonical.*

Lemma 15.8.2. *For every information algebra Δ the following conditions are satisfied:*

(I) $(\Delta^c)^{\neg} = (\Delta^{\neg})^c;$
(II) $\neg(\Delta^c) = (\neg\Delta)^c;$
(III) $(\Delta^c)^d = (\Delta^d)^c.$

The proof follows from Lemma 15.6.3.

The following theorem shows how canonicity results with respect to various classes of information algebras are related.

Theorem 15.8.2. *For all information terms t_1 and t_2 the following conditions are equivalent:*

(I) $t_1 = t_2$ is MOA-canonical [resp. DMOA-canonical];
(II) $t_1^\neg = t_2^\neg$ is DSUA-canonical [resp. SUA-canonical];
(III) $\neg t_1 = \neg t_2$ is SUA-canonical [resp. DSUA-canonical];
(IV) $t_1^d = t_2^d$ is DMOA-canonical [resp. DSUA-canonical].

Proof. By way of example we prove that (I) implies (III). Assume that $t_1 = t_2$ is MOA-canonical and $\neg t_1 = \neg t_2$ is true in a SUA algebra Δ'. By Lemma 15.7.1(II,V), Δ can be presented in the form $\neg\Delta$ for some $\Delta \in$ MOA. So if $t_1 = t_2$ is true in MOA, then $t_1 = t_2$ is true in Δ^c. By Lemma 15.7.2(III), $\neg t_1 = \neg t_2$ is true in $\neg(\Delta^c)$. By Lemma 15.8.2(II), $\neg t_1 = \neg t_2$ is true in $(\neg\Delta)^c = (\Delta')^c$. The proofs of the converse implication and the remaining equivalences are similar. *Q.E.D.*

The following theorem presents some canonical classes of information algebras.

Theorem 15.8.3. *The following classes of information algebras are canonical:*

(I) AW-IND, AW-SIM-TOT, AW-SIM, AW-IN;
(II) AS-DIV, AS-RORT, AS-RLNIM.

Proof. (I) Observe that all the axioms of WMOA algebras are strictly positive identities, so by Theorem 15.8.1(I) they are canonical with respect to every class of (I). In the following discussion we will drop indices of relative operators. The axioms of the form $x \leq f(x)$ are MOA-equivalent to the identities of the form $x \cdot -f(x) = 0$. Since x is a special term and $f(x)$ is a positive term, $x \cdot -f(x)$ is a Sahlqvist term. By Theorem 15.8.1(II), the respective axiom is MOA-canonical and by Lemma 15.8.1 it is AW-IND-canonical, AW-SIM-TOT-canonical, and AW-IN-canonical. By similar reasoning we can show the appropriate canonicity of the axioms of the form $x \cdot f(1) \leq f(x)$, $f(f(x)) \leq f(x)$, $f(g^d(x)) \leq x$, and $g(f^d(x)) \leq x$. By Lemma 15.2.6 the axioms of the form $x \leq f^d(f(x))$ say that f is an autoconjugated operator. Hence, by Lemma 15.6.4(III), the axiom is AW-SIM-canonical.

(II) To prove this part we will use Theorem 15.8.2. By way of example we show that $f(x) \leq -x$ is SUA-canonical. Observe that $-f(x) \cdot x = 0$ is a Sahlqvist identity, and hence it is MOA-canonical. By Theorem 15.8.2(III), $(-(-f(x))) \cdot x = 0$ is SUA-canonical. This identity is SUA-equivalent to $f(x) \cdot x = 0$ which, in turn, is SUA-equivalent to $f(x) \leq -x$. By Lemma 15.8.1, the axioms $f(x) \leq -x$ are AS-DIV-canonical and AS-RLNIM-canonical. For the remaining axioms the proofs are similar. *Q.E.D.*

The canonicity of the remaining classes of information algebras is problematic, since the identities that hold for the atoms of an algebra Δ do not necessarily hold for the atoms of the algebra Δ^c.

15.9 Relationship Between Information Algebras and the Frames Determined by Their Canonical Extensions

In this section we present relationships between some classes of information algebras and the frames determined by the canonical extensions of these algebras. These results extend the results of Sect. 15.4 to the information algebras that are not necessarily complete.

Lemma 15.9.1. *Let $\Delta = \langle \mathcal{B}, (f_P)_{P \subseteq PAR} \rangle$ be an information algebra and let $\Delta^c = \langle \mathcal{B}^c, (f_P^c)_{P \subseteq PAR} \rangle$ be its canonical extension. Then for all $F, F' \in U_\mathcal{B}$, the following conditions hold:*

(I)   if f_P is a modal operator, then $\langle F, F' \rangle \in |f_P^c|$ iff for every $x \in F'$, $f_P(x) \in F$;

(II) if f_P is a sufficiency operator, then $\langle F, F' \rangle \in |f_P^c|$ iff there is an $x \in F'$ such that $f_P(x) \in F$;

(III) if f_P is a dual modal operator, then $\langle F, F' \rangle \in |f_P^c|^d$ iff for every $x \notin F'$, $f_P(x) \notin F$;

(IV) if f_P is a dual sufficiency operator, then $\langle F, F' \rangle \in |f_P^c|^d$ iff there is an $x \notin F'$ such that $f_P(x) \notin F$.

Proof. By way of example we prove condition (III). We have $\langle F, F' \rangle \in |f_P^c|^d$ iff $F \notin f_P^c(-\{F'\})$ iff $F \notin inf(\{sup(\{s(f_P(x)) : x \notin t\})\} : t \notin -\{F'\})$ iff $F \notin sup(\{s(f_P(x)) : x \notin F'\})$ iff for all $x \notin F'$, $F \notin s(f_P(x))$ iff for all $x \notin F'$, $f_P(x) \notin F$.   *Q.E.D.*

Lemma 15.9.2. *Let $\Delta = \langle \mathcal{B}, (f_P)_{P \subseteq PAR} \rangle$ be an information algebra. Then the following conditions hold:*

(I)   if $\Delta \in$ MOA, then $f_P(x) = 1$ iff for every $F \in U_\mathcal{B}$ there is an $F' \in U_\mathcal{B}$ such that $x \in F'$ and $\langle F, F' \rangle \in |f_P^c|$;

(II) if $\Delta \in$ SUA, then $f_P(x) = 1$ iff for every $F \in U_\mathcal{B}$ and for every $F' \in U_\mathcal{B}$, if $x \in F'$, then $\langle F, F' \rangle \in |f_P^c|$;

(III) if $\Delta \in$ DMOA, then $f_P(x) = 1$ iff for every $F \in U_\mathcal{B}$ and for every $F' \in U_\mathcal{B}$, if $\langle F, F' \rangle \in |f_P^c|^d$, then $x \in F'$;

(IV) if $\Delta \in$ DSUA, then $f_P(x) = 1$ iff for every $F \in U_\mathcal{B}$ there is an $F' \in U_\mathcal{B}$ such that $\langle F, F' \rangle \notin |f_P^c|^d$ and $x \notin F'$.

Proof. By way of example we show that condition (II) holds. In the proof we use the complete coadditivity of sufficiency operators f_P^c. Observe that $f_P(x) = 1$ iff $s(f_P(x)) = U_\mathcal{B}$ iff $f_P^c(s(x)) = U_\mathcal{B}$ iff $f_P^c(sup(\{\{F'\} : F' \in$

$s(x)\})) = U_B$ iff $inf(\{f_P^c(\{F'\}) : F' \in s(x)\}) = U_B$. In other words, for every $F \in U_B$, $F \in f_P^c(s(x))$ iff for every $F \in U_B$, and for every $F' \in s(x)$ we have $F \in f_P^c(\{F'\})$ iff for every $F \in U_B$, and for every $F' \in U_B$, if $x \in F'$, then $\langle F, F' \rangle \in |f_P^c|$. $Q.E.D.$

Lemma 15.9.3. *Let $\Delta = \langle \mathcal{B}, (f_P)_{P \subseteq PAR} \rangle$ be an information algebra. Then the following conditions hold:*

(I) if $\Delta \in$ WMOA $\cup$ SDSUA, then $f_\emptyset^c(X) = \emptyset$ for every $X \subseteq U_B$;
(II) if $\Delta \in$ WDMOA $\cup$ SSUA, then $f_\emptyset^c(X) = U_B$ for every $X \subseteq U_B$.

Proof. We show condition (II) for a SSUA algebra; that is we assume that $f_\emptyset(x) = 1$. Then for every $F \in U_B$, we have $f_\emptyset^c(\{F\}) = sup(\{s(f_\emptyset(x)) : x \in F\}) = sup(\{s(1) : x \in F\}) = s(1) = U_B$. $Q.E.D.$

Theorem 15.9.1. *Let $\Delta = \langle \mathcal{B}, (f_P)_{P \subseteq PAR} \rangle$ be an information algebra. Then the following conditions hold:*

(I) if $\Delta \in$ MOA, then Δ is an AW-algebra iff $|\Delta^c| \in$ FW;
(II) if $\Delta \in$ DMOA, then Δ is an AW-algebra iff $|\Delta^c|^d \in$ FW;
(III) if $\Delta \in$ SUA, then Δ is an AS-algebra iff $|\Delta^c| \in$ FS;
(IV) if $\Delta \in$ DSUA, then Δ is an AS-algebra iff $|\Delta^c|^d \in$ FS.

Proof. We show condition (IV). $|\Delta^c|^d$ is a frame with strong relations iff the following conditions are satisfied:

(i) $|f_\emptyset^c|^d = U_B \times U_B$;
(ii) $|f_{P \cup Q}^c|^d = |f_P^c|^d \cap |f_Q^c|^d$.

By Lemma 15.9.3(I) we have $\langle F, F' \rangle \in |f_\emptyset^c|^d$ iff $F \notin f_\emptyset^c(-\{F'\})$ iff $F \notin \emptyset$.
Similarly, using Lemma 15.9.1, we get $\langle F, F' \rangle \in |f_{P \cup Q}^c|^d$ iff $F \notin f_{P \cup Q}^c(-\{F'\})$ iff $F \notin f_P^c(-\{F'\}) \cup f_Q^c(-\{F'\})$ iff $F \notin f_P^c(-\{F'\})$ and $F \notin f_Q^c(-\{F'\})$ iff $\langle F, F' \rangle \in |f_P^c|^d \cap |f_Q^c|^d$. $Q.E.D.$

It is an open problem whether similar results hold for SMOA, SDMOA, WSUA, WDSUA. Now we consider canonical extensions of complex algebras of relative frames.

Theorem 15.9.2. *Let $F = \langle W, (\mathcal{R}_P)_{P \subseteq PAR} \rangle$ be a relative frame. Then we have:*

(I) $\langle x, y \rangle \in \mathcal{R}_P$ iff $\langle \uparrow \{x\}, \uparrow \{y\} \rangle \in |\langle \mathcal{R}_P \rangle^c|$;
(II) $\langle x, y \rangle \in \mathcal{R}_P$ iff $\langle \uparrow \{x\}, \uparrow \{y\} \rangle \in |[[\mathcal{R}_P]]^c|$;
(III) $\langle x, y \rangle \in \mathcal{R}_P$ iff $\langle \uparrow \{x\}, \uparrow \{y\} \rangle \in |[\mathcal{R}_P]^c|^d$;
(IV) $\langle x, y \rangle \in \mathcal{R}_P$ iff $\langle \uparrow \{x\}, \uparrow \{y\} \rangle \in |\langle \langle \mathcal{R}_P \rangle \rangle^c|^d$.

Proof. (I) By definition $\uparrow \{x\} = \{X \subseteq W : x \in X\}$ and it is a maximal filter in the Boolean algebra of the subsets of W. By Lemma 15.9.1(I) we have $\langle \uparrow \{x\}, \uparrow \{y\}\rangle \in |\langle \mathcal{R}_P \rangle^c|$ iff for every $Z \subseteq W$, if $Z \in \uparrow \{y\}$, then $\langle \mathcal{R}_P \rangle Z \in \uparrow \{x\}$ iff (i) for every $Z \subseteq W$, if $y \in Z$, then $x \in \langle \mathcal{R}_P \rangle Z$. In particular, for $Z = \{y\}$ we get $x \in \langle \mathcal{R}_P \rangle \{y\}$, which is equivalent to: there is a $t \in W$ such that $\langle x, t \rangle \in \mathcal{R}_P$ and $t \in \{y\}$. We conclude that $\langle x, y \rangle \in \mathcal{R}_P$. Conversely, if $\langle x, y \rangle \in \mathcal{R}_P$, then (i) is true.

(II) By Lemma 15.9.1(II), we have $\langle \uparrow \{x\}, \uparrow \{y\}\rangle \in |[[\mathcal{R}_P]]^c|$ iff there is $Z \in \uparrow \{y\}$ such that $[[\mathcal{R}_P]]Z \in \uparrow \{x\}$ iff (ii) there is a $Z \subseteq W$ such that $y \in Z$ and $x \in [[\mathcal{R}_P]]Z$. The latter means that for every $t \in W$, if $t \in Z$, then $\langle x, t \rangle \in \mathcal{R}_P$. In particular, taking $t = y$, we get $\langle x, y \rangle \in \mathcal{R}_P$. Conversely, if $\langle x, y \rangle \in \mathcal{R}_P$, then (ii) is true.

(III) By Lemma 15.9.1(III) we have $\langle \uparrow \{x\}, \uparrow \{y\}\rangle \in |[\mathcal{R}_P]^c|^d$ iff for all $Z \subseteq W$, if $Z \notin \uparrow \{y\}$, then $[\mathcal{R}_P]Z \notin \uparrow \{x\}$ iff (iii) for every $Z \subseteq W$, if $y \notin Z$, then $x \notin [\mathcal{R}_P]Z$. In particular, for $Z = -\{y\}$ we get: there is a $t \in W$ such that $\langle x, t \rangle \in \mathcal{R}_P$ and $t \notin -\{y\}$, which yields $\langle x, y \rangle \in \mathcal{R}_P$. Conversely, if $\langle x, y \rangle \in \mathcal{R}_P$, then (iii) is true.

The proof of (IV) is similar.   Q.E.D.

It follows that there are one-to-one correspondences between a frame and the canonical frames derived from its complex algebras.

15.10 Relationship Between Information Logics and Information Algebras

Let $\mathcal{L}$ be a Rare-logic whose modal connectives are $\langle A \rangle$ [resp. $[A]$, $[[A]]$, $\langle\langle A \rangle\rangle$] for parameter expressions A, and whose $\mathcal{L}$-frames are of the form $\langle W, (\mathcal{R}_p)_{p \subseteq PAR}\rangle$. Any formula ϕ of the language of $\mathcal{L}$ can be viewed as an information term. Namely, the Boolean connectives of ϕ are treated as Boolean operators of information algebras and the modal connectives of ϕ play the role of the additional unary information operators of these algebras. We denote the respective term by t_ϕ.

In analogy to the relationship between modal logics and modal algebras, relationships between information logics and information algebras are of the following two kinds.

First of all, it is easy to see that we have the following theorem.

Theorem 15.10.1. *Let $\mathcal{L}$ be a Rare-logic as above and let F be an $\mathcal{L}$-frame. For every formula ϕ of $\mathrm{LAN}(\mathcal{L})$, the following conditions are equivalent:*

(I) $F \models \phi$;
(II) $t_\phi = 1$ is true in $\langle F \rangle$ [resp. $[F]$, $[[F]]$, $\langle\langle F \rangle\rangle$].

Second, given an information algebra Δ and a term t of Δ such that $t = 1$ is true in Δ, we wish to verify whether $t = 1$ is true in the respective complex algebra of $|\Delta|$ or $|\Delta|^d$. Equivalently, if t is of the form t_ϕ for some formula ϕ of a Rare-logic, the question is whether truth of t_ϕ in Δ implies $|\Delta| \models \phi$ [resp. $|\Delta|^d \models \phi$]. Due to Theorem 15.6.1 and Theorem 15.10.1 the latter problem is equivalent to the problem of preservation of the respective identities by the canonical extensions. A systematic exploration of these problems in connection with information algebras requires further studies.

15.11 Notes

Modal algebras are introduced in [JT51] under the name Boolean algebras with operators (BAO). The results concerning MOA algebras are reformulations of the results presented there. Further development of the BAO theory can be found in [Gol89] (see also [Gol00]). Extensions of the notion of BAO to distributive lattices with operators is presented in [GJ94] and [SS00a, SS00b]. Sufficiency and mixed algebras are introduced in [DO01a, DO01b]. In these papers the algebras are defined without assuming that the underlying Boolean algebra is complete and atomic. The axioms referring to the atoms are replaced by the corresponding conditions on the canonical extensions of the respective Boolean algebras. Boolean algebras with relative operators are introduced in [DO01b]. Information algebras originated in [Orło95]. The classes defined there correspond to SMOA, WMOA, SDSUA, and WDSUA. The further development of their theory can be found in [SI98, SI01]. This chapter contains all the results from these papers. We also follow the style and notation of these papers. Algebras similar to AS-IND and AS-SIM are presented in [Com93] and [Pom94], respectively. A discussion of the preservation of identities holding in a Boolean algebra under forming of the canonical extension can be found in [KM82, Gol89, Jón94].

Lemma 15.6.4(I) is proved in [JT51], (II) is proved in [DO01b], and (III) is proved in [Jón82]. Theorem 15.8.1(II) in the context of modal logics is proved in [Sah75], and it is reformulated in the context of Boolean algebras with operators in [RV95]. Theorem 15.8.1(I) is proved in [Jón94].

References

[AB01] C. Areces and P. Blackburn. Bringing them all together. *Journal of Logic and Computation*, 11(5):657–669, 2001. (Cited on page 115)

[ABM00] C. Areces, P. Blackburn, and M. Marx. Complexity of hybrid temporal logics. *Journal of the IGPL*, 8(5):653–679, 2000. Available via http://www3.oup.co.uk/igpl/contents/ on WWW. (Cited on page 136)

[AHU74] A. Aho, J. Hopcroft, and J. Ullman. *The Design and Analysis of Computer Algorithms*. Addison-Wesley, Reading, MA, 1974. (Cited on page 136)

[ANB98] H. Andréka, I. Németi, and J. van Benthem. Modal languages and bounded fragments of predicate logic. *Journal of Philosophical Logic*, 27(3):217–274, 1998. (Cited on page 241)

[Are00] C. Areces. *Logic Engineering: The Case of Description and Hybrid Logics*. PhD thesis, University of Amsterdam, 2000. (Cited on page 115)

[Arm74] W. Armstrong. Dependency structures of database relationships. In *IFIP'74*, pages 580–583, 1974. (Cited on page 68)

[AT89] D. Archangelsky and M. Taitslin. A logic for data description. In A. Meyer and M. Taitslin, editors, *Symposium on Logic Foundations of Computer Science, Pereslavl Zalessky*, pages 2–11. Lecture Notes in Computer Science, Vol. 363. Springer, Berlin, 1989. (Cited on pages 116, 192, 266)

[AT97] D. Archangelsky and M. Taitslin. A logic for information systems. *Studia Logica*, 58(1):3–16, 1997. (Cited on pages 170, 192)

[Aum76] R. Aumann. Agreeing to disagree. *Annals of Statistics*, 4(3):1236–1239, 1976. (Cited on page 215)

[Bal96a] Ph. Balbiani. A modal logic for data analysis. In W. Penczek and A. Szalas, editors, *21st Symposium on Mathematical Foundations of Computer Sciences, Krakow, Poland*, pages 167–179. Lecture Notes in Computer Science, Vol. 1113. Springer, Berlin, 1996. (Cited on pages 67, 116, 136, 241)

[Bal96b] Ph. Balbiani. Modal logics with relative accessibility relations. In D. Gabbay and H. J. Ohlbach, editors, *Conference on Formal and Applied Practical Reasoning, Bonn, Germany*, pages 29–41. Lecture Notes in Artificial Intelligence, Vol. 1085. Springer, Berlin, 1996. (Cited on pages 136, 241)

[Bal98] Ph. Balbiani. Axiomatization of logics based on Kripke models with relative accessibility relations. In *[Oe98a]*, pages 553–578, 1998. (Cited on pages 67, 116, 136, 170, 215, 216, 241)

[Bal01] Ph. Balbiani. Emptiness relations in property systems. In H. de Swart, editor, *6th International Workshop on Relational Methods in Computer Science - RelMiCS'6, Oisterwijk, The Netherlands*, pages 47–61, 2001. (Cited on page 67)

[Ban97] M. Banerjee. Rough sets and 3-valued Łukasiewicz logic. *Fundamenta Informaticae*, 31:213–220, 1997. (Cited on page 353)

[BBR58]   A. Białynicki-Birula and H. Rasiowa. On constructible falsity in the constructive logic with strong negation. *Colloquium Mathematicum*, 6:287–310, 1958.   (Cited on page 353)

[BC93]   M. Banerjee and M. Chakraborty. Rough algebra. *Bulletin of the Polish Academy of Sciences, Mathematics*, 41(4):293–297, 1993.   (Cited on page 354)

[BC96]   M. Banerjee and M. Chakraborty. Rough sets through algebraic logic. *Fundamenta Informaticae*, 28(3–4):211–221, 1996.   (Cited on page 353)

[BD74]   R. Balbes and Ph. Dwinger. *Distributive Lattices*. University of Missouri Press, Columbia, MO, 1974.   (Cited on page 12)

[Ben84]   J. van Benthem. Correspondence theory. In D. Gabbay and F. Günthner, editors, *Handbook of Philosophical Logic, Vol. II*, pages 167–247. Reidel, Dordrecht, 1984.   (Cited on pages 90, 136)

[Ben85]   J. van Benthem. *Modal logic and Classical Logic*. Bibliopolis, Naples, 1985.   (Cited on pages 136, 266)

[BG00]   T. Burns and A. Gomolińska. The theory of socially embedded games: the mathematics of social relationships, rule complexes, and action modalities. *Quality and Quantity: International Journal of Methodology*, 34(4):379–406, 2000.   (Cited on page 68)

[BH83]   J. van Benthem and L. Humberstone. The logic of non-contingency. *Notre Dame Journal of Formal Logic*, 24(4):426–430, 1983.   (Cited on page 215)

[Bir84]   G. Birkhoff. *Lattice Theory*. American Mathematical Society Colloquium Publications, Providence, RI, 3rd edition, 1984.   (Cited on page 12)

[BK95]   M. Białasik and B. Konikowska. Reasoning with nondeterministic specifications. Technical Report 795, Institute of Computer Science, Polish Academy of Sciences, 1995.   (Cited on page 169)

[Bla90]   P. Blackburn. *Nominal Tense Logic and Other Sorted Intensional Frameworks*. PhD thesis, University of Edinburgh, 1990.   (Cited on page 115)

[Bla93]   P. Blackburn. Nominal tense logic. *Notre Dame Journal of Formal Logic*, 34(1):56–83, 1993.   (Cited on page 115)

[Bla00a]   P. Blackburn. Internalizing labelled deduction. *Journal of Logic and Computation*, 10(1):137–168, 2000.   (Cited on page 170)

[Bla00b]   P. Blackburn. Representation, reasoning, and relational structures: a hybrid logic manifesto. *Logic Journal of the IGPL*, 8(3):339–365, 2000.   (Cited on page 115)

[BO98]   W. Buszkowski and E. Orłowska. Indiscernibility-based formalization of dependencies in information systems. In *[Oe98a]*, pages 293–315, 1998.   (Cited on page 68)

[BO99]   Ph. Balbiani and E. Orlowska. A hierarchy of modal logics with relative accessibility relations. *Journal of Applied Non-Classical Logics, special issue in the Memory of George Gargov*, 9:303–328, 1999.   (Cited on pages 116, 136, 241)

[Boh58]   N. Bohr. Quantum physics and philosophy: causality and complementarity. In R. Klibanski, editor, *Philosophy of the Mid-Century*, pages 308–314. La Nuova Italia, Florence, 1958.   (Cited on page 67)

[Bon94]   Z. Bonikowski. Algebraic structures of rough sets. In *Rough Sets, Fuzzy Sets and Knowledge Discovery (RSKD'93). Workshops in Computing*, pages 242–247. Springer and British Computer Society, Berlin, London, 1994.   (Cited on page 354)

[Bro96]   M. Brown. A logic of comparative obligation. *Studia Logica*, 57:117–137, 1996.   (Cited on page 68)

[BRV01]   P. Blackburn, M. de Rijke, and Y. Venema. *Modal Logic*. Cambridge University Press, 2001.   (Cited on pages 115, 292)

[BS81] S. Burris and H. R. Sankappanavar. *A Course in Universal Algebra.* Graduate Texts in Mathematics. Springer, Heidelberg, 1981. (Cited on page 12)

[BS84] R. Bull and K. Segerberg. Basic modal logic. In D. Gabbay and F. Günthner, editors, *Handbook of Philosophical Logic, Vol. II*, pages 1–88. Reidel, Dordrecht, 1984. (Cited on page 115)

[BS01] F. Baader and U. Sattler. An overview of tableau algorithms for description logics. *Studia Logica*, 69:5–40, 2001. (Cited on page 292)

[Bul70] R. Bull. An approach to tense logic. *Theoria*, 36(3):282–300, 1970. (Cited on page 115)

[BV01] Ph. Balbiani and D. Vakarelov. First order characterization and modal analysis of indiscernibility and complementarity in information systems. In *ECSQARU'01*, pages 772–781. Lecture Notes in Computer Science, Vol. 2143. Springer, Berlin, 2001. (Cited on page 192)

[Cat97] G. Cattaneo. Generalized rough sets. Preclusivity fuzzy-intuitionistic (BZ) lattices. *Studia Logica*, 58:47–77, 1997. (Cited on page 354)

[Cat98] G. Cattaneo. Abstract approximation spaces for rough theories. In *[Pe98]*, pages 59–98, 1998. (Cited on page 354)

[CCM97] S. Cerrito and M. Cialdea Mayer. A polynomial translation of S4 into T and contraction-free tableaux for S4. *Logic Journal of the IGPL*, 5(2):287–300, 1997. Available via http://www3.oup.co.uk/igpl/contents/ on WWW. (Cited on page 292)

[CDGLN01] D. Calvanese, g. De Giacomo, M. Lenzerini, and D. Nardi. Reasoning in expressive description logics. In A. Robinson and A. Voronkov, editors, *Handbook of Automated Reasoning*, pages 1581–1634. MIT Press, Cambridge, MA, 2001. (Cited on page 116)

[Cer94] C. Cerrato. Decidability by filtrations for graded normal logics (graded modalities V). *Studia Logica*, 53(1):61–73, 1994. (Cited on pages 136, 191)

[CG69] C. Chen and G. Grätzer. Stone lattices I. *Canadian Journal of Mathematics*, 21:884–894, 1969. (Cited on page 353)

[Cha94] Ph. Chatalic. Viewing hypothesis theories as constrained graded theories. In C. MacNish, D. Pearce, and L. Pereira, editors, *4th Workshop on Logics in Artificial Intelligence, York, UK*, pages 261–278. Lecture Notes in Artificial Intelligence, Vol. 838. Springer, Berlin, 1994. (Cited on page 191)

[Che92] A. Chemicka. Elementary properties of knowledge operators (in Polish), 1992. Master's thesis, Department of Mathematics, University of Warsaw. (Cited on pages 89, 352)

[Chu56] A. Church. *Introduction to Mathematical Logic: Part I*. Princeton University Press, NJ, 2nd edition, 1956. (Cited on page 135)

[Cie80] K. Ciesielski. Generalized threshold logic. *Bulletin of the Polish Academy of Sciences, Mathematics*, 28(5–6):219–228, 1980. (Cited on page 169)

[CK73] C. Chang and H. Keisler. *Model Theory*. North-Holland, Amsterdam, 1973. (Cited on pages 115, 136)

[CL94] C. Chen and I. Lin. The complexity of propositional modal theories and the complexity of consistency of propositional modal theories. In A. Nerode and Yu. V. Matiyasevich, editors, *3rd Conference on Logical Foundations of Computer Science, St. Petersburg*, pages 69–80. Lecture Notes in Computer Science, Vol. 813. Springer, Berlin, 1994. (Cited on page 292)

[CM77] A. Chandra and P. Merlin. Optimal implementation of conjunctive queries in relational databases. In *9th ACM Symposium on Theory of Computing*, pages 77–90, 1977. (Cited on page 135)

[CM86] K. M. Chandy and J. Misra. How processes learn. *Distributed Computing*, 1:40–52, 1986. (Cited on page 215)

[Cod70] E. Codd. A relational model for large shared data banks. *Communications of the ACM*, 13:377–387, 1970.   (Cited on page 68)

[Com91] S. Comer. An algebraic approach to the approximation of information. *Fundamenta Informaticae*, 14:492–502, 1991.   (Cited on page 353)

[Com93] S. Comer. On connections between information systems, rough sets and algebraic logic. In C. Rauszer, editor, *Algebraic Methods in Logic and Computer Science*. Banach Center Publications, Vol. 28, Warsaw, 1993.   (Cited on pages 353, 377)

[Coo71] S. Cook. The complexity of theorem-proving procedures. In *3rd Annual ACM Symposium on Theory of Computing, Shaker Heights, OH, USA*, pages 151–158, 1971.   (Cited on pages 134, 136)

[Cre67] M. Cresswell. A Henkin theorem for T. *Notre Dame Journal of Formal Logic*, 8(3):186–190, 1967.   (Cited on page 136)

[Cre88] M. Cresswell. Necessity and contingency. *Studia Logica*, 47(2):145–149, 1988.   (Cited on pages 115, 215)

[CZ97] A. Chagrov and M. Zakharyaschev. *Modal Logic*. Clarendon Press, Oxford, 1997.   (Cited on page 115)

[Dan84] R. Danecki. Nondeterministic propositional dynamic logic with intersection is decidable. In A. Skowron, editor, *5th Symposium on Computation Theory, Zaborów, Poland*, pages 34–53. Lecture Notes in Computer Science, Vol. 208. Springer, Berlin, 1984.   (Cited on page 136)

[DEG+95] D. Dubois, F. Esteva, P. García, L. Godo, and H. Prade. Similarity-based consequence relations. In C. Froidevaux and J. Kohlas, editors, *Symbolic and Quantitative Approaches to Uncertainty*, pages 171–179. Lecture Notes in Artificial Intelligence, Vol. 946. Springer, Berlin, 1995.   (Cited on page 170)

[Dem96a] S. Demri. A class of information logics with a decidable validity problem. In W. Penczek and A. Szalas, editors, *21st Symposium on Mathematical Foundations of Computer Sciences, Krakow, Poland*, pages 291–302. Lecture Notes in Computer Science, Vol. 1113. Springer, Berlin, 1996.   (Cited on pages 67, 191)

[Dem96b] S. Demri. The validity problem for the logic DALLA is decidable. *Bulletin of the Polish Academy of Sciences, Mathematics*, 44(1):79–86, 1996.   (Cited on page 266)

[Dem97a] S. Demri. A completeness proof for a logic with an alternative necessity operator. *Studia Logica*, 58(1):99–112, 1997.   (Cited on pages 67, 216)

[Dem97b] S. Demri. Extensions of modal logic S5 preserving NP-completeness. *Bulletin of the Section of Logic*, 26(2):73–84, 1997.   (Cited on page 136)

[Dem98] S. Demri. A class of decidable information logics. *Theoretical Computer Science*, 195(1):33–60, 1998.   (Cited on pages 136, 266)

[Dem99a] S. Demri. A logic with relative knowledge operators. *Journal of Logic, Language and Information*, 8(2):167–185, 1999.   (Cited on pages 136, 216, 241)

[Dem99b] S. Demri. Sequent calculi for nominal tense logics: a step towards mechanization? In N. Murray, editor, *International Conference on Theorem Proving with Analytic Tableaux and Related Methods, Saratoga Springs, USA*, pages 140–154. Lecture Notes in Artificial Intelligence, Vol. 1617. Springer, Berlin, 1999.   (Cited on page 170)

[Dem00] S. Demri. The nondeterministic information logic NIL is PSPACE-complete. *Fundamenta Informaticae*, 42(3–4):211–234, 2000.   (Cited on page 292)

[Dem02] S. Demri. A polynomial space construction of tree-like models for logics with local chains of modal connectives. *Theoretical Computer Science*, 2002. To appear.   (Cited on page 293)

[DG97] I. Düntsch and G. Gediga. Algebraic aspects of attribute dependencies in information systems. *Fundamenta Informaticae*, 29:119–133, 1997. (Cited on page 68)

[DG00a] S. Demri and D. Gabbay. On modal logics characterized by models with relative accessibility relations: Part I. *Studia Logica*, 65(3):323–353, 2000. (Cited on page 241)

[DG00b] S. Demri and D. Gabbay. On modal logics characterized by models with relative accessibility relations: Part II. *Studia Logica*, 66(3):349–384, 2000. (Cited on page 241)

[DG00c] S. Demri and R. Goré. Display calculi for logics with relative accessibility relations. *Journal of Logic, Language and Information*, 9(2):213–236, 2000. (Cited on page 216)

[DGO01] I. Düntsch, G. Gediga, and E. Orłowska. Relational attribute systems. *International Journal of Human–Computer Studies*, 55:293–309, 2001. (Cited on page 35)

[Did87] E. Diday. Introduction à l'approche symbolique en analyse des données. In *Journées Symboliques-umériques pour l'apprentissage des Connaissances à Partir des Données, Paris, France*, 1987. (Cited on page 89)

[DK98] S. Demri and B. Konikowska. Relative similarity logics are decidable: reduction to FO^2 with equality. In *8th Workshop on Logics in Artificial Intelligence, Dagsthul, Germany*, pages 279–293. Lecture Notes in Artificial Intelligence, Vol. 1489. Springer, Berlin, 1998. Available via http://lsv.ens-cachan.fr/~demri on WWW. (Cited on page 266)

[DO96] S. Demri and E. Orłowska. Logical analysis of demonic nondeterministic programs. *Theoretical Computer Science*, 166:173–202, 1996. (Cited on pages 67, 169)

[DO98a] S. Demri and E. Orłowska. Complementarity relations: reduction of decision rules and informational representability. In *[Pe98]*, pages 99–106, 1998. (Cited on pages 67, 320)

[DO98b] S. Demri and E. Orłowska. Informational representability of models for information logics. In *[Oe98b]*, pages 383–409, 1998. (Cited on page 320)

[DO00] I. Düntsch and E. Orłowska. A proof system for contact relation algebras. *Journal of Philosophical Logic*, 29:241–262, 2000. (Cited on page 169)

[DO01a] I. Düntsch and E. Orlowska. Beyond modalities: sufficiency and mixed algebras. In *[OSe01]*, pages 263–285, 2001. (Cited on page 377)

[DO01b] I. Düntsch and E. Orlowska. Boolean algebras arising from information systems. In *Proceedings of the Tarski Centenary Conference, Warsaw, Poland, June 2001*, 2001. To appear. (Cited on page 377)

[DOR94] S. Demri, E. Orłowska, and I. Rewitzky. Towards reasoning about Hoare relations. *Annals of Mathematics and Artificial Intelligence*, 12:265–289, 1994. (Cited on page 169)

[DOV99] S. Demri, E. Orłowska, and D. Vakarelov. Indiscernibility and complementarity relations in Pawlak's information systems. In J. Gerbrandy, M. Marx, M. de Rijke, and Y. Venema, editors, *JFAK. Essays Dedicated to Johan van Benthem on the Occasion of his 50th Birthday*, 1999. Available via http://www.illc.uva.nl/~j50/ on WWW. (Cited on pages 192, 292, 320)

[DP90a] B. Davey and H. Priestley. *Introduction to Lattices and Order*. Cambridge Mathematical Textbooks. Cambridge University Press, 1990. (Cited on page 35)

[DP90b] D. Dubois and H. Prade. Rough fuzzy sets and fuzzy rough sets. *International Journal of General Systems*, 17:191–209, 1990. (Cited on page 90)

[DP91] D. Dubois and H. Prade. Putting rough sets and fuzzy sets together. In R. Słowinski, editor, *Intelligent Decision Support. Handbook of Applications and*

Advances of the Rough Set Theory, pages 203–232. Kluwer, Dordrecht, 1991. (Cited on page 90)

[DS00] S. Demri and J. Stepaniuk. Computational complexity of multimodal logics based on rough sets. *Fundamenta Informaticae*, 44(4):373–396, 2000. (Cited on page 292)

[Dün80] I. Düntsch. *Projektivität Primideale und Kettenbedingungen von Stone Algebren*. PhD thesis, Free University of Berlin, 1980. (Cited on page 353)

[Dün94] I. Düntsch. Rough relation algebra. *Fundamenta Informaticae*, 21:321–331, 1994. (Cited on page 353)

[Dün97] I. Düntsch. A logic for rough sets. *Theoretical Computer Science*, 179:427–436, 1997. (Cited on page 353)

[EG01] F. Esteva and L. Godo. On complete residuated many-valued logics with t-norm conjuction. In *31st IEEE International Symposium on Multiple Valued Logic, Warsaw, Poland*, pages 81–86, 2001. (Cited on page 36)

[EGG99] F. Esteva, P. García, and L. Godo. Similarity-based logical systems. In D. Dubois and H. Prade, editors, *Logics and Knowledge-based Systems*, pages 269–288. Kluwer, Dordrecht, 1999. (Cited on page 170)

[EGG00] F. Esteva, P. García, and L. Godo. Similarity-based reasoning. In V. Novak and I. Prefilieva, editors, *Discovering the World with Fuzzy Logic*, pages 367–393. Physica Verlag, Berlin, 2000. (Cited on page 170)

[EGGR97] F. Esteva, P. García, L. Godo, and R. Rodríguez. A modal account of similarity-based reasoning. *International Journal of Approximate Reasoning*, 16:235–260, 1997. (Cited on pages 116, 170, 191)

[End72] H. Enderton. *A Mathematical Introduction to Logic*. Academic, New York, 1972. (Cited on page 115)

[Eps90] R. Epstein. *The Semantic Foundation of Logic Vol. 1: Propositional Logics*. Kluwer, Dordrecht, 1990. (Cited on page 241)

[ER64] C. Elgot and A. Robinson. Random access stored program machine. *Journal of the Association for Computing Machinery*, 11:365–399, 1964. (Cited on page 136)

[FdCO85] L. Fariñas del Cerro and E. Orłowska. DAL – A logic for data analysis. *Theoretical Computer Science*, 36:251–264, 1985. (Cited on pages 116, 215)

[FHMV95] R. Fagin, J. Halpern, Y. Moses, and M. Vardi. *Reasoning About Knowledge*. MIT Press, Cambridge, MA, 1995. (Cited on page 215)

[Fit88] M. Fitting. First-order modal tableaux. *Journal of Automated Reasoning*, 4:191–213, 1988. (Cited on page 292)

[FL79] M. Fischer and R. Ladner. Propositional dynamic logic of regular programs. *Journal of Computer and System Sciences*, 18:194–211, 1979. (Cited on pages 116, 135, 136, 266)

[FO95] M. Frias and E. Orłowska. A proof system for fork algebras and its applications to reasoning in logics based on intuitionism. *Logique et Analyse*, 150–151–152:239–284, 1995. (Cited on page 169)

[FS92] K. Fine and G. Schurz. Transfer theorems for multimodal logics. In J. Copland, editor, *Logic and Reality. Essays in Pure and Applied Logic. In Memory of Arthur Prior*. Oxford University Press, 1992. (Cited on page 241)

[Für81] M. Fürer. The computational complexity of the unconstrained limited domino problem (with implications for logical decision problems). In *Logical Machines: Decision Problems and Complexity*, pages 312–319. Lecture Notes in Computer Science, Vol. 171. Springer, Berlin, 1981. (Cited on page 135)

[Fur98] H. Furusawa. *Algebraic Formalisations of Fuzzy Relations and Their Representation Theorems*. PhD thesis, Department of Informatics, Kyushu University, Fukuoka, 1998. (Cited on page 353)

[FV86a] R. Fagin and M. Vardi. Knowledge and implicit knowledge in a distributed environment: preliminary report. In J. Halpern, editor, *Theoretical Aspects of Reasoning About Knowledge*, pages 187–206. Morgan Kaufmann, San Francisco, CA, 1986. (Cited on page 215)

[FV86b] R. Fagin and M. Vardi. The theory of data dependencies: a survey. In M. Anshel and W. Gewirtz, editors, *Mathematics of Information Processing. Symposia in Applied Mathematics, Vol. 34*, pages 19–71. American Mathematical Society, Providence, RI, USA, 1986. (Cited on page 68)

[Gab72] D. Gabbay. A general filtration method for modal logics. *Journal of Philosophical Logic*, 1:29–34, 1972. (Cited on page 136)

[Gar86] G. Gargov. Two completeness theorems in the logic for data analysis. Technical Report 581, Institute of Computer Science, Polish Academy of Sciences, Warsaw, 1986. (Cited on pages 115, 116, 191)

[GG93] G. Gargov and V. Goranko. Modal logic with names. *Journal of Philosophical Logic*, 22(6):607–636, 1993. (Cited on pages 115, 266)

[GHE01] L. Godo, P. Hájek, and F. Esteva. A fuzzy modal logic for belief functions. In *IJCAI'01, Seattle, USA*, pages 723–732. Morgan Kaufmann, San Francisco, CA, 2001. (Cited on page 116)

[GHOS96] J. Green, N. Horn, E. Orłowska, and P. Siemers. A rough set model of information retrieval. *Fundamenta Informaticae*, 28:273–298, 1996. (Cited on page 89)

[Gia95] G. de Giacomo. *Decidability of Class-Based Knowledge Representation Formalisms*. PhD thesis, Universita Degli Studi Di Roma "La Sapienza", Dipartimento Di Informatica E Sistemistica, 1995. (Cited on pages 115, 136)

[GJ79] M. Garey and D. S. Johnson. *Computers and Intractability: a Guide to the Theory of NP-completeness*. Freeman, San Francisco, CA, 1979. (Cited on page 136)

[GJ94] M. Gehrke and B. Jonsson. Bounded distributive lattices with operators. *Mathematica Japonica*, 40:207–214, 1994. (Cited on page 377)

[GKV97] E. Grädel, Ph. Kolaitis, and M. Vardi. On the decision problem for two-variable first-order logic. *The Bulletin of Symbolic Logic*, 3(1):53–69, 1997. (Cited on page 135)

[GO99] E. Grädel and M. Otto. On logics with two variables. *Theoretical Computer Science*, 224(1–2):73–113, 1999. (Cited on page 266)

[Gol75] R. Goldblatt. First-order definability in modal logic. *The Journal of Symbolic Logic*, 40(1):35–40, 1975. (Cited on page 136)

[Gol89] R. Goldblatt. Varieties of complex algebras. *Annals of Pure and Applied Logic*, 44(3):153–301, 1989. (Cited on page 377)

[Gol97a] M. Golovanov. Bimodal propositional logic $S5_2Cn$. *Bulletin of the Section of Logic*, 26(3):118–125, 1997. (Cited on page 191)

[Gol97b] M. Golovanov. Finite bases of admissible rules for the logic $S5_2C$. In *4th Conference on Logical Foundations of Computer Science*, pages 119–129. Lecture Notes in Computer Science, Vol. 1234. Springer, Berlin, 1997. (Cited on page 191)

[Gol00] R. Goldblatt. Algebraic polymodal logic: a survey. *Logic Journal of the IGPL*, 8(4):393–450, 2000. (Cited on page 377)

[Gor90a] V. Goranko. Completeness and incompleteness in the bimodal base L(R,-R). In P. Petkov, editor, *Mathematical Logic*, pages 311–326. Plenum, New York, 1990. (Cited on pages 115, 216)

[Gor90b] V. Goranko. Modal definability in enriched languages. *Notre Dame Journal of Formal Logic*, 31:81–105, 1990. (Cited on pages 90, 115)

[Gou67] J. A. Gougen. L-fuzzy sets. *Journal of Mathematical Analysis and Applications*, 18:145–174, 1967. (Cited on page 36)

[GP90] G. Gargov and S. Passy. A note on Boolean modal logic. In P. Petkov, editor, *Summer School and Conference on Mathematical Logic '88*, pages 299–309. Plenum, New York, 1990. (Cited on pages 115, 136, 216, 292)

[GP92] V. Goranko and S. Passy. Using the universal modality: gains and questions. *Journal of Logic and Computation*, 2(1):5–30, 1992. (Cited on pages 115, 241)

[GPT87] G. Gargov, S. Passy, and T. Tinchev. Modal environment for Boolean speculations. In D. Skordev, editor, *Mathematical logic and its applications*, pages 253–263. Plenum, New York, 1987. (Cited on pages 115, 136)

[Grä99a] E. Grädel. On the restraining power of guards. *The Journal of Symbolic Logic*, 64(4):1719–1742, 1999. (Cited on page 135)

[Grä99b] E. Grädel. Why are modal logics so robustly decidable? *Bulletin of the EATCS*, 68:90–103, 1999. Available via http://www-mgi.informatik.rwth.aachen.de/Publications on WWW. (Cited on page 241)

[GT75] R. Goldblatt and S. Thomason. Axiomatic classes in propositional modal logic. In J. Crossley, editor, *Algebra and Logic*, pages 163–173. Lecture Notes in Mathematics, Vol. 450. Springer, Berlin, 1975. (Cited on page 115)

[GW92] M. Gehrke and E. Walker. On the structure of rough sets. *Bulletin of the Polish Academy of Sciences, Mathematics*, 40:235–255, 1992. (Cited on page 353)

[Hal62] P. Halmos. *Algebraic Logic*. Chelsea, New York, 1962. (Cited on page 353)

[Hal87] J. Halpern. Using reasoning about knowledge to analyze distributed systems. *Annual Review of Computer Science*, 2:37–68, 1987. (Cited on page 215)

[Har84] D. Harel. Dynamic logic. In D. Gabbay and F. Günthner, editors, *Handbook of Philosophical Logic, Vol. II*, pages 497–604. Reidel, Dordrecht, 1984. (Cited on page 136)

[HC68] G. Hughes and M. Cresswell. *An Introduction to Modal Logic*. Methuen, London, 1968. (Cited on page 115)

[HC84] G. Hughes and M. Cresswell. *A Companion to Modal Logic*. Methuen, London, 1984. (Cited on page 115)

[Hem96] E. Hemaspaandra. The price of universality. *Notre Dame Journal of Formal Logic*, 37(2):173–203, 1996. (Cited on pages 115, 292)

[HHE+94] P. Hájek, D. Harmancova, F. Esteva, P. García, and L. Godo. On modal logics for qualitative possibility in a fuzzy setting. In R. Lopez de Mantars and D. Poole, editors, *Uncertainty in Artificial Intelligence*, pages 278–285. Morgan Kaufmann, San Francisco, CA, 1994. (Cited on pages 116, 191)

[Hin62] J. Hintikka. *Knowledge and Belief*. Cornell University Press, London, 1962. (Cited on pages 115, 215)

[HKT00] D. Harel, D. Kozen, and J. Tiuryn. *Dynamic Logic*. MIT Press, Cambridge, MA, 2000. (Cited on page 116)

[HM80] M. Hennessy and R. Milner. On observing nondeterminism and concurrency. In *7th International Symposium on Automata, Languages and Programming, Noordwijkerhout*, pages 299–309. Lecture Notes in Computer Science, Vol. 85. Springer, Berlin, 1980. (Cited on page 136)

[HM85] J. Halpern and Y. Moses. A guide to the modal logics of knowledge and belief: preliminary draft. In *9th International Joint Conference on Artificial Intelligence*, pages 480–490. Morgan Kaufmann, San Francisco, CA, 1985. (Cited on page 215)

[HM91] W. van der Hoek and J.-J. Meyer. Graded modalities in epistemic logic. *Logique et Analyse*, 133–134:251–270, 1991. (Cited on page 191)

[HM92] J. Halpern and Y. Moses. A guide to completeness and complexity for modal logics of knowledge and belief. *Artificial Intelligence*, 54:319–379, 1992. (Cited on pages 136, 215, 216, 266, 292)

[HM97] W. van der Hoek and J.-J. Meyer. A complete epistemic logic for multiple agents – combining distributed and common knowledge. In P. Mongin, M. Bacharach, L. Gerard-Valet, and H. Shin, editors, *Epistemic Logic and the Theory of Games and Decisions*, pages 35–68. Kluwer, Dordrecht, 1997. (Cited on page 116)

[HM99] W. van der Hoek and J.-J. Meyer. A postscript to a completeness proof for Johan. In J. Gerbrandy, M. Marx, M. de Rijke, and Y. Venema, editors, *JFAK. Essays Dedicated to Johan van Benthem on the Occasion of his 50th Birthday*, 1999. Available via http://www.illc.uva.nl/~j50/ on WWW. (Cited on page 116)

[HO95] M. Herment and E. Orłowska. Handling information logics in a graphical proof editor. *Computational Intelligence*, 11(2):297–322, 1995. (Cited on page 169)

[Hod84] W. Hodges. Elementary predicate logic. In D. Gabbay and F. Günthner, editors, *Handbook of Philosophical Logic, Vol. I*, pages 1–131. Reidel, Dordrecht, 1984. (Cited on page 115)

[Höh96] U. Höhle. Commutative, residuated l-monoids. In U. Höhle and E. P. Klement, editors, *Non-Classical Logics and their Applications to Fuzzy Subsets*, pages 53–106. Kluwer, Dordrecht, 1996. (Cited on page 36)

[HS65] J. Hartmanis and R. Stearns. On the computational complexity of algorithms. *Transactions of the American Mathematical Society*, 117:285–306, 1965. (Cited on page 136)

[HST00] I. Horrocks, U. Sattler, and S. Tobies. Practical reasoning for very expressive description logics. *Logic Journal of the IGPL*, 8(3):239–263, 2000. (Cited on page 116)

[Hum83] L. Humberstone. Inaccessible worlds. *Notre Dame Journal of Formal Logic*, 24(3):346–352, 1983. (Cited on page 115)

[Hum87] L. Humberstone. The modal logic of "all and only". *Notre Dame Journal of Formal Logic*, 28(2):177–188, 1987. (Cited on page 115)

[Hum95] L. Humberstone. The logic of non-contingency. *Notre Dame Journal of Formal Logic*, 36(2):214–229, 1995. (Cited on pages 115, 215)

[Imm86] N. Immerman. Relational queries computable in polynomial-time. *Information and Computation*, 68:86–104, 1986. (Cited on page 136)

[Itu98] L. Iturrioz. Rough sets and three-valued structures. In *[Oe98b]*, pages 596–603, 1998. (Cited on page 353)

[Iwi87] T. Iwinski. Algebraic approach to rough sets. *Bulletin of the Polish Academy of Sciences, Mathematics*, 35:673–683, 1987. (Cited on page 352)

[Iwi88] T. Iwinski. Contraction of attributes. *Bulletin of the Polish Academy of Sciences, Mathematics*, 36(9–10):623–632, 1988. (Cited on page 69)

[Iwi91] T. Iwinski. Rough analysis in lattices. Working papers of the University of Carlos III, Madrid, No. 91–23, 1991. (Cited on page 353)

[Jär97] J. Järvinen. Representation of information systems and dependence spaces, and some basic algorithms. Licentiate's thesis. University of Turku, Department of Mathematics, Finland, 1997. (Cited on pages 67, 352)

[Joh90] D. Johnson. A catalog of complexity classes. In J. van Leeuwen, editor, *Handbook of Theoretical Computer Science, Vol. A, Algorithms and Complexity*, pages 68–161. North-Holland, Amsterdam, 1990. (Cited on page 136)

[Jón82] B. Jónsson. The theory of binary relations. In H. Andréka, D. Monk, and I. Németi, editors, *Algebraic logic. Colloquia Mathematica Societatis Janos*

Bolyai, Vol. 54, pages 245–292. North-Holland, Amsterdam, 1982.   (Cited on pages 12, 377)

[Jón94] B. Jónsson. On the canonicity of Sahlqvist identities. *Studia Logica*, 53:473–491, 1994.   (Cited on page 377)

[JT51] B. Jónsson and A. Tarski. Boolean algebras with operators. Part I. *American Journal of Mathematics*, 73:891–936, 1951.   (Cited on pages 115, 377)

[Kan57] S. Kanger. *Provability in Logic*. Stockholm Studies in Philosophy, University of Stockholm. Almqvist and Wiksell, 1957.   (Cited on page 115)

[Kat74a] T. Katrinak. Construction of regular double p-algebras. *Bulletin de la Société Royale de Science de Liège*, 43:294–301, 1974.   (Cited on page 353)

[Kat74b] T. Katrinak. Injective double Stone algebras. *Algebra Universalis*, 4:259–267, 1974.   (Cited on page 353)

[Ken93] R. Kent. Rough concept analysis. In *International Conference on Rough Sets and Knowledge Discovery, Banff, Canada*, pages 245–253, 1993.   (Cited on page 35)

[KF99] Y. Kawahara and H. Furusawa. An algebraic formalization of fuzzy relations. *Fuzzy Sets and Systems*, 101:125–135, 1999.   (Cited on page 353)

[KM82] R. Kramer and R. Maddux. Equations not preserved by complete extensions. *Algebra Universalis*, 15:86–89, 1982.   (Cited on page 377)

[KMO98] B. Konikowska, Ch. Morgan, and E. Orłowska. A relational formalisation of arbitrary finite valued logic. *Logic Journal of the IGPL*, 6(5):755–774, 1998. Available via http://www3.oup.co.uk/igpl/contents/ on WWW.   (Cited on page 169)

[Kon87] B. Konikowska. A formal language for reasoning about indiscernibility. *Bulletin of the Polish Academy of Sciences*, 35:239–249, 1987.   (Cited on pages 67, 191)

[Kon97] B. Konikowska. A logic for reasoning about relative similarity. *Studia Logica*, 58(1):185–226, 1997.   (Cited on pages 67, 115, 169, 215, 216)

[Kon98] B. Konikowska. A logic for reasoning about similarity. In *[Oe98a]*, pages 462–491, 1998.   (Cited on pages 67, 115, 169, 241)

[Kon00] B. Konikowska. Rasiowa–Sikorski deduction systems – Foundations and applications. In R. Dyckhoff, editor, *Automated Reasoning with Analytic Tableaux and Related Methods, St Andrews, Scotland, UK*, pages 22–68. Tutorial paper in Research Report CS/00/001, University of St Andrews, UK, 2000.   (Cited on page 169)

[KOP81] E. Konrad, E. Orłowska, and Z. Pawlak. Knowledge representation systems. Technical Report 433, Institute of Computer Science, Polish Academy of Sciences, 1981.   (Cited on pages 67, 89)

[Koy92] R. Koymans. *Specifying Message Passing and Time-critical Systems with Temporal Logic*. Lecture Notes in Computer Science, Vol. 651. Springer, Berlin, 1992.   (Cited on page 115)

[Kri63] S. Kripke. Semantical analysis of modal logic I: normal modal propositional calculi. *Zeitschrift für Mathematische Logik und Grundlagen der Mathematik*, 9:67–96, 1963.   (Cited on page 115)

[KS98] M. Krynicki and L. Szczerba. On the logic with rough quantifier. In *[Oe98a]*, pages 601–613, 1998.   (Cited on page 192)

[KT90] D. Kozen and J. Tiuryn. Logics of programs. In J. van Leeuwen, editor, *Handbook of Theoretical Computer Science*, pages 790–840. North-Holland, Amsterdam, 1990.   (Cited on page 241)

[KT91] M. Krynicki and H. Tuschik. An axiomatization of the logic with rough quantifier. *The Journal of Symbolic Logic*, 56:608–617, 1991.   (Cited on page 192)

[Kuh95] S. Kuhn. Minimal logic of non-contingency. *Notre Dame Journal of Formal Logic*, 36(2):230–234, 1995.   (Cited on pages 115, 215)

[Lad77] R. Ladner. The computational complexity of provability in systems of modal propositional logic. *SIAM Journal of Computing*, 6(3):467–480, 1977. (Cited on pages 134, 135, 136, 266, 292)

[Lem65] E. Lemmon. *Beginning Logic*. Chapman and Hall, London, 1965.   (Cited on pages 169, 216)

[Len78] W. Lenzen. Recent work in epistemic logic. *Acta Philosophica Fennica*, 30:1–219, 1978.   (Cited on page 215)

[Lev73] L. Levin. Universal sorting problems. *Problems of Information Transmissions*, 9(3):265–266, 1973.   (Cited on pages 134, 136)

[Lew80] H. Lewis. Complexity results for classes of quantificational formulas. *Journal of Computer and System Sciences*, 21:317–353, 1980.   (Cited on page 135)

[Lip76] W. Lipski. Informational systems with incomplete information. In *3rd International Symposium on Automata, Languages and Programming, Edinburgh, Scotland*, pages 120–130, 1976.   (Cited on page 35)

[Lip79] W. Lipski. On semantic issues connected with incomplete information databases. *ACM Transactions on Database Systems*, 4(3):262–296, 1979. (Cited on page 35)

[LR96] R. Lassaigne and M. de Rougemont. *Logique et Complexité*. Hermès, Paris, 1996.   (Cited on page 136)

[LS77] E. Lemmon and D. Scott. *An Introduction to Modal Logic*. American Philosophical Quarterly, 1977.   (Cited on pages 115, 136)

[LS00] C. Lutz and U. Sattler. The complexity of reasoning with Boolean modal logics. In *Advances in Modal Logics*. CSLI, Stanford, 2000. To appear,.   (Cited on page 292)

[Łuka20] J. Łukasiewicz. O logice trójwartościowej. *Ruch Filozoficzny*, 5:169–171, 1920.   (Cited on page 353)

[Lux98] M. Luxenburger. Dependencies between many-valued attributes. In *[Oe98a]*, pages 316–343, 1998.   (Cited on page 68)

[Lyn77] N. Lynch. Log Space recognition and translation of parentheses languages. *Journal of the Association for Computing Machinery*, 24(4):583–590, 1977.   (Cited on page 291)

[Mac97] W. MacCaull. Relational proof systems for linear and substructural logics. *Logic Journal of the IGPL*, 5(5):673–697, 1997. Available via http://www3.oup.co.uk/igpl/contents/ on WWW.   (Cited on page 169)

[Mac98a] W. MacCaull. A relational approach to association rules and functional dependencies. In E. Orłowska and A. Szałas, editors, *4th International Seminar on Relational Methods in Logic, Algebra and Computer Science, Warsaw, Poland*, pages 159–164, 1998.   (Cited on page 169)

[Mac98b] W. MacCaull. Relational tableaux for tree models, language models and information networks. In *[Oe98b]*, pages 344–382, 1998.   (Cited on page 169)

[Mac00] W. MacCaull. A proof system for dependencies for information relations. *Fundamenta Informaticae*, 34:1–28, 2000.   (Cited on page 68)

[Mac01] W. MacCaull. A tableaux procedure for the implication problem for association rules. In *[OSe01]*, pages 77–95, 2001.   (Cited on page 68)

[Mad97] R. Maddux. Relation algebras. In C. Brink, W. Kahl, and G. Schmidt, editors, *Relational Methods in Computer Science*, pages 22–38, 1997.   (Cited on page 12)

[Mak66] D. Makinson. On some completeness theorems in modal logic. *The Journal of Symbolic Logic*, 12:379–384, 1966.   (Cited on page 136)

[Mak90] D. Makinson. Logique modale: quelques jalons essentiels. In L. Iturrioz and A. Dussauchoy, editors, *Modèles Logiques et Systèmes d'intelligence Artificielle*, pages 75–97. Hermès, 1990. (Cited on page 115)

[Mar97] M. Marx. Complexity of modal logics of relations. Technical report, ILLC, 1997. Available via http://turing.wins.uva.nl/~marx/ on WWW. (Cited on page 292)

[Mik95] S. Mikulás. *Taming Logics*. PhD thesis, Amsterdam University, ILLC, 1995. (Cited on page 191)

[MMN95] M. Marx, S. Mikulás, and I. Németi. Taming Logic. *Journal of Logic, Language and Information*, 4:207–226, 1995. (Cited on page 191)

[Moi72] G. Moisil. *Essais sur les Logiques Non-chrysipiennes*. Editions de l'Academie de la Republique de Roumanie, Bucharest, 1972. (Cited on page 353)

[Mon68] A. Monteiro. Construction des algèbres de Łukasiewicz trivalentes dans les algèbres de Boole monadiques. *Mathematica Japonicae*, 12:1–23, 1968. (Cited on page 353)

[Mon74] M. Montalbano. *Decision Tables*. Science Research Associates, Chicago, 1974. (Cited on page 36)

[Mon89] (editor) D. Monk. *Handbook on Boolean Algebras*. North-Holland, Amsterdam, 1989. (Cited on page 12)

[Mor75] M. Mortimer. On language with two variables. *Zeitschrift für Mathematische Logik und Grundlagen der Mathematik*, 21:135–140, 1975. (Cited on page 135)

[MR66] H. Montgomery and R. Routley. Contingency and non-contingency bases for normal modal logics. *Logique et Analyse*, 9:318–328, 1966. (Cited on page 215)

[MR68] H. Montgomery and R. Routley. Non-contingency axioms for S4 and S5. *Logique et Analyse*, 11:422–424, 1968. (Cited on pages 215, 216)

[MR89] W. Marek and H. Rasiowa. On reaching consensus by groups of intelligent agents. In *International Symposium on Methodologies for Intelligent Systems*, pages 234–243. North-Holland, Amsterdam, 1989. (Cited on page 215)

[Nak92] A. Nakamura. On a logic based on fuzzy modalities. In *22nd International Symposium on Multiple-Valued Logic, Sendai, Japan*, pages 460–466. IEEE Computer Society Press, 1992. (Cited on page 191)

[Nak93] A. Nakamura. On a logic based on graded modalities. *IEICE Transactions*, E76-D(5):527–532, 1993. (Cited on page 191)

[Nel49] D. Nelson. Constructible falsity. *The Journal of Symbolic Logic*, 14:16–26, 1949. (Cited on page 353)

[NG91] A. Nakamura and J.-M. Gao. A logic for fuzzy data analysis. *Fuzzy Sets and Systems*, 39:127–132, 1991. (Cited on page 192)

[NP85a] M. Novotný and Z. Pawlak. Characterization of rough top equalities and rough bottom equalities. *Bulletin of the Polish Academy of Sciences, Mathematics*, 33:91–97, 1985. (Cited on page 89)

[NP85b] M. Novotný and Z. Pawlak. On rough equalities. *Bulletin of the Polish Academy of Sciences, Mathematics*, 33:99–104, 1985. (Cited on page 89)

[NS98] A. Nonnengart and A. Szałas. A fixpoint approach to second order quantifier elimination with applications to correspondence theory. In *[Oe98b]*, pages 89–108, 1998. (Cited on page 90)

[Oe98a] E. Orłowska (ed.). *Incomplete Information: Rough Set Analysis*, volume 13 of *Studies in Fuzziness and Soft Computing*. Physica, Heidelberg, 1998. (Cited on pages 67, 379, 380, 388, 389, 392, 397)

[Oe98b] E. Orłowska (ed.). *Logic at work. Essays dedicated to the Memory of Helena Rasiowa*, volume 24 of *Studies in Fuzziness and Soft Computing*. Physica, Heidelberg, 1998.   (Cited on pages 383, 387, 389, 390)

[Ohl91] H. J. Ohlbach. Semantics based translation methods for modal logics. *Journal of Logic and Computation*, 1(5):691–746, 1991.   (Cited on page 241)

[ONdRG01] H.J. Ohlbach, A. Nonnengart, M. de Rijke, and D. Gabbay. Encoding two-valued non-classical logics in classical logic. In A. Robinson and A. Voronkov, editors, *Handbook of Automated Reasoning*, pages 1403–1486. MIT Press, Cambridge, MA, 2001.   (Cited on page 241)

[OP81] E. Orłowska and Z. Pawlak. Expressive power of knowledge representation system. Technical Report 432, Institute of Computer Science, Polish Academy of Sciences, 1981.   (Cited on page 116)

[OP84] E. Orłowska and Z. Pawlak. Representation of nondeterministic information. *Theoretical Computer Science*, 29:27–39, 1984.   (Cited on page 169)

[OR01] E. Orłowska and A. Radzikowska. Double residuated lattices. In H. de Swart, editor, *6th International Workshop on Relational Methods in Computer Science - RelMiCS'6, Oisterwijk, The Netherlands*, pages 185–199, 2001. (Cited on page 36)

[Orło74] E. Orłowska. Threshold logic. *Studia Logica*, 33(1):1–9, 1974.   (Cited on page 169)

[Orło83] E. Orłowska. Semantics of vague concepts. In G. Dorn and P. Weingartner, editors, *Foundations of Logic and Linguistics. Problems and Solutions. Selected contributions to the 7th International Congress of Logic, Methodology, and Philosophy of Science, Salzburg, Austria*, pages 465–482. Plenum, London, New York, 1983.   (Cited on page 89)

[Orło84a] E. Orłowska. Logic of indiscernibility relations. In A. Skowron, editor, *5th Symposium on Computation Theory, Zaborów, Poland*, pages 177–186. Lecture Notes in Computer Science, Vol. 208. Springer, Berlin, 1984.   (Cited on pages 67, 115, 192)

[Orło84b] E. Orłowska. Modal logics in the theory of information systems. *Zeitschrift für Mathematische Logik und Grundlagen der Mathematik*, 30(1):213–222, 1984.   (Cited on page 116)

[Orło85a] E. Orłowska. Logic of nondeterministic information. *Studia Logica*, 44:93–102, 1985.   (Cited on page 67)

[Orło85b] E. Orłowska. Semantics of nondeterministic possible worlds. *Bulletin of the Polish Academy of Sciences*, 33(9–10):453–458, 1985.   (Cited on page 192)

[Orło87a] E. Orłowska. Algebraic approach to database constraints. *Fundamenta Informaticae*, 10:57–68, 1987. See also: Report 182, Langages et Systèmes Informatiques, Toulouse, 1983.   (Cited on page 68)

[Orło87b] E. Orłowska. Logic for reasoning about knowledge. *Bulletin of the Section of Logic*, 16(1):26–38, 1987.   (Cited on page 67)

[Orło88a] E. Orłowska. Kripke models with relative accessibility and their applications to inferences from incomplete information. In G. Mirkowska and H. Rasiowa, editors, *Mathematical Problems in Computation Theory*, pages 329–339. Banach Center, Vol. 21 PWN–Polish Scientific, Warsaw, 1988.   (Cited on pages 67, 116, 241)

[Orło88b] E. Orłowska. Logical aspects of learning concepts. *Journal of Approximate Reasoning*, 2:349–364, 1988.   (Cited on pages 215, 241)

[Orło88c] E. Orłowska. Relational interpretation of modal logics. In H. Andréka, D. Monk, and I. Németi, editors, *Algebraic logic. Colloquia Mathematica Societatis Janos Bolyai 54*, pages 443–471. North-Holland, Amsterdam, 1988. (Cited on page 169)

[Orło88d] E. Orłowska. Representation of vague information. *Information Systems*, 13:167–174, 1988. (Cited on page 192)

[Orło89] E. Orłowska. Logic for reasoning about knowledge. *Zeitschrift für Mathematische Logik und Grundlagen der Mathematik*, 35:559–568, 1989. (Cited on pages 67, 89, 215, 216, 241)

[Orło90] E. Orłowska. Kripke semantics for knowledge representation logics. *Studia Logica*, 49(2):255–272, 1990. (Cited on page 241)

[Orło91] E. Orłowska. Relational proof systems for some AI logics. In Ph. Jorrand and J. Kelemen, editors, *FAIR'91*, pages 33–47. Lecture Notes in Artificial Intelligence, Vol. 535. Springer, Berlin, 1991. (Cited on page 169)

[Orło92] E. Orłowska. Relational proof system for relevant logics. *The Journal of Symbolic Logic*, 57(4):1425–1440, 1992. (Cited on page 169)

[Orło93a] E. Orłowska. Dynamic logic with program specifications and its relational proof system. *Journal of Applied Non-Classical Logics*, 3(2):147–171, 1993. (Cited on page 169)

[Orło93b] E. Orłowska. Reasoning with incomplete information: rough set based information logics. In V. Alagar, S. Bergler, and F.Q. Dong, editors, *Incompleteness and Uncertainty in Information Systems Workshop*, pages 16–33. Springer, Berlin, October 1993. (Cited on pages 116, 215, 241)

[Orło93c] E. Orłowska. Rough set semantics for non-classical logics. In W. Ziarko, editor, *2nd International Workshop on Rough Sets and Knowledge Discovery, Banff, Canada*, pages 143–148, 1993. (Cited on page 320)

[Orło95] E. Orłowska. Information algebras. In *AMAST'95, Montreal, Canada*, pages 50–65. Lecture Notes in Computer Science, Vol. 639. Springer, Berlin, 1995. (Cited on pages 241, 377)

[Orło99] E. Orłowska. Many-valuedness and uncertainty. *International Journal of Multiple Valued Logic*, 4:207–227, 1999. (Cited on pages 36, 68, 69)

[OSe01] E. Orłowska and A. Szałas (eds.). *Relational Methods for Computer Science Applications*, volume 65 of *Studies in Fuzziness and Soft Computing*. Physica, Heidelberg, 2001. (Cited on pages 383, 389, 395)

[Pag93] P. Pagliani. From concept lattices to approximation spaces: algebraic structures of some spaces of partial objects. *Fundamenta Informaticae*, 18:1–25, 1993. (Cited on page 35)

[Pag95] P. Pagliani. Towards a logic of rough set systems. In T. Lin and A. Wildberger, editors, *Soft Computing*, pages 59–62. The Society of Computer Simulation, San Diego, CA, USA, 1995. (Cited on page 353)

[Pag96] P. Pagliani. Rough sets and Nelson algebras. *Fundamenta Informaticae*, 27(2–3):205–219, 1996. (Cited on page 353)

[Pag98] P. Pagliani. Rough set theory and logic-algebraic structures. In *[Oe98a]*, pages 109–192, 1998. (Cited on pages 35, 353)

[Pap94] Ch. Papadimitriou. *Computational Complexity*. Addison-Wesley, Reading, MA, 1994. (Cited on page 136)

[Par81] D. Park. Concurrency and automata on infinite sequences. In *5th GI Conference on Theoretical Computer Science, Karlsruhe, Germany*, pages 167–183. Lecture Notes in Computer Science, Vol. 104. Springer, Berlin, 1981. (Cited on page 136)

[Paw81a] Z. Pawlak. Classification of objects by means of attributes. Technical Report 429, Institute of Computer Science, Polish Academy of Sciences, Warsaw, 1981. (Cited on page 89)

[Paw81b] Z. Pawlak. Rough relations. Technical Report 435, Institute of Computer Science, Polish Academy of Sciences, Warsaw, 1981. (Cited on page 353)

[Paw82] Z. Pawlak. Rough sets. *International Journal of Information and Computer Sciences*, 11:341–356, 1982. Also available as a technical report (No. 435), Institute of Computer Science, Polish Academy of Sciences, Warsaw, 1981. (Cited on pages 35, 89)

[Paw85] Z. Pawlak. Rough sets and fuzzy sets. *Fuzzy Sets and Systems*, 17:99–102, 1985. (Cited on pages 36, 68)

[Paw87] Z. Pawlak. Rough functions. *Bulletin of the Polish Academy of Sciences*, 35(5–6):249–251, 1987. (Cited on page 36)

[Paw91] Z. Pawlak. *Rough Sets - Theoretical Aspects of Reasoning about Data*. Kluwer Academic, Dordrecht, 1991. (Cited on pages 36, 67)

[Pe98] L. Polkowski and A. Skowron (editors). *Rough Sets in Knowledge Discovery*. Studies in Fuzziness and Soft Computing. Physica, Heidelberg, 1998. (Cited on pages 381, 383, 395)

[Pen88] W. Penczek. A temporal logic for event structures. *Fundamenta Informaticae*, 11:297–326, 1988. (Cited on page 136)

[Pen89] W. Penczek. A temporal logic for the local specification of concurrent systems. In *Information Processing'89*, pages 857–862. North-Holland, Amsterdam, 1989. (Cited on page 136)

[PF77] A. Prior and K. Fine. *Worlds, Times and Selves*. University of Massachusetts Press, 1977. (Cited on page 115)

[Pom87] J. Pomykala. Approximation operations in approximation space. *Bulletin of the Polish Academy of Sciences, Mathematics*, 35(9–10):653–662, 1987. (Cited on page 89)

[Pom88] J. Pomykala. On definability in nondeterministic information system. *Bulletin of the Polish Academy of Sciences, Mathematics*, 36(3–4):193–210, 1988. (Cited on page 89)

[Pom94] J. Pomykala. On similarity-based approximation of information. *Demonstratio Mathematica*, 27(3–4):663–671, 1994. (Cited on page 377)

[PP88] J. Pomykala and J. A. Pomykala. The Stone algebra of rough sets. *Bulletin of the Polish Academy of Sciences, Mathematics*, 36:495–508, 1988. (Cited on page 353)

[Pra76] V. Pratt. Semantical considerations on Floyd–Hoare logic. In *17th IEEE Symposium on Foundations of Computer Science*, pages 109–121, 1976. (Cited on page 116)

[Pra79] V. Pratt. Models of program logics. In *20th IEEE Symposium on Foundations of Computer Science*, pages 115–122, 1979. (Cited on pages 135, 266, 292)

[Pra80] V. Pratt. Applications of modal logic to programming. *Studia Logica*, 39:257–274, 1980. (Cited on page 116)

[Pri67] A. Prior. *Past, Present and Future*. Oxford University Press, 1967. (Cited on page 115)

[PSe99] S. Pal and A. Skowron (eds.). *Rough Fuzzy Hybridization: A New Trend in Decision-making*. Springer, Berlin, 1999. (Cited on page 36)

[PT85] S. Passy and T. Tinchev. PDL with data constants. *Information Processing Letters*, 20:35–41, 1985. (Cited on page 115)

[PT91] S. Passy and T. Tinchev. An essay in combinatory dynamic logic. *Information and Computation*, 93:263–332, 1991. (Cited on pages 115, 136, 170)

[Ras73] H. Rasiowa. *Introduction to Modern Mathematics*. North-Holland PWN, Amsterdam, Warsaw, 1973. (Cited on page 12)

[Rau74] C. Rauszer. Semi-Boolean algebras and their applications to intuitionistic logic with dual operations. *Fundamenta Mathematicae*, 83:219–249, 1974. (Cited on page 36)

[Rau84] C. Rauszer. An equivalence between indiscernibility relations in information systems and a fragment of intuitionistic logic. In A. Skowron, editor, *5th Symposium on Computation Theory, Zaborów, Poland*, pages 298–317. Lecture Notes in Computer Science, Vol. 208. Springer, Berlin, 1984. (Cited on pages 191, 192)

[Rau85] C. Rauszer. An equivalence between theory of functional dpendencies and fragment of intutionistic logic. *Bulletin of the Polish Academy of Sciences, Mathematics*, 33:571–579, 1985. (Cited on page 68)

[Rau88] C. Rauszer. Algebraic properties of functional dependencies. *Bulletin of the Polish Academy of Sciences, Mathematics*, 33:561–569, 1988. (Cited on page 68)

[Rau92] C. Rauszer. Rough logic for multi-agent systems. In M. Masuch and L. Pólos, editors, *Knowledge Representation and Reasoning Under Uncertainty, Logic at Work*, pages 161–181. Lecture Notes in Computer Science, Vol. 808. Springer, Berlin, 1992. (Cited on pages 89, 192)

[Rau93] C. Rauszer. Knowledge representation systems for groups of agents. In J. Wolenski, editor, *Philosophical Logic in Poland*, pages 217–238. Kluwer, Dordrecht, 1993. (Cited on page 215)

[RdS95] C. Rauszer and H. de Swart. Different approaches to common knowledge and Auman's theorem. In A. Laux and H. Wansing, editors, *Knowledge and Belief in Philosophy and Artificial Intelligence*, pages 87–112. Akademie, Berlin, 1995. (Cited on page 215)

[Rij93] M. de Rijke. *Extending Modal Logic*. PhD thesis, ILLC, Amsterdam University, 1993. (Cited on page 136)

[RK01a] A. Radzikowska and E. Kerre. A comparative study of fuzzy rough sets. *Fuzzy Sets and Systems*, 2001. To appear. (Cited on pages 36, 90)

[RK01b] A. Radzikowska and E. Kerre. A general calculus of fuzzy rough sets. 2001. submitted. (Cited on page 90)

[RK01c] A. Radzikowska and E. Kerre. On some classes of fuzzy information relations. In *31st IEEE International Symposium on Multiple Valued Logic, Warsaw, Poland*, pages 75–80, 2001. (Cited on page 69)

[RS63] H. Rasiowa and R. Sikorski. *The Mathematics of Metamathematics*. PWN–Polish Scientific, Warsaw, 1963. (Cited on pages 12, 169)

[RS91] C. Rauszer and A. Skowron. The discernibility matrices and functions in information systems. In R. Słowinski, editor, *Intelligent decision support. Handbook of Applications and Advances in the Rough Set Theory*, pages 331–362. Kluwer, Dordrecht, 1991. (Cited on page 67)

[RV95] M. de Rijke and Y. Venema. Sahlqvist theorem for Boolean algebras with operators. *Studia Logica*, 54:61–78, 1995. (Cited on page 377)

[Sah75] H. Sahlqvist. Completeness and correspondence in the first and second order semantics for modal logics. In S. Kanger, editor, *3rd Scandinavian Logic Symposium, Uppsala, Sweden, 1973*, pages 110–143. North-Holland, Amsterdam, 1975. (Cited on pages 136, 377)

[Sai88] I. Sain. Is "some-other-time" sometimes better than "sometime" for proving partial correctness of programs. *Studia Logica*, 47(3):278–301, 1988. (Cited on page 115)

[Sal72] Z. Saloni. Gentzen rules for the m-valued logic. *Bulletin of the Polish Academy of Sciences, Mathematics*, 20:819–826, 1972. (Cited on page 169)

[Sch91] K. Schild. A correspondence theory for terminological logics: preliminary report. In *12th International Joint Conference on Artificial Intelligence*, pages 466–471, 1991. (Cited on page 241)

[Sco82] D. Scott. Domains for denotational semantics. In M. Nielsen and E. Schmidt, editors, *International Symposium on Automata, Languages and*

Programming, pages 577–613. Lecture Notes in Computer Science, Vol. 140. Springer, Berlin, 1982.   (Cited on page 35)

[Seg71] K. Segerberg. An essay in classical modal logic (three volumes). Technical Report Filosofiska Studier No. 13, Uppsala Universitet, 1971.   (Cited on pages 115, 136)

[Seg76] K. Segerberg. "somewhere else" and "some other time". In *Wright and wrong. Mini-essays in honor of Georg Henrik von Wright on his sixtieth birthday*, pages 61–69. Abo Akademi, Finland, 1976.   (Cited on page 115)

[Seg82] K. Segerberg. A completeness theorem in the modal logic of programs. In T. Traczyk, editor, *Universal Algebra and Applications*, pages 31–46. Banach Center Publications, Vol. 9, Warsaw, 1982.   (Cited on page 135)

[Sen84] A. Sendlewski. Some investigations of varieties of N-lattices. *Studia Logica*, 43:257–280, 1984.   (Cited on page 353)

[Sen90] A. Sendlewski. Nelson algebras through Heyting ones I. *Studia Logica*, 49:105–126, 1990.   (Cited on page 353)

[She56] J. Sheperdson. On the interpretation of Aristotelian syllogistic. *The Journal of Symbolic Logic*, 21:137–147, 1956.   (Cited on page 68)

[SI98] E. SanJuan and L. Iturrioz. Duality and informational representability of some information algebras. In *[Pe98]*, pages 233–247, 1998.   (Cited on page 377)

[SI01] E. SanJuan and L. Iturrioz. An application of standard BAO theory to some abstract information algebras. In *[OSe01]*, pages 203–215, 2001.   (Cited on page 377)

[SM73] L. Stockmeyer and A. Meyer. Word problems requiring exponential-time. In *5th ACM Symposium on the Theory of Computing*, pages 1–9, 1973.   (Cited on page 135)

[Smu68] R. Smullyan. *First-Order Logic*. Springer, Berlin, 1968.   (Cited on page 169)

[Spa93a] E. Spaan. *Complexity of Modal Logics*. PhD thesis, ILLC, Amsterdam University, 1993.   (Cited on pages 115, 135)

[Spa93b] E. Spaan. The complexity of propositional tense logics. In M. de Rijke, editor, *Diamonds and Defaults*, pages 287–309. Kluwer Academic Dordrecht, Series Studies in Pure and Applied Intensional Logic, Vol. 229, 1993.   (Cited on page 292)

[SS63] J. Shepherdson and H. Sturgis. Computability of recursive functions. *Journal of the Association for Computing Machinery*, 10:217–255, 1963.   (Cited on page 136)

[SS83] B. Schweizer and A. Sklar. *Probabilistic Metric Space*. North-Holland, Amsterdam, 1983.   (Cited on page 36)

[SS00a] V. Sofronie-Stokkermans. Duality and canonical extensions of bounded distributive lattices with operators, and applications to the semantics of nonclassical logics I. *Studia Logica*, 64:93–132, 2000.   (Cited on page 377)

[SS00b] V. Sofronie-Stokkermans. Duality and canonical extensions of bounded distributive lattices with operators, and applications to the semantics of nonclassical logics II. *Studia Logica*, 64:151–172, 2000.   (Cited on page 377)

[Sta79] R. Statman. Intuitionistic propositional logic is polynomial-space complete. *Theoretical Computer Science*, 9:67–72, 1979.   (Cited on page 135)

[Ste98] J. Stepaniuk. Rough relations and logics. In *[Pe98]*, pages 248–260, 1998.   (Cited on pages 292, 353)

[Sto77] L. Stockmeyer. The polynomial-time hierarchy. *Theoretical Computer Science*, 3:1–21, 1977.   (Cited on page 135)

[Sto87] L. Stockmeyer. Classifying the computational complexity of problems. *The Journal of Symbolic Logic*, 52(1):1–43, 1987.   (Cited on page 136)

[SV89] G. Sambin and V. Vaccaro. A new proof of Sahlqvist's theorem on modal definability and completeness. *The Journal of Symbolic Logic*, 54(3):992–999, 1989. (Cited on page 136)

[Szc87a] L. Szczerba. Rough quantifiers. *Bulletin of the Polish Academy of Sciences, Mathematics*, 35:251–254, 1987. (Cited on page 192)

[Szc87b] L. Szczerba. Rough quantifiers have no Tarski property. *Bulletin of the Polish Academy of Sciences, Mathematics*, 35:663–665, 1987. (Cited on page 192)

[Tar41] A. Tarski. On the calculus of relations. *The Journal of Symbolic Logic*, 6(3):73–89, 1941. (Cited on page 12)

[Tar53] A. Tarski. *Undecidable Theories*. Studies in Logic and the Foundations of Mathematics. North-Holland, Amsterdam, 1953. In collaboration with A. Mostowski and R. Robinson. (Cited on page 241)

[Thi97] H. Thiele. Fuzzy rough sets versus rough fuzzy sets - an interpretation and a comparative study using concepts of modal logics. In *5th European Congress on Intelligent Techniques and Soft Computing (EUFIT'97), Vol. 1, Aachen, Germany*, pages 159–167, 1997. (Cited on page 90)

[TS96] A. Troelstra and H. Schwichtenberg. *Basic Proof Theory*. Cambridge Tracts in Theoretical Computer Science 43. Cambridge University Press, 1996. (Cited on page 135)

[Tur37] A. Turing. On computable numbers with an application to the Entscheidungsproblem. *Proceedings London Mathematical Society*, 42:230–265, 1937. Correction, ibid 43 (1937), 544–546. (Cited on page 136)

[Tza99] M. Tzakova. Tableau calculi for hybrid logics. In N. Murray, editor, *International Conference on Theorem Proving with Analytic Tableaux and Related Methods, Saratoga Springs, USA*, pages 278–292. Lecture Notes in Artificial Intelligence, Vol. 1617. Springer, Berlin, 1999. (Cited on page 170)

[Vak77] D. Vakarelov. Notes on N-lattices and constructive logic with strong negation. *Studia Logica*, 36:109–125, 1977. (Cited on page 353)

[Vak87] D. Vakarelov. Abstract characterization of some knowledge representation systems and the logic NIL of nondeterministic information. In Ph. Jorrand and V. Sgurev, editors, *Artificial Intelligence: Methodology, Systems, Applications*, pages 255–260. North-Holland, Amsterdam, 1987. (Cited on pages 67, 136, 169, 320)

[Vak89] D. Vakarelov. Modal logics for knowledge representation systems. In A. R. Meyer and M. Taitslin, editors, *Symposium on Logic Foundations of Computer Science, Pereslavl-Zalessky*, pages 257–277. Lecture Notes in Computer Science, Vol. 363. Springer, Berlin, 1989. (Cited on pages 67, 136, 169, 320)

[Vak90] D. Vakarelov. Modal characterization of the classes of finite and infinite quasi-ordered sets. In P. Petkov, editor, *Mathematical Logic*, pages 373–387. Plenum, New York, 1990. (Cited on page 136)

[Vak91a] D. Vakarelov. Logical analysis of positive and negative similarity relations in property systems. In M. de Glas and D. Gabbay, editors, *First World Conference on the Fundamentals of Artificial Intelligence, Paris, France*, 1991. (Cited on pages 67, 320)

[Vak91b] D. Vakarelov. A modal logic for similarity relations in Pawlak knowledge representation systems. *Fundamenta Informaticae*, 15:61–79, 1991. (Cited on pages 136, 170, 320)

[Vak91c] D. Vakarelov. Modal logics for knowledge representation systems. *Theoretical Computer Science*, 90:433–456, 1991. (Cited on pages 67, 136, 169, 192, 215, 216, 320)

[Vak95] D. Vakarelov. A duality between Pawlak's information systems and bi-consequence systems with applications to first-order and modal characterizations of some informational relations. In M. de Glas and Z. Pawlak, editors, *Second World Conference on the Fundamentals of Artificial Intelligence, Paris, France*, pages 417–429. Angkor, Paris, 1995. (Cited on page 320)

[Vak96] D. Vakarelov. *Applied Modal Logic: Modal Logics for Information Science.* Kluwer, 1996. Forthcoming. Preprint available as a Technical Report No. X-1997-02 from the ILLC. (Cited on pages 169, 170, 266)

[Vak98] D. Vakarelov. Information systems, similarity and modal logics. In *[Oe98a]*, pages 492–550, 1998. (Cited on pages 35, 68, 170, 320)

[Val88] M. Valiev. Interpretation of modal logics as epistemic logics (In Russian). In *Conference of Borzomi*, pages 76–77, 1988. (Cited on pages 215, 216)

[Var68] J.C. Varlet. Algèbres de Lukasiewicz trivalentes. *Bulletin de la Société Royale des Sciences de Liège*, 9–10:399–408, 1968. (Cited on page 353)

[Var82] M. Vardi. The complexity of relational query languages. In *14th Annual ACM Symposium on Theory of Computing*, pages 137–146, 1982. (Cited on page 136)

[Var97] M. Vardi. Why is modal logic so robustly decidable? In *DIMACS Series in Discrete Mathematics and Theoretical Computer Science 31, American Mathematical Society*, pages 149–183, 1997. Available via http://www.cs.rice.edu/~vardi/ on WWW. (Cited on page 241)

[Ven93] Y. Venema. Derivation rules as anti-axioms in modal logic. *The Journal of Symbolic Logic*, 58(3):1003–1034, 1993. (Cited on page 136)

[VW94] M. Vardi and P. Wolper. Reasoning about infinite computations. *Information and Computation*, 115:1–37, 1994. (Cited on page 292)

[Was71] A. Wasilewska. A formalization of the modal propositional S4 calculus. *Studia Logica*, 27:133–147, 1971. (Cited on page 169)

[Was97] A. Wasilewska. Topological rough algebras. In T.Y. Lin and N. Cercone, editors, *Rough Sets and Data Mining*, pages 411–425. Kluwer, Dordrecht, 1997. (Cited on page 354)

[WB95] A. Wasilewska and M. Banerjee. Rough sets and topological quasi-Boolean algebras. In T.Y. Lin, editor, *Workshop on Rough Sets and Data Mining at 23rd Annual Computer Science Conference, Nashville, TN, USA*, pages 61–67, 1995. (Cited on page 354)

[WD39] M. Ward and R. Dilworth. Residuated lattices. *Transactions of the American Mathematical Society*, 45:335–354, 1939. (Cited on page 36)

[Wed48] A. Wedberg. The Aristotelian theory of classes. *Ajatus*, 15:299–314, 1948. (Cited on page 68)

[Wil82] R. Wille. Restructuring lattice theory. In I. Rival, editor, *Ordered Sets*, pages 445–470. Reidel, Dordrecht, 1982. (Cited on page 35)

[Wil88] R. Wille. Dependencies of many-valued attributes. In H. Block, editor, *Classification and Related Methods of Data Analysis*, pages 581–586. North-Holland, Amsterdam, 1988. (Cited on page 68)

[Wój88] R. Wójcicki. *Theory of Logical Calculi.* Kluwer, Dordrecht, 1988. (Cited on page 241)

[Wri51] G. von Wright. *An Essay in Modal Logic.* North-Holland, Amsterdam, 1951. (Cited on page 215)

[WV95] A. Wasilewska and L. Vigneron. Rough equality algebras. In *Annual Joint Conference on Information Sciences, Wrightsville Beach, North Carolina, USA*, pages 26–30, 1995. (Cited on pages 89, 354)

[Yin88] M.-S. Ying. On standard models of fuzzy modal logics. *Fuzzy Sets and Systems*, 26:357–363, 1988. (Cited on page 191)

[Ż83] W. Żakowski. Approximations in the space (U,π). *Demonstratio Mathematicae*, 16, 1983.   (Cited on page 89)

[Zad65] L. Zadeh. Fuzzy sets. *Information and Control*, 8:338–353, 1965.   (Cited on page 36)

[Zad71] L. Zadeh. Similarity relations and fuzzy orderings. *Information Systems*, 3:177–200, 1971.   (Cited on page 191)

Index

Former volumes appeared as
EATCS Monographs on Theoretical Computer Science